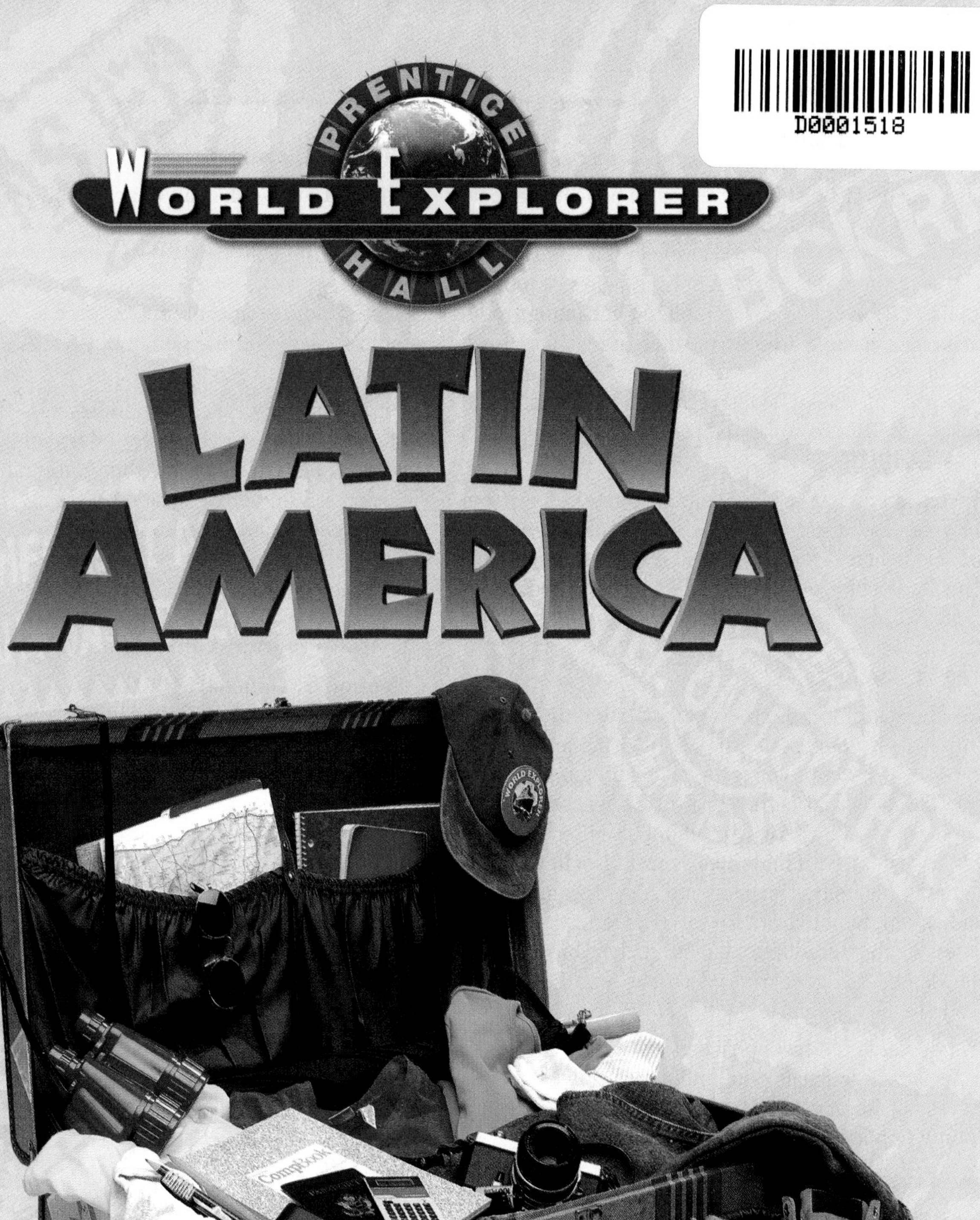

LATIN AMERICA

PRENTICE HALL
Needham, Massachusetts
Upper Saddle River, New Jersey

Program Authors

Heidi Hayes Jacobs

Heidi Hayes Jacobs has served as an educational consultant to more than 500 schools across the nation. Dr. Jacobs is an adjunct professor in the Department of Curriculum on Teaching at Teachers College, Columbia University. She completed her undergraduate studies at the University of Utah in her hometown of Salt Lake City. She received an M.A. from the University of Massachusetts, Amherst, and completed her doctoral work at Columbia University's Teachers College in 1981.

The backbone of Dr. Jacobs's experience comes from her years as a teacher of high school, middle school, and elementary school students. As an educational consultant, she works with K–12 schools and districts on curriculum reform and strategic planning.

Brenda Randolph

Brenda Randolph is the former Director of the Outreach Resource Center at the African Studies Program at Howard University, Washington, D.C. She is the Founder and Director of Africa Access, a bibliographic service on Africa for schools. She received her B.A. in history with high honors from North Carolina Central University, Durham, and her M.A. in African studies with honors from Howard University. She completed further graduate studies at the University of Maryland, College Park, where she was awarded a Graduate Fellowship.

Brenda Randolph has published numerous articles in professional journals and bulletins. She currently serves as library media specialist in Montgomery County Public Schools, Maryland.

Michal L. LeVasseur

Michal LeVasseur is an educational consultant in the field of geography. She is an adjunct professor of geography at the University of Alabama, Birmingham, and serves with the Alabama Geographic Alliance. Her undergraduate and graduate work is in the fields of anthropology (B.A.), geography (M.A.), and science education (Ph.D.).

Dr. LeVasseur's specialization has moved increasingly into the area of geography education. In 1996, she served as Director of the National Geographic Society's Summer Geography Workshop. As an educational consultant, she has worked with the National Geographic Society as well as with schools to develop programs and curricula for geography.

Special Program Consultant

Yvonne S. Gentzler, Ph.D.
School of Education
University of Idaho, Moscow, Idaho

Content Consultant on Latin America

Daniel Mugan
Center for Latin American Studies
University of Florida
Gainesville, Florida

PRENTICE HALL
Upper Saddle River, New Jersey
Needham, Massachusetts

Student Edition ISBN: 0-13-433704-2

10 01 00

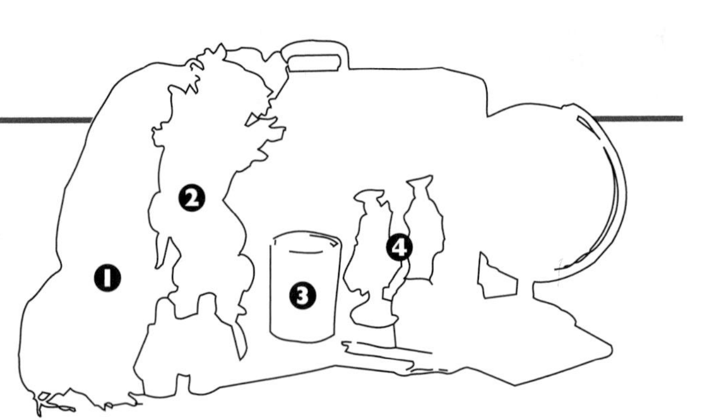

On the Cover

1. Woven blanket from Mexico
2. Mexican wood carving of an ancient Mayan snake god
3. Reproduction of Mayan pottery
4. Family of dolls from Peru dressed in traditional clothing

Content Consultants for the World Explorer Program

Africa
Barbara Brown
Africa Studies Center
Boston University
Boston, Massachusetts

Ancient World
Maud Gleason
Department of Classics
Stanford University
Stanford, California

East Asia
Leslie Swartz
Harvard University East Asian Outreach Program at the Children's Museum of Boston
Boston, Massachusetts

Middle East
Elizabeth Barlow
Center for Middle Eastern and North African Studies
University of Michigan
Ann Arbor, Michigan

North Africa
Laurence Michalak
Center for Middle East Studies
University of California
Berkeley, California

Religion
Michael Sells
Department of Religion
Haverford College
Haverford, Pennsylvania

Russia, Eastern Europe, Central Asia
Janet Valliant
Center for Russian, Eastern European, and Central Asian Studies
Harvard University
Cambridge, Massachusetts

South Asia
Robert Young
South Asia Regional Studies
University of Pennsylvania
Philadelphia, Pennsylvania

Western Europe
Ruth Mitchell-Pitts
Center for West European Studies
University of North Carolina
Chapel Hill, North Carolina

Teacher Advisory Board

Jerome Balin
Lincoln Junior High School
Naperville, Illinois

Linda Boaen
Baird School
Fresno, California

Nikki L. Born
Harllee Middle School
Bradenton, Florida

Carla Bridges
Concord Middle School
Concord, North Carolina

Bruce L. Campbell
Walled Lake Middle School
Walled Lake, Michigan

Barbara Coats Grabowski
Russell Middle School
Omaha, Nebraska

David Herman
North Carroll Middle School
Hampstead, Maryland

Fred Hitz
Wilson Middle School
Muncie, Indiana

William B. Johnson
La Mesa Junior High School
Canyon Country, California

Kristi Karis
West Ottawa Middle School
Holland, Michigan

Kristen Koch
Discovery Middle School
Orlando, Florida

Peggy McCarthy
Beulah School
Beulah, Colorado

Deborah J. Miller
Whitney Young Middle School
Detroit, Michigan

Lawrence Peglow
Greenway Middle School
Pittsburgh, Pennsylvania

Lyn Shiver
Northwestern Middle School
Alpharetta, Georgia

The World Explorer Team

The editors, designers, marketer, market researcher, manager, production buyer, and manufacturing buyer who made up the World Explorer team are listed below.

Jackie Bedoya, Bruce Bond, Ellen Brown, David Lippman, Catherine Martin-Hetmansky, Nancy Rogier, Olena Serbyn, Carol Signorino, John Springer, Susan Swan

TABLE OF CONTENTS

LATIN AMERICA 1

ACTIVITY ATLAS 2

CHAPTER 1 **Latin America: Physical Geography** 8

1 Land and Water 9
2 Climate and Vegetation 14
Skills Activity Using Regional Maps to Show Climate 20
3 Natural Resources 22
Chapter 1 Review and Activities 28
Literature *The Surveyor* by Alma Flor Ada 30

CHAPTER 2 **Latin America: Shaped by Its History** 34

1 Early Civilizations of Middle America 35
2 The Incas: People of the Sun 39
3 European Conquest 43
Skills Activity Using a Time Line 48
4 Independence 50
5 Issues in Latin America Today 55
Chapter 2 Review and Activities 60

CHAPTER 3 **Cultures of Latin America** 62

1 The Cultures of Mexico and Central America 63
2 The Cultures of the Caribbean 68
3 The Cultures of South America 73
Skills Activity Distinguishing Facts From Opinions 78
Chapter 3 Review and Activities 80

CHAPTER 4 **Exploring Mexico and Central America** 82
1 Mexico: One Family's Move to the City 83
2 Guatemala: Descendants of an Ancient People 89
Skills Activity Previewing a Reading Selection 94
3 Panama: Where Two Oceans Meet 96
Chapter 4 Review and Activities 102
Activity Shop Lab Making a Model Canal Lock 104

CHAPTER 5 **Exploring the Caribbean** 106
1 Cuba: Clinging to Communism 107
2 Haiti: The Road to Democracy 113
Skills Activity Locating Information 118
3 Puerto Rico: Cultural Identity of a People 120
Chapter 5 Review and Activities 126

CHAPTER 6 **Exploring South America** 128
1 Brazil: Resources of the Rain Forest 129
2 Peru: Life in the Altiplano 135
Skills Activity Using Isolines to Show Elevation 140
3 Chile: A Growing Economy Based on Agriculture 142
4 Venezuela: Oil Powers the Economy 148
Chapter 6 Review and Activities 154
Activity Shop Interdisciplinary Rain Forest Resources 156
Literature From the *Question Book* by Pablo Neruda 158

PROJECT POSSIBILITIES 160

REFERENCE 162
Map and Globe Handbook 163
Atlas 180
World View 196
Glossary of Geographic Terms 204
Gazetteer 206
Glossary 208
Index 211
Acknowledgments 214

OF SPECIAL INTEREST

A hands-on, active approach to practicing and applying key social studies skills

Using Regional Maps to Show Climate	20
Using a Time Line	48
Distinguishing Facts From Opinions	78
Previewing a Reading Selection	94
Locating Information	118
Using Isolines to Show Elevation	140

Engaging, step-by-step activities for exploring important topics in Latin America

Lab: Making a Model Canal Lock	104
Interdisciplinary: Rain Forest Resources	156

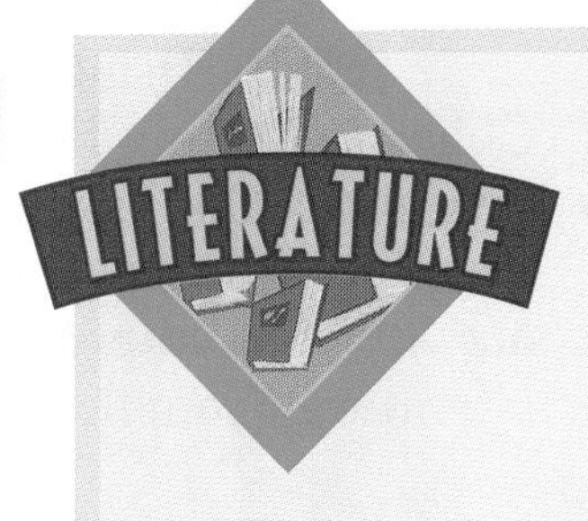

High-interest selections written by Latin American authors that shed light on the region's varied cultures

The Surveyor by Alma Flor Ada	30
From the *Question Book* by Pablo Neruda	158

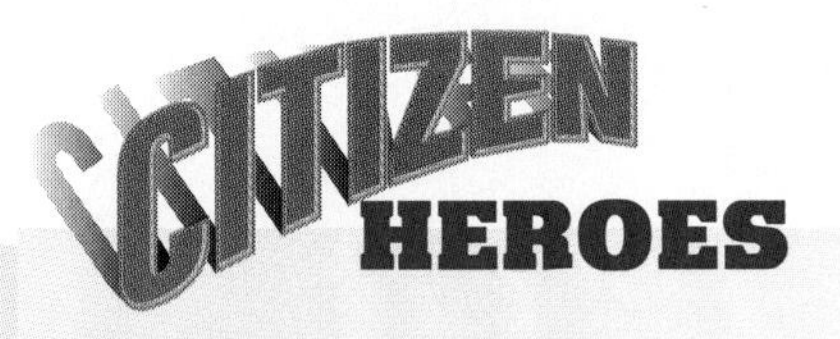

Sor Juana Inez de la Cruz	65
Mothers and Grandmothers of Argentina	77
Justina Tzoc	92
José Martí	109
Hector Turrini	133

Tenochtitlán	37
Brasília	76

Student Art From Peru	75
Student Art From Haiti	116

MAPS

Latin America: Relative Location 2
Latin America: Relative Size 2
Latin America: Political 3
Latin America: Physical 4
Latin America: Natural Vegetation 5
Latin America: Major Hydroelectric Plants 6
The Regions of Latin America 10
Latin America: Climate Regions 15
Latin America: Vegetation Regions 18
Latin America: Climates 20
Latin America: Natural Resources 24
Latin America: Place Location 29
Early Civilizations of Latin America 34
Spanish Conquest 44
Spanish and Portuguese Empires in the Americas 46
South America: Independence 52
Latin America: Place Location 61
Latin America: Place Location 81
Mexico and Central America: Political 82
Country Profile: Mexico 84
Mexico: Volcanoes and Earthquake Faults 86
The Growth of Mexico City 87
Country Profile: Guatemala 90
Country Profile: Panama 97
Shipping Routes and the Panama Canal 98
Mexico and Central America: Place Location 103
Country Profile: Cuba 108
Country Profile: Haiti 114
Country Profile: Puerto Rico 121
The Caribbean: Place Location 127
South America: Political 128
Country Profile: Brazil 130
Country Profile: Peru 136
Peru: Contour Map 141
Country Profile: Chile 143
Country Profile: Venezuela 149
South America: Place Location 155
Earth's Revolution and the Seasons 166
Mercator Projection 170
Equal-Area Projection 171
Robinson Projection 171
Azimuthal Projection 171
West Africa: Population Density 172
Russia: Political 174
Hawaii: Physical 175
North Africa and the Middle East: Oil Production 176
Atlas 180

CHARTS, GRAPHS, AND TABLES

Biggest Hydroelectric Dams 7
Sources of Energy 7
Vertical Climate Zones 17
The Columbian Exchange 47
Debts of Latin American Nations 56
A Growing Population 65
Caribbean Customs 69
Mexico's Population 83
Country Profile: Mexico 84
Country Profile: Guatemala 90
Country Profile: Panama 97
Country Profile: Cuba 108
Country Profile: Haiti 114
Country Profile: Puerto Rico 121
Puerto Ricans in the Mainland United States 122
Country Profile: Brazil 130
Two Cities, Two Climates 133
Country Profile: Peru 136
Country Profile: Chile 143
Country Profile: Venezuela 149
U.S. Petroleum Imports From Venezuela, 1984–1996 151
Climate Regions 178
Natural Vegetation Regions 179

How can I get the most out of my social studies book? How does my reading relate to my world? Answering questions like these means that you are an active reader, an involved reader. As an active reader, you are in charge of the reading situation!

The following strategies tell how to think and read as an active reader. You don't need to use all of these strategies all the time. Feel free to choose the ones that work best in each reading situation. You might use several at a time, or you might go back and forth among them. They can be used in any order.

Give yourself a purpose

The sections in this book begin with a list called "Questions to Explore." These questions focus on key ideas presented in the section. They give you a purpose for reading. You can create your own purpose by asking questions like these: How does the topic relate to your life? How might you use what you learn at school or at home?

Preview

To preview a reading selection, first read its title. Then look at the pictures and read the captions. Also read any headings in the selection. Then ask yourself: What is the reading selection about? What do the pictures and headings tell about the selection?

Reach into your background

What do you already know about the topic of the selection? How can you use what you know to help you understand what you are going to read?

Ask questions

Suppose you are reading about the continent of South America. Some questions you might ask are: Where is South America? What countries are found there? Why are some of the countries large and others small? Asking questions like these can help you gather evidence and gain knowledge.

Predict

As you read, make a prediction about what will happen and why. Or predict how one fact might affect another fact. Suppose you are reading about South America's climate. You might make a prediction about how the climate affects where people live. You can change your mind as you gain new information.

Connect

Connect your reading to your own life. Are the people discussed in the selection like you or someone you know? What would you do in similar situations? Connect your reading to something you have already read. Suppose you have already read about the ancient Greeks. Now you are reading about the ancient Romans. How are they alike? How are they different?

Visualize

What would places, people, and events look like in a movie or a picture? As you read about India, you could visualize the country's heavy rains. What do they look like? How do they sound? As you read about geography, you could visualize a volcanic eruption.

Respond

Talk about what you have read. What did you think? Share your ideas with your classmates.

Assess yourself

What did you find out? Were your predictions on target? Did you find answers to your questions?

Follow up

Show what you know. Use what you have learned to do a project. When you do projects, you continue to learn.

The ancient peoples of Latin America built great civilizations from the riches of their land. Today, their descendants have mixed with newcomers from around the world to create a modern society with new traditions. Cities of steel and glass rise alongside ancient ruins. From villages in the rain forests, mountains, and countryside, people move to the thriving cities. Every day more families arrive, hoping to make a new life.

Guiding Questions

The readings and activities in this book will help you discover answers to these Guiding Questions.

- What are the main physical features of Latin America?
- What factors have affected cultures in Latin America?
- Why have many Latin Americans been moving to cities in recent years?
- What is the relationship of the nations of Latin America with the United States and the world?
- How has geography influenced the ways in which Latin Americans make a living?

Project Preview

You can also discover answers to the Guiding Questions by working on projects. Preview the following projects and choose one that you might want to do. For more details, see page 160.

A Latin American Concert Research Latin American music and find some examples on tape to play for your class.

Visions of Latin America Create a diorama and write a short report to show how Latin America's geography affects the way people live.

Latin America in the News Collect articles on Latin America from magazines and newspapers for a bulletin board display.

Explorer's Dictionary Create an illustrated dictionary of important terms translated from Latin American languages.

The woman in the photo above left lives in Jamaica. In the photo above, the colorful clothing of people in Guatemala shows their famous skill with weaving. Students at a school in Lima, Peru, are shown in the photo at left.

EXPLORER'S JOURNAL

A journal can be your personal book of discovery. As you explore Latin America, you can use your journal to keep track of things you learn and do. You can also record your thoughts about your journey. For your first entry, write your thoughts on where in Latin America you would like to go and what you would want to see there.

DISCOVERY ACTIVITIES ABOUT

Latin America

Learning about Latin America means being an explorer and a geographer. No explorer would start out without first checking some facts. Begin by exploring the maps of Latin America on the following pages.

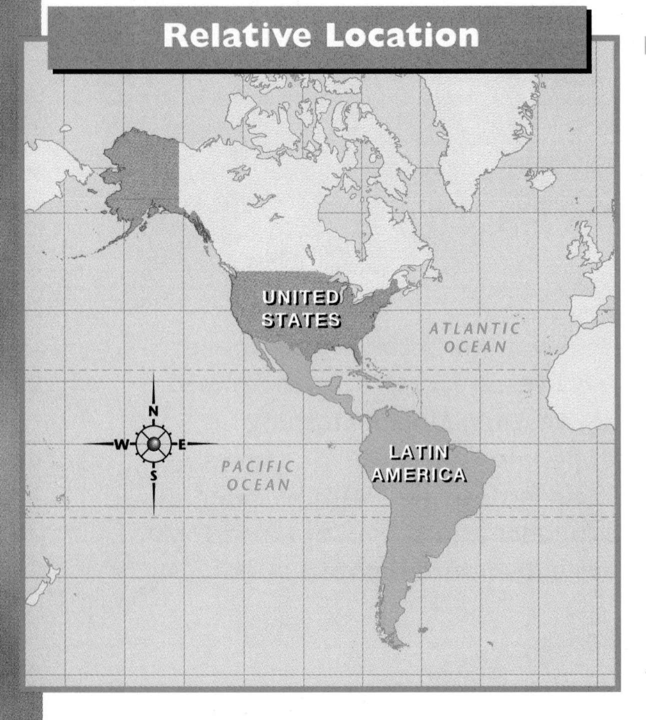

LOCATION

1. **Explore Latin America's Location** Notice where the United States and Latin America are located relative to the Equator. On the other side of the Equator, seasons come at the opposite time of year. For example, when it's summer here, it's winter there. Think about the season your birthday falls in. In what season would it fall if you lived in Argentina? What if you lived in Panama? How about in Bogotá, the capital city of Colombia? Or in Brasília, the capital of Brazil?

REGIONS

2. **Estimate Latin America's Size** How long is Latin America's west coast? To get an idea, curve a piece of string along the edge of the United States' west coast on the map above. Cut the string the same length as the coast. Now see how many string-lengths fit along the west coast of Latin America. Begin at the edge of the Pacific Ocean where Mexico borders California. Finish at the southern tip of South America. About how many times longer is Latin America's Pacific Coast than that of the United States?

LOCATION

3. Compare the Size of Countries The map below shows the countries that make up Latin America. Which two countries are the biggest in land area? Study the map to make your estimates. Check your answers in the World View section at the back of your textbook.

MOVEMENT

4. Investigate the Languages of Latin America The languages people speak give us clues about their history. Long ago, settlers from other countries took control of Latin America. Where were they from? Here are your clues: Portuguese is the official language of Brazil, and Spanish is spoken in most other Latin American countries.

PLACE

5. Examine the Physical Features of Latin America Volcanoes created many of Latin America's dramatic features. Long ago, volcanoes erupting along the west coast of South America formed the Andes Mountains. Volcanoes that exploded under the Caribbean Sea became a chain of islands called the Lesser Antilles. Central America has volcanic mountains, too. Some are still active! Trace the Andes Mountains, the Lesser Antilles, and the mountains in Central America with your finger. Which of these areas has the highest altitude?

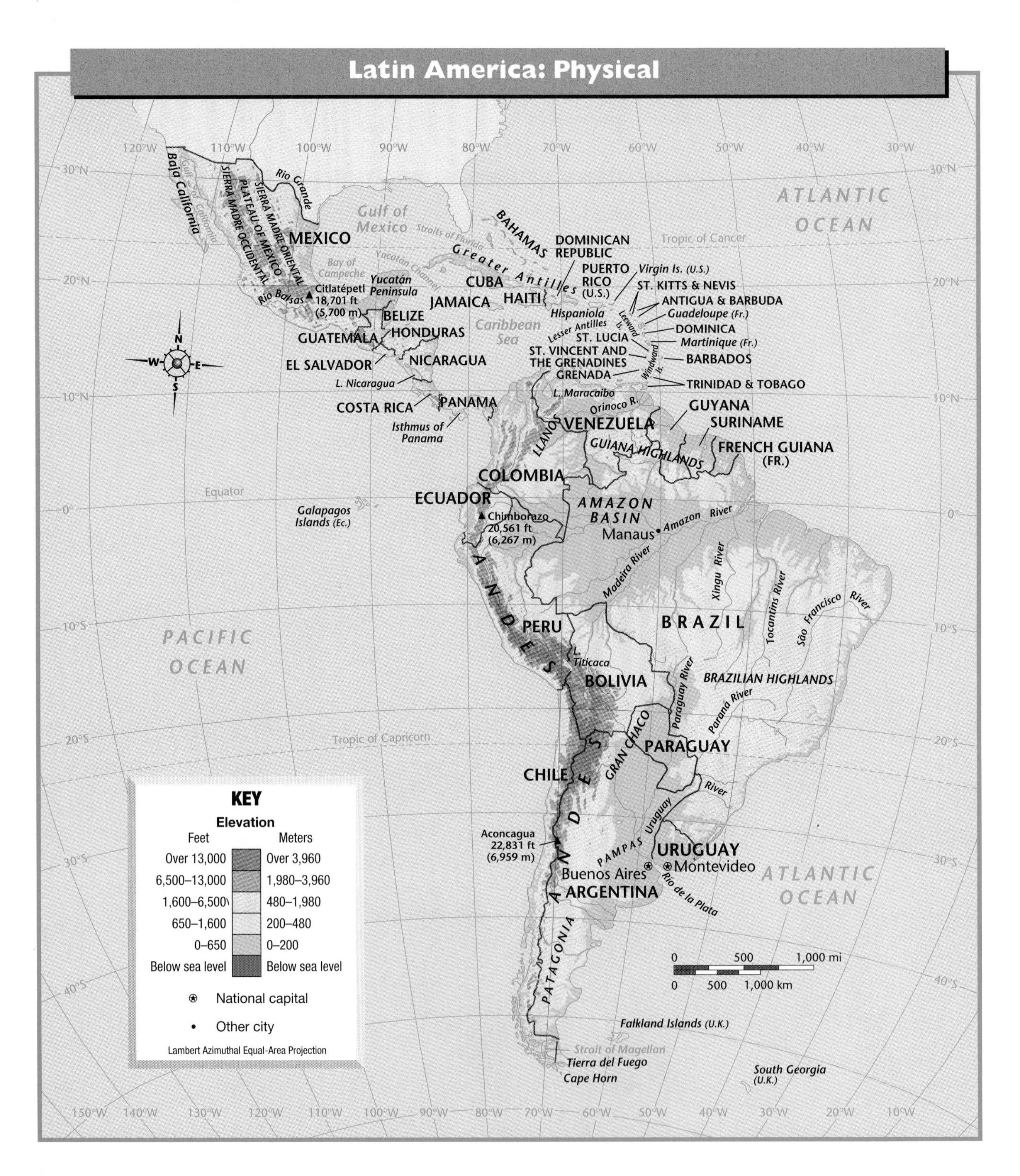

REGIONS

6. Guide Geo Leo Geo Leo is exploring Latin America by boat, and he's taking you along to navigate. Read the passages below. To answer Geo Leo's questions, use the map below and the map on the opposite page.

A. *We board our ship on the south side of the island of Hispaniola. A dense rain forest covers the island's mountain slopes. Which way to the Panama Canal?*

B. *We are sailing south past one of the Earth's driest deserts. It is in a long, skinny South American country that extends north and south along the continent's west coast. Steep mountains rise to the east. Where are we?*

C. *From the Falkland Islands, we travel north. For days we sail past desert. Finally, we see tropical rain forest along the coast. What two major cities will we come to next?*

D. *We continue sailing north, past grassland. We reach more rain forest and sail down a river through a low-lying area. Just ahead the Madeira River joins the one we are traveling on. Which way to the city of Manaus, our final destination?*

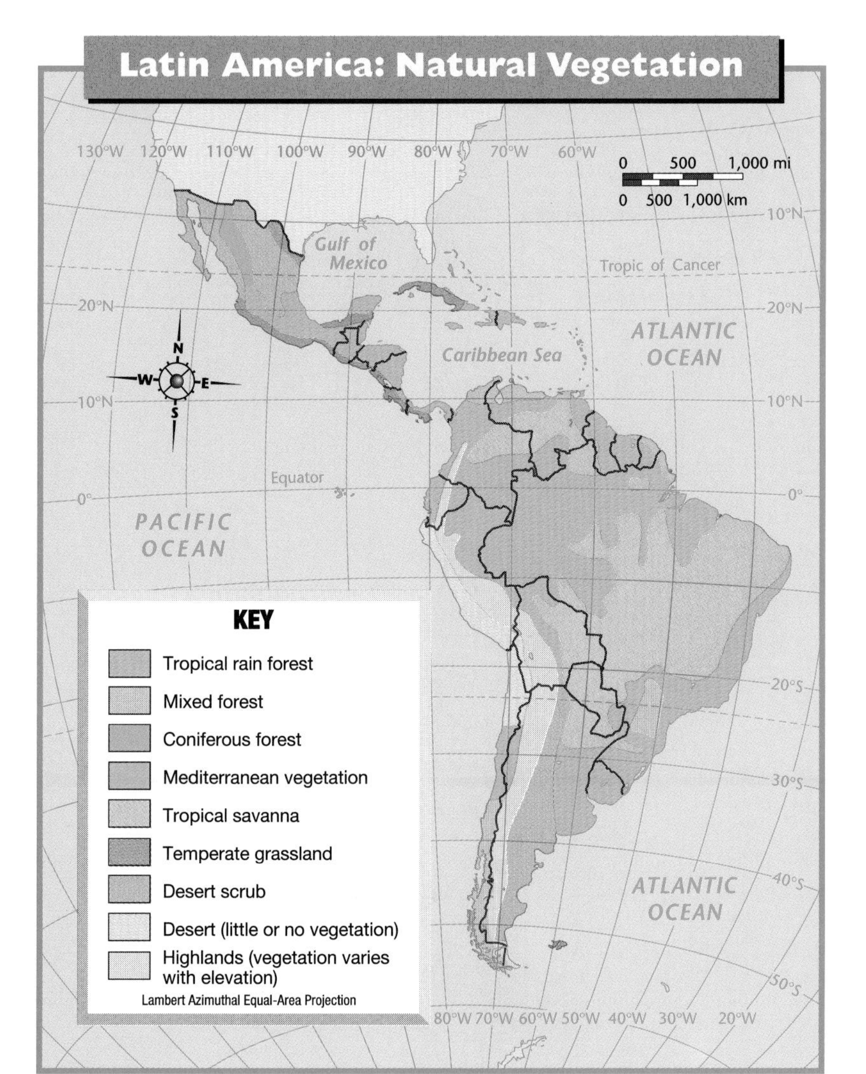

GEO LEO

BONUS

List each body of water you and Geo Leo traveled over.

LOCATION

7. Investigate Latin America's Use of Hydroelectricity Hydroelectricity is electric power that is made by harnessing the power of water. One way to build a hydroelectric power plant is to build a dam across a river. The dam creates a large lake of water. To make electricity, the plant releases water from the lake into the river. As the water moves into the river, it turns a wheel. In some places, hydroelectric plants harness the power of ocean tides. Some of the largest hydroelectric plants are in Latin America. The world's largest is located on the border of Brazil and Paraguay. Look at the map below. What places in Latin America do you think would be good spots to build new hydroelectric power plants?

Biggest Hydroelectric Dams

Name of Dam	Location
1. Itaipú	**Brazil/Paraguay**
2. Grand Coulee	United States
3. Guri (Raul Leoni)	**Venezuela**
4. Tucuruíi	**Brazil**
5. Sayano-Shushensk	Russia
6. Krasnoyarsk	Russia
7. Corpus-Posadas	**Argentina/Paraguay**
8. LaGrande 2	Canada
9. Churchill Falls	Canada
10. Bratsk	Russia

INTERACTION

8. Explore the Effects of a River Dam Unlike coal and petroleum, water power cannot be used up. It also does not cause air pollution. But building a dam does affect the environment of a river. It creates a large, artificial lake. It also reduces the amount of water that is in the river below the dam. What do you think are some advantages of building a dam across a river? What are some disadvantages?

◀ ▼ What percentage of its energy does Latin America get from hydroelectricity? How does this compare to energy use around the world?

Sources of Energy

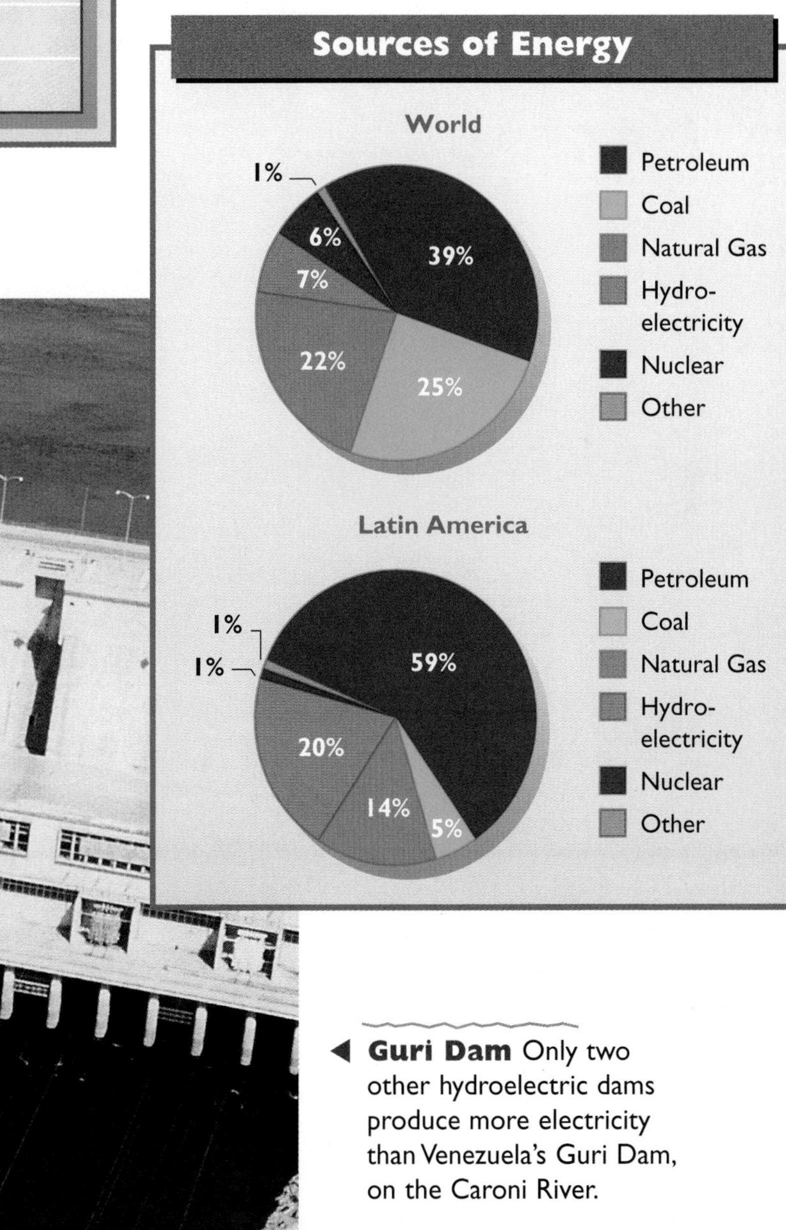

◀ **Guri Dam** Only two other hydroelectric dams produce more electricity than Venezuela's Guri Dam, on the Caroni River.

LATIN AMERICA

Physical Geography

SECTION 1
Land and Water

SECTION 2
Climate and Vegetation

SECTION 3
Natural Resources

These rugged mountains are the Andes (AN deez). *They run the length of South America. To help you get to know this part of Latin America, do the following.*

Study the picture

What do you think it would be like to live in or near the Andes? Based on what you see in the photograph, where would be the best area to live?

Think about the climate

Have you ever climbed in the mountains? How did the temperature change as you climbed higher? Based on your experience, do you think the climate is the same at the top of the Andes as at the bottom? Where would it be colder? Where would it be warmer?

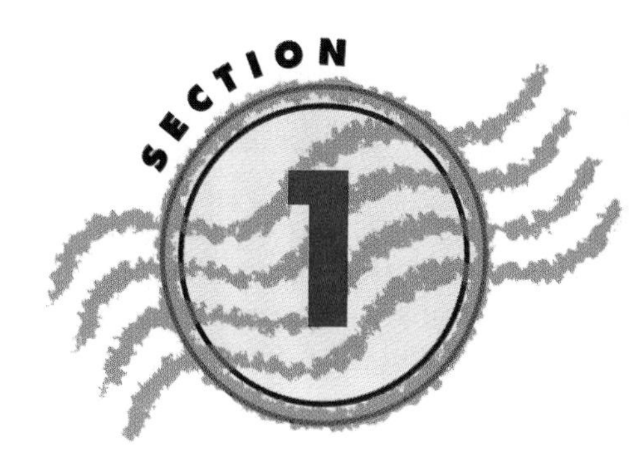

Land and Water

Reach Into Your Background
No two places in the world are exactly the same. Think about the state in which you live. What features set it apart from other states? List some features that make your state special.

Questions to Explore

1. What are the main geographic regions of Latin America?
2. How do Latin America's geographic features affect the lives of the people?

Key Terms
plateau
isthmus
coral
pampas
tributary

Key Places
Mexico
Central America
Caribbean
South America

High in the Andes Mountains, planes take off and land at El Alto airport. *El Alto* (ehl AHL toh) is Spanish for "the high one." It is an accurate name, for El Alto is the highest airport in the world. El Alto is the airport for La Paz, Bolivia.

Shortly after leaving the plane, tourists may get mountain sickness. The "thin" air of the Andes contains less oxygen than most people are used to. Oxygen starvation makes visitors' hearts beat faster and leaves them short of breath. Later on in the day, they may get terrible headaches. It takes a few days for visitors' bodies to get used to the mountain air. But the people who live in the Andes do not have these problems. Their bodies are used to the mountain environment.

The Andes mountain range is one of Latin America's major landforms. In this section, you will learn about Latin America's other landforms and about the people who live there.

Where Is Latin America?

Latin America is located in the Western Hemisphere south of the United States. Look at the map in the Activity Atlas. You will see that Latin America includes all the nations from Mexico to the tip of South America. It also includes the islands that dot the Caribbean (ka ruh BEE un) Sea.

Geographic features divide Latin America into three smaller regions. They are (1) Mexico and Central America, (2) the Caribbean, and (3) South America. South America is so large that geographers classify it as a continent. Look at the physical map in the Activity Atlas. Can you identify the geographic features that separate these three areas?

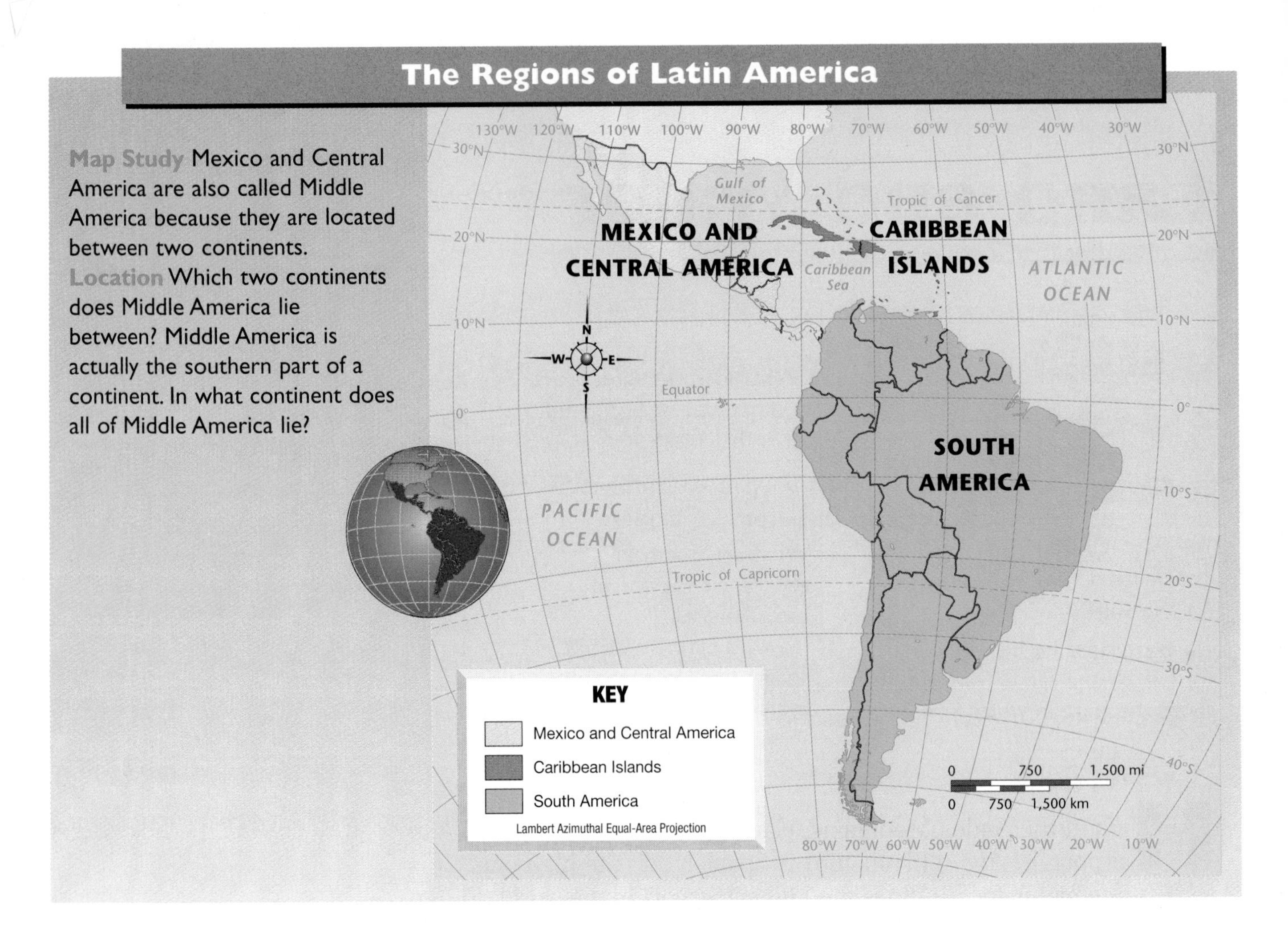

The Regions of Latin America

Map Study Mexico and Central America are also called Middle America because they are located between two continents. **Location** Which two continents does Middle America lie between? Middle America is actually the southern part of a continent. In what continent does all of Middle America lie?

Perhaps you are wondering how Latin America got its name. About 500 years ago, Europeans sailed to Latin America. Most came from Spain and Portugal. European colonists brought their own languages and ways of life with them. Today, most Latin Americans speak Spanish, Portuguese, or French. These languages have their roots in the ancient language of Latin. As a result, the region is known as Latin America.

READ ACTIVELY

Predict How do you think the physical features of Latin America might be like those of the United States?

Landforms of Latin America

Imagine mountains that pierce the clouds and grassy plains that never seem to end. Picture wet rain forests and sunbaked deserts. This is Latin America, a region of variety and contrast.

Mexico and Central America Mexico and Central America stretch 2,500 miles (4,023 km) from the U.S. border to South America. It is a distance that is almost equal to the width of the mainland United States. Mountains dominate this region. These mountains are part of a long system of mountain ranges. This huge system extends from Canada through the United States all the way to the tip of South America.

Between the mountains in Mexico lies Mexico's Central Plateau. A **plateau** (pla TOH) is a large raised area of mostly level land. Mexico's Central Plateau makes up more than half of the country's area. Most of Mexico's people live here. However, the surrounding mountains make it hard for people to travel to and from the Central Plateau. Another major landform in Mexico is the narrow coastal plains.

Central America, located south of Mexico, is an isthmus. An **isthmus** is a narrow strip of land that has water on both sides and joins two larger bodies of land. Find Central America on the map in the Activity Atlas. What two large bodies of land does the isthmus of Central America connect? As in Mexico, narrow plains run along Central America's coasts. Between these coastal plains are rugged, steep mountains. More than a dozen of these mountains are active volcanoes. Volcanic ash has made the soil fertile. As a result, many people tend farms in the region.

The Caribbean Imagine islands made of skeletons. Imagine other islands that are the tops of underwater mountains. The Caribbean is made up of these two types of islands. The smaller islands are made up of the skeletons of tiny sea animals. Over hundreds of years, the skeletons meld together to form a rocklike substance called **coral.**

The larger islands of the Caribbean are the tops of huge underwater mountains. These include Cuba, Jamaica (juh MAY kuh), Hispaniola (his pun YOH luh), and Puerto Rico. Most people on the islands make a living farming.

The Tlaloques According to Aztec religion, a group of rain gods lived on the tops of mountains. They were called the Tlaloques. Tlaloc, the leader of the Tlaloques, was responsible for rain and lightning. The Aztecs were right, in a way—mountains affect rainfall. Clouds cool off and drop rain when they rise over the mountains.

Harvesting Alfalfa in Mexico

In Mexico, farming is an important way of making a living, even in the drier areas of the country. Raising crops requires fertile soil, a source of fresh water, and a long growing season. As in Central America, much of Mexico's fertile soil is the result of volcanic activity.

South America South America contains many types of landforms. Perhaps the most impressive landform is the Andes Mountains. The Andes run some 4,500 miles (7,250 km) along the western coast of South America. In some places, the Andes rise to heights of more than 20,000 feet (6,100 m). That's about the same height as twenty 100-story buildings stacked one on top of another. Except for the Himalaya Mountains in Asia, the Andes are the highest mountains in the world.

The Andes are steep and difficult to cross. But their rich soil has drawn farmers to the region. East of the Andes are rolling highlands. These highlands spread across parts of Brazil, Venezuela (ven uh ZWAY luh), Guyana (gy AN uh), and other South American countries. Farther south are the Pampas (PAHM puz), a large plains area that stretches through Argentina (ar jun TEE nuh) and Uruguay (YOOR uh gway). **Pampas** are flat grassland regions that are very similar to the Great Plains in the United States.

The Pampas and other plains areas, the eastern highlands, and the Andes frame the Amazon River Basin. The Amazon River Basin contains the largest tropical rain forest in the world. This dense forest covers more than a third of the continent.

The Rivers of Latin America

Latin America is famous for its rivers and lakes. They are some of the longest and largest bodies of water in the world. Latin America's waters are important to the people of the region. Rivers serve as natural

Herding Cattle on the Pampas

Grasslands known as the Pampas can also be found in Brazil. These grasslands are perfect for raising cattle. **Critical Thinking** How are these grasslands similar to the Great Plains in the United States?

highways in places where it is hard to build roads. The fish that swim the waters of Latin America provide food. Rushing water from large rivers provides electric power.

Amazon: The Ocean River Latin America's Amazon (AM uh zahn) River is the second-longest river in the world. Only the Nile in Africa is longer. The Amazon flows 4,000 miles (6,437 km) from Peru across Brazil into the Atlantic Ocean.

How large is the Amazon? The Amazon River carries more water than any other river in the world. It contains about 20 percent of all the fresh river water on Earth. The Amazon River gathers power from the more than 1,000 tributaries (TRIB yoo tehr eez) that spill into it. **Tributaries** are the rivers and streams that flow into a larger river. With its tributaries, the Amazon drains an area of more than two million square miles. No wonder people call the Amazon the "Ocean River."

An Amazon Scene

The people who live near the Amazon River in Brazil rely on it for transportation, fish, and water. Families also wash their laundry right at the river bank.

Other Rivers and Lakes Latin America has many other bodies of water besides the Amazon. The Paraná (pah rah NAH), Paraguay, and Uruguay rivers form the Río de la Plata system. The Río de la Plata separates Argentina and Uruguay. In Venezuela, people travel on the Orinoco River and Lake Maracaibo (mar uh KY boh). Lake Titicaca is the highest lake in the world on which ships can travel. It lies high in the Andes Mountains.

Visualize How could a ship sail on a lake? What would the lake have to be like?

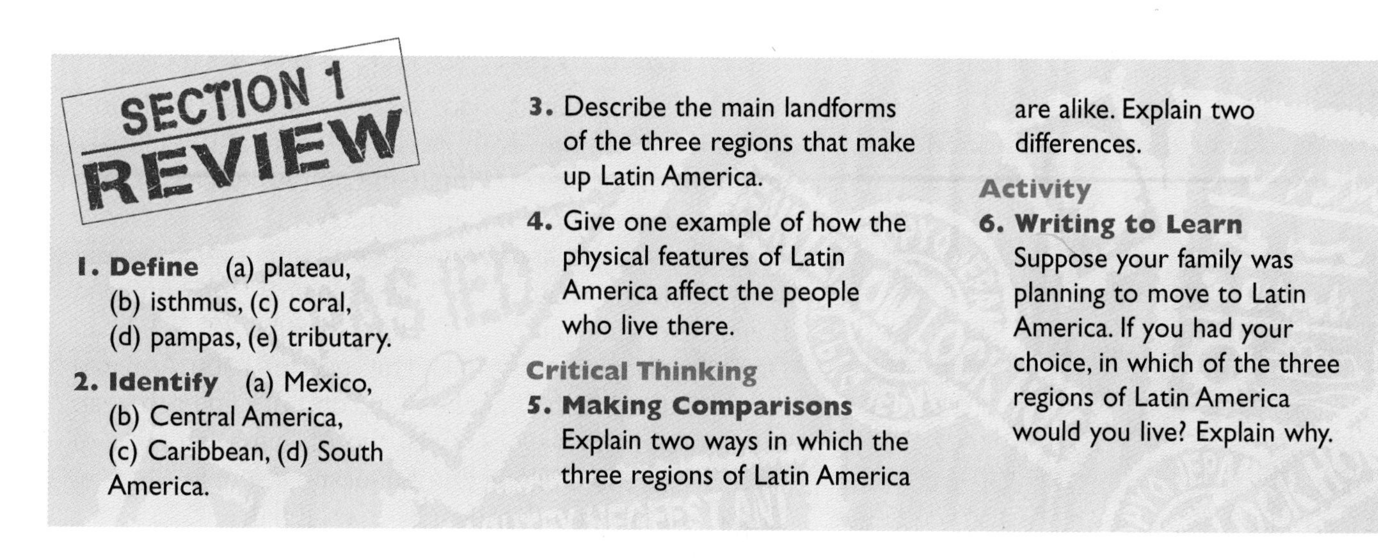

SECTION 1 REVIEW

1. **Define** (a) plateau, (b) isthmus, (c) coral, (d) pampas, (e) tributary.
2. **Identify** (a) Mexico, (b) Central America, (c) Caribbean, (d) South America.
3. Describe the main landforms of the three regions that make up Latin America.
4. Give one example of how the physical features of Latin America affect the people who live there.

Critical Thinking

5. **Making Comparisons** Explain two ways in which the three regions of Latin America are alike. Explain two differences.

Activity

6. **Writing to Learn** Suppose your family was planning to move to Latin America. If you had your choice, in which of the three regions of Latin America would you live? Explain why.

Section 2: Climate and Vegetation

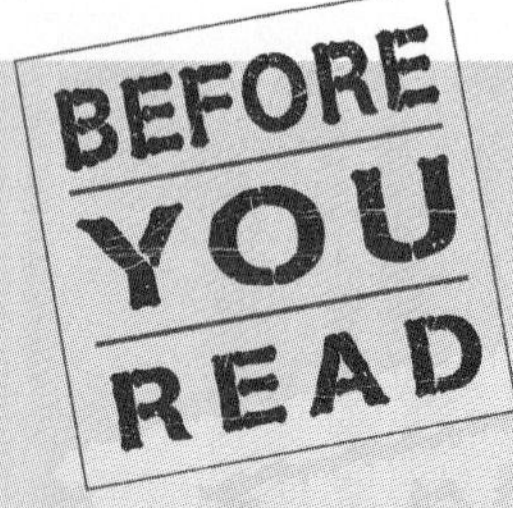

Reach Into Your Background

Suppose the temperature outside is 90°F (32°C). Would you feel more comfortable lying on a sandy beach or sitting under a tree in the woods? In what type of climate would you want to vacation someday?

Questions to Explore

1. What kinds of climate and vegetation does Latin America have?
2. In what ways do climate and vegetation affect how Latin Americans live?

Key Terms

El Niño
elevation

Key Places

Andes
Atacama Desert
Patagonia
Amazonian rain forest

Every few years, a warm ocean current flows along the western coast of South America. This warm current drives away fish that thrive in the cold waters of the Pacific Ocean. The current brings other changes to Latin America, too. Instead of dry weather, heavy rains pour down and low-lying regions are flooded. In other places, drought plagues the land and the people.

Just what is this strange ocean current that brings disaster? It is **El Niño** (el NEEN yoh). Because it usually strikes near Christmas time, Latin Americans named the phenomena El Niño, Spanish for "the Christ child." El Niño is one of many factors that affect climate in Latin America.

▼ Mexico's Sonoran Desert shows that even a hot, dry desert can be full of plant life.

Climate: Hot, Cold, and Mild

What's the climate like where you live? Is it hot? Cold? Rainy? If you lived in Latin America, the climate might be any of these. Climate in Latin America can vary greatly even within the same country.

In parts of the Andes, below-zero temperatures would set your teeth chattering. Travel down to the Amazon Basin, and you may be sweating in 80°F (27°C) heat. Don't forget your umbrella: This part of Latin America receives more than 80 inches (203 cm) of rain each year. If you prefer dry weather, visit the Atacama (ah tah KAH mah) Desert in Chile or the Sonoran Desert in Mexico. These are two of the driest places on Earth.

Map Study The Equator passes through the country of Ecuador, which was named for it. Countries south of the Equator have seasons that are the reverse of seasons in the Northern Hemisphere. **Regions** When it is winter in the United States, what season is it in Paraguay? What is the climate in most parts of Paraguay? In what other South American countries would you find this climate region?

Sugar Cane Farming

People in the Dominican Republic grow much of their own food, but they also grow sugar cane to export. **Regions** How does the climate in the Caribbean make the area good for farming? How is the climate in the Caribbean dangerous for farms?

The Climate and the People The climate in the Caribbean is usually sunny and warm. From June to November, however, the region is often hit with fierce hurricanes. In 1988, Hurricane Gilbert shattered the sunny Caribbean weather like an atom bomb. Winds howled at over 180 miles per hour (300 km/hr). Waves nearly 20 feet (6 m) high smashed into the coast. The storm tore roofs off houses, shattered windows, and yanked huge trees from the ground. Gilbert turned out to be the strongest hurricane to strike the Western Hemisphere this century.

Hurricanes are a part of life for people living in the Caribbean. But climate affects the people of Latin America in other ways, too. For example, people who live in the mountains need warm clothing and shelter to protect them against falling temperatures. That's because the higher up the mountains you go, the cooler it gets. Those who live in the sunny, warm tropics think more about cooling sea breezes than chilling winter winds.

Climate Regions of Latin America Look at the climate regions map on the previous page. You will notice that many parts of Latin America have a tropical wet climate. A tropical wet climate means hot, humid, rainy weather all year round. Rain forests thrive in this type of climate.

Other parts of Latin America have a tropical wet and dry climate. These areas are equally hot, but the rainy season does not last all year long. Parts of Mexico and Brazil and most of the Caribbean have a tropical wet and dry climate.

Much of Argentina, Uruguay, and Paraguay has a humid subtropical climate, similar to that of parts of the southern United States. People living in this climate usually have hot, wet summers and cool winters. Farmers in these areas can raise such crops as wheat and apples, which need a cold season to grow well. Farther south, the climate turns arid. Farmers raise sheep on the plains of this colder, drier area, called Patagonia (pat uh GOH nee uh).

What Factors Affect Climate? Have you ever hiked in the mountains? If you have, you probably noticed that as you climbed higher the temperature dropped. At some point during your hike, you may have stopped to put on a sweatshirt or jacket.

Elevation, the height of land above sea level, is a key factor in the climate of mountainous Latin America. Look at the diagram below. It shows how elevation affects climate. The higher the elevation, the colder the temperature. Suppose it is a warm 80°F (27°C) at sea level. At 3,000 feet (914 m), the temperature may be 72°F (25°C). Continue up to 6,000 feet (1,829 m), and the temperature may now be only about 65°F (13°C). Above 10,000 feet (3,048 m), the temperature may remain below freezing—too cold for people to live. Temperature also affects what crops people can grow in each region.

Other factors also affect Latin America's climate. Regions close to the Equator are generally warmer than those farther away. Look at the Latin America: Climate Regions map. Find the Equator. Which parts of Latin America are closest to the Equator? Which are farthest away?

Visualize Suppose that you were climbing a mountain. How would the vegetation you see change as you climb higher?

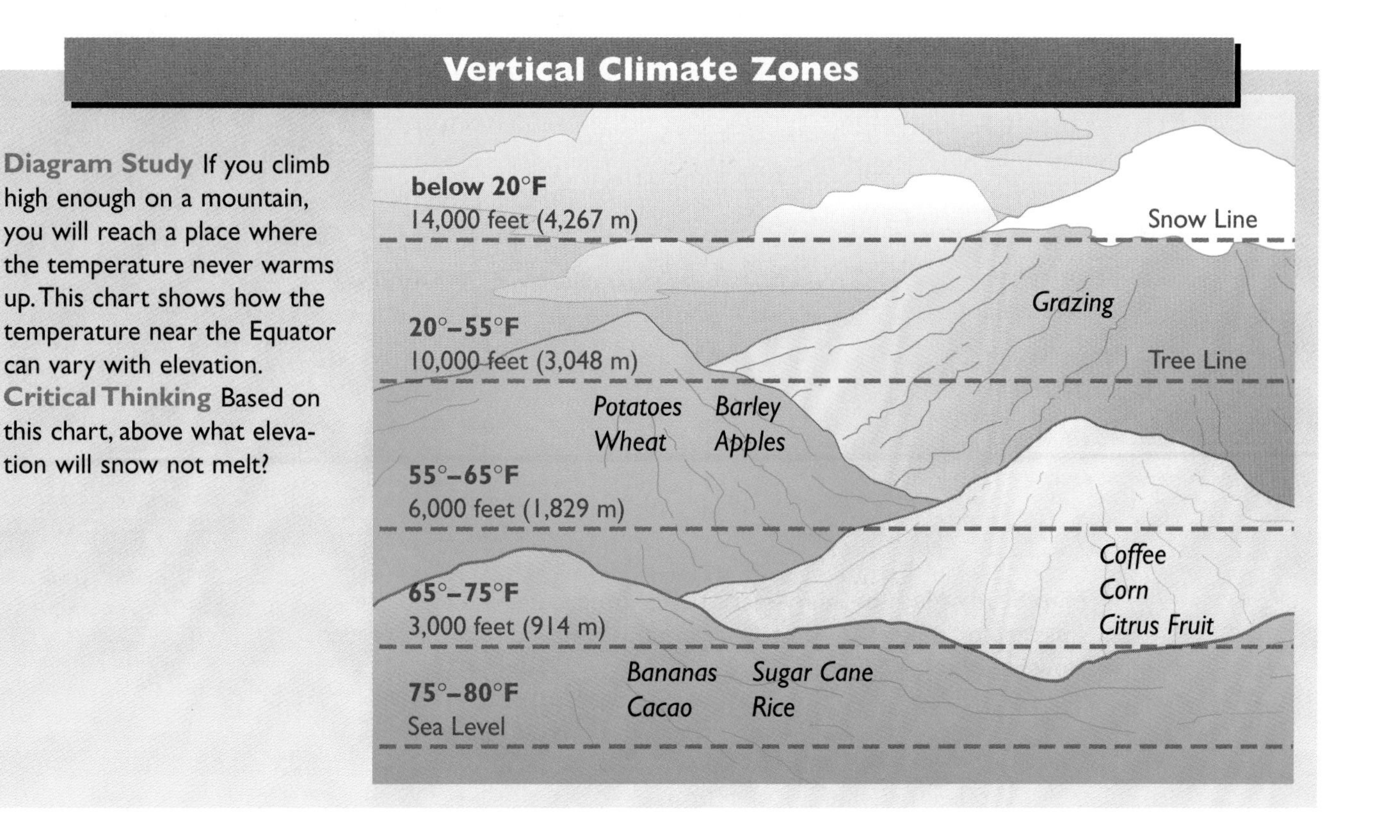

Diagram Study If you climb high enough on a mountain, you will reach a place where the temperature never warms up. This chart shows how the temperature near the Equator can vary with elevation. **Critical Thinking** Based on this chart, above what elevation will snow not melt?

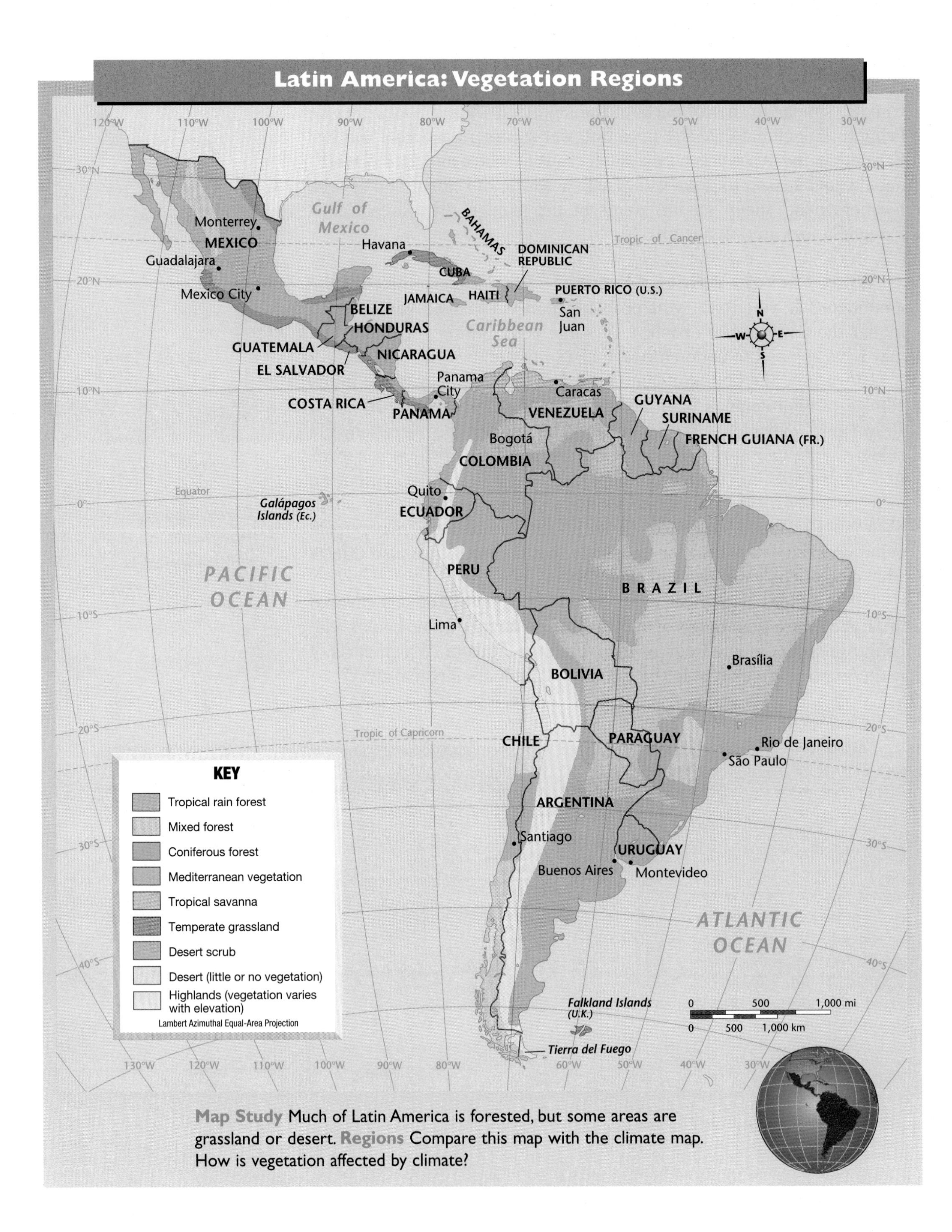

Map Study Much of Latin America is forested, but some areas are grassland or desert. **Regions** Compare this map with the climate map. How is vegetation affected by climate?

Wind patterns affect the climate too. Winds move cold air from the North and South Poles toward the Equator. They also move warm air from the Equator toward the Poles. In the Caribbean, sea breezes blowing toward shore help to keep temperatures moderate. Winds also affect rainfall in the Caribbean. More rain falls on the sides of islands facing the wind than on sides facing away.

Ask Questions What would you like to know about living in the rain forest?

Natural Vegetation and Climate

Imagine a forest so dense and lush that almost no sunlight reaches the ground. Broad green leaves, tangled vines, and thousands of species of trees and plants surround you. The air is hot and heavy with moisture. Welcome to the Amazonian rain forest.

Now, suppose you have traveled to the coast of northern Chile. You're in the Atacama Desert. Winds carry no moisture to this barren land, and there is little sign of life. The Andes shield this parched region from rain. Parts of the desert have never felt a single raindrop.

Latin America's varied climate and physical features make such extremes possible. Look at the natural vegetation map on the previous page. How many different kinds of vegetation does the map show? Note which countries in Latin America have areas of tropical rain forest. Now, find these countries on the climate map. How do the tropical climate and heavy rainfall in these countries contribute to the vegetation that grows there?

Find Uruguay on the vegetation map and on the climate map. Uruguay's climate and vegetation have helped make sheep and cattle raising a key part of the country's economy.

Elevation also affects vegetation. For example, palm trees and fruit trees that grow well in the coastal plains of Mexico and Central America would not survive high in the Andes. To grow at higher elevations, plants must be able to withstand cooler temperatures, chill winds, and irregular rainfall.

▲Tree sloths live in the rain forest trees. They rarely descend from the trees.

1. **Define** (a) El Niño, (b) elevation.
2. **Identify** (a) Andes, (b) Atacama Desert, (c) Patagonia, (d) Amazonian rain forest.
3. Describe two climates in Latin America. Then explain how climate affects the vegetation that grows in those regions.
4. How do Latin America's climate and vegetation affect how and where the people live?

Critical Thinking

5. **Drawing Conclusions** In what ways would the life of a family living on a Caribbean island be different from a family living high in the Andes?

Activity

6. **Writing to Learn** Latin America has been called a land of extremes. Do you agree or disagree? Write a paragraph or more telling why. Begin with the following sentences: "Many people have called Latin America a land of extremes. I believe that . . ." Support your opinion with examples.

SKILLS ACTIVITY

Using Regional Maps to Show Climate

If you could follow the Earth's weather for many years, no two years would look exactly alike. Think how the weather in your own location varies. Some years are colder, warmer, wetter, or drier than others. The same is true for every place on the planet.

Still, you could notice patterns in the weather. For example, one place may tend to have hot, rainy summers and cold, dry winters. Another place might be hot and dry all year round. The typical weather patterns in a location are called its climate.

Traveling across the Earth, you would find that no two places have exactly the same climate. Even the next town might be a degree cooler than your own. Still, you would find some similarities. Places in a large area that have similar weather make up a climate region.

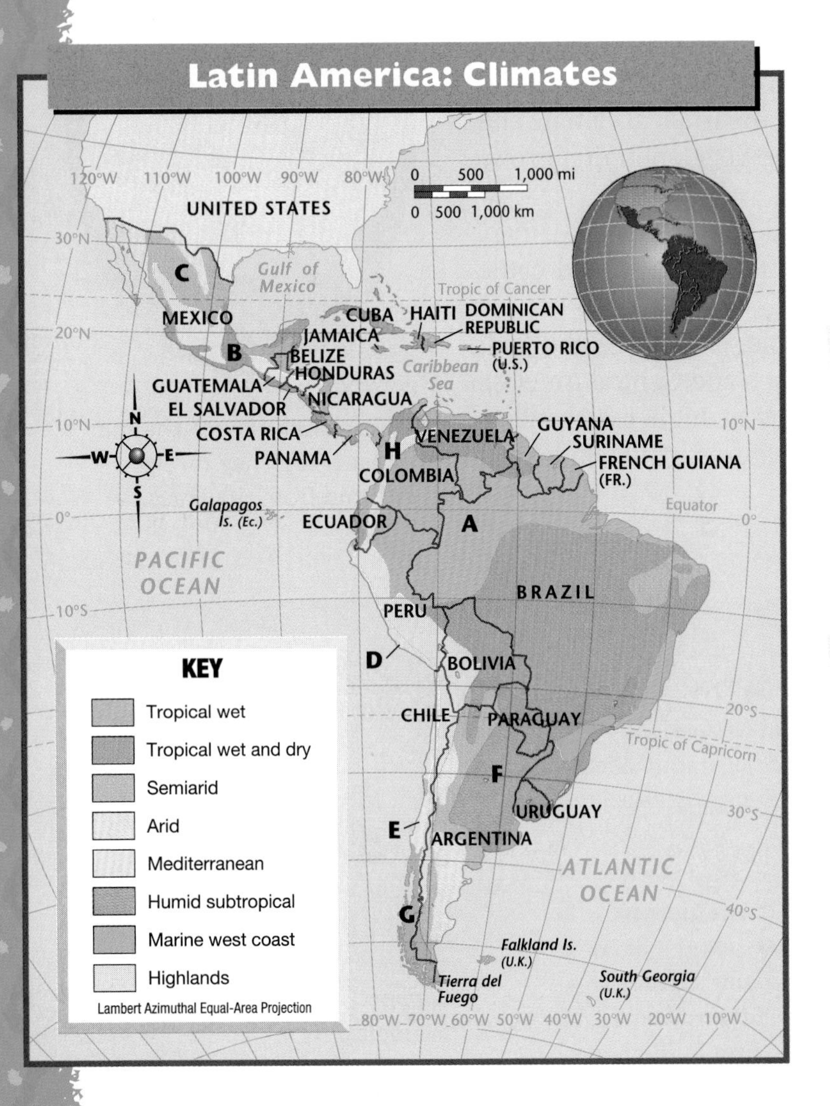

Get Ready

A region's climate affects how its inhabitants live. Learning to read a climate map can help you understand what life is like in different regions of the world.

Try It Out

Climates in Latin America fall into four general categories: *tropical, dry, mild,* and *highland.* Read about the climates described below. Use the map to answer each question.

A. Find a tropical climate zone. Tropical climates are hot year round. There are two types. Tropical wet zones have rain nearly every day. Tropical wet and dry zones have a wet season and a dry season. Where are tropical wet and dry zones usually located in relation to tropical wet zones?

B. Find a dry climate. Dry climates have little rain. There are two types. Arid zones may go years without rain. Semiarid zones receive enough rain for short grasses to grow. Where are semiarid zones usually located in relation to arid zones?

C. Find a mild climate. Mild climates are more comfortable than tropical or dry climates. There are three types. Marine climates are wet and have only moderate changes in temperature during the year. Humid subtropical areas are also wet but warmer than marine climates. Mediterranean climates are warm, too, but only rainy in the winter. Where are mild climate regions usually located in relation to large bodies of water?

D. Find a highland climate. Highland climates are found in mountainous regions. In a highland climate, temperatures vary. The higher you climb up a mountain, the colder it gets. Where is South America's highland climate located?

Apply the Skill

A region's climate can affect the kind of homes people build, the jobs they do, and the food they eat. Read the descriptions that follow. Then match each description with a letter on the map.

1. Few trees grow in Mexico's dry central region. Instead of building homes from wood, farmers often use sun-dried brick called adobe. Flat roofs are sometimes made of tile, straw, or sheet metal.

2. In the south of Mexico, more rain falls. The rain would eventually wash away an adobe home. So instead, some farmers build with wooden poles coated with a lime and clay mixture that keeps out the rain. Roofs are slanted so that rain water runs off.

3. Peru's west coast has one of the Earth's driest climates. To raise crops, farmers channel mountain streams to bring water to their fields.

4. Near the base of the Andes Mountains in Colombia, the weather is hot. High in the mountain peaks the climate is cold. In between, the mountain slopes have a mild climate perfect for growing coffee—one of Columbia's leading crops.

5. The Yanomamo are an Indian people living on the border between Brazil and Venezuela. A dense forest grows here. To clear land for crops, the Yanomamo must slash and burn trees. In addition to crops, they eat food found in the forest—anteaters, armadillos, and roasted caterpillars.

Natural Resources

Reach Into Your Background

Do you know what natural resources are? They are things found in nature that people can use to meet their needs. For example, trees are a natural resource. List two other natural resources. Describe how people use each one.

Questions to Explore

1. What are Latin America's important natural resources?
2. Why is it important for Latin American nations to have more than one source of income?

Key Terms

hydroelectricity
diversify

Key Places

Jamaica
Venezuela
Brazil
Colombia
Chile

Bolivia has always depended on mineral resources for wealth. At first, silver helped to bring money into Bolivia's treasury. Soon, however, another metal became even more important than silver. That metal was tin.

For many years, Bolivia enjoyed the good times that wealth from tin brought. Then, in the 1920s and 1930s, a world-wide economic crisis hit. Industries stopped buying tin, as well as other natural resources. Bolivia suffered as its main resource failed to bring money into the economy. This economic crisis hit all of Latin America hard. It brought home a problem many Latin American nations have: They rely too much on one resource.

▼ Latin America has about 12 percent of the world's petroleum.

Latin America's Resources

What do the following items have in common? Fish, petroleum, water, silver, and bananas. You have probably guessed that all these items are natural resources of Latin America. Latin America's resources are as varied as its physical features and climate.

Mexico and Central America: Riches of Land and Sea Mexico is a treasure chest of minerals. The country has deposits of silver, gold, copper, coal, iron ore, and just about any other mineral you can name. How many of these mineral resources can you find on the map on the next page? Mexico also has huge amounts of oil and natural gas. In addition, trees cover nearly a quarter of Mexico's land. Wood from these trees is turned into lumber and paper products.

Central America's climate and rich soil are good for farming. The people grow coffee, cotton, sugar cane, and bananas. They also plant cacao trees. Cacao seeds are made into chocolate and cocoa.

Not all of Central America's resources are on land. People catch fish and shellfish in the region's waters. Central Americans use the power of rushing water to produce electricity. This type of power is called **hydroelectricity** (hy droh ee lek TRIS ih tee). Countries build huge dams to harness and control the energy that rushing water produces.

The Caribbean: Sugar, Coffee, and More Caribbean countries also have rich soil and a good climate for farming. Farmers grow sugar cane, coffee, bananas, cacao, citrus fruits, and other crops on the islands.

The Caribbean has other resources as well. For example, Jamaica is one of the world's main producers of bauxite—a mineral used to make aluminum. Cuba and the Dominican Republic have nickel deposits. Trinidad is rich in oil.

Drilling for Oil

Some of Mexico's petroleum reserves can only be reached through offshore drilling, or drilling into the ocean floor. **Interaction** What special precautions do you think that offshore drillers might have to take to avoid harming the environment?

Map Study Natural resources are important to a country's economy because they can be sold to other countries or used to make products that can be sold. **Movement** Which countries have natural resources that are located close to waterways? How would this location make the resources more useful?

Harnessing Water Power

The hydroelectric power plant at Itaipú Dam is the largest in the world. It harnesses the energy of the Paraná River to provide electric power to Paraguay and Brazil. **Critical Thinking** What detail in this picture is a clue that the dam is used to produce electricity?

South America: A Wealth of Resources Like Mexico, South America is rich in minerals. It contains gold, copper, tin, bauxite, and iron ore. Businesses drill for oil in many South American countries. Much of South America's oil is found in Venezuela.

South America's plants and fish are natural resources, too. Forests cover about half the continent. Trees from these forests provide everything from wood for building to coconuts for eating. People harvest many rain forest plants to make medicines. Tuna, anchovies, and other fish are plentiful in the waters off the Pacific Coast.

Like other parts of Latin America, South America has rich soil. Farmers grow many different crops there. For example, coffee is a key crop in Brazil and Colombia. Wheat is important in Argentina. Many South American economies rely on the production of sugar cane, cotton, and rice.

Natural Resources and Latin America's Economy

Not every country shares in the wealth of Latin America's resources. Some Latin American countries have many resources, while others have few. Some countries do not have the money they need to develop all of their resources. Other countries rely too much on one resource or crop.

Sailors of the Seventh Century South Americans have been trading with the people of Mexico since at least A.D. 600. They sailed north from Ecuador, Colombia, and Peru on rafts. These adventurers traded not only goods, such as tweezers and bells, but also skills and ideas. For example, they taught people of Mexico how to make metal objects such as needles.

Cash Crop Farming

Many Latin American economies are based on agriculture. Half of Colombia's exports are coffee, and one third of Honduras' exports are bananas. **Critical Thinking** What problems do you think one-crop economies face?

Prices, Weather, and Other Factors Depending on one resource or crop can lead to problems. For example, when world copper prices are high, the copper mining industry is very successful. But suppose copper prices drop sharply. Then copper exports are not worth as much. When this happens, the mining industry loses money. Mining workers may lose their jobs. Chile is the leading producer of copper in the world. When prices plunge, Chile's economy suffers.

Many people in Latin America make their living by farming. Some Latin American countries depend on one or two crops, such as coffee, bananas, or sugar. When the price of a crop goes down, exports of that crop bring less money into the country. As a result, workers' wages may drop, and some workers may lose their jobs.

Visualize How would the crops in a field look after a hurricane? How would they look after a drought?

Weather and disease also cause people and businesses to lose money. Hurricanes, droughts, and plant disease can damage crops. Weather sometimes hurts the fishing industry. The warm ocean current El Niño affects the fish that live in South America's coastal waters. Usually, the cold water of the Pacific supports a large number of small water plants on which the fish feed. When El Niño strikes, the warm water kills the plants and the fish die or move to other areas. Peru is among the countries affected by El Niño. Peruvian fishers have suffered great economic losses due to El Niño effects.

Depending on Oil Oil is one of Latin America's most valuable resources. But it is risky to depend on oil. Oil prices increase and decrease. Sometimes they change suddenly. Mexico, like Venezuela, is a major oil producer. In the mid-1980s, oil companies produced more oil than the world needed. As a result, prices dropped. Mexico earned much less income than it had expected. The same thing happened to Trinidad.

There are other problems as well. In the 1960s, people discovered oil in Ecuador. Soon, oil became the country's main export. But in 1987, earthquakes destroyed Ecuador's major oil pipeline. The country's income was slashed.

Avoiding the Problems of a One-Resource Country Latin American nations know the risks of depending on one resource or crop. They are trying to diversify their economies. To **diversify** is to add variety. When Latin American nations try to diversify their economies, it means that they are looking for other ways to make money. Many are building factories. Factories make products that can be sold to bring more money into the economy. Factories also provide jobs for people.

Venezuela has been trying to set up more factories and farms. Venezuela is also improving its bauxite and iron mines. Ecuador passed a law to encourage industry. Businesses there built factories to make cloth, electrical appliances, and other products.

Brazil has also been building up its industries. That way Brazil does not have to depend on agriculture. Brazil now exports machinery, steel, and chemicals. Brazil has also encouraged cotton farming. As a result, cotton weaving has become a successful industry.

El Salvador used to depend too heavily on its coffee crop. Now, cotton, sugar, corn, and other crops play an important role in the nation's economy. Trinidad has also encouraged its farmers to raise more kinds of crops. The government realizes that the country depends too much on oil and sugar.

1. **Define** (a) hydroelectricity, (b) diversify.
2. **Identify** (a) Jamaica, (b) Venezuela, (c) Brazil, (d) Colombia, (e) Chile.
3. Describe the important natural resources of Latin America.
4. Why is it important for Latin American nations to diversify their economies?

Critical Thinking

5. **Recognizing Cause and Effect** Suppose a disease destroyed Colombia's coffee crop. How would this loss affect coffee-plantation workers and their families? How would it affect Colombia's economy?

Activity

6. **Writing to Learn** Imagine that you are the president of a Latin American country. Your nation depends on bananas for nearly all of its income. What arguments would you use to persuade people to diversify?

CHAPTER 1

Review and Activities

Reviewing Main Ideas

1. List the three main regions of Latin America. Then choose two and describe their features.
2. In what ways do the physical features of Latin America affect the people and their way of life?
3. How does elevation affect climate?
4. (a) Give an example of how climate in one region of Latin America affects the vegetation that grows there.
   (b) How does this affect the way in which people live?
5. How are a country's natural resources tied to its economy?
6. What problems arise when a country depends too heavily on a single source of income? Support your answer with one or two examples.
7. How are the nations of Latin America trying to avoid the problems of relying on a single source of income?

Reviewing Key Terms

Match the definitions in Column I with the key terms in Column II

Column I

1. height of land above sea level
2. plains in Argentina and Uruguay
3. to add variety
4. river or stream that flows into a larger body of water
5. electricity generated by the power of moving water
6. large raised area of mostly level land
7. narrow strip of land that has water on both sides and joins two larger bodies of land

Column II

a. **isthmus**
b. **pampas**
c. **plateau**
d. **tributary**
e. **elevation**
f. **diversify**
g. **hydro-electricity**

Critical Thinking

1. **Identifying Central Issues** Explain the meaning of this statement, and give examples: "The weather in Latin America is a great friend to the people, but also a terrible enemy."
2. **Drawing Conclusions** "How a country uses its natural resources affects the well-being of its people." Do you agree or disagree with this statement? Explain your answer.

Graphic Organizer

Copy the chart to the right onto a separate sheet of paper. Then fill in the empty boxes to complete the chart. Use the maps in this chapter to help you.

	Physical Features	Climate	Vegetation	Natural Resources
Mexico and Central America				
The Caribbean				
South America				

Map Activity

For each place listed below, write the letter from the map that shows its location.

1. Colombia
2. Brazil
3. Jamaica
4. Mexico
5. Venezuela

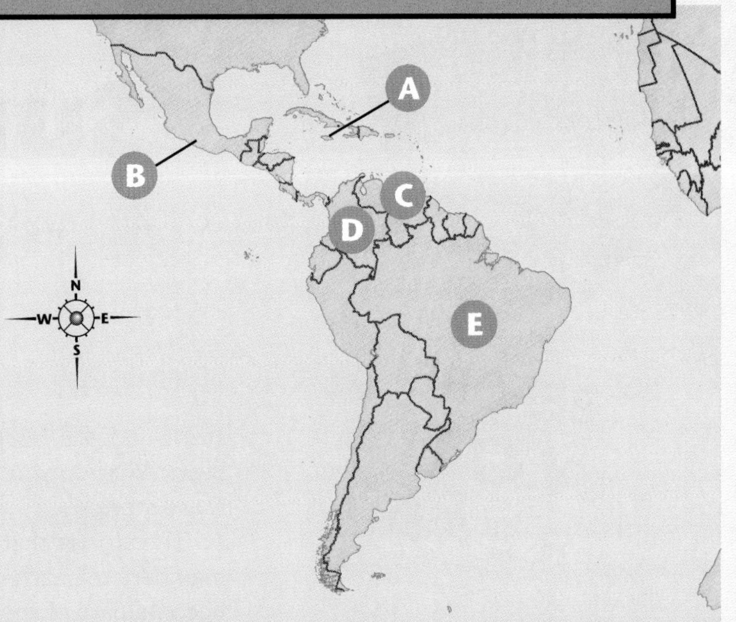

Writing Activity

Writing a Letter
Imagine that you are a visitor to Latin America. You are touring the whole region: Mexico, Central America, the Caribbean, and South America. Write a letter home, describing your trip. Write about such items as these: impressive sights, the weather, interesting facts you've learned, places you liked or didn't like.

Internet Activity

Use a search engine to find **The Green Arrow Guide to Central America.** Click on **El Salvador.** Click on **An Introduction to El Salvador** and read about El Salvador's geography and climate. Use the information to make a physical map of El Salvador.

Skills Review

Turn to the Skill Activity.

Review the steps for reading a regional map. Then complete the following: (a) In your own words, describe two factors that vary from climate to climate. (b) What types of climates can be found in Latin America?

How Am I Doing?

Answer these questions to help you check your progress.

1. Can I identify and describe the main regions of Latin America?
2. Do I understand how Latin America's physical features, climate, and vegetation affect the people who live in the region?
3. Can I identify important natural resources of Latin America?
4. Can I explain why Latin American countries want to diversify their economies?
5. What information from this chapter can I use in my book project?

The Surveyor

BY ALMA FLOR ADA

Reach Into Your Background

Do people in your family tell you stories about interesting or exciting events that have happened to them? What stories do you remember the best? What do you learn from these stories?

The stories that family members tell each other become part of the family history. Family stories are important because they teach people about their cultural heritage. Alma Flor Ada grew up in Cuba. The following story shows what Ada learned from one of the stories her father used to tell her.

Questions to Explore

1. What can you learn from this story about family life in Cuba?
2. What does this story tell you about how geography affects people's lives in Cuba?

My father, named Modesto after my grandfather, was a surveyor. Some of the happiest times of my childhood were spent on horseback, on trips where he would allow me to accompany him as he plotted the boundaries of small farms in the Cuban countryside. Sometimes we slept out under the stars, stringing our hammocks between the trees, and drank fresh water from springs. We always stopped for a warm greeting at the simple huts of the neighboring peasants, and my eyes would drink in the lush green forest crowned by the swaying leaves of the palm trees.

surveyor (sir VAY ur) *n.:* a person who measures land and geographic features

Since many surveying jobs called for dividing up land that a family had inherited from a deceased parent or relative, my father's greatest concern was that justice be achieved. It was not enough just to divide the land into equal portions. He also had to ensure that all parties would have access to roads, to water sources, to the most fertile soil. While I was able to join him in some trips, other surveying work involved large areas of land. On these jobs, my father was part of a team, and I would stay home, eagerly awaiting to hear the stories from his trip on his return.

◀ The equipment that surveyors use must be strong and lightweight.

Latin American families tend not to limit their family boundaries to those who are born or have married into it. Any good friend who spends time with the family and shares in its daily experiences is welcomed as a member. The following story from one of my father's surveying trips is not about a member of my blood family, but instead concerns a member of our extended family.

Félix Caballero, a man my father always liked to recruit whenever he needed a team, was rather different from the other surveyors. He was somewhat older, unmarried, and he kept his thoughts to himself. He came to visit our house daily. Once there, he would sit silently in one of the living room's four rocking chairs, listening to the lively conversations all around him. An occasional nod or a single word were his only contributions to those conversations. My mother and her sisters sometimes made fun of him behind his back. Even though they never said so, I had the impression that they questioned why my father held him in such high regard.

Then one day my father shared this story.

"We had been working on foot in mountainous country for most of the day. Night was approaching. We still had a long way to go to return to where we had left the horses, so we decided to cut across to the other side of the mountain, and soon found ourselves facing a deep gorge. The gorge was spanned by a railroad bridge, long and narrow, built for the sugarcane trains. There were no side rails or walkways, only a set of tracks resting on thick, heavy crossties suspended high in the air.

"We were all upset about having to climb down the steep gorge and up the other side, but

Predict Why do you think that Ada's father admires Félix so much?

recruit (ree KROOT) *v.:* to enlist or hire to join a group
gorge (gorj) *n.:* a narrow canyon with steep walls
span (span) *v.:* to extend across a space

▶ Walking across a railroad bridge is dangerous, because most are just wide enough for a train to pass.

dissuade (dis SWAYD) *v.*: to persuade not to do something
ominous (OM ih nus) *adj.*: threatening

the simpler solution, walking across the bridge, seemed too dangerous. What if a cane train should appear? There would be nowhere to go. So we all began the long descent . . . all except for Félix. He decided to risk walking across the railroad bridge. We all tried to dissuade him, but to no avail. Using an old method, he put one ear to the tracks to listen for vibrations. Since he heard none, he decided that no train was approaching. So he began to cross the long bridge, stepping from crosstie to crosstie between the rails, balancing his long red-and-white surveyor's poles on his shoulder.

"He was about halfway across the bridge when we heard the ominous sound of a steam engine. All eyes rose to Félix. Unquestionably he had heard it, too, because he had stopped in the middle of the bridge and was looking back.

"As the train drew closer, and thinking there was no other solution, we all shouted, 'Jump! Jump!', not even sure our voices would carry to where he stood, so high above us. Félix did look down at the rocky riverbed, which, as it was the dry season, held little water. We tried to encourage him with gestures and more shouts, but he had stopped looking down. We could not imagine what he was doing next, squatting down on the tracks, with the engine of the train already visible. And then, we understood. . . .

"Knowing that he could not manage to hold onto the thick wooden crossties, Félix laid his thin but resilient surveyor's poles across the ties, parallel to the rails. Then he let his body slip down between two of the ties, as he held onto the poles. And there he hung, below the bridge, suspended over the gorge but safely out of the train's path.

"The cane train was, as they frequently are, a very long train. To us, it seemed interminable. . . . One of the younger men said he counted two hundred and twenty cars. With the approaching darkness, and the smoke and shadows of the train, it was often difficult to see our friend. We had heard no human sounds, no screams, but could we have heard anything at all, with the racket of the train crossing overhead?

"When the last car began to curve around the mountain, we could just make out Félix's lonely figure still hanging beneath the bridge. We all watched in relief and amazement as he pulled himself up and at last finished walking, slowly and calmly, along the tracks to the other side of the gorge."

After I heard that story, I saw Félix Caballero in a whole new light. He still remained as quiet as ever, prompting a smile from my mother and her sisters as he sat silently in his rocking chair. But in my mind's eye, I saw him crossing that treacherous bridge, stopping to think calmly of what to do to save his life, emerging all covered with soot and smoke but triumphantly alive—a lonely man, hanging under a railroad bridge at dusk, suspended from his surveyor's poles over a rocky gorge.

If there was so much courage, such an ability to calmly confront danger in the quiet, aging man who sat rocking in our living room, what other wonders might lie hidden in every human soul?

resilient (rih ZIL yunt) *adj.:* able to withstand shock and bounce back from changes
treacherous (TRECH ur us) *adj.:* dangerous

Visualize Visualize the team of surveyors as they watch the train go by. How do you think they looked? How might they have acted?

EXPLORING YOUR READING

Look Back

1. How does this story change the way the author feels about Félix Caballero?

Think It Over

2. Why is surveying land important in Cuba?
3. Why do you think that the author's family accepts Félix Caballero as a member of their extended family?
4. What lesson does the author of this story hope to teach?

Go Beyond

5. What does this story tell you about the character traits that help a person to act in an emergency?

Ideas for Writing: A Short Story

6. Choose a story that has been told to you by a family member or friend. Or, choose a story that you have told others about an event that happened to you. Write the story. Include an introduction and conclusion that explain why the story is important to you.

Latin America
Shaped by Its History

SECTION 1
Early Civilizations of Middle America

SECTION 2
The Incas
People of the Sun

SECTION 3
European Conquest

SECTION 4
Independence

SECTION 5
Issues in Latin America Today

This map shows the location of three civilizations in Latin America that existed before Europeans arrived in the region.

Study the map
(a) What are the names of the civilizations shown on the map? (b) Which civilization is the oldest?

Consider the geography
Which civilization do you think was the most difficult to defend from invaders? Explain your answer.

Early Civilizations of Middle America

Reach Into Your Background

What does the word *pyramid* bring to mind? Write down three things you know about pyramids. Then, compare what you know about pyramids with the pyramids you will read about in this section.

Questions to Explore

1. What were the chief characteristics and accomplishments of Mayan and Aztec civilizations?
2. How have Latin America's early civilizations affected present-day cultures in Latin America?

Key Terms

maize
hieroglyphics

Key Places

Copán
Tikal
Valley of Mexico
Tenochtitlán

Fans cheered as the players brought the ball down the court. Suddenly, the ball flew into the air and sailed through the hoop. Fans and players shouted and screamed. Although this may sound like a championship basketball game, it is actually a moment of a game played over 1,000 years ago. The game was called pok-a-tok.

Pok-a-tok was a game played by the ancient Mayas. Using only their leather-padded hips and elbows, players tried to hit a five-pound (1.9 kg), six-inch (15.2 cm) rubber ball through a stone hoop mounted 30 feet (9.1 m) above the ground.

▼ This pok-a-tok court is in Copán, Honduras. How is it similar to a basketball court?

Mayan Civilization

How do we know about this ancient game? Crumbling ruins of pok-a-tok courts and ancient clay statues of players have been found at sites in Central America and southern Mexico. In these areas, Mayan civilization thrived from about A.D. 300 to A.D. 900. By studying ruins, scientists have learned much about Mayan civilization.

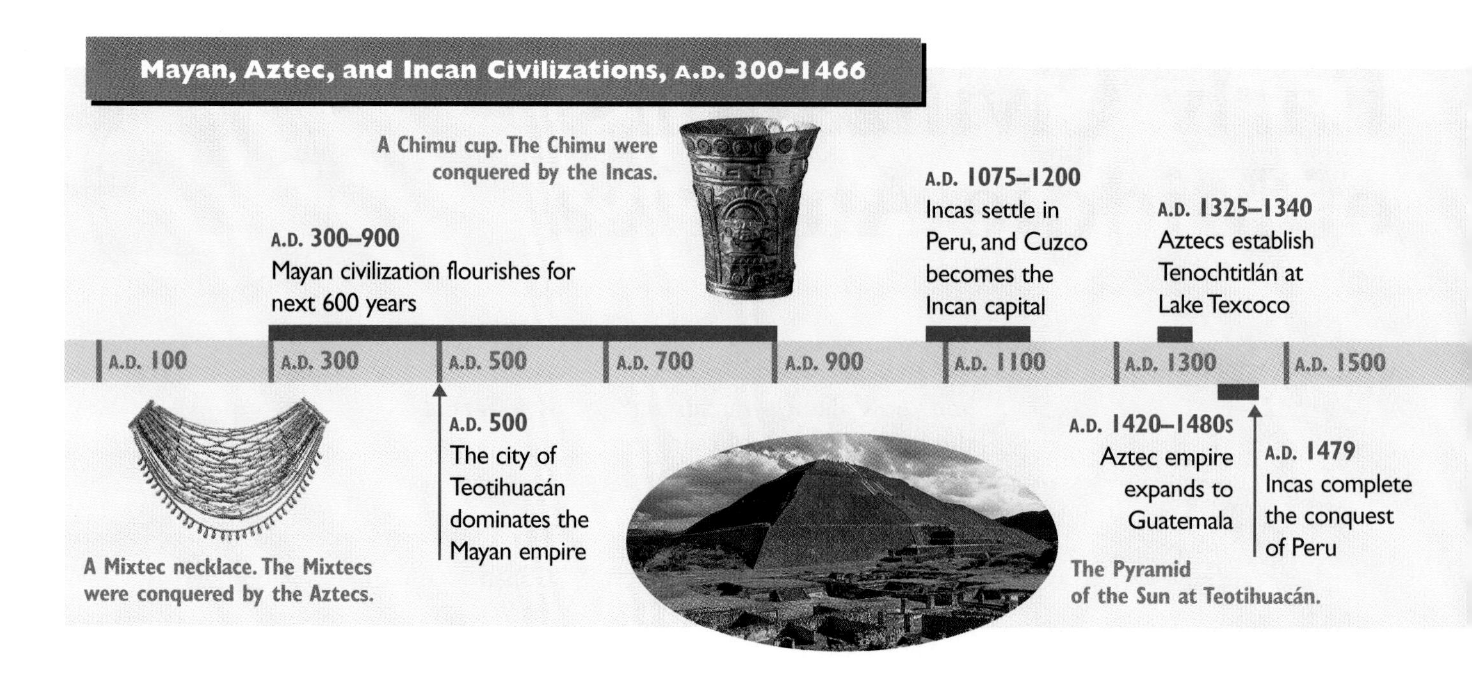

Mayan, Aztec, and Incan Civilizations, A.D. 300–1466
A.D. 300–900
Mayan civilization flourishes for next 600 years
A.D. 1075–1200
Incas settle in Peru, and Cuzco becomes the Incan capital
A.D. 1325–1340
Aztecs establish Tenochtitlán at Lake Texcoco
A.D. 100
A.D. 300
A.D. 500
A.D. 700
A.D. 900
A.D. 1100
A.D. 1300
A.D. 1500
A.D. 500
The city of Teotihuacán dominates the Mayan empire
A.D. 1420–1480s
Aztec empire expands to Guatemala
A.D. 1479
Incas complete the conquest of Peru

A Chimu cup. The Chimu were conquered by the Incas.

A Mixtec necklace. The Mixtecs were conquered by the Aztecs.

The Pyramid of the Sun at Teotihuacán.

The Mayas built great cities. One such city was Copán (ko PAHN) in the present-day country of Honduras. Another was Tikal (tee KAHL) in present-day Guatemala. Mayan cities were religious centers. A large pyramid-shaped temple stood in the center of the city. The Mayas worshipped their gods there. Farmers worked in fields surrounding the cities. Past the fields lay the dense tropical rain forest.

Mayan Farming and Science The Mayan farmers' most important crop was **maize,** or corn. Maize was the main food of the Mayas. They also grew beans, squash, peppers, avocados, and papayas. Mayan priests studied the stars and planets. They designed an accurate calendar, which they used to decide when to hold religious ceremonies. The Mayan calendar was more accurate than any used in Europe until the 1700s. The Mayas developed a system of writing using signs and symbols called **hieroglyphics** (hy ur oh GLIF iks). They also developed a number system that is similar to the present-day decimal system.

LINKS
TO
MATH

The Concept of Zero The Mayas created a numbering system that included the idea of zero. Zero is important in math because it is a symbol that shows that there is none of something. For example, to write the number 308, you need a symbol to show that there are no tens. Mathematicians consider the idea of zero to be one of the world's greatest inventions.

The Great Mystery of the Mayas About A.D. 900, the Mayas suddenly left their cities. No one knows why. Crop failures, war, disease, drought, or famine may have killed many Mayas. Or perhaps people rebelled against the control of the priests and nobles. The Mayas left their cities, but stayed in the region. Millions of Mayas still live in the countries of Mexico, Belize, Guatemala, Honduras, and El Salvador.

Aztec Civilization

Another ancient civilization of Middle America is that of the Aztecs. They arrived in the Valley of Mexico in the 1100s. The Valley of Mexico is in Central Mexico and includes the site of present-day Mexico City.

The Aztecs wandered about the valley looking for a permanent home until 1325. They finally settled on an island in Lake Texcoco. They changed the swampy lake into a magnificent city, which they called Tenochtitlán (tay nawch tee TLAHN). Tenochtitlán stood on the site of present-day Mexico City.

Tenochtitlán

Tenochtitlán, the Aztec capital, was built in the center of a lake. The Aztecs built floating islands by piling rich earth from the bottom of the lake onto rafts made of wood. After a while, the roots of plants and trees grew down to the lake bottom, anchoring the rafts. Some islands were the size of football fields. What do you think it would be like to live on a lake?

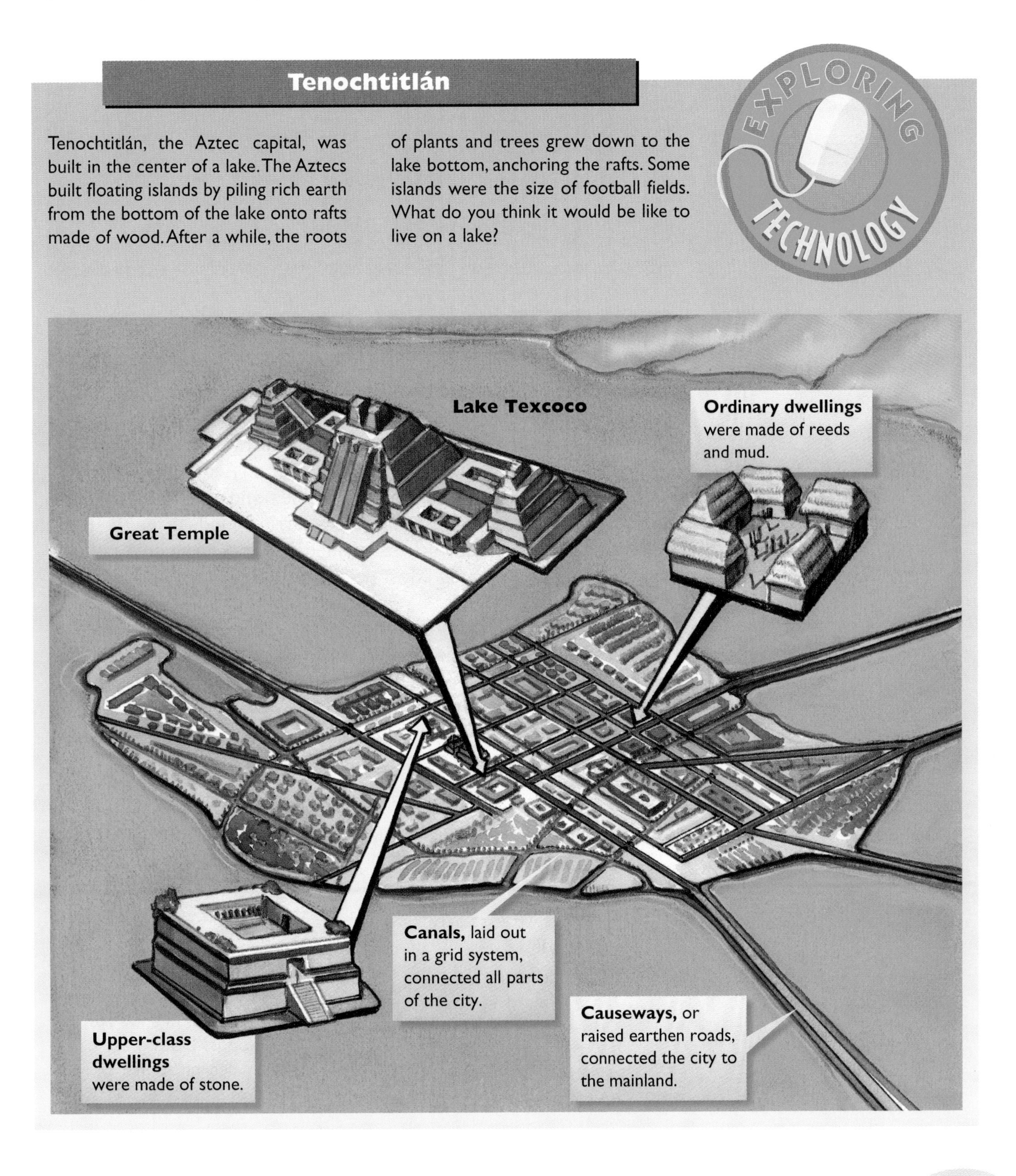
EXPLORING
TECHNOLOGY
Lake Texcoco
Ordinary dwellings were made of reeds and mud.
Great Temple
Canals, laid out in a grid system, connected all parts of the city.
Causeways, or raised earthen roads, connected the city to the mainland.
Upper-class dwellings were made of stone.

Aztec Astronomy

The Aztecs observed the stars and planets carefully. They named them after their gods, like Quetzalcoatl, shown at right. The Aztecs used their knowledge of astronomy to make calendars like the one below.

The Aztecs Expand Their Empire In the 1400s, Aztec warriors began conquering the other people in the region. They forced the people they conquered to pay tribute, or taxes. Tribute could be paid in food, cotton, gold, or slaves. The Aztecs grew rich from the tribute.

The Aztecs had an emperor who ruled over all Aztec lands. The rest of Aztec society had several classes. Nobles and priests helped the emperor. Warriors fought battles. Traders carried goods throughout the empire and beyond. Craftworkers created jewelry, garments, pottery, sculptures, and other goods. Most people, however, were farmers.

Other Aztec Accomplishments Tenochtitlán was a center of trade and learning. Aztec doctors made more than 1,000 medicines from plants. They used the medicines to lower fevers, cure stomachaches, and heal wounds. Like the Mayas, Aztec astronomers predicted eclipses and the movements of planets. Aztec priests kept records using hieroglyphics similar to those used by the Mayas.

1. **Define** (a) maize, (b) hieroglyphics.
2. **Identify** (a) Copán, (b) Tikal, (c) Valley of Mexico, (d) Tenochtitlán.
3. What were the main features of Mayan civilization?
4. How was Aztec society organized?

Critical Thinking

5. **Distinguishing Fact From Opinion** Tell if the following statements are facts or opinions. Explain why. (a) Mayan calendars were very accurate. (b) Aztec civilization was more advanced than Mayan civilization.

Activity

6. **Writing to Learn** What are some reasons for the decline of Mayan and Aztec civilizations? Does every society decline sooner or later?

The Incas

People of the Sun

Reach Into Your Background

The United States has roads that run from state to state. These roads are called interstate highways. Think about some ways that interstate highways are useful. Then, compare what you know about interstate highways with the roads you will read about in this section.

Questions to Explore

1. What was Incan civilization like?
2. How did the Incas interact with and change their environment to increase farmland and farm production?

Key Terms

aqueduct
quipu

Key People and Places

Pachacuti
Cuzco
Topa Inca

The runner sped along the mountain road. He lifted a horn made from a shell to his lips and blew. A second runner appeared and began running beside him. Without stopping, the first runner relayed to the second runner the message he carried. The second runner took off like the wind. He would not stop until he reached the next runner.

The Incas used runners to spread news from one place in their empire to another. Incan messengers carried news at a rate of 250 miles (402 km) a day. Without these runners, controlling the vast empire would have been very difficult.

The Rise of the Incas

This great and powerful empire had small beginnings. In about 1200, the Incas settled in Cuzco (KOOS koh), a village in the Andes that is now a city in the country of Peru. Most Incas were farmers. They grew maize and other crops. Through wars and conquest, the Incas won control of the entire Cuzco valley, one of many valleys that extend from the Andes to the Pacific Ocean.

In 1438, Pachacuti (PAHTCH an koo tee) became ruler of the Incas. The name Pachacuti means "he who shakes the earth." Pachacuti conquered the people who lived near the Pacific Ocean, from Lake Titicaca north to the city of Quito.

▼ The Incas shaped their stones so well that they did not need cement to hold a wall together.

Pachacuti demanded loyalty from the people he conquered. If they proved disloyal, he forced them off their land. He replaced them with people loyal to the Incas.

Pachacuti's son, Topa Inca, expanded the empire. In time, it stretched some 2,500 miles (4,023 km) from what is now Ecuador south along the Pacific coast through Peru, Bolivia, Chile, and Argentina. The 12 million people ruled by the Incas lived mostly in small villages.

Incan Accomplishments

Connect How do your family and community depend on roads?

The Incas were excellent farmers, builders, and managers. Their capital, Cuzco, was the center of government, trade, learning, and religion. In the 1500s, one of the first Spaniards to visit Cuzco described it as "large enough and handsome enough to compare to any Spanish city."

The emperor, and the nobles who helped him run the empire, lived in the city near the central plaza. They wore special headbands and earrings that showed their high rank. Most of the farmers and workers outside Cuzco lived in mud huts.

Roads and Aqueducts The Incas built more than 19,000 miles (30,577 km) of roads. The roads went over some of the most mountainous land in the world. The road system helped the Incas to govern their vast empire. Not only did runners use the roads to deliver messages, but Incan armies and trade caravans also used the roads for speedy travel.

▼Pachacuti built many cities. The most famous one is the "lost city" of Machu Picchu. It lies high in the Andes Mountains, 54 miles (87 km) northwest of Cuzco. **Interaction** Look closely at the picture. How did the Incas adapt their city to the mountains?

History on a String

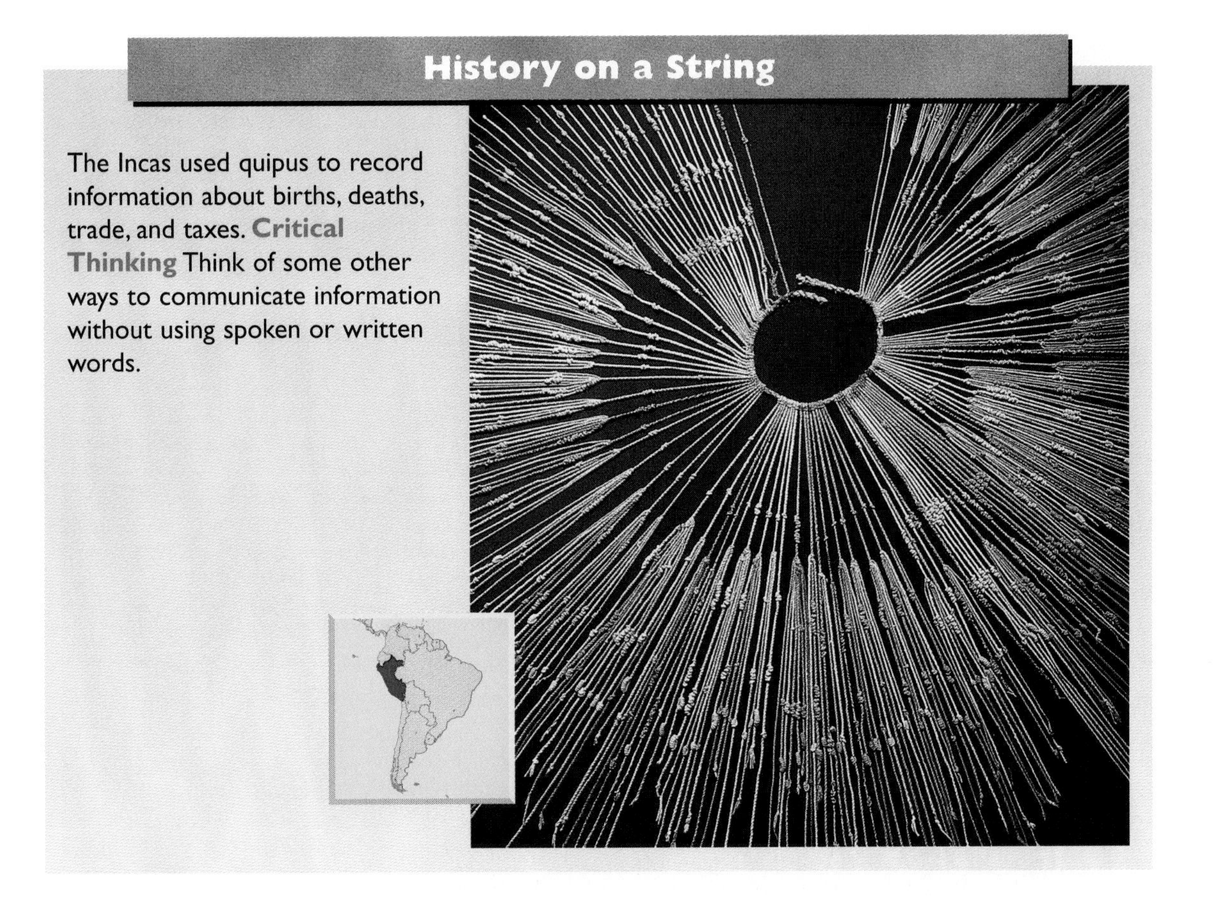

The Incas used quipus to record information about births, deaths, trade, and taxes. **Critical Thinking** Think of some other ways to communicate information without using spoken or written words.

The Incas also built canals and aqueducts to carry water to dry areas. An **aqueduct** is a pipe or channel designed to carry water from a distant source. One stone aqueduct carried water from a mountain lake almost 500 miles (805 km) to its destination. The system of canals and aqueducts allowed the Incas to irrigate land that was otherwise too dry to grow crops.

Government and Records The Incas organized their government carefully. The emperor chose nobles to govern each province. Each noble conducted a census to count people so they could be taxed. Local officials collected some of each village's crops as a tax. The villagers also had to work on government building projects. However, the government took care of the poor, the sick, and the elderly.

The Incas did not have a written language. Incan government officials and traders recorded information on knotted strings called **quipus** (KEE poos). Every quipu had a main cord with several colored strings attached to it. Each color represented a different item, and knots of different sizes at certain intervals stood for numbers.

Religion Like the Mayas and the Aztecs, the Incas worshipped many gods. The sun god, Inti, was an important god of the Incas. They believed Inti was their parent. They referred to themselves as "children of the sun." Another important Incan god was Viracocha (vee ra KOCH ah), the creator of all the people of the Andes.

Earthquake-proof Buildings Incan stone walls were so firmly constructed that even violent earthquakes could not knock them down. The walls swayed but did not crumble the way some modern buildings do. Engineers today are learning to make buildings that can resist an earthquake.

Farming in the Mountains

The Incas increased the amount of farmland in hilly areas by building terraces into the sides of steep slopes. The terraces helped keep soil from washing down the mountain. These terraces are at Pasaq, an ancient Incan fortress in Peru. **Interaction** Think of some other reasons why farming in the mountains might be hard.

Quechua Descendants of the Incas The Spanish conquered the Incan empire in the 1500s. However, descendants of the Incas still live in present-day Peru, Ecuador, Bolivia, Chile, and Colombia. They speak Quechua (KECH wah), the Incan language.

They use farming methods that are like those of the ancient Incas. The Incan culture also survives in the poncho and in other clothing styles, as well as in cloth woven into brightly colored complex patterns.

1. **Define** (a) aqueduct, (b) quipu.
2. **Identify** (a) Pachacuti, (b) Topa Inca, (c) Cuzco.
3. Why was a good network of roads important to the Incan empire?
4. Describe a few features of the Incan religion.

Critical Thinking

5. **Drawing Conclusions** Look at the shape of the Incan empire on the map on the opening page of this chapter. In an attack, what features would make the empire difficult to defend? What features would help defend the empire?

Activity

6. **Writing to Learn** Make a list of some of the ways the Incas used land for farming. Do you think the Incas made good use of farmland? Why or why not?

European Conquest

Reach Into Your Background
How do you decide what is right and what is wrong? Think of a time when you were not sure what was the right thing to do. As you read this section, notice how the people made decisions. Think about whether or not you agree with the decisions they made.

Questions to Explore

1. Why did Europeans sail to the Americas?
2. What were the effects of European rule on Native Americans in the region?

Key Terms
Treaty of Tordesillas
treaty
Line of Demarcation
conquistador
mestizo
hacienda
encomienda

Key People
Hernan Cortés
Malinche
Christopher Columbus
Moctezuma
Francisco Pizarro

Hernan Cortés was the Spanish soldier who conquered the Aztecs. He landed in Mexico in 1519 and soon met Malinche (mah LIHN chay). She was the daughter of a Mayan leader. Malinche, whom Cortés called Doña Marina, spoke several languages in addition to Mayan. She quickly learned Spanish. Malinche became Cortés's main translator. She also kept an eye on Aztec spies. Without Malinche, Cortés could not have conquered the Aztecs. Why did European explorers, like Cortés, want to conquer Native Americans? Why did some Native Americans, like Malinche, help the conquerers?

▼Sailors in the 1400s guided their ships using only the stars, a compass, and an astrolabe. Below is a drawing of an astrolabe.

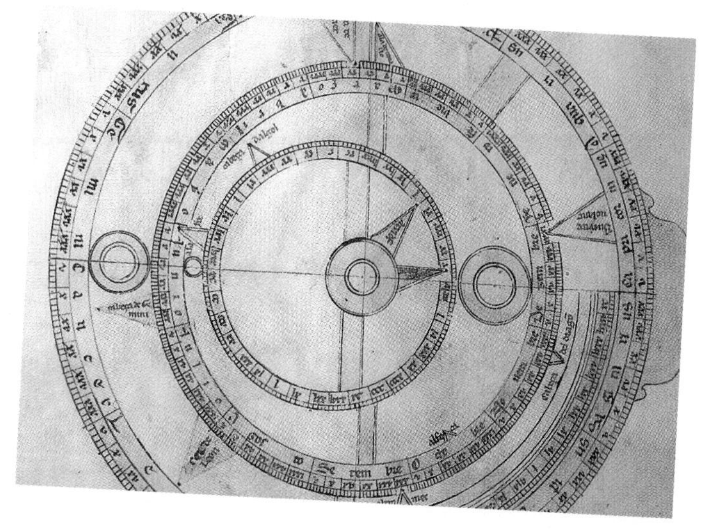

Europeans Arrive in the Americas

In the 1400s, Spain and Portugal searched for new trade routes to Asia. They knew that in Asia they would find expensive goods such as spices and silks. These goods could be traded for a profit.

Columbus Reaches America Christopher Columbus thought he could reach Asia by sailing west across the Atlantic Ocean. Columbus knew the world was round, as did most educated

Spanish Conquest and Colonization of the Americas

Map Study Columbus sailed to the Americas in 1492, 1493, 1498, and 1502. His 1502 voyage is shown here. Cortés sailed to the Americas in 1504 and conquered the Aztecs in 1519. Pizarro sailed in 1502 and conquered the Incas in 1533. **Movement** Once they reached the Caribbean, what factors do you think helped the Spanish to find the Aztec and Incan empires so quickly? **Regions** South America has two major language regions: Spanish and Portuguese. How did the Line of Demarcation create these regions?

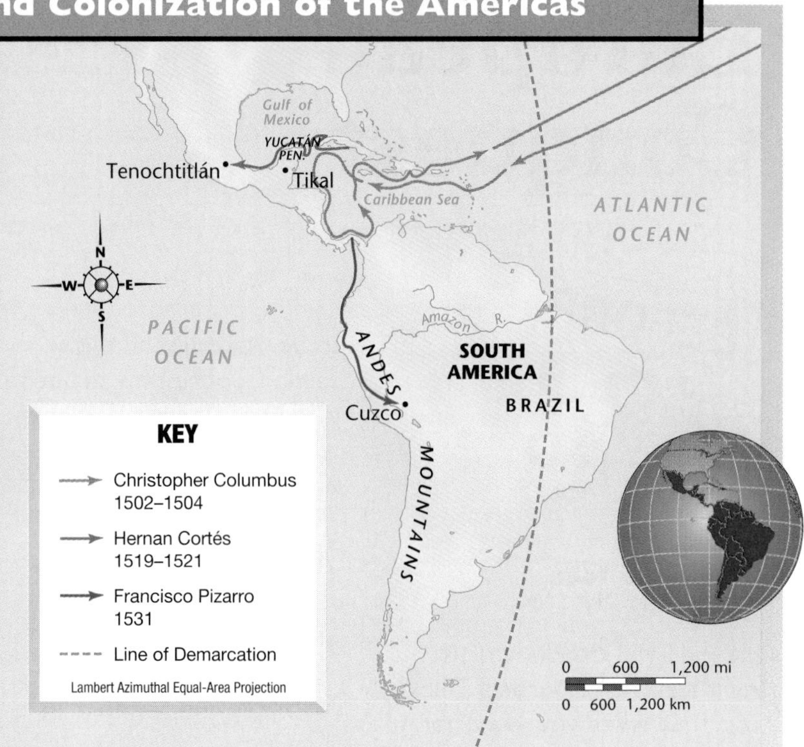

Navigating Without Modern Instruments
Explorers like Columbus did not have radar, satellites, and computers to guide their ships. They used the stars as a reference. Sailors imagined a triangle with a straight line from the ship to the horizon, and a line from the horizon to a star. Measuring the angle between the line to the star and the horizon helped them figure out their location.

Europeans. But Columbus believed the distance around the world was shorter than it was. First Columbus asked Portugal to sponsor his voyage. Then he asked Spain. Queen Isabella of Spain finally agreed.

Columbus set sail in early August, 1492. Some 10 weeks later, on October 12, he spotted land. Columbus thought he had reached the East Indies in Asia, so he described the people there as Indians.

Dividing the World Spain and Portugal soon became fierce rivals. Each country tried to stop the other from claiming land in the Americas. In 1494, Spain and Portugal signed the **Treaty of Tordesillas** (tor day SEE yas). A **treaty** is an agreement in writing made between two or more countries. The treaty set an imaginary line from North Pole to South Pole at about 50° longitude, called the **Line of Demarcation.** It gave Spain the right to settle and trade west of the line. Portugal could do the same east of the line. The only part of South America that is east of the line is roughly the eastern half of present-day Brazil. Because of the Treaty of Tordesillas, the language and background of Brazil are Portuguese.

A Clash of Cultures

Spanish explorers heard stories of wealthy kingdoms in the Americas. They hoped to find gold and other treasures. Spanish rulers did not pay for the trips of the explorers. Instead, they gave the **conquistadors** (kon KEES ta dors), or conquerors, the right to hunt for treasure. The conquistadors could also settle in America. In exchange, conquistadors agreed to give Spain one fifth of any treasures they found. If a conquistador failed, he lost his own fortune. If he succeeded, both he and Spain gained fame, wealth, and glory.

Cortés Conquers the Aztecs In 1519, Hernan Cortés sailed to the coast of Mexico in search of treasure. He brought a small army with him. The Aztec ruler Moctezuma (mahk the ZOOM uh) heard that a strange ship was offshore. He sent spies to find out about it. The spies reported back to Moctezuma:

> "We must tell you that we saw a house in the water, out of which came white men, with white hands and faces, and very long, bushy beards, and clothes of every color: white, yellow, red, green, blue, and purple, and on their heads they wore round hats."

The Aztecs demanded heavy tribute from the peoples who lived near them, so these groups disliked the Aztecs. Cortés made agreements with these groups. Then he headed for Tenochtitlán with 500 soldiers and 16 horses. Aztec spies told Moctezuma that the Spanish were coming. The Aztecs had never seen horses before. Moctezuma's spies described the Spanish as "supernatural creatures riding on hornless deer, armed in iron, fearless as gods." Moctezuma thought Cortés might be the god Quetzalcoatl (ket sahl koh AHTL). According to Aztec legend, Quetzalcoatl had promised to return to rule the Aztecs.

With a heavy heart, Moctezuma welcomed Cortés and his soldiers. Cortés tried to convince Moctezuma to surrender to Spain. After several months, Moctezuma agreed. But the peace did not last long. Spanish soldiers killed some Aztecs. Then the Aztecs began to fight against the Spanish. The battle was fierce and bloody. Moctezuma was killed, and Cortés and his army barely escaped.

With the help of the Aztecs' enemies, Cortés surrounded and attacked Tenochtitlán. In 1521, the Aztecs finally surrendered. By then, about 240,000 Aztecs had died and 30,000 of Cortés's allies had been killed. Tenochtitlán and the Aztec empire lay in ruins.

Pizarro Conquers the Incas Francisco Pizarro (fran SIS koh pih ZAR oh), like Cortés, was a Spanish conquistador. He heard stories about the rich Incan kingdom. Pizarro planned to attack the Pacific coast of South America. In 1531, Pizarro set sail with a small force of 180 Spanish soldiers. Pizarro captured and killed the Incan

A Court Welcome

This historical painting shows Moctezuma welcoming Cortés to his court. **Critical Thinking** Based on this painting, what conclusions can you draw about Aztec wealth?

Connect How would you feel if you saw people riding on a large animal that you had never seen before?

Ask Questions Suppose that you were a doctor living in South America at the time of the Conquest. What questions would you ask to discover why so many Native Americans were dying of European diseases?

emperor. He also killed many other Incan leaders. By 1535, Pizarro had conquered most of the Incan empire, including the capital, Cuzco.

The conquistadors defeated the two most powerful empires in the Americas. It took them only 15 years. How did they do it? The Spanish had guns and cannons that the Native Americans had never seen. They also rode horses. At first, horses terrified Native Americans. The Europeans also carried diseases such as smallpox, measles, and chicken pox. These diseases wiped out entire villages. And, because of local rivalry, some Native Americans like Malinche helped the Spanish conquistadors.

Colonization

By the 1540s, Spain claimed land throughout much of the Americas. Spain's lands stretched from what today is Kansas all the way south to the tip of South America. Brazil was claimed by Portugal.

Spain Organizes Its Empire Spain divided its territory into provinces. Spain also set up a strong government. The two most important provinces were New Spain and Peru. The capital of New Spain was Mexico City. Lima became the capital city of Peru.

Lima's geographic layout was based on the Spanish social classes. The most powerful citizens lived in the center of Lima. They either came from Spain or had Spanish parents. **Mestizos,** people of mixed Spanish and Native American descent, lived on the outskirts of the city. Many

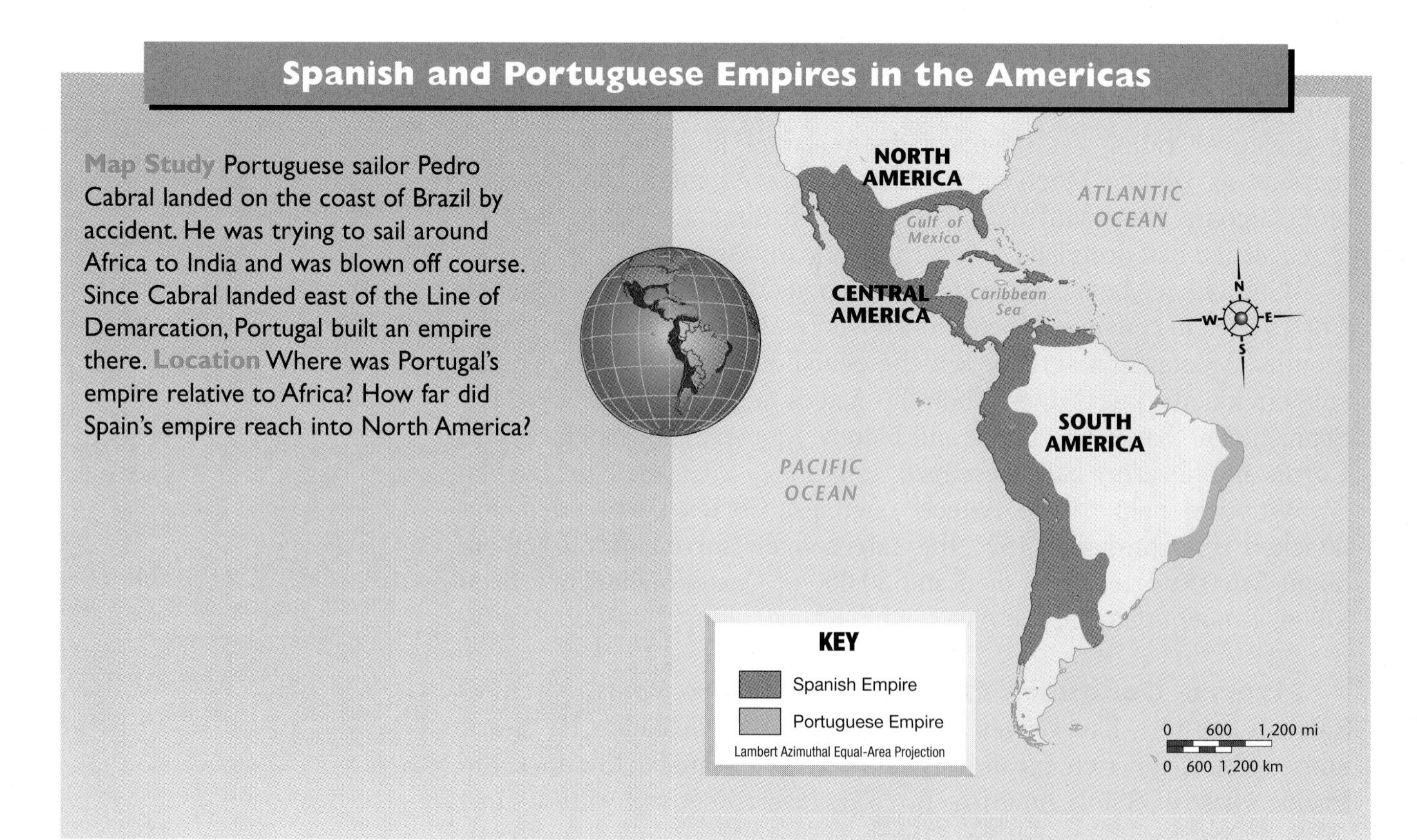

Map Study Portuguese sailor Pedro Cabral landed on the coast of Brazil by accident. He was trying to sail around Africa to India and was blown off course. Since Cabral landed east of the Line of Demarcation, Portugal built an empire there. **Location** Where was Portugal's empire relative to Africa? How far did Spain's empire reach into North America?

mestizos were poor. But some were middle class or quite wealthy. Native Americans were the least powerful class. Most Native Americans continued to live in the countryside. The Spanish forced them to work on haciendas. A **hacienda** (hah see EN duh) was a plantation owned by Spaniards or the Catholic Church.

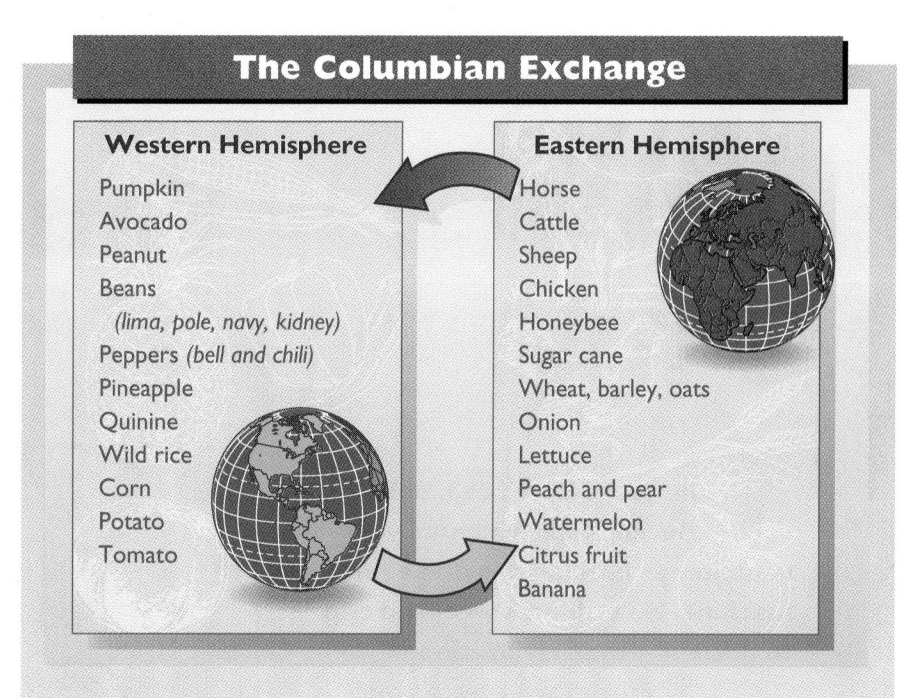

The Columbian Exchange
Western Hemisphere
Pumpkin
Avocado
Peanut
Beans
(lima, pole, navy, kidney)
Peppers (bell and chili)
Pineapple
Quinine
Wild rice
Corn
Potato
Tomato
Eastern Hemisphere
Horse
Cattle
Sheep
Chicken
Honeybee
Sugar cane
Wheat, barley, oats
Onion
Lettuce
Peach and pear
Watermelon
Citrus fruit
Banana

Chart Study Goods, as well as people, crossed the Atlantic in the years after the conquest. Do you think that the Eastern and Western hemispheres benefitted equally from the Columbian Exchange? Why or why not?

The Effect of European Rule Spain gave its settlers **encomiendas** (en KOH mee en dus), which were rights to demand taxes or labor from Native Americans. Native Americans were allowed to stay on their own land, so the Spanish claimed that encomiendas protected Native Americans. In fact, encomiendas forced Native Americans to work for the settlers. At first, the Native Americans worked only on the haciendas. But when silver was discovered in Mexico and Peru, the Spanish forced Native Americans to also work in the mines. Some died from overwork and malnutrition. Many died from European diseases. In 1519, New Spain had a Native American population of 25 million. Only 3 million survived the first 50 years of Spanish rule. In 1532, 12 million Native Americans lived in Peru. Fifty years later, there were fewer than 2 million.

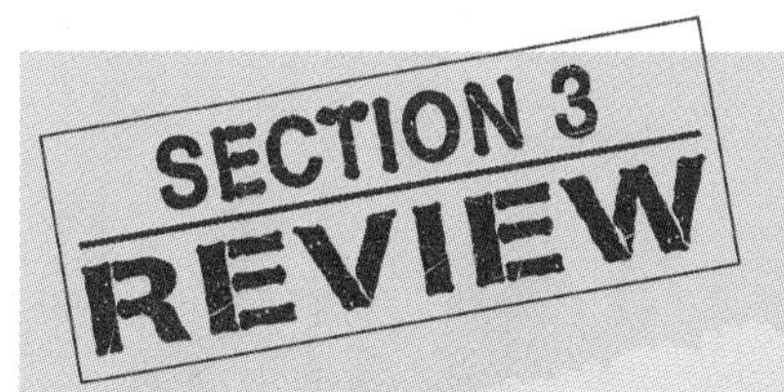

1. **Define** (a) Treaty of Tordesillas, (b) treaty, (c) Line of Demarcation, (d) conquistador, (e) mestizo, (f) hacienda, (g) encomienda.
2. **Identify** (a) Hernan Cortés, (b) Malinche, (c) Christopher Columbus, (d) Moctezuma, (e) Francisco Pizarro.
3. What was the effect of the Treaty of Tordesillas on the European settlement of the Americas?
4. How did the Spanish conquest affect Native Americans?

Critical Thinking

5. **Recognizing Bias** The Treaty of Tordesillas affected the lives of millions of Native Americans. However, Native Americans were not asked about the treaty. What do you think this says about European attitudes toward Native Americans?

Activity

6. **Writing to Learn** Write two paragraphs: one by a Native American who has just seen a European for the first time and another by a European who has just seen a Native American for the first time.

Using a Time Line

The year is A.D. 2098. Biff Bucko, a star geography student, jumps into his shiny new time machine. He's off on a weekend trip to ancient Mayan civilization.

The centuries whiz by. As our hero approaches the year A.D. 1000, he slows to a stop. "When was Mayan culture at its height?" he wonders. Biff looks to the left and right. "Hmm . . . I think it's this way." Biff should have checked the time line in his glove compartment. If he had, he would have known that Mayan civilization declined after A.D. 900. Instead, he's landed in the 1400s where the Aztecs are busy conquering Middle America. "Oops," thinks Biff as a band of Aztec warriors descends upon him.

Studying the past makes you a kind of time traveler, too. Still, it's always best to know where you're going. Creating a time line can help.

Get Ready

A time line is like a map of the past. It keeps important dates in order so you don't get lost in time. Keep yours handy while you study for a test, research a report, or read for fun.

To make a time line you'll need:

- two sheets of paper
- thirteen paper clips

Try It Out

A. Make a paper ruler. Fold one sheet of paper in half the long way. Now fold it over again. You'll use this paper as a ruler to measure your time line.

B. Mark the divisions of time periods. Attach three paper clips along the top edge of your paper ruler. Slide one to the left corner, one to the right corner, and one to the exact center.

C. Look at dates for your time line. Your time line will cover a span of about 1,200 years. Label the left paper clip on your ruler with the year 300. Label the right paper clip 1500 and the middle one 900.

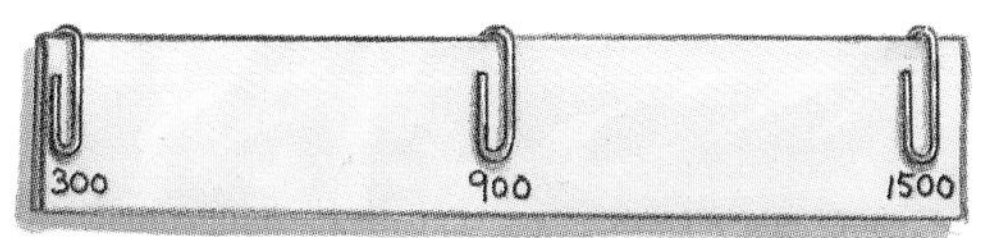

D. Figure out time intervals. Space your other paper clips evenly across the top of the ruler. The space between each will stand for 100 years. Label your clips with the years 400, 500, and so on.

E. Locate the dates on your time line. Turn your other paper so the long side is on top. Draw a straight line across it. Using your ruler, mark the 100-year intervals. Then mark where each of the four time line dates belongs on the line. (Estimate for the dates 1345 and 1438.) Label each mark with its date and event.

Dates for Your Time Line			
300	**900**	**1385**	**1438**
Mayan civilization rises	Mayas leave their cities	Aztecs found the city of Tenochtitlán	Pachacuti founds the Incan Empire

Apply the Skill

Now choose some other dates in Latin American history that you want to remember. Follow the steps below to create a time line.

1. **Design a time line ruler.** First look at the dates you've selected. What time span will your time line cover? For a long span, each paper clip could mark 100 years. For a shorter span, you could mark every 50 years, 10 years, or 1 year. Choose a measurement that makes sense.
2. **Find a date to start your ruler.** Take the earliest date you chose for your time line. Round it to a lower number. For example, if you are measuring every 50 years, round the date 1492 down to 1450.
3. **Find a date to end your ruler.** Take your last date. Round it up.
4. **Count the paper clips you'll need.** Say your ruler starts at 1450, ends at 1650, and marks every 50 years. Count: 1450, 1500, 1550, 1600, 1650. That's five clips.
5. **Put a clip at each end of the ruler.** Space the others evenly. Label each with its year. Now use the ruler to mark points on your time line. Label each point with its date and event.

Independence

Reach Into Your Background

What qualities do you think make a hero? What about bravery, or doing the right thing no matter what the personal cost? Jot down at least three qualities that you think a hero should have.

Questions to Explore

1. How did Latin American nations win independence from their European rulers?
2. How did the American and French revolutions influence events in Latin America?

Key Terms

revolution
criollo
caudillo

Key People

Miguel Hidalgo
Agustín de Iturbide
Simón Bolívar
José de San Martín
Dom Pedro

On August 24, 1791, the night sky over Saint-Domingue (san duh MANG) glowed red and gold. The French Caribbean colony was on fire. The slaves were sick of being mistreated by their white masters. They finally had rebelled. Now they were burning every piece of white-owned property they could find. This Night of Fire was the beginning of the first great fight for freedom in Latin America. Toussaint L'Ouverture (too SAN loo vur TOOR), a former slave, led the people of Saint-Domingue in this fight for more than 10 years. Eventually they won. They founded the independent country of Haiti (HAY tee) in 1804.

The flame of liberty lit in Haiti soon spread across Latin America. By 1825, most of the region was independent. Latin Americans would no longer be ruled by Europe.

▼ Toussaint L'Ouverture was captured by the French, but his followers won Haiti's independence.

Independence in Mexico

Haiti's leaders drew encouragement from two famous revolutions. A **revolution** is a political movement in which the people overthrow the government and set up another. During the 1770s and early 1780s, the 13 British colonies in North America fought a war to free themselves from Britain's rule. In 1789, the ordinary people of France staged a violent uprising against their royal rulers. These actions inspired not only the people of Haiti, but also people across Latin America.

Criollos (kree OH yohz) paid particular attention to these events. A **criollo** had Spanish parents, but had been born in Latin America.

Criollos often were the wealthiest and best-educated people in the Spanish colonies. Few criollos had any political power, however. Only people born in Spain could hold government office. Many criollos attended school in Europe. There, they learned about the ideas that inspired revolution in France and the United States. The criollos especially liked the idea that people had the right to govern themselves.

The "Cry of Dolores" Mexico began its struggle for self-government in 1810. Miguel Hidalgo (mee GEHL ee DAHL goh) led the way. He was a criollo priest in the town of Dolores. With other criollos in Dolores, he planned to begin a revolution.

In September 1810, the Spanish government discovered Hidalgo's plot. But before the authorities could arrest him, Hidalgo took action. He wildly rang the church bells. A huge crowd gathered. "Recover from the hated Spaniards the land stolen from your forefathers," he shouted. "Long live America, and death to the bad government!"

Hidalgo's call for revolution became known as the "Cry of Dolores." It attracted some 80,000 fighters in a matter of weeks. This army consisted mostly of mestizos and Native Americans. They were angry. They wanted revenge against anybody connected with the Spanish government. The rebels won some victories. Their luck, however, soon changed. By the beginning of 1811, they were in full retreat. Hidalgo tried to flee the country. However, government soldiers soon captured him. He was put on trial and convicted of treason. Hidalgo was executed by firing squad in July 1811.

Ask Questions What would you like to know about the attitudes of Mexican criollos toward the revolution?

The Cry of Dolores

Hidalgo made the "Cry of Dolores" on September 16. Mexico celebrates its independence every year on that day. **Critical Thinking** Why do you think that the painter of this mural included so many people in the background behind Hidalgo?

African Independence
Although Africa is closer to Europe than to Latin America, Europeans began to colonize Africa later. Europeans began claiming parts of Africa in the 1880s. Like the people of Latin America, many people in Africa later were inspired by the ideas of self-government and independence. African countries began to achieve independence in the 1950s and 1960s.

Independence Finally Comes The Spanish could execute the revolution's leaders, but they could not kill its spirit. Small rebel groups kept fighting. Then Agustín de Iturbide (ee toor BEE day) joined the rebels. He was a high-ranking officer in the Spanish army. Many people who had opposed the rebellion changed their minds. They had viewed Hidalgo as a dangerous hothead. But Iturbide was different. He was a criollo and an army officer. They could trust Iturbide to protect their interests. They decided to support the rebellion. In 1821, Iturbide declared Mexico independent.

South American Independence

Simón Bolívar (see MOHN boh LEE vahr) was not the first Latin American revolutionary leader. Almost certainly, however, he was the greatest. He was born in the country of Venezuela in 1783. His family was one of the richest and most important families in Latin America. Like most wealthy Latin Americans, he went to school in Spain. There, he met Prince Ferdinand, the heir to the Spanish throne. They decided to play a game similar to present-day badminton. Custom required that Bolívar show respect for the prince by losing. Instead, Bolívar played hard and tried to win. He even knocked the prince's hat off with his racquet! The angry prince demanded an apology. Bolívar refused. He claimed it was an accident. Furious, the prince insisted that they fight a duel. He soon calmed down, however.

South America: Independence

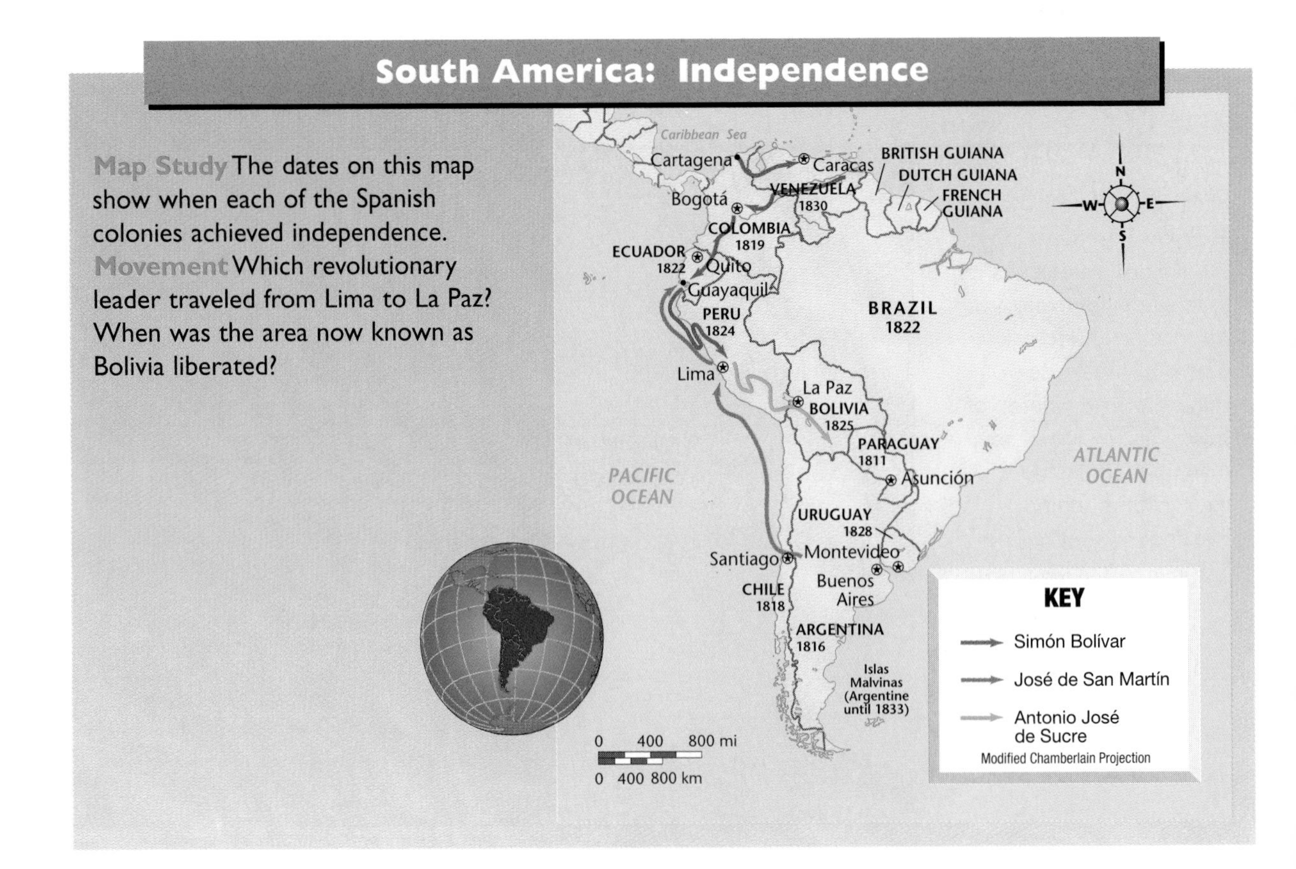

Map Study The dates on this map show when each of the Spanish colonies achieved independence. **Movement** Which revolutionary leader traveled from Lima to La Paz? When was the area now known as Bolivia liberated?

Many years later, these two faced off again. This time, Bolívar knocked Spanish America from under Ferdinand's feet.

Bolívar and San Martín: The Liberators Bolívar joined the fight for Venezuelan independence in 1804. Six years later he became its leader. Bolívar was completely certain that he would win. His confidence, courage, and daring inspired his soldiers. They enjoyed victory after victory. By 1822, Bolívar's troops had freed a large area from Spanish rule (the future countries of Colombia, Venezuela, Ecuador, and Panama). This newly liberated region formed Gran Colombia. Bolívar became its president. Even though his country was free, Bolívar did not give up the cause of independence. "The Liberator," as he was now known, turned south toward Peru.

José de San Martín (san mahr TEEN), an Argentine, had lived in Spain and served in the Spanish army. When Argentina began its fight for freedom, he quickly offered to help. San Martín took good care of his troops. He shared each hardship they had to suffer. They loved him for it. Many said they would follow San Martín anywhere—even over the snow-capped Andes Mountains. In 1817, his soldiers had to do just that. He led them through high passes in the Andes into Chile. This bold action took the Spanish completely by surprise. In a matter of months, Spain was defeated. San Martín declared Chile's independence. Then he turned his attention to Peru.

Again, San Martín took an unexpected action. This time, he attacked from the sea. The Spanish were not prepared for San Martín's tactics. Spanish defenses quickly collapsed. In July 1821, San Martín pushed inland and seized Lima, the capital of Peru.

▶ Nearly every town or city in South America has a central square with a statue of Bolívar or San Martín. These high school girls are visiting the statue of Bolívar in Meridá, Venezuela.

A year later, San Martín met with Bolívar to discuss the fight for independence. Historians do not know what happened in that meeting. But afterward, San Martín suddenly gave up his command. He left Bolívar to continue the fight alone. This Bolívar did. Eventually, he drove the remaining Spanish forces out of South America altogether. By 1825, only Cuba and Puerto Rico were still ruled by Spain.

Brazil Takes a Different Route to Freedom Portugal's colony, Brazil, became independent without fighting a war. In the early 1800s, French armies invaded Spain and Portugal. Portugal's royal family fled to Brazil for safety. The king returned to Portugal in 1821. However, he left his son, Dom Pedro, to rule the colony. Dom Pedro used more power than the king expected. He declared Brazil independent in 1822. Three years later, Portugal quietly admitted that Brazil was independent.

Ask Questions What questions would you ask Simón Bolívar about his dream of a "United States of South America"?

Challenges of Independence

After winning independence, Latin American leaders faced hard challenges. They had to decide how to govern their nations. Also, after years of fighting, Latin American nations were very poor.

Simón Bolívar dreamed of uniting South America as one country. Gran Colombia was the first step. Bolívar hoped it would become the "United States of South America." In trying to govern Gran Colombia, however, Bolívar found that his dream was impossible. Latin America was a huge area, divided by the Andes and dense rain forests. Also, the leaders of the countries in Gran Columbia wanted little to do with Bolívar. In poor health, he retired from politics.

Even though he did not last long in office, Bolívar set the standard for Latin American leaders. Most were **caudillos** (kow DEE yohs), military officers who ruled very strictly. Bolívar cared about the people he governed. Many other caudillos did not. These others just wanted to stay in power and get rich.

SECTION 4 REVIEW

1. **Define** (a) revolution, (b) criollo, (c) caudillo.
2. **Identify** (a) Miguel Hidalgo, (b) Agustín de Iturbide, (c) Simón Bolívar, (d) José de San Martín, (e) Dom Pedro.
3. What world events influenced the independence movement in Latin America?
4. How was Brazil's path to independence different from that of the rest of South America?

Critical Thinking

5. **Identifying Central Issues** What do you think Simón Bolívar had in mind when he wanted South America to become the "United States of South America"?

Activity

6. **Writing to Learn** Imagine you are a journalist with Bolívar's or San Martín's army. Describe the army's main actions.

Issues in Latin America Today

Reach Into Your Background

Most people like the feeling of being able to take care of themselves. What could you do now to prepare for your own independence?

Questions to Explore

1. How are Latin American nations trying to improve their economies?
2. What issues has the move to the cities created in Latin America?

Key Terms

invest
economy
campesino
rural
urban

Key Places

Brazil

Samuel Zemurray came from Russia to the United States in 1892. He worked for his aunt and uncle, who owned a store in Alabama. As part of his job, Zemurray sometimes traveled to the port city of Mobile. He noticed that fruit and vegetable traders there often threw away ripe bananas. They knew the bananas would spoil before reaching stores. Zemurray bought the ripe bananas and delivered them to stores overnight. The quick delivery meant that the fruit was still fit to be sold. Zemurray's business was so successful that he decided to expand. He did this by buying land in the country of Honduras, where bananas were grown. Zemurray soon became a leading banana grower.

▼ Many large-scale farming operations in Latin America are still foreign-owned.

Foreign Investment

In the 1900s, many companies like Zemurray's invested in Latin America. To **invest** means to spend money to earn more money. Some companies owned farms and grew crops such as sugar and bananas. Other foreign companies ran mines. By the mid-1900s, most businesses in Latin America were owned by or did work for foreign companies. As a result, foreign companies became powerful in Latin American economies. A country's **economy** is made up of the ways that goods and services are produced and made available to people. When money from the sale of goods and services comes into or goes out of a country, it affects the country's economy.

Predict What steps do you think Latin American countries took to balance their economies?

Foreign companies made huge profits from their businesses in Latin America. However, these companies did little to help Latin American countries build their economies. Many Latin Americans realized that it was important to improve their economies. They needed to build factories so that they could make their own manufactured goods. They also needed to grow many different kinds of crops and to develop a wide range of resources.

Some Latin American countries soon took steps to carry out these economic building plans. And they proved successful. During the 1960s and early 1970s, the economies of many Latin American countries grew. However, in the early 1980s, oil prices went up. Latin American countries needed oil to run their factories—and they had to pay higher and higher prices for it. At the same time, the prices of Latin American products fell. Latin American countries had to spend more money, but they were making less and less. To make up the difference, they borrowed money from wealthy countries such as the United States. By the 1980s, many Latin American countries had huge foreign debts.

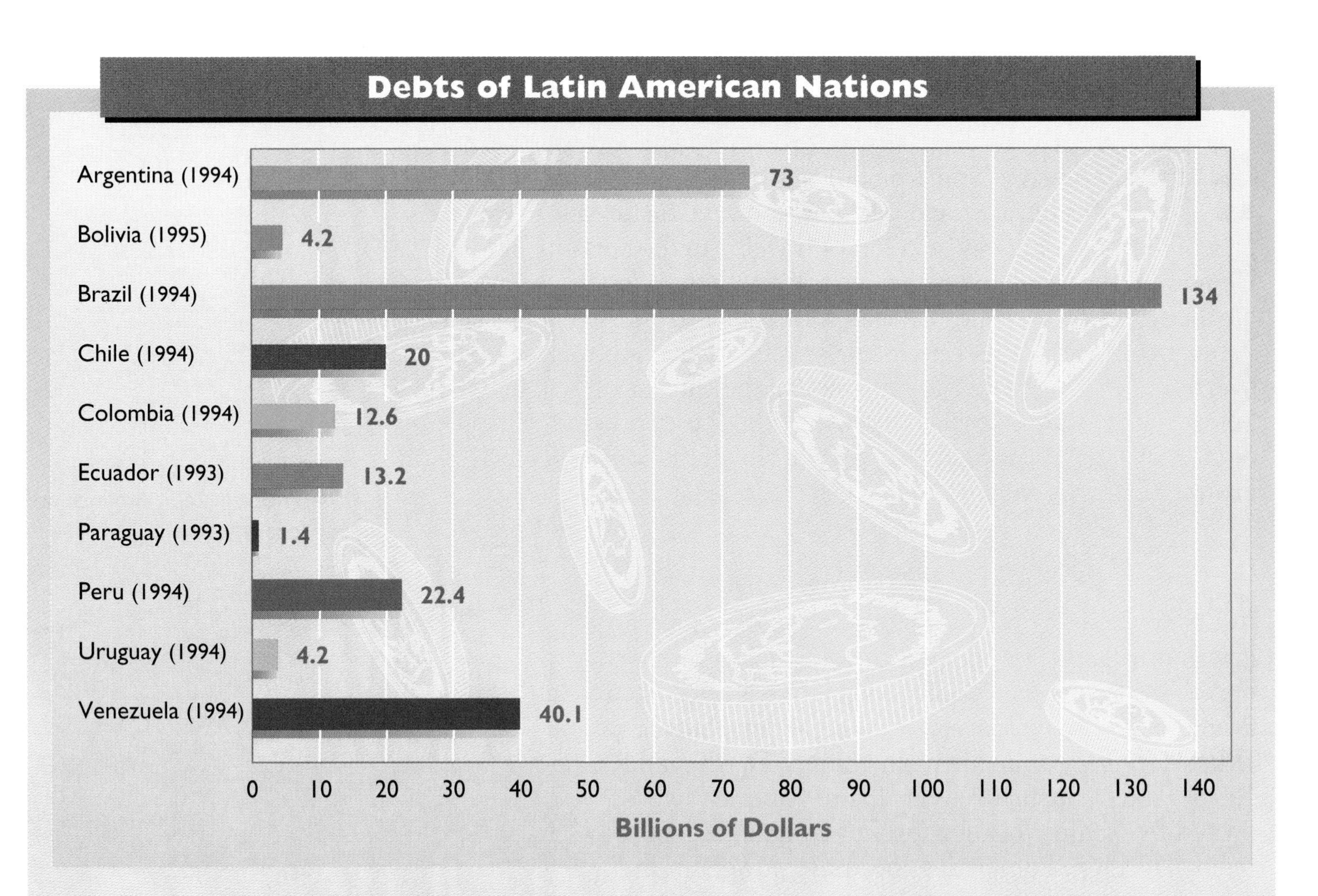

Chart Study Argentina and Brazil are the two Latin American countries with the most industry. They also have the most foreign debt. **Critical Thinking** Why do you think that Argentina and Brazil have more debt than other countries?

Facing Economic Challenges

People in Latin American countries have expanded their economies by building more factories and growing different kinds of crops. And they have taken other steps to improve their economies.

Foreign companies still invest in Latin America. But most Latin American countries limit how investments can be made. They want to prevent foreign countries from having too much control over important parts of their economies. Some countries, for instance, have tried to stop foreign companies from acquiring too much land.

Latin American countries have tried to improve their economies by cooperating with one another. For a long time, most Latin American countries did not trade with one another. They did not need to because, for the most part, they all produced the same kinds of goods. Recently, however, some countries have developed new industries. The products these countries make can be traded to other countries in the region. This kind of trade has increased in the last few years. Latin American countries also have formed several organizations that encourage cooperation in the region.

African Economies Many African countries are also trying to improve their economies with less foreign investment. Africans are trying to earn more money by growing more types of cash crops. They are also working to build their own industries and mine their own resources without help from foreign companies.

Land Distribution

The issue of how land is used greatly affects the future of Latin America's economies. Land is one of Latin America's most important resources. Some people and companies own great amounts of land in

Building Televisions on an Assembly Line

In the last 50 years, Latin American countries have begun to produce many more products in factories like this one in Brazil. **Critical Thinking** What skills do you think these factory workers need?

A Farm in El Salvador

In El Salvador, many farmers do not have modern farming equipment. They use traditional wooden plows and oxen. **Critical Thinking** What would it cost a farmer to own oxen? How would this cost compare to the cost of owning a tractor?

Latin America but most people in the region do not own any land. In Brazil, for example, 45 percent of the land is owned by only 1 percent of the population.

Dividing the Land Much of the farmland in Latin America is owned by a few wealthy families. This land is occupied by haciendas where crops are grown to sell abroad. In contrast, many poor farmers—known as **campesinos** (kahm peh SEE nohs)—own only small tracts of land. They often grow enough only to meet their own needs.

Starting in the 1930s, many Latin American countries tried to help the campesinos by dividing the land more equally. These programs have met with mixed success. In some cases, the land given to the campesinos was of poor quality. No matter how hard they tried, they could not make a living from it. In other cases, the campesinos struggled because they had neither the money to buy seeds and equipment nor the skills necessary for success. Many Latin American countries have begun to see that taking land from one person and giving it to another does not necessarily improve people's lives or the economy.

Using and Protecting the Land Dividing up the land has raised other issues. Brazil gave land to landless peasants by moving them to the Amazonian rain forest. The peasants burned down trees to clear the land for farming. After a few years, however, the soil in the rain forest became unfit for farming.

Many people around the world expressed worries about the clearing of the rain forest. Some believed that this would hurt the environment. Others said that it would change the way of life of the Native Americans who live there. Some people, however, have challenged this view. Economic progress, they say, will come only if Brazil uses all its resources. Brazilian leaders are looking for a balance. They want to find ways to help the economy and the campesinos without destroying the rain forest.

Farming in a Rain Forest

This pepper farmer has cleared land on an island in the Amazon River, in northern Brazil. **Critical Thinking** How does pepper farming contribute to Brazil's economy?

The Move to the City

Many campesinos have decided that making a living from the land is just too difficult. They have left the land and gone to the cities in search of different economic opportunities. This move has resulted in the rapid growth of the populations of large cities. Since the 1950s, many Latin American countries have had a population explosion. The population has increased dramatically in both the **rural,** or countryside, and the **urban,** or city, areas of Latin America. The population of urban areas, however, has gone up the most.

Many Latin Americans who move to the cities are looking for better jobs. They also want to improve the quality of their lives. They hope to find comfortable homes, better medical care, and good schools for their children. However, they do not always realize their hopes. As Latin American countries strive to build their economies, there will be greater opportunities for people to have a better life.

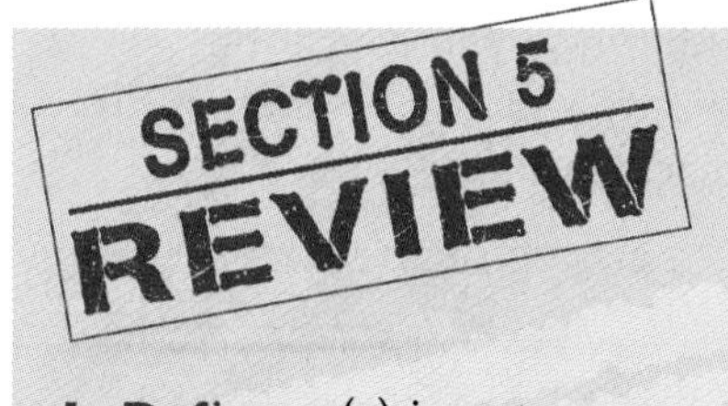

1. **Define** (a) invest, (b) economy, (c) campesino, (d) rural, (e) urban.
2. **Identify** Brazil.
3. What steps have Latin American countries taken to improve their economies?
4. How have Latin American countries tried to change the landowning system in the region?

Critical Thinking

5. **Recognizing Cause and Effect** How has the increase in population contributed to the growth of cities in Latin America?

Activity

6. **Writing to Learn** You have read that many people oppose Brazil's plans to move poor farmers to the rain forest. Write a paper that explores both the pro and the con sides of the following statement: "A country has the right to use its resources as it sees fit."

CHAPTER 2

Review and Activities

Reviewing Main Ideas

1. Why was an accurate calendar important to Mayan priests?
2. How did the Aztecs expand their empire?
3. How were the Incas able to change their environment in order to grow more food?
4. Give two examples of how the Mayan, Aztec, or Incan empires affect culture in Latin America today.
5. Why was Hernan Cortés able to persuade many Native Americans in the region to fight the Aztecs?
6. (a) Why did Spain gain control over most of Latin America?
   (b) How did Portugal come to control Brazil?
7. What role did the criollos play in the fight for Latin American independence?
8. How did José de San Martín surprise the Spanish in Chile and Peru?
9. How have many Latin American countries been trying to improve their economies in recent years?

Reviewing Key Terms

Use each key term below in a sentence that shows the meaning of the term.

1. maize
2. hieroglyphics
3. aqueduct
4. quipu
5. Line of Demarcation
6. conquistador
7. mestizo
8. hacienda
9. encomienda
10. criollo
11. caudillo
12. invest
13. economy
14. campesino
15. rural
16. urban

Critical Thinking

1. **Recognizing Cause and Effect** What were two causes of the fall of the Aztec and Incan empires? What were two effects on the Native American people of the region?
2. **Making Comparisons** Compare the way in which Mexico gained its independence with the way in which the countries of South America gained theirs.

Graphic Organizer

Copy this tree map onto a separate sheet of paper. Then use the empty boxes to outline Latin American history from Mayan civilization through the Spanish conquest.

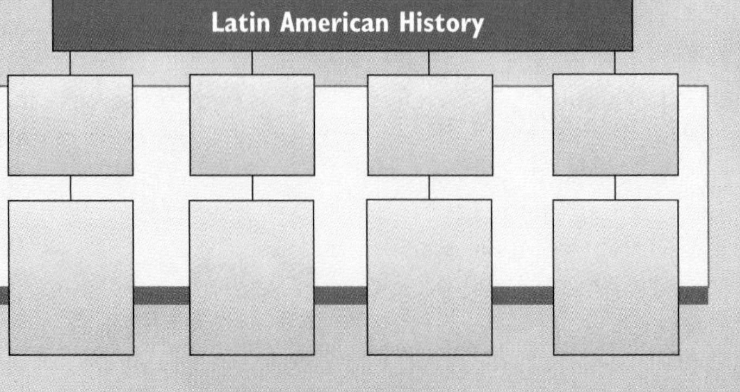

Map Activity

For each place listed below, write the letter from the map that shows its location.

1. Brazil
2. Guatemala
3. Mexico
4. Chile
5. Peru
6. Andes
7. Mexico City

Latin America: Place Location

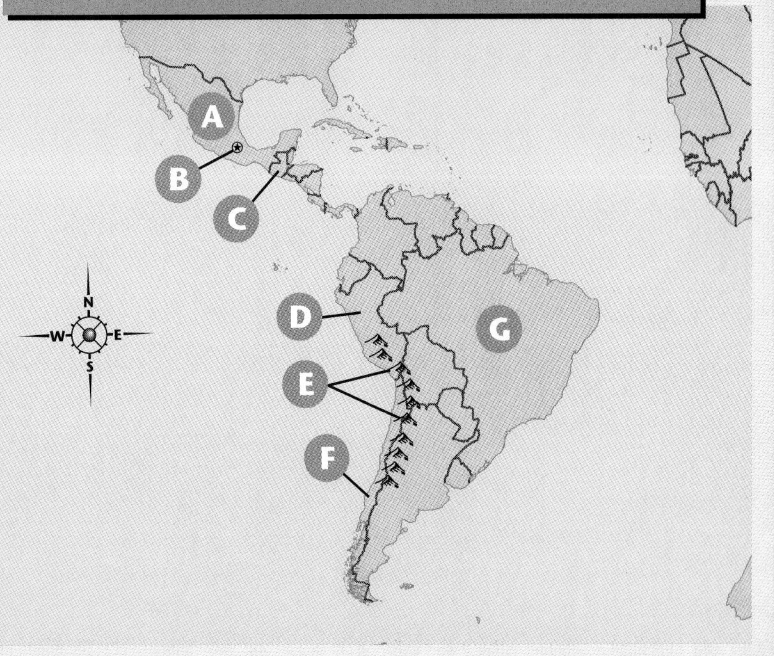

Writing Activity

Writing a Story

The Mayas, Aztecs, and Incas had spoken histories. Information was passed from generation to generation in stories and songs. Suppose that you lived at the time of the Spanish conquest. Write a story or a song that tells about the conquest.

Internet Activity

Use a search engine to find the site **Rabbit in the Moon: Mayan Glyphs and Architecture.** Explore and learn about the ancient Mayan civilization. Then, click on **How to Write Your Name in Mayan Glyphs.** Write your name in Mayan hieroglyphics, or play Bul, the on-line Mayan Game of Chance.

Skills Review

Turn to the Skill Activity.

Review the steps for using a time line. Then: (a) Explain in your own words how using a time line can help you to understand history. (b) What kinds of events should you list on a time line?

How Am I Doing?

Answer these questions to help you check your progress.

1. Can I identify and describe characteristics of the Mayan, Aztec, and Incan civilizations?
2. Can I explain how European rule affected Native Americans?
3. Can I explain how Latin American countries achieved independence?
4. Can I explain how foreign investment has affected Latin America?
5. What information from this chapter can I use in my book project?

Cultures of Latin America

SECTION 1
The Cultures of Mexico and Central America

SECTION 2
The Cultures of the Caribbean

SECTION 3
The Cultures of South America

These people are attending a festival in Peru. Get to know more about the people of Latin America by completing the following.

Link culture and history

Look at the people in this scene. Based on what you know about the history of Latin America, what do you think is the ethnic background of the people in the picture.

Compare regions

The cultures of Latin America are a unique blend of Native American, African, and European influences. How do you think the variety of peoples found in Latin America compares with that in the United States?

The Cultures of Mexico and Central America

Reach Into Your Background

What are your hopes and dreams for the future? Do you hope to work in a particular profession? Do you plan to go to college? Many Mexicans and Central Americans have the same kinds of dreams.

Questions to Explore

1. What is the ethnic heritage of the people of Mexico and Central America?
2. Why have many people in this region been moving from the country to the city?
3. What are the causes of Mexican and Central American immigration to the United States?

Key Terms

diversity
indigenous
injustice
maquiladora
emigrate
immigrant

Key Places

Mexico City

Elvia Alvarado (el VEE ah ahl vah RAH doh) walks the back roads of rural Honduras. She helps poor campesinos make a living. Honduran campesinos are like rural people in all of Central America. Many have little land of their own. It is hard for them to make enough money to support their families.

Alvarado is a mother and grandmother. She works for an organization of campesinos. She helps people get loans to buy seeds and farm machinery. Alvarado also helps them get more land. She works with community groups.

Alvarado's work is not easy. "The communities we work in are hard to get to," she says. "Sometimes I don't eat all day, and in the summertime the streams dry up and there's often no water to drink." Sometimes Alvarado does not get paid. "But I couldn't be happy if my belly was full while my neighbors didn't have a plate of beans and tortillas to put on the table," she says. "My struggle is for a better life for all Hondurans."

Cultural Heritage

Alvarado lives and works in Honduras, in Central America. It is one of seven nations in this area. Together they form a crooked, skinny isthmus. The isthmus links Mexico and South America.

One Region, Many Faces There is much diversity, or variety, among the people of Central America. Hondurans, like Alvarado, are mostly mestizo. They have both Spanish and indigenous ancestors. Indigenous (in DIJ uh nus) people are descendants of the people who first lived in a region. In Latin America, indigenous people are also called Native Americans or Indians. About half of Guatemala's people are mestizo. The other half are indigenous. Many Costa Ricans are direct descendants of Spaniards. And more than half the people of Belize are of African or mixed African and European descent.

These countries have many languages, too. Guatemala is home to more than 20 languages. Spanish is the language of government and business. But the indigenous people in Guatemala speak their own languages. So do indigenous people in Panama, El Salvador, and Nicaragua. Spanish is the main language in six of the seven countries. People in Belize speak English.

Huipiles Huipiles, or Mayan blouses, are works of art as well as clothing. The beautiful designs in a huipile have existed for thousands of years. Diamond-shaped designs stand for the universe. Other designs identify the weaver.

Mexico's Heritage Mexico blends Native American and Spanish influences. Spanish is the first language for most Mexicans, and Mexico is the largest Spanish-speaking country. Some Mexicans speak Native American languages. About 30 percent of the people of Mexico are indigenous, and some Mexicans are mestizos.

The Church Religion is important to the people of Mexico and Central America. In the 1500s and 1600s, Spanish missionaries converted many Native Americans to Christianity. The Roman Catholic Church has been important to this region ever since. Most of the people are Catholic. Native Americans have blended many elements of their religions with Christianity.

▶ The people of El Salvador are mostly mestizo, and their mixed heritage is reflected in their paintings. **Critical Thinking** What in this painting illustrates the Salvadorans' Spanish heritage?

A Growing Population

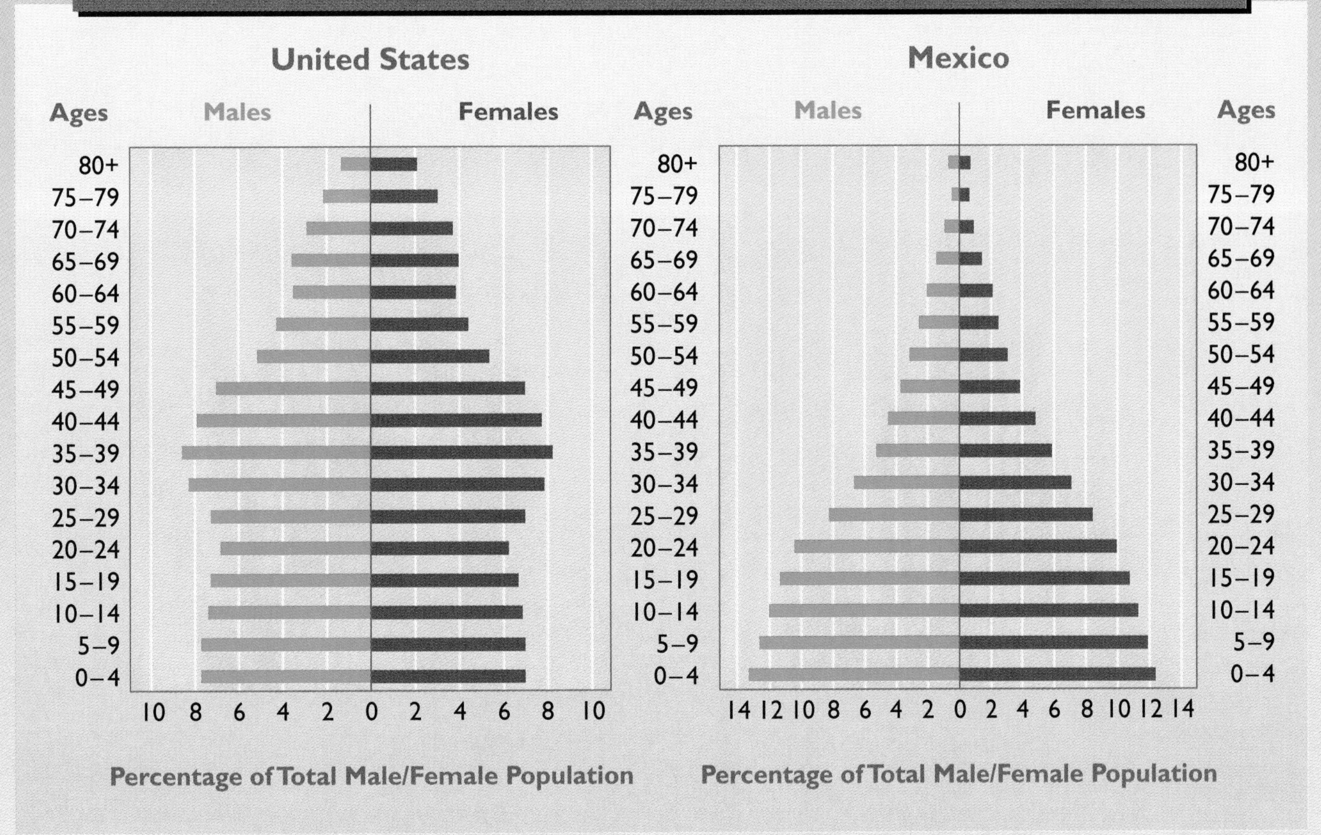

Chart Study Unlike the United States, Mexico is a nation of young people. **Critical Thinking** Think about what different skills and needs people have at different ages. What challenges do you think Mexico faces because so many of its people are very young?

Often, the Roman Catholic Church has fought injustice. **Injustice** is the unfair treatment of people. There are many examples of injustice. Injustice occurs when people have their property taken from them unfairly. It also occurs when people are imprisoned without first having a trial. Injustice often happens in countries that have undemocratic governments. Priests and bishops have called for all people to be treated fairly.

Following the Church's lead, many citizens have taken their own steps to end poverty and injustice. People have started their own health clinics, farms, and organizations. Like Elvia Alvarado and her campesino families, they hope that by working together they will be able to create a better way of life.

Looking for Work

The population of Mexico and Central America is growing rapidly. If it continues at the current rate, it will double in 20 to 30 years. Rapid population growth has made it hard for young people in rural areas to

A Voice of Protest In the late 1600s, Mexican nun Sor Juana Inez de la Cruz was punished by her bishop for writing a letter defending women's right to learn. Sor Juana was a published poet, but the bishop took away her books and writing materials. However, Sor Juana's essay inspired later generations of women to stand up for their rights.

Dawn to Dusk

Many Mexican and Central American immigrants to the United States find jobs on farms, picking crops. The farm workers on the right are picking strawberries near Salinas, California. The worker below is harvesting broccoli in Texas' Rio Grande Valley.

find jobs. Many have left their homes to look for work in the city. Today, most people in Mexico and Central America live in cities.

In Mexico, some people move to towns along the border with the United States. There, they can work in factories owned by American companies. These companies place their factories in Mexico because wages are lower there. Border factories are called **maquiladoras** (ma kee la DOR as).

Ask Questions What questions about maquiladoras would you like answered?

Life in the City In many cities in the region, there are big contrasts between the lives of the wealthy and the lives of the poor. Wealthy people live in big houses on wide streets. They go to good schools and can afford to pay for medical care. Many of them have a lifestyle similar to that of wealthy people in the United States.

For the poor, however, life in the city can be hard. There is a shortage of housing. It is not easy to find work. Sometimes, the only job available is selling fruit or soda on street corners. It is hard to feed a family on the wages such work commands. Yet people are willing to live with hardships they find in the city. Cecilia Cruz can explain why. She moved with her husband and their two sons to Mexico City from the southern state of Oaxaca (wah HAH kah). They live in a two-room house made of cinder blocks. It is on the outermost boundary of the city. "We came here for the schools," says Cruz. "There are more choices here. The level of education is much higher." Most newcomers to the city would agree.

Visualize What would a house made of cinder blocks look like? What problems might you notice if you went inside a cinder block house?

Moving to the United States Most people in Mexico and Central America move somewhere else within their own country if they cannot find work. Some move to cities or border towns. In addition, however, thousands of people emigrate. To **emigrate** means to move out of one country into another. Most leave because they cannot find work at home. Also, rising prices have made living more expensive. Many people emigrate to the United States.

Fermin Carrillo (fair MEEN kah REE yoh) is one worker who did just that. He left his home town of Huaynamota, Mexico. There were no more jobs at home, and his parents needed food and medical care. Carrillo moved to a town in Oregon. Now he works in a fish processing plant. He sends most of the money he earns home to his parents. Carrillo hopes one day to become a U.S. citizen. Other immigrants are different. They want to return home after earning some money to help their families. An **immigrant** is a person who has moved into one country from another.

Many Mexicans and Central Americans, like Fermin Carrillo, have left the region in search of a better life. Many more have followed Elvia Alvarado's example. They have stayed and begun to build a better life for themselves at home.

1. **Define** (a) diversity, (b) indigenous, (c) injustice, (d) maquiladora, (e) emigrate, (f) immigrant.
2. **Identify** Mexico City.
3. (a) What is the main language and religion of the people of Mexico and Central America? (b) How do the languages and religions of the region reflect its history?
4. What is one reason that rural people in Mexico and Central America are moving to the cities?

Critical Thinking

5. **Recognizing Cause and Effect** Explain several reasons for Mexican and Central American immigration to the United States.

Activity

6. **Writing to Learn** Write a journal entry from the point of view of one of the people mentioned in this section. Write about that person's hopes and dreams. How are they like your own? How are they different?

The Cultures of the Caribbean

Reach Into Your Background

Have you ever been on an island? Have you ever read a story about someone who lived on an island? What was the island like? What do you remember most about life there?

Questions to Explore

1. How did European, African, and Native American cultures blend to create unique Caribbean cultures?
2. What are the key characteristics of Caribbean cultures?

Key Terms

ethnic group
Carnival

Key Places

Jamaica
Cuba
Hispaniola
Trinidad and Tobago

Dorothy Samuels is a ten-year-old from Jamaica, a tropical island in the Caribbean Sea. She lives in a village near the ocean and goes to a village school. Dorothy is a good student. She hopes one day to go to college in Kingston, Jamaica's capital city. Jamaican laws require that women have as much opportunity to educate themselves as men do. Equality of women is important to Jamaican culture because many Jamaican women are independent farmers and business owners.

▼ Many Jamaican women carry goods on their heads. This practice came to the Caribbean from Africa.

Dorothy's family are farmers. They plant yams and other vegetables and fruits. They also plant cocoa beans. Every Saturday, Dorothy's mother and grandmother take their fruits and vegetables to the market to sell. All the traders at the market are women.

The People of the Caribbean

People in the Caribbean can make a living farming because most Caribbean islands have very fertile soil. These islands stretch over 2,000 miles (3,219 km) from Florida to the northeast coast of South America. As you might expect, a variety of peoples and cultures live within this large area.

The First People of the Caribbean The Caribbean islands are also called the West Indies because when Christopher Columbus arrived there, he thought he had reached the Indies in Asia.

The first people to live in the Caribbean were Native Americans, the Ciboney (SEE boh nay). The Ciboney lived on the islands for thousands of years. In about 300 B.C., they were joined by another indigenous group, the Arawaks (AR ah wahks), who came from South America. In about 1000, the Caribs (KA ribz), another South American group, arrived.

The Caribs gave the region its name. They lived there for more than 400 years before the first Europeans came to the area. Christopher Columbus and other Spaniards enslaved the Native Americans. Almost all of the Caribs, Arawaks, and other groups died of overwork and of diseases the Spanish brought with them. Today, just a few hundred Caribs still live on the island of Dominica.

Other Europeans followed the Spanish. They hoped to make money from the region's wealth of natural resources. Dutch, French, and English colonists began claiming territory in the 1600s. They built large sugar plantations and brought many enslaved Africans to work on them.

Predict What ethnic groups do you think live in the Caribbean today?

Caribbean Customs

	Jamaica	Puerto Rico	Dominican Republic
Greetings	A handshake; "Good morning/ afternoon/evening"; use Mr., Mrs., Miss.	A handshake. Women kiss each other on the cheek.	Shake hands. Greet everyone when you enter a room. Ask about people's families.
Gestures	Show approval of an idea by touching fists. Suck air through your teeth to mean "Give me a break."	Wiggle your nose to mean, "What's going on?" Point with puckered lips.	Point with puckered lips. Clap hands to request your check in a restaurant.
Table Manners	Keep the fork in the left hand. If you buy food from a street cart, eat it on the spot.	Keep both hands above the table. Stay at the table after the meal to relax and chat.	Guests are served first and sometimes separately. They often are given more elaborate food than the hosts.
Clothing	Women wear colorful skirts and matching headdresses. Many people have tailors make their clothes. Jewelry is common.	Casual clothing is worn for everyday occasions. Parties and social events require formal clothing.	Dressing well is considered important. Clothing is always clean and well-pressed. Men have a traditional suit called a chacabana, which is a white shirt over dark trousers.

Chart Study When you visit another culture, knowing the local customs can help you understand what you see. **Critical Thinking** Name some customs that are unique to the United States.

Most of the Caribbean people today are descended from these Africans. Immigrants from China, India, and the Middle East also came to the area to work.

People in the Caribbean Today Since slavery was legally ended in the Caribbean, its population has grown to about 36 million. Nearly one third of these people live on the region's largest island, Cuba.

Because so many people came to the Caribbean as colonists, slaves, or immigrants, the area has great ethnic variety. An **ethnic group** is a group of people who share race, language, religion, or cultural traditions. The ethnic groups of the Caribbean are Native American, African, European, Asian, and Middle Eastern.

Depending on their island's history, the people of a Caribbean island may speak one of several European languages. Their language may also be a mixture of European and African languages. For example, two countries and two cultures exist on the island of Hispaniola. On the eastern half is one country, the Dominican Republic. Its population is Spanish-speaking and mostly mestizo. West of the Dominican Republic is the country of Haiti. Nearly all of Haiti's people are descended from Africans. They speak French and Creole, which is a blend of French and African languages.

Most West Indians are Christians, but there are also small groups of Hindus, Muslims, and Jews. Some people practice traditional African religions.

A Caribbean Family

Family life is very important to people in the Caribbean. This family, from Montserrat, British West Indies, is made up of parents and their children. Many people in the Caribbean live in family groups that also include grandparents, uncles, aunts, and cousins.

Vibrant Colors

Haiti was one of the first places where the work of folk artists was recognized as real art. Large, colorful murals comment on religious and political themes. Bus drivers gain prestige by painting public buses, called taptaps.

Food, Music, Art, and Fun

Caribbean culture is known for its liveliness. People play music, dance, and tell stories. People also play many sports. Baseball, soccer, and track and field are popular. On some islands, people also play cricket, which is a British game similar to baseball. Dominoes is a popular game throughout the region.

Food Caribbean food is a mixture from all the cultures of the islands. Caribbean people can enjoy many types of seafood that are not found in U.S. waters. For instance, the people of Barbados love to eat flying fish and sea urchin eggs. Bammy—a bread made from the cassava plant—is still made the way the Arawaks made it. People also cook spicy curries from India, sausages from England, and Chinese dishes. Many tropical fruits grow on the islands. West Indians use the fruit to make many juices and other drinks that are not readily available in the United States.

Music Caribbean music is famous around the world. Calypso is a form of song that uses humor in its lyrics. You may have heard reggae (REG ay) music. It is from Jamaica. Steel drums are Caribbean musical instruments. They are made from recycled oil drums. A steel drum can be "tuned" so that different parts of it play different notes. Players strike the instruments with rubberized drumsticks. The rubber hitting the drum makes an almost liquid sound.

Soca—Calypso with Soul
In the 1970s, a new form of Caribbean music evolved. It blended calypso with two other styles—funk and ska. Funk is an earthy, blues music. Ska is similar to reggae. The first song to use this music was Lord Shorty's "Soul Calypso." The name of the new musical form comes from the title "Soul Calypso." It is called *soca.*

Carnival at Port of Spain, Trinidad

Many people in Caribbean countries dress in lavish, colorful costumes to celebrate before Lent. **Critical Thinking** What similar celebrations take place in the United States?

Carnival Many islanders observe the Roman Catholic tradition of Lent, which is the period of 40 days before Easter Sunday. People consider Lent to be a very solemn time, so just before Lent they throw a huge party. The party is called **Carnival.**

Different countries celebrate Carnival in different ways. The biggest Carnival takes place in Trinidad and Tobago. People spend all year making costumes and floats. Lent always starts on a Wednesday. At 5 A.M. the Monday before, people go into the streets in their costumes. Calypso bands play. Thousands of fans follow the bands through the streets, dancing and celebrating. At the stroke of midnight Tuesday, the party stops. Lent has begun.

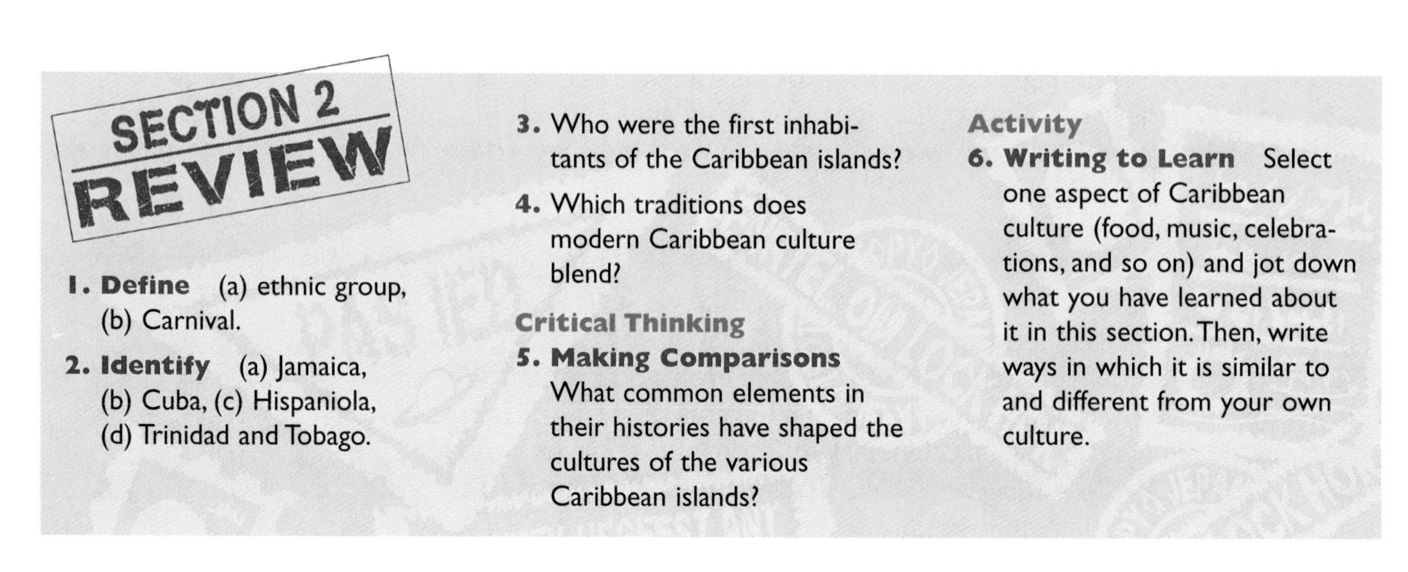

SECTION 2 REVIEW

1. **Define** (a) ethnic group, (b) Carnival.
2. **Identify** (a) Jamaica, (b) Cuba, (c) Hispaniola, (d) Trinidad and Tobago.
3. Who were the first inhabitants of the Caribbean islands?
4. Which traditions does modern Caribbean culture blend?

Critical Thinking

5. **Making Comparisons** What common elements in their histories have shaped the cultures of the various Caribbean islands?

Activity

6. **Writing to Learn** Select one aspect of Caribbean culture (food, music, celebrations, and so on) and jot down what you have learned about it in this section. Then, write ways in which it is similar to and different from your own culture.

The Cultures of South America

Reach Into Your Background

Think about the books you read, the music you like to listen to, and the clothes you wear. These things are all part of your culture. How is your culture related to the history of your family and your region? How does the geography in your region affect your culture?

Questions to Explore

1. What major cultural groups live in South America?
2. How has geography created diversity in this region?

Key Terms

subsistence farming
import

Key Places

Andes
Chile
Argentina
Brazil

Between Peru and Bolivia is the deep lake called Lake Titicaca. It lies high in the Andes Mountains. This area is bitterly cold. There are few trees. Native Americans here make their living from totora reeds, a kind of thick, hollow grass that grows on the lakeshore. They use these reeds to make houses, mats, hats, ropes, sails, toys, roofs, and floors. They eat the reeds, feed them to livestock, and brew them into tea. Totora reeds can even be made into medicine. Long ago, some Native American groups built floating islands with tortora reeds. They used the islands to hide from the Incas. Today, some Native Americans live on floating islands.

▼ The Native Americans who live on Lake Titicaca in Peru use tortora reeds to make boats.

The People of South America

Most South Americans today are descended from Native Americans, Africans, or Europeans. In this way, they are like the people of Mexico and Central America. South America's history is also like that of its neighbors to the north. It was colonized mainly by Spain. Most South Americans speak Spanish and are Catholic. Each nation has its own unique culture, however.

Regions Within South America There are four cultural regions in South America. The first region includes Colombia, Venezuela, Guyana, Suriname, and French Guiana, which are in the northern part of South America. They each border the Caribbean Sea. The cultures of these countries are like those of the Caribbean islands.

To the south and west, the culture is very different. Peru, Ecuador, and Bolivia are Andean countries. Many Native Americans live high in the Andes. In Bolivia, there are more indigenous people than mestizos. The Quechua and Aymara (eye muh RAH) people each speak their own languages.

Connect How are the Pampas of Argentina like the plains of the United States?

The third cultural region consists of Chile, Argentina, and Uruguay. The long, thin country of Chile has mountains, beaches, deserts, forests, and polar regions. Although its geography is diverse, its people are not. Most people in Chile are mestizos. The big cities of Argentina and Uruguay, however, are very diverse. Many different ethnic groups live there. Another culture exists on Argentina's Pampas, or plains. On the Pampas, gauchos (GOW chohz), or cowhands, herd cattle.

Brazil is South America's largest country. Brazil was a colony of Portugal. Its people speak Portuguese. However, Brazil is culturally diverse. Many Native Americans live in Brazil. So do people of African and European descent. Some Brazilians are of mixed descent. Many people have moved to Brazil from other countries. Brazil's largest city, São Paulo (sow PAW loh), is home to more Japanese than any other place in the world except Japan!

Herding Llamas in Peru

Some of the indigenous people of the Andes raise llamas, a relative of the camel. **Interaction** How do you think the people of the Andes use llamas?

A Peruvian Scene

Yhaninc Puelles Enriquez
age 12
Cuzco, Peru

The scene shown by this student artist is similar to the photograph on the previous page. **Critical Thinking** How are the scenes in the art and the photograph alike and different?

Art and Literature in South America South America has produced many famous artists, novelists, filmmakers, and poets. Chilean poets Pablo Neruda (PAH bloh nay ROO duh) and Gabriela Mistral (gah bree AY lah mees TRAHL) both were awarded the Nobel Prize for their work. Neruda wrote about everyday objects, including rain, tomatoes, and socks. Mistral wrote for and about children. Colombian Gabriel García Márquez (gah bree EL gar SEE uh MAR kays) and Chilean Isabel Allende (EES uh bel ah YEN day) both are famous for writing novels telling about several generations of life in one family. García Márquez was awarded the Nobel Prize.

Gabriela Mistral Chilean poet Gabriela Mistral was awarded the Nobel Prize for Literature in 1945. But Mistral considered herself to be more a teacher than a writer. Mistral taught school in rural Chile in the early 1900s, but she was frustrated by the low quality of the textbooks that were available. In response, Mistral began to write poetry and prose for children.

Country and City Life

South America contains cities with millions of people, but it also has vast areas with hardly any people at all. Many people still live in the countryside. Others are leaving farms and moving to cities.

Farming in South America Outside of Chile, Argentina, and Uruguay, most rural people with land of their own do **subsistence farming.** That means they grow only enough food for their families to eat. They only have small plots of land. Farmers plant corn, beans, potatoes, and rice.

Very large farms grow crops to export to other countries. The main export crops of South America are coffee, sugar, cocoa, and bananas. Export farming uses so much land for cash crops that South America has to import food to eat. To **import** means to buy from another country.

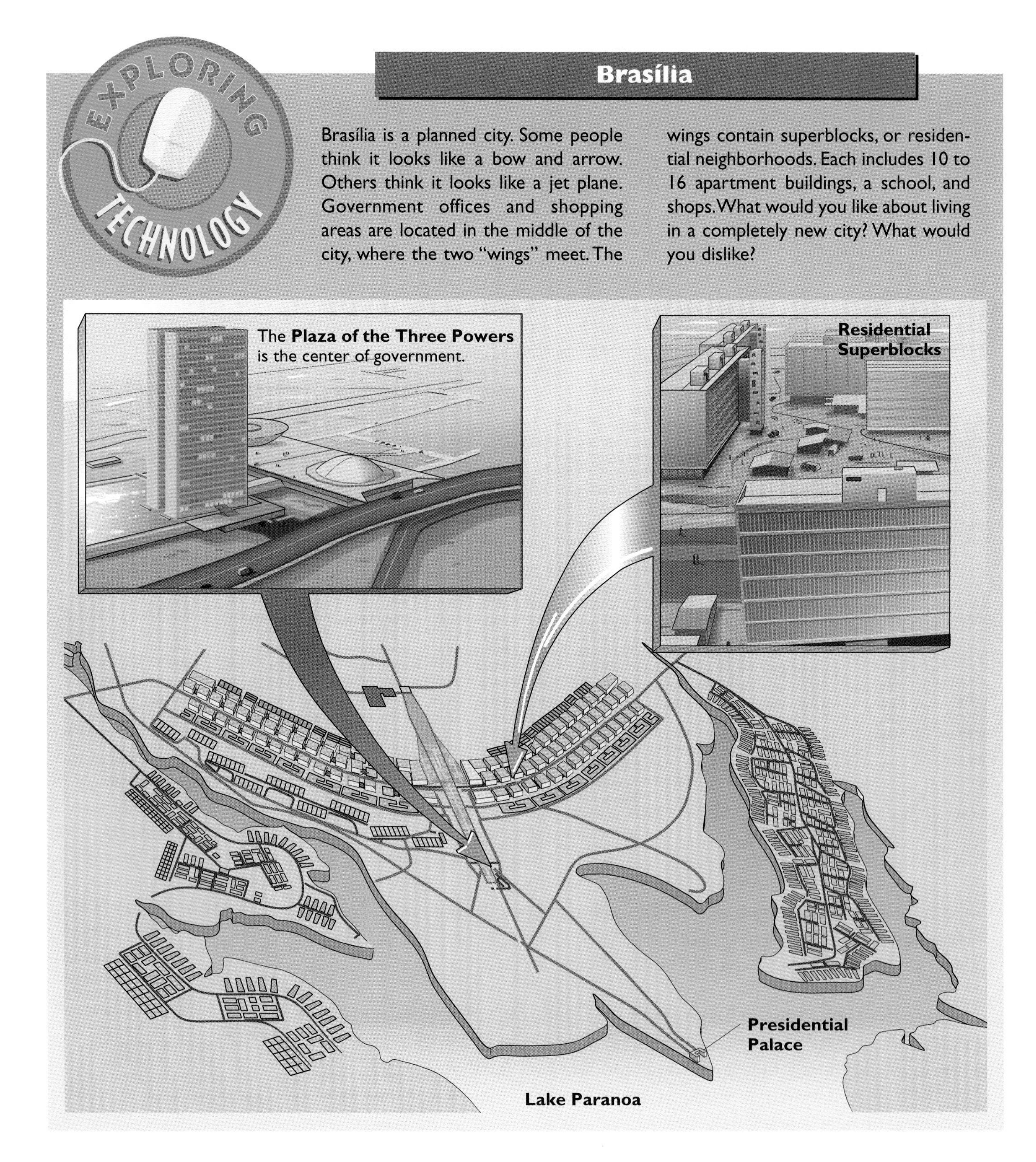
EXPLORING
TECHNOLOGY
The **Plaza of the Three Powers** is the center of government.
Residential Superblocks
Presidential Palace
Lake Paranoa

Brasília

Brasília is a planned city. Some people think it looks like a bow and arrow. Others think it looks like a jet plane. Government offices and shopping areas are located in the middle of the city, where the two "wings" meet. The wings contain superblocks, or residential neighborhoods. Each includes 10 to 16 apartment buildings, a school, and shops. What would you like about living in a completely new city? What would you dislike?

The population of South America is booming. Latin America is the fastest-growing region in the world. Like Mexicans and Central Americans, South Americans cannot find enough jobs in rural areas. Every day, thousands of rural South Americans move to the cities looking for work.

South America's Cities The cities of South America illustrate the region's mix of cultures. Many major cities—Lima, Peru, and Buenos Aires, Argentina, for example—were built by Spanish colonists more than 400 years ago. Some of the buildings in these older cities follow Native American designs. In contrast, modern office blocks and apartment buildings of concrete, steel, and glass tower above the downtown areas. One or two cities were built quite recently. Brasília, the Brazilian capital, was constructed in the 1950s. It was a completely planned city, designed to draw people to the country's interior.

By contrast, one of the unplanned things about many South American cities is the slums. They are called *favelas* (fuh VEH luz) in Brazil and *barrios* (BAR ee ohs) in Venezuela. More and more people have migrated into the cities in recent years. Usually they have ended up in poor neighborhoods. City governments try to provide electricity and running water to everyone. But people move into cities so quickly that it is hard for city governments to keep up.

The Role of Women In some ways, women do not yet play a role equal to that of men in South America. Women in South America are more likely than men to be poor. They also do not attend school for as many years as men do.

More and more women in South America today are fighting to make a living for themselves and their children. They are demanding equal rights. Women are struggling for the rights to go to school, to get into different types of jobs, to have good health care, and to have a voice in government. Some women are getting bank loans to start small businesses. These businesses are sometimes based on traditional skills such as sewing, weaving, or preparing food.

Working Together From 1976 to 1983, Argentina had a military government. The government took thousands of people prisoner. Many were never seen again. The mothers and grandmothers of the "disappeared" marched in protest every day for six years in Buenos Aires. Their actions forced the government to explain what happened to the missing people.

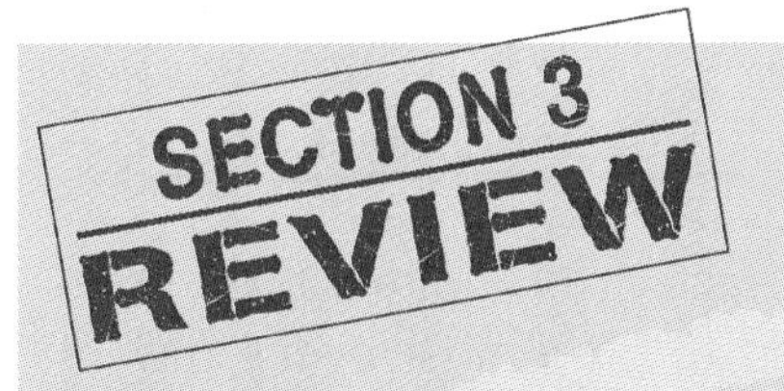

1. **Define** (a) subsistence farming, (b) import.
2. **Identify** (a) Andes, (b) Chile, (c) Argentina, (d) Brazil.
3. What pressures does rapid population growth place on the countries of South America?
4. Name two ways in which the geography of South America has shaped how people live.

Critical Thinking

5. **Recognizing Cause and Effect** What is one cause of rapid population growth in the cities? What is one effect?

Activity

6. **Writing to Learn** Choose one region of South America you'd like to visit, and write a paragraph explaining why.

Distinguishing Facts From Opinions

Kate was nervous, but excited. This was her first trip out of the United States. For two weeks, she had seen more fantastic things in Mexico than she could have dreamed of: beautiful countryside, ancient ruins . . . the list was endless. Now, she was about to start a new adventure.

Today, she would travel from Mexico City to Paplanta, a small town near the coast to the east. A fellow traveler had discouraged her. "The train trip is very long," she had said.

The train trip is very long and boring!
GUIDE BOOK
The train ride to Paplanta is three hours long.

"And boring. There's nothing to look at out the windows. The town is not interesting, either. You should skip that trip altogether."

"Hmmm," Kate thought as she pulled out her guidebook and train schedule. The guidebook said that the ruins of an old Spanish mission were located at Paplanta. The El Tajin ruins were also there. On Sundays, the town hosted an open-air market. The train schedule said it was only a three-hour train ride away, through mountainous country. "A long trip? Nothing to look at? Ha!" More determined than ever, Kate headed to the train station.

Get Ready

Kate decided to go to Paplanta because she relied on facts instead of opinions. Facts are statements that can be proved true. Opinions are beliefs. That the train ride was three hours long is a fact. The traveler's statement that the train ride "is very long" is an opinion. Distinguishing facts from opinions, as Kate found out, is a valuable skill.

Distinguishing facts from opinions is something you will need to do almost every day of your life. You will do it as you watch television, read books and magazines, and—like Kate—as you reach your own decisions.

Ladinos make up about 50 percent of the population of Guatemala.

F

Guatemala is the most beautiful country in Latin America.

O

How can you distinguish, or tell the difference between, facts and opinions? It's as simple as A-B-C:

A. Facts can be proved true.

B. Opinions cannot be proved true.

C. Opinions are often indicated by words and phrases like "I think," "I believe," "should," and "ought to," and by adjectives like "beautiful" or "ugly."

Try It Out

Learn to distinguish facts from opinions by playing a simple game. All you need are some note cards, a couple of pens, and a partner.

A. Deal the cards. Deal ten note cards to your partner and ten to yourself. Each of you should then write one fact or one opinion about Latin America on each of your note cards. You can get the facts from your textbook. The opinions should be your own beliefs. On the back of each note card, write an F if you wrote a fact and an O if you wrote an opinion. Don't let your partner see these!

B. Shuffle the cards. Shuffle your cards, and give them to your partner. Challenge him or her to identify each sentence as a fact or an opinion. Award one point for each correct answer. Give a bonus point if your partner can explain how the statement could be proved true if it is a fact or how your partner knew it was an opinion. Total your partner's score, and write it down.

C. Switch cards. Now try your hand at your partner's note cards. Compare scores. Which of you won? The winner should help the loser learn more about distinguishing fact from opinion.

Apply the Skill

Now distinguish facts from opinions in a real case.

1. **Read for understanding.** Read the paragraph in the box below once or twice, until you are sure you understand its meaning.

2. **Read for facts and opinions.** Now reread *one sentence at a time.* For each sentence, apply the A-B-C method of distinguishing facts from opinions. Ask yourself: A) Is this a fact that *can* be proved true? B) Is this an opinion that *cannot* be proved true? C) Are there words in the sentence that identify it as an opinion? Which sentences are facts and which are opinions? How could you prove the facts true? How do you know the other sentences express opinions?

> Urbanization takes place when people move from rural areas to urban areas. I believe that urbanization in Mexico is a bad thing. First, the cities are already too crowded. There are thousands of homeless people in urban areas. Lots of people can't find jobs. Second, the city streets were not designed for so many cars. Traffic jams are a huge headache. Finally, the water and electric systems do not have the capacity to serve more people. I think the time has come for the government to try to stop urbanization.

CHAPTER 3

Review and Activities

Reviewing Main Ideas

1. (a) What are maquiladoras?
   (b) Why are they important to the economy of Mexico?
2. To which country are some Mexicans and Central Americans emigrating to find jobs?
3. (a) Who were the first people on the Caribbean islands?
   (b) What happened to those people?
4. What are some of the musical styles that began in the Caribbean?
5. How do some of the people of the Andes make a living?
6. (a) How is the country of Chile geographically diverse?
   (b) How is Brazil culturally diverse?

Reviewing Key Terms

Decide whether each statement is true or false. If it is true, write "true." If it is false, change the underlined term to make the statement true.

1. Border factories are called <u>mestizos.</u>
2. <u>Indigenous</u> people are descendants of a region's first inhabitants.
3. To <u>emigrate</u> is to move from one's home country to another country.
4. Many Mexicans become <u>pampas</u> in the United States because they cannot find jobs in their home countries.
5. Ethnic <u>diversity</u> refers to people with a variety of cultures, customs, religions, or languages.
6. <u>Imports</u> occur when a government does not respect people's human rights.
7. To <u>immigrate</u> means to buy from another country.

Critical Thinking

1. **Making Comparisons** Consider these three regions: Mexico and Central America; the Caribbean; South America. What do the cultures of these regions have in common? How are they different?
2. **Recognizing Cause and Effect** What is the main reason that many Latin Americans move from one region or one country to another?

Graphic Organizer

Copy the chart to the right onto a separate sheet of paper. Then fill in the empty boxes to complete the chart.

	Mexico and Central America	The Caribbean	South America
Languages			
Religions			
Ethnic Background			
Special Features			

Map Activity

For each place listed below, write the letter from the map that shows its location.

1. Andes
2. Argentina
3. Brazil
4. Honduras
5. Jamaica
6. Mexico City
7. Trinidad and Tobago

Latin America: Place Location

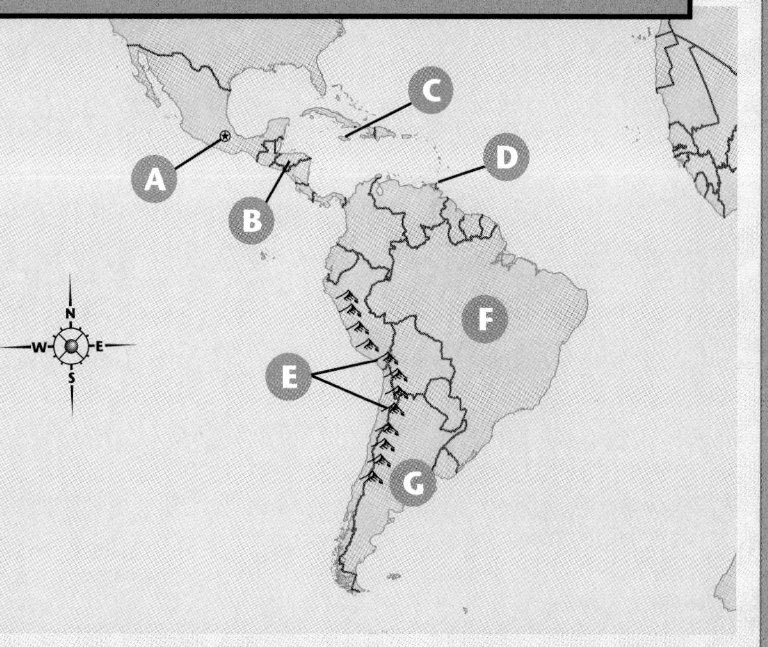

Writing Activity

Writing a Magazine Article
In this chapter, you've taken a guided tour of the cultures of Latin America. Write an article for a travel magazine describing the "high points" of your tour. As you write, consider how historical events and geography influenced the region's culture.

Internet Activity

Use a search engine to find the site **amigo! Mexican Art & Culture.** Explore several links to learn about various aspects of Mexican culture. Make a travel brochure highlighting some of your favorite findings, create a portfolio of Mexican culture, or give a class presentation on the aspect that interested you the most.

Skills Review

Turn to the Skill Activity.

Review the steps for distinguishing facts from opinions. Then, write a brief paragraph about the cultures of Latin America that includes both facts and opinions.

How Am I Doing?

Answer these questions to help you check your progress.

1. Can I explain how the cultures in a region reflect its history?
2. Can I explain how most people make a living in the countryside?
3. Can I identify the reasons why many people in Latin America are moving from rural to urban areas?
4. What information from this chapter can I use in my book project?

CHAPTER 4

Exploring Mexico and Central America

SECTION 1
Mexico
ONE FAMILY'S MOVE TO THE CITY

SECTION 2
Guatemala
DESCENDANTS OF AN ANCIENT PEOPLE

SECTION 3
Panama
WHERE TWO OCEANS MEET

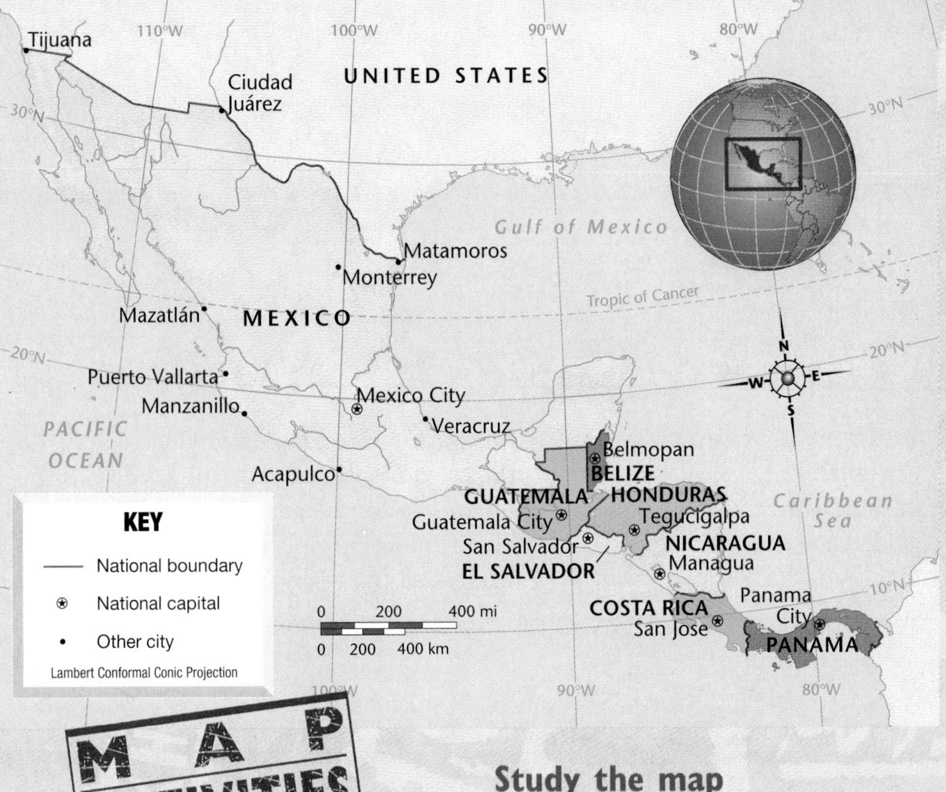

MAP ACTIVITIES

Look at the map above. Notice that the shape of Mexico and Central America is like a funnel, wide at the top and narrowing to a point. To learn more about this region, complete the following activities.

Study the map

How many countries are there in Central America? What bodies of water do they border?

Consider the geography

Mexico is a large country, while the countries of Central America are small. How do you think geography helped divide Central America into small countries?

Mexico

One Family's Move to the City

Reach Into Your Background

Have you ever moved from one house to another or from one city to another? Did you have to change schools? Think about what the move was like and make a few notes about how you felt at the time.

Questions to Explore

1. Why have many Mexicans been moving from the countryside to the city?
2. What challenges do Mexicans from the country face when they build new lives in the city?

Key Terms

squatter
plaza
migrant farmworker

Key Places

Mexico City

Ramiro Avila (rah MEE roh ah VEE lah) is one of seven children. He grew up in the state of Guanajuato (gwah nuh HWAH toh), in central Mexico. In his small village, Ramiro knew everyone and everyone knew him.

Ramiro's family were campesinos who owned no land. Even as a young child, Ramiro had to work to help support the family. He and his father had jobs as farm laborers. They worked on someone else's farm. They made less than a dollar a day.

The Move to Mexico City

Ramiro's village is located in the southern part of the Mexican Plateau. This area has Mexico's best farmland. It also is home to more than half of the country's people. Not surprisingly, it is the location of Mexico's largest city—Mexico City. Find Mexico City on the map on the previous page.

When Ramiro was 13, his parents decided to move the family to Mexico City. They hoped to find better work. The city was far away and their lives would be completely different. But moving offered them a chance to make a decent living.

Mexico's Population

Chart Study What pattern of population movement does this chart show?

	Total Population	Urban (%)	Rural (%)
1995	93,986,000	71.0	29.0
2000*	102,912,000	77.7	22.3
2010*	120,115,000	81.6	18.4

*Projected population

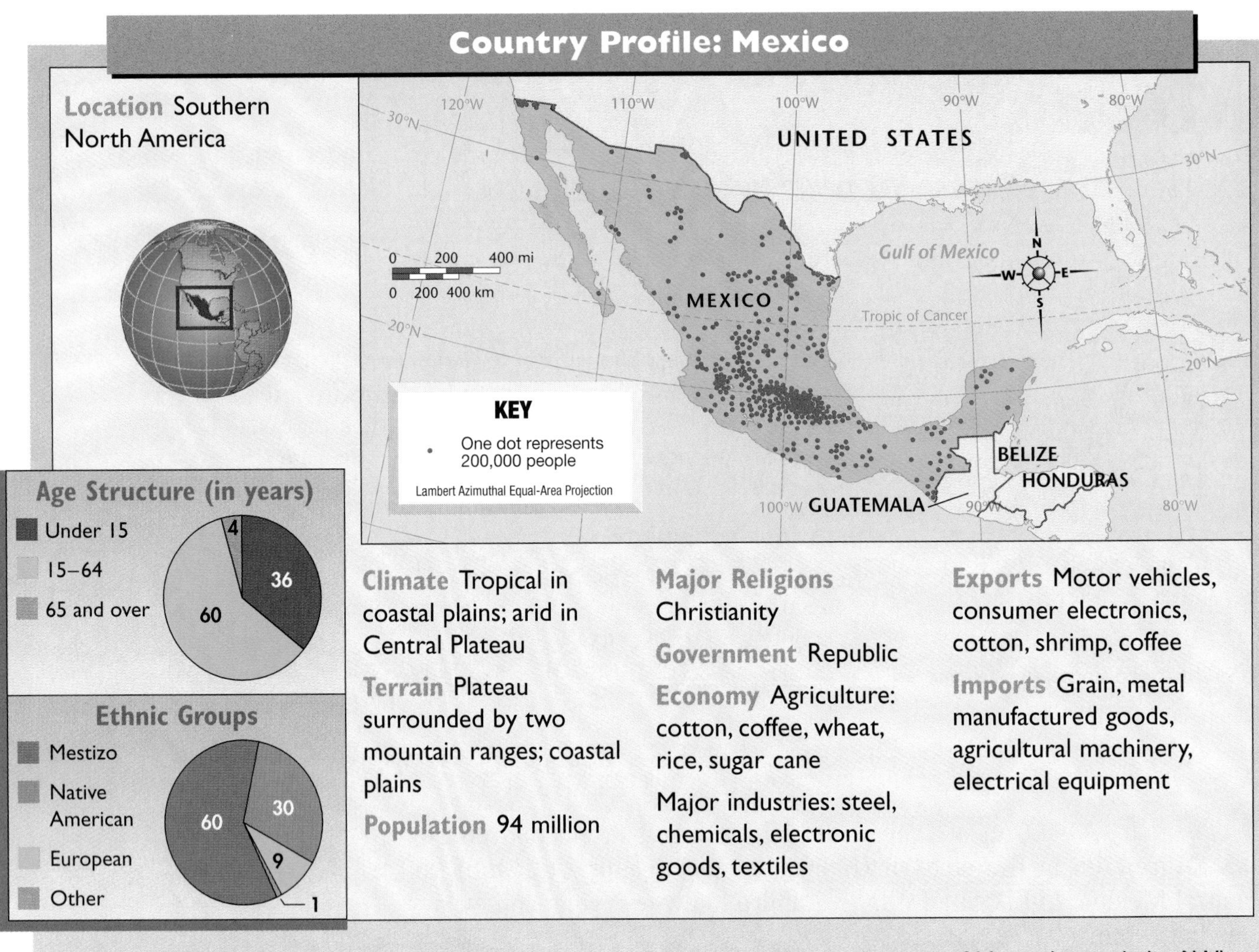

Map Study The map above shows Mexico's population distribution. Some parts of Mexico are sparsely populated, while others are very crowded. **Location** Where do most of Mexico's people live? Why do you think that they live in that area and not elsewhere?

Housing in the City Like thousands of other campesino families coming to the city, Ramiro's family did not have much money. When they arrived in Mexico City, they could not afford a house. They went to live in Colonia Zapata, which is one of many neighborhoods where poor people become **squatters.** That means they settle on someone else's land without permission. Many small houses of squatters cling to the sides of a steep hill in the Colonia. The older houses near the bottom of the hill are built of concrete. However, most people cannot afford to make sturdy houses when they first arrive. Therefore, many of the newer houses higher up the hill are constructed of scrap metal.

Ramiro's family made a rough, one-room house of rock. Ramiro felt that his new house was ugly. He and his family hoped that soon they would be able to buy land from the government. Then they could build a real house with a garden and a patio.

Ask Questions What would you like to know about campesinos who move to the city from the countryside?

Work and School Ramiro went to school in Mexico City, but he also worked as a cook in a tiny restaurant. He started work at 7 A.M. and worked until 2 P.M., preparing scrambled eggs and sausage. For these seven hours of work he earned about $3. His mother and some of his brothers and sisters worked, too. Ramiro went to a school that held night classes, attending classes until 9:30 at night.

Ramiro's father could not get a job in Mexico City. He decided to go to Texas in the United States. He found work as a farm laborer there. He sent money home every month. The move to Mexico City brought a lot of responsibilities for Ramiro. It became his job to look after his younger brothers and sisters while his father was gone. Ramiro's life was very different from how it had been in his village.

Life in Rural Mexico

Before Ramiro's family moved, they lived in a village where life has changed little over the years. Every village has a church and a market. At the center of most villages is a public square called a **plaza.** Farm families grow their own food. If they have extra food, they sell it at the market. Rural people buy nearly everything they need—clothing, food, toys, housewares—at the market rather than in stores.

Markets of Rural Mexico

This photograph shows a market in Oaxaca, Mexico. People in rural Mexico buy many of their groceries and housewares from markets like these. **Critical Thinking** What details in this photograph show similarities between rural markets and urban supermarkets? What details show differences?

Farm Work Most farm families in Mexico and Central America are poor. Many campesinos work their own small farms. They often plow the land and harvest their crops by hand because they cannot afford expensive equipment. **Migrant farmworkers** do not own land. Like Ramiro and his father, they work on large farms owned by rich landowners. Migrants travel from one area to another, picking the crops that are in season.

READ ACTIVELY

Predict What problems might occur as more people move into a city?

Lack of Jobs Mexico's population has risen dramatically over the last 20 years. The country's population is growing at a rate of more than two percent each year—one of the highest rates in the world. There is not enough farm work for so many people. A large family cannot support itself on a small farm. And there are not enough jobs for all the migrant workers. Many people move to the cities because they cannot find work in the countryside.

About 70 percent of Mexico's people now live in cities and large towns. Many of them live in Mexico City. If you count the people in all the outlying areas, Mexico City has over 23 million people. Only Tokyo, Japan, has more people than Mexico City.

Mexico City: A Megacity

Mexico City is huge. Its population sprawls over a large area. It is a megacity, an urban center where many of Mexico's people live. Unlike most big cities, Mexico City does not have many skyscrapers and major streets. Two- and three-story buildings still form its downtown. Only a

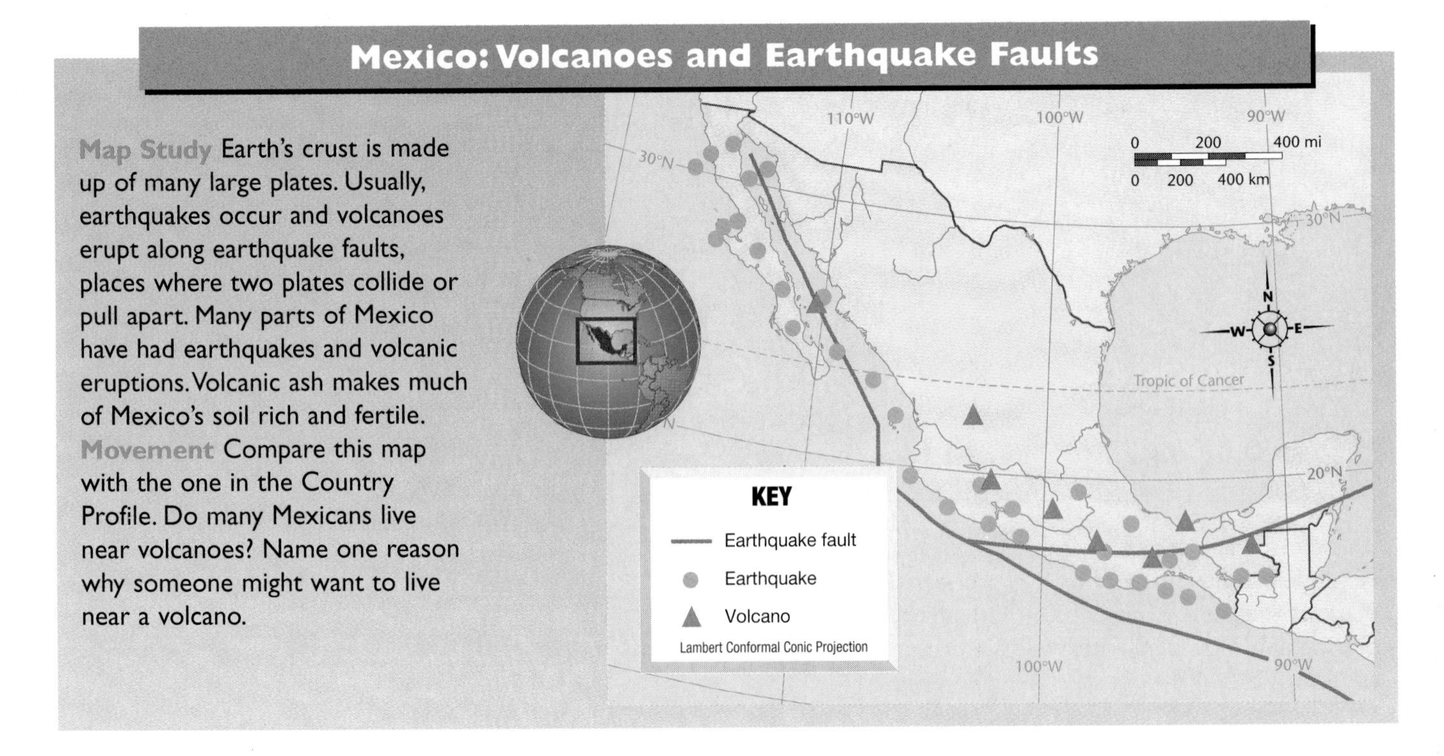

Mexico: Volcanoes and Earthquake Faults

Map Study Earth's crust is made up of many large plates. Usually, earthquakes occur and volcanoes erupt along earthquake faults, places where two plates collide or pull apart. Many parts of Mexico have had earthquakes and volcanic eruptions. Volcanic ash makes much of Mexico's soil rich and fertile. **Movement** Compare this map with the one in the Country Profile. Do many Mexicans live near volcanoes? Name one reason why someone might want to live near a volcano.

The Growth of Mexico City

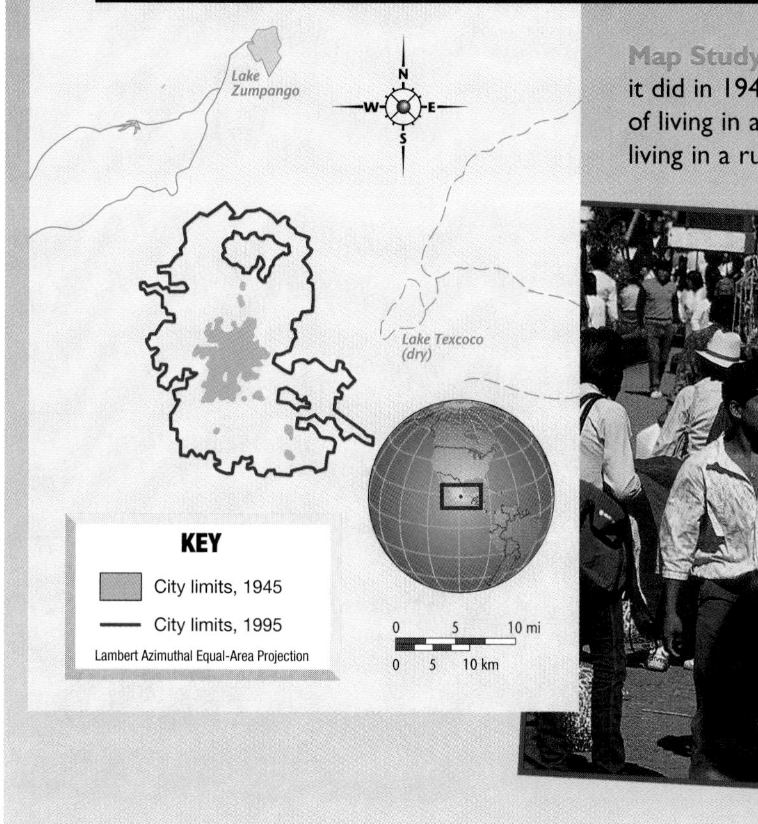

Map Study Mexico City covers more than twice the land that it did in 1945. **Interaction** How do you think the challenges of living in a city might be different from the challenges of living in a rural area?

few streets are wide enough for the city's traffic. The subway, the underground railroad system, carries thousands of people each day.

Small neighborhoods of very wealthy people are tucked away from the rest. But most of Mexico City's residents are not wealthy. They live in all areas of the city. The poorest, like Ramiro and his family, live on the outskirts. Some must travel several hours a day to get to their jobs and back.

Pollution and Geography Because the cities have grown so large, Mexico's capital and other large cities in the region are facing problems of pollution and traffic jams. Four million cars and trucks jam Mexico City's narrow streets. They compete with taxis, trolleys, and buses. Mexico City's location traps pollution close to the city. The city spreads across a bowl-shaped valley. The mountains surrounding the valley stop winds from carrying away factory smoke, automobile exhaust fumes, and other pollution. The pollution creates smog. It hangs over the city like a black cloud.

Making a Living Large cities offer many ways to make a living. Factories and offices employ millions of people. Thousands more sell goods from stalls in the street. Ramiro's sister, Carmela, is a street vendor. She sells juice at a stand in the bus station near their neighborhood.

Tenochtitlán—A Clean City Tenochtitlán, the Aztec capital, did not have a pollution problem. In fact, the first Europeans to visit Tenochtitlán were amazed at how clean the city was. At least 1,000 workers cleaned and swept the city's streets. Clean water was piped in from springs. At the time, European cities did not have fresh, clean water.

Smog Over Mexico City

Even on a sunny day, buildings a few blocks away appear dim and blurry in Mexico City because of smog. **Interaction** Why do you think Mexico City has so much smog? How do you think the smog affects the way people in Mexico City live?

Every morning, she gets up at 5:30 to make juice from oranges and carrots. People on their way to work buy her juice for their long trip into the city.

Mexico City is not the only city that is growing. All of Mexico's major cities are becoming more crowded. City life is not easy for most Mexicans. Hard work and hope are what keep people going.

1. **Define** (a) squatter, (b) plaza, (c) migrant farmworker.
2. **Identify** Mexico City.
3. What is the main reason that rural people from all over Mexico have been moving to the cities?
4. What difficulties do rural people face when they move to Mexico City?

Critical Thinking

5. **Expressing Problems Clearly** How do the lives of rural Mexicans improve when they move to the city? How do their lives continue to be difficult?

Activity

6. **Writing to Learn** Write an entry in your journal comparing and contrasting Ramiro's life with your own. How are your lives different? What similarities do you notice?

Guatemala

DESCENDANTS OF AN ANCIENT PEOPLE

Reach Into Your Background

Each year the Nobel Peace Prize is awarded to someone who has worked for peace in the world. What qualities do you think a person should have in order to receive such a prize?

Questions to Explore

1. How are the indigenous people of Guatemala a unique culture?
2. What are the main issues that indigenous people face?
3. How did Rigoberta Menchú become a leader of her people?

Key Terms

ladino
ethnic group
strike

Key People and Places

Rigoberta Menchú
Guatemala

"Where I live is practically a paradise, the country is so beautiful. There are no big roads and no cars. Only people can reach it." These are the words of a Guatemalan woman named Rigoberta Menchú (ree goh BEHR tah men CHOO). Menchú is a Mayan woman. She was born in 1959. She speaks a language called Quiché (kee CHAY). In 1984, Menchú wrote a book about her life in Guatemala.

The mountains where Menchú was born are beautiful. But Menchú's family was very poor. They farmed their land, but the soil was not good. "Where we live in the mountains," Menchú wrote, "you can barely grow maize and beans. The land isn't fertile enough for anything else."

▼ Most Mayas who live in the highlands of Guatemala have only small plots of land to farm.

The Struggle for Land

Menchú's mountain home is in the country of Guatemala. This southern neighbor of Mexico is "first" in Central America in many categories. For example, it has the largest population among Central American countries. To learn more about Guatemala, study the Country Profile on the next page.

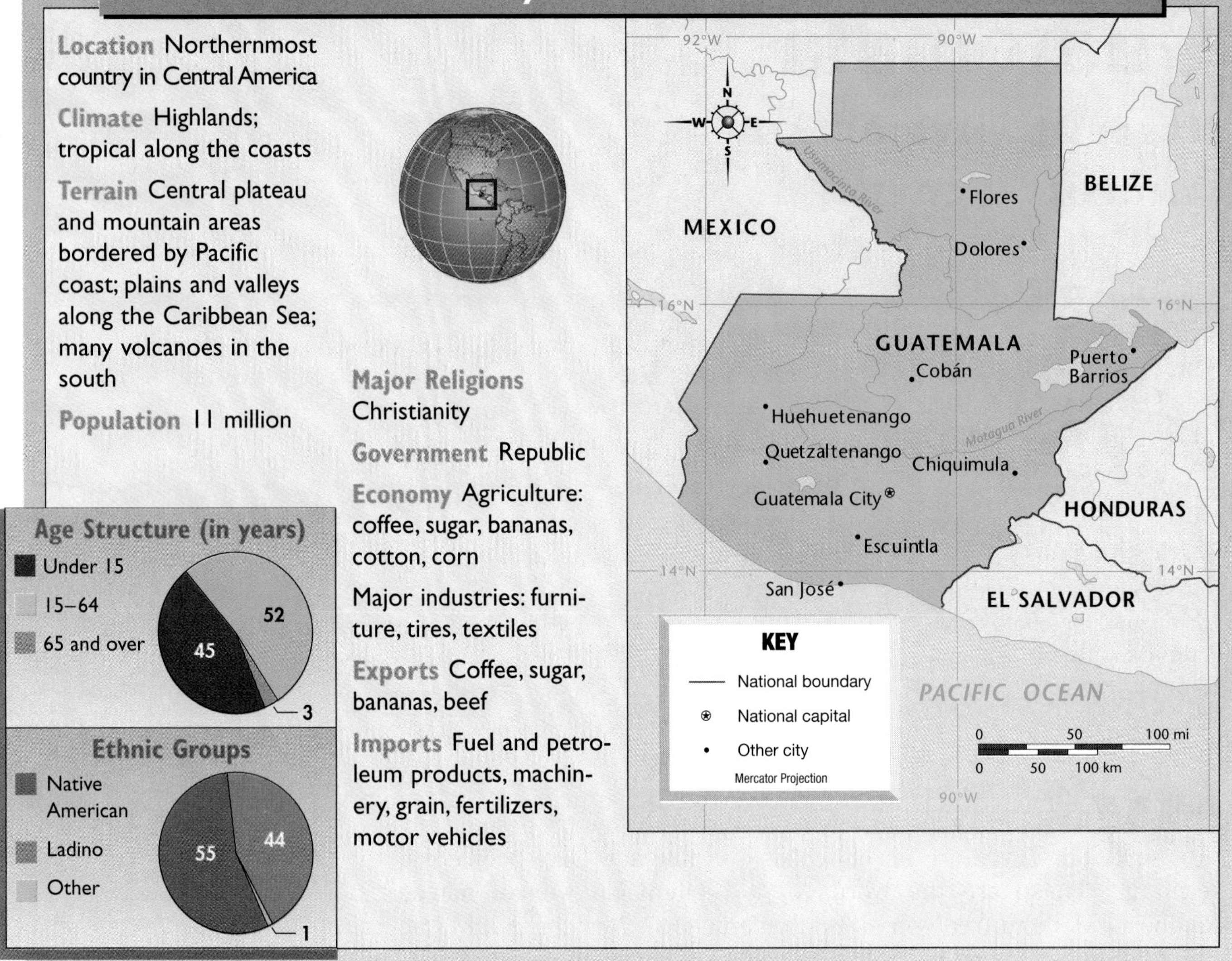

Map Study This map shows the country of Guatemala. **Location** What four countries border Guatemala? **Chart Study** The chart on the bottom left shows the percentages of ethnic groups in Guatemala. Most Mayas live in rural communities, speak a Mayan language, and follow Mayan customs. Ladinos speak Spanish, have adopted Spanish customs, and often live in towns or cities. **Critical Thinking** Which ethnic group do you think has been more involved in Guatemala's government? Why?

Menchú's parents lived in the mountains because it was the only land available to Native Americans. Most land in Guatemala belongs to a few rich families. The rich landowners of Guatemala are **ladinos** (luh DEE nohs), mestizos who are descended from Native Americans and Spaniards. Native Americans who follow European ways are also considered to be ladinos.

Menchú's parents worked hard to make their land produce crops. "You had to pay a fee so that you could clear the land," she wrote. "Of course, it's not very easy to make things grow on land that's just been cleared. You don't get a good yield for at least eight or nine years."

Losing a Home During most of Menchú's childhood, there was a civil war going on in Guatemala. The Mayas were caught in the middle. Indigenous people do not always think of themselves as citizens of the country in which they live. A Mayan woman is more likely to think of herself as a Maya than as a Guatemalan.

Also, most Native Americans in Guatemala cannot read or write. Most Mayas have not filed any papers with the government showing that they own land. The Mayas often have no way to prove that their land belongs to them. The people of Menchú's village worked hard for many years, and soon the land began to produce crops. But then the civil war and landowners caught up with Menchú's village.

Menchú wrote that when she was twelve years old, the landowners came with soldiers. They disagreed with the village's claim to the land. Now that it was cleared and producing crops, they wanted it. They forced Menchú's family and their neighbors to leave.

"First they went into our houses without permission and got all the people out," Menchú remembered. Then, the soldiers were ordered to throw away each family's belongings. The soldiers took all the corn the people had stored. The villagers had nowhere to go but out into the rain.

The Sami The Sami, or Lapps, live in the far north of Norway, Sweden, Finland, and Russia. The governments of these countries consider the Sami their citizens. Most Sami, however, look upon themselves as part of a separate nation. In recent years, the Sami have won some degree of self-government. The Sami of Norway, for example, have their own elected assembly.

A Guatemalan Market

Mayas in rural Guatemala do much of their shopping at open-air markets like this one. **Movement** What types of goods are being traded or sold at this market?

Colorful Clothing

Mayan communities each have their own hand-woven style of clothing. **Critical Thinking** What skills do you think are needed to weave cloth into a certain pattern?

Overcoming Obstacles
Justina Tzoc travels through rural Guatemala, teaching Quiché Maya women about their rights and teaching them to read. Her work is dangerous, because she sometimes travels through areas that are torn by civil war. But Tzoc is determined to help every woman she can reach.

A 500-Year-Old Struggle Menchú's story is a common one. The indigenous people of Guatemala have fought against injustice for 500 years. They started when the Spanish first arrived.

The Spanish conquered Native Americans by force. Many were killed. Others died of hunger or the hardships of slavery. Still others died from European diseases. In many Latin American countries, there are few indigenous people left.

But in Guatemala, Native Americans are the majority of the population. They form 23 ethnic groups. An **ethnic group** is a group of people who share language, religion, and cultural traditions. The indigenous groups of Guatemala are related to each other. However, each group is different. Each has its own language and customs. Rigoberta Menchú comes from the largest group, the Quiché Maya.

Rigoberta Menchú Takes a Stand

Rigoberta Menchú began working with campesinos all over the country. She learned several other indigenous languages. She also learned Spanish. She wanted to be able to work with ladinos who supported Native American land rights. Menchú became part of a nationwide political movement, which is a large group of people who work together to defend their rights or to change the leaders in power. This political movement was to defend campesino rights. Menchú helped villages plan ways to protect themselves. She taught people how to read. She also taught people about the history of their land. Menchú helped the movement organize meetings, protests, and **strikes,** or work stoppages. She was determined to defend Native American land rights.

Menchú's mother, father, and brother were killed fighting against the landowners. But Menchú continued to fight for the rights of her people. Her life, too, was in danger. For her own safety, Menchú had to leave the country. She went to live in Mexico.

Rigoberta Menchú

Rigoberta Menchú never went to school. Instead, she worked on farms and as a maid. Later, she taught herself to speak and read several languages. She knew that command of these languages would help her get her message to all Guatemalans.

Peace in Guatemala In 1992, Rigoberta Menchú was awarded the Nobel Peace Prize. She was the first indigenous person in the world ever to win the prize. Since 1992, Menchú has continued to work for justice in Guatemala. Her efforts have brought important changes. Recently, Guatemala's government appointed 21 Mayan priests to advise officials about Mayan culture. New Mayan organizations are being formed every day. In addition, Mayan languages are being used in books, newspapers, and radio programs. Government officials and Mayan leaders hope these changes will bring peace to Guatemala.

Ask Questions What questions would you like to ask Rigoberta Menchú about her activities?

1. **Define** (a) ladino, (b) ethnic group, (c) strike.
2. **Identify** (a) Rigoberta Menchú, (b) Guatemala.
3. How does Rigoberta Menchú describe the land where she was born?
4. How do most indigenous people in Guatemala make a living? What difficulties do they face?

Critical Thinking

5. **Identifying Cause and Effect** Explain the main reason that Guatemala's indigenous people and other farmers have formed a political movement.

Activity

6. **Writing to Learn** Write a short essay explaining what you would have done if you were in Rigoberta Menchú's position. Then, explain what you would do if you were the president of Guatemala.

Previewing a Reading Selection

Sean asked his mom if he could go for a bike ride before it got dark. His mom said, "Sure, if you finish your homework first." Sean didn't have much homework. "If I can finish it in an hour," Sean thought to himself, "I'll have a whole hour for a killer mountain bike adventure."

He settled down to study. His assignment was to answer ten questions about the Panama Canal using two books he had checked out from the school library. He read the first question: "What are three obstacles workers faced when building the Panama Canal?" He picked up the first book and began reading on page 1. Five pages and 10 minutes later he didn't have his answer. He tried the other book. Ten pages and 20 minutes later he still hadn't found what he was looking for. "Half an hour gone and not one question answered!" he thought, disgustedly. "No bike ride tonight!"

Sean missed out on his bike ride because he forgot to apply an important skill: previewing. Previewing means looking over a book or chapter before you read it or try to find information in it. Previewing is a valuable study skill that will help you read more efficiently.

Get Ready

How do you preview? You might be surprised to learn that this is one skill you already know! If you've ever seen a preview for a movie, you've "previewed" that movie. You have a general idea what the movie is about. If you've ever looked over a menu, you've "previewed" your meal. You have a general idea of what the food will be like.

Of course, previewing a reading selection is a little different from previewing a movie or meal. Previewing means looking over something you are about to read in a general way to become familiar with it. The idea is to get a "sense" of the material. To get a sense of what a book is about, you can use five things: the title, the table of contents, the illustrations, the index, and sample paragraphs. To do this with a chapter, you can use titles, subtitles, illustrations, and captions.

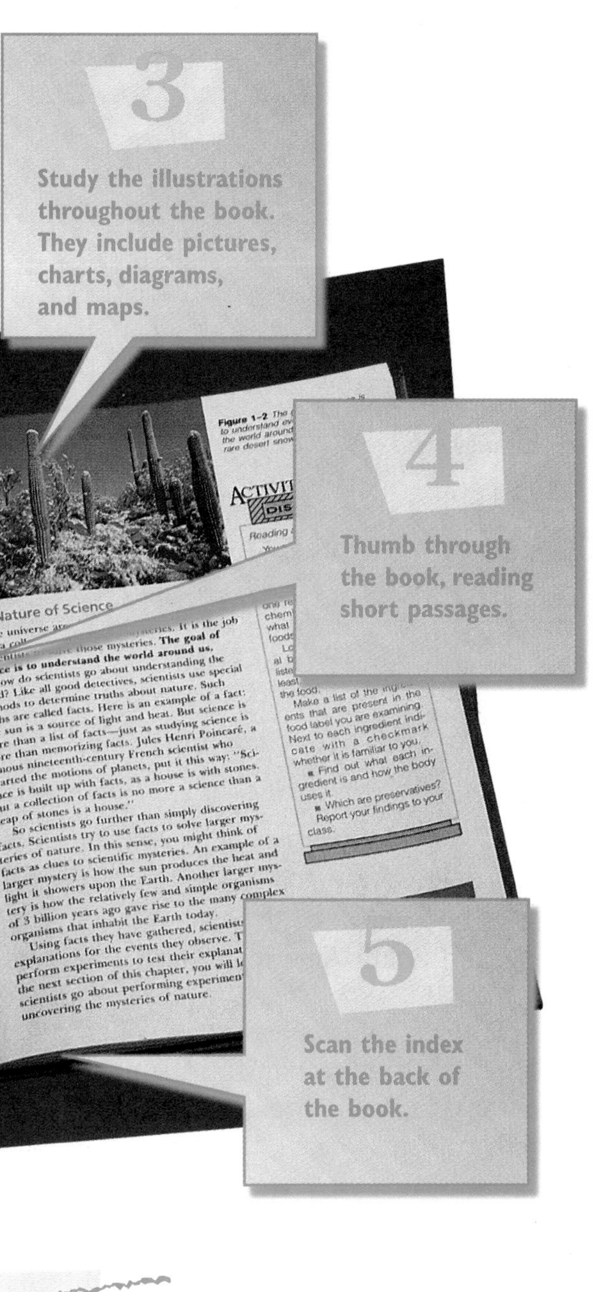
3
Study the illustrations throughout the book. They include pictures, charts, diagrams, and maps.
4
Thumb through the book, reading short passages.
5
Scan the index at the back of the book.
The Nature of Science

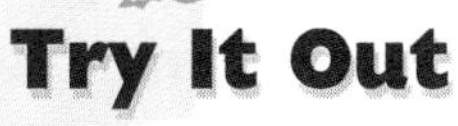

Try It Out

You can practice previewing a book in a fun and easy way by playing a "What Does It Tell Us?" game with a group of six students. Choose your group members, and choose a book. Then sit down and preview it together. Your group will follow the script to the right. After each person reads his or her part to the group, the other group members should work together to answer the question. Group Member 6 is the group secretary, who writes the answers down.

Group Member 1: "The title indicates the main subject of the book. Many books have a subtitle that gives even more information. What does the title of our book tell us?"

Group Member 2: "The table of contents is like a menu at a restaurant. It tells us what general topics are available in the book. What does the table of contents tell us?"

Group Member 3: "The illustrations in a book provide clues to the subjects discussed in the book. What do the illustrations tell us about the book?"

Group Member 4: "The index lists the specific topics in a book and the pages where they are discussed. What does the index tell us about the content of our book?"

Group Member 5: "By thumbing through a book and reading a few paragraphs here and there, you can get an idea of how a book is written. You can see if there are special headings in the book. What does a little reading tell us about our book?"

When you've completed this process, use the secretary's notes to find specific information in the book. If you are going to read the whole book, this process can help you get the most out of your reading.

Apply the Skill

Now that you know how to preview, practice by previewing Chapter 4. What do the titles and subtitles tell you about the chapter? How about the illustrations and captions? Take notes as you preview the chapter. Then, use your notes to write a short description of the chapter. Finally, as you read through the chapter, see how it matches your description.

Panama

Where Two Oceans Meet

Reach Into Your Background

Have you ever agreed to a deal or given away something and then wondered if you made the best choice? Think about how you felt. Write down some ways you might try to undo the deal.

Questions to Explore

1. What geographic and political factors made Panama a good site for a canal?
2. How was the Panama Canal built?
3. How did Panama gain control of the Panama Canal?

Key Term

lock

Key Places

Panama Canal
Canal Zone

The Panama Canal is the shortcut of the Western Hemisphere. It's the only way to get from the Pacific Ocean to the Atlantic by ship without going all the way around South America. That's a savings of 7,800 miles (12,553 km).

But be prepared to wait. Traffic jams can leave you bobbing in the ocean for up to 20 hours. Then the trip through the 40-mile (64.4-km) canal takes another eight hours. That's about walking speed. Then there is the toll: as much as $34,000.

Going Through the Canal

Cruising through the Pacific Ocean, a tanker approaches the city of Balboa, in the country of Panama. It is heading for the Panama Canal. The ship is loaded with petroleum. Other ships sailing toward the canal carry lumber, metal ores, and other cargo. Ships pass through the Panama Canal 24 hours a day, 365 days a year. The canal is crowded. The tanker must get in line.

The tanker enters the canal at sea level. But parts of the canal go through mountains and are not at sea level. The tanker will need to be raised and lowered several times as it travels toward the Atlantic Ocean.

Miraflores Lock The ship sails north to Miraflores (mee ruh FLOR uhs) Lock. A **lock** is a section of waterway in which ships are raised or lowered by adjusting the water level. The tanker passes through a set of gates into a lock chamber. The water in the chamber is still at sea level. Then, more water comes pouring into the chamber

Country Profile: Panama

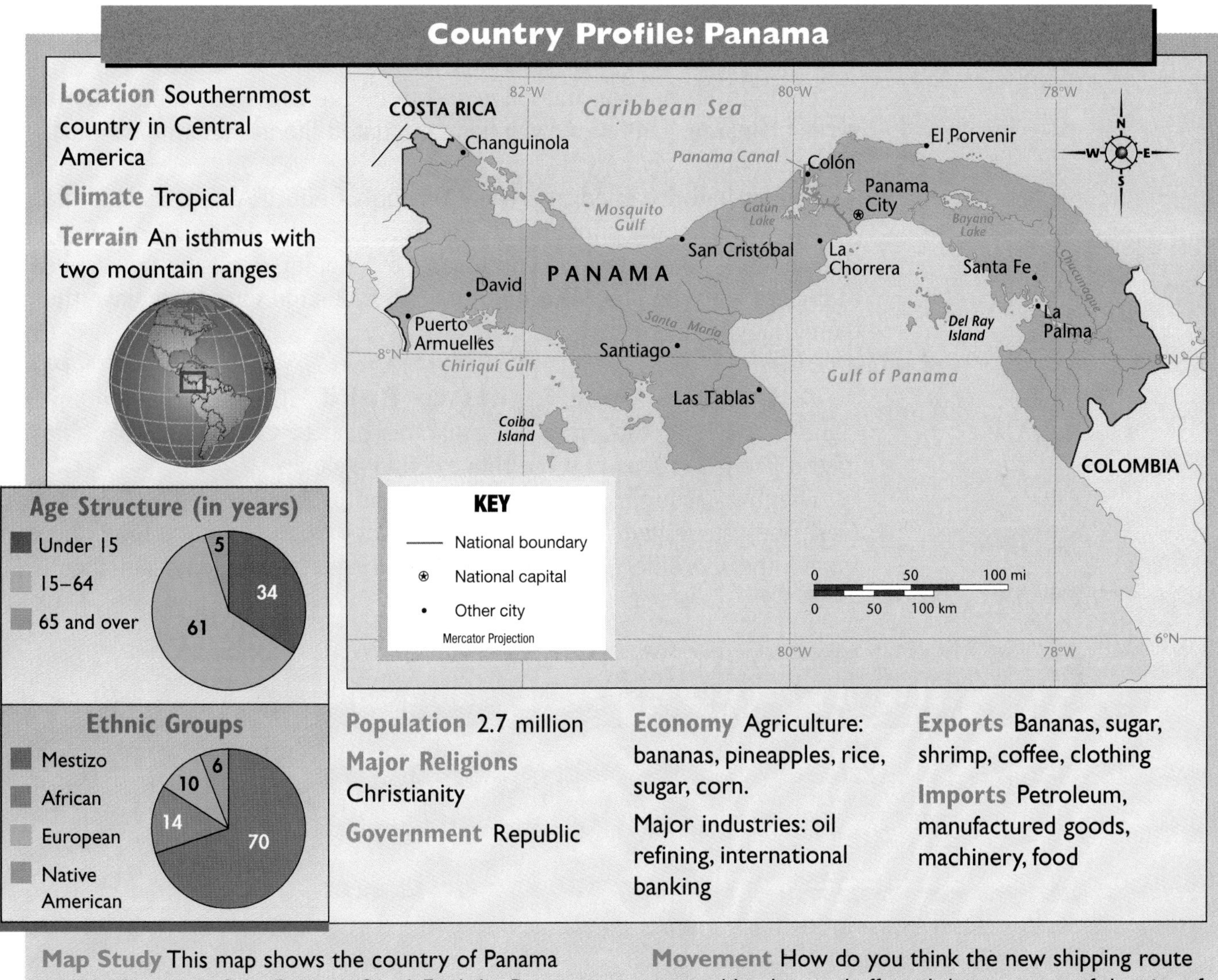

Location Southernmost country in Central America

Climate Tropical

Terrain An isthmus with two mountain ranges

Population 2.7 million

Major Religions Christianity

Government Republic

Economy Agriculture: bananas, pineapples, rice, sugar, corn.
Major industries: oil refining, international banking

Exports Bananas, sugar, shrimp, coffee, clothing

Imports Petroleum, manufactured goods, machinery, food

Map Study This map shows the country of Panama and the location of the Panama Canal. Find the Panama Canal on the map.

Movement How do you think the new shipping route created by the canal affected the economy of the city of Colón? Explain your answer.

through valves. The tanker rises like a toy boat in a bathtub filling with water. When the water rises high enough, the ship passes through a second set of gates and enters a small lake. It proceeds to the next lock, and the water level is raised again.

Galliard Cut During the voyage, the tanker will pass through two more sets of locks. It will zigzag through the eight-mile (13-km) Galliard (GAL yurd) Cut. The Galliard Cut was blasted through the hard rock of Panama's mountains. The tanker will sail through a huge artificial lake and past an island that is home to a wild game preserve. Finally, eight hours after entering the canal, the tanker exits at Limón (lih MOHN) Bay in the city of Colón (kuh LOHN). It has traveled only 40 miles (64 km), but it is now in the Atlantic Ocean.

The Idea for a Canal Takes Hold

Look at the map on this page and trace the route the canal follows across Panama. This waterway has dominated life in Panama for much of the twentieth century.

Sailors had dreamed of a canal through Central America since the 1500s. A canal could shorten the trip from the Atlantic to the Pacific by thousands of miles. It would cut the cost of shipping goods by thousands of dollars for each ship. But not until the 1900s did engineers have the technology to make such a canal.

A Struggle Over Rights to Build The first real attempt came in 1881. At that time, Panama was part of Colombia. Colombia gave a French company the rights to build a canal.

Digging through Panama posed several problems for the builders. First, they struggled with mud slides as they dug. Second, a mountain range, the Cordillera de San Blas (kord ul YEHR uh day san blas),

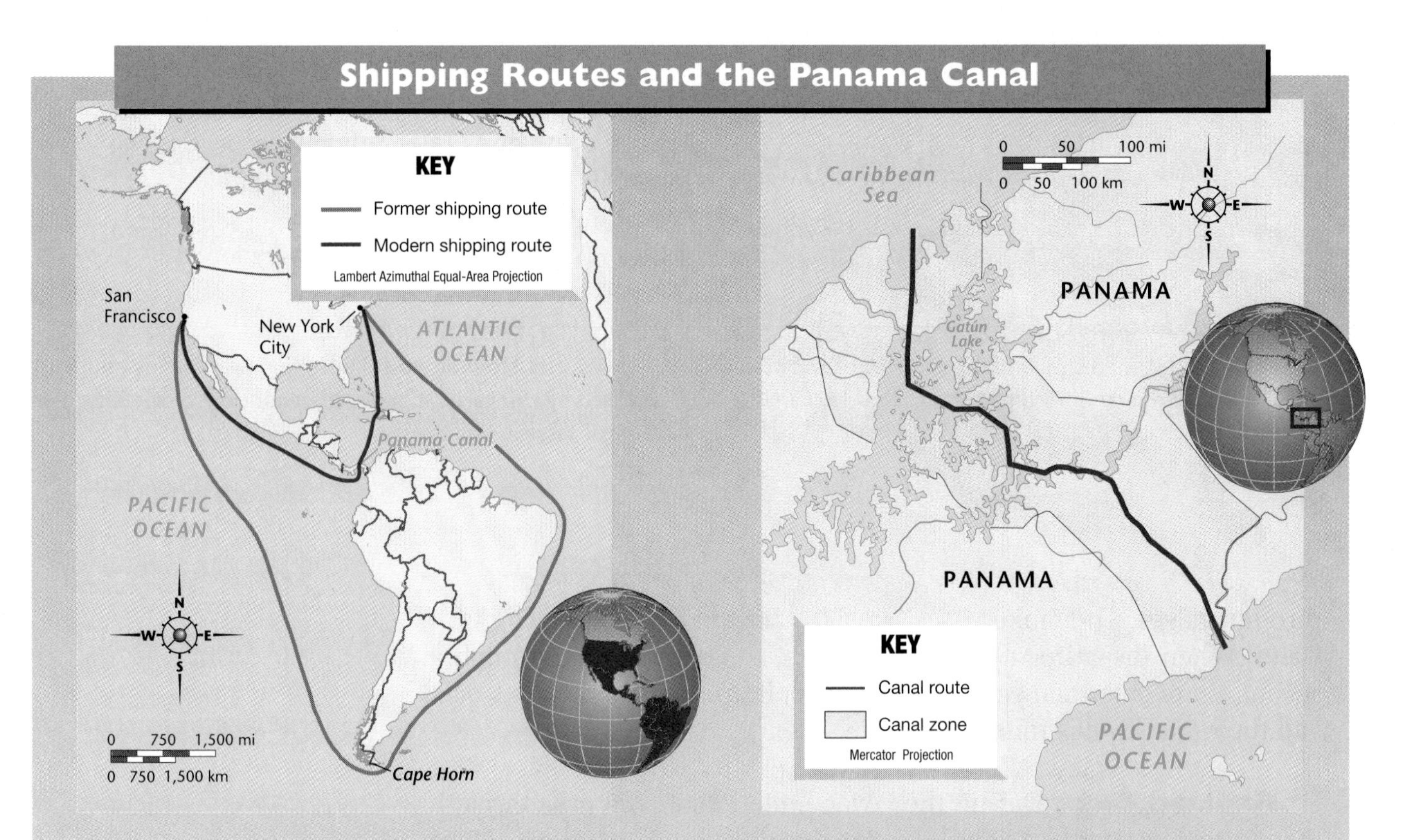

Map Study The map on the left shows shipping routes from New York to San Francisco before and after construction of the Panama Canal. The map on the right is a close up of the Panama Canal route. Before the Panama Canal was built, ships had to travel more than 13,000 miles (20,900 km) around South America. After the Canal was built, ships only had to travel 5,200 miles (8,370 km). **Movement** Why do you think that Panama and the United States both wanted to control the Canal Zone?

Panama's Tropical Rain Forest

Panama's Barro Colorado rain forest is inside the Canal Zone. **Critical Thinking** This photograph shows a trail through the rain forest. Where is it? Based on this photograph, think of some difficulties that might have faced the Panama Canal workers.

blocked the way. Disease was also a problem. Much of Panama is covered with dense tropical forest. Tropical diseases such as malaria and yellow fever killed many workers. After several years of digging and blasting, the French company went bankrupt. Work on the canal stopped.

In 1902, the United States government bought what was left of the French company. Then, the United States began talks with Colombia about getting the rights to continue building a canal.

Colombia refused to grant the United States rights to build the canal. The businesspeople of Panama were disappointed. They knew that a canal would bring business to Panama. They wanted the canal to be built as soon as possible. Also, many Panamanians wanted to be free of Colombia's rule. They saw the canal as a chance to win independence.

In November 1903, the United States helped Panama revolt against Colombia. Two weeks after Panama declared its independence, the United States received the rights needed to build the canal.

Not Made in Panama You would assume the "Panama hat," a hand-woven straw hat, is made in Panama. However, you would be wrong—the hats were originally made in Ecuador. They were named for Panama because it was a shipping center for hats in the 1800s. Ecuadorans still make the Panama hat. But today, many hats are made even farther from Panama—in Asia.

Like Digging Through Sand

The cut through Panama's soft earth hills was the hardest part of the canal to build. Earth still slides into the canal there today. **Movement** Based on the picture on the left, how were workers and supplies moved to and from the canal?

Building the Canal The builders of the canal faced numerous problems. They had to scoop out and remove mountains of earth and rock. The hills were made of soft earth. Whenever the diggers carved out a hole, more earth would slide into its place. The project called for a dam to be built to form a lake. There were locks to design and build.

While the work was difficult and slow, by far the biggest problem facing the project was disease. Some 25,000 workers had died of malaria and yellow fever while the French worked on the canal. Scientists did not know what caused these diseases, so they could do little to prevent them.

In the early 1900s, doctors discovered that malaria and yellow fever were both carried by mosquitoes. The mosquitoes bred in swamps and also in people's drinking water. In 1904, the Panama Canal Company hired a doctor and a large crew to deal with the mosquito problem. It took one year, 1,000 tons (907 metric tons) of timber, 200 tons (181 metric tons) of wire mesh, and 4,500 workers to do the job. Workers burned sulfur in every house to kill mosquitoes. They covered

Predict How do you think workers overcame problems to build the Panama Canal?

every water vessel with mesh so mosquitoes could not get in. They filled in swampy breeding grounds with dirt. Without this effort, the Panama Canal probably could not have been built.

Modern medicine and machinery were important to the project. So was good planning. Still, it took eight years and the sweat of 45,000 workers, mostly Caribbean islanders, to make the waterway. The Panama Canal remains one of the greatest engineering feats of modern times.

Control of the Canal

When the United States gained rights to build a canal, it signed a treaty with Panama. The treaty gave the United States the right to build the Panama Canal, and to control it forever.

Ask Questions What would you like to know about life near the Canal Zone?

The Canal Zone The United States also controlled an area called the Canal Zone. The Canal Zone included the land on either side of the canal, the ports, the port cities, and the railroad. The treaty allowed the United States to run the Zone according to its laws, and gave the United States the right to invade Panama to protect the canal.

Many Panamanians felt this was too high a price to pay for the privilege of having the canal in their country. The canal gave the United States a great deal of power in Panama. The United States built 14 military bases in the Canal Zone and stationed thousands of soldiers there.

For years, Panama talked with the United States about regaining control of the canal. In the 1960s and 1970s, many Panamanians grew angry. They rioted to protest U.S. control.

A Change of Ownership In 1978, after years of talks, U.S. President Jimmy Carter signed two new treaties with Panama's government. The Panama Canal Neutrality Treaty and the Panama Canal Treaty gave Panama more control over the canal. In 1999, the Panama Canal will belong to Panama for the first time.

1. **Define** lock.
2. **Identify** (a) Panama Canal, (b) Canal Zone.
3. How did a canal come to be built in Panama?
4. What difficulties did the builders of the canal face?
5. How did the United States gain control of rights to build the canal?
6. Two sets of treaties have determined the control of the Panama Canal, the original treaty of 1903 and two in 1978. Describe the terms of these treaties.

Critical Thinking

7. **Identifying Central Issues** It has been very important to Panamanians to regain control of the canal. Explain why, in both political and economic terms.

Activity

8. **Writing to Learn** Imagine that you are a newspaper editor in 1900. Decide whether you think Panama or Nicaragua is a better choice for the location of the canal, and write a short editorial defending your position.

CHAPTER 4

Review and Activities

Reviewing Main Ideas

1. Describe the movement of Mexicans from one area to another—rural to rural, rural to urban. Why do many people make these moves?
2. What problems has Mexico City experienced as a result of its rapid population growth?
3. How are the indigenous cultures of Guatemala distinct from the ladino culture?
4. What are the main challenges that indigenous Guatemalans face?
5. How did the United States gain the rights to build a canal in Panama?
6. (a) Why was the canal important to the United States and Panama?
   (b) How is control of the canal currently changing?

Reviewing Key Terms

Match the definitions in Column I with the key terms in Column II.

Column I

1. a landless person who travels from one area to another working other people's land
2. a section of a waterway in which ships are raised or lowered by adjusting the water level
3. a person who settles on someone else's land without permission
4. a work stoppage
5. a public square
6. people who share race, language, religion, and cultural traditions

Column II

a. **squatter**
b. **plaza**
c. **migrant farmworker**
d. **ethnic group**
e. **strike**
f. **lock**

Critical Thinking

1. **Identifying Central Issues** What are the main demands that Rigoberta Menchú and others like her have made of the government and landowners? How has the government responded?
2. **Drawing Conclusions** Over the years, the United States has exercised a great deal of economic and political influence in Central America. How does the Panama Canal demonstrate U.S. influence in the region? What do you think the changes taking place over the control of the canal say about U.S. influence in the region today?

Graphic Organizer

Copy the tree map onto a piece of paper. In the first set of boxes, note the three kinds of population movement. In the second set, note details about these movements.

Population Movements in Mexico

Map Activity

For each place listed below, write the letter from the map that shows its location.

1. Guatemala
2. Colón, Panama
3. Panama
4. Mexico City

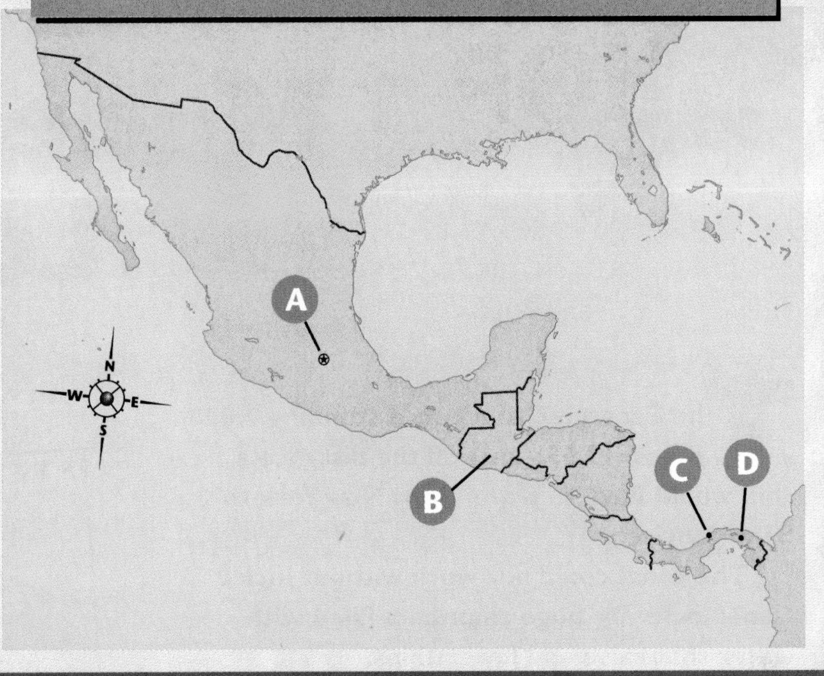

Internet Activity

Use a search engine to find the site **Ancient Guatemala.** Read **Our Mayan Legacy**. Then, click on **Guatemalan Home Page.** Click on the links **Modern Guatemala and Our People.** Make a chart comparing the architecture, language, people, and culture of ancient and modern Guatemala.

Writing Activity

Writing News Stories
Imagine you are a writer for a radio news program. Write brief news stories on population movements in Mexico, the work of Rigoberta Menchú, and the history of the Panama Canal. Be sure that each of your stories can be read in two to three minutes.

Skills Review

Turn to the Skill Activity.

Review the steps for previewing. Then use these steps to preview Chapter 5. Based on your preview, write a brief paragraph describing what you expect to read in the chapter.

How Am I Doing?

Answer these questions to help you check your progress.

1. Can I explain why a Mexican family might decide to leave the countryside for the city?
2. Do I understand the major challenges that face the indigenous peoples of Guatemala?
3. Can I describe the building of the Panama Canal and its impact on the Panamanian people?
4. What information from this chapter can I use in my book project?

LAB ACTIVITY SHOP

Making a Model Canal Lock

The Panama Canal cuts a stunning 7,800 miles (12,553 km) off the distance a ship would have to travel from New York to San Francisco.

The canal could not work without locks. Canal locks are huge chambers filled with water that raise and lower ships.

The Panama Canal needs locks because the sea level at the Atlantic and the Pacific entrances to the canal is not the same. Also, the path of the canal is not level—it goes up one slope to the continental divide and down the other.

Purpose

The best way to understand how canal locks work is to build a model of one. As you complete this activity, you will understand how a real ship travels through a real canal.

Materials

- two half-gallon cardboard juice or milk cartons
- modelling wax
- scissors
- duct tape
- a ballpoint pen
- a cork
- a paper clip
- a pitcher of water

Procedure

STEP ONE

Construct a model canal and lock. Follow the illustrations. Cut the cartons in half lengthwise. Line up three of the four halves lengthwise and connect them on the outside with duct tape. Then carefully cut out the walls of cardboard that separate the boxes and divide your canal. Line three edges of each cut-out wall with modelling wax. Then replace the walls. Use

enough wax to make a watertight seal. These are the gates in the canal lock.

STEP TWO

Use the pen, cork, and paper clip to make a model ship. Look at the picture for an example. Stick the paper clip into the bottom of the ship to make it float upright.

STEP THREE

Fill your canal with water. Fill one end and the middle of the carton with water about one inch deep. Fill the other end with water almost to the top. Float your boat in the end of the canal with the lower water level.

STEP FOUR

Operate the canal lock to raise your ship to the higher water level. Remove the gate that separates your ship from the middle chamber. Sail your ship into the middle chamber and close the gate behind it by carefully replacing it. To raise your ship to the next level, slowly pour water into the middle chamber until the water level matches the level in the last chamber. Remove the second gate, sail your ship into the last chamber, and replace the gate. You have successfully navigated a canal!

Observations

1. How did you raise your ship from one level to a higher level?
2. Why does the canal lock need gates to work?

ANALYSIS AND CONCLUSION

1. How do you think the water level is raised in a real lock?
2. Repeat the activity in reverse. How will you lower your ship?

Exploring the Caribbean

SECTION 1
Cuba
CLINGING TO COMMUNISM

SECTION 2
Haiti
THE ROAD TO DEMOCRACY

SECTION 3
Puerto Rico
CULTURAL IDENTITY OF A PEOPLE

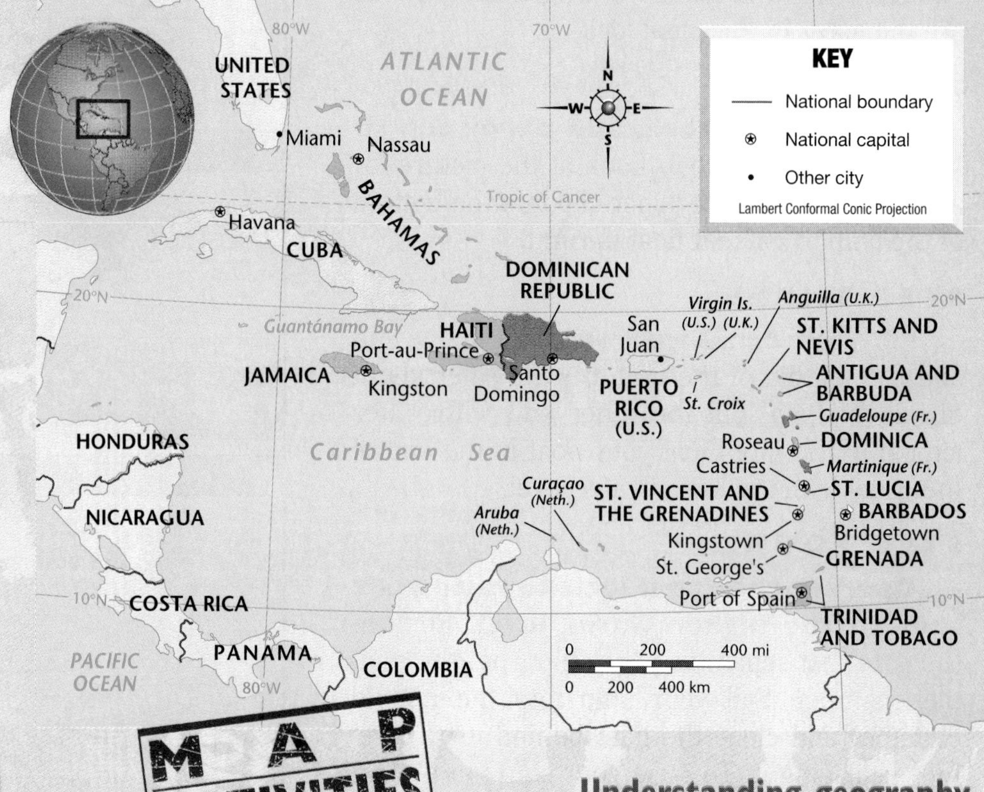

MAP ACTIVITIES

The islands of the Caribbean stretch about 1,500 miles (2,414 km) across blue-green waters. Each island has its own traditions and cultures. To learn more about the Caribbean, complete the following activities.

Understanding geography

How do you think the sea may have affected the economies of the Caribbean islands?

Study the map

Before the Europeans arrived in the region, how do you think the sea may have served as both a highway and a barrier to contact with other people?

Cuba

Clinging to Communism

Reach Into Your Background

Suppose that you had to move tomorrow and you could pack exactly one suitcase. You could never come back for the things you left behind. What would you pack?

Questions to Explore

1. What is life in Cuba like today?
2. What ties do Cuban Americans have to Cuba?

Key Terms

dictator
communist
exile
illiterate

Key People and Places

Fidel Castro
Fulgencio Batista
Miami

Twelve-year-old Venesa Alonso (vuh NEH suh uh LAHN zoh) lives in Miami, Florida. Her home is just a few miles away from the ocean. Venesa hardly ever goes to the beach, however. The blue waves and roaring surf remind her of her trip from Cuba to the United States. The memory still gives her nightmares.

Venesa and her family left Cuba in the summer of 1994. They built a rickety raft and carried it to the ocean. They were among the 35,000 Cubans who took to the sea that summer. They sailed on anything that would float—rubber tires, old boats, and home-made rafts. One hope kept them going. It was the thought of making it to the United States. They planned to apply to enter the United States as immigrants.

Venesa's family and thousands of others left Cuba for two main reasons. The first reason was that Cuba's economy was in bad shape. People often did not have enough food to eat. Clothing, medicine, and other basic necessities were hard to get. A desire for freedom was the second reason why many people left. Cuba's leader, Fidel Castro (fee DEL KAS troh), does not allow Cubans to speak out against government policies they disagree with.

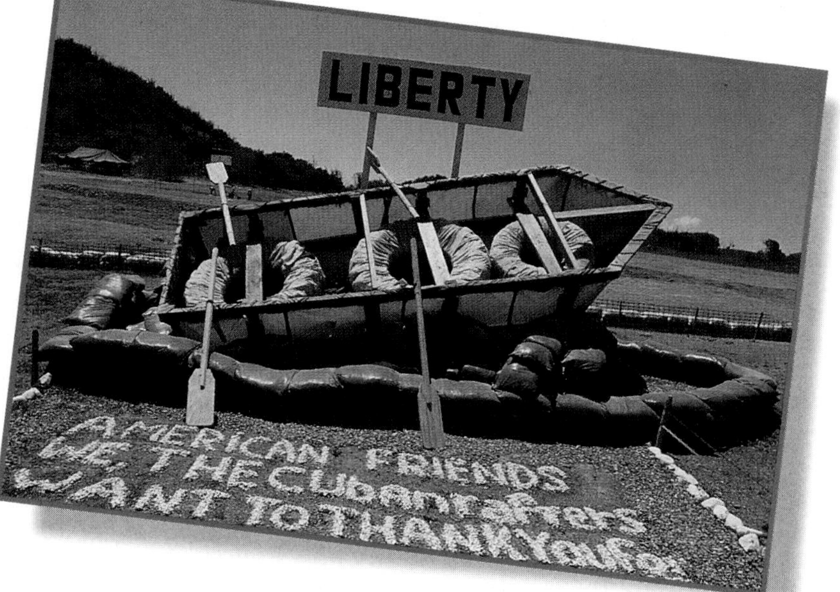

▼ Cubans trying to reach the United States in 1995 took to the sea in boats like this one.

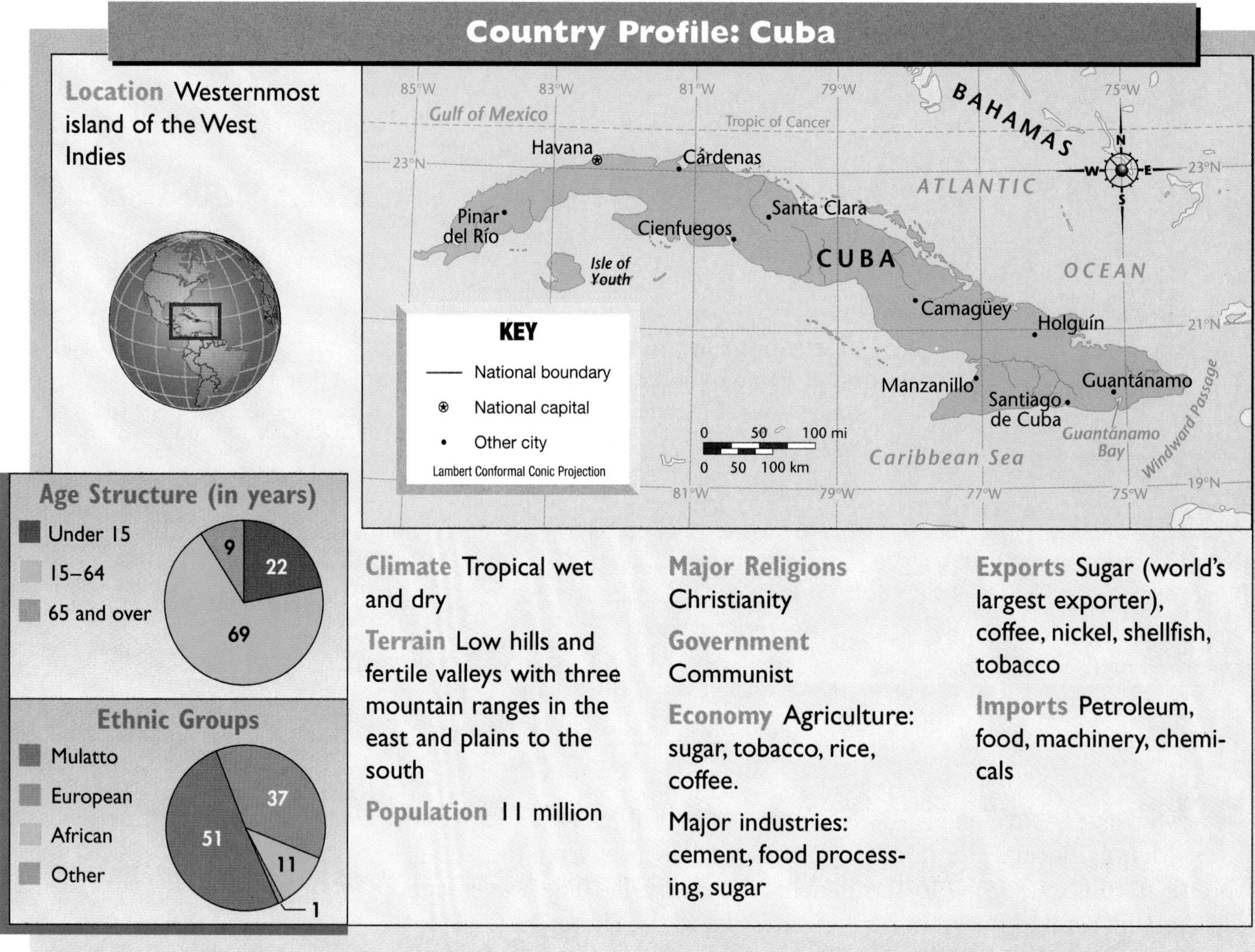

Map Study Hundreds of thousands of Cubans have left Cuba in recent years. Many Cubans traveled on small boats and on rafts made of plywood and inner tubes. They were trying to cross 90 miles (145 km) of ocean to reach Florida. **Location** What is the capital of Cuba? Where are Cuba's capital and most of its major cities located?

Cuba's History

Cuba is a small country. It is about the size of the state of Pennsylvania. Cuba's farmland is fertile, and Cuba is the third largest sugar producer in the world. Look at the political map in the Activity Atlas in the front of your book. Cuba is located between the two entrances to the Gulf of Mexico. It also has excellent harbors. This makes it a good place to trade with the United States and other parts of the Caribbean. But Cuba's relationship with the United States and many of its neighbors has not been friendly since the 1960s.

Cuban Independence Cuba's government and economy were not always like they are now. Cuba was a Spanish colony. In 1898, the United States defeated Spain in the Spanish-American War, and Cuba won its independence. In the years that followed, Cuba became the richest country in the Caribbean. Sugar planters made money

A Fiery Speechmaker

Fidel Castro led the revolution in Cuba. After the revolution, Cuba's friendly relationship with the United States ended. **Critical Thinking** Why do you think the United States is opposed to Castro's rule as Cuba's communist dictator?

Ask Questions If you could interview Fidel Castro, what questions would you ask him?

selling to people in the United States. Hotels were built, and tourists came to Cuba to enjoy its beautiful beaches and great climate. Many Cubans became businesspeople, teachers, doctors, and lawyers.

Not all Cubans shared the country's wealth, however. Most farm and factory workers earned low wages. Cuba also had many harsh leaders who ruled as dictators. A **dictator** is a ruler who has complete power. In the 1950s, Fulgencio Batista (fool HEN see yoh bah TEE stah) was Cuba's leader. During his rule, some people formed rebel groups to remove Batista and change the country.

Communism in Cuba A young lawyer named Fidel Castro led one of these small rebel groups. He tried three times to overthrow the government during the 1950s. By his third attempt, he had gained many supporters. Finally, Batista gave up and left the country in 1959.

When Batista left, Fidel Castro took control of Cuba. He still holds power today. Castro's government is **communist.** In a communist country, the government owns all large businesses and most of the country's land. Under Castro, the Cuban government took over private businesses and land. Further, Castro said that newspapers and books could print only information supporting his government. Anyone who disagreed with government policy was put in jail. Huge numbers of Cubans fled the island. Many settled in Miami, Florida.

Cuba became a communist country in the early 1960s. At the same time, it became friendly with the Soviet Union. The Soviet Union was then the most powerful communist nation in the world. It sent money and supplies to Cuba. The United States and the Soviet Union, however, were not friendly. As a result, Cuba's relationship with the United States became tense. Relations grew worse when the United States openly welcomed the people who fled from Cuba.

To Be a Leader When José Martí grew up in Cuba in the 1800s, it was still a colony of Spain. At age 16, he started a newspaper dedicated to Cuban independence. Martí later became famous for his poems and essays. In 1895, he led the revolution that eventually liberated Cuba. By the time independence was achieved, however, Martí had died in a battle with the Spanish.

Cuban Americans Relax in Miami

There is a large Cuban American community in Miami, Florida. These men are playing dominoes in a Miami park. Behind them is a mural showing the presidents of many countries in the Western Hemisphere.

Cubans Leaving Cuba

Lydia Martin left Cuba in 1970. She was only six years old. Her mother had grown tired of the limits on freedom and lack of opportunity in communist Cuba. She wanted to take Lydia to the United States with her. Lydia's father begged her to stay.

> "For years [my mother] had been anxious to leave Cuba . . . to take me to a place where I could learn about freedom. Her exit papers had finally arrived, but my father wouldn't let me go. . . . There was no talking sense into a man who feared losing his little girl forever. . . . While my mother was away at the church, I called him.
>
> "I'm leaving with my mother," I told him with all the bravery a six-year-old could muster. . . .
>
> "Have you stopped to think you may never see me again?" my father asked. . . ."

Cuban Exiles Many Cuban exiles tell stories like Lydia's. An **exile** is a person who leaves his or her homeland for another country because of political problems. From the 1960s onwards, large numbers of people left Cuba. Many families were torn apart.

Dreams of Returning to Cuba Some Cubans never got over the loss of their home. In the 1970s, relations between the United States and Cuba grew worse. Even if she wanted to, Lydia Martin could not write to her father. The government might punish him if he got a letter from the United States. Still, Lydia hoped to reunite with him one day. Lydia's mother now spoke of Cuba with longing. She said that in Cuba, the sky was bluer, the sand whiter, and the palm trees greener.

In 1991, the government of the Soviet Union collapsed and could no longer help Cuba. Food, medicine, tools, and other necessities became more scarce. Lydia began worrying about her father and her other relatives. In 1995, she flew back to the island for the first time. Visitors from the United States are not always welcome in Cuba, especially if they once fled the island. Lydia was nervous.

Livan Hernandez At 21 years old, Livan Hernandez was close to becoming a star pitcher in the Cuban Baseball League. He left Cuba for a chance to make millions of dollars pitching for a major league team in the United States. If that decision sounds easy, consider that Hernandez left behind everyone who is dear to him in Cuba. Hernandez hopes his family can one day enjoy the same freedom he has found.

Cuba: Today and Tomorrow

When Lydia stood on the beach in Cuba, she thought of her mother. Her mother had been right. The sky did seem bluer here, the sand whiter, and the palm trees greener.

Lydia had heard about the food shortages in Cuba, but she had not known how bad they were. Her father's new family sometimes had little more than rice to eat. When Lydia unpacked the shoes, soap, powdered milk, and underwear she had brought, her father and his new family took them with joy. They cooked her a delicious meal of lobster and rice on her first night. They had been saving money for it for months.

◀ After Lydia Martin (left) departed from Cuba, she did not see or talk to her father (right) again for 25 years.

A Cuban High School

At many of Cuba's rural schools, students spend four hours in the classroom and four hours doing manual labor. **Critical Thinking** How is this school similar to yours? How is it different?

One thing that Cubans do not need to save money for is education. In the 1960s and 1970s, Castro overhauled Cuba's schools. At the time, many Cubans were **illiterate,** or unable to read and write. Castro sent students and teachers into the countryside to teach. Soon, more Cubans could read and write than ever before. Today, about 95 percent of Cubans can read and write.

Schools in Cuba may have helped many Cubans to learn how to read. However, they teach only communist ideas. But because Cuba is close to the United States, Cubans can tune in to American radio stations. Cuban teenagers listen to popular American dance music. They wear jeans from the United States whenever they can get them. Castro has allowed some businesses to be privately owned. The tourist industry is growing.

No one knows what Cuba's future will bring. Many think the time is near when those who left Cuba will be able to return home to visit or live there in freedom.

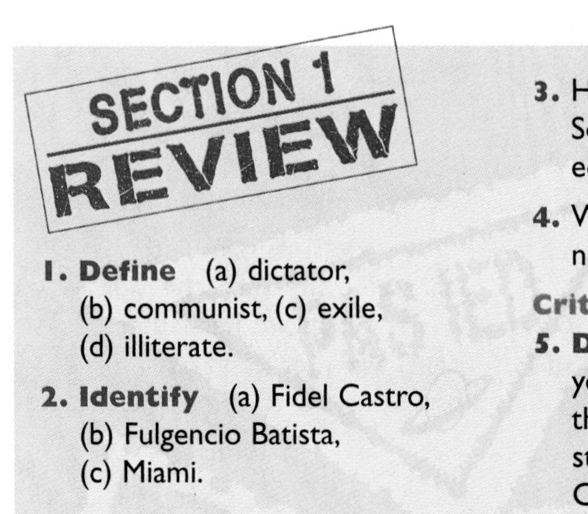

1. **Define** (a) dictator, (b) communist, (c) exile, (d) illiterate.
2. **Identify** (a) Fidel Castro, (b) Fulgencio Batista, (c) Miami.
3. How did the collapse of the Soviet Union affect Cuba's economy?
4. What problems did communism bring to Cuba?

Critical Thinking

5. **Drawing Conclusions** Do you think that Cubans born in the United States feel as strongly about Cuba as their Cuban-born parents do? Why or why not?

Activity

6. **Writing to Learn** Work with a partner. One of you will write a letter to a relative in Cuba from the point of view of a Cuban exile in the United States. The other will write a response from the point of view of a Cuban who has never left Cuba.

Haiti

The Road to Democracy

Reach Into Your Background
Is there something in your life that you have had to try many times to achieve? What strategies did you use to try to get what you wanted? Did they work? Why or why not?

Questions to Explore

1. How did Haiti's struggle for democracy affect people's lives?
2. How does the history of Haiti affect the culture of its people?

Key Terms
Creole
dialect

Key People and Places
Jean-Bertrand Aristide
Toussaint L'Ouverture
François Duvalier
Jean-Claude Duvalier
Port-au-Prince

The plane dipped toward Port-au-Prince (port oh PRINS), the capital of Haiti. It flew over a spreading slum. The slum was a neighborhood of crumbling cardboard huts with tin roofs. In the streets, people were jammed into a solid mass. All heads turned up toward the sky.

As if in one voice, a cheer of joy rose from the crowd. In the plane, Haiti's president, Jean-Bertrand Aristide (zhan behr TRAHND uh ris TEED), was returning to his country after a three-year exile. He had been elected by the people, but Haiti's military had forced him to leave. Then, a group of generals had taken over the country. The United States and other nations had pressured the military to give power back to Aristide. Many hoped that Aristide's return would also bring back democracy.

▼ After his exile, Haitian President Jean-Bertrand Aristide returned to Haiti amid cheers of support.

Haiti's Struggle for Democracy

Aristide was the first president to be elected democratically in many years. This does not mean that most Haitians did not want democracy. Their country was born out of a desperate struggle for freedom. Haiti is the only nation in the Americas formed from a successful revolt of enslaved Africans.

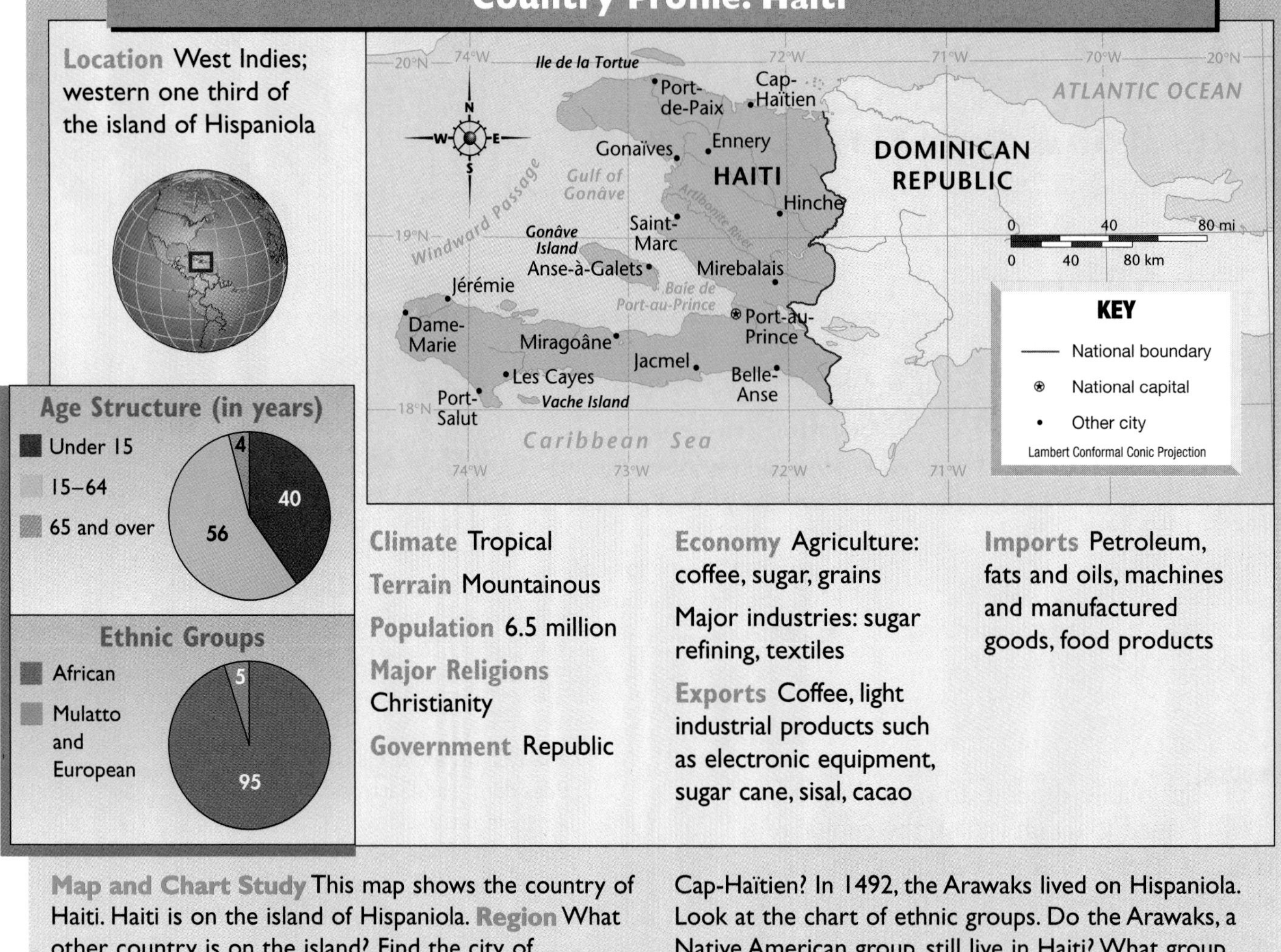

Map and Chart Study This map shows the country of Haiti. Haiti is on the island of Hispaniola. **Region** What other country is on the island? Find the city of Cap-Haïtien. This is near the spot where Columbus landed in 1492. **Location** On what side of the island is Cap-Haïtien? In 1492, the Arawaks lived on Hispaniola. Look at the chart of ethnic groups. Do the Arawaks, a Native American group, still live in Haiti? What group makes up the largest part of the population?

The Birth of Haiti As you can see on the Country Profile above, Haiti lies on the western third of the island of Hispaniola. Haiti was once a colony of France. Europeans brought enslaved Africans to Haiti to work on sugar cane and coffee plantations. In the 1790s, slave revolts began. A Haitian leader named Toussaint L'Ouverture helped banish slavery from Haiti in 1801. He also offered Haitians a new way of life, based on the idea that all people could live as equals.

Troubled Years In the years that followed, Toussaint L'Ouverture's goal of freedom and equality was never fully realized. Most of Haiti's presidents became dictators once they got into power. One of the worst was François Duvalier (frahn SWAH doo VAHL yay), who took power in 1957. Because Duvalier had been a country doctor, Haitians called him "Papa Doc."

Papa Doc died in 1971. He was followed by his son, Jean-Claude Duvalier (zhan KLAHD doo VAHL yay), or "Baby Doc." Both Papa Doc and Baby Doc were cruel leaders. They stole government funds and used violence to keep power. During their rule, Haiti became the poorest country in the Western Hemisphere.

In 1986, rebels forced Baby Doc to leave the country. Many Haitians thought a period of freedom and prosperity was about to begin. But this was not to be. Haiti was ruled by one military leader after another. And most Haitians still made a living trying to farm small plots of land.

Connect How do most people in the United States make a living?

Life on a Farm When farmer Pierre Joseph stands at the top of his land, he can see the calm waters of the Caribbean. When he looks down, he sees the dry, cracked earth of his one acre.

About two thirds of the people in Haiti make their living by farming. The land has been overused. Most trees have been cut. Rains wash the topsoil into the sea. Joseph is thin because he rarely gets enough to eat. "The land just doesn't yield enough," he says. He points to the few rows of corn and beans that he can grow on his one acre.

Farmers like Pierre Joseph can barely make a living, but many feel they are rich in other ways. Haitian culture blends African, French, and West Indian tradition. The blend of traditions gives Haiti a Creole culture. **Creole** is a word referring to people of mixed ancestry.

Creole also refers to the dialect spoken in Haiti. A **dialect** is the different version of a language that is spoken in a particular region. The Creole dialect is based on both French and African languages.

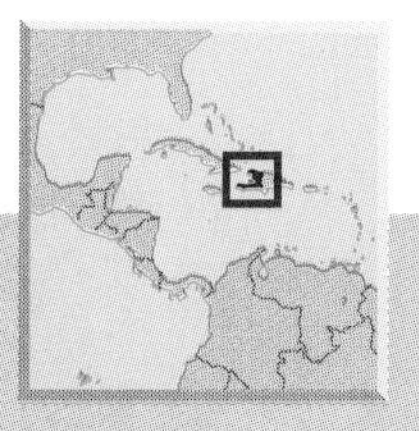

Papa Doc and Baby Doc

François (left) and Jean-Claude Duvalier (right) often used violence to rule Haiti. The country also became much poorer during their rule. By the time Baby Doc was forced from power, the average Haitian earned only about $300 a year.

Life in the City Haiti's capital, Port-au-Prince, is a blend not only of cultures, but also of rich and poor. The wealthy live in spacious wooden houses on the hills overlooking the city. There is a small middle class of doctors, lawyers, teachers, and owners of small businesses, that also live fairly well. Many poor people from the country live in tiny homes of crumbling concrete.

Predict Why do you think that Haitians were so glad to see Jean-Bertrand Aristide?

Hopes for the Future

In December 1990, Jean-Bertrand Aristide was elected president. Haitians held high hopes for the future. Aristide was a Catholic priest who had long defended the rights of the poor. He took office in February 1991.

A Military Takeover Aristide served as president for seven months. Then Haiti's military forced him to leave the country. The military also attacked his supporters. "We have been in hiding since police shot up our house in October," an Aristide supporter told reporters in 1991. "We got away because people warned us they were coming."

The year after the election, thousands of Aristide supporters fled the capital. They feared for their lives. They squeezed into trucks by the dozen and went to hide in the hills. Others tore their homes apart to make rafts. Then they took to the sea. Many headed for the United States. Some were sent back.

A Rural Village in Haiti

Cange Walthe
age 12
Haiti

This student drawing of rural Haiti contrasts with the urban scene on the next page. **Critical Thinking** What clues does this student provide to show that this village is in a rural area? What clues show that the village is in a place that has a tropical climate?

Dancing in the Streets

Haiti's people danced in the streets of Port-au-Prince when they heard that Aristide was returning to the country. They hoped that peace would return to Haiti along with Aristide.

Hundreds of children also left Haiti on rafts. Fifteen-year-old Fresenel Pierre (frehz uh NEL pea EHR) was one. He had an older brother waiting for him in Miami, where there is a large Haitian community. The children Fresenel sailed with were the children of Aristide supporters. Many were coming to the United States with no one to take them in.

Returning to Roots In 1994, Aristide came back to Haiti. Since his return, a new spirit seems to be everywhere in Haiti. It has led to a movement to return to Haiti's Creole roots. For many Haitians, the idea of Creole has become an idea of equality. It suggests that people of different races and cultures must all work together to give Haiti its special identity.

1. **Define** (a) Creole, (b) dialect.
2. **Identify** (a) Jean-Bertrand Aristide, (b) Toussaint L'Ouverture, (c) François Duvalier, (d) Jean-Claude Duvalier, (e) Port-au-Prince.
3. How did Haiti win its independence?
4. What obstacles to making a living do farmers like Pierre Joseph face?

Critical Thinking

5. **Making Comparisons** Give an example of how Haitian culture blends African and European traditions.

Activity

6. **Writing to Learn** Write a diary entry from the point of view of Pierre Joseph about how economic and political conditions in Haiti affect his life.

Locating Information

Marisol felt like a sailor lost at sea.

She was surrounded by an ocean of information. Shelves overflowing with books towered above her. Beyond the bookshelves, more shelves loomed, filled with magazines. Past the magazines were computer terminals. Enough information to fill millions of pages could be accessed through them. Although she was in her community library, Marisol felt just as lost as if she were adrift in a lifeboat.

Marisol had gone to the library to find information about Toussaint L'Ouverture. Marisol had read in her textbook how L'Ouverture had led the Haitian people to freedom more than 200 years ago. Marisol's assignment was to write a one-page biography, or life story, about L'Ouverture. One question loomed in her mind: Where should she begin?

Get Ready

Locating information is an essential skill. Throughout your school career, you will need to locate information to complete homework assignments and class projects. As an adult, you will need to locate information to help you decide many things such as where to live, what job to do, and how to do it.

The first rule about locating information is *Don't panic!* Marisol felt lost in the library. But libraries and other sources of information are carefully designed to make your search for information as easy as possible. Just like a sailor at sea, it's a matter of choosing your destination, planning your route, and finally sailing to the one little island where the information you need is located.

Try It Out

Locating the information you need can be an exciting adventure. When you locate the information you've been searching for, you will feel the satisfaction and excitement of an explorer who finds the right island. Work with a partner to plan a voyage out into the Sea of Information:

A. Choose your destination. Your destination is the information you need. You and your partner should pick one now, and write it down. It might look like this: *"Destination: Information about how many Cubans live in the United States."*

B. Determine the best way to get there. Just as there are many ways to travel, there are many ways to locate information. Five important routes to information are listed in the box to the right. Discuss each source of information with your partner. Choose the source most likely to have the information you seek.

C. Prepare for your journey. You're about to depart, so pack your bags! You'll need a notebook and a pencil to jot down information. You might need a few coins for the copy machine.

D. Use signposts. Just as signposts can help you find your way on a real journey, different "signposts" can help you on your journey to find information. Read about these "signposts" in the box.

Five Important Routes To Information

Libraries Most of the world's information is stored in libraries. *Signposts:* the card catalog and librarians.

Books There are books about nearly every subject. *Signposts:* book titles and tables of contents.

Periodicals Magazines and newspapers can provide up-to-date information on a huge range of topics. *Signposts:* magazine indexes and newspaper indexes found in libraries.

The Internet The Internet is a worldwide network of computers containing information. *Signposts:* special electronic search indexes on the Internet.

People By interviewing experts, you can learn what they know about their specialties. *Signposts:* the telephone directory to locate appropriate people to interview.

Apply the Skill

Now that you've made an information-seeking journey with a partner, it's time to do it alone. Choose one of the following destinations:

- Destination: Information that identifies the chief agricultural product grown in Cuba.
- Destination: Information that identifies the President of Haiti.
- Destination: Information that identifies three historic sites you could visit in Puerto Rico.

Once you have reached your destination by locating the information, draw a map to show how you found it.

Puerto Rico

Cultural Identity of a People

Reach Into Your Background

Do you ever feel that you have "two selves"? One that acts a certain way with some people? And another that comes out when you are with other people? Are both of them the real you?

Questions to Explore

1. What factors influenced Puerto Rican culture?
2. What is Puerto Rico's relationship with the United States?

Key Terms

citizen
commonwealth
constitution

Key Places

San Juan
Condado

Puerto Rican Esmeralda Santiago (ez mur EL duh sant ee AHG oh) can never forget the first time she saw the movie *West Side Story.* She was living in New York. It was 1961 and she was 13 years old. The movie was about Puerto Ricans living in New York, but most of the actors who played them were English-speaking whites. To her, they just didn't seem like Puerto Rican people.

Seeing the movie was a turning point in Esmeralda's life. She knew the movie was not about her. But she did not know what the film should have been like. Realizing this made her feel confused.

▼ Esmeralda Santiago moved from Puerto Rico to New York City when she was 13 years old.

> "I had no sense of Puerto Rican culture or what it was to me. Where did I come from? Who is this person who calls herself a Puerto Rican and what does that mean? . . . [W]hen I think Puerto Rican, there's this big void, this empty space where my history should be."

Puerto Rican and American

Even though Esmeralda felt confused about who she was, she remembered her early days in Puerto Rico vividly. When Esmeralda's mother brought her to New York City, everything changed.

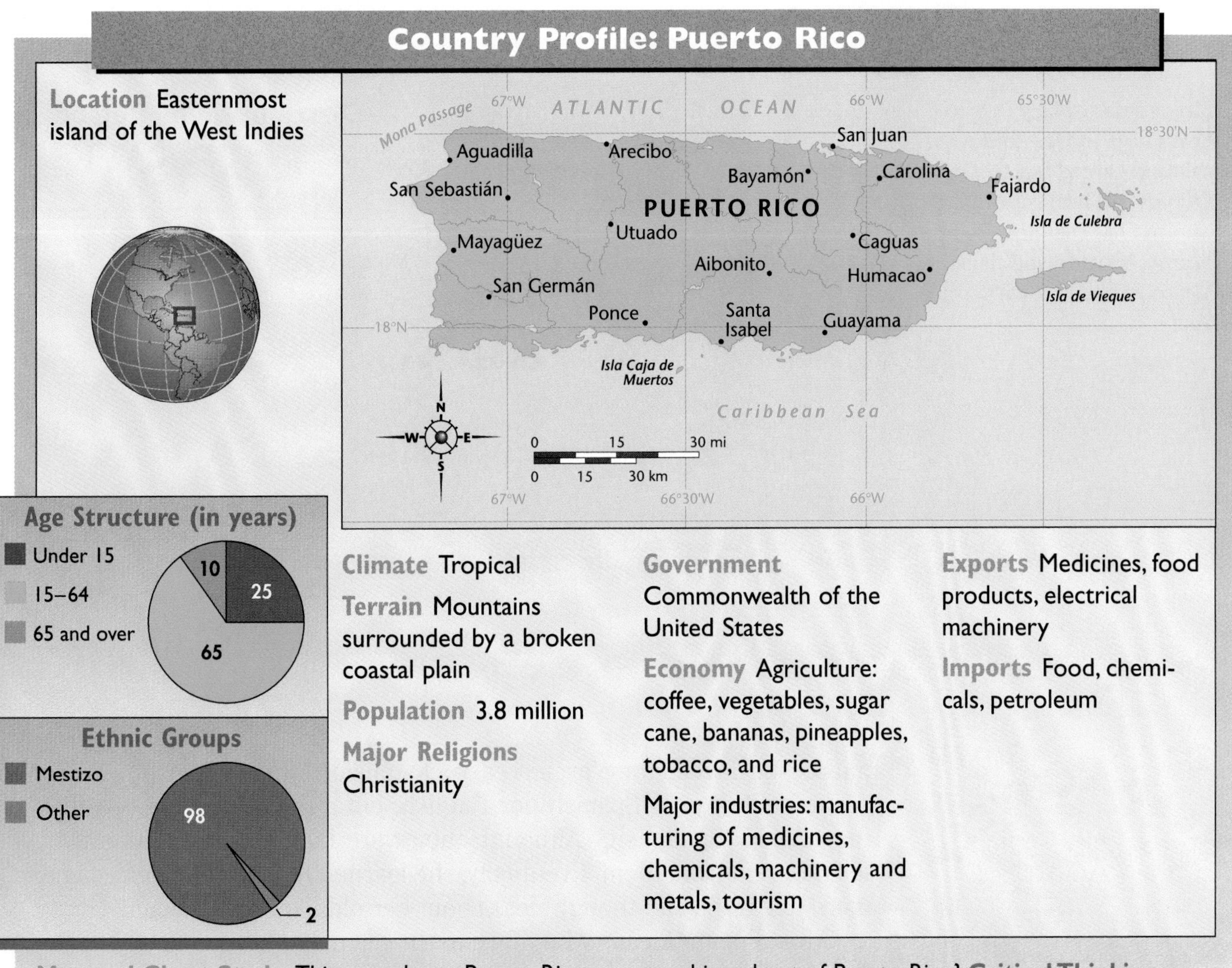

Map and Chart Study This map shows Puerto Rico. **Location** Read the description of Puerto Rico's terrain. Where are Puerto Rico's mountains located? How do you know? **Movement** How do you think most exports are shipped out of Puerto Rico? **Critical Thinking** Look at the chart that shows age structure. Would you say that Puerto Rico's population is old, young, or evenly balanced? Why?

It was not that Esmeralda was completely separated from her people. Puerto Ricans are U.S. citizens. **Citizens** are individuals with certain rights and responsibilities under a particular government. However, Puerto Ricans cannot vote in U. S. presidential elections. They do not pay U.S. taxes. And they have only a non-voting representative in the U.S. Congress. Puerto Rico is a commonwealth of the United States. A **commonwealth** is a place that has its own government but also has strong ties to another country. Esmeralda had the right to return to Puerto Rico whenever she chose.

Esmeralda found life on the mainland strange and confusing. One problem was that to succeed in school, she had to improve her English. Esmeralda was also confused by her new group of friends. She found that Puerto Ricans living on the mainland were different from her friends on the island of Puerto Rico. Instead of the salsa and merengue

Puerto Ricans in the Mainland United States

Chart Study Many Puerto Ricans have moved to the mainland United States. **Critical Thinking** Which region of the mainland has the most Puerto Ricans? What do you think draws Puerto Ricans to a particular area?

Population	
Total	2,728,000
Northeast	1,872,000
Midwest	258,000
South	406,000
West	192,000

Distribution by Region

Northeast	68.6%
Midwest	9.4%
South	14.9%
West	7.0%

Connect What kind of music do you listen to? Does the music you listen to reflect your feelings about your life and your community? Why or why not?

music she loved, they preferred rock music. Most of the time they spoke neither pure Spanish nor English, but a mixture of the two that they called "Spanglish." Although they were Puerto Rican, Esmeralda felt different from them. Eventually, she learned their ways. She became more like them and thought less about her old life on the island.

Most Puerto Ricans who move to the mainland keep connections to Puerto Rico. As people travel back and forth between the mainland and Puerto Rico, they bring customs and products with them. If you visited Puerto Rico, you would see many influences from the U.S. mainland. You would also see that in Puerto Rico, there is a strong cultural connection to the Caribbean. Most people are a mix of Spanish and African ancestry. Some Puerto Ricans like to look even further back into their history by calling themselves "Boricuas" (bohr ee KOO uhs). The name comes from the Boriqueno (bohr ee KAY noh), an indigenous farming people who lived on the island before the Spanish arrived.

More Than the Four Walls

The land of Puerto Rico is a memory no Puerto Rican forgets. Some, like Esmeralda Santiago, never go back to it. But others return, longing for the familiar ways they left behind. Julia de Jesus Chaparro (HOO lee a day HAY soos sha PAHR ro) moved back to a small mountain village in Puerto Rico after more than 14 years in Boston. She is fond of saying that where she lives now there are "more than the four walls of the city." To prove what she means, she takes visitors to her back porch. Outside it, one can see a row of steep mountains. Peeking between them is the bright blue of the Caribbean Sea. The mountain slopes steeply down from her back porch, but she has managed to clear some land. Her garden of mangoes, coconuts, grapefruit, and lemons thrives in the sun. Behind a nearby tree, a hen and six chickens are pecking in the dirt.

On other parts of the island, farmers ride horses through fields of tall sugar cane. Higher in the hills, Puerto Rican cowhands, called *jíbaros* (HEE bahr ohs), hunt, fish, and raise chickens, pigs, and cattle. To the southwest, where the land gets lower, fishing villages dot the coast.

Puerto Rico is an island of cities as well as countryside. Puerto Rican cities show influences of Spanish, Caribbean, and U.S. mainland cultures. About 70 percent of Puerto Ricans live in cities. Many city people work in factories. Others work in the hotels and restaurants that draw many tourists. Puerto Rico's capital, San Juan (san HWAHN), has a large waterfront area known as the Condado (kohn DAH do). It is packed with luxury hotels. Not far away, modern skyscrapers pierce the brilliant sky. In the old section of San Juan, Spanish-style buildings are everywhere. A 450-year-old Catholic church built by the Spanish has been carefully restored. Not far from it sit ancient houses graced with iron balconies in lacy Spanish style.

Visualize What might you see if you looked out the back door of an apartment in the city? What might you see if you looked out the back door of a house in the countryside?

A Commonwealth in Question

In 1951, Puerto Ricans voted to adopt their own constitution. A **constitution** is a statement of a country's basic laws and values. This gave Puerto Rico its own group of lawmakers. But it was still connected

New York City's Spanish Harlem

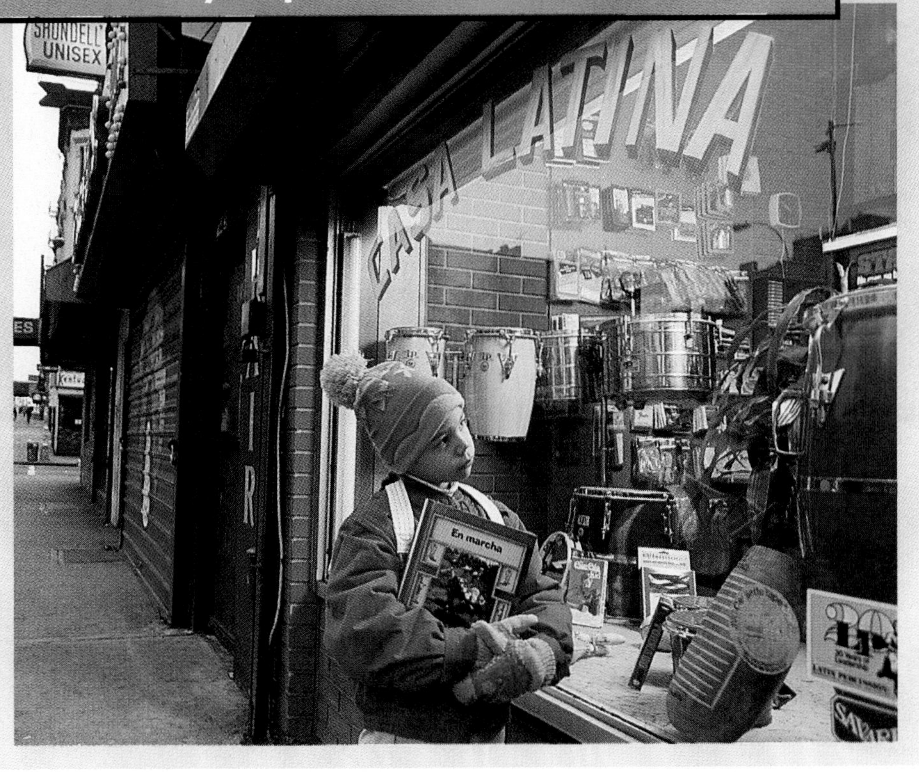

Puerto Ricans are the largest ethnic group in New York City's Lower East Side, and they make up about 12 percent of the city's total population.

to the United States. Puerto Rico is bound by many United States laws. Puerto Ricans have many questions about this. Is it good for Puerto Rico? Should Puerto Rico become independent? Or should it become a state of the United States?

Connect Would people in your area want to become part of another state? Why or why not?

What Direction to Take? Puerto Ricans have many disagreements over the answers to these questions. Many feel that having "one foot" in Puerto Rico and "one foot" in the United States can lead to problems. Others point out how the relationship with the United States has helped Puerto Rico. U.S. businesses on the island have raised the standard of living. Each year, the U.S. government sends millions of dollars to the island to help people in need.

Some people still feel that Puerto Rico has a disadvantage because people there cannot vote in U.S. elections. They say Puerto Rico should try to become a state. But if it does, it will become the poorest state in the union. Puerto Ricans earn more money than people in other Caribbean countries. However, they earn less than people on the U.S. mainland. Also, if Puerto Rico becomes a state, Puerto Ricans will have

San Juan: Old and New

San Juan, Puerto Rico's oldest city, is famous for historic forts and the wrought iron balconies of its oldest neighborhoods. But San Juan is also a vacation spot for tourists, with modern hotels lining its sandy beaches.

▶ These women are celebrating Puerto Rico's Spanish heritage. Puerto Ricans celebrate many holidays with traditional music and dancing.

to pay U.S. taxes. This could lower the earnings of many who have little to spare. For these reasons, in 1993, Puerto Ricans voted not to become the 51st state of the United States.

The Question of Independence Some people who voted against statehood have even bigger dreams for the country. They want Puerto Rico to become a separate nation. If not, they fear that Puerto Ricans will become confused about their identity, just as Esmeralda Santiago became confused about hers. They stress Puerto Rico's connection to other Caribbean nations. They want to make sure that Puerto Ricans always identify with the Spanish language and Spanish culture. But for now, Puerto Rico will keep its links to the mainland. Many Puerto Ricans hope that their relationship with the United States will lead to a profitable and peaceful future.

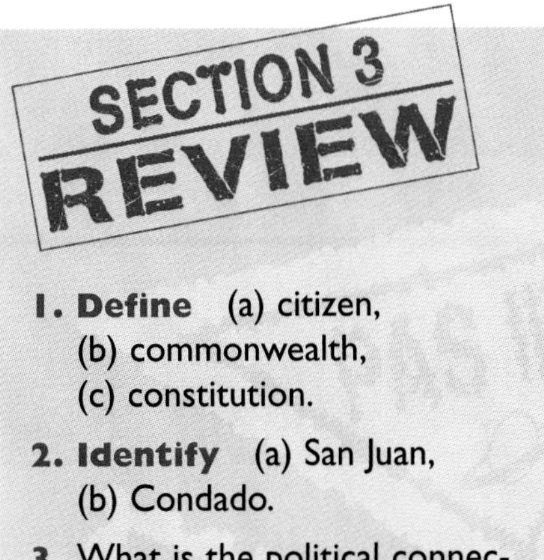

1. **Define** (a) citizen, (b) commonwealth, (c) constitution.
2. **Identify** (a) San Juan, (b) Condado.
3. What is the political connection between Puerto Rico and the United States?
4. Compare life in the mainland United States with life in Puerto Rico.

Critical Thinking

5. **Identifying Central Issues** What are the three options Puerto Ricans consider in terms of their relationship with the United States? What are the benefits and drawbacks of each?

Activity

6. **Writing to Learn** Try to put yourself in Esmeralda Santiago's place. Write a paragraph telling what it was like to move to New York from Puerto Rico.

CHAPTER 5

Review and Activities

Reviewing Main Ideas

1. What happened to Cuba when the communist regime in the Soviet Union fell?
2. What changes did Lydia Martin notice when she visited Cuba in 1995?
3. How is Haiti's history unique?
4. What were two results of Jean-Bertrand Aristide's forced exile from Haiti?
5. How do the cultures of Spain and the United States influence Puerto Rico? Give one example of how each has influenced Puerto Rico.
6. How have frequent trips to the U.S. mainland affected some Puerto Rican families?

Reviewing Key Terms

Use each key term below in a sentence that shows the meaning of the term.

1. communist
2. dictator
3. exile
4. illiterate
5. Creole
6. dialect
7. commonwealth
8. citizen
9. constitution

Critical Thinking

1. **Making Comparisons** Both Cubans and Puerto Ricans have settled in the United States. How has the experience been similar for both? How has it been different?
2. **Drawing Conclusions** How do you think Toussaint L'Ouverture's fight for independence inspires Haitians to fight for democracy?

Graphic Organizer

Copy the chart to the right onto a piece of paper, then fill in the empty boxes to complete the chart.

	Cuba	Haiti	Puerto Rico
Form of government			
United States Influence			

Map Activity

For each place listed below, write the letter from the map that shows its location.

1. Port-au-Prince
2. San Juan
3. Havana
4. Miami
5. Gulf of Mexico
6. Guantánamo Bay
7. Dominican Republic

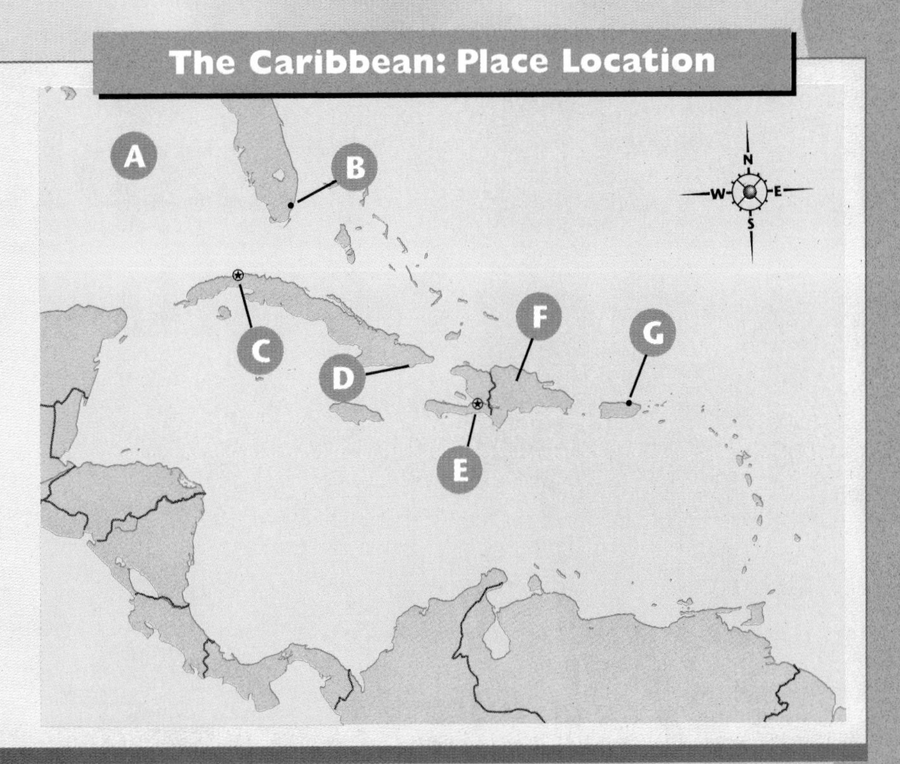

Writing Activity

Writing a Poem
Write a poem describing the culture in your region. Does your region have a blend of cultures, like Haiti? Why or why not? How does the culture in your region affect the way you feel about yourself?

Internet Activity

Use a search engine to find the site **Nueva Vista: Latino/Puerto Rican Home Page.** Click on **Viewpoint.** Then, click on **The 51st State: the State of Confusion** and read one person's view on Puerto Rico's status as a U.S. commonwealth. Use this information to debate the issue with your classmates.

Skills Review

Turn to the Skill Activity.

Review the steps for locating information. Then write a one page biography of Fidel Castro. Make a list of four routes you could take to find information.

How Am I Doing?

Answer these questions to help you check your progress.

1. Do I understand why many Cubans have emigrated to the United States?
2. Can I explain how Haiti's people have struggled for democracy?
3. Do I understand Puerto Rico's relationship with the United States?
4. Can I describe what factors have affected culture in the Caribbean islands?
5. What information from this chapter can I use in my book project?

CHAPTER 6

Exploring South America

SECTION 1
Brazil
RESOURCES OF THE RAIN FOREST

SECTION 2
Peru
LIFE IN THE ALTIPLANO

SECTION 3
Chile
A GROWING ECONOMY BASED ON AGRICULTURE

SECTION 4
Venezuela
OIL POWERS THE ECONOMY

MAP ACTIVITIES

South America is more than two times as large as the mainland United States. Because it is so large, its geography and cultures are diverse. To learn more about South America, complete the following activities.

Understanding geography

Much of South America is located south of the Equator. If you were to start at the Equator and travel south, how do you think the climate would change? Why?

Study the map

How do you think the Andes Mountains may have affected political boundaries in South America?

Brazil

Resources of the Rain Forest

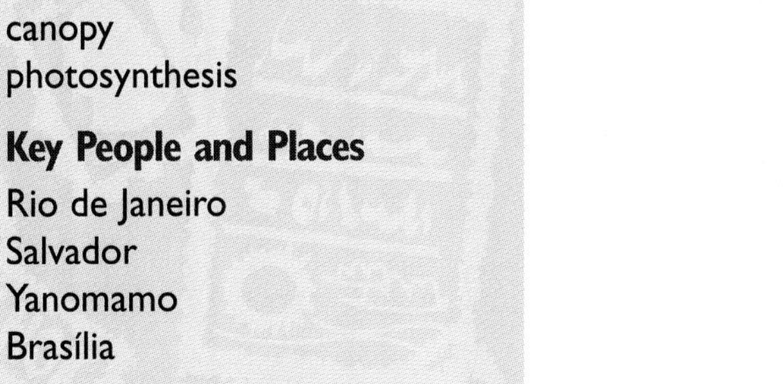

Reach Into Your Background

In this section, you will learn about the rain forests in Brazil. List three things you already know or can guess about the rain forests.

Questions to Explore

1. Why are the rain forests in Brazil a global issue?
2. How does what happens to the rain forests affect Brazil's economy?

Key Terms

canopy
photosynthesis

Key People and Places

Rio de Janeiro
Salvador
Yanomamo
Brasília

Deep in the rain forest in Brazil, the light barely penetrates. At the top of the trees, the leaves form a dense mass called a **canopy.** Sun and rain beat down upon the canopy. But on the ground, the air feels almost chilly. The only sounds are the calls of birds, monkeys, and insects.

▼ The canopy of Brazil's rain forest parts only where rivers slice through it.

Brazil and Its Rain Forests

Brazil, the largest country in South America, is nearly as large as the United States. It is also one of the richest countries in the world in land and resources. Until recently, its immense rain forests remained undisturbed. Only the few Native American groups that had lived in them for centuries ever explored them.

Brazil's Geography Brazil's rain forests take up about one half of the country. Look at the map in the Country Profile. In the southeast, the forests give way to a large plateau divided by mountain ranges and river valleys. The plateau reaches Brazil's long coast. Many harbors lie along the coast. Large cities, such as Rio de Janeiro (ree oh day zhuh NER oh), grew up around harbors. Most of Brazil's people live near the coast, far from the rain forests.

Country Profile: Brazil

Location Eastern half of South America

Climate Tropical wet along the Amazon and southeast coast. Tropical wet and dry in the southeast interior

Terrain Long Atlantic coastline, Amazon rain forest covering one half of the country, hilly upland plateaus and low mountains

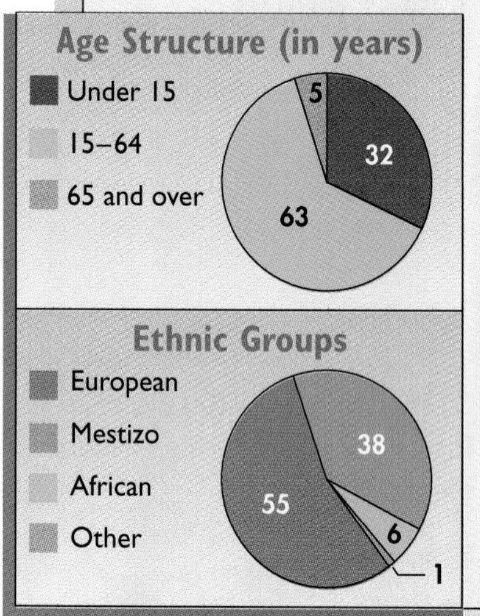

Population 161 million

Major Religions Christianity

Government Republic

Economy Agriculture: coffee (world's largest grower), cotton, soybeans, sugar, rice

Major industries: steel, automobiles, appliances, chemicals, machinery, textiles, mining

Exports Coffee, iron ore, soybeans, motor vehicle parts

Imports Petroleum, coal, food, chemical products

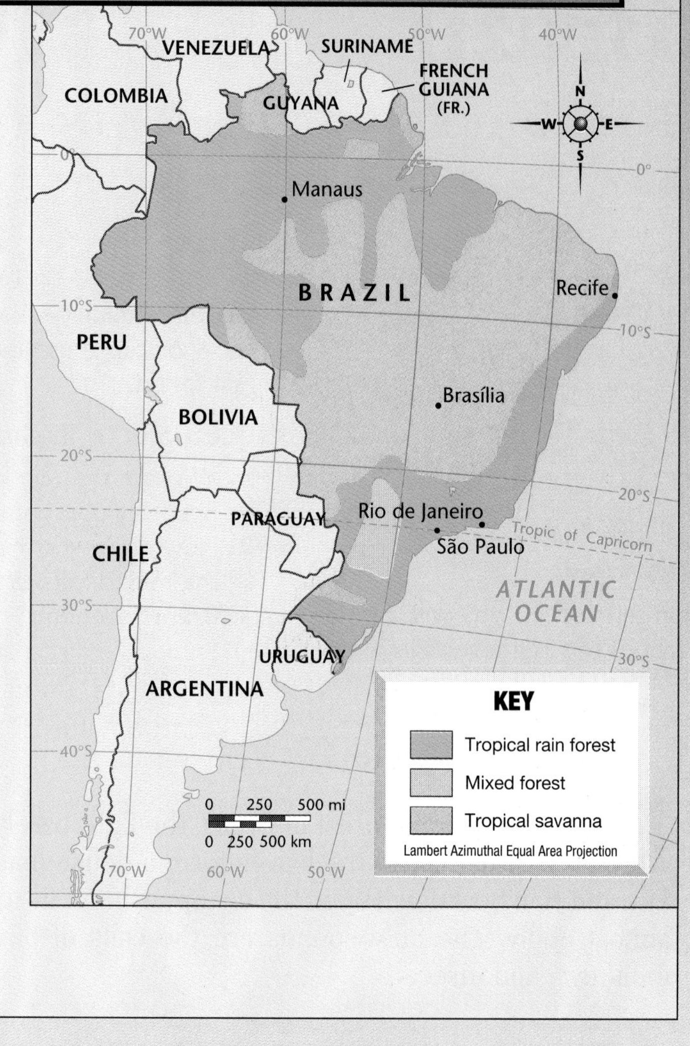

Map Study This map shows the vegetation regions of Brazil. Brazil contains over 1 million square miles (2,589,900 sq km) of rain forest. Northern Brazil contains part of the largest rain forest in the world, the Amazonian rain forest. Alaska could fit inside Brazil's Amazonian rain forest twice. Texas could fit inside it five times. **Location** What four Brazilian cities are located in the rain forest?

The People of Brazil

The Native Americans living in the rain forest were some of the first people to live in Brazil. Today, most Brazilians are a mix of Native American, African, and European heritages.

Many parts of African culture still flourish in Brazil. The most African of Brazilian cities, Salvador, lies on the coastal plains. Visitors are surprised by how much Salvador is like a town in Africa. Most of the people who live here descend from the millions of Africans brought to Brazil as slaves.

Working on Farms and in Factories Many Africans in Brazil were forced to work the coffee plantations. Brazil used their labor to become the world's largest coffee grower. When the slaves were freed in the late 1800s, they became paid but cheap labor.

Coffee prices dropped in the first few years of the 1900s. Brazilians realized that they could not depend on one or two crops to survive. In the 1930s, the government discouraged coffee production and tried to diversify the economy by building more factories. Today, Brazil produces many goods, including iron and steel, cars, and electrical equipment. Since 1960, about 30 million people have left farms and plantations to get jobs in these new industries. They moved into the cities.

READ ACTIVELY

Connect How is the history of Africans in Brazil like the history of Africans brought to the United States?

A Brazilian City Brazilian cities are home to the rich and the very poor. Rio de Janeiro is a good example of these contrasts. It lies on the coast, surrounded by huge mountains that dip to the sea. If you climbed to the top of one, you could see the whole city. To the south, you would see expensive hotels and shops for tourists. In the downtown area, you would see old palaces and government buildings.

But to the north, you would see clusters of small houses where factory workers live. Below this neighborhood is an even poorer one, crowded with homes that have no electricity or running water. About a quarter of Rio's 12 million people live in these neighborhoods known as *favelas* (fuh VEH lus). However, most of Rio's people live in well-built houses with electricity and running water.

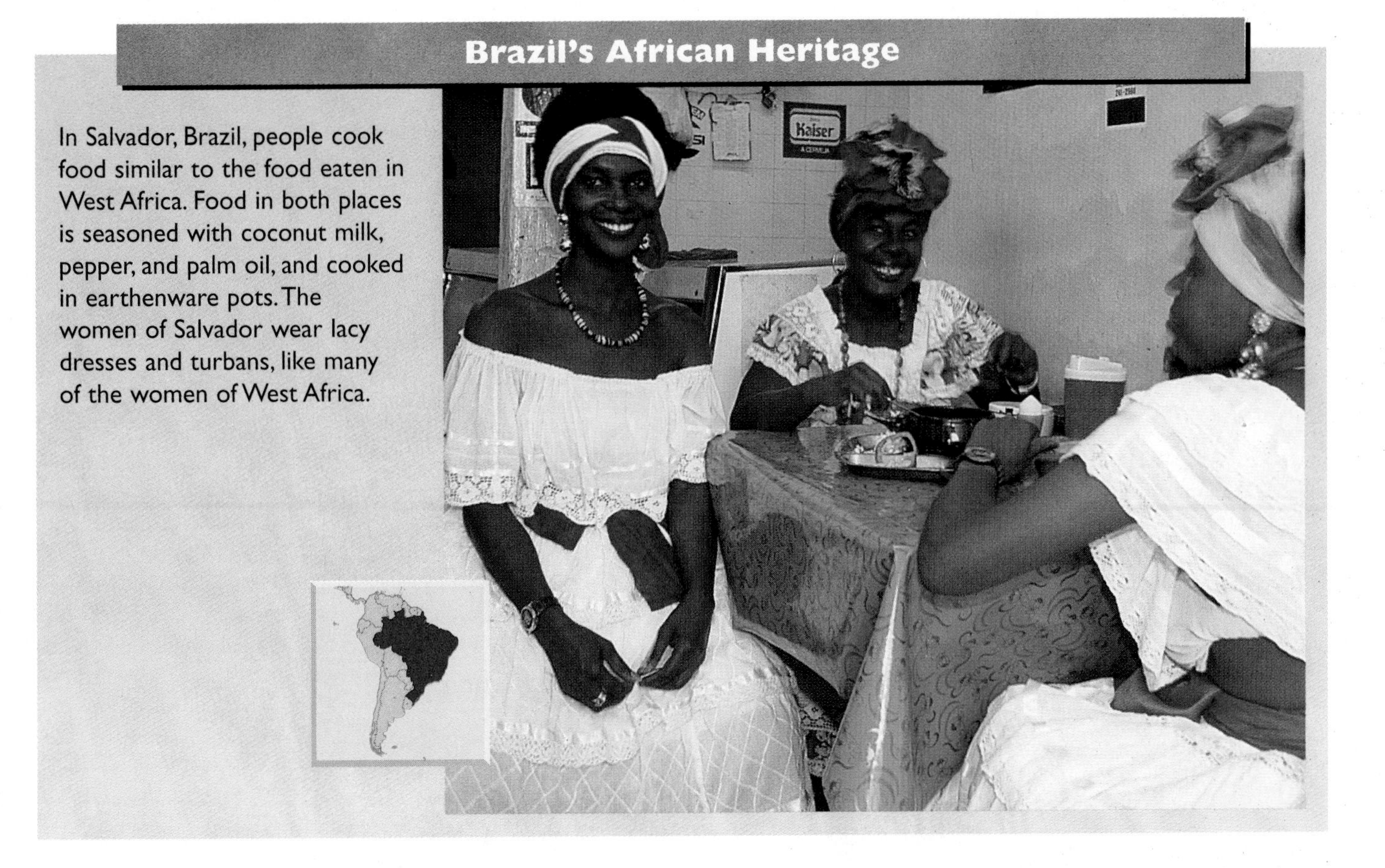

Brazil's African Heritage

In Salvador, Brazil, people cook food similar to the food eaten in West Africa. Food in both places is seasoned with coconut milk, pepper, and palm oil, and cooked in earthenware pots. The women of Salvador wear lacy dresses and turbans, like many of the women of West Africa.

Visualize What do you think you would see if you climbed to the top of a tree in the rain forest?

Using the Rain Forest's Resources

On a sunny January in 1994, two boys who lived in the rain forest scrambled up the trees. The boys were Yanomamos. The Yanomamo are a Native American group that lives in the rain forests. The boys pointed to a plane soaring close to the treetops. The plane dipped down and landed on a dirt strip. "Foreign visitors!" the boys called excitedly.

Brazil's New Capital: Brasília The visitors were from Brasília (bruh ZIL yuh), the capital city of Brazil. Brasília is closer to the rain forest than the coastal cities are. On the vast interior plain where Brasília now stands, there used to be nothing but a savanna called the Cerrado (suh RAH doh). The Cerrado was a region 10 times larger than the state of Kansas. The government thought that moving the capital there would attract some people from the coastal areas.

The government wanted to develop Brazil's interior region using the resources of the rain forest. The rain forests are important to Brazil's economy because people cut timber, mine for gold, and farm there. Now, the government hoped to develop industry using the resources of the rain forest.

Worldwide Impact of the Rain Forest The rain forest where the Yanomamo live is very important to life all around the Earth. Scientists estimate that rain forests produce about one third of the world's oxygen. Green plants and trees produce their own food using

▼São Paulo is the largest city in Brazil. It contains more than 20,000 factories, which provide jobs for 600,000 workers.

Two Cities, Two Climates

Brasília: A City of the Savanna

Manaus: A City of the Rain Forest

Curved lines show temperatures in Fahrenheit degrees. **Bars** show rainfall in inches.

Chart Study A climate graph shows rainfall and temperature in the same space. The bars show rainfall, while the curved lines show temperature. **Critical Thinking** How are the seasons in Brasília and Manaus different from each other?

water, carbon dioxide, and sunlight. This process is called **photosynthesis** (foht oh SIN thuh sis). In the process of photosynthesis, oxygen is given off. All people and animals need oxygen to breathe.

The rain forest also holds about one fifth of the world's fresh water. Many scientists think that when people come to the rain forest, they may upset the delicate balance of nature.

Protecting the Rain Forest Brazil's government is taking care to use the rain forest's resources without upsetting this balance. The government has started using satellites to keep an eye on the rain forest. That way, the government can respond fast to protect the rain forest from the following dangers.

First, if too much timber is cut down, there will not be enough trees to absorb the carbon dioxide in the atmosphere. The carbon dioxide layer may trap heat near the Earth, changing the world's climate. When part of the forest is destroyed, the animals and plants that live there may not survive. When plant life is destroyed, less oxygen is produced.

A Voice of Protest Friar Hector Turrini moved from Italy to Brazil more than 45 years ago. At that time, there were so few roads that Turrini had to learn to fly a plane to get around his parish. He dedicated himself to protecting the Native Americans and rubber tappers who depend on the rain forest. Now Turrini is working to protect the rain forest.

Amazon Fruit What is green and bumpy, round like a softball, and looks like the sole of a shoe? It is a conde (KON day). Scientists in Brazil have discovered more than 40 types of fruits growing in the Amazon rain forest. Besides being high in vitamins and protein, these fruits taste good. Scientists hope to persuade Amazon farmers to stop clearing rain forest land and begin planting these fruits instead.

Second, there is the problem of smuggling. Each year, Brazil loses about 12 million animals to smugglers. Many of these animals are endangered. Smugglers look for monkeys, parrots, and other animals. One parrot can be sold for $10,000. One woolly monkey can be sold for as much as $50,000. It is illegal to capture or kill these animals, but the smugglers often get away with it.

Third, development can cause pollution. In the late 1980s, the discovery of gold attracted many miners to the rain forest. Mining gold involves mixing the gold with mercury. The mercury polluted streams in the forest. It made people in several Yanomamo villages sick.

The gold mining in the rain forest attracted the attention of the world. The government of Brazil passed strict laws about mining in the rain forest. Sometimes the government insisted that the miners leave. At times, military police had to be called in to make sure they did.

Giving Land to the Poor One of the main reasons that people come to the rain forest is the lack of land to farm. This may seem strange when one considers Brazil's large size. However, most of Brazil's land is owned by a few people who may choose not to farm their land. About one third of Brazil's farmland is unused. This represents about 300 million acres (122 million hectares) of crop and ranch land.

In 1995, Brazil's president gave some of this unused land to poor farmers. The goal is to resettle more than 3,600 poor families who want a new place to live and who want to return to farming. The process is a slow one. However, life for some resettled Brazilians is improving.

People are starting small farms just north of Rio de Janeiro. The farms help people make a living for themselves. On a balmy July day in 1995, farmer Joe Brum showed a reporter his farm. Brum had received the 17-acre plot from the government. Now his tin-roofed house was shaded by the coconut and banana trees he had planted. He had a couple of pigs and had earned enough money to buy a satellite dish and a television.

Brum's eyes gleamed as he pointed to the rows of vegetables. "What I have here," he explained to the reporter, "I made myself."

1. **Define** (a) canopy, (b) photosynthesis.
2. **Identify** (a) Rio de Janeiro, (b) Salvador, (c) Yanomamo, (d) Brasília.
3. Why are Brazil's rain forests important to the whole world?
4. In what ways does Brazil depend on its rain forest?

Critical Thinking

5. **Expressing Problems Clearly** Some people want Brazil to stop using rain forests completely. Is this reasonable? What do you think it would do to Brazil's economy?

Activity

6. **Writing a Journal Entry** Use what you know about the rain forest to write a journal entry about a visit to it.

Peru

Life in the Altiplano

Reach Into Your Background

Did you choose your clothing according to the weather report this morning? The decision you make is affected by climate. Think of other ways that climate affects your life.

Questions to Explore

1. How has geography affected the lifestyle of Native Americans of the altiplano?
2. How do people on the altiplano survive?

Key Terms

altiplano
sierra
montaña
tundra

Key People and Places

Lake Titicaca
Aymara
Quechua
Cuzco

When people on Tribuna, an island in Lake Titicaca, play soccer, they must be careful. That's because the island is made of straw. The ground is uneven, and when they walk on it they can feel the water shifting below. "It seems crazy to play soccer on water," says Luis Colo, who lives on Tribuna. "We don't jump on each other after a goal, or we'd probably fall through the field."

Tribuna is one of about 70 islands made by the Aymara (eye muh RAH). The Aymara have adapted to the geography of Lake Titicaca. The Aymara make their islands out of tortora reeds. They join the floating roots of tortora reeds together and then lay cut reeds on top. This process creates an island that is firm enough to support small communities of people with huts and livestock. When the Aymara need more land, they build another island.

▲ When the wind comes up, the Aymara must anchor their islands to keep them from being swept away.

Peru's Three Geographic Regions

The Aymara live on Lake Titicaca. Find Lake Titicaca on the map in the Country Profile. Lake Titicaca lies high in Peru's **altiplano** (al tih PLAH noh), a high plateau region in the Andes. The altiplano is about 12,000 feet (3,658 m) above sea level. It lies in the southern part of Peru near the Bolivian border.

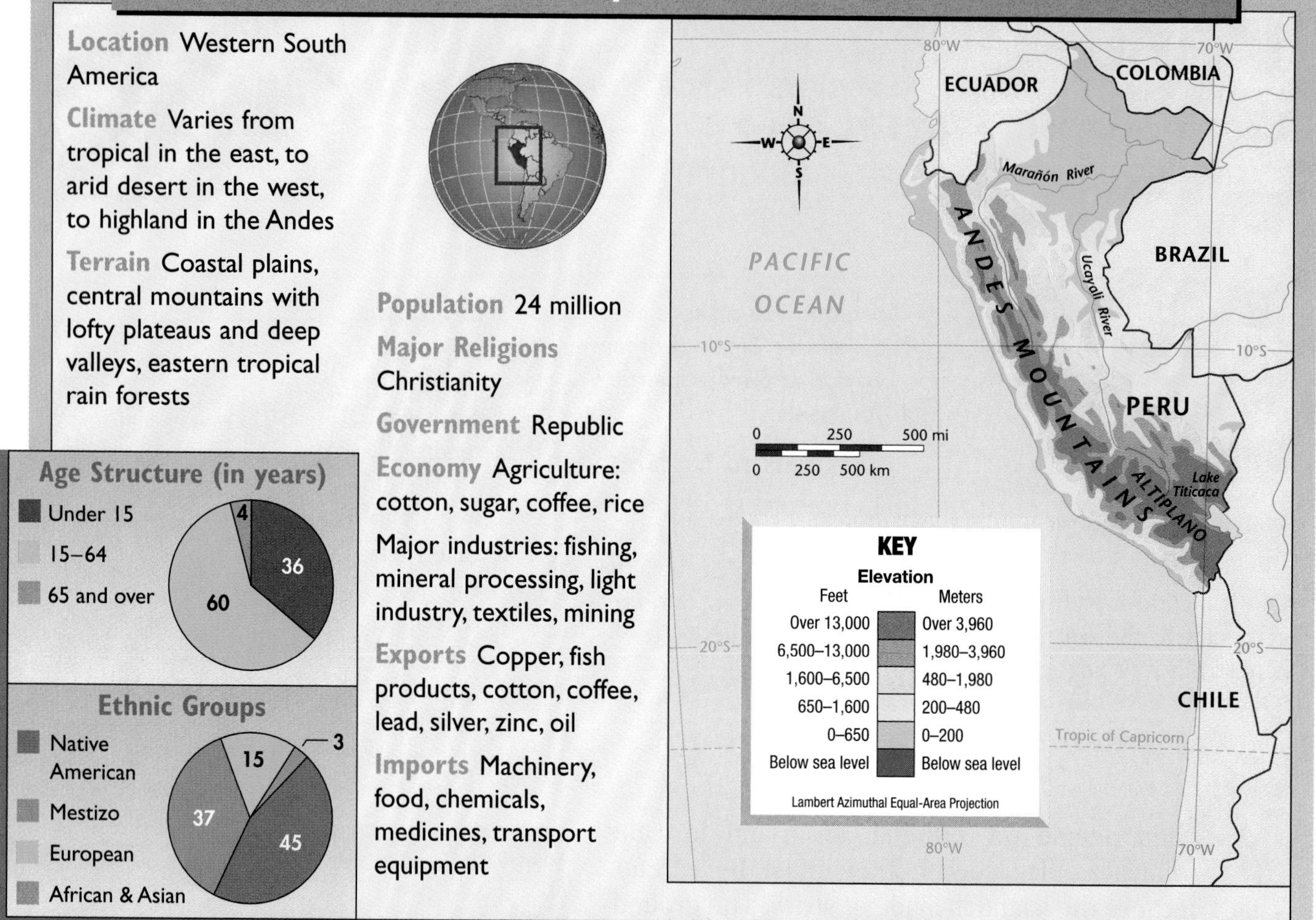

Map Study This map shows the elevation of land in Peru. The higher you climb in the mountains, the colder the climate gets. In the Andes Mountains, trees will not grow above 10,000 feet (3,048 m) because it is too cold. But east of the Andes, the elevation is lower. Much of the eastern lowlands is covered with a dense tropical rain forest. **Location** How high in the mountains is Lake Titicaca? What direction do the rivers on this map flow? How can you tell?

Peru's mountains divide the country into three geographic regions. The altiplano and Peru's highest mountains are in the **sierra,** the mountains that run from northwest to southeast Peru. The mountains are so high that the temperature can drop as low as 20°F (–7°C). People who live in this region must sleep under many blankets. They sometimes wear sweaters to bed.

Their life is far different from the lives of those who live on the coastal plain, which is Peru's second geographical region. This dry region is warmed by the sun and cooled by sea breezes. Several cities, including Trujillo (troo HEE yoh), Chimbote (chim BOH tay), and Lima (LEE muh), dot the coast.

The third region is called the **montaña.** The montaña is made of large stretches of tropical forests on the lower slopes of mountains in northeast Peru. Here the weather is warm and humid all year round.

Peru's People

Native Americans make up almost half of Peru's population. Most Native Americans living in Peru are Quechua. About 15 percent of Peruvians are of European descent. Another 37 percent are mestizo. The remaining Peruvians are of African and Asian descent.

Peru's Cities The altiplano contains cities and isolated towns. City life is very different from village life. Most city dwellers have electricity. The streets are paved, and there are telephones. But in Peru's cities, the old mixes with the new.

One Peruvian city, Cuzco, is the site of the ancient Incan capital. Parts of the old Incan wall that once surrounded the city are still standing. Today's modern houses are made of adobe, with red tile roofs. But their foundations are the remains of Incan stonework. There are buildings from the time of the Spanish colonists as well.

Spanish conquistador Francisco Pizarro founded Peru's largest city and capital, Lima, in 1535. Lima lies on the coastal plain. Like Cuzco, Lima is a mix of old and new. Historic Spanish cathedrals and government buildings from the 1600s and 1700s stand next to modern skyscrapers.

Bridging Canyons The Incas invented the technology for building suspension bridges. First, they built stone towers on each side of a canyon. They suspended cables woven from plants from the stone towers. Then, they laid wooden slats across the cables to make a bridge. They used smaller cables for railings. People still use Incan bridges today. Modern suspension bridges have steel cables and are reinforced with iron beams.

◀ Lima is the busiest and most modern of Peru's cities. What details in the photo are modern? What details are more traditional?

Life in Rural Areas In the isolated towns of the altiplano, life is very different from life in the city. There are no telephones to ring. Few buses drive through the villages. Most people are Quechua or Aymara.

Predict How do you think the Quechuas of the altiplano make a living?

A Day in a Quechua Village Modesto Mamani (moh DES toh muh MAN ee) is a 13-year-old Quechua boy. He wakes before dawn to the freezing mountain air. He eats breakfast as soon as the sun comes up. Breakfast is always the same: a couple of rolls, coffee with sugar, and whole wheat kernels that can be eaten like popcorn. The only other meal may be lunch. It is usually potato and barley soup with chunos—freeze-dried potato skins.

For much of the day, Modesto works in the field with his father and brothers. On other days, he looks after the sheep or goes with his mother to the market. Despite all of these chores, Modesto finds time to play soccer on the tundra in back of his house. A **tundra** is an area where no trees grow because the soil is always cold.

Modesto Mamani at School and at Work

Modesto's life mixes the modern and the traditional. He wants to study to become an engineer so that he can bring technology to the altiplano. But even when he is studying, Modesto is never far from his soccer ball. He also spends a lot of time tending sheep and knitting wool sweaters. Sometimes he even knits when he is playing soccer!

The Straw People Modesto's village is not far from the Aymara islands on Lake Titicaca. The people there live on one of the 70 tortora reed islands that float on the lake. The islanders use tortora reeds for many other purposes besides building islands. They weave it to make boats. They use it as fuel for cooking. They eat the soft inside of the reeds. Most important, though, they use the reeds to repair the islands. Tortora reeds last only a few months before they start to rot. A person who slipped through them could die in the lake's icy waters.

On the straw islands, women wake at dawn to get water from the lake for cooking and washing. They spend the rest of the day washing clothes, untangling fishing nets, and making new homes out of reeds. Once or twice a week they go to market to trade fish for rice, potatoes, and sugar. Meanwhile, the men fish and help to repair the straw islands.

Quechua Market Day

On market days, Quechua from several communities gather together to buy and sell goods. What kinds of goods are being sold at this market?

A Modern Future Quechuas and other Native Americans living on the altiplano follow traditions that are hundreds of years old. Their communities, however, are slowly changing. Thousands of Native Americans have left for jobs in the city. Life is changing even for those who stay in the village. The future holds a promising mix of old and new ways.

1. **Define** (a) altiplano, (b) sierra, (c) moñtana, (d) tundra.
2. **Identify** (a) Lake Titicaca, (b) Aymara, (c) Quechua, (d) Cuzco.
3. How is the daily life of the Quechua affected by the high altitude of the altiplano?
4. Describe people's lives on the straw islands of Lake Titicaca.

Critical Thinking

5. **Recognizing Bias** Do you think the Quechua see their way of life as outsiders see it? Explain.

Activity

6. **Writing to Learn** Compare life in a Peruvian city with life in a rural Quechua or Aymara community.

Using Isolines to Show Elevation

Climb straight up, hike over the side, or walk all the way around? That was the question Melissa and José faced.

They stared up at the huge hill in front of them. According to the map, the campsite they were hiking to was exactly on the opposite side of the hill. What was the best route to take?

Melissa spread the map out on a fallen log. "Look," she said, pointing at the map. "This hill is steep on this side, but we can climb it." She traced the route on the map. "But look what we'd run into on the other side!"

"A cliff!" José responded. "We'd never be able to get down. It's way too steep. I guess we'll have to walk around the hill."

"Not so fast. If we head to our left, we can climb up a gentle slope and work our way past the cliff down the hill on the other side. It's kind of steep, but at least we'll be going downhill!"

Get Ready

How could Melissa tell from the map how steep different parts of the hill were? The answer is that the map showed isolines. The word *isolines* comes from the Greek word *iso,* which means "equal," and our word *lines.* Isolines link together equal parts of a map. On the map Melissa and José used, every part of the hill that was the same elevation was linked by an isoline. By studying the pattern of the isolines, Melissa could figure out the best route to take.

Isolines that show elevation are also called contour lines, because their pattern shows the contour, or shape, of the land.

You can make your own contour map. To do this, you will need:

- an irregularly shaped rock, about the size of a cantaloupe
- a pan of water big enough and deep enough to submerge the rock
- a crayon or waterproof marker
- a sheet of blank paper and a pencil

Try It Out

A. Fill the pan with water deep enough to cover the rock.

B. Holding the top of the rock, dip the bottom of it evenly about one inch into the water. Don't drop it! Remove the rock. Use the crayon or marker to trace the waterline all the way around the rock.

C. Dip the rock again, about one inch deeper. The waterline will now be about one inch higher up on the rock. Trace the new waterline with the crayon or marker, all the way around the rock.

D. Continue this process, dipping the rock about one inch deeper each time. Do this until you can go no farther.

E. Now, put the rock on the floor, and look at it from above. Can you see how each crayon or marker line connects the parts of the rock that are the same height? These are isolines. Using a pencil, copy the pattern you see looking down on the rock onto to your piece of paper. Next, label each of your isolines from the outside in. The outside line should be marked "1 inch," the next line "2 inches," and so on.

You have just drawn a map of the top of the rock using isolines.

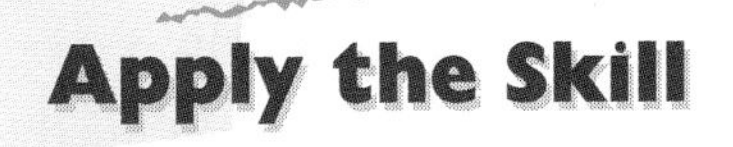

Apply the Skill

The map on this page shows isolines of a region around the city of Lima, Peru. Use the map to visualize the shape of the land.

1 Remember that isolines connect places of equal elevation. Just like the isolines you made on the rock, the isolines on this map connect places of equal elevation. The lines are numbered to show their elevation. What is the lowest elevation shown on the map? What is the highest elevation?

2 Use the isolines to get useful information from the map. Remember that where the land is steep, isolines are close together. Where the land is flatter, isolines are farther apart. As you head east from Lima, does the elevation increase or decrease? Now sketch a side view of the map. What is the highest point? What is the lowest? How can you tell?

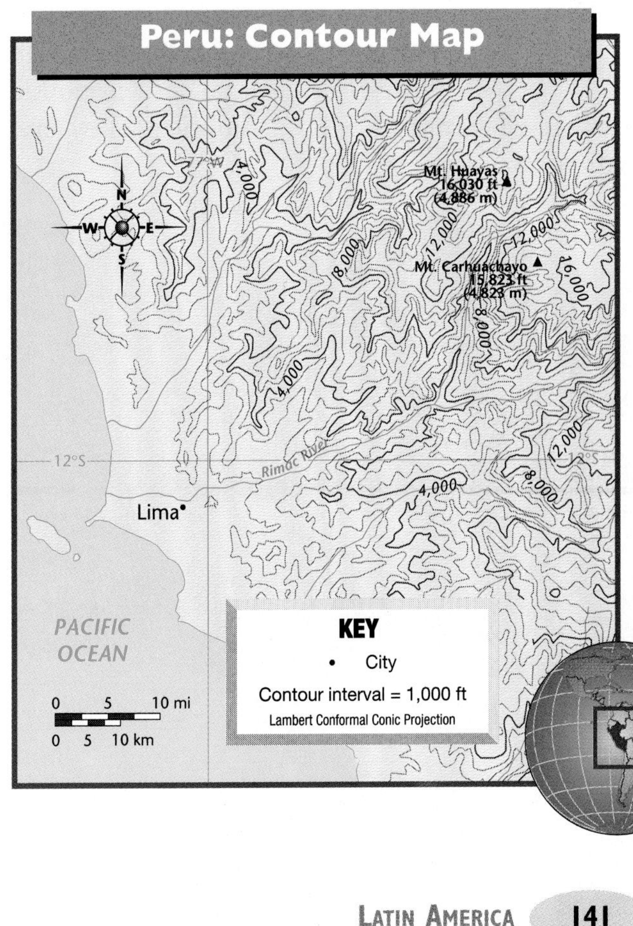

Chile

A Growing Economy Based on Agriculture

Reach Into Your Background
Do you like eating fresh fruit in summer? What if you could have fresh, juicy strawberries and peaches in the middle of winter? Think of ways to make this possible.

Questions to Explore

1. How does Chile's location affect the crops it grows?
2. How does producing more crops help Chile?

Key Terms
pesticide

Key Places
Santiago
Andes
Atacama Desert

It was a fairly quiet day at the airport of Santiago (san tee AH goh), the capital of Chile. Two passengers from Venezuela stepped off a plane. They had their carry-on luggage and a couple of maracas. A maraca is a musical instrument that sounds like a rattle. It is made from a hollow gourd filled with dried-out seeds or pebbles.

There is nothing very surprising about seeing maracas in South America. They are used in many orchestras and bands to play Latin music. So why was the customs officer staring at them suspiciously? Before the travelers had time to pass through customs, the officer grabbed the maracas and X-rayed them. Then he broke them open. Just as he thought, they did not contain dried-up seeds or pebbles. They were full of new seeds that were good for planting.

▼ Maracas are normally used to play music.

Life in Chile

Chile may be the only country in the world that inspects maracas brought into its borders. In recent years, Chile's agriculture has been booming. Chile makes millions of dollars a year by exporting peaches, grapes, cherries, and other

Country Profile: Chile

Location Western coast of southern South America

Climate Arid in north, Mediterranean in central regions

Terrain Central valley bordered by Andes Mountains in the east, a narrow plain along the coast

Population 14 million

Major Religions Christianity

Government Republic

Economy Agriculture: grains, grapes, beans, potatoes

Major industries: fish processing, wood products, iron, steel

Mining: copper (world's largest), molybdenum, iodine (half of world output)

Exports Copper, iron ore, paper and wood products, fruits

Imports Wheat, vehicles, petroleum, spare parts, raw materials

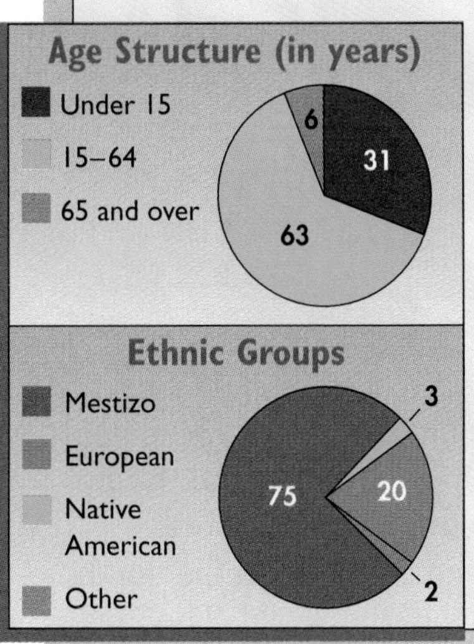

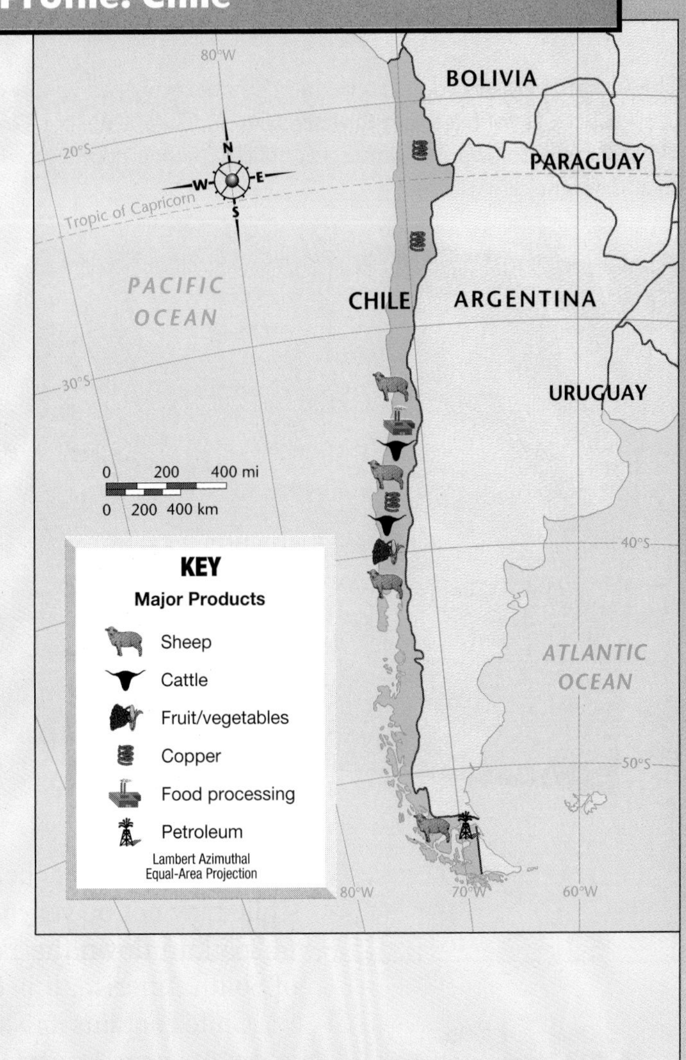

Map Study This map shows the major products of each region in Chile. Most of Chile's people live in its central valley. Read the description of the climate and terrain in central Chile. **Place** How do the climate and terrain of central Chile make it a good region for farming? **Movement** The Andes Mountains run down the whole length of Chile. What do you think would be the easiest way to ship Chile's products out of the country?

fruits and vegetables. Their country is protected by the Andes mountains, so some of the insect pests and animal diseases that plague other countries never reach Chile. That is why the government is so concerned about what enters now. Protecting Chile's crops is very important. No plant or animal matter from foreign places is allowed because it might bring disease to the crops.

The Geography of Chile Look at the physical map of Latin America in the Activity Atlas at the front of your book. Find the Andes Mountains. They run down the whole length of this long country like a giant spine. Chile is narrow. On average, it is about 100 miles (161 km) wide. If Chile were flat, it would take less than two hours to drive

A Study in Contrasts

The Atacama Desert looks barren and empty compared to Cerro Santa Lucia, a park in Santiago. But they are both in Chile. **Critical Thinking** What factors do you think make it possible for one country to have such different climates?

across it. However, because of the mountains, it takes much longer. Chile may not be very wide, but it is extremely long. It runs 2,650 miles (4,265 km) down the Pacific Coast. Chile reaches all the way to the tip of South America. It is the longest, narrowest country in the world.

Chile contains an amazing variety of lands and climates. In the north is the Atacama Desert, one of the driest regions in the world. The long central valley near the coast has rolling hills, high grasses, and dense forests. This is the region where most of the people live.

What Makes a Poem? What do you think is a proper topic for a poem? Chilean poet Pablo Neruda was willing to write a poem about anything. He wrote many poems about everyday subjects, like dusty wheels, sweat, and his socks. He even wrote a poem about a person wearing out a pair of shoes. He called it "You Flame Foot!"

The People of Chile Chile's early Spanish settlers married Native Americans already living there. Today, mestizos make up about 75 percent of the population. Only 3 percent of Chileans are Native Americans.

The lifestyles of Chileans vary from region to region. In the far south, sheep herders in heavy wool sweaters brave the strong winds. Farther north in the central valley, farmers grow wheat, potatoes, sugar beets, corn, tomatoes, and many fruits. In the cities, people in business suits hurry in and out of tall skyscrapers. Few people live in the Atacama Desert of the far north. Not many plants or animals can survive here either. But the desert is rich in copper, so the region is dotted with mines. Chile exports more copper than any country in the world.

A Chilean City A visit to Santiago is unforgettable. Old Spanish buildings stand near gleaming skyscrapers. The city is in the valley of the central plain, so the altitude is low enough to produce mild weather.

The sea makes the air humid. Palm trees grow in the public parks. The snowcapped Andes lie to the east.

The beautiful sights of Santiago are sometimes blocked by a thick layer of smog. Pollution has become so bad that it makes many small children and old people sick. The signs of pollution are everywhere. On a bad day, people wear surgical masks in order to breathe, or they press scarves to their faces. Few mothers bring their babies out on a day like this. If they do, the babies may have to be rushed to the hospital to receive oxygen.

Connect What cities in the United States have problems with pollution? Which of these cities, like Santiago, are surrounded by mountains?

The Problems of Industry How did pollution get to be so bad in Santiago? One cause is the city's location. It is surrounded by the Andes on three sides. The mountains trap the exhaust from vehicles and smoke from factories in the valley. This is especially true during the winter, when there is not much wind.

Another reason for the increase in pollution is the economy. Before the 1980s, Chile's economy depended mostly on its copper exports. Part of the copper industry was owned by the government. The profits went into projects that were supposed to help everyone in the country.

▼ German architecture can be found in many parts of southern Chile. German immigrants arrived here more than 100 years ago.

Net Fishing Off Chile's Coast

In northern Chile, the soil is not very good for farming. Many people here fish for a living. Chile's fishing industry is one of the largest in the world. **Critical Thinking** What difference do you see between people who fish for a living and those who fish for fun?

Falling Copper Prices Other countries besides Chile suffered when copper prices dropped in the 1980s. Zaire, in Central Africa, paid all its trade bills in 1980, mostly from the money it earned selling copper. By 1990, however, Zaire was heavily in debt because of the fall in copper prices.

In the early 1980s, world copper prices began to drop. The government tried to solve the problem by encouraging industry. The government relaxed the laws that protected the environment from pollution. Government leaders thought that if the laws were too strict, some private industries would not survive. Encouraging private industry did save Chile's economy. It was easier to mine and process copper. Tons of steel, cement, glass, and electronic equipment were made and sold.

The standard of living rose. But so did pollution levels. Also, more people moved to the cities to get jobs in the new industries. More than 80 percent of Chile's people now live in cities.

During the 1990s, Chile's government took action to reduce the problems of pollution in the city. On days when the wind does not blow, industries are shut down. And only a limited number of cars may enter the city. Further, the government may also require new cars to have special exhaust systems that do not produce much pollution. No one knows how well these solutions will work. But most Chileans are hoping for a cleaner and healthier future.

Chile's Agricultural Revolution

The drop in copper prices in the early 1980s made it clear that Chile could not depend on copper to survive. Chile decided that one way to improve the economy was to sell more crops.

Pest-Free Produce Chile's fruits and vegetables are free of many common plant pests. As a result, these products are welcome in many other countries. To supply the demands of these countries, about 15 percent of Chile's people farm. Chilean workers are also employed at packing plants for fruits and vegetables. Modern farming methods help grow even more crops.

By the late 1980s, agriculture was especially important for Chile. It had become a billion dollar industry, providing jobs for about 900,000 Chileans. Chile shipped wheat, potatoes, sugar beets, corn, grapes, melons, apples, peaches, apricots, cherries, and other fruits and vegetables around the world.

The United States, Japan, and Europe are an especially good market for Chilean produce from October through May. These months are winter in the Northern Hemisphere, but summer in the Southern Hemisphere. This means that Chile can provide fruits and vegetables to the United States, for example, during the months when American farmers cannot.

Although the Andes mountains protect Chile from many common plant pests and diseases, Chile has some pests of its own. To prevent them from destroying the fruits and vegetables, Chilean farmers use different kinds of pesticides. A **pesticide** (PES tuh syd) is a chemical used to kill insects and stop diseases that can hurt crops. Pesticides have helped farmers to increase crop production. But some people think that the pesticides may have caused certain kinds of illness in young children. As a result, Chilean scientists and farmers are trying to find ways to control pests without using chemicals. They want to make sure that Chilean fruits and vegetables are the tastiest and healthiest that people can buy.

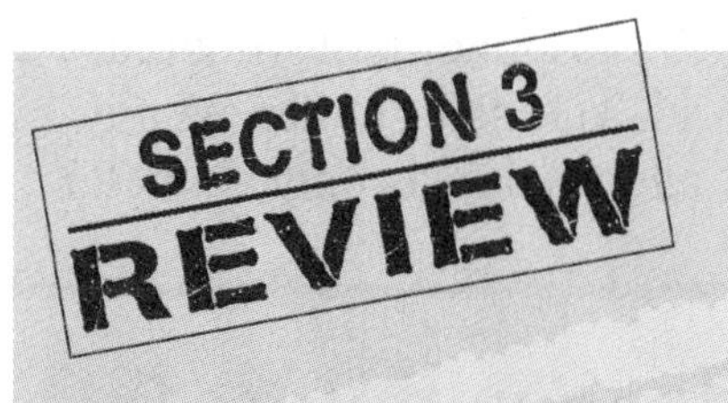

1. **Define** pesticide.
2. **Identify** (a) Santiago, (b) Andes, (c) Atacama Desert.
3. What aspect of Chile's location gives it an advantage in agriculture?
4. How has the growth of agriculture helped Chileans?

Critical Thinking

5. **Expressing Problems Clearly** Industries can cause pollution, but when industries close down, people lose their jobs. If you were the mayor of an industrial city with a pollution problem, what would you do?

Activity

6. **Writing to Learn** Like many places around the world, Chile is a popular tourist destination. Think about the reasons why a tourist might like to visit Chile. Describe the country's most interesting features. Present these paragraphs in the form of a tourist brochure.

Venezuela

Oil Powers the Economy

Reach Into Your Background

There are some things in life that people can control and others that they cannot. Think of at least one thing in your life that you can control. Think of another thing that is beyond your control.

Questions to Explore

1. How was Venezuela affected by the oil boom?
2. How is Venezuela trying to change its economy for the future?

Key Terms

boom
privatization

Key Places

Caracas
Lake Maracaibo

Welcome to Caracas (kuh RAHK us), population about 3.3 million. The view from a high-rise apartment can be breathtaking. At night, thousands of lights dot the surrounding hills. Below, on the street, fashionable-looking people walk by on their way to dinner or a movie.

Outside, the air is balmy. You won't find much pollution in the air, either. The city is in a valley that runs from east to west. Winds blow through it. They sweep the exhaust of the many cars out of the city.

Why not visit one of the cafes? Or if you're lucky, you might find a party for teenagers going on right in the street. They may be listening to American-style rap music. But the words will be in Spanish. If you have the time, take the Caracas subway. It cost the government millions to build, more than any other subway in the world. You can get almost anywhere in the city on it, and the fare is only about 25 cents.

▼ Many of Venezuela's largest petroleum deposits lie beneath the floor of Lake Maracaibo.

A Land Made Wealthy by Oil

Venezuela's government could pay for the subways because of money it made from the sale of oil. Venezuela has vast supplies of oil. The Country Profile map shows where Venezuela's oil is located. Venezuela's oil has earned millions of dollars on the world market. People migrated from the countryside to work for the oil companies.

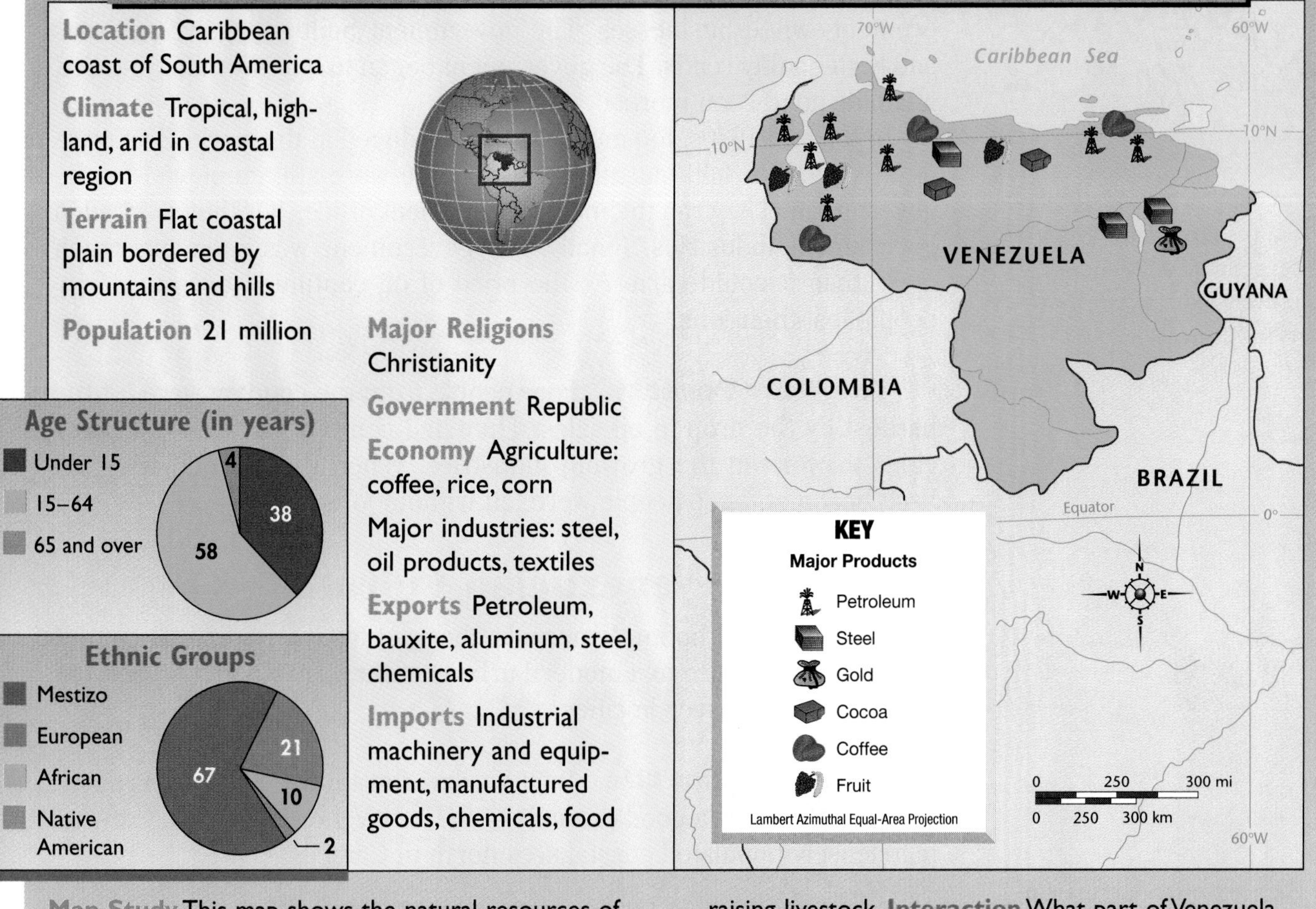

Map Study This map shows the natural resources of Venezuela. Venezuela is famous for its deposits of petroleum. However, Venezuela also has many other resources, including soil that is good for farming and raising livestock. **Interaction** What part of Venezuela has the most natural resources? What area do you think has the most cities?

They helped maintain the giant oil rigs in Lake Maracaibo. They also worked in oil refineries.

Both the government and individuals own oil companies in Venezuela. They have grown rich mining, processing, and selling oil. By the early 1980s, Venezuela was the richest country in Latin America. Much of the money has gone to Caracas, where most Venezuelans live.

Ups and Downs of Oil Prices Venezuela's oil was discovered about 75 years ago. Since then, Venezuela has pumped about 67 billion barrels of oil. There seemed to be no end to the money that could be made in the oil industry. Except for the Persian Gulf region, Venezuela has the biggest oil reserves in the world.

During the 1970s, the price of oil went up. An oil boom began. A **boom** is a period of increased prosperity during which more of a product is produced and sold. The standard of living of many Venezuelans went up, too. That is when the government started spending huge sums

Predict Do you think that one resource, such as oil, can support a country forever? Why or why not?

of money. Many people were hired to run government agencies and government-owned businesses. The government built expensive subways and high-quality roads. The government began to borrow money so that it could spend even more.

In the mid-1980s, too much oil was produced in the world. The price of oil started to fall, but millions of people were still employed by the government. They ran the many government offices. Or they worked in government industries. Finally, the government was spending much more than it could earn. As the price of oil continued to drop, many people lost their jobs.

The New Poverty Poor people from the country were hit the hardest by the drop in oil sales. They had come to Caracas and other cities to work in the growing industries. When the oil industries cut back, many of these people were left without jobs.

Venezuelan Culture

During the oil boom, Venezuela changed from a traditional culture based on agriculture to a modern urban country. Now about 80 percent of the population lives in cities.

A Venezuelan Life Juan Varderi (hwahn var DEHR ee) is about 28 years old. He is a good example of the new Venezuelan. Juan grew up in a densely populated coastal area north of Caracas.

▼Caracas is the largest city in Venezuela. It is also the country's capital.

U.S. Petroleum Imports From Venezuela, 1984–1996

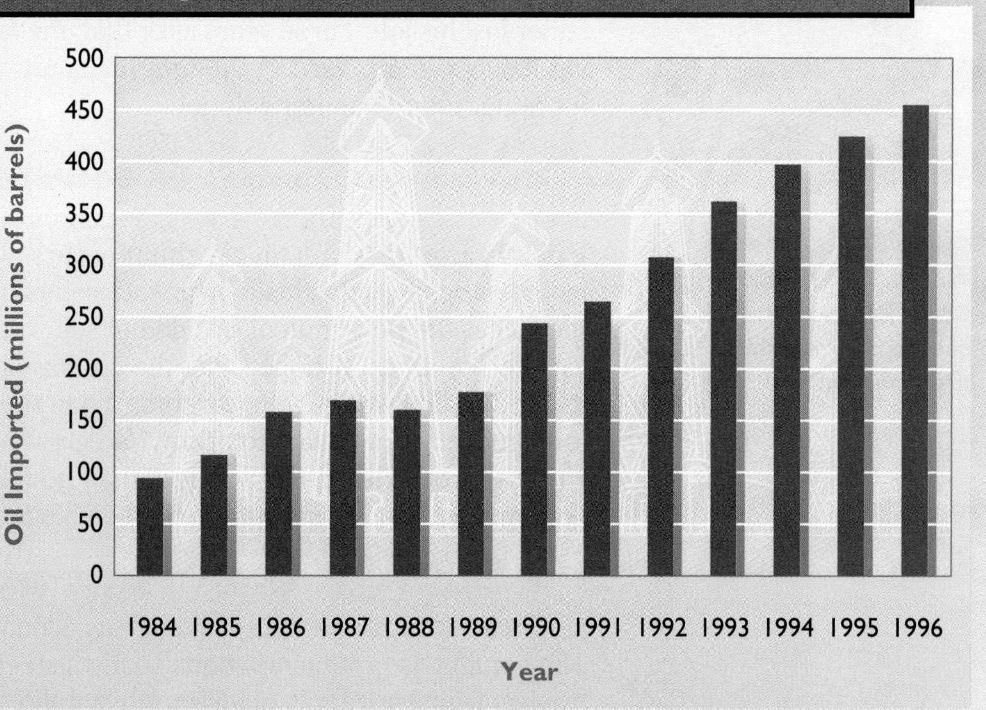

Chart Study The United States has several major petroleum deposits, but still uses more petroleum than it produces. The United States imports petroleum from Canada, Mexico, Nigeria, Saudi Arabia, and Venezuela. **Critical Thinking** When did the United States import the least amount of petroleum from Venezuela? When did it import the most?

Juan's grandfather raised sheep on a ranch east of Lake Maracaibo. He made a fairly good living selling wool and meat to people in Caracas. He fully expected that his son, Juan's father, would work with him, so he never encouraged him to go to school. But in the 1970s, Juan's father was lured by the oil industry, which was beginning to boom.

Varderi's father left the ranch at age 16. He went to work on an oil rig that was owned by the government. By the time Juan was born, the family was living in Caracas in a small apartment. They had a radio but no telephone. Juan Varderi grew up playing baseball on the streets of Caracas. Baseball is very popular in Venezuela.

By the early 1980s, Juan's father was making more money. The family bought a television. Televisions had become popular. Varderi remembers those years as the most exciting time of his life.

> "There were American programs you could watch on television, dubbed into Spanish. My friends and I paid attention to the clothes that the Americans wore. We tried to dress like them. We thought their music was the coolest in the world. We used to watch rock videos and try to learn the words of songs. In the early 1980s, we thought we could live just like rich Americans seemed to live. We didn't understand it was only taking place on TV. We didn't know what was going to happen to us in just a few years."

Germany in Venezuela In 1843, the Venezuelan government recruited almost 400 Germans to live in the mountains west of Caracas. For over 100 years their colony, Colonia Tovar, was isolated. The people spoke German, ate German food, and married only Germans. The town is still so different from the rest of the country that it deserves its nickname, "Germany in Venezuela."

Ask Questions If you had a chance to meet Juan Varderi, what questions would you ask? What questions do you think that Juan would ask you?

A few years later, when Juan Varderi turned 15, oil prices fell. His father lost his job. Three years after that, the family was in danger of losing its apartment. Varderi thought his family would have to move. But his father found another solution.

Government Businesses Go Public The solution Juan's father found lay in a new government policy of privatization. **Privatization** (pry vuh tih ZAY shun) occurs when the government sells its industries to individuals or private companies. In the late 1980s and the 1990s, the government decided to sell some of its businesses to private corporations. It hoped that the corporations would make big profits. The profits would help workers. When the government turned over an oil refinery to a private company, Varderi's father applied for a job there. He was hired. The salary was less than he had earned working for the government, but it was enough to keep his family in their apartment.

Finding Other Ways to Make Money Venezuela started new industries in an attempt to make its economy less dependent on oil. The country is producing goods such as steel, gold, cocoa, coffee, and tropical fruits. Varderi's oldest brother, Julio, received money from the government to start a small fruit orchard. This year he made enough money to support his family and help pay for a ticket for Juan to visit New York City. It was a trip Juan had always dreamed of.

Planting Corn in Venezuela

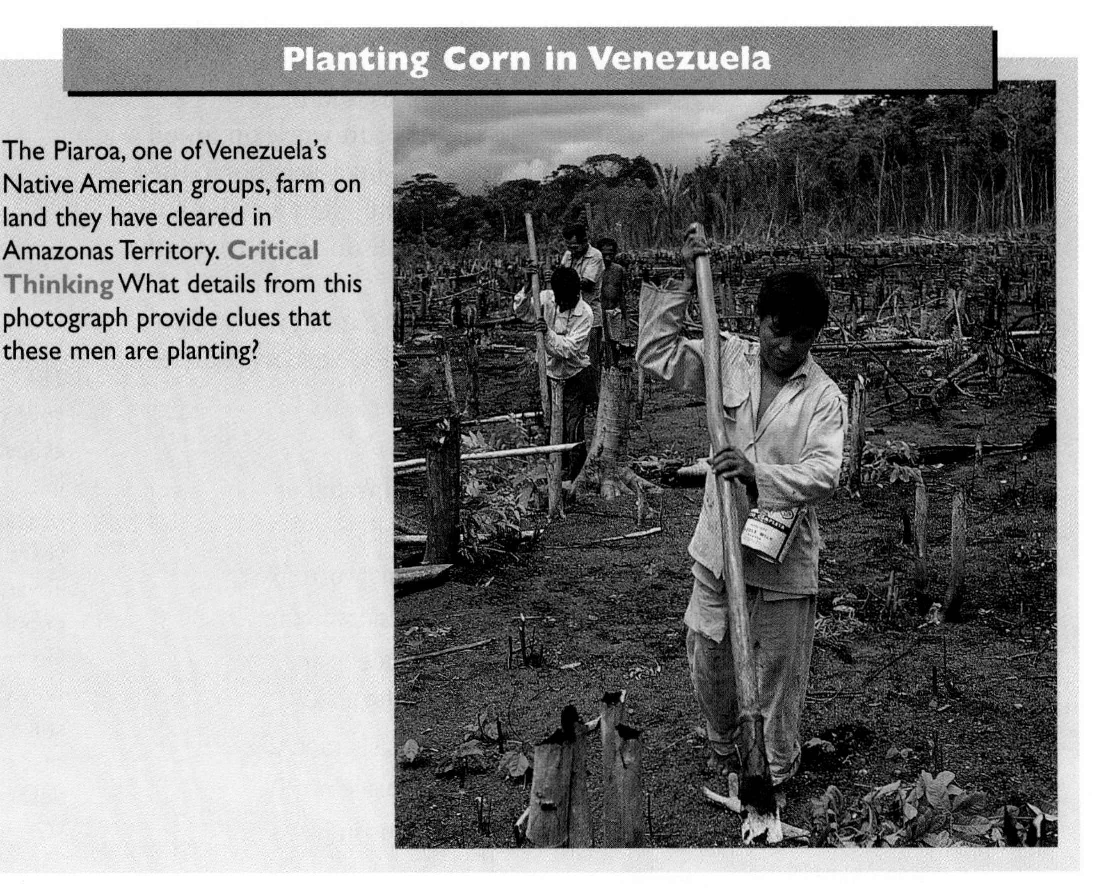

The Piaroa, one of Venezuela's Native American groups, farm on land they have cleared in Amazonas Territory. **Critical Thinking** What details from this photograph provide clues that these men are planting?

Teenagers in Caracas

Many Venezuelans like to wear fashions from the United States, especially jeans. They also like to meet each other in plazas, or public squares. In fact, addresses in Caracas are given by plazas and corners, not streets.

A Changed Venezuela Whatever Venezuela's economic fortune is, one thing is certain. The oil boom brought Venezuela into the modern world. When televisions, cellular phones, and other conveniences came into Venezuelan homes, life changed permanently. Juan Varderi dreams of having these things again in the future. And he is willing to work as hard as necessary to get them.

1. **Define** (a) boom, (b) privatization.
2. **Identify** (a) Caracas, (b) Lake Maracaibo.
3. (a) What happened to many Venezuelans during the oil boom? (b) What happened to them after?
4. Explain how Venezuela is trying to improve its economy.

Critical Thinking

5. **Drawing Conclusions** (a) Why did the drop in oil prices affect Venezuela so much? (b) What do you think Venezuela should do to avoid economic problems in the future?

Activity

6. **Writing Activity** Juan Varderi learned about United States culture from television programs. Describe America as shown on television.

CHAPTER 6

Review and Activities

Reviewing Main Ideas

1. Why are the rain forests so important for the environment?
2. In what ways does the Brazilian economy depend upon the rain forest?
3. (a) What challenges does life on the altiplano present?
   (b) How do the people who live there overcome these challenges?
4. Why are many Quechua and Aymara moving to the cities of Peru?
5. Why does Chile have such strict customs laws?
6. (a) How does geography contribute to Chile's pollution problem?
   (b) How does it contribute to its agricultural boom?
7. What type of lifestyle changes did many Venezuelans make during the oil boom of the 1970s?
8. Why is it important for Venezuela to develop new ways to boost its economy?

Reviewing Key Terms

Use each key term below in a sentence that shows the meaning of the term.

1. canopy
2. photosynthesis
3. altiplano
4. sierra
5. montaña
6. tundra
7. pesticide
8. boom
9. privatization

Critical Thinking

1. **Making Comparisons** In what ways have Chile's and Venezuela's economic histories been similar? How have they differed?
2. **Recognizing Cause and Effect** How do you think the coming of modern conveniences like electricity will change life for the Quechua?

Graphic Organizer

Copy the chart onto a piece of paper. Then fill in the empty boxes to complete the chart.

	Brazil	Peru	Chile	Venezuela
Important exports				
Major cities				

Map Activity

For each place listed below, write the letter from the map that shows its location.

1. Amazon River
2. Rio de Janeiro
3. Brasília
4. Cuzco
5. Lake Titicaca
6. Santiago
7. Andes
8. Caracas
9. Orinoco River

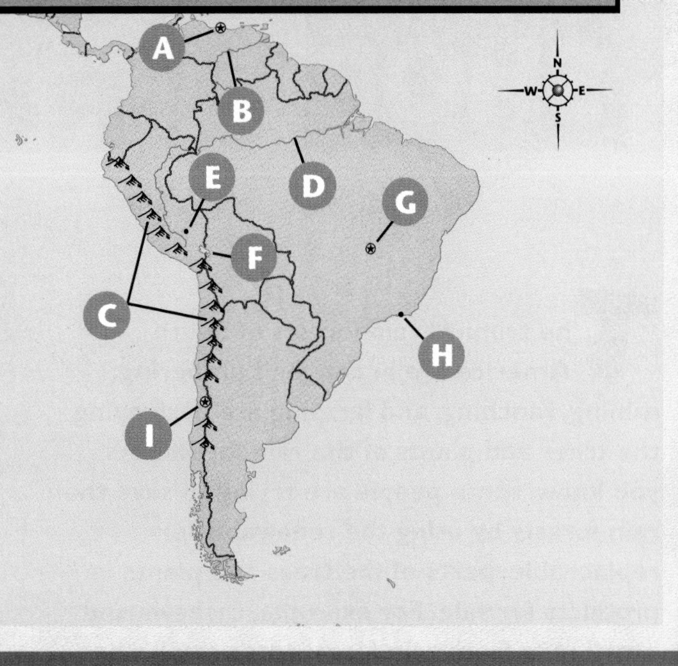

Writing Activity

Writing a Test

Write your own test about the economies of Chile and Venezuela. You may include multiple choice, true/false, fill in the blank, and essay questions on your test. Ask questions about how natural resources are important in each country's economy. Ask about benefits and problems that have affected each economy. Write an answer key to go with your test. Then trade tests with a partner. Take each other's tests. How did you do?

Internet Activity

Use a search engine to find the site **Rainforest Action Network.** Click on **Kid's Corner.** Here you can learn about life in the rain forest, issues of concern, and action that you can take. After exploring, click the BACK button on your browser. Click on **Rainforest Information.** Then click on **Take a Rainforest Quiz** to take a fun, on-line quiz.

Skills Review

Turn to the Skill Activity.

Review the steps for making a contour map. Then answer the following: (a) What are isolines? (b) Explain in your own words how you can use isolines to get useful information from a map.

How Am I Doing?

Answer these questions to help you check your progress.

1. Can I explain how changes in Brazil's rain forests affect the rest of the world?
2. Do I understand how geography has affected the lifestyles of Native Americans in Peru?
3. Can I explain why agriculture is important to Chile's economy?
4. Do I understand how the oil boom affected Venezuela's economy?
5. What information from this chapter can I use in my book project?

Rain Forest Resources

The tropical rain forests of South America are in danger. Lumbering, mining, ranching, and farming are destroying the trees and plants of the rain forests. As you know, some people are trying to save the rain forests by using the renewable, or replaceable, parts of the trees and plants in products for sale. For example, cashews and brazil nuts from rain forest trees can be harvested without harming the trees themselves. Oils from rain forest plants and nuts can be used in lotions and shampoos. If people can make money from a rain forest without cutting or burning it, people will have reasons to preserve the forests.

Purpose

In this activity, you will invent a new rain forest product. As you work on this activity, you will discover how rain forest products can be used without destroying rain forest resources.

Invent a Product

Think of a product that can be made with a renewable rain forest resource. Rain forest nuts are used in candy, ice cream, and cookies. Natural rubber from rubber trees is used to make bath toys. Use encyclopedias and other references to find out about the fruits of the assai tree, the oil of the babacu tree, and the resin of the copaiba tree. Think of something from the rain forest that many people need. Once you decide on your product, give it a name that people will remember.

Design a Package

When you have a product in mind, decide how it should look in a store. Should it come in a bag, a box, a can, or a bottle? Design the package, including art work and a product description.

Set a Price

Do some research to find out what products like yours cost. Visit or call a store. Then decide on the price for your product that is in the range of similar products. Put the price on your package.

Figure Your Costs

Now figure out how much money is needed to make your product. Assume that your costs are half of the selling price. For example, if your selling price is $6.50, then your manufacturing cost is $3.25. Divide your total manufacturing cost into the categories listed below.

- 50 percent for labor
- 25 percent for materials
- 10 percent for transportation
- 10 percent for advertising
- 5 percent for taxes

Then make a circle graph showing the percentage and dollar amount for each type of expense.

Make a Poster

Make a poster showing the layers of rain forest life: herb layer, shrub layer, understory, canopy, and emergent layer. Use encyclopedias and reference books such as *Usborne Science and Experiments: Ecology* (Usborne Publishing, 1988). Show the different kinds of creatures that live at each level and explain how they survive.

Links to Other Subjects

Designing a package for a new product	**Art**
Making a circle graph	**Math**
Doing research on the layers of the rain forest	**Science**
Writing a script	**Language Arts**
Writing a song	**Music**

Create a Commercial

You can make a commercial to advertise your rain forest product. Use the poster you made as a prop for your commercial. Write a short script that explains why it is important to protect rain forests and how your product helps in that effort. Write and perform an original jingle or music for the commercial. You can produce your commercial on computer or shoot it with a video camera. Or, you can perform your commercial for the rest of the class. Remember that your commercial should make people want to buy your product.

Write a summary that describes the process you used to create your product. Be sure to answer the following questions in your summary.

1. What did you learn about using rain forest resources?
2. How can rain forest resources be used without destroying them?
3. Do you think it is possible for people to protect rain forests by using their renewable resources?

Question Book

BY PABLO NERUDA

Reach Into Your Background

Do you pay close attention to the world around you? Describe a plant, a building, or a person that you saw on your way to school today. Remember as many details as you can. If you saw a tree, try to remember the shape of its leaves and whether its roots were visible above the ground. If you saw a person, try to remember what the person was wearing and how old the person seemed to be.

Many of Pablo Neruda's poems help readers pay more attention to the world around them. Neruda, who lived in Chile, often wrote about subjects that people take for granted. The following poem is from a book of Neruda's poetry called *Question Book.*

Questions to Explore

1. How does this poem help you look more closely at the changes of the seasons?
2. Because Chile is in the Southern Hemisphere, its seasons are the reverse of the seasons in the United States. Does knowing this change your understanding of the poem? Why or why not?

Ask Questions If you were going to write a poem of questions, what questions would you ask?

LXXII

Si todos los ríos son dulces
de dónde saca sal el mar?

Cómo saben las estaciones
que deben cambiar de camisa?

Por qué tan lentas en invierno
y tan palpitantes después?

Y cómo saben las raíces
que deben subir a la luz?

Y luego saludar al aire
con tantas flores y colores?

Siempre es la misma
primavera
la que repite su papel?

LXXII

If all rivers are sweet
where does the sea get its salt?

How do the seasons discover
it's time to change shirts?

Why are winters so slow
and the aftermaths, volatile?

How do the roots know
they must climb toward the light?

And then greet the air
with such colors and flowers?

Is it always the same spring,
repeating the same role?

aftermath (AF ter math) *n.:* the period that comes after an event
volatile (VOL a til) *adj.:* explosive
role (roll) *n.:* a part played by an actor

◀▲ These photos show winter and summer in Chile's Patagonian Andes. How can you tell which season is which?

Visualize What does a root look like as it pushes away from a seed and up toward the sky?

EXPLORING YOUR READING

Look Back

1. What do all the questions in this poem have in common?

Think It Over

2. Seasons don't wear shirts. What does Neruda mean when he refers to the seasons changing their shirts?
3. How is spring like an actor playing a role in a play?
4. Based on this poem, does Neruda seem to think that nature is friendly or unfriendly? Explain your answer.

Go Beyond

5. How can paying attention to details around you help you appreciate nature?

Ideas for Writing: Answer Poem

6. The questions that Neruda asks all have scientific explanations. Find out the scientific answer to Neruda's questions. Then, write an answer poem in response to Neruda's.

As you study Latin America, you will be reading and thinking about these important questions.

- **What are the main physical features of Latin America?**
- **What factors have affected cultures in Latin America?**
- **Why have many Latin Americans been moving to cities in recent years?**
- **What is the relationship of the nations of Latin America with the United States and the world?**
- **How has geography influenced the ways in which Latin Americans make a living?**

Doing a project shows what you know! Are you doing this project? **Muy bueno!**

GEO LEO

Project Menu

The chapters in this book have some answers to these questions. Now it's time for you to find your own answers by doing projects on your own or with a group. Here are some ways to make your own discoveries about Latin America.

A Latin American Concert As you study Latin America, find out about the music of each region. Find out what kinds of instruments people play and what the instruments are made of. Then try to find examples of each kind of music. You might find some in public libraries, which usually have a music collection. Play the music for your class. You might explain how history and geography had an effect on the development of each kind of music. For example, in the Andes, people make a kind of rattle out of llamas' hooves. Talk about the roles of different types of music. For example, merengue is dance music, and reggae often serves as political protest.

From Questions to Careers

INTERPRETER

When people who speak different languages need to talk to each other, they often need an interpreter. An interpreter is someone who speaks both languages and can translate for both people as they talk.

In the United States, most interpreters work for the government. They translate during meetings between U.S. officials and visitors from other countries. Interpreters are especially important when there is an emergency. For example, when a major earthquake struck San Francisco in 1989, interpreters helped Spanish speakers get medical attention and talk to telephone operators.

Interpreters also work for companies doing business in other countries. Large corporations often have a whole team of interpreters.

Many interpreters have a degree in their second language and additional training in interpreting. However, some bilingual people are able to become interpreters for small companies or agencies without training.

Visions of Latin America Create a diorama showing the effect of geography on the way people live in Latin America. Your diorama can be realistic or it can show a symbol. Work in groups of three or four.

After you finish your diorama, write a short report to explain how the subject of your diorama affects the people of Latin America today. Display the whole set of dioramas with the reports. Invite other students to look at them. You might also display them at parents' night.

Latin America in the News As you read about Latin America, keep a bulletin board display called *Latin America in the News.* Look in magazines and newspapers for articles that describe life in Latin America. For example, when you study Mexico, you can collect articles about Mexican culture, politics, or economics.

When you have finished your study of Latin America, choose the articles that you want to keep. Make a scrapbook to contain the articles. Display the scrapbook in the school library or resource center.

Explorer's Dictionary Many languages are spoken in Latin America. As you work on this book, create a dictionary of important terms. Use a foreign-language dictionary to translate your terms into Spanish or another Latin American language.

Illustrate your dictionary with drawings or pictures cut out from magazines or travel brochures. Bind the pages together with yarn or staples. Display your dictionary so other students can use it.

WORLD EXPLORER
PRENTICE HALL

Reference

TABLE OF CONTENTS

Map and Globe Handbook **163**

How do you find your way around the world? The Map and Globe Handbook features the skills every geographer needs.

Atlas **180**

Where in the world is it? The Atlas provides physical and political maps of the world and its continents.

The World: Political 180
The World: Physical 182
United States: Political 184
North and South America: Political 186
North and South America: Physical 187
Europe: Political 188
Europe: Physical 189
Africa: Political 190
Africa: Physical 191
Asia: Political 192
Asia: Physical 193
Australia, New Zealand, and the Pacific Islands: Physical-Political 194
The Arctic and Antarctica 195

World View **196**

What's your favorite country? World View lists information about every country in the world!

Glossary of Geographic Terms **204**
Gazetteer **206**
Glossary **208**
Index **211**
Acknowledgments **214**

This Map and Globe Handbook is designed to help you develop some of the skills you need to be a world explorer. These can help you whether you explore from the top of an elephant in India or from a computer at school.

You can use the information in this handbook to improve your map and globe skills. But the best way to sharpen your skills is to practice. The more you practice, the better you'll get.

GEO CLEO and GEO LEO

Table of Contents

Five Themes of Geography	**164**
Understanding Movements of the Earth	**166**
Maps and Globes Represent the Earth	**167**
Locating Places on a Map or a Globe	**168**
Map Projections	**170**
Parts of a Map	**172**
Comparing Maps of Different Scale	**173**
Political Maps	**174**
Physical Maps	**175**
Special Purpose Maps	**176**
Landforms, Climate Regions, and Natural Vegetation Regions	**177**

Five Themes of Geography

Studying the geography of the entire world can be a huge task. You can make that task easier by using the five themes of geography: location, place, human-environment interaction, movement, and regions. The themes are tools you can use to organize information and to answer the where, why, and how of geography.

1. Location
Chicago, Illinois, occupies one location on the Earth. No other place has exactly the same absolute location.

1 Location answers the question, "Where is it?" You can think of the location of a continent or a country as its address. You might give an absolute location such as "22 South Lake Street" or "40°N and 80°W." You might also use a relative address, telling where one place is by referring to another place. "Between school and the mall" and "eight miles east of Pleasant City" are examples of relative locations.

2 Place identifies the natural and human features that make one place different from every other place. You can identify a specific place by its landforms, climate, plants, animals, people, or cultures. You might even think of place as a geographic signature. Use the signature to help you understand the natural and human features that make one place different from every other place.

2. Place
Ancient cultures in Egypt built distinctive pyramids. Use the theme of place to help you remember features that exist only in Egypt.

3 Human-Environment Interaction focuses on the relationship between people and the environment. As people live in an area, they often begin to make changes to it, usually to make their lives easier. For example, they might build a dam to control flooding during rainy seasons. Also, the environment can affect how people live, work, dress, travel, and communicate.

4 Movement answers the question "How do people, goods, and ideas move from place to place?" Remember that, often, what happens in one place can affect what happens in another. Use the theme of movement to help you trace the spread of goods, people, and ideas from one location to the next.

5 Region is the last geographic theme. A region is a group of places that share common features. Geographers divide the world into many types of regions. For example, countries, states, and cities are political regions. The people in these places live under the same type of government. Other features can be used to define regions. Places that have the same climate belong to a particular climate region. Places that share the same culture belong to a cultural region. The same place can be found in more than one region. The state of Hawaii is in the political region of the United States. Because it has a tropical climate, Hawaii is also part of a tropical climate region.

3. Human-Environment Interaction
Peruvians have changed steep mountain slopes into terraces suitable for farming. Think how this environment looked before people made changes.

1. What is the absolute location of your school? What is one way to describe its relative location?
2. What might be a "geographic signature" of the town or city you live in?
3. Give an example of human-environment interaction where you live.
4. Name at least one thing that comes into your town or city and one that goes out. How is each moved? Where does it come from? Where does it go?
5. What are several regions you think your town or city belongs in?

4. Movement
Arab traders brought not only goods to Kuala Lumpur, Malaysia, but also Arab building styles and the Islamic religion.

5. Regions
Wheat farming is an important activity in Kansas. This means that Kansas is part of a farming region.

Understanding Movements of the Earth

Planet Earth is part of our solar system. The Earth revolves around the sun in a nearly circular path called an orbit. A revolution, or one complete orbit around the sun, takes 365 1/4 days, or a year. As the Earth revolves around the sun, it is also spinning around in space. This movement is called a rotation. The Earth rotates on its axis—an invisible line through the center of the Earth from the North Pole to the South Pole. The Earth makes one full rotation about every 24 hours. As the Earth rotates, it is daytime on the side facing the sun. It is night on the side away from the sun.

The Earth's axis is tilted at an angle. Because of this tilt, sunlight strikes different parts of the Earth at certain points in the year, creating different seasons.

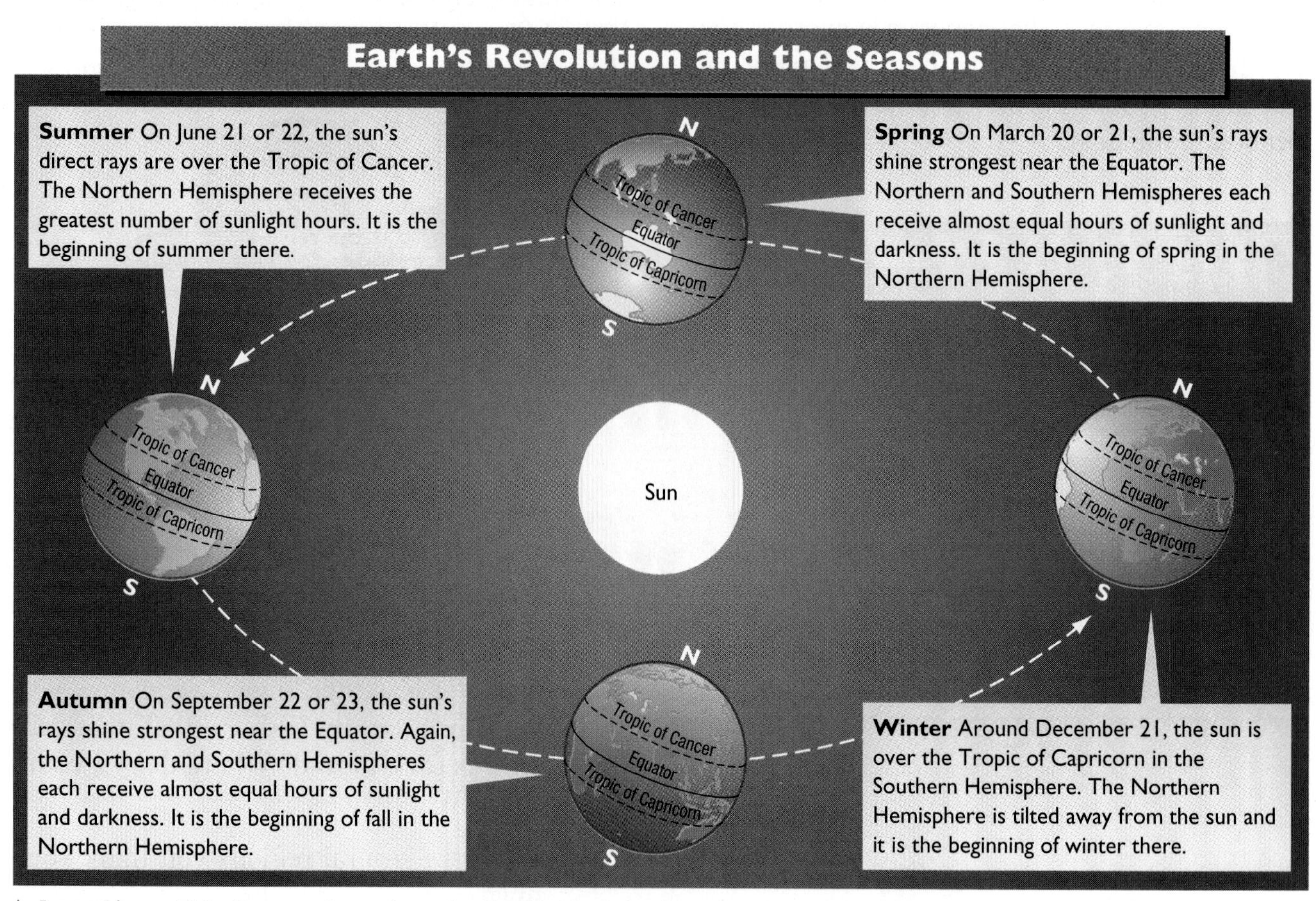

Earth's Revolution and the Seasons
Summer On June 21 or 22, the sun's direct rays are over the Tropic of Cancer. The Northern Hemisphere receives the greatest number of sunlight hours. It is the beginning of summer there.
Spring On March 20 or 21, the sun's rays shine strongest near the Equator. The Northern and Southern Hemispheres each receive almost equal hours of sunlight and darkness. It is the beginning of spring in the Northern Hemisphere.
N
Tropic of Cancer
Equator
Tropic of Capricorn
S
Sun
Autumn On September 22 or 23, the sun's rays shine strongest near the Equator. Again, the Northern and Southern Hemispheres each receive almost equal hours of sunlight and darkness. It is the beginning of fall in the Northern Hemisphere.
Winter Around December 21, the sun is over the Tropic of Capricorn in the Southern Hemisphere. The Northern Hemisphere is tilted away from the sun and it is the beginning of winter there.

▲ **Location** This diagram shows how the Earth's tilt and orbit around the sun combine to create the seasons. Remember, in the Southern Hemisphere the seasons are reversed.

1. What causes the seasons in the Northern Hemisphere to be the opposite of those in the Southern Hemisphere?
2. During which two months of the year do the Northern and Southern Hemispheres have about equal hours of daylight and darkness?

Maps and Globes Represent the Earth

Globes

A globe is a scale model of the Earth. It shows the actual shapes, sizes, and locations of all the Earth's landmasses and bodies of water. Features on the surface of the Earth are drawn to scale on a globe. This means a smaller unit of measure on the globe stands for a larger unit of measure on the Earth.

Because a globe is made in the true shape of the Earth, it offers these advantages for studying the Earth.

- The shape of all land and water bodies are accurate.
- Compass directions from one point to any other point are correct.
- The distance from one location to another is always accurately represented.

However, a globe presents some disadvantages for studying the Earth. Because a globe shows the entire Earth, it cannot show small areas in great detail. Also, a globe is not easily folded and carried from one place to another. For these reasons, geographers often use maps to learn about the Earth.

Maps

A map is a drawing or representation, on a flat surface, of a region. A map can show details too small to be seen on a globe. Floor plans, mall directories, and road maps are among the maps we use most often.

While maps solve some of the problems posed by globes, they have some disadvantages of their own. Maps flatten the real round world. Mapmakers cut, stretch, push, and pull some parts of the Earth to get it all flat on paper. As a result, some locations may be distorted. That is, their size, shape, and relative location may not be accurate. For example, on most maps of the entire world, the size and shape of the Antarctic and Arctic regions are not accurate.

1. What is the main difference between a globe and a map?
2. What is one advantage of using a globe instead of a map?

Global Gores

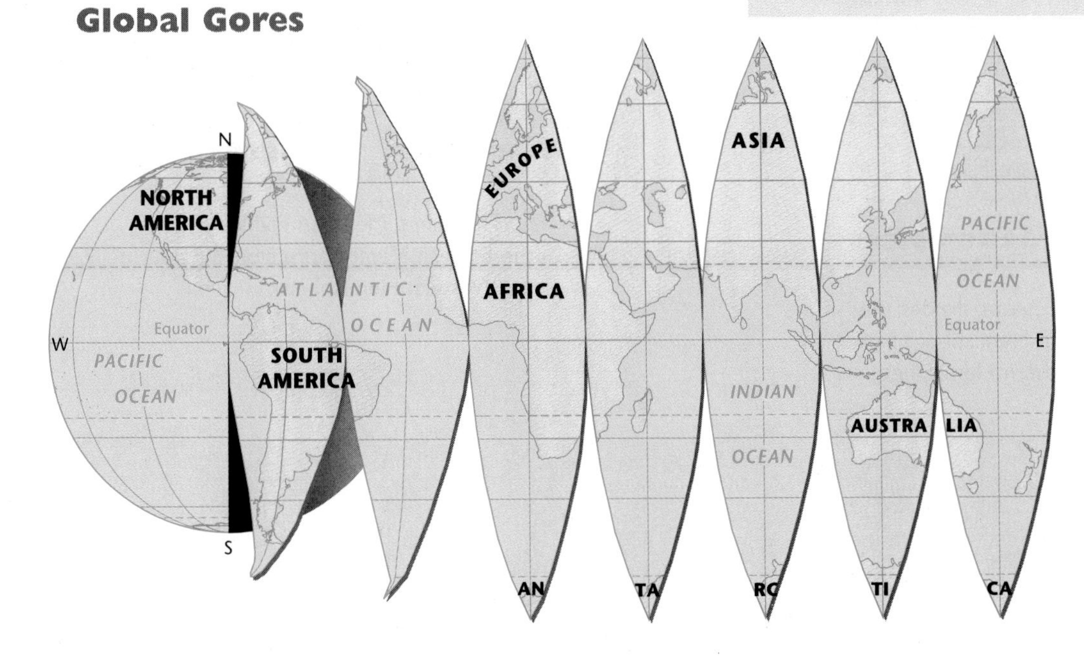

◀ Location When mapmakers flatten the surface of the Earth, curves become straight lines. As a result, size, shape, and distance are distorted.

Locating Places on a Map or a Globe

The Hemispheres

Another name for a round ball like a globe is a sphere. The Equator, an imaginary line halfway between the North and South Poles, divides the globe into two hemispheres. (The prefix *hemi* means "half.") Land and water south of the Equator are in the Southern Hemisphere. Land and water north of the Equator are in the Northern Hemisphere.

Mapmakers sometimes divide the globe along an imaginary line that runs from North Pole to South Pole. This line, called the Prime Meridian, divides the globe into the Eastern and Western Hemispheres.

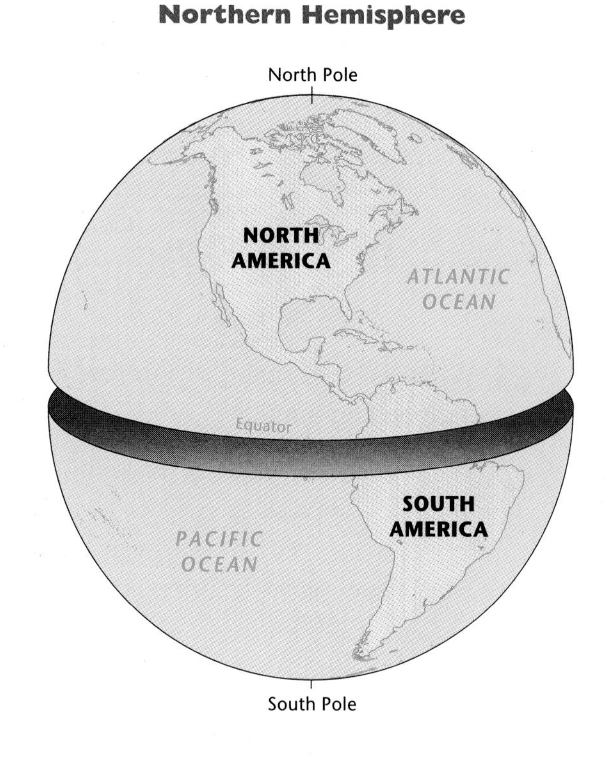

▲ The Equator divides the Northern Hemisphere from the Southern Hemisphere.

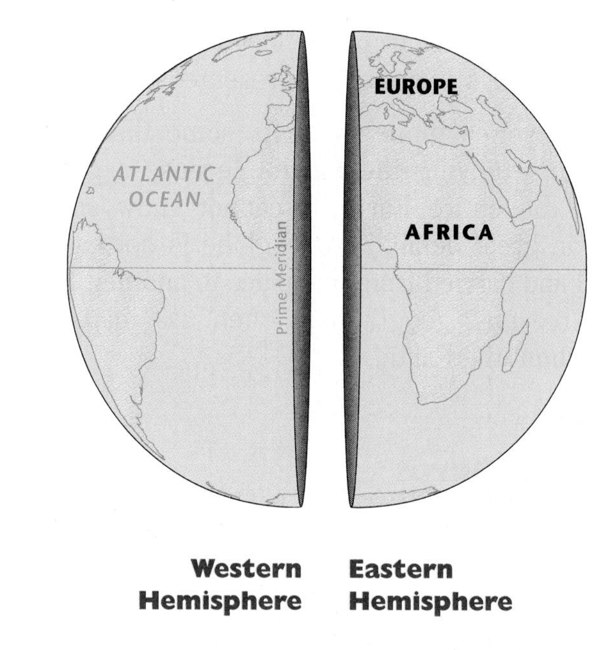

▲ The Prime Meridian divides the Eastern Hemisphere from the Western Hemisphere.

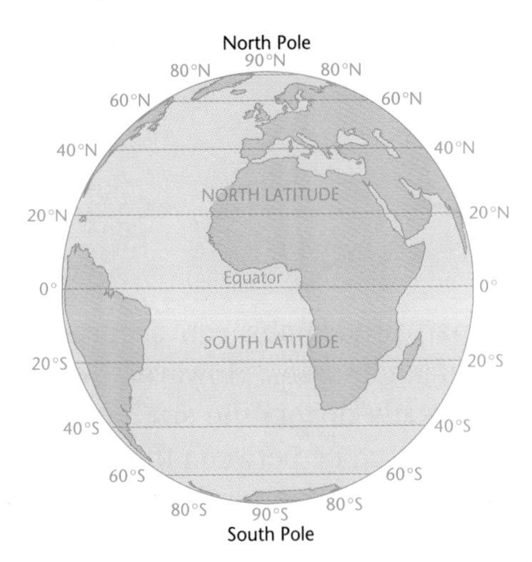

Parallels of Latitude

The Equator, at 0° latitude, is the starting place for measuring latitude or distances north and south. Most globes do not show every parallel of latitude. They may show every 10, 20, or even 30 degrees.

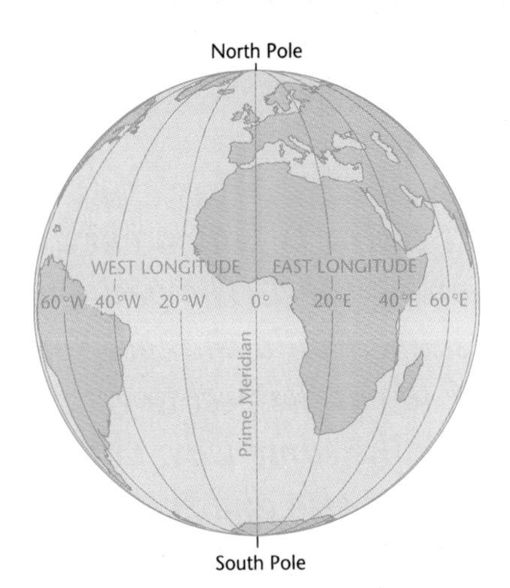

Meridians of Longitude

The Prime Meridian, at 0° longitude, runs from pole to pole through Greenwich, England. It is the starting place for measuring longitude or distances east and west. Each meridian of longitude meets its opposite longitude at the North and South Poles.

Two sets of lines cover most globes. One set of lines runs parallel to the Equator. These lines, including the Equator, are called *parallels of latitude.* They are measured in degrees (°). One degree of latitude represents a distance of about 70 miles (112 km). The Equator has a location of 0°. The other parallels of latitude tell the direction and distance from the Equator to another location.

The second set of lines runs north and south. These lines are called *meridians of longitude.* Meridians show the degrees of longitude east or west of the Prime Meridian, which is located at 0°. A meridian of longitude tells the direction and distance from the Prime Meridian to another location. Unlike parallels, meridians are not the same distance apart everywhere on the globe.

Together the pattern of parallels of latitude and meridians of longitude is called the global grid. Using the lines of latitude and longitude, you can locate any place on Earth. For example, the location of 30° north latitude and 90° west longitude is usually written as 30°N, 90°W. Only one place on Earth has these coordinates—the city of New Orleans, in the state of Louisiana.

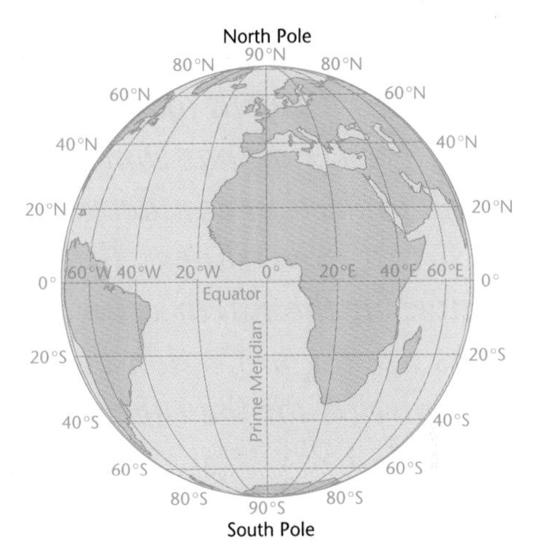

The Global Grid

By using lines of latitude and longitude, you can give the absolute location of any place on the Earth.

1. Which continents lie completely in the Northern Hemisphere? The Western Hemisphere?
2. Is there land or water at 20°S latitude and the Prime Meridian? At the Equator and 60°W longitude?

Map Projections

Imagine trying to flatten out a complete orange peel. The peel would split. The shape would change. You would have to cut the peel to get it to lie flat. In much the same way, maps cannot show the correct size and shape of every landmass or body of water on the Earth's curved surface. Maps shrink some places and stretch others. This shrinking and stretching is called distortion—*a change made to a shape.*

To make up for this disadvantage, mapmakers use different map projections. Each map projection is a way of showing the round Earth on flat paper. Each type of projection has some distortion. No one projection can accurately show the correct area, shape, distance, and direction for the Earth's surface. Mapmakers use the projection that has the least distortion for the information they are studying.

Same-Shape Maps

Some map projections can accurately show the shapes of landmasses. However, these projections often greatly distort the size of landmasses as well as the distance between them.

One of the most common same-shape maps is a Mercator projection, named for the mapmaker who invented it. The Mercator projection accurately shows shape and direction, but it distorts distance and size. In this projection, the northern and southern areas of the globe appear stretched more than areas near the Equator. Because the projection shows true directions, ships' navigators use it to chart a straight line course between two ports.

Mercator Projection

Equal-Area Maps

Some map projections can show the correct size of landmasses. Maps that use these projections are called equal-area maps. In order to show the correct size of landmasses, these maps usually distort shapes. The distortion is usually greater at the edges of the map and less at the center.

Robinson Maps

Many of the maps in this book use the Robinson projection. This is a compromise between the Mercator and equal-area projections. It gives a useful overall picture of the world. The Robinson projection keeps the size and shape relationships of most continents and oceans but does distort size of the polar regions.

Azimuthal Maps

Another kind of projection shows true compass direction. Maps that use this projection are called azimuthal maps. Such maps are easy to recognize—they are usually circular. Azimuthal maps are often used to show the areas of the North and South Poles. However, azimuthal maps distort scale, area, and shape.

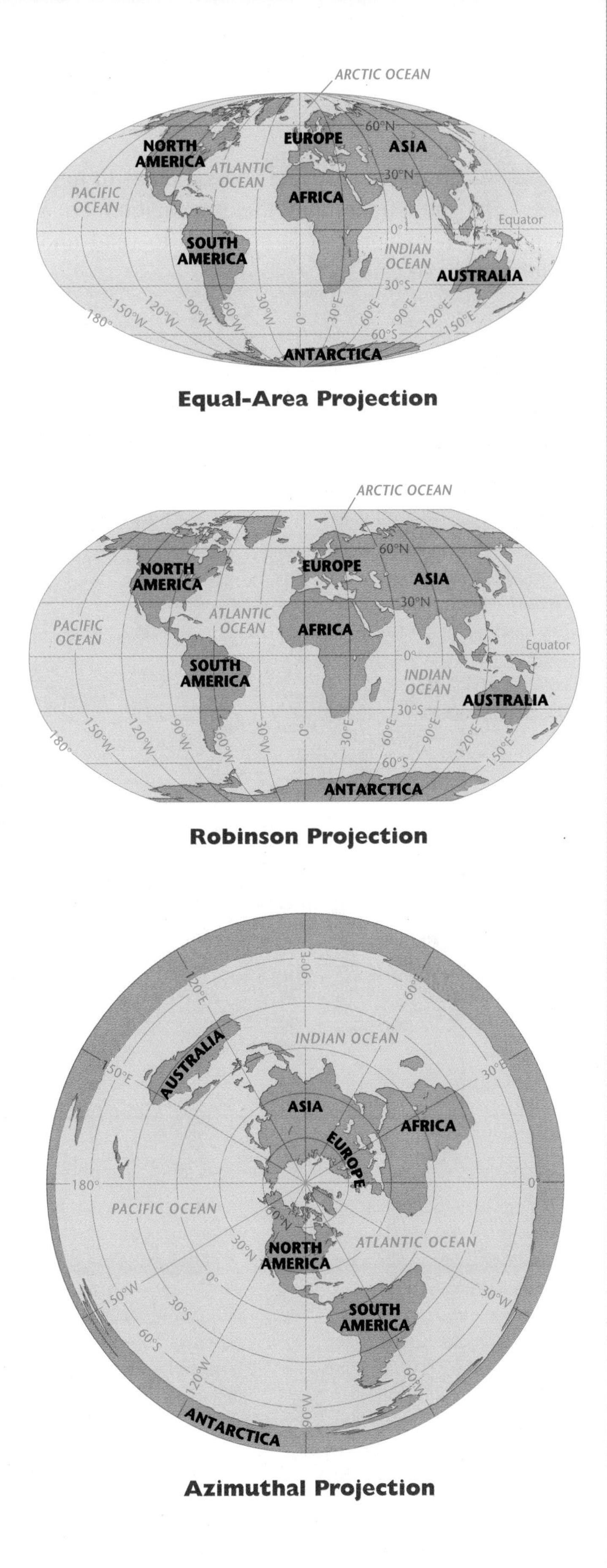

Equal-Area Projection

Robinson Projection

Azimuthal Projection

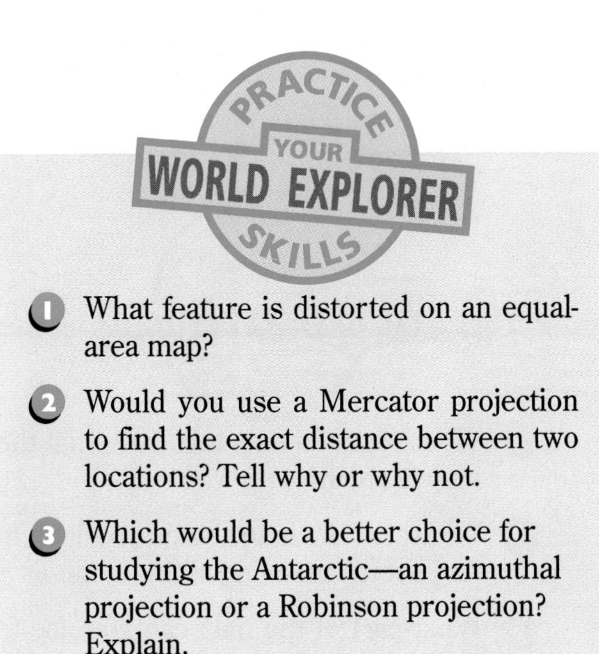

1. What feature is distorted on an equal-area map?
2. Would you use a Mercator projection to find the exact distance between two locations? Tell why or why not.
3. Which would be a better choice for studying the Antarctic—an azimuthal projection or a Robinson projection? Explain.

Parts of a Map

Mapmakers provide several clues to help you understand the information on a map. As an explorer, it is your job to read and interpret these clues.

Compass

Many maps show north at the top of the map. One way to show direction on a map is to use an arrow that points north. There may be an N shown with the arrow. Many maps give more information about direction by displaying a compass showing the directions, north, east, south, and west. The letters N, E, S, and W are placed to indicate these directions.

Title

The title of a map is the most basic clue. It signals what kinds of information you are likely to find on the map. A map titled *West Africa: Population Density* will be most useful for locating information about where people live in West Africa.

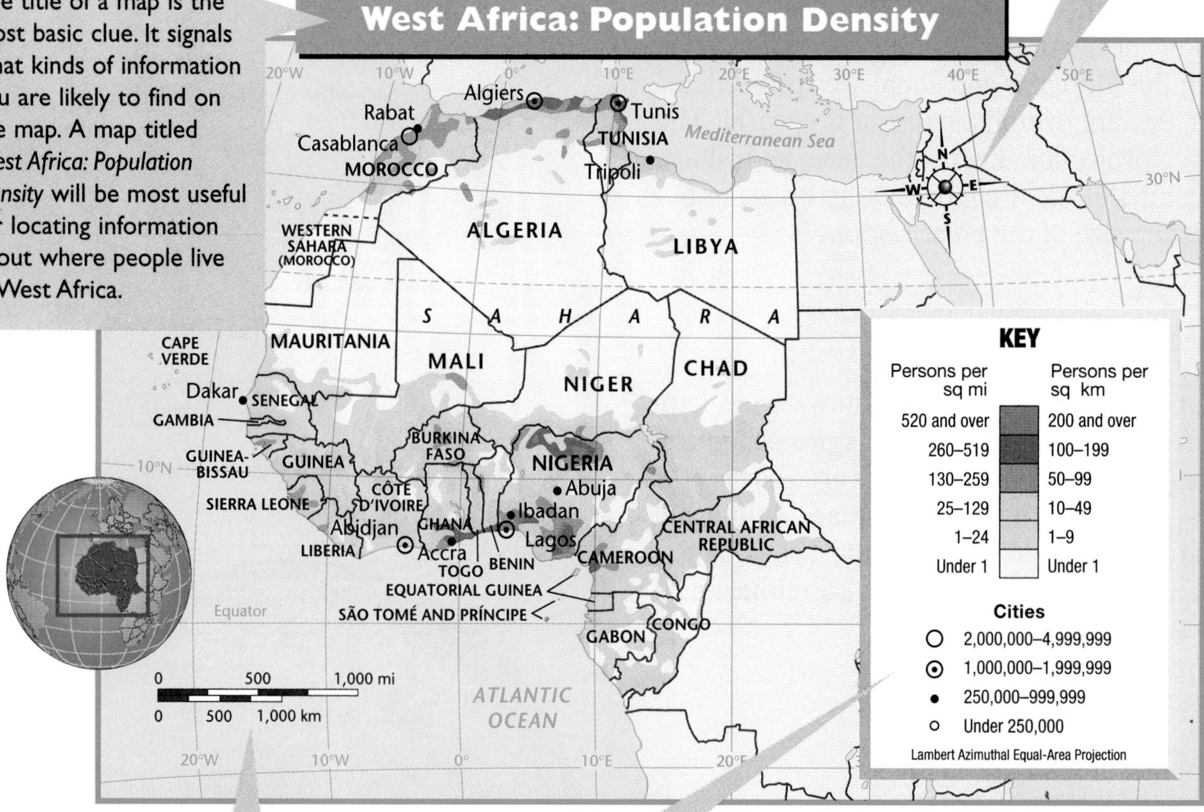

Scale

A map scale helps you find the actual distances between points shown on the map. You can measure the distance between any two points on the map, compare them to the scale, and find out the actual distance between the points. Most map scales show distances in both miles and kilometers.

Key

Often a map has a key, or legend, that shows the symbols used on the map and what each one means. On some maps, color is used as a symbol. On those maps, the key also tells the meaning of each color.

Practice Your World Explorer Skills

1. What part of a map tells you what the map is about?
2. Where on the map should you look to find out the meaning of this symbol? •
3. What part of the map can you use to find the distance between two cities?

Comparing Maps of Different Scale

Here are three maps drawn to three different scales. The first map shows Moscow's location in the northeastern portion of Russia. This map shows the greatest area—a large section of northern Europe. It has the smallest scale (1 inch = about 900 miles) and shows the fewest details. This map can tell you what direction to travel to reach Moscow from Finland.

Find the red box on Map 1. It shows the whole area covered by Map 2. Study Map 2. It gives a closer look at the city of Moscow. It shows the features around the city, the city's boundary, and the general shape of the city. This map can help you find your way from the airport to the center of town.

Now find the red box on Map 2. This box shows the area shown on Map 3. This map moves you closer into the city. Like the zoom on a computer or camera, Map 3 shows the smallest area but has the greatest detail. This map has the largest scale (1 inch = about 0.8 miles). This is the map to use to explore downtown Moscow.

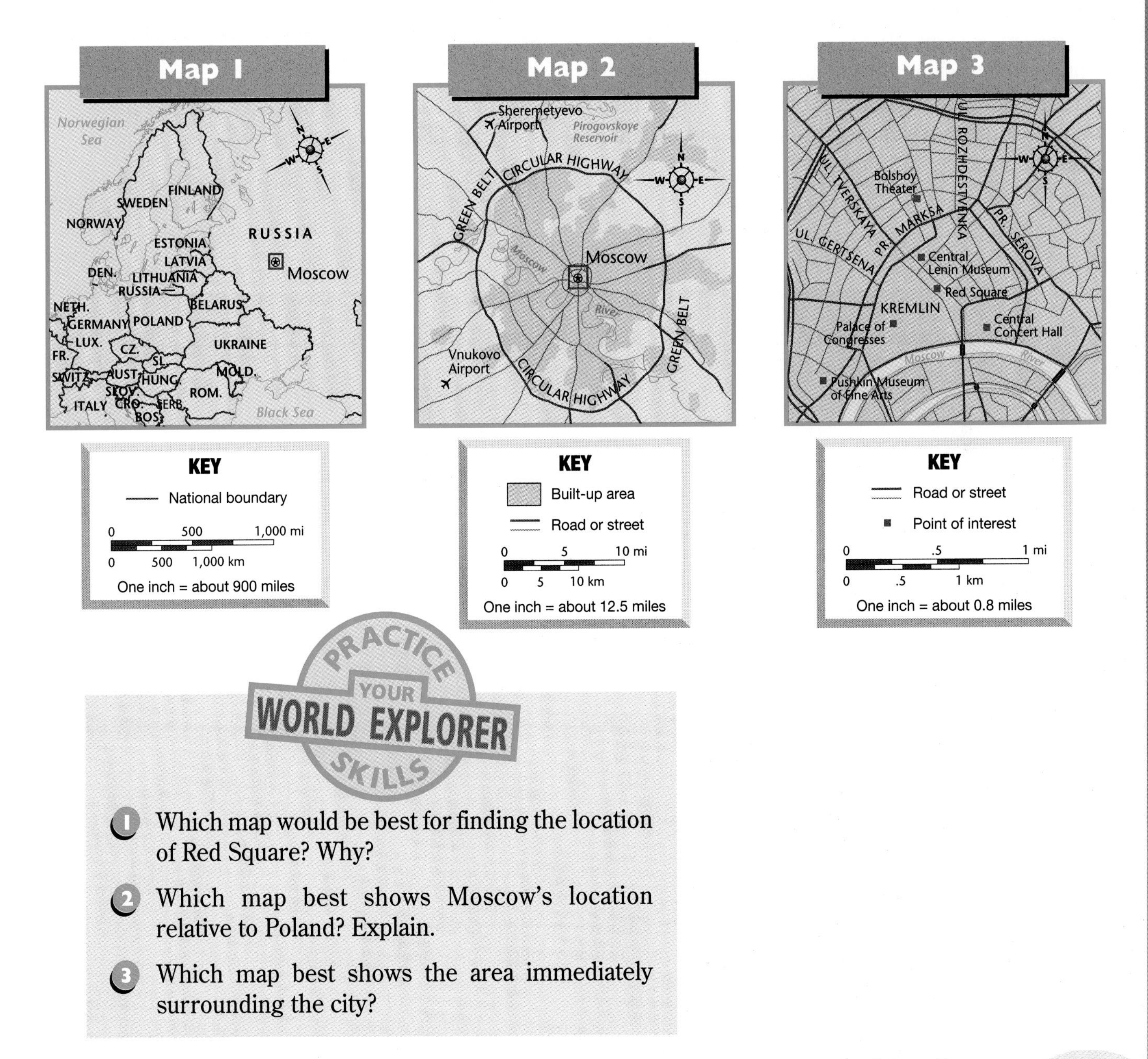

1. Which map would be best for finding the location of Red Square? Why?
2. Which map best shows Moscow's location relative to Poland? Explain.
3. Which map best shows the area immediately surrounding the city?

Political Maps

Mapmakers create maps to show all kinds of information. The kind of information presented affects the way a map looks. One type of map is called a political map. Its main purpose is to show continents, countries, and divisions within countries such as states or provinces. Usually different colors are used to show different countries or divisions within a country. The colors do not have any special meaning. They are used only to make the map easier to read.

Political maps also show where people have built towns and cities. Symbols can help you tell capital cities from other cities and towns. Even though political maps do not give information that shows what the land looks like, they often include some physical features such as oceans, lakes, and rivers.

Political maps usually have many labels. They give country names, and the names of capital and major cities. Bodies of water such as lakes, rivers, oceans, seas, gulfs, and bays are also labeled.

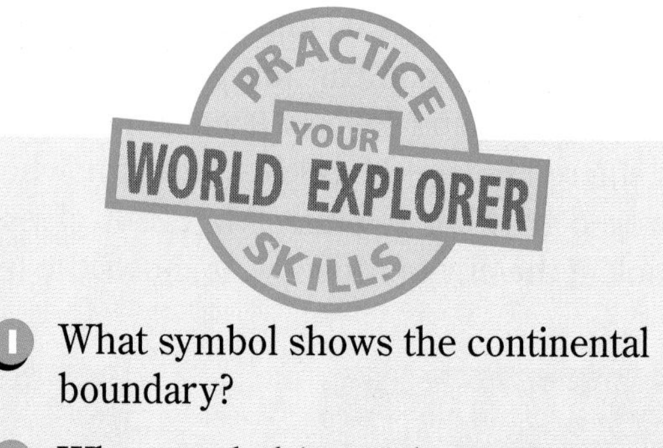

1. What symbol shows the continental boundary?
2. What symbol is used to indicate a capital city? A major city?
3. What kinds of landforms are shown on this map?

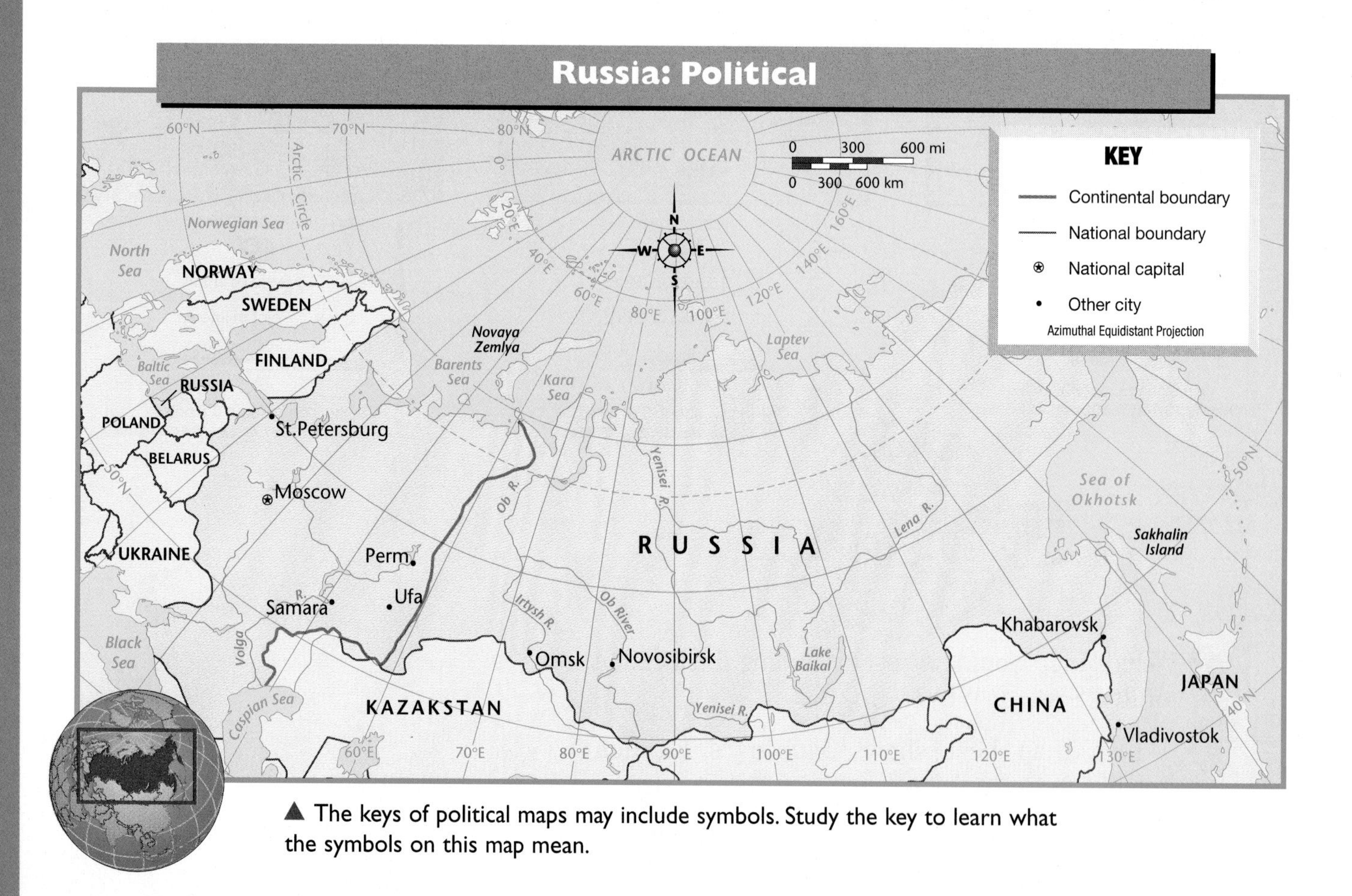

▲ The keys of political maps may include symbols. Study the key to learn what the symbols on this map mean.

Physical Maps

Like political maps, physical maps show country labels and labels for capital cities. However, physical maps also show what the land of a region looks like by showing the major physical features such as plains, hills, plateaus, or mountains. Labels give the names of features such as mountain peaks, mountains, plateaus, and river basins.

In order to tell one landform from another, physical maps often show elevation and relief. Elevation is the height of the land above sea level. Physical maps in this book use color to show elevation. Browns and oranges show higher lands while blues and greens show lands that are at or below sea level.

Relief shows how quickly the land rises or falls. Hills, mountains, and plateaus are shown on relief maps using shades of gray. Level or nearly level land is shown without shading. Darkly shaded areas indicate steeper lands.

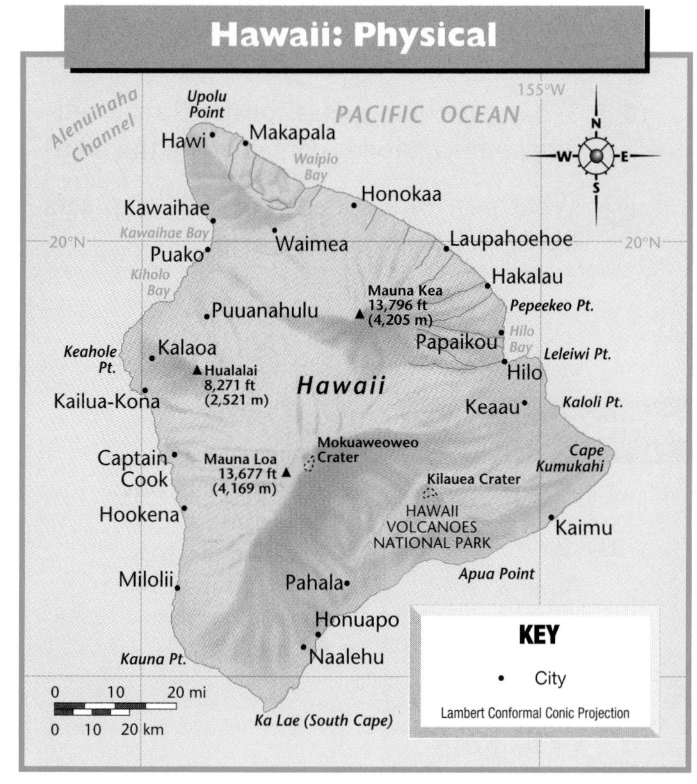

▲ On a physical map, shading is sometimes used to show relief. Use the shading to locate the moutains in Hawaii.

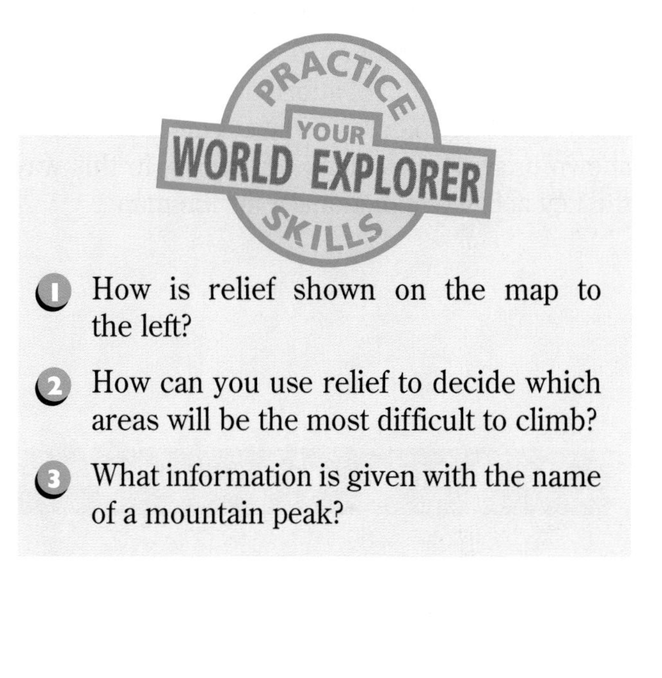

1. How is relief shown on the map to the left?
2. How can you use relief to decide which areas will be the most difficult to climb?
3. What information is given with the name of a mountain peak?

▼ Mauna Kea, an extinct volcano, is the highest peak in the state of Hawaii. Find Mauna Kea on the map.

Special Purpose Maps

As you explore the world, you will encounter many different kinds of special purpose maps. For example, a road map is a special purpose map. The title of each special purpose map tells the purpose and content of the map. Usually a special purpose map highlights only one kind of information. Examples of special purpose maps include land use, population distribution, recreation, transportation, natural resources, or weather.

The key on a special purpose map is very important. Even though a special purpose map shows only one kind of information, it may present many different pieces of data. This data can be shown in symbols, colors, or arrows. In this way, the key acts like a dictionary for the map.

Reading a special purpose map is a skill in itself. Look at the map below. First, try to get an overall sense of what it shows. Then, study the map to identify its main ideas. For example, one main idea of this map is that much of the petroleum production in the region takes place around the Persian Gulf.

1. What part of a special purpose map tells what information is contained on the map?
2. What part of a special purpose map acts like a dictionary for the map?

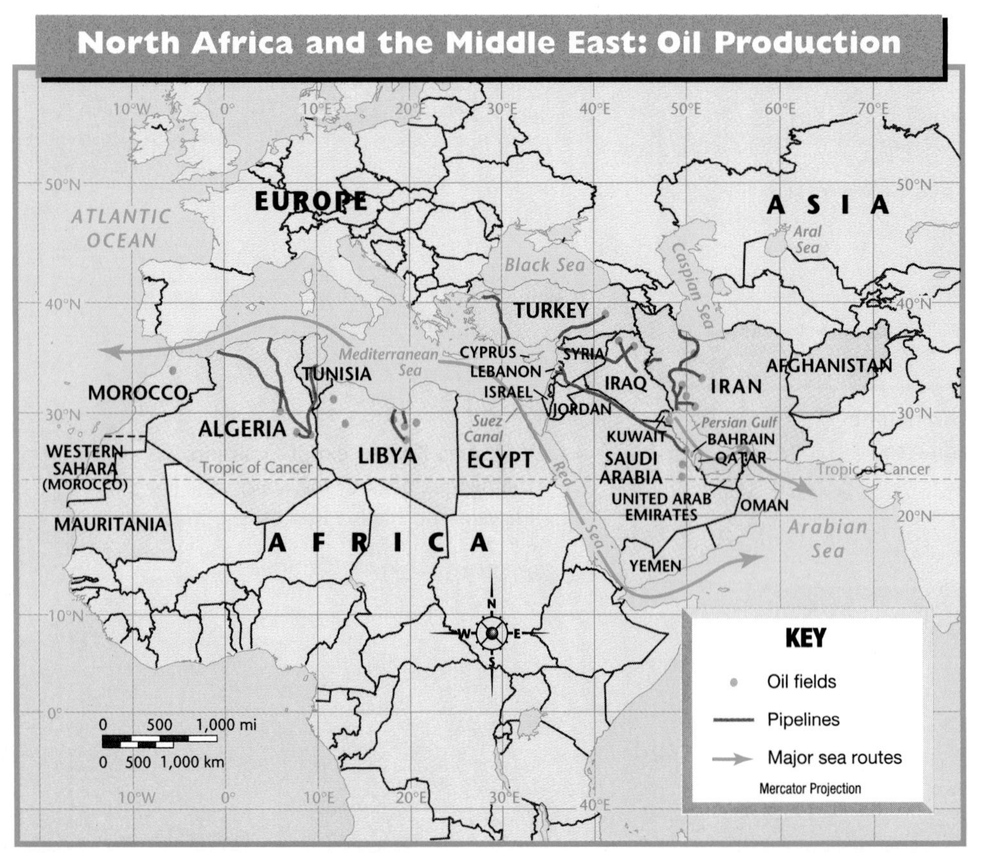

◀ The title on a special purpose map indicates what information can be found on the map. The symbols used on the map are explained in the map's key.

Landforms, Climate Regions, and Natural Vegetation Regions

Maps that show landforms, climate, and vegetation regions are special purpose maps. Unlike the boundary lines on a political map, the boundary lines on these maps do not separate the land into exact divisions. A tropical wet climate gradually changes to a tropical wet and dry climate. A tundra gradually changes to an ice cap. Even though the boundaries between regions may not be exact, the information on these maps can help you understand the region and the lives of people in it.

Landforms

Understanding how people use the land requires an understanding of the shape of the land itself. The four most important landforms are mountains, hills, plateaus, and plains. Human activity in every region in the world is influenced by these landforms.

- **Mountains** are high and steep. Most are wide at the bottom and rise to a narrow peak or ridge. Most geographers classify a mountain as land that rises at least 2,000 feet (610 m) above sea level. A series of mountains is called a mountain range.
- **Hills** rise above surrounding land and have rounded tops. Hills are lower and usually less steep than mountains. The elevation of surrounding land determines whether a landform is called a mountain or a hill.
- A **plateau** is a large, mostly flat area of land that rises above the surrounding land. At least one side of a plateau has a steep slope.
- **Plains** are large areas of flat or gently rolling land. Plains have few changes in elevation. Many plains areas are located along coasts. Others are located in the interior regions of some continents.

▶ A satellite view of the Earth showing North and South America. What landforms are visible in the photograph?

Climate Regions

Another important influence in the ways people live their lives is the climate of their region. Climate is the weather of a given location over a long period of time. Use the descriptions in the table below to help you visualize the climate regions shown on maps.

Climate	Temperatures	Precipitation
Tropical		
Tropical wet	Hot all year round	Heavy all year round
Tropical wet and dry	Hot all year round	Heavy when sun is overhead, dry other times
Dry		
Semiarid	Hot summers, mild to cold winters	Light
Arid	Hot days, cold nights	Very light
Mild		
Mediterranean	Hot summers, cool winters	Dry summers, wet winters
Humid subtropical	Hot summers, cool winters	Year round, heavier in summer than in winter
Marine west coast	Warm summers, cool winters	Year round, heavier in winter than in summer
Continental		
Humid continental	Hot summers, cold winters	Year round, heavier in summer than in winter
Subarctic	Cool summers, cold winters	Light
Polar		
Tundra	Cool summers, very cold winters	Light
Ice Cap	Cold all year round	Light
Highlands	Varies, depending on altitude and direction of prevailing winds	Varies, depending on altitude and direction of prevailing winds

Natural Vegetation Regions

Natural vegetation is the plant life that grows wild without the help of humans. A world vegetation map tells what the vegetation in a place would be if people had not cut down forests or cleared grasslands. The table below provides descriptions of natural vegetation regions shown on maps. Comparing climate and vegetation regions can help you see the close relationship between climate and vegetation.

Vegetation	Description
Tropical rain forest	Tall, close-growing trees forming a canopy over smaller trees, dense growth in general
Deciduous forest	Trees and plants that regularly lose their leaves after each growing season
Mixed forest	Both leaf-losing and cone-bearing trees, no type of tree dominant
Coniferous forest	Cone-bearing trees, evergreen trees and plants
Mediterranean vegetation	Evergreen shrubs and small plants
Tropical savanna	Tall grasses with occasional trees and shrubs
Temperate grassland	Tall grasses with occasional stands of trees
Desert scrub	Low shrubs and bushes, hardy plants
Desert	Little or no vegetation
Tundra	Low shrubs, mosses, lichens; no trees
Ice Cap	Little or no vegetation
Highlands	Varies, depending on altitude and direction of prevailing winds

 How are mountains and hills similar? How are they different?

2 What is the difference between a plateau and a plain?

Atlas

The World: Political

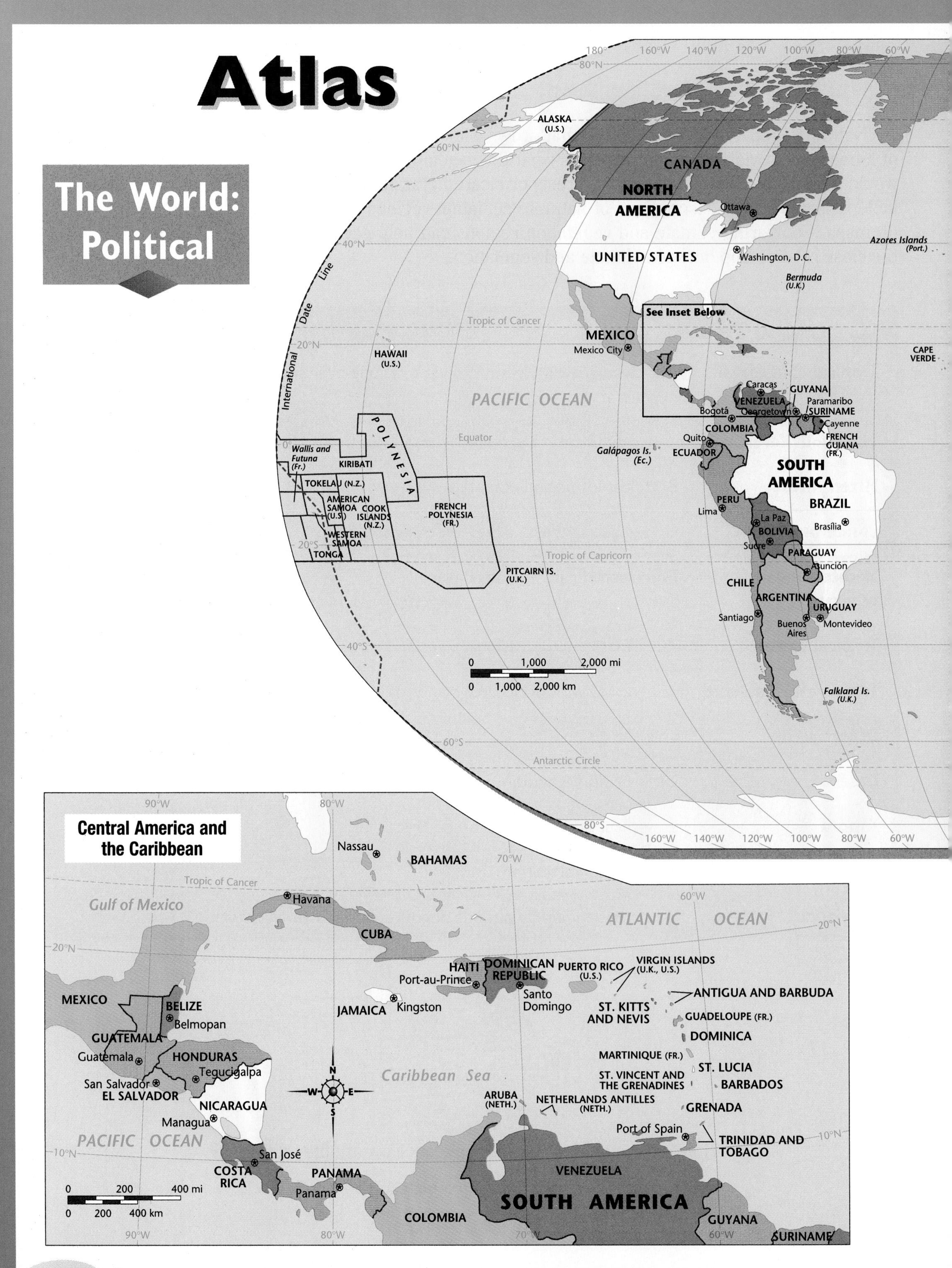

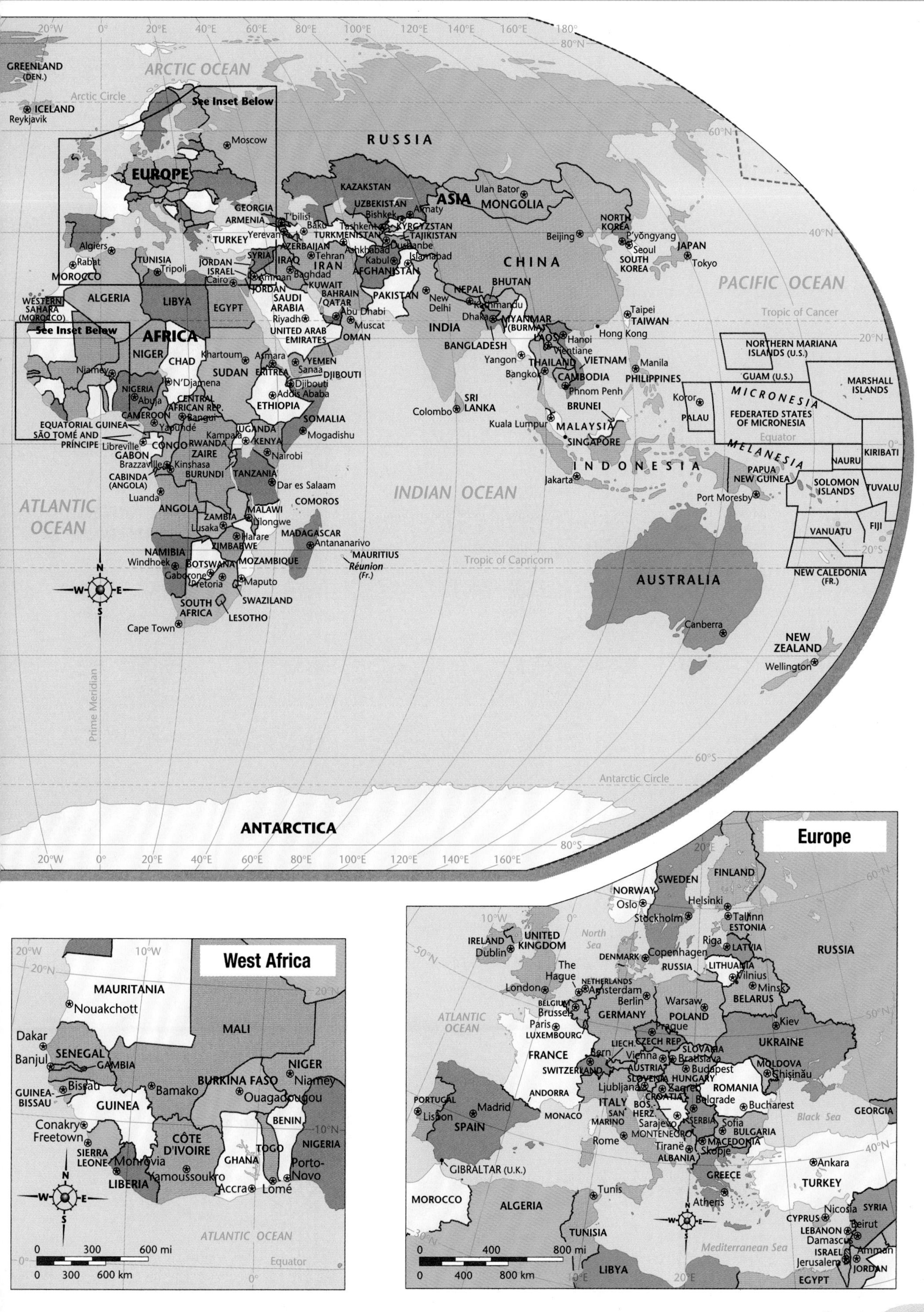

ARCTIC OCEAN
GREENLAND (DEN.)
ICELAND
Reykjavik
Arctic Circle
See Inset Below
RUSSIA
Moscow
EUROPE
KAZAKSTAN
ASIA
MONGOLIA
Ulan Bator
UZBEKISTAN
Bishkek
Almaty
KYRGYZSTAN
GEORGIA
T'bilisi
ARMENIA
Baku
Tashkent
TAJIKISTAN
TURKEY
Yerevan
TURKMENISTAN
AZERBAIJAN
Dushanbe
Ashkhabad
Tehran
IRAN
Kabul
Islamabad
AFGHANISTAN
Algiers
Rabat
MOROCCO
TUNISIA
Tripoli
SYRIA
JORDAN
ISRAEL
Amman
IRAQ
Baghdad
KUWAIT
Cairo
BAHRAIN
QATAR
SAUDI ARABIA
Riyadh
UNITED ARAB EMIRATES
Abu Dhabi
Muscat
OMAN
PAKISTAN
New Delhi
NEPAL
Kathmandu
BHUTAN
Dhaka
MYANMAR (BURMA)
INDIA
BANGLADESH
CHINA
Beijing
NORTH KOREA
P'yŏngyang
Seoul
SOUTH KOREA
JAPAN
Tokyo
PACIFIC OCEAN
Taipei
TAIWAN
Hong Kong
Tropic of Cancer
Hanoi
LAOS
Vientiane
VIETNAM
Yangon
THAILAND
Bangkok
CAMBODIA
Phnom Penh
Manila
PHILIPPINES
NORTHERN MARIANA ISLANDS (U.S.)
GUAM (U.S.)
MARSHALL ISLANDS
MICRONESIA
FEDERATED STATES OF MICRONESIA
Koror
PALAU
Equator
WESTERN SAHARA (MOROCCO)
ALGERIA
LIBYA
EGYPT
AFRICA
NIGER
CHAD
Khartoum
Asmara
ERITREA
SUDAN
YEMEN
Sanaa
DJIBOUTI
Djibouti
Addis Ababa
ETHIOPIA
SOMALIA
Mogadishu
Niamey
N'Djamena
NIGERIA
Abuja
CENTRAL AFRICAN REP.
Bangui
CAMEROON
Yaoundé
EQUATORIAL GUINEA
SÃO TOMÉ AND PRÍNCIPE
Libreville
GABON
CONGO
Brazzaville
Kinshasa
UGANDA
Kampala
KENYA
RWANDA
Nairobi
ZAIRE
BURUNDI
TANZANIA
Dar es Salaam
CABINDA (ANGOLA)
Luanda
ANGOLA
COMOROS
ZAMBIA
MALAWI
Lilongwe
Lusaka
Harare
ZIMBABWE
MADAGASCAR
Antananarivo
MAURITIUS
Réunion (Fr.)
NAMIBIA
Windhoek
BOTSWANA
Gaborone
Pretoria
MOZAMBIQUE
Maputo
SWAZILAND
SOUTH AFRICA
LESOTHO
Cape Town
ATLANTIC OCEAN
INDIAN OCEAN
Colombo
SRI LANKA
Kuala Lumpur
BRUNEI
MALAYSIA
SINGAPORE
INDONESIA
Jakarta
PAPUA NEW GUINEA
Port Moresby
MELANESIA
NAURU
KIRIBATI
SOLOMON ISLANDS
TUVALU
VANUATU
FIJI
NEW CALEDONIA (FR.)
Tropic of Capricorn
AUSTRALIA
Canberra
NEW ZEALAND
Wellington
Prime Meridian
Antarctic Circle
ANTARCTICA
20°W 0° 20°E 40°E 60°E 80°E 100°E 120°E 140°E 160°E 180°
80°N 60°N 40°N 20°N 0° 20°S 60°S 80°S
N S E W
West Africa
MAURITANIA
Nouakchott
MALI
Dakar
SENEGAL
Banjul
GAMBIA
NIGER
Niamey
Bissau
GUINEA-BISSAU
GUINEA
Bamako
BURKINA FASO
Ouagadougou
BENIN
Conakry
Freetown
SIERRA LEONE
Monrovia
LIBERIA
CÔTE D'IVOIRE
Yamoussoukro
GHANA
TOGO
NIGERIA
Porto-Novo
Accra
Lomé
ATLANTIC OCEAN
Equator
0 300 600 mi
0 300 600 km
Europe
SWEDEN
FINLAND
NORWAY
Oslo
Helsinki
Stockholm
Tallinn
ESTONIA
RUSSIA
IRELAND
Dublin
UNITED KINGDOM
North Sea
Riga
LATVIA
DENMARK
Copenhagen
LITHUANIA
Vilnius
Minsk
BELARUS
The Hague
NETHERLANDS
Amsterdam
London
Berlin
Warsaw
POLAND
BELGIUM
Brussels
GERMANY
Paris
LUXEMBOURG
Prague
Kiev
ATLANTIC OCEAN
LIECH.
CZECH REP.
SLOVAKIA
UKRAINE
FRANCE
Bern
Vienna
Bratislava
MOLDOVA
Chişinău
SWITZERLAND
AUSTRIA
Budapest
SLOVENIA
HUNGARY
Ljubljana
Zagreb
ROMANIA
ANDORRA
CROATIA
PORTUGAL
Lisbon
Madrid
SPAIN
ITALY
BOS. HERZ.
Belgrade
Bucharest
MONACO
SAN MARINO
Sarajevo
SERBIA
Sofia
BULGARIA
Black Sea
GEORGIA
MONTENEGRO
Rome
Tiranë
ALBANIA
MACEDONIA
Skopje
GIBRALTAR (U.K.)
GREECE
Ankara
TURKEY
MOROCCO
ALGERIA
Tunis
Athens
TUNISIA
CYPRUS
Nicosia
SYRIA
LEBANON
Beirut
Damascus
ISRAEL
Amman
Jerusalem
JORDAN
EGYPT
LIBYA
Mediterranean Sea
0 400 800 mi
0 400 800 km

The World: Physical

ARCTIC OCEAN
Beaufort Sea
Yukon R.
Mackenzie R.
Bering Sea
Aleutian Islands
ROCKY MOUNTAINS
NORTH AMERICA
CANADIAN SHIELD
Hudson Bay
GREENLAND (DEN.)
GREAT PLAINS
Missouri R.
Great Lakes
St. Lawrence R.
Colorado R.
Mississippi R.
APPALACHIAN MTS.
Rio Grande
SIERRA MADRE OCCIDENTAL
SIERRA MADRE ORIENTAL
Gulf of Mexico
ATLANTIC OCEAN
Hawaiian Islands
Tropic of Cancer
West Indies
Caribbean Sea
PACIFIC OCEAN
POLYNESIA
Equator
Orinoco R.
GUIANA HIGHLANDS
AMAZON BASIN
Amazon R.
SOUTH AMERICA
ANDES MOUNTAINS
BRAZILIAN HIGHLANDS
Tropic of Capricorn
PAMPAS
Rio de la Plata
PATAGONIA
Cape Horn
Drake Passage
Antarctic Circle
ANTARCTIC PENINSULA

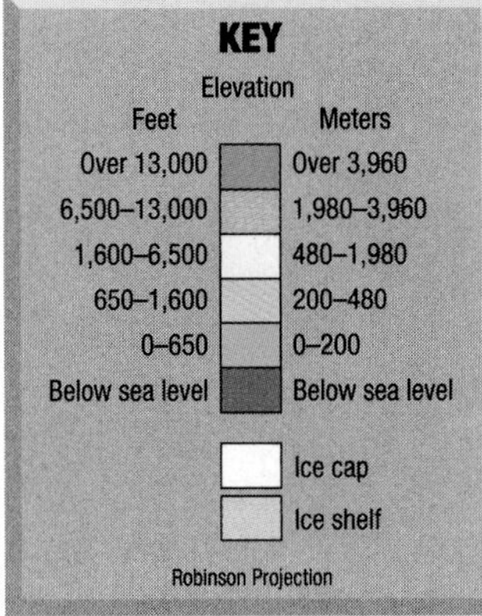

KEY
Elevation
Feet
Meters
Over 13,000
Over 3,960
6,500–13,000
1,980–3,960
1,600–6,500
480–1,980
650–1,600
200–480
0–650
0–200
Below sea level
Below sea level
Ice cap
Ice shelf
Robinson Projection

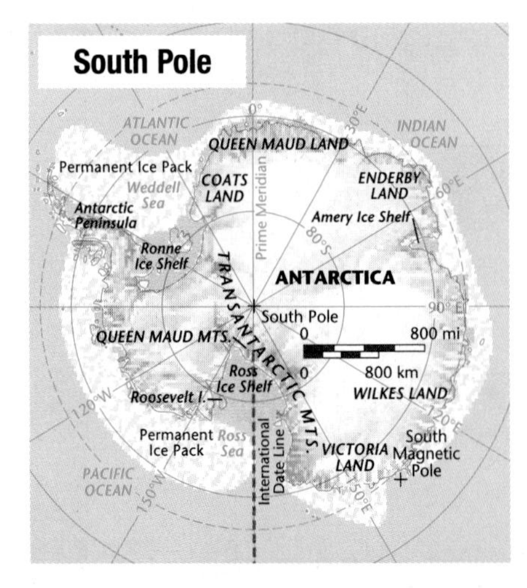

South Pole
ATLANTIC OCEAN
INDIAN OCEAN
QUEEN MAUD LAND
Permanent Ice Pack
Weddell Sea
COATS LAND
ENDERBY LAND
Antarctic Peninsula
Amery Ice Shelf
Prime Meridian
Ronne Ice Shelf
ANTARCTICA
TRANSANTARCTIC MTS.
South Pole
QUEEN MAUD MTS.
0
800 mi
800 km
Ross Ice Shelf
Roosevelt I.
WILKES LAND
Permanent Ice Pack
Ross Sea
International Date Line
VICTORIA LAND
South Magnetic Pole
PACIFIC OCEAN

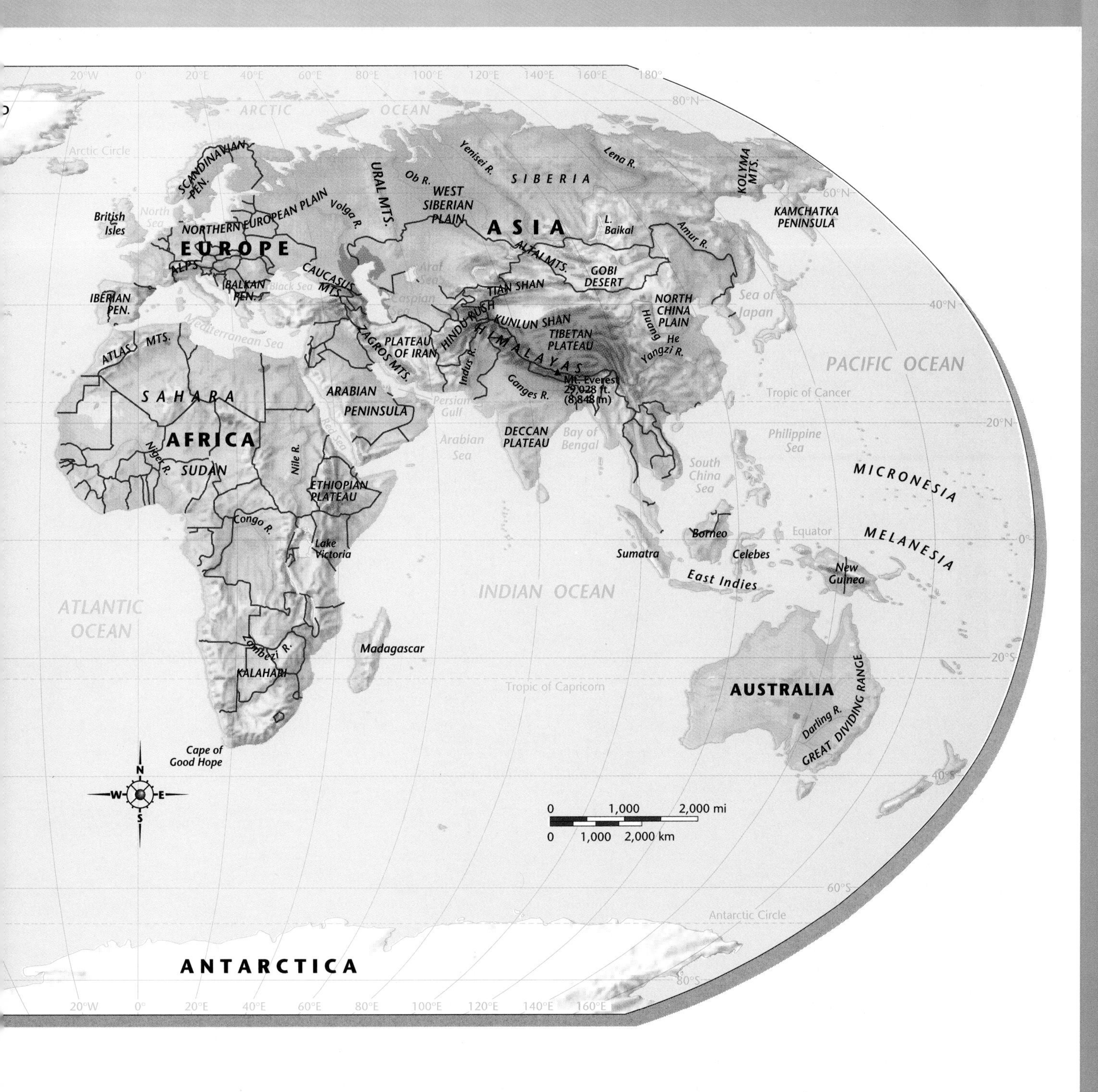
ARCTIC OCEAN
Arctic Circle
SCANDINAVIAN PEN.
British Isles
North Sea
NORTHERN EUROPEAN PLAIN
EUROPE
ALPS
BALKAN PEN.
Black Sea
IBERIAN PEN.
Mediterranean Sea
ATLAS MTS.
SAHARA
AFRICA
Niger R.
SUDAN
Nile R.
Red Sea
ETHIOPIAN PLATEAU
Congo R.
Lake Victoria
ATLANTIC OCEAN
Zambezi R.
KALAHARI
Madagascar
Cape of Good Hope
Volga R.
URAL MTS.
CAUCASUS MTS.
Aral Sea
Caspian Sea
ZAGROS MTS.
PLATEAU OF IRAN
ARABIAN PENINSULA
Persian Gulf
Arabian Sea
Ob R.
WEST SIBERIAN PLAIN
Yenisei R.
SIBERIA
ASIA
Lena R.
KOLYMA MTS.
KAMCHATKA PENINSULA
L. Baikal
Amur R.
ALTAI MTS.
GOBI DESERT
TIAN SHAN
HINDU KUSH
KUNLUN SHAN
TIBETAN PLATEAU
HIMALAYAS
Indus R.
Mt. Everest 29,028 ft. (8,848 m)
Ganges R.
DECCAN PLATEAU
Bay of Bengal
NORTH CHINA PLAIN
Huang He
Yangzi R.
Sea of Japan
PACIFIC OCEAN
Tropic of Cancer
Philippine Sea
South China Sea
MICRONESIA
MELANESIA
Borneo
Sumatra
Celebes
Equator
East Indies
New Guinea
INDIAN OCEAN
AUSTRALIA
GREAT DIVIDING RANGE
Darling R.
Tropic of Capricorn
0 1,000 2,000 mi
0 1,000 2,000 km
Antarctic Circle
ANTARCTICA
N
S
E
W

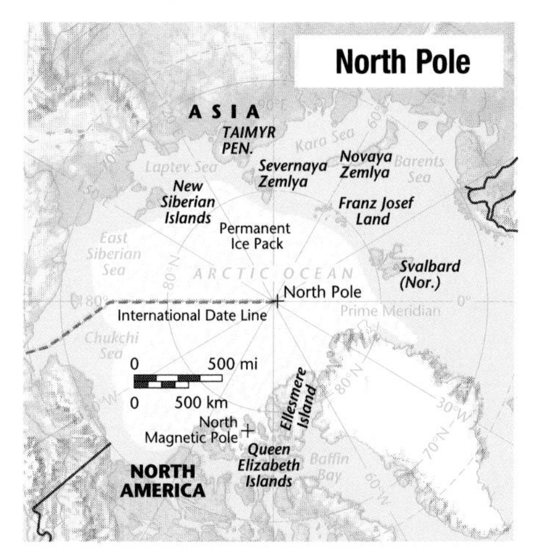
North Pole
ASIA
TAIMYR PEN.
Kara Sea
Laptev Sea
Severnaya Zemlya
Novaya Zemlya
Barents Sea
New Siberian Islands
Franz Josef Land
Permanent Ice Pack
East Siberian Sea
Svalbard (Nor.)
ARCTIC OCEAN
North Pole
International Date Line
Prime Meridian
Chukchi Sea
0 500 mi
0 500 km
Ellesmere Island
North Magnetic Pole
Queen Elizabeth Islands
Baffin Bay
NORTH AMERICA

United States: Political

CANADA
90°W
80°W
70°W
0 150 300 mi
0 150 300 km
Lake Superior
Lake Huron
Lake Michigan
Lake Ontario
Lake Erie
NORTH DAKOTA
SOUTH DAKOTA
MINNESOTA
WISCONSIN
MICHIGAN
IOWA
ILLINOIS
INDIANA
OHIO
PENNSYLVANIA
NEW YORK
VERMONT
NEW HAMPSHIRE
MAINE
MASSACHUSETTS
RHODE ISLAND
CONNECTICUT
NEW JERSEY
DELAWARE
MARYLAND
WEST VIRGINIA
VIRGINIA
KENTUCKY
TENNESSEE
NORTH CAROLINA
SOUTH CAROLINA
GEORGIA
FLORIDA
ALABAMA
MISSISSIPPI
LOUISIANA
ARKANSAS
MISSOURI
KANSAS
OKLAHOMA
TEXAS
Presque Isle
Augusta
Portland
Montpelier
Concord
Boston
Providence
Albany
Hartford
New Haven
Buffalo
New York City
Trenton
Philadelphia
Harrisburg
Pittsburgh
Dover
Baltimore
Annapolis
Washington, D.C.
Richmond
Norfolk
Cleveland
Columbus
Cincinnati
Charleston
Frankfort
Louisville
Raleigh
Charlotte
Columbia
Charleston
Savannah
Atlanta
Columbus
Jacksonville
Tallahassee
Tampa
Miami
Lake Okeechobee
Birmingham
Montgomery
Jackson
Hattiesburg
New Orleans
Baton Rouge
Shreveport
Memphis
Nashville
Little Rock
Pine Bluff
St. Louis
Jefferson City
Kansas City
Springfield
Indianapolis
Chicago
Milwaukee
Madison
Lansing
Detroit
Sault Ste. Marie
Duluth
Minneapolis
St. Paul
Cedar Rapids
Des Moines
Omaha
Lincoln
Topeka
Wichita
Tulsa
Oklahoma City
Dallas
Austin
Houston
San Antonio
Missouri River
Mississippi River
Ohio River
Tennessee River
Kansas River
Red River
Rio Grande
ATLANTIC OCEAN
Gulf of Mexico
40°N
30°N
N
E
S
W
KEY
National boundary
State boundary
National capital
State capital
Other city
Transverse Mercator Projection

North and South America: Political

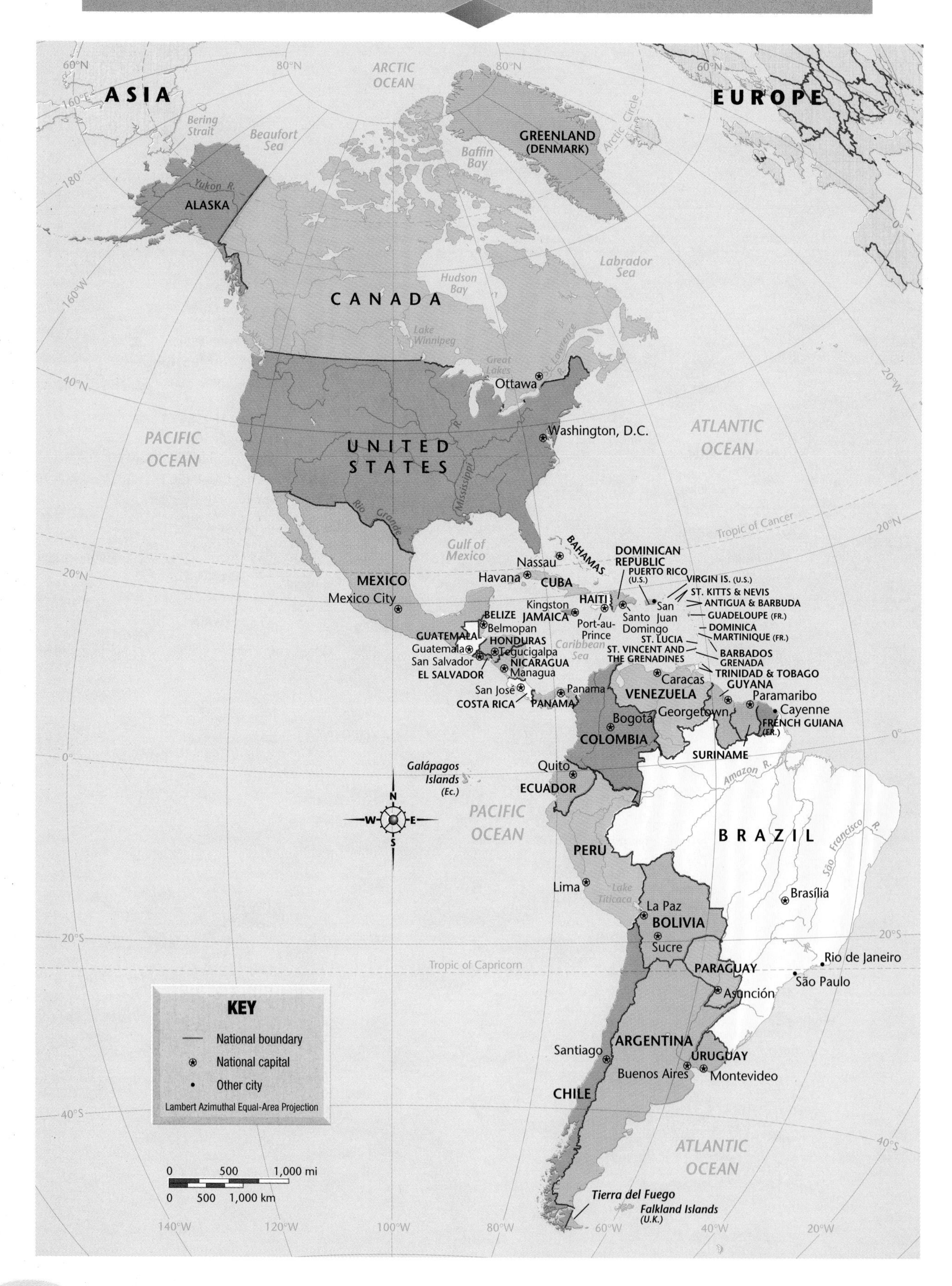

North and South America: Physical

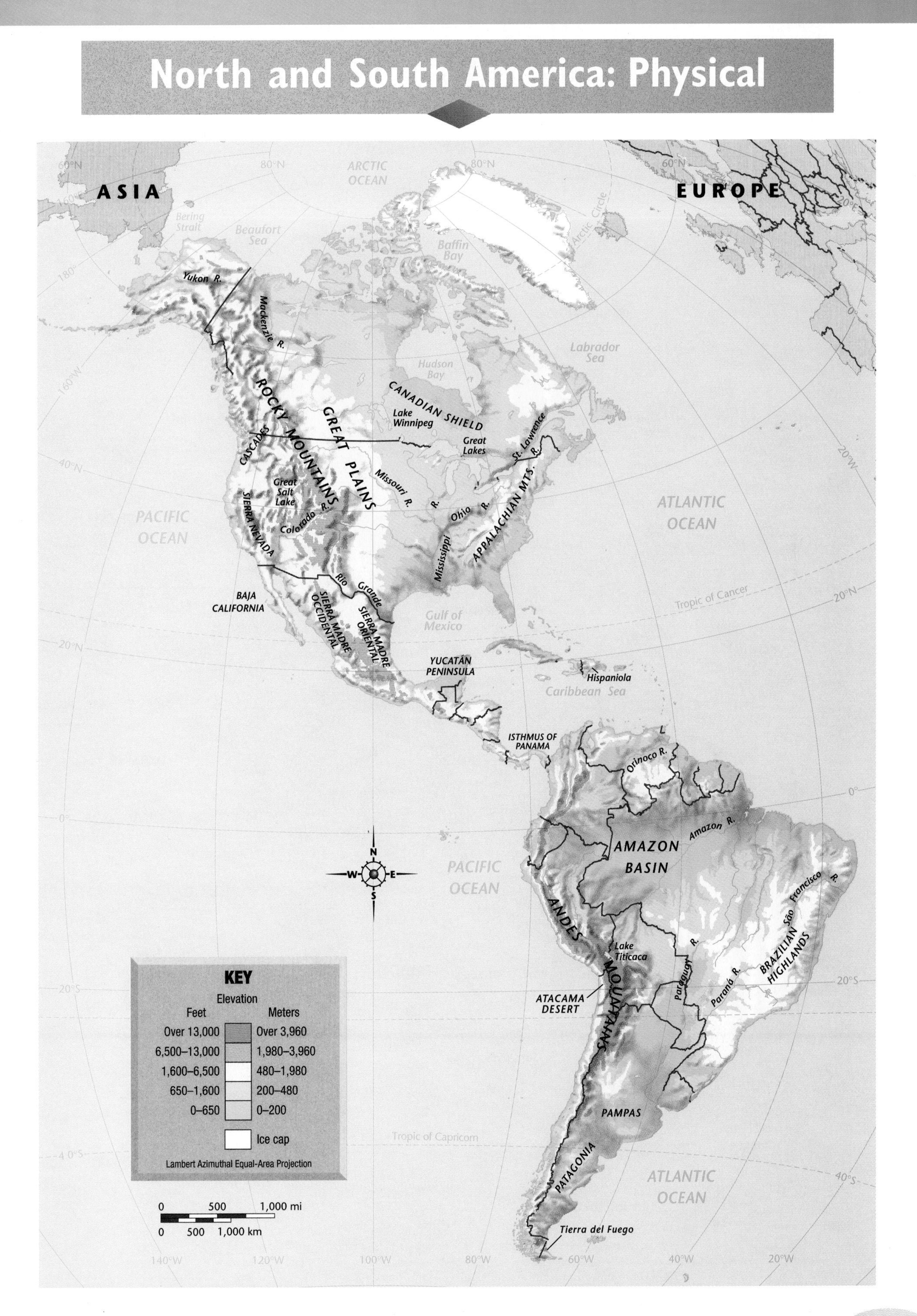

ASIA
EUROPE
ARCTIC OCEAN
Bering Strait
Beaufort Sea
Baffin Bay
Labrador Sea
Hudson Bay
Arctic Circle
Yukon R.
Mackenzie R.
ROCKY MOUNTAINS
CANADIAN SHIELD
GREAT PLAINS
Lake Winnipeg
Great Lakes
St. Lawrence R.
CASCADES
Great Salt Lake
SIERRA NEVADA
Colorado R.
Missouri R.
Ohio R.
Mississippi R.
APPALACHIAN MTS.
PACIFIC OCEAN
ATLANTIC OCEAN
Tropic of Cancer
BAJA CALIFORNIA
Rio Grande
SIERRA MADRE OCCIDENTAL
SIERRA MADRE ORIENTAL
Gulf of Mexico
YUCATÁN PENINSULA
Hispaniola
Caribbean Sea
ISTHMUS OF PANAMA
Orinoco R.
Amazon R.
AMAZON BASIN
ANDES MOUNTAINS
São Francisco R.
BRAZILIAN HIGHLANDS
Lake Titicaca
ATACAMA DESERT
Paraguay R.
Paraná R.
PAMPAS
PATAGONIA
Tropic of Capricorn
Tierra del Fuego
N
S
E
W
KEY
Elevation
Feet
Meters
Over 13,000
Over 3,960
6,500–13,000
1,980–3,960
1,600–6,500
480–1,980
650–1,600
200–480
0–650
0–200
Ice cap
Lambert Azimuthal Equal-Area Projection
0 500 1,000 mi
0 500 1,000 km
60°N
80°N
40°N
20°N
0°
20°S
40°S
180°
160°W
140°W
120°W
100°W
80°W
60°W
40°W
20°W

Europe: Political

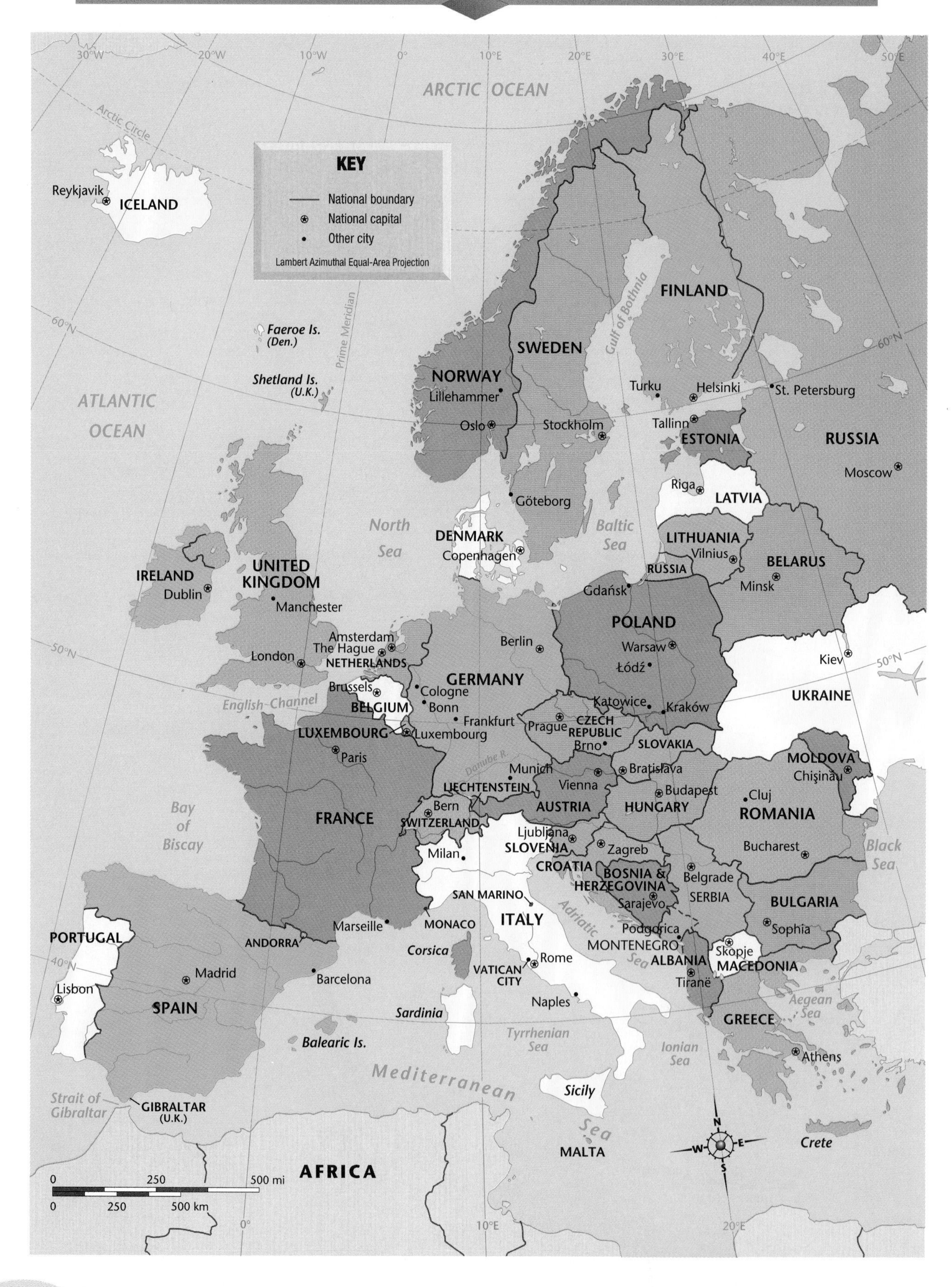

Europe: Physical

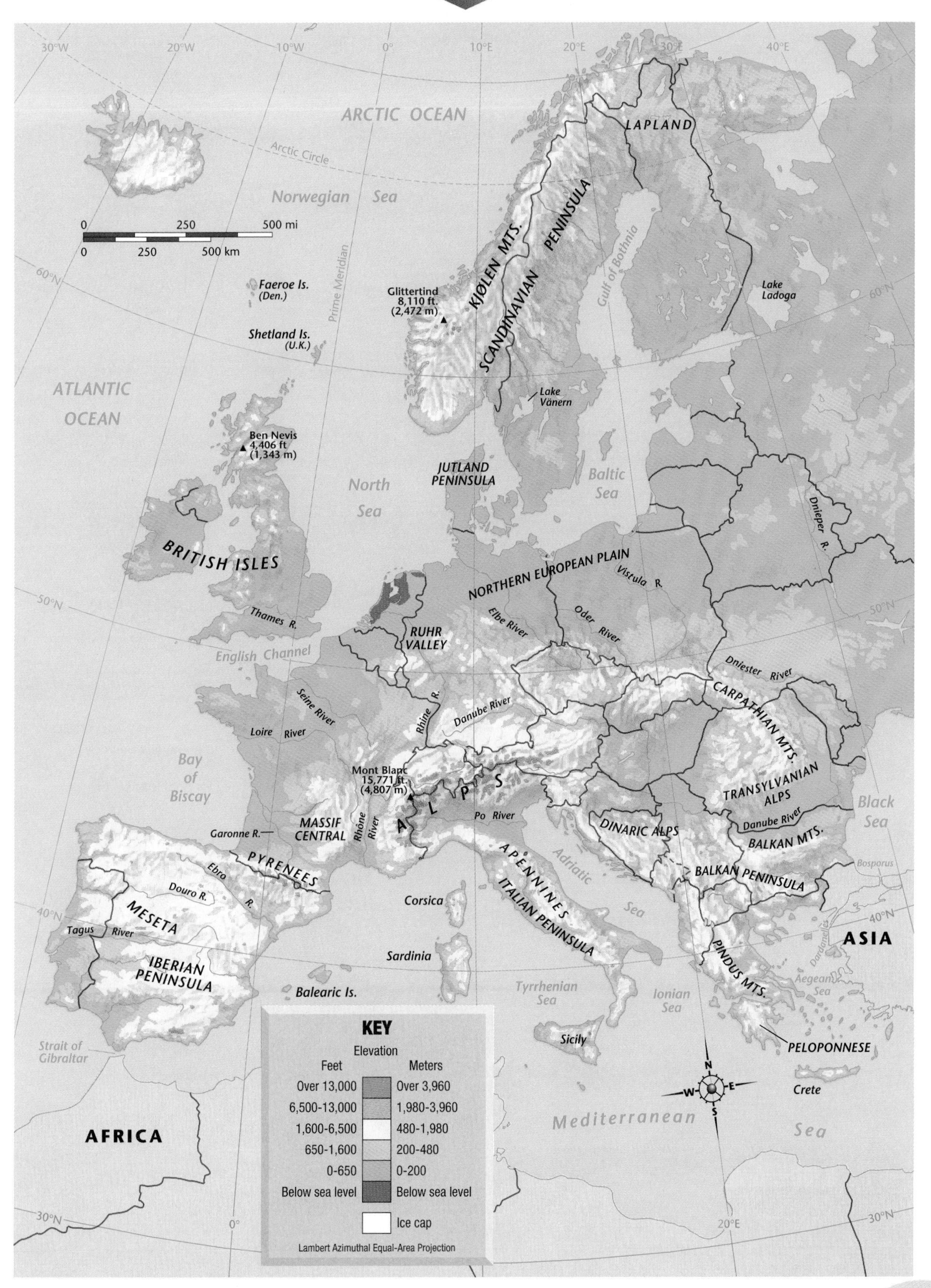

ARCTIC OCEAN
Arctic Circle
Norwegian Sea
0 250 500 mi
0 250 500 km
Faeroe Is. (Den.)
Shetland Is. (U.K.)
Prime Meridian
Glittertind 8,110 ft. (2,472 m)
KJØLEN MTS.
SCANDINAVIAN PENINSULA
LAPLAND
Gulf of Bothnia
Lake Ladoga
Lake Vänern
ATLANTIC OCEAN
Ben Nevis 4,406 ft (1,343 m)
JUTLAND PENINSULA
North Sea
Baltic Sea
Dnieper R.
BRITISH ISLES
NORTHERN EUROPEAN PLAIN
Vistula R.
Thames R.
Elbe River
Oder River
RUHR VALLEY
English Channel
Dniester River
Seine River
Rhine R.
Danube River
CARPATHIAN MTS.
Loire River
Bay of Biscay
Mont Blanc 15,771 ft. (4,807 m)
ALPS
TRANSYLVANIAN ALPS
Black Sea
MASSIF CENTRAL
Rhône River
Po River
Garonne R.
DINARIC ALPS
Danube River
BALKAN MTS.
PYRENEES
Ebro R.
APENNINES
Adriatic Sea
Bosporus
BALKAN PENINSULA
Douro R.
MESETA
Corsica
ITALIAN PENINSULA
Tagus River
ASIA
PINDUS MTS.
Dardanelles
IBERIAN PENINSULA
Sardinia
Balearic Is.
Tyrrhenian Sea
Ionian Sea
Aegean Sea
Sicily
PELOPONNESE
Strait of Gibraltar
Crete
Mediterranean Sea
AFRICA
KEY
Elevation
Feet Meters
Over 13,000 Over 3,960
6,500-13,000 1,980-3,960
1,600-6,500 480-1,980
650-1,600 200-480
0-650 0-200
Below sea level Below sea level
Ice cap
Lambert Azimuthal Equal-Area Projection

Africa: Political

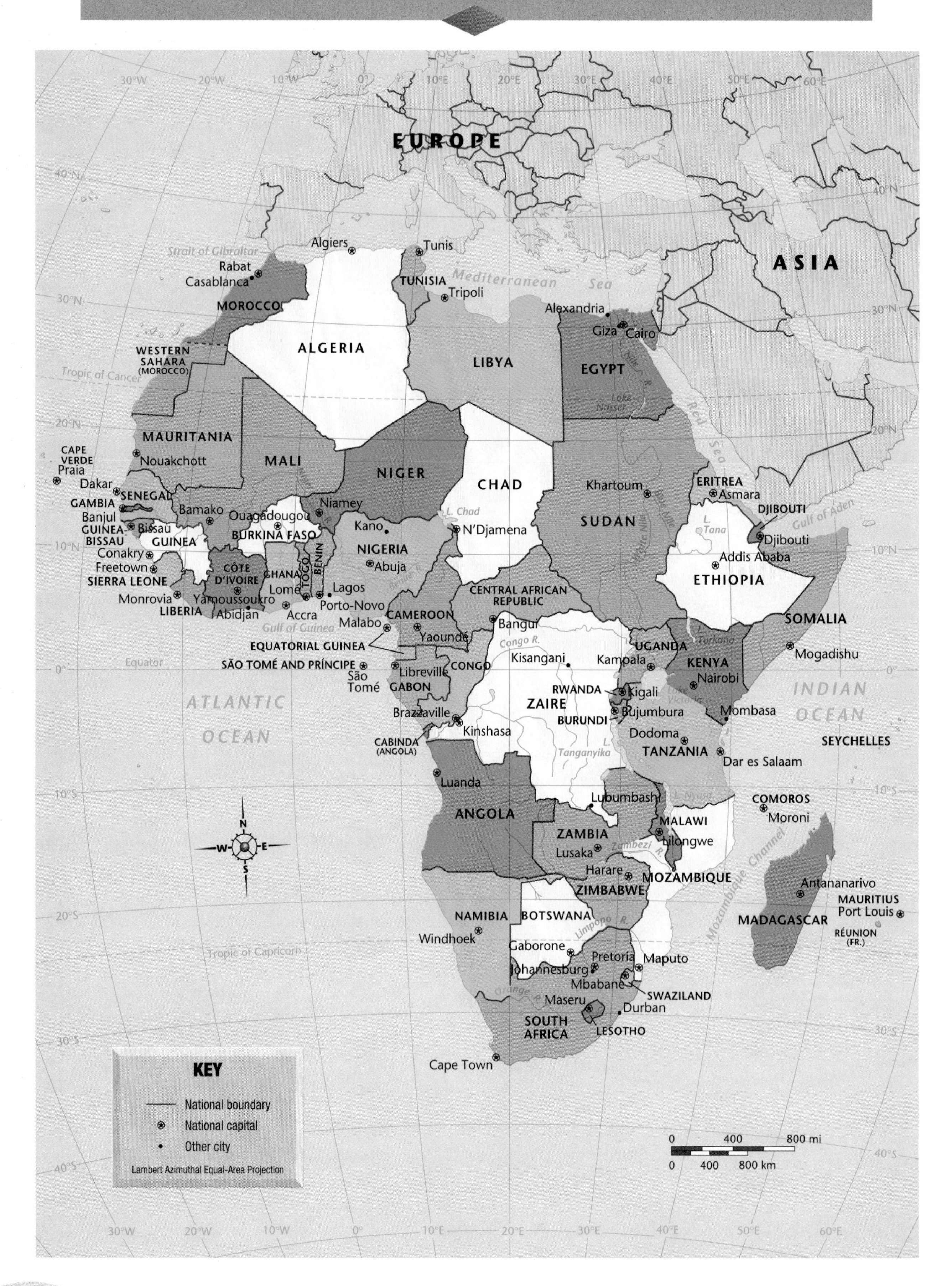

Africa: Physical

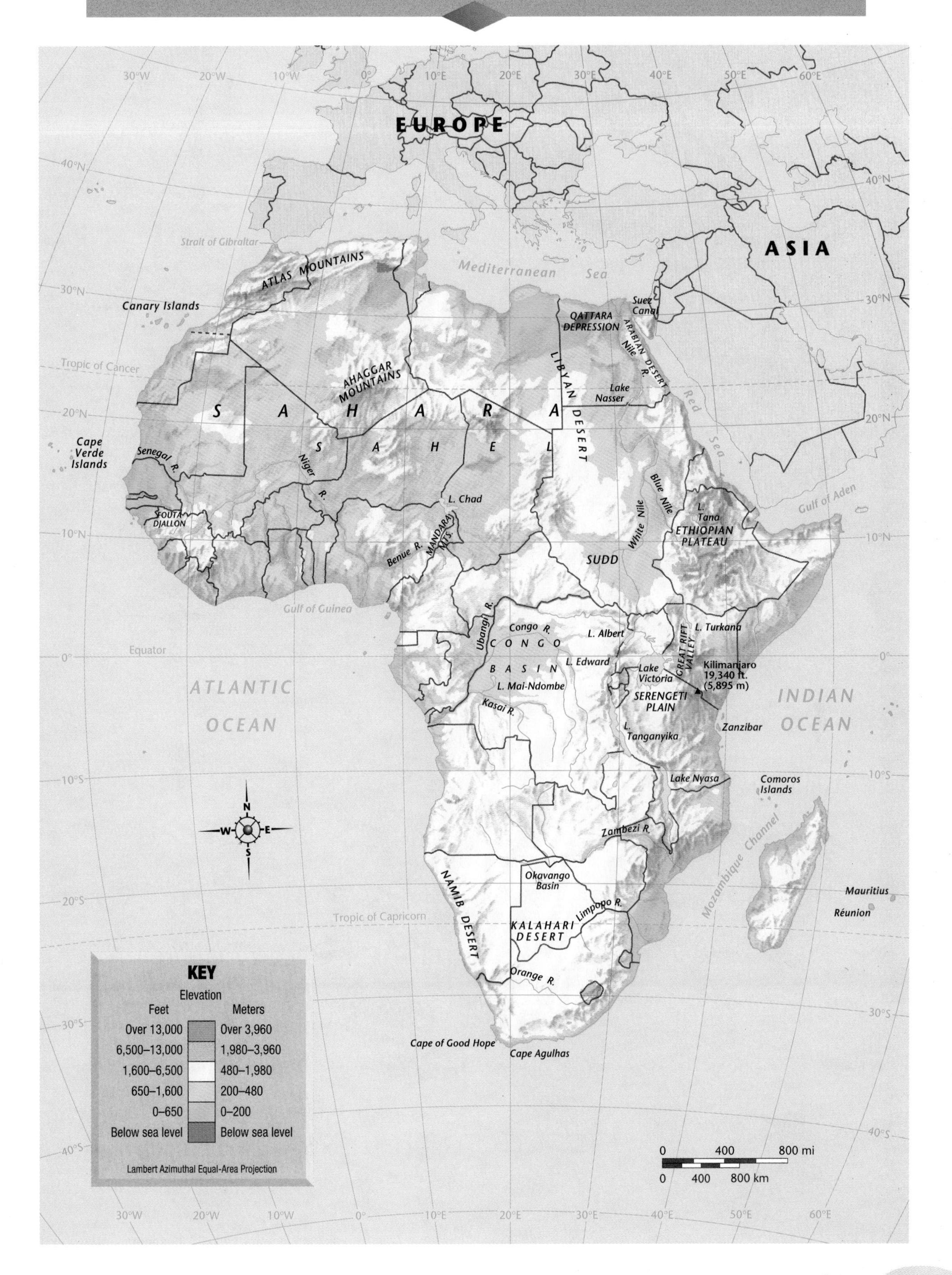

EUROPE
ASIA
Strait of Gibraltar
Mediterranean Sea
ATLAS MOUNTAINS
Canary Islands
Tropic of Cancer
AHAGGAR MOUNTAINS
S A H A R A
QATTARA DEPRESSION
Suez Canal
ARABIAN DESERT
Nile R.
LIBYAN DESERT
Lake Nasser
Red Sea
Cape Verde Islands
Senegal R.
Niger R.
S A H E L
L. Chad
Blue Nile
White Nile
L. Tana
ETHIOPIAN PLATEAU
Gulf of Aden
FOUTA DJALLON
Benue R.
MANDARA MTS.
SUDD
Gulf of Guinea
Ubangi R.
Congo R.
CONGO BASIN
L. Albert
L. Edward
L. Turkana
GREAT RIFT VALLEY
Lake Victoria
Kilimanjaro 19,340 ft. (5,895 m)
L. Mai-Ndombe
Equator
ATLANTIC OCEAN
INDIAN OCEAN
Kasai R.
SERENGETI PLAIN
L. Tanganyika
Zanzibar
Lake Nyasa
Comoros Islands
Zambezi R.
Mozambique Channel
NAMIB DESERT
Okavango Basin
Limpopo R.
KALAHARI DESERT
Tropic of Capricorn
Mauritius
Réunion
Orange R.
Cape of Good Hope
Cape Agulhas
N
W
E
S
KEY
Elevation
Feet
Meters
Over 13,000
Over 3,960
6,500–13,000
1,980–3,960
1,600–6,500
480–1,980
650–1,600
200–480
0–650
0–200
Below sea level
Below sea level
Lambert Azimuthal Equal-Area Projection
0 400 800 mi
0 400 800 km
30°W 20°W 10°W 0° 10°E 20°E 30°E 40°E 50°E 60°E
40°N 30°N 20°N 10°N 0° 10°S 20°S 30°S 40°S

Asia: Political

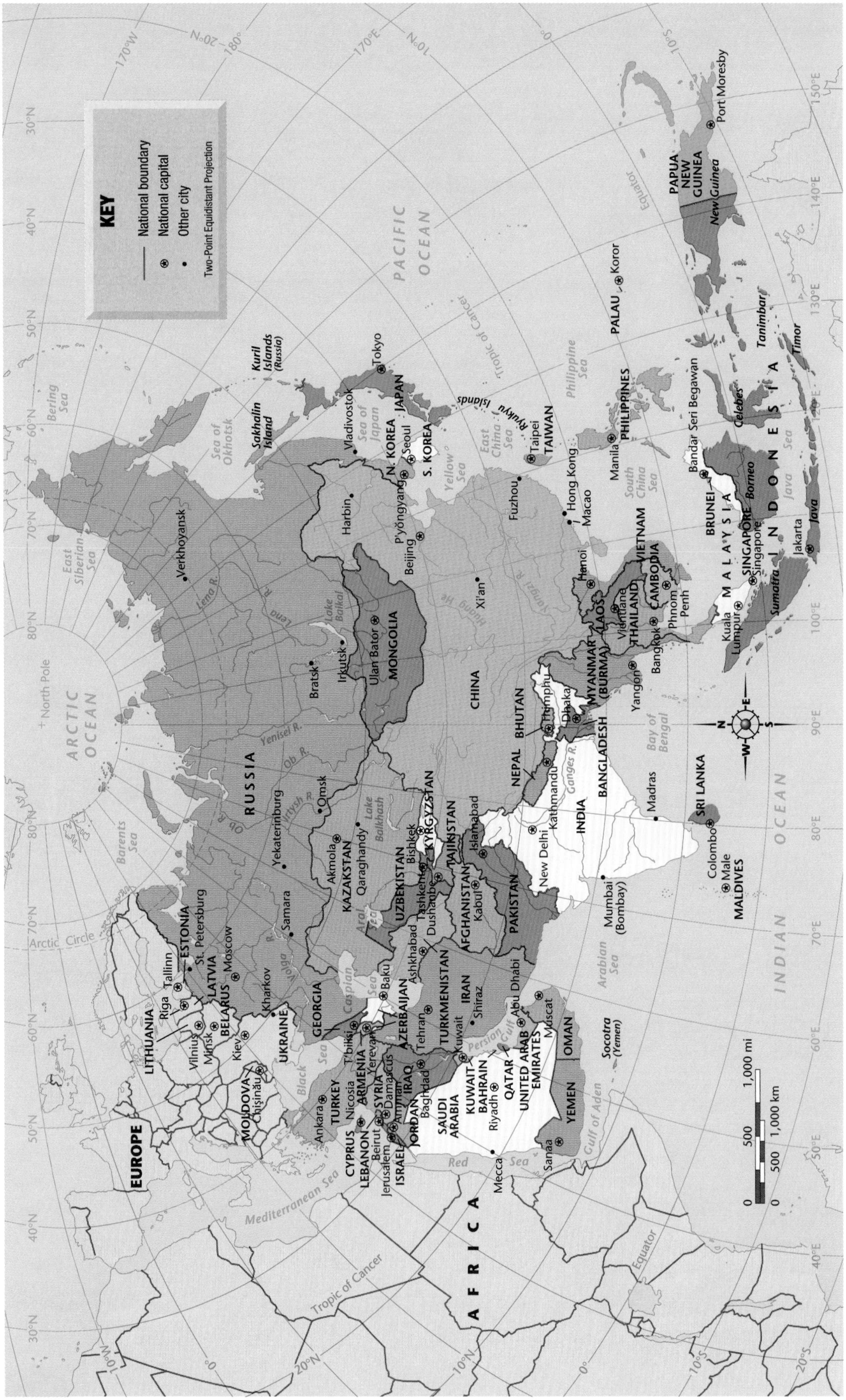

KEY

- National boundary
- National capital
- Other city

Two-Point Equidistant Projection

0 500 1,000 mi
0 500 1,000 km

ARCTIC OCEAN
North Pole
PACIFIC OCEAN
INDIAN OCEAN
EUROPE
AFRICA
Barents Sea
East Siberian Sea
Bering Sea
Sea of Okhotsk
Sakhalin Island
Kuril Islands (Russia)
Mediterranean Sea
Black Sea
Caspian Sea
Aral Sea
Lake Balkhash
Lake Baikal
Red Sea
Persian Gulf
Gulf of Aden
Arabian Sea
Bay of Bengal
Sea of Japan
Yellow Sea
East China Sea
South China Sea
Philippine Sea
Java Sea
Ryukyu Islands
Socotra (Yemen)
Arctic Circle
Tropic of Cancer
Equator
Volga R.
Ob R.
Irtysh R.
Yenisei R.
Lena R.
Huang He
Yangzi R.
Ganges R.
LITHUANIA
Riga
Tallinn
ESTONIA
St. Petersburg
Vilnius
Minsk
LATVIA
BELARUS
Moscow
MOLDOVA
Chişinău
Kiev
Kharkov
UKRAINE
RUSSIA
Samara
Yekaterinburg
Omsk
Verkhoyansk
Bratsk
Irkutsk
Ankara
TURKEY
GEORGIA
CYPRUS
Nicosia
T'bilisi
LEBANON
ARMENIA
Yerevan
Beirut
SYRIA
Jerusalem
Damascus
ISRAEL
Amman
JORDAN
IRAQ
Baghdad
AZERBAIJAN
Baku
Ashkhabad
Akmola
KAZAKSTAN
Qaraghandy
UZBEKISTAN
Bishkek
Tashkent
Dushanbe
KYRGYZSTAN
TAJIKISTAN
Tehran
TURKMENISTAN
SAUDI ARABIA
Kuwait
KUWAIT
BAHRAIN
IRAN
Shiraz
AFGHANISTAN
Kabul
Islamabad
Mecca
Riyadh
QATAR
UNITED ARAB EMIRATES
Abu Dhabi
PAKISTAN
Muscat
Sanaa
YEMEN
OMAN
NEPAL
BHUTAN
New Delhi
Kathmandu
Thimphu
INDIA
Dhaka
BANGLADESH
Mumbai (Bombay)
Madras
Colombo
SRI LANKA
Male
MALDIVES
Ulan Bator
MONGOLIA
CHINA
Xi'an
Beijing
Harbin
Vladivostok
P'yŏngyang
N. KOREA
Seoul
S. KOREA
JAPAN
Tokyo
Fuzhou
Taipei
TAIWAN
Hong Kong
Macao
Hanoi
MYANMAR (BURMA)
LAOS
Vientiane
Yangon
THAILAND
VIETNAM
Bangkok
CAMBODIA
Phnom Penh
Manila
PHILIPPINES
PALAU
Koror
Bandar Seri Begawan
BRUNEI
Kuala Lumpur
MALAYSIA
SINGAPORE
Singapore
Borneo
Celebes
Sumatra
INDONESIA
Jakarta
Java
Tanimbar
Timor
PAPUA NEW GUINEA
New Guinea
Port Moresby

Asia: Physical

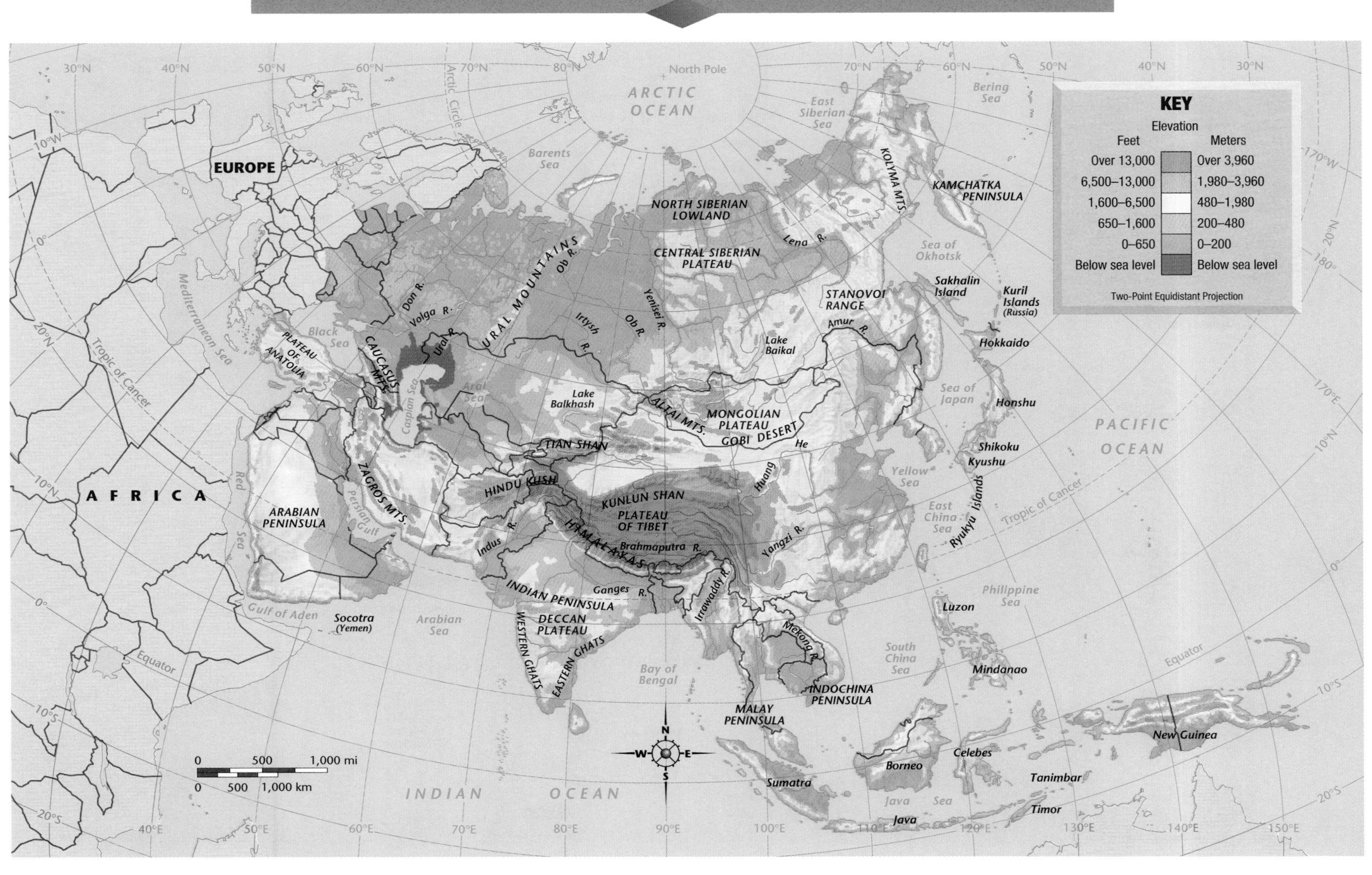
KEY
Elevation
Feet
Meters
Over 13,000
Over 3,960
6,500–13,000
1,980–3,960
1,600–6,500
480–1,980
650–1,600
200–480
0–650
0–200
Below sea level
Below sea level
Two-Point Equidistant Projection
EUROPE
AFRICA
ARCTIC OCEAN
North Pole
PACIFIC OCEAN
INDIAN OCEAN
Arctic Circle
Tropic of Cancer
Equator
Barents Sea
East Siberian Sea
Bering Sea
Sea of Okhotsk
Sea of Japan
Yellow Sea
East China Sea
Philippine Sea
South China Sea
Java Sea
Bay of Bengal
Arabian Sea
Gulf of Aden
Red Sea
Persian Gulf
Mediterranean Sea
Black Sea
Caspian Sea
Aral Sea
NORTH SIBERIAN LOWLAND
CENTRAL SIBERIAN PLATEAU
KOLYMA MTS.
KAMCHATKA PENINSULA
STANOVOI RANGE
URAL MOUNTAINS
CAUCASUS MTS.
PLATEAU OF ANATOLIA
ARABIAN PENINSULA
ZAGROS MTS.
HINDU KUSH
TIAN SHAN
ALTAI MTS.
MONGOLIAN PLATEAU
GOBI DESERT
KUNLUN SHAN
PLATEAU OF TIBET
HIMALAYAS
INDIAN PENINSULA
DECCAN PLATEAU
WESTERN GHATS
EASTERN GHATS
MALAY PENINSULA
INDOCHINA PENINSULA
Lena R.
Ob R.
Yenisei R.
Irtysh R.
Don R.
Volga R.
Ural R.
Amur R.
Lake Baikal
Lake Balkhash
He
Huang
Yangzi R.
Brahmaputra R.
Ganges R.
Indus R.
Irrawaddy R.
Mekong R.
Sakhalin Island
Kuril Islands (Russia)
Hokkaido
Honshu
Shikoku
Kyushu
Ryukyu Islands
Luzon
Mindanao
Celebes
Borneo
Sumatra
Java
Tanimbar
Timor
New Guinea
Socotra (Yemen)
0 500 1,000 mi
0 500 1,000 km
N
S
E
W
30°N
40°N
50°N
60°N
70°N
80°N
20°N
10°N
0°
10°S
20°S
10°W
170°W
180°
170°E
40°E
50°E
60°E
70°E
80°E
90°E
100°E
110°E
120°E
130°E
140°E
150°E

Australia, New Zealand, and the Pacific Islands: Physical–Political

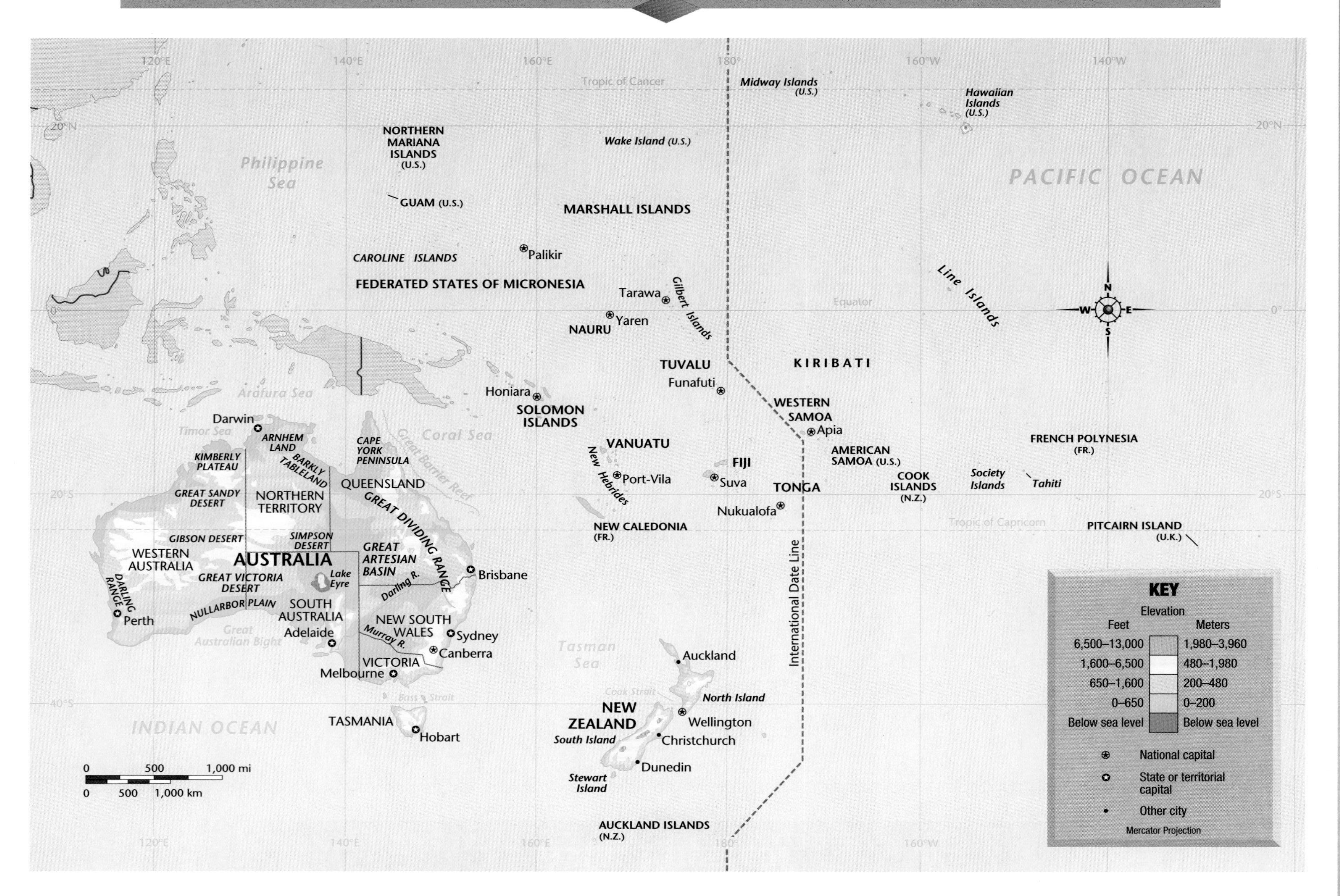

120°E
140°E
160°E
180°
160°W
140°W
20°N
0°
20°S
40°S
Tropic of Cancer
Equator
Tropic of Capricorn
International Date Line
PACIFIC OCEAN
INDIAN OCEAN
Philippine Sea
Arafura Sea
Timor Sea
Coral Sea
Tasman Sea
Great Australian Bight
Great Barrier Reef
Cook Strait
Bass Strait
NORTHERN MARIANA ISLANDS (U.S.)
GUAM (U.S.)
Wake Island (U.S.)
Midway Islands (U.S.)
Hawaiian Islands (U.S.)
MARSHALL ISLANDS
CAROLINE ISLANDS
FEDERATED STATES OF MICRONESIA
Palikir
Tarawa
Gilbert Islands
Line Islands
NAURU
Yaren
TUVALU
Funafuti
KIRIBATI
Honiara
SOLOMON ISLANDS
WESTERN SAMOA
Apia
AMERICAN SAMOA (U.S.)
FRENCH POLYNESIA (FR.)
VANUATU
New Hebrides
Port-Vila
FIJI
Suva
TONGA
Nukualofa
COOK ISLANDS (N.Z.)
Society Islands
Tahiti
NEW CALEDONIA (FR.)
PITCAIRN ISLAND (U.K.)
Darwin
ARNHEM LAND
KIMBERLY PLATEAU
BARKLY TABLELAND
CAPE YORK PENINSULA
QUEENSLAND
GREAT SANDY DESERT
NORTHERN TERRITORY
GREAT DIVIDING RANGE
GIBSON DESERT
SIMPSON DESERT
WESTERN AUSTRALIA
AUSTRALIA
GREAT ARTESIAN BASIN
Lake Eyre
Brisbane
DARLING RANGE
GREAT VICTORIA DESERT
Darling R.
Perth
NULLARBOR PLAIN
SOUTH AUSTRALIA
NEW SOUTH WALES
Adelaide
Murray R.
Sydney
Canberra
VICTORIA
Melbourne
TASMANIA
Hobart
Auckland
North Island
NEW ZEALAND
Wellington
South Island
Christchurch
Dunedin
Stewart Island
AUCKLAND ISLANDS (N.Z.)
0
500
1,000 mi
0
500
1,000 km
KEY
Elevation
Feet
Meters
6,500–13,000
1,980–3,960
1,600–6,500
480–1,980
650–1,600
200–480
0–650
0–200
Below sea level
Below sea level
National capital
State or territorial capital
Other city
Mercator Projection

The Arctic

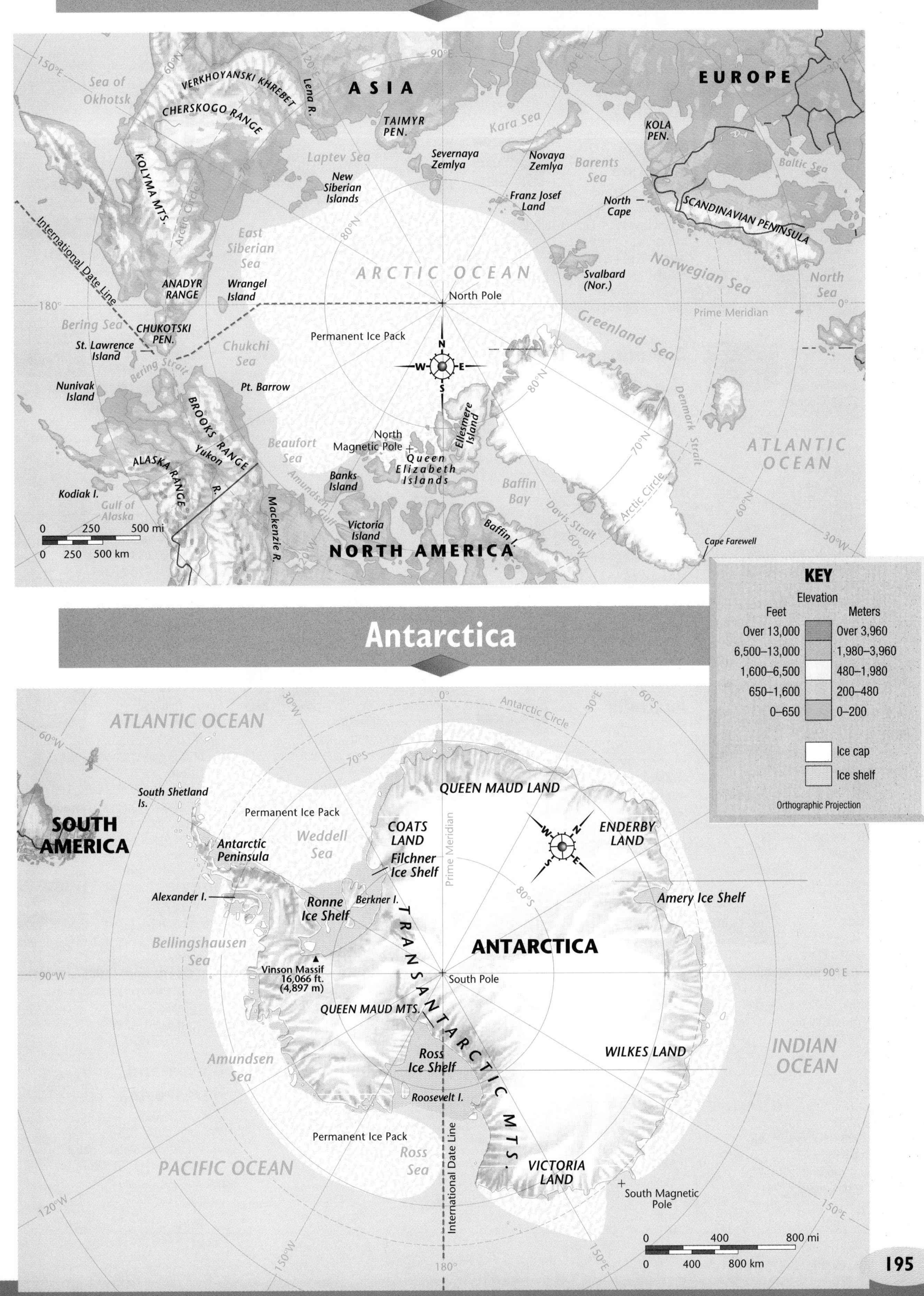

Antarctica

World View

Afghanistan

CAPITAL: Kabul
POPULATION: 21,251,821
MAJOR LANGUAGES: Pashtu, Afghan Persian, Turkic, and 30 various languages
AREA: 250,010 sq mi; 647,500 sq km
LEADING EXPORTS: fruits and nuts, handwoven carpets, and wool
CONTINENT: Asia

Albania

CAPITAL: Tiranë
POPULATION: 3,413,904
MAJOR LANGUAGES: Albanian, Tosk dialect, and Greek
AREA: 11,101 sq mi; 28,750 sq km
LEADING EXPORTS: asphalt, metals and metallic ores, and electricity
CONTINENT: Europe

Algeria

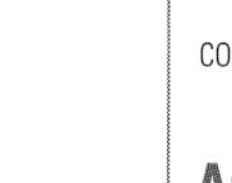

CAPITAL: Algiers
POPULATION: 28,539,321
MAJOR LANGUAGES: Arabic (official), French, and Berber dialects
AREA: 919,626 sq mi; 2,381,740 sq km
LEADING EXPORTS: petroleum and natural gas
CONTINENT: Africa

Andorra

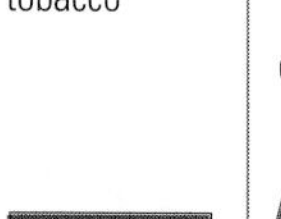

CAPITAL: Andorra La Vella
POPULATION: 65,780
MAJOR LANGUAGES: Catalan (official), French, and Castilian
AREA: 174 sq mi; 450 sq km
LEADING EXPORTS: electricity, tobacco products, and furniture
CONTINENT: Europe

Angola

CAPITAL: Luanda
POPULATION: 10,069,501
MAJOR LANGUAGES: Portuguese (official), Bantu, and various languages
AREA: 481,370 sq mi; 1,246,700 sq km
LEADING EXPORTS: oil, diamonds, and refined petroleum products
CONTINENT: Africa

Anguilla

CAPITAL: The Valley
POPULATION: 7,099
MAJOR LANGUAGE: English (official)
AREA: 35 sq mi; 91 sq km
LEADING EXPORTS: lobster and salt
LOCATION: Caribbean Sea

Antigua and Barbuda

CAPITAL: Saint John's
POPULATION: 65,176
MAJOR LANGUAGES: English (official) and various dialects
AREA: 170 sq mi; 440 sq km
LEADING EXPORTS: petroleum products and manufactures
LOCATION: Caribbean Sea

Argentina

CAPITAL: Buenos Aires
POPULATION: 34,292,742
MAJOR LANGUAGES: Spanish (official), English, Italian, German, and French
AREA: 1,068,339 sq mi; 2,766,890 sq km
LEADING EXPORTS: meat, wheat, corn, oilseed, and manufactures
CONTINENT: South America

Armenia

CAPITAL: Yerevan
POPULATION: 3,557,284
MAJOR LANGUAGES: Armenian and Russian
AREA: 11,506 sq mi; 29,800 sq km
LEADING EXPORTS: gold and jewelry, and aluminum
CONTINENT: Asia

Australia

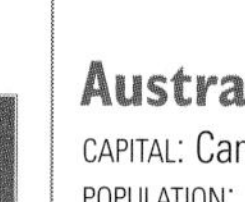

CAPITAL: Canberra
POPULATION: 18,322,231
MAJOR LANGUAGES: English and various languages
AREA: 2,968,010 sq mi; 7,686,850 sq km
LEADING EXPORTS: coal, gold, meat, wool, and alumina
CONTINENT: Australia

Austria

CAPITAL: Vienna
POPULATION: 7,986,664
MAJOR LANGUAGE: German
AREA: 32,376 sq mi; 83,850 sq km
LEADING EXPORTS: machinery and equipment, and iron and steel
CONTINENT: Europe

Azerbaijan

CAPITAL: Baku
POPULATION: 7,789,886
MAJOR LANGUAGES: Azeri, Russian, Armenian, and various languages
AREA: 33,438 sq mi; 86,600 sq km
LEADING EXPORTS: oil and gas, chemicals, and oil field equipment
CONTINENT: Asia

Bahamas

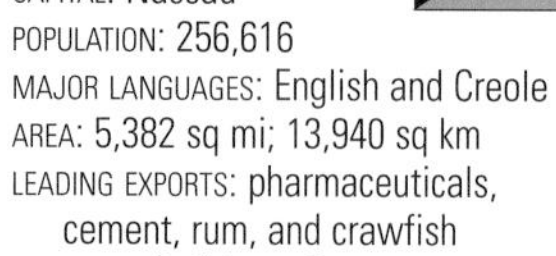

CAPITAL: Nassau
POPULATION: 256,616
MAJOR LANGUAGES: English and Creole
AREA: 5,382 sq mi; 13,940 sq km
LEADING EXPORTS: pharmaceuticals, cement, rum, and crawfish
LOCATION: Caribbean Sea

Bahrain

CAPITAL: Manama
POPULATION: 575,925
MAJOR LANGUAGES: Arabic, English, Farsi, and Urdu
AREA: 239 sq mi; 620 sq km
LEADING EXPORTS: petroleum and petroleum products
CONTINENT: Asia

Bangladesh

CAPITAL: Dhaka
POPULATION: 128,094,948
MAJOR LANGUAGES: Bangla and English
AREA: 55,600 sq mi; 144,000 sq km
LEADING EXPORTS: garments, jute and jute goods, and leather
CONTINENT: Asia

Barbados

CAPITAL: Bridgetown
POPULATION: 256,395
MAJOR LANGUAGE: English
AREA: 166 sq mi; 430 sq km
LEADING EXPORTS: sugar and molasses, and rum
LOCATION: Caribbean Sea

Belarus

CAPITAL: Minsk
POPULATION: 10,437,418
MAJOR LANGUAGES: Byelorussian and Russian
AREA: 79,926 sq mi; 207,600 sq km
LEADING EXPORTS: machinery and transportation equipment
CONTINENT: Europe

Belgium

CAPITAL: Brussels
POPULATION: 10,081,880
MAJOR LANGUAGES: Dutch, French, and German
AREA: 11,780 sq mi; 30,510 sq km
LEADING EXPORTS: iron and steel, and transportation equipment
CONTINENT: Europe

Belize

CAPITAL: Belmopan
POPULATION: 214,061
MAJOR LANGUAGES: English (official), Spanish, Maya, and Garifuna
AREA: 8,865 sq mi; 22,960 sq km
LEADING EXPORTS: sugar, citrus fruits, bananas, and clothing
CONTINENT: North America

Benin

CAPITAL: Porto-Novo
POPULATION: 5,522,677
MAJOR LANGUAGES: Fon, Yoruba, and at least 6 various languages
AREA: 43,484 sq mi; 112,620 sq km
LEADING EXPORTS: cotton, crude oil, palm products, and cocoa
CONTINENT: Africa

Bermuda

CAPITAL: Hamilton
POPULATION: 61,629
MAJOR LANGUAGE: English
AREA: 19.3 sq mi; 50 sq km
LEADING EXPORTS: semitropical produce and light manufactures
LOCATION: Atlantic Ocean

Bhutan

CAPITAL: Thimphu
POPULATION: 1,780,638
MAJOR LANGUAGES: Dzongkha (official), Tibetan dialects, and Nepalese dialects
AREA: 18,147 sq mi; 47,000 sq km
LEADING EXPORTS: cardamon, gypsum, timber, and handicrafts
CONTINENT: Asia

Bolivia

CAPITAL: La Paz
POPULATION: 7,896,254
MAJOR LANGUAGES: Spanish, Quechua, and Aymara
AREA: 424,179 sq mi; 1,098,580 sq km
LEADING EXPORTS: metals, natural gas, soybeans, jewelry, and wood
CONTINENT: South America

Bosnia and Herzegovina

CAPITAL: Sarajevo
POPULATION: 3,201,823
MAJOR LANGUAGE: Serbo-Croatian
AREA: 19,782 sq mi; 51,233 sq km
LEADING EXPORTS: none
CONTINENT: Europe

Botswana

CAPITAL: Gaborone
POPULATION: 1,392,414
MAJOR LANGUAGES: English and Setswana
AREA: 231,812 sq mi; 600,370 sq km
LEADING EXPORTS: diamonds, copper and nickel, and meat
CONTINENT: Africa

Brazil

CAPITAL: Brasília
POPULATION: 160,737,489
MAJOR LANGUAGES: Portuguese, Spanish, English, and French
AREA: 3,286,600 sq mi; 8,511,965 sq km
LEADING EXPORTS: iron ore, soybean, bran, and orange juice
CONTINENT: South America

British Virgin Islands

CAPITAL: Road Town
POPULATION: 13,027
MAJOR LANGUAGE: English
AREA: 58 sq mi; 150 sq km
LEADING EXPORTS: rum, fresh fish, gravel, sand, and fruits
LOCATION: Caribbean Sea

Brunei

CAPITAL: Bandar Seri Begawan
POPULATION: 292,266
MAJOR LANGUAGES: Malay, English, and Chinese
AREA: 2,228 sq mi; 5,770 sq km
LEADING EXPORTS: crude oil and liquefied natural gas
LOCATION: South China Sea

Bulgaria

CAPITAL: Sofia
POPULATION: 8,775,198
MAJOR LANGUAGE: Bulgarian
AREA: 42,824 sq mi; 110,910 sq km
LEADING EXPORTS: machinery and agricultural products
CONTINENT: Europe

Burkina Faso

CAPITAL: Ouagadougou
POPULATION: 10,422,828
MAJOR LANGUAGES: French (official) and Sudanic languages
AREA: 105,873 sq mi; 274,200 sq km
LEADING EXPORTS: cotton, gold, and animal products
CONTINENT: Africa

Burundi

CAPITAL: Bujumbura
POPULATION: 6,262,429
MAJOR LANGUAGES: Kirundi, French, and Swahili
AREA: 10,746 sq mi; 27,830 sq km
LEADING EXPORTS: coffee, tea, cotton, and hides and skins
CONTINENT: Africa

Cambodia

CAPITAL: Phnom Penh
POPULATION: 10,561,373
MAJOR LANGUAGES: Khmer and French
AREA: 69,902 sq mi; 181,040 sq km
LEADING EXPORTS: timber, rubber, soybeans, and sesame
CONTINENT: Asia

Cameroon

CAPITAL: Yaounde
POPULATION: 13,521,000
MAJOR LANGUAGES: 24 various languages, English, and French
AREA: 183,574 sq mi; 475,440 sq km
LEADING EXPORTS: petroleum products and lumber
CONTINENT: Africa

Canada

CAPITAL: Ottawa
POPULATION: 28,434,545
MAJOR LANGUAGES: English and French
AREA: 3,851,940 sq mi; 9,976,140 sq km
LEADING EXPORTS: newsprint, wood pulp, timber, and crude petroleum
CONTINENT: North America

Cape Verde

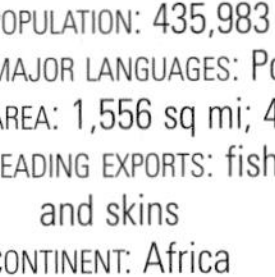
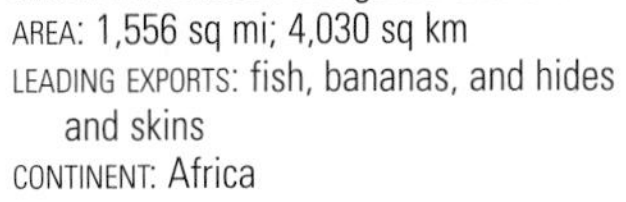

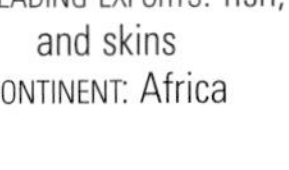
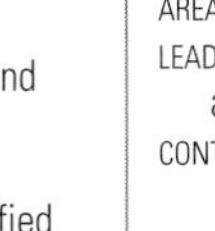

CAPITAL: Praia
POPULATION: 435,983
MAJOR LANGUAGES: Portuguese and Crioulo
AREA: 1,556 sq mi; 4,030 sq km
LEADING EXPORTS: fish, bananas, and hides and skins
CONTINENT: Africa

Cayman Islands

CAPITAL: George Town
POPULATION: 33,192
MAJOR LANGUAGE: English
AREA: 100 sq mi; 260 sq km
LEADING EXPORTS: turtle products and manufactured goods
LOCATION: Caribbean Sea

Central African Republic

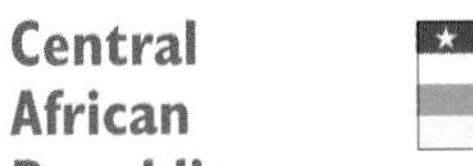

CAPITAL: Bangui
POPULATION: 3,209,759
MAJOR LANGUAGES: French, Sangho, Arabic, Hunsa, and Swahili
AREA: 240,542 sq mi; 622,980 sq km
LEADING EXPORTS: diamonds, timber, cotton, coffee, and tobacco
CONTINENT: Africa

Chad

CAPITAL: N'Djamena
POPULATION: 5,586,505
MAJOR LANGUAGES: French, Arabic, Sara, Songo, and over 100 various languages and dialects
AREA: 495,772 sq mi; 1,284,000 sq km
LEADING EXPORTS: cotton, cattle, textiles, and fish
CONTINENT: Africa

Chile

CAPITAL: Santiago
POPULATION: 14,161,216
MAJOR LANGUAGE: Spanish
AREA: 292,269 sq mi; 756,950 sq km
LEADING EXPORTS: copper and other metals and minerals
CONTINENT: South America

China

CAPITAL: Beijing
POPULATION: 1,203,097,268
MAJOR LANGUAGES: Mandarin, Putonghua, Yue, Wu, Minbei, Minnan, Xiang, and Gan and Hakka dialects
AREA: 3,705,533 sq mi; 9,596,960 sq km
LEADING EXPORTS: textiles, garments, footwear, and toys
CONTINENT: Asia

Colombia

CAPITAL: Bogota
POPULATION: 36,200,251
MAJOR LANGUAGE: Spanish
AREA: 439,751 sq mi; 1,138,910 sq km
LEADING EXPORTS: petroleum, coffee, coal, and bananas
CONTINENT: South America

Comoros

CAPITAL: Moroni
POPULATION: 549,338
MAJOR LANGUAGES: Arabic, French, and Comoran
AREA: 838 sq mi; 2,170 sq km
LEADING EXPORTS: vanilla, ylang-ylang, cloves, and perfume oil
LOCATION: Indian Ocean

Congo

CAPITAL: Brazzaville
POPULATION: 2,504,996
MAJOR LANGUAGES: French, Lingala, Kikongo, and other languages
AREA: 132,051 sq mi; 342,000 sq km
LEADING EXPORTS: crude oil, lumber, plywood, sugar, and cocoa
CONTINENT: Africa

Cook Islands

CAPITAL: Avarua
POPULATION: 19,343
MAJOR LANGUAGES: English and Maori
AREA: 95 sq mi; 240 sq km
LEADING EXPORTS: copra, fresh and canned fruit, and clothing
LOCATION: Pacific Ocean

Costa Rica

CAPITAL: San José
POPULATION: 3,419,114
MAJOR LANGUAGES: Spanish and English
AREA: 19,730 sq mi; 51,100 sq km
LEADING EXPORTS: coffee, bananas, textiles, and sugar
CONTINENT: North America

Côte d'Ivoire

CAPITAL: Yamoussoukro
POPULATION: 14,791,257
MAJOR LANGUAGES: French, Dioula, and 59 other dialects
AREA: 124,507 sq mi; 322,460 sq km
LEADING EXPORTS: cocoa, coffee, tropical woods, and petroleum
CONTINENT: Africa

Croatia

CAPITAL: Zagreb
POPULATION: 4,665,821
MAJOR LANGUAGE: Serbo-Croatian
AREA: 21,830 sq mi; 56,538 sq km
LEADING EXPORTS: machinery and transportation equipment
CONTINENT: Europe

Cuba

CAPITAL: Havana
POPULATION: 10,937,635
MAJOR LANGUAGE: Spanish
AREA: 42,805 sq mi; 110,860 sq km
LEADING EXPORTS: sugar, nickel, shellfish, and tobacco
LOCATION: Caribbean Sea

Cyprus

CAPITAL: Nicosia
POPULATION: 736,636
MAJOR LANGUAGES: Greek, Turkish, and English
AREA: 3,572 sq mi; 9,250 sq km
LEADING EXPORTS: citrus, potatoes, grapes, wines, and cement
LOCATION: Mediterranean Sea

Czech Republic

CAPITAL: Prague
POPULATION: 10,432,774
MAJOR LANGUAGES: Czech and Slovak
AREA: 30,388 sq mi; 78,703 sq km
LEADING EXPORTS: manufactured goods
CONTINENT: Europe

Denmark

CAPITAL: Copenhagen
POPULATION: 5,199,437
MAJOR LANGUAGES: Danish, Faroese, Greenlandic, and German
AREA: 16,630 sq mi; 43,070 sq km
LEADING EXPORTS: meat and meat products, and dairy products
CONTINENT: Europe

Djibouti

CAPITAL: Djibouti
POPULATION: 421,320
MAJOR LANGUAGES: French, Arabic, Somali, and Afar
AREA: 8,495 sq mi; 22,000 sq km
LEADING EXPORTS: hides and skins, and coffee (in transit)
CONTINENT: Africa

Dominica

CAPITAL: Roseau
POPULATION: 82,608
MAJOR LANGUAGES: English and French patois
AREA: 290 sq mi; 750 sq km
LEADING EXPORTS: bananas, soap, bay oil, and vegetables
LOCATION: Caribbean Sea

Dominican Republic

CAPITAL: Santo Domingo
POPULATION: 7,511,263
MAJOR LANGUAGE: Spanish
AREA: 18,815 sq mi; 48,730 sq km
LEADING EXPORTS: ferronickel, sugar, gold, coffee, and cocoa
LOCATION: Caribbean Sea

Ecuador

CAPITAL: Quito
POPULATION: 10,890,950
MAJOR LANGUAGES: Spanish, Quechua, and various languages
AREA: 109,487 sq mi; 283,560 sq km
LEADING EXPORTS: petroleum, bananas, shrimp, and cocoa
CONTINENT: South America

Egypt

CAPITAL: Cairo
POPULATION: 62,359,623
MAJOR LANGUAGES: Arabic, English, and French
AREA: 386,675 sq mi; 1,001,450 sq km
LEADING EXPORTS: crude oil and petroleum products
CONTINENT: Africa

El Salvador

CAPITAL: San Salvador
POPULATION: 5,870,481
MAJOR LANGUAGES: Spanish and Nahua
AREA: 8,124 sq mi; 21,040 sq km
LEADING EXPORTS: coffee, sugar cane, and shrimp
CONTINENT: North America

Equatorial Guinea

CAPITAL: Malabo
POPULATION: 420,293
MAJOR LANGUAGES: Spanish, Pidgin English, Fang, Bubi, and Ibo
AREA: 10,831 sq mi; 28,050 sq km
LEADING EXPORTS: coffee, timber, and cocoa beans
CONTINENT: Africa

Eritrea

CAPITAL: Asmara
POPULATION: 3,578,709
MAJOR LANGUAGES: Tigre, Kunama, Cushitic dialects, Nora Bana, and Arabic
AREA: 46,844 sq mi; 121,320 sq km
LEADING EXPORTS: salt, hides, cement, and gum arabic
CONTINENT: Africa

Estonia

CAPITAL: Tallinn
POPULATION: 1,625,399
MAJOR LANGUAGES: Estonian, Latvian, Lithuanian, and Russian
AREA: 17,414 sq mi; 45,100 sq km
LEADING EXPORTS: textiles, food products, vehicles, and metals
CONTINENT: Europe

Ethiopia

CAPITAL: Addis Ababa
POPULATION: 55,979,018
MAJOR LANGUAGES: Amharic, Tigrinya, Orominga, Guaraginga, Somali, Arabic, English, and various languages
AREA: 435,201 sq mi; 1,127,127 sq km
LEADING EXPORTS: coffee, leather products, and gold
CONTINENT: Africa

Fiji

CAPITAL: Suva
POPULATION: 772,891
MAJOR LANGUAGES: English, Fijian, and Hindustani
AREA: 7,054 sq mi; 18,270 sq km
LEADING EXPORTS: sugar, clothing, gold, processed fish, and lumber
LOCATION: Pacific Ocean

Finland

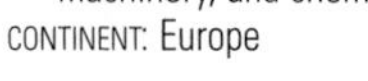

CAPITAL: Helsinki
POPULATION: 5,085,206
MAJOR LANGUAGES: Finnish, Swedish, Lapp, and Russian
AREA: 130,132 sq mi; 337,030 sq km
LEADING EXPORTS: paper and pulp, machinery, and chemicals
CONTINENT: Europe

France

CAPITAL: Paris
POPULATION: 58,109,160
MAJOR LANGUAGES: French and regional dialects and languages
AREA: 211,217 sq mi; 547,030 sq km
LEADING EXPORTS: machinery and transportation equipment
CONTINENT: Europe

Gabon

CAPITAL: Libreville
POPULATION: 1,185,749
MAJOR LANGUAGES: French, Fang, Myene, Bateke, Bapounou/Eschira, and Bandjabi
AREA: 103,351 sq mi; 267,670 sq km
LEADING EXPORTS: crude oil, timber, manganese, and uranium
CONTINENT: Africa

The Gambia

CAPITAL: Banjul
POPULATION: 989,273
MAJOR LANGUAGES: English, Mandinka, Wolof, Fula, and various languages
AREA: 4,363 sq mi; 11,300 sq km
LEADING EXPORTS: peanuts and peanut products, and fish
CONTINENT: Africa

Georgia

CAPITAL: T'bilisi
POPULATION: 5,725,972
MAJOR LANGUAGES: Armenian, Azeri, Georgian, Russian, and various languages
AREA: 26,912 sq mi; 69,700 sq km
LEADING EXPORTS: citrus fruits, tea, and wine
CONTINENT: Asia

Germany

CAPITAL: Berlin
POPULATION: 81,337,541
MAJOR LANGUAGE: German
AREA: 137,808 sq mi; 356,910 sq km
LEADING EXPORTS: machines and machine tools, and chemicals
CONTINENT: Europe

Ghana

CAPITAL: Accra
POPULATION: 17,763,138
MAJOR LANGUAGES: English, Akan, Moshi-Dagomba, Ewe, Ga, and various languages
AREA: 92,104 sq mi; 238,540 sq km
LEADING EXPORTS: cocoa, gold, timber, tuna, and bauxite
CONTINENT: Africa

Greece

CAPITAL: Athens
POPULATION: 10,647,511
MAJOR LANGUAGES: Greek, English, and French
AREA: 50,944 sq mi; 131,940 sq km
LEADING EXPORTS: manufactured goods, foodstuffs, and fuels
CONTINENT: Europe

Grenada

CAPITAL: Saint George's
POPULATION: 94,486
MAJOR LANGUAGES: English and French patois
AREA: 131 sq mi; 340 sq km
LEADING EXPORTS: bananas, cocoa, nutmeg, and fruits and vegetables
LOCATION: Caribbean Sea

Guatemala

CAPITAL: Guatemala
POPULATION: 10,998,602
MAJOR LANGUAGES: Spanish, Quiche, Cakchiquel, Kekchi, and various languages and dialects
AREA: 42,044 sq mi; 108,890 sq km
LEADING EXPORTS: coffee, sugar, bananas, cardamom, and beef
CONTINENT: North America

Guinea

CAPITAL: Conakry
POPULATION: 6,549,336
MAJOR LANGUAGES: French and various languages
AREA: 94,930 sq mi; 245,860 sq km
LEADING EXPORTS: bauxite, alumina, diamonds, gold, and coffee
CONTINENT: Africa

Guinea Bissau

CAPITAL: Bissau
POPULATION: 1,124,537
MAJOR LANGUAGES: Portuguese, Criolo, and various languages
AREA: 13,946 sq mi; 36,210 sq km
LEADING EXPORTS: cashews, fish, peanuts, and palm kernels
CONTINENT: Africa

Guyana

CAPITAL: Georgetown
POPULATION: 723,774
MAJOR LANGUAGES: English and various dialects
AREA: 83,003 sq mi; 214,970 sq km
LEADING EXPORTS: sugar, bauxite/alumina, rice, and shrimp
CONTINENT: South America

Haiti

CAPITAL: Port-au-Prince
POPULATION: 6,539,983
MAJOR LANGUAGES: French and Creole
AREA: 8,784 sq mi; 22,750 sq km
LEADING EXPORTS: light manufactures and coffee
LOCATION: Caribbean Sea

Holy See (Vatican City)

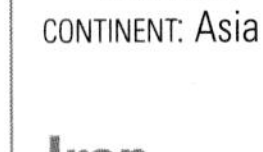

CAPITAL: Vatican City
POPULATION: 830
MAJOR LANGUAGES: Italian, Latin, and various languages
AREA: 17 sq mi; 44 sq km
LEADING EXPORTS: none
CONTINENT: Europe

Honduras

CAPITAL: Tegucigalpa
POPULATION: 5,549,743
MAJOR LANGUAGES: Spanish and various dialects
AREA: 43,280 sq mi; 112,090 sq km
LEADING EXPORTS: bananas, coffee, shrimp, lobsters, and minerals
CONTINENT: North America

Hungary

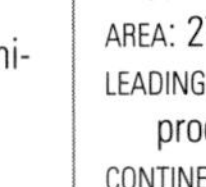

CAPITAL: Budapest
POPULATION: 10,318,838
MAJOR LANGUAGES: Hungarian and various languages
AREA: 35,920 sq mi; 93,030 sq km
LEADING EXPORTS: raw materials and semi-finished goods
CONTINENT: Europe

Iceland

CAPITAL: Reykjavik
POPULATION: 265,998
MAJOR LANGUAGE: Icelandic
AREA: 39,770 sq mi; 103,000 sq km
LEADING EXPORTS: fish and fish products, and animal products
LOCATION: Atlantic Ocean

India

CAPITAL: New Delhi
POPULATION: 936,545,814
MAJOR LANGUAGES: English, Hindi, Bengali, Telugu, Marathi, Tamil, Urdu, Gujarati, Malayam, Kannada, Oriya, Punjabi, Assamese, Kashmiri, Sindhi, Sanskrit, and Hindustani (all official)
AREA: 1,269,389 sq mi; 3,287,590 sq km
LEADING EXPORTS: clothing, and gems and jewelry
CONTINENT: Asia

Indonesia

CAPITAL: Jakarta
POPULATION: 203,583,886
MAJOR LANGUAGES: Bahasa Indonesia, English, Dutch, Javanese, and various dialects
AREA: 741,052 sq mi; 1,919,251 sq km
LEADING EXPORTS: manufactures, fuels, and foodstuffs
CONTINENT: Asia

Iran

CAPITAL: Tehran
POPULATION: 64,625,455
MAJOR LANGUAGES: Farsi (official) and Turkic languages
AREA: 634,562 sq mi; 1,643,452 sq km
LEADING EXPORTS: petroleum, carpets, fruit, nuts, and hides
CONTINENT: Asia

Iraq

CAPITAL: Baghdad
POPULATION: 20,643,769
MAJOR LANGUAGES: Arabic, Kurdish, Assyrian, and Armenian
AREA: 168,760 sq mi; 437,072 sq km
LEADING EXPORTS: crude oil and refined products, and fertilizers
CONTINENT: Asia

Ireland

CAPITAL: Dublin
POPULATION: 3,550,448
MAJOR LANGUAGES: Irish Gaelic and English
AREA: 27,136 sq mi; 70,280 sq km
LEADING EXPORTS: chemicals and data processing equipment
CONTINENT: Europe

Israel

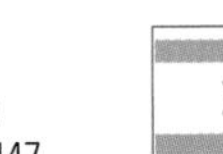

CAPITAL: Jerusalem
POPULATION: 7,566,447
MAJOR LANGUAGES: Hebrew, Arabic, and English
AREA: 10,421 sq mi; 26,990 sq km
LEADING EXPORTS: machinery and equipment, and cut diamonds
CONTINENT: Asia

Italy

CAPITAL: Rome
POPULATION: 58,261,971
MAJOR LANGUAGES: Italian, German, French, and Slovene
AREA: 116,310 sq mi; 301,230 sq km
LEADING EXPORTS: metals, and textiles and clothing
CONTINENT: Europe

Jamaica

CAPITAL: Kingston
POPULATION: 2,574,291
MAJOR LANGUAGES: English and Creole
AREA: 4,243 sq mi; 10,990 sq km
LEADING EXPORTS: alumina, bauxite, sugar, bananas, and rum
LOCATION: Caribbean Sea

Japan

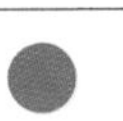

CAPITAL: Tokyo
POPULATION: 125,506,492
MAJOR LANGUAGE: Japanese
AREA: 145,888 sq mi; 377,835 sq km
LEADING EXPORTS: machinery, motor vehicles, and electronics
CONTINENT: Asia

Jordan

CAPITAL: Amman
POPULATION: 4,100,709
MAJOR LANGUAGES: Arabic and English
AREA: 34,447 sq mi; 89,213 sq km
LEADING EXPORTS: phosphates, fertilizers, and potash
CONTINENT: Asia

Kazakhstan

CAPITAL: Almaty
POPULATION: 17,376,615
MAJOR LANGUAGES: Kazakh and Russian
AREA: 1,049,191 sq mi; 2,717,300 sq km
LEADING EXPORTS: oil, and ferrous and nonferrous metals
CONTINENT: Asia

Kenya

CAPITAL: Nairobi
POPULATION: 28,817,227
MAJOR LANGUAGES: English, Swahili, and various languages
AREA: 224,970 sq mi; 582,650 sq km
LEADING EXPORTS: tea, coffee, and petroleum products
CONTINENT: Africa

Kiribati

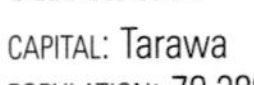

CAPITAL: Tarawa
POPULATION: 79,386
MAJOR LANGUAGES: English and Gilbertese
AREA: 277 sq mi; 717 sq km
LEADING EXPORTS: copra, seaweed, and fish
LOCATION: Pacific Ocean

Korea, North

CAPITAL: P'yongyang
POPULATION: 23,486,550
MAJOR LANGUAGE: Korean
AREA: 46,542 sq mi; 120,540 sq km
LEADING EXPORTS: minerals and metallurgical products
CONTINENT: Asia

Korea, South

CAPITAL: Seoul
POPULATION: 45,553,882
MAJOR LANGUAGES: Korean and English
AREA: 38,025 sq mi; 98,480 sq km
LEADING EXPORTS: electronic and electrical equipment
CONTINENT: Asia

Kuwait

CAPITAL: Kuwait
POPULATION: 1,817,397
MAJOR LANGUAGES: Arabic and English
AREA: 6,881 sq mi; 17,820 sq km
LEADING EXPORT: oil
CONTINENT: Asia

Kyrgyzstan

CAPITAL: Bishkek
POPULATION: 4,769,877
MAJOR LANGUAGES: Kyrgyz and Russian
AREA: 76,644 sq mi; 198,500 sq km
LEADING EXPORTS: wool, chemicals, cotton, metals, and shoes
CONTINENT: Asia

Laos

CAPITAL: Vientiane
POPULATION: 4,837,237
MAJOR LANGUAGES: Lao, French, English, and various languages
AREA: 91,432 sq mi; 236,800 sq km
LEADING EXPORTS: electricity, wood products, coffee, and tin
CONTINENT: Asia

Latvia

CAPITAL: Riga
POPULATION: 2,762,899
MAJOR LANGUAGES: Lettish, Lithuanian, Russian, and various languages
AREA: 24,750 sq mi; 64,100 sq km
LEADING EXPORTS: oil products, timber, and ferrous metals
CONTINENT: Europe

Lebanon

CAPITAL: Beirut
POPULATION: 3,695,921
MAJOR LANGUAGES: Arabic, French, Armenian, and English
AREA: 4,016 sq mi; 10,400 sq km
LEADING EXPORTS: agricultural products, chemicals, and textiles
CONTINENT: Asia

Lesotho

CAPITAL: Maseru
POPULATION: 1,992,960
MAJOR LANGUAGES: Sesotho, English, Zulu, and Xhosa
AREA: 11,719 sq mi; 30,350 sq km
LEADING EXPORTS: wool, mohair, wheat, cattle, and peas
CONTINENT: Africa

Liberia

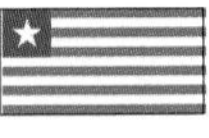

CAPITAL: Monrovia
POPULATION: 3,073,245
MAJOR LANGUAGES: English and Niger-Congo
AREA: 43,002 sq mi; 111,370 sq km
LEADING EXPORTS: iron ore, rubber, timber, and coffee
CONTINENT: Africa

Libya

CAPITAL: Tripoli
POPULATION: 5,248,401
MAJOR LANGUAGES: Arabic, Italian, and English
AREA: 679,385 sq mi; 1,759,540 sq km
LEADING EXPORTS: crude oil and refined petroleum products
CONTINENT: Africa

Liechtenstein

CAPITAL: Vaduz
POPULATION: 30,654
MAJOR LANGUAGES: German and Alemannic
AREA: 62 sq mi; 160 sq km
LEADING EXPORTS: small specialty machinery and dental products
CONTINENT: Europe

Lithuania

CAPITAL: Vilnius
POPULATION: 3,876,396
MAJOR LANGUAGES: Lithuanian, Polish, and Russian
AREA: 25,175 sq mi; 65,200 sq km
LEADING EXPORTS: electronics, petroleum products, and food
CONTINENT: Europe

Luxembourg

CAPITAL: Luxembourg
POPULATION: 404,660
MAJOR LANGUAGES: Luxembourgisch, German, French, and English
AREA: 998 sq mi; 2,586 sq km
LEADING EXPORTS: finished steel products and chemicals
CONTINENT: Europe

Macedonia

CAPITAL: Skopje
POPULATION: 2,159,503
MAJOR LANGUAGES: Macedonian, Albanian, Turkish, Serb, Gypsy, and various languages
AREA: 9,781 sq mi; 25,333 sq km
LEADING EXPORTS: manufactured goods and machinery
CONTINENT: Europe

Madagascar

CAPITAL: Antananarivo
POPULATION: 13,862,325
MAJOR LANGUAGES: French and Malagasy
AREA: 226,665 sq mi; 587,040 sq km
LEADING EXPORTS: coffee, vanilla, cloves, shellfish, and sugar
CONTINENT: Africa

Malawi

CAPITAL: Lilongwe
POPULATION: 9,808,384
MAJOR LANGUAGES: English, Chichewa, and various languages
AREA: 45,747 sq mi; 118,480 sq km
LEADING EXPORTS: tobacco, tea, sugar, coffee, and peanuts
CONTINENT: Africa

Malaysia

CAPITAL: Kuala Lumpur
POPULATION: 19,723,587
MAJOR LANGUAGES: Malay, English, Mandarin, Tamil, Chinese dialects, and various languages and dialects
AREA: 127,322 sq mi; 329,750 sq km
LEADING EXPORTS: electronic equipment
CONTINENT: Asia

Maldives

CAPITAL: Male
POPULATION: 261,310
MAJOR LANGUAGES: Divehi dialect and English
AREA: 116 sq mi; 300 sq km
LEADING EXPORTS: fish and clothing
CONTINENT: Asia

Mali

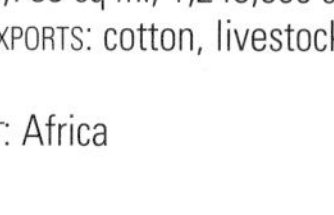

CAPITAL: Bamako
POPULATION: 9,375,132
MAJOR LANGUAGES: French, Bambara, and various languages
AREA: 478,783 sq mi; 1,240,000 sq km
LEADING EXPORTS: cotton, livestock, and gold
CONTINENT: Africa

Malta

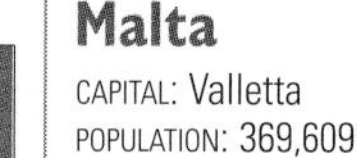

CAPITAL: Valletta
POPULATION: 369,609
MAJOR LANGUAGES: Maltese and English
AREA: 124 sq mi; 320 sq km
LEADING EXPORTS: machinery and transportation equipment
LOCATION: Mediterranean Sea

Marshall Islands

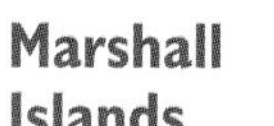

CAPITAL: Majuro
POPULATION: 56,157
MAJOR LANGUAGES: English, Marshallese dialects, and Japanese
AREA: 70 sq mi; 181.3 sq km
LEADING EXPORTS: coconut oil, fish, live animals, and trichus shells
LOCATION: Pacific Ocean

Mauritania

CAPITAL: Nouakchott
POPULATION: 2,263,202
MAJOR LANGUAGES: Hasaniya Arabic, Wolof, Pular, and Soninke
AREA: 397,969 sq mi; 1,030,700 sq km
LEADING EXPORTS: iron ore, and fish and fish products
CONTINENT: Africa

Mauritius

CAPITAL: Port Louis
POPULATION: 1,127,068
MAJOR LANGUAGES: English (official), Creole, French, Hindi, Urdu, Hakka, and Bojpoori
AREA: 718 sq mi; 1,860 sq km
LEADING EXPORTS: textiles, sugar, and light manufactures
LOCATION: Indian Ocean

Mayotte

CAPITAL: Mamoutzou
POPULATION: 97,088
MAJOR LANGUAGES: Mahorian and French
AREA: 145 sq mi; 375 sq km
LEADING EXPORTS: ylang-ylang and vanilla
CONTINENT: Africa

Mexico

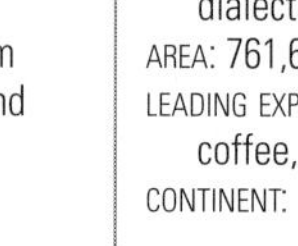
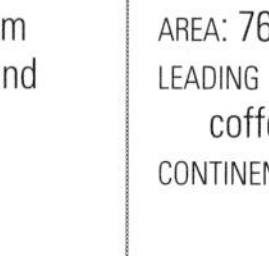
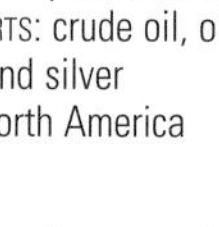

CAPITAL: Mexico City
POPULATION: 93,985,848
MAJOR LANGUAGES: Spanish and Mayan dialects
AREA: 761,632 sq mi; 1,972,550 sq km
LEADING EXPORTS: crude oil, oil products, coffee, and silver
CONTINENT: North America

Micronesia

CAPITAL: Federated states of Kolonia (on the Island of Pohnpei)
*a new capital is being built about 10 km southwest in the Palikir Valley
POPULATION: 122,950
MAJOR LANGUAGES: English, Turkese, Pohnpeian, Yapese, and Kosrean
AREA: 271 sq mi; 702 sq km
LEADING EXPORTS: fish, copra, bananas, and black pepper
LOCATION: Pacific Ocean

Moldova

CAPITAL: Chisinau
POPULATION: 4,489,657
MAJOR LANGUAGES: Moldovan (official), Russian, and Gagauz dialect
AREA: 13,012 sq mi; 33,700 sq km
LEADING EXPORTS: foodstuffs, wine, and tobacco
CONTINENT: Europe

Monaco

CAPITAL: Monaco
POPULATION: 31,515
MAJOR LANGUAGES: French (official), English, Italian, and Monegasque
AREA: .73 sq mi; 1.9 sq km
LEADING EXPORTS: exports through France
CONTINENT: Europe

Mongolia

CAPITAL: Ulaanbaatar
POPULATION: 2,493,615
MAJOR LANGUAGES: Khalkha Mongol, Turkic, Russian, and Chinese
AREA: 604,270 sq mi; 1,565,000 sq km
LEADING EXPORTS: copper, livestock, animal products, and cashmere
CONTINENT: Asia

Morocco

CAPITAL: Rabat
POPULATION: 29,168,848
MAJOR LANGUAGES: Arabic (official), Berber dialects, and French
AREA: 172,420 sq mi; 446,550 sq km
LEADING EXPORTS: food and beverages
CONTINENT: Africa

Mozambique

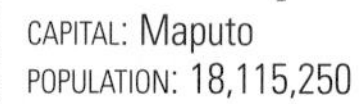

CAPITAL: Maputo
POPULATION: 18,115,250
MAJOR LANGUAGES: Portuguese and various dialects
AREA: 309,506 sq mi; 801,590 sq km
LEADING EXPORTS: shrimp, cashews, cotton, sugar, copra, and citrus
CONTINENT: Africa

Myanmar (Burma)

CAPITAL: Rangoon
POPULATION: 45,103,809
MAJOR LANGUAGE: Burmese
AREA: 261,979 sq mi; 678,500 sq km
LEADING EXPORTS: pulses and beans, teak, rice, and hardwood
CONTINENT: Asia

Namibia

CAPITAL: Windhoek
POPULATION: 1,651,545
MAJOR LANGUAGES: English (official), Afrikaans, German, Oshivambo, Herero, Nama, and various languages
AREA: 318,707 sq mi; 825,418 sq km
LEADING EXPORTS: diamonds, copper, gold, zinc, and lead
CONTINENT: Africa

Nauru

CAPITAL: Government offices in Yaren District
POPULATION: 10,149
MAJOR LANGUAGES: Nauruan and English
AREA: 8 sq mi; 21 sq km
LEADING EXPORTS: phosphates
LOCATION: Pacific Ocean

Nepal

CAPITAL: Kathmandu
POPULATION: 21,560,869
MAJOR LANGUAGES: Nepali (official) and 20 various languages divided into numerous dialects
AREA: 54,365 sq mi; 140,800 sq km
LEADING EXPORTS: carpets, clothing, and leather goods
CONTINENT: Asia

Netherlands

CAPITAL: Amsterdam
POPULATION: 15,452,903
MAJOR LANGUAGE: Dutch
AREA: 14,414 sq mi; 37,330 sq km
LEADING EXPORTS: metal products and chemicals
CONTINENT: Europe

New Caledonia

CAPITAL: Noumea
POPULATION: 184,552
MAJOR LANGUAGES: French and 28 Melanesian-Polynesian dialects
AREA: 7,359 sq mi; 19,060 sq km
LEADING EXPORTS: nickel metal and nickel ore
LOCATION: Pacific Ocean

New Zealand

CAPITAL: Wellington
POPULATION: 3,407,277
MAJOR LANGUAGES: English and Maori
AREA: 103,741 sq mi; 268,680 sq km
LEADING EXPORTS: wool, lamb, mutton, beef, fish, and cheese
LOCATION: Pacific Ocean

Nicaragua

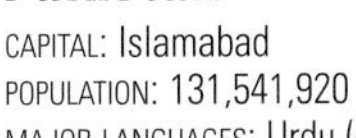

CAPITAL: Managua
POPULATION: 4,206,353
MAJOR LANGUAGES: Spanish (official), English, and various languages
AREA: 50,000 sq mi; 129,494 sq km
LEADING EXPORTS: meat, coffee, cotton, sugar, seafood, and gold
CONTINENT: North America

Niger

CAPITAL: Niamey
POPULATION: 9,280,208
MAJOR LANGUAGES: French (official), Hausa, and Djerma
AREA: 489,208 sq mi; 1,267,000 sq km
LEADING EXPORTS: uranium ore and livestock products
CONTINENT: Africa

Nigeria

CAPITAL: Abuja
POPULATION: 101,232,251
MAJOR LANGUAGES: English (official), Hausa, Yoruba, Ibo, and Fulani
AREA: 356,682 sq mi; 923,770 sq km
LEADING EXPORTS: oil, cocoa, and rubber
CONTINENT: Africa

Niue

CAPITAL: (Free association with New Zealand)
POPULATION: 1,837
MAJOR LANGUAGES: Polynesian and English
AREA: 100 sq mi; 260 sq km
LEADING EXPORTS: canned coconut cream, copra, and honey
LOCATION: Pacific Ocean

Norway

CAPITAL: Oslo
POPULATION: 4,330,951
MAJOR LANGUAGES: Norwegian (official), Lapp, and Finnish
AREA: 125,186 sq mi; 324,220 sq km
LEADING EXPORTS: petroleum and petroleum products
CONTINENT: Europe

Oman

CAPITAL: Muscat
POPULATION: 2,125,089
MAJOR LANGUAGES: Arabic (official), English, Baluchi, Urdu, and Indian dialects
AREA: 82,034 sq mi; 212,460 sq km
LEADING EXPORTS: petroleum, re-exports, and fish
CONTINENT: Asia

Pakistan

CAPITAL: Islamabad
POPULATION: 131,541,920
MAJOR LANGUAGES: Urdu (official), English (official), Punjabi, Sindhi, Pashtu, Urdu, Balochi, and other languages
AREA: 310,414 sq mi; 803,940 sq km
LEADING EXPORTS: cotton, textiles, clothing, rice, and leather
CONTINENT: Asia

Palau

CAPITAL: Koror
POPULATION: 16,661
MAJOR LANGUAGES: English (official), Sonsorolese, Angaur, Japanese, Tobi, and Palauan
AREA: 177 sq mi; 458 sq km
LEADING EXPORTS: trochus, tuna, copra, and handicrafts
LOCATION: Pacific Ocean

Panama

CAPITAL: Panama
POPULATION: 2,680,903
MAJOR LANGUAGES: Spanish (official) and English
AREA: 30,194 sq mi; 78,200 sq km
LEADING EXPORTS: bananas, shrimp, sugar, clothing, and coffee
CONTINENT: North America

Papua New Guinea

CAPITAL: Port Moresby
POPULATION: 4,294,750
MAJOR LANGUAGES: English, pidgin English, and Motu
AREA: 178,266 sq mi; 461,690 sq km
LEADING EXPORTS: gold, copper ore, oil, logs, and palm oil
LOCATION: Pacific Ocean

Paraguay

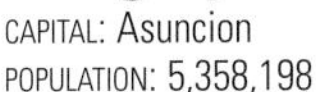

CAPITAL: Asuncion
POPULATION: 5,358,198
MAJOR LANGUAGES: Spanish (official) and Guarani
AREA: 157,052 sq mi; 406,750 sq km
LEADING EXPORTS: cotton, soybeans, timber, and vegetable oils
CONTINENT: South America

Peru

CAPITAL: Lima
POPULATION: 24,087,372
MAJOR LANGUAGES: Spanish (official), Quechua (official), and Aymara
AREA: 496,243 sq mi; 1,285,220 sq km
LEADING EXPORTS: copper, zinc, and fish meal
CONTINENT: South America

Philippines

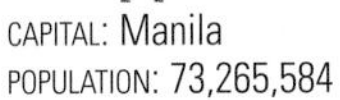

CAPITAL: Manila
POPULATION: 73,265,584
MAJOR LANGUAGES: Pilipino and English (official)
AREA: 115,834 sq mi; 300,000 sq km
LEADING EXPORTS: electronics, textiles, and coconut products
CONTINENT: Asia

Poland

CAPITAL: Warsaw
POPULATION: 38,792,442
MAJOR LANGUAGE: Polish
AREA: 120,731 sq mi; 312,680 sq km
LEADING EXPORTS: intermediate goods
CONTINENT: Europe

Portugal

CAPITAL: Lisbon
POPULATION: 10,562,388
MAJOR LANGUAGE: Portuguese
AREA: 35,553 sq mi; 92,080 sq km
LEADING EXPORTS: clothing and footwear, and machinery
CONTINENT: Europe

Qatar

CAPITAL: Doha
POPULATION: 533,916
MAJOR LANGUAGES: Arabic (official) and English
AREA: 4,247 sq mi; 11,000 sq km
LEADING EXPORTS: petroleum products, steel, and fertilizers
CONTINENT: Asia

Romania

CAPITAL: Bucharest
POPULATION: 23,198,330
MAJOR LANGUAGES: Romanian, Hungarian, and German
AREA: 91,702 sq mi; 237,500 sq km
LEADING EXPORTS: metals and metal products, and mineral products
CONTINENT: Europe

Russia

CAPITAL: Moscow
POPULATION: 149,909,089
MAJOR LANGUAGES: Russian and various languages
AREA: 6,952,996 sq mi; 17,075,200 sq km
LEADING EXPORTS: petroleum and petroleum products
CONTINENT: Europe and Asia

Rwanda

CAPITAL: Kigali
POPULATION: 8,605,307
MAJOR LANGUAGES: Kinyarwanda (official), French (official), and Kiswahili
AREA: 10,170 sq mi; 26,340 sq km
LEADING EXPORTS: coffee, tea, cassiterite, and wolframite
CONTINENT: Africa

Saint Kitts and Nevis

CAPITAL: Basseterre
POPULATION: 40,992
MAJOR LANGUAGE: English
AREA: 104 sq mi; 269 sq km
LEADING EXPORTS: machinery, food, and electronics
LOCATION: Caribbean Sea

Saint Lucia

CAPITAL: Castries
POPULATION: 156,050
MAJOR LANGUAGES: English and French patois
AREA: 239 sq mi; 620 sq km
LEADING EXPORTS: bananas, clothing, cocoa, and vegetables
LOCATION: Caribbean Sea

Saint Vincent and the Grenadines

CAPITAL: Kingstown
POPULATION: 117,344
MAJOR LANGUAGES: English and French patois
AREA: 131 sq mi; 340 sq km
LEADING EXPORTS: bananas, and eddoes and dasheen (taro)
LOCATION: Caribbean Sea

San Marino

CAPITAL: San Marino
POPULATION: 24,313
MAJOR LANGUAGE: Italian
AREA: 23 sq mi; 60 sq km
LEADING EXPORTS: building stone, lime, wood, and chestnuts
CONTINENT: Europe

Sao Tome and Principe

CAPITAL: Sao Tome
POPULATION: 140,423
MAJOR LANGUAGE: Portuguese (official)
AREA: 371 sq mi; 960 sq km
LEADING EXPORTS: cocoa, copra, coffee, and palm oil
CONTINENT: Africa

Saudi Arabia

CAPITAL: Riyadh
POPULATION: 18,729,576
MAJOR LANGUAGE: Arabic
AREA: 757,011 sq mi; 1,960,582 sq km
LEADING EXPORTS: petroleum and petroleum products
CONTINENT: Asia

Senegal

CAPITAL: Dakar
POPULATION: 9,007,080
MAJOR LANGUAGES: French (official), Wolof, Pulaar, Diola, and Mandingo
AREA: 75,752 sq mi; 196,190 sq km
LEADING EXPORTS: fish, ground nuts, and petroleum products
CONTINENT: Africa

Serbia and Montenegro

CAPITAL: Belgrade
POPULATION: 11,101,833
MAJOR LANGUAGES: Serbo-Croatian and Albanian
AREA: 39,436 sq mi; 102,350 sq km
LEADING EXPORTS: none
CONTINENT: Europe

Seychelles

CAPITAL: Victoria
POPULATION: 72,709
MAJOR LANGUAGES: English (official), French (official), and Creole
AREA: 176 sq mi; 455 sq km
LEADING EXPORTS: fish, cinnamon bark, and copra
CONTINENT: Africa

Sierra Leone

CAPITAL: Freetown
POPULATION: 4,753,120
MAJOR LANGUAGES: English (official), Mende, Temne, and Krio
AREA: 27,700 sq mi; 71,740 sq km
LEADING EXPORTS: rutile, bauxite, diamonds, coffee, and cocoa
CONTINENT: Africa

Singapore

CAPITAL: Singapore
POPULATION: 2,890,468
MAJOR LANGUAGES: Chinese, Malay, Tamil, and English
AREA: 244 sq mi; 633 sq km
LEADING EXPORTS: computer equipment
CONTINENT: Asia

Slovakia

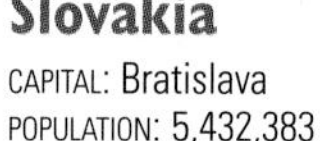

CAPITAL: Bratislava
POPULATION: 5,432,383
MAJOR LANGUAGES: Slovak and Hungarian
AREA: 18,860 sq mi; 48,845 sq km
LEADING EXPORTS: machinery and transportation equipment
CONTINENT: Europe

Slovenia

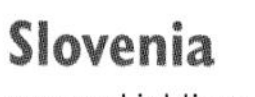

CAPITAL: Ljubljana
POPULATION: 2,051,522
MAJOR LANGUAGES: Slovenian, Serbo-Croatian, and various languages
AREA: 7,837 sq mi; 20,296 sq km
LEADING EXPORTS: machinery and transportation equipment
CONTINENT: Europe

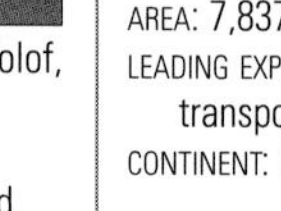

Solomon Islands

CAPITAL: Honiara
POPULATION: 399,206
MAJOR LANGUAGES: Melanesian pidgin and English
AREA: 10,985 sq mi; 28,450 sq km
LEADING EXPORTS: fish, timber, palm oil, cocoa, and copra
LOCATION: Pacific Ocean

Somalia

CAPITAL: Mogadishu
POPULATION: 7,347,554
MAJOR LANGUAGES: Somali (official), Arabic, Italian, and English
AREA: 246,210 sq mi; 637,660 sq km
LEADING EXPORTS: bananas, live animals, fish, and hides
CONTINENT: Africa

South Africa

CAPITAL: Pretoria (administrative), Cape Town (legislative), Bloemfontein (judicial)
POPULATION: 45,095,459
MAJOR LANGUAGES: Afrikaans, English, Ndebele, Pedi, Sotho, Swazi, Tsonga, Tswana, Venda, Xhosa, and Zulu (all official)
AREA: 471,027 sq mi; 1,219,912 sq km
LEADING EXPORTS: gold, other minerals and metals, and food
CONTINENT: Africa

Spain

CAPITAL: Madrid
POPULATION: 39,404,348
MAJOR LANGUAGES: Spanish, Catalan, Galician, and Basque
AREA: 194,892 sq mi; 504,750 sq km
LEADING EXPORTS: cars and trucks, and semifinished goods
CONTINENT: Europe

Sri Lanka

CAPITAL: Colombo
POPULATION: 18,342,660
MAJOR LANGUAGES: Sinhala (official) and Tamil
AREA: 25,333 sq mi; 65,610 sq km
LEADING EXPORTS: garments and textiles, teas, and diamonds
CONTINENT: Asia

Sudan

CAPITAL: Khartoum
POPULATION: 30,120,420
MAJOR LANGUAGES: Arabic (official), Nubian, Ta Bedawie, Nilotic, Nilo-Hamitic, and Sudanic dialects
AREA: 967,532 sq mi; 2,505,810 sq km
LEADING EXPORTS: gum arabic, livestock/meat, and cotton
CONTINENT: Africa

Suriname

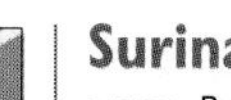

CAPITAL: Paramaribo
POPULATION: 429,544
MAJOR LANGUAGES: Dutch (official), English, Sranang, Tongo, Hindustani, and Japanese
AREA: 63,041 sq mi; 163,270 sq km
LEADING EXPORTS: alumina, aluminum, and shrimp and fish
CONTINENT: South America

Swaziland

CAPITAL: Mbabane
POPULATION: 966,977
MAJOR LANGUAGES: English (official) and SiSwati (official)
AREA: 6,641 sq mi; 17,360 sq km
LEADING EXPORTS: sugar, edible concentrates, and wood pulp
CONTINENT: Africa

Sweden

CAPITAL: Stockholm
POPULATION: 8,821,759
MAJOR LANGUAGES: Swedish, Lapp, and Finnish
AREA: 173,738 sq mi; 449,964 sq km
LEADING EXPORTS: machinery, motor vehicles, and paper products
CONTINENT: Europe

Switzerland

CAPITAL: Bern
POPULATION: 7,084,984
MAJOR LANGUAGES: German, French, Italian, Romansch, and various languages
AREA: 15,943 sq mi; 41,290 sq km
LEADING EXPORTS: machinery and equipment
CONTINENT: Europe

Syria

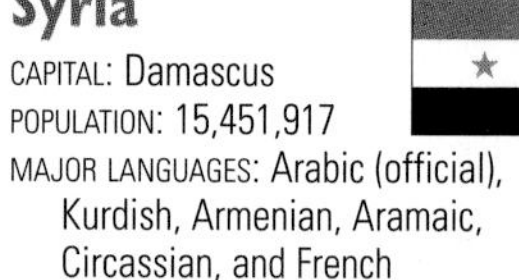

CAPITAL: Damascus
POPULATION: 15,451,917
MAJOR LANGUAGES: Arabic (official), Kurdish, Armenian, Aramaic, Circassian, and French
AREA: 71,501 sq mi; 185,180 sq km
LEADING EXPORTS: petroleum, textiles, cotton, and fruits
CONTINENT: Asia

Taiwan

CAPITAL: Taipei
POPULATION: 21,500,583
MAJOR LANGUAGES: Mandarin Chinese (official), Taiwanese, and Hakka dialects
AREA: 13,892 sq mi; 35,980 sq km
LEADING EXPORTS: electrical machinery and electronics
CONTINENT: Asia

Tajikistan

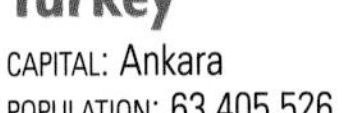

CAPITAL: Dushanbe
POPULATION: 6,155,474
MAJOR LANGUAGES: Tajik (official) and Russian
AREA: 55,253 sq mi; 143,100 sq km
LEADING EXPORTS: cotton, aluminum, fruits, and vegetable oil
CONTINENT: Asia

Tanzania

CAPITAL: Dar Es Salaam
POPULATION: 28,701,077
MAJOR LANGUAGES: Swahili, English, and various languages
AREA: 364,914 sq mi; 945,090 sq km
LEADING EXPORTS: coffee, cotton, tobacco, tea, and cashew nuts
CONTINENT: Africa

Thailand

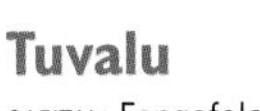

CAPITAL: Bangkok
POPULATION: 60,271,300
MAJOR LANGUAGES: Thai and English
AREA: 198,463 sq mi; 511,770 sq km
LEADING EXPORTS: machinery and manufactures
CONTINENT: Asia

Togo

CAPITAL: Lome
POPULATION: 4,410,370
MAJOR LANGUAGES: French, Ewe and Mina, Dagomba, and Kabye
AREA: 21,927 sq mi; 56,790 sq km
LEADING EXPORTS: phosphates, cotton, cocoa, and coffee
CONTINENT: Africa

Tonga

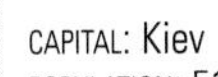

CAPITAL: Nukualofa
POPULATION: 105,600
MAJOR LANGUAGES: Tongan and English
AREA: 289 sq mi; 748 sq km
LEADING EXPORTS: squash, vanilla, fish, root crops, and coconut oil
LOCATION: Pacific Ocean

Trinidad and Tobago

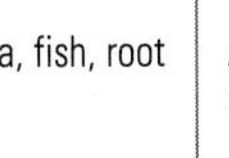
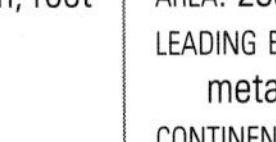

CAPITAL: Port-of-Spain
POPULATION: 1,271,159
MAJOR LANGUAGES: English, Hindu, French, and Spanish
AREA: 1,981 sq mi; 5,130 sq km
LEADING EXPORTS: petroleum and petroleum products
LOCATION: Caribbean Sea

Tunisia

CAPITAL: Tunis
POPULATION: 8,879,845
MAJOR LANGUAGES: Arabic and French
AREA: 63,172 sq mi; 163,610 sq km
LEADING EXPORTS: hydrocarbons and agricultural products
CONTINENT: Africa

Turkey

CAPITAL: Ankara
POPULATION: 63,405,526
MAJOR LANGUAGES: Turkish, Kurdish, and Arabic
AREA: 301,394 sq mi; 780,580 sq km
LEADING EXPORTS: manufactured products, and foodstuffs
CONTINENT: Europe and Asia

Turkmenistan

CAPITAL: Ashgabat
POPULATION: 4,075,316
MAJOR LANGUAGES: Turkmen, Russian, Uzbek, and various languages
AREA: 188,463 sq mi; 488,100 sq km
LEADING EXPORTS: natural gas, cotton, and petroleum products
CONTINENT: Asia

Tuvalu

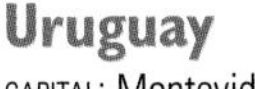

CAPITAL: Fongafale, on Funafuti atoll
POPULATION: 9,991
MAJOR LANGUAGES: Tuvaluan and English
AREA: 10 sq mi; 26 sq km
LEADING EXPORT: copra
LOCATION: Pacific Ocean

Uganda

CAPITAL: Kampala
POPULATION: 19,573,262
MAJOR LANGUAGES: English, Luganda, Swahili, Bantu languages, and Nilotic languages
AREA: 91,139 sq mi; 236,040 sq km
LEADING EXPORTS: coffee, cotton, and tea
CONTINENT: Africa

Ukraine

CAPITAL: Kiev
POPULATION: 51,867,828
MAJOR LANGUAGES: Ukranian, Russian, Romanian, Polish, and Hungarian
AREA: 233,098 sq mi; 603,700 sq km
LEADING EXPORTS: coal, electric power, and metals
CONTINENT: Europe

United Arab Emirates

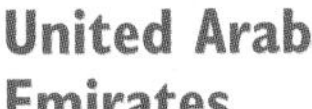

CAPITAL: Abu Dhabi
POPULATION: 2,924,594
MAJOR LANGUAGES: Arabic, Persian, English, Hindi, and Urdu
AREA: 29,183 sq mi; 75,581 sq km
LEADING EXPORTS: crude oil, natural gas, re-exports, and dried fish
CONTINENT: Asia

United Kingdom

CAPITAL: London
POPULATION: 58,295,119
MAJOR LANGUAGES: English, Welsh, and Scottish Gaelic
AREA: 94,529 sq mi; 244,820 sq km
LEADING EXPORTS: manufactured goods, machinery, and fuels
CONTINENT: Europe

United States

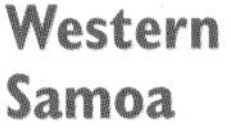

CAPITAL: Washington, D.C.
POPULATION: 263,814,032
MAJOR LANGUAGES: English and Spanish
AREA: 3,618,908 sq mi; 9,372,610 sq km
LEADING EXPORTS: capital goods and automobiles
CONTINENT: North America

Uruguay

CAPITAL: Montevideo
POPULATION: 3,222,716
MAJOR LANGUAGES: Spanish and Brazilero
AREA: 68,041 sq mi; 176,220 sq km
LEADING EXPORTS: wool and textile manufactures
CONTINENT: South America

Uzbekistan

CAPITAL: Tashkent
POPULATION: 23,089,261
MAJOR LANGUAGES: Uzbek, Russian, Tajik, various languages
AREA: 172,748 sq mi; 447,400 sq km
LEADING EXPORTS: cotton, gold, natural gas, and minerals
CONTINENT: Asia

Vanuatu

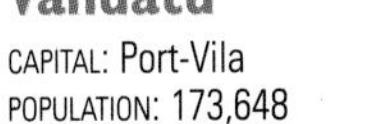

CAPITAL: Port-Vila
POPULATION: 173,648
MAJOR LANGUAGES: English, French, pidgin, and Bislama
AREA: 5,699 sq mi; 14,760 sq km
LEADING EXPORTS: copra, beef, cocoa, timber, and coffee
LOCATION: Pacific Ocean

Venezuela

CAPITAL: Caracas
POPULATION: 21,004,773
MAJOR LANGUAGES: Spanish and various languages
AREA: 352,156 sq mi; 912,050 sq km
LEADING EXPORTS: petroleum, bauxite and aluminum, and steel
CONTINENT: South America

Vietnam

CAPITAL: Hanoi
POPULATION: 74,393,324
MAJOR LANGUAGES: Vietnamese, French, Chinese, English, Khmer, and various languages
AREA: 127,248 sq mi; 329,560 sq km
LEADING EXPORTS: petroleum, rice, and agricultural products
CONTINENT: Asia

Western Samoa

CAPITAL: Apia
POPULATION: 209,360
MAJOR LANGUAGES: Samoan and English
AREA: 1,104 sq mi; 2,860 sq km
LEADING EXPORTS: coconut oil and cream, taro, copra, and cocoa
LOCATION: Pacific Ocean

Yemen

CAPITAL: Sanaa
POPULATION: 14,728,474
MAJOR LANGUAGE: Arabic
AREA: 203,857 sq mi; 527,970 sq km
LEADING EXPORTS: crude oil, cotton, coffee, hides, and vegetables
CONTINENT: Asia

Zaire (Democratic Republic of Congo)

CAPITAL: Kinshasa
POPULATION: 44,060,636
MAJOR LANGUAGES: French, Lingala, Swahili, Kingwana, Kikongo, and Tshiluba
AREA: 905,599 sq mi; 2,345,410 sq km
LEADING EXPORTS: copper, coffee, diamonds, cobalt, and crude oil
CONTINENT: Africa

Zambia

CAPITAL: Lusaka
POPULATION: 9,445,723
MAJOR LANGUAGES: English (official) and about 70 various languages
AREA: 290,594 sq mi; 752,610 sq km
LEADING EXPORTS: copper, zinc, cobalt, lead, and tobacco
CONTINENT: Africa

Zimbabwe

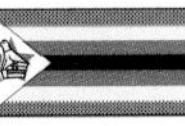

CAPITAL: Harare
POPULATION: 11,139,961
MAJOR LANGUAGES: English, Shona, and Sindebele
area: 150,809 sq mi; 390,580 sq km
LEADING EXPORTS: agricultural products and manufactures
CONTINENT: Africa

Glossary of Geographic Terms

basin
a depression in the surface of the land; some basins are filled with water

bay
a part of a sea or lake that extends into the land

butte
a small raised area of land with steep sides

▲ butte

canyon
a deep, narrow valley with steep sides; often has a stream flowing through it

cataract
a large waterfall; any strong flood or rush of water

◀ cataract

delta
a triangular-shaped plain at the mouth of a river, formed when sediment is deposited by flowing water

flood plain
a broad plain on either side of a river, formed when sediment settles on the riverbanks

glacier
a huge, slow-moving mass of snow and ice

hill
an area that rises above surrounding land and has a rounded top; lower and usually less steep than a mountain

island
an area of land completely surrounded by water

isthmus
a narrow strip of land that connects two larger areas of land

mesa
a high, flat-topped landform with cliff-like sides; larger than a butte

mountain
an area that rises steeply at least 2,000 feet (300 m) above surrounding land; usually wide at the bottom and rising to a narrow peak or ridge

▶ glacier

◀ delta

mountain pass
a gap between mountains

peninsula
an area of land almost completely surrounded by water and connected to the mainland by an isthmus

plain
a large area of flat or gently rolling land

plateau
a large, flat area that rises above the surrounding land; at least one side has a steep slope

river mouth
the point where a river enters a lake or sea

strait
a narrow stretch of water that connects two larger bodies of water

tributary
a river or stream that flows into a larger river

volcano
an opening in the Earth's surface through which molten rock, ashes, and gasses from the Earth's interior escape

▶ volcano

Gazetteer

A

Amazon Rain Forest a large tropical rain forest occupying the drainage basin of the Amazon River in northern South America and covering an area of 2,700,000 square miles, p. 19

Andes Mountains (13°S, 75°W) a mountain system extending along the western coast of South America, p. 8

Argentina (35.3°S, 67°W) a country in South America, p. 12

Atacama Desert (23.5°S, 69°W) a desert in Chile, South America; the driest place on the Earth, p. 14

B

Bolivia (17°S, 64°W) a country in South America, p. 3

Brasília (15.49°S, 47.39°W) the capital city of Brazil, p. 76

Brazil (9°S, 53°W) the largest country in South America, p. 12

C

Canal Zone a 10-mile strip of land along the Panama Canal, stretching from the Atlantic Ocean to the Pacific Ocean, p. 101

Caracas (10.3°N, 66.58°W) the capital city of Venezuela, p. 148

Caribbean (14.3°N, 75.3°W) a part of the southern Atlantic Ocean, p. 9

Central America (10.45°N, 87.15°W) the part of Latin America that includes the seven republics of Guatemala, Honduras, El Salvador, Nicaragua, Costa Rica, Panama, and Belize, p. 9

Chile (35°S, 72°W) a country in South America, p. 14

Colombia (3.3°N, 72.3°W) a country in South America, p. 25

Condado a waterfront area of San Juan, Puerto Rico, p. 123

Copán (14.5°N, 89.1°W) a ruined ancient Mayan city in western Honduras, p. 36

Cuba (22°N, 79°W) an island country, the largest of the Caribbean islands, p. 11

Cuzco (13.36°S, 71.52°W) a city in Peru; capital of the Incan empire, p. 39

G

Guatemala (15.45°N, 91.45°W) a country in Central America, p. 36

H

Haiti (19°N, 72.15°W) a country in the Caribbean Sea, on the island of Hispaniola, p. 50

Hispaniola (17.3°N, 73.15°W) an island in the Caribbean Sea, divided between Haiti in the west and the Dominican Republic in the east, p. 11

J

Jamaica (17.45°N, 78°W) an island country in the Caribbean Sea, p. 11

L

Lake Maracaibo (9.55°N, 72.13°W) a lake in northwestern Venezuela, p. 13

Lake Titicaca (16.12° S, 70.33° W) the world's largest lake, in the Andes Mountains in South America, p. 13

M

Mexico (23.45°N, 104°W) a country in North America, p. 9

Mexico City (19.28°N, 99.09°W) the capital of and largest city in Mexico; one of the largest urban areas in the world, p. 36

Miami (25.45°N, 80.11°W) a city in southeastern Florida, p. 107

P

Panama (9°N, 80°W) a country in Central America, p. 53

Panama Canal (9.2°N, 79.55°W) an important shipping canal across the Isthmus of Panama, linking the Caribbean Sea (and the Atlantic Ocean) to the Pacific Ocean, p. 96

Paraguay (24°S, 57°W) a country in South America, p. 3

Patagonia (46.45°S, 69.3°W) a desert in southern Argentina; the largest desert in the Americas, p. 17

Peru (10°S, 75°W) a country in South America, p. 13

Port-au-Prince (18.35°N, 72.2°W) the capital city and chief port of Haiti, p. 113

Puerto Rico (18.16°N, 66.5°W) an island commonwealth of the United States in the Caribbean Sea, p. 11

R

Rio de Janeiro (22.5°S, 43.2°W) a major city in Brazil, p. 129

S

Salvador (12.59°S, 38.27°W) the capital city and major port of Bahia state, in northeastern Brazil, p. 130

San Juan (18.3°N, 66.10°W) the capital and largest city in Puerto Rico, p. 123

Santiago (33.26°S, 70.4°W) the capital city of Chile, p. 142

São Paulo (23.34°S, 46.38°W) the largest city in Brazil, p. 74

South America (15°S, 60°W) the world's fourth-largest continent, bounded by the Caribbean Sea, the Atlantic Ocean, and the Pacific Ocean, and linked to North America by the Isthmus of Panama, p. 9

T

Tenochtitlán Aztec metropolis covering more than five square miles near modern Mexico City; originally located on two small islands in Lake Texcoco, it gradually grew; one of two Aztec capitals, its name means "stone rising in the water," p. 37

Tikal (17.16°N, 89.49°W) the largest Mayan city in the northern part of Guatemala, p. 36

Trinidad and Tobago (11°N, 61°W) republic of the West Indies, on the two islands called Trinidad and Tobago, p. 3

V

Valley of Mexico the area in Mexico where Lake Texcoco, Tenochtitlán, and modern Mexico City are located, p. 36

Venezuela (8°N, 65°W) a country in South America, p. 12

W

West Indies (19°N, 78°W) the islands of the Caribbean, p. 3

Glossary

A

altiplano [al tih PLAH noh] a high plateau region; a region of high plateaus in the Andes, p. 135

aqueduct a pipe or channel used to carry water from a distant source to dry areas, p. 41

B

boom a period of increased prosperity an economic activity when more of a product is produced and sold, p. 149

C

campesino [kahm pe SEE noh] a poor Latin American farmer, p. 58

canopy a dense mass of leaves forming the top layer of a forest, p.129

Carnival an annual celebration in Latin America with music, dances, and parades, p. 72

caudillo [kow DEE yoh] a military officer who rules strictly, p. 54

citizen an individual with certain rights and responsibilities under a particular government, p. 121

commonwealth a self-governing political unit with strong ties to a particular country, p. 121

communist having an economic system in which the government owns all large businesses and most of a country's land, p. 109

conquistador [kon KEES ta dor] 16th-century conquerors working for the Spanish government who were in charge of gaining land and wealth in the Americas, p. 44

constitution a statement of a country's basic laws and values, p. 123

coral a rock-like substance formed from the skeletons of tiny sea animals, p. 11

Creole a person, often of European and African descent, born in the Caribbean or other parts of the Americas, whose culture has strong French and African influence; a dialect spoken by Creoles, p. 115

criollo [kree OH yoh] a person born of Spanish parents born outside Spain; often among the best-educated and wealthiest people in the Spanish colonies, p. 50

D

dialect a version of a language that is spoken in a particular region, p. 115

dictator a ruler of a country who has complete power, p. 109

diversify to add variety; to expand, p. 27

diversity variety, p. 64

E

economy the ways that goods and services are produced and made available to people, p. 55

elevation height of land above sea level, p. 17

El Niño [el NEEN yoh] a warm ocean current that flows along the western coast of South America; this current influences global weather patterns, p. 14

emigrate move out of one country into another, p. 67

encomienda [en KOH mee en duh] a right that was granted by the Spanish government to its settlers in the Americas to demand taxes or labor from Native Americans, p. 47

ethnic group group of people who share language, religion, and cultural traditions, pp. 70, 92

exile a person who leaves or is forced to leave his or her homeland for another country because of political reasons, p. 110

H

hacienda [hah see EN duh] plantation owned by the Spanish settlers or the Catholic Church in Spanish America, p. 47

hieroglyphics [hy ur oh GLIF iks] a system of writing using signs and symbols, used by the Maya and other cultures, p. 36

hydroelectricity [hy droh ee lek TRIS ih tee] electricity produced by rushing water, p. 23

I

illiterate unable to read or write, p. 112

immigrant a person who has moved into one country from another, p. 67

import to bring products into one country from another to sell, p. 76

indigenous [in DIJ uh nus] describes people who are descendants of the people who first lived in a region, p. 64

injustice lack of fairness, p. 65

invest to spend money to earn more money, p. 55

isthmus narrow strip of land that has water on both sides and joins two larger bodies of land, p. 11

L

ladino [luh DEE noh] in Guatemala, a mestizo, p. 90

Line of Demarcation an imaginary line from the North Pole to the South Pole (at about 50° longitude) set forth in the 1494 Treaty of Tordesillas; Spain had the right to settle and trade west of the line and Portugal had the right to settle and trade east of the line, p. 44

lock a section of waterway in which ships are raised or lowered by adjusting the water level, p. 96

M

maize both the plant and the kernel of corn, p. 36

maquiladora [ma kee la DOR a] a U.S.-owned factory in Mexico that is located close to the U.S.-Mexico border, p. 66

mestizo a person of mixed Spanish and Native American ancestry, p. 46

migrant farmworker a laborer who travels from one area to another, picking crops that are in season, p. 86

montaña in northeast Peru, large stretches of tropical forests on the lower slopes of mountains, p. 136

P

pampas [PAHM puhs] flat grassland regions in the southern part of South America; a region similar to the Great Plains in the United States, p.12

pesticide [PES tuh syd] a chemical used to kill insects and diseases that can attack crops, p. 147

photosynthesis [foht oh SIN thuh sis] the process by which green plants and trees produce their own food using water, carbon dioxide, and sunlight; oxygen is released as a result of photosynthesis, p. 133

plateau [pla TOH] large raised area of mostly level land, p. 11

plaza public square at the center of a village, town, or city, p. 85

privatization [pry vuh tih ZAY shun] a policy by a government to sell its industries to individuals or private companies, p. 152

Q

quipu [KEE poo] a knotted string used by Incan government officials and traders for record keeping, p. 41

R

revolution a political movement in which people overthrow the existing government and set up another, p. 50

rural having to do with the countryside, p. 59

S

sierra a group of mountains, such as the one that runs from northwest to southeast Peru, p. 136

squatter a person who settles on someone else's land without permission, p. 84

strike work stoppage; a refusal to continue to work until certain demands of workers are met, p. 93

subsistence farming the practice of growing only as much food as a group of people needs to survive, p. 75

T

treaty an agreement in writing made between two or more countries, p. 44

Treaty of Tordesillas [tor day SEE yas] the 1494 treaty setting up the Line of Demarcation, giving Spain the right to settle and trade west of the line and Portugal the same rights east of the line, p. 44

tributary [TRIB yoo tehr ee] river or stream that flows into a main river, p. 13

tundra a cold region with little vegetation; in mountains, the area above the tree line, p. 138

U

urban having to do with cities, p. 59

The *italicized* page numbers refer to illustrations. The *m, c, p,* or *t* preceding the number refers to maps *(m)*, charts *(c)*, pictures *(p)*, or tables *(t)*.

Index

A

Activity Atlas, 2–7
Activity Shop: Interdisciplinary, 156–157; Lab, 104–105
Africans: in Brazil, 74, 130–131; culture in the Caribbean, 70; enslavement of, 69, 113–114, 130–131; in Haiti, 113–114; language of, 70, 115; heritage in Peru, 137; heritage in Puerto Rico, 122; religion of, 70
agriculture: in Chile, 142, 147
altiplano, 135; Andes, 135; life in cities and towns of the, 137–138
Amazon River, 13, *p 13*
Amazon River Basin, 12; climate of, 14; rain forest in, 12
Andean countries, 74
Andes Mountains, 8, *p 8*, 9, 12, 14, 39, 73, 74, 143–144, 145; altiplano, 135; climate of, 14; farming in, 12; Native Americans in, 73–74; soil in, 12
aqueduct, 41
Arawaks, 69
Argentina, *m 15, m 18*, 25, 40, 53, 74, 75, *m 128*; climate of, *m 15*, 17; farming in, 75; natural vegetation of, *m 18*; Pampas in, 12, 74
Aristide, Jean-Bertrand, 113, 116, 117
Asians: culture in the Caribbean, 70; heritage in Peru, 137
Atacama Desert, 144; climate of, 14, 19; copper in, 144; natural vegetation of, 19
Atlantic Ocean, 13, 43, 96
Aymara, 74, 135, 138, 139; Lake Titicaca, 135, 139; tortora reeds, 135, 139
Aztec civilization, *m 34*, 36–38, *c 36*; accomplishments of, 38; beginnings of, 36–37; rulers of, 45; social structure of, 38; Tenochtitlán, 37

B

Batista, Fulgencio, 109
Belize, *m 15, m 18*, 36; language of, 64
Bolívar, Simón, 52–54
Bolivia, *m 15, m 18*, 40, 42, 73, 74, *m 128*; altiplano of, 135; economy of, 22; natural resources of, 22
boom, 149
Boricuas (Boriqueno), 122
Brasília, Brazil, *p 76*, 77, 132, *c 133*
Brazil, 12, 13, *m 15, m 18*, 25, *p 25*, 44, 54, 74, *m 128*, 129–134; ancestry of, 130; Cerrado of, 132; climate of, *m 15*, 16; coffee plantations in, 131; coffee production in, 25, 131; Country Profile of, 130; diversification in, 27, 131; economy of, 27, 131, 132; enslavement of Africans in, 74, 130–131; factories in, 131; farming in, 131, 134; geography of, 129; government in, 132, 133–134; industry in, 27, 132; land in, 58, 129, 134; language of, 44, 74; Native Americans in, 74, 129, 130, 132; natural vegetation of, *m 18*; people of, 129, 130; rain forests of, 58–59, 129–134; resources of, 129; urbanization in, 131; Yanomamo in, 132
Buenos Aires, Argentina, 77

C

campesino, 58, 59
canopy, 129
Caracas, Venezuela, 148; subway in, 148
Caribbean, 9, *m 10*, 11, 23, 68–72, 74, 106–125, *m 106*; Carnival in, 72; climate of, 16, *p 16*; culture in, 68–72, *c 69*; Europeans in, 69; farming in, 23, 68; food and music in, 71; landforms of, 9, 11; languages of, 70; migration from other countries to, 70; name origination, 69; natural resources of, 23, *m 24*; people of, 68–70; and Puerto Rico, 122; religion in the, 70, 72
Caribs, 69
Carnival, 72
Castro, Fidel, 107, 109, 112; Cuba's education system, 112
Catholicism: in the Caribbean, 72; in Mexico and Central America, 65; Roman Catholic Church, 64–65; in South America, 73
caudillo, 54
Central America, *m 10*, 11, 35, 63, 82, *m 82*, 89–101; Aztec civilization in, 36–38; culture in, 63–65; employment in, 66, 67; farming in, 11, 23, 86; hydroelectricity in, 23; landforms of, 9, 10–11; languages of, 64; location of, 10–11; Mayan civilization in, 35–36; and Mexico, 9, 10–11, 23, 35, 36, 63–65, 66, 67, 82, *m 82*, 86; natural resources of, 23, *m 24*; natural vegetation of, 21; population of, 66; religion in, 64–65; urbanization in, 66–67
Cerrado, 132
charts: Caribbean customs, 69; climate regions, 178; elevation, 17; natural vegetation regions, 179; oil imported in Venezuela, 151; population growth, 65; population of Puerto Rico, 122; precipitation and rainfall in Brasília and Manaus, Brazil, 133; time line, 36; urban versus rural, 83
Chile, *m 15, m 18*, 40, 74, 75, *m 128*, 142–147; agriculture in, 142, 147; ancestry of, 144; Andes in, 143–144, 145; Atacama Desert in, 14, 19, 144; climate of, 14, 144; Country Profile of, 143; copper in, 26, 144, 145–147; descendants of Incas in, 42; economy of, 26, 142, 145–147; environment in, 146; and Europe, 147; exports of, 142, 144, 145, 147; farming and crops in, 75, 143, 144, 147; geography of, 143–144; government in, 143, 146; independence in, 53; industry in, 146; and Japan, 147; lifestyles of people in, 144; Native Americans in, 144; people of, 144; pesticide, 147; pollution in, 146; Spanish influence on, 144; and United States, 147
Chimbote, Peru, 136
China: migration to the Caribbean, 70
Christianity, 64, 65, 70
Ciboney, 69
citizen, 121
climate, 14–19, *m 15, p 16, m 20, c 178*; in the Amazon River Basin, 14; in the Andes Mountains, 14; in the Atacama Desert, 14; and elevation, 17, *c 17*, 19; El Niño, 14; Equator, 17; hurricanes, 16; of Latin America, 16–17; Patagonia, 17; regions, 16, *c 178*; in the Sonoran Desert, 14; wind patterns, 19
coastal plain, 136
coffee: plantations, 114, 131; production, 25, 131
Colombia, *m 15, m 18*, 42, 53, 74, 98–99, *m 128*; coffee, 25
Colón, 97
Colonia Zapata, 84
Columbus, Christopher, 43–44, 69
commonwealth, 121
communist, 109
Condado, 123
conquistador, 44–45, 137
constitution, 123
Copán, Honduras, 36
copper: in Chile, 26, 144, 145–147
coral, 11
Cortés, Hernán, 43, 45
Costa Rica, *m 15, m 18*, 64
Country Profile: of Brazil, 130; of Chile, 143; of Cuba, 108; of Guatemala, 90; of Haiti, 114; of Mexico, 84; of Panama, 97; of Peru, 136; of Puerto Rico, 121; of Venezuela, 149
Creole: culture, 115; dialect, 115; language, 70; traditions, 117
criollo, 50–51
"Cry of Dolores," 51
Cuba, 11, *m 15, m 18*, 70, *m 106*, 107–112; communism in, 109; Country Profile of, 108; economy of, 107, 108; education system/literacy, 112; exiles from, 110; farming in, 107; government in, 108–109; independence in, 108; location of, 108; nickel in, 23; reasons for leaving, 107; sugar production in, 107, 108; and Soviet Union, 109, 111; and trade, 108–109; and United States, 108–109, 111
culture: in the Caribbean, 68–72; in Central America, 63–65; in Latin America, 62; in Mexico, 63–65; in South America, 73–77
Cuzco, Peru, 39, 40, 46; Incas in, 137; Spanish influences on, 137

D

deserts: Atacama, 14, 19, 144; Sonoran, 14, *p 14*
dialect, 115
dictator, 109; of Cuba, 109; of Haiti, 114–115
diversify, 27, 131, 152
diversity, 64
Dominica, 69
Dominican Republic, *m 15, m 18*, 70, *m 106*; language of, 70; sugar cane in, *p 16*
Dom Pedro, 54
Doña Marina. *See* Malinche
Dutch colonists, 69
Duvalier, François ("Papa Doc"), 114
Duvalier, Jean-Claude ("Baby Doc"), 115

E

economy, 55; in Bolivia, 22; in Brazil, 27, 131, 132; in Chile, 26, 142, 145–147; in Latin America, 25–27, 55–59
Ecuador, *m 15, m 18*, 42, 53, 74, *m 128*; economy of, 27; oil in, 27; education, 85, 112
elevation, 17, *c 17*, 19
El Niño, 14

El Salvador, *m 15*, *m 18*, 36; economy of, 27; farming in, *p 58;* language of, 64
emigrate, 67
***encomienda* system,** 47
English colonists, 69
environment, 59; in Brazil, 129–134; in Chile, 146. *See also* rain forest
Equator, 17
ethnic group, 70, 92
Europe: and Chile, 147
Europeans: in the Americas, 43–47; conquerors, 43–46; culture in the Caribbean, 70; heritage in Brazil, 74, 130; heritage in Haiti, 114; heritage in Peru, 137; language, 70
exile, 110

F

farming, 36; in the Andes, 12; in Brazil, 131, 134; in Chile, 144, 147; in the Caribbean, *p 16*, 23, 68; in Central America, 11, 23, 86; and the Incas, 39, 41; in Latin America, 26, 58; in Mexico, *p 11*, *p 55*, 83, 86; modern methods in, 147; in the rain forest, 58, 134; in South America, 17, 25, 75–76; subsistence, 75
foreign debt, 56, *t 56*
foreign investment, 55–56; limitations of, 57
French Guiana, *m 15*, *m 18*, *m 128*
French: colonies, 114; colonists, 69; language, 10, 70, 115

G

Galliard Cut, 97
gauchos, 74
gold mining: in Brazil's rain forest, 134
Gran Colombia, 53, 54
Guatemala, *m 15*, *m 18*, *m 82*, 89–93; civil war in, 91; Country Profile of, 90; fight against injustice, 92; ladino, 90; landowners of, 90, 91; land rights in, 92–93; languages of, 64, 89; location of, 89; Mayas in, 36; Native Americans in, 90–93; peace in, 93; people of, 64; population of, 89, 92
Gulf of Mexico, 108
Guyana, 12, *m 15*, *m 18*, 74, *m 128*

H

hacienda, 47
Haiti, *m 15*, *m 18*, 50, *m 106*, 113–117; Country Profile of, 114; Creole, 115, 117; culture in, 115; democracy in, 113; enslavement of Africans in, 50, 113–114; farming in, 115; language of, 70; L'Ouverture, Toussaint, 50, 114; military, 116; Night of Fire in, 50; revolution in, 50, 113; sugar cane and coffee plantations in, 114; and United States, 113, 116–117
Hidalgo, Miguel, 51
hieroglyphics, 36
Hindus, 70
Hispañiola, 11, 70, 114
Honduras, *m 15*, *m 18*, 36, 63, 64
hydroelectricity, 13, 23, *p 25*
hydroelectric plants, *m 6*

I

illiterate, 112
immigrant, 67
import, 76
Incan empire, *m 34*, 39–42, *c 36*; accomplishments of, 40; beginnings of, 39; Cuzco, Peru, 39, 40, 46, 137; farming in, 39, 41, 42, *p 42*; government and records of, 41; Incan culture today, 42; language of, 42; religion in, 41; roads in, 40; rulers of, 39–40; Spanish conquest of, 42
independence, 50–54; challenges of, 54; in Mexico, 50–52; in South America, 52–54, *m 52*
India: migration to the Caribbean, 70
indigenous, 64
injustice, 65
invest, 55
islands: formation of the Caribbean, 11
isthmus, 11, 63
Iturbide, Agustín de, 52

J

Jamaica, 11, *m 15*, *m 18*, 23, 68
Japan: and Chile, 147
Japanese: in São Paulo, Brazil, 74
Jewish people, 70

K

Kingston, Jamaica, 68

L

ladino, 90
Lake Maracaibo, 13, 149
Lake Texcoco, 37
Lake Titicaca, 13, 39, 73, 135, 139; altiplano, 135; Aymara, 135, 139; Tribuna, 135
land: in Latin America, 57–58
landforms, *m 4*, 9–12, 177; of the Caribbean, 9, 11; of Central America, 9, 10–11; of Mexico, 9, 10–11; of South America, 9, 12
languages: Creole, 70; English, 64; French, 10, 70, 115; Latin, 10; Portuguese, 10, 44, 74; Quechua, 42, 74; Quiche, 89; Spanglish, 122; Spanish, 10, 64, 70, 73, 125, 148
Latin America, 9, 10, *m 10*; climate regions of, 14, *m 15*, 16–17, *m 20*, *c 178*; cultures in, 62–77; current issues in, 55–59; economy in, 25–27, 55–59; farming in, 26, 58; foreign investment in, 55–56, 57; history of, 34–59; hydroelectric plants in, *m 6*; land in, 57–58; landforms of, 9, 10; languages of, 10; location of, *m 2*, 9; name origination, 10; natural resources of, 22, *m 24*; natural vegetation regions of, *m 5*, *m 18*, *c 179*; new industries in, 57; oil in, 23, 25, 27, 56, 148–153; physical features of, *m 4;* physical geography of, 8–27; project possibilities, 160–161; rivers and lakes in, 12–13; trade in, 57; urbanization in, 59
latitude, 169
Lima, Peru, 46, 53, 77, 136, 137; Pizarro, Francisco, 137; Spanish influence on, 137
Limón Bay, 97
Line of Demarcation, 44, *m 44*
literature, 30–33, 158–159
lock, 96–97, 104–105
longitude, 169
L'Ouverture, Toussaint, 50, 114; slavery, 114

M

maize, 36
Malinche (Doña Marina), 43
Manaus, Brazil, *c 133*
maps: of ancient civilizations, 34; of the Caribbean, 106; of Central America, 82; of climate regions in Latin America, 15, 20; of empires, 46; of hydroelectric plants in Latin America, 6; of location of Latin America, 2; of Mexico, 82, 84; of Mexico City, 82; of natural resources, 24; of natural vegetation regions of Latin America, 5, 18; of physical features (landforms) of Latin America, 4; of regions, 10; of South America, 128; of South American independence, 52; of Spanish conquest, 44
maps and globes, 163–179; comparing maps of different scale, 173; five themes of geography, 164–165; landforms, climate regions, and natural vegetation regions, 177–179; locating places on a map or a globe, 168–169; maps and globes represent the Earth, 167; map projections, 170–171; parts of a map, 172; physical maps, 175; political maps, 174; special purpose maps, 176; understanding movements of the Earth, 166
maquiladora, 66
Mayan civilization, *m 34*, 35–36, *c 36*; accomplishments of, 36; beginnings of, 35–36; disappearance of, 36; farming in, 36; hieroglyphics, 36; religion in, 36
Mayas, 89, 91–93; land rights of, 92–93; language of, 89
Menchú, Rigoberta, 89–93; fighting against injustice, 92–93; Quiché Maya, 92; Nobel Peace Prize, 93
mestizo, 46–47, 64, 74, 137, 144
Mexican Plateau, 83
Mexico, *m 10*, 11, *p 11*, 14, 35, 50–52, 63–65, 82, *m 82*, 83–88; Aztec civilization in, 36–38; and Central America, 9, 10–11, 23, 35, 36, 63–65, 66, 67, 82, *m 82*, 86; Central Plateau of, 11; city life in, 66–67; climate of, 16; Country Profile of, 84; culture in, 63–65; employment in, 66–67, 85, 87; farming in, *p 11*, 83, 86; housing in, 84; independence in, 50–52; landforms of, 9, 10–11; language of, 64; location of, 10; Mayan civilization in, 35–36; natural resources of, 23, *m 24*; oil in, 27; population growth in, c 65, 66, 83, 86; and United States, 66, 67; religion in, 64–65; rural life in, 85–86; school in, 85; unemployment in, 86; urbanization in, 66, 67, 83–88; vegetation of, 21
Mexico City, Mexico, 36, 37, 46, 83, *m 82*, 86–88, *m 87*; employment in, 87; pollution in, 87
Middle America, 36
Middle East: migration to the Caribbean, 70
migrant farmworker, 86
Miraflores Lock, 96
Moctezuma, 45
montaña, 137
mountains: Andes, 8, *p 8*, 9, 12, 14, 39, 73, 74, 143–144, 145
Muslims, 70

N

Native Americans: in the Andes, 73–74; in Brazil, 74, 129, 130, 132; in Chile, 144; culture in the Caribbean, 70; in Guatemala, 90–93; in Mexico, 51; in Peru, 47, 137, 139; in the rain forest, 59; in South America, 73

natural resources, 22–27, *m 24*; of Bolivia, 22, *m 24*; of the Caribbean, 23, *m 24*; of Central America, 23, *m 24*; of Cuba, 23, *m 24*; land, 57–58; of Mexico, 23, *m 24*; oil, 23, 25, 27, 148–153; of the rain forest, 129, 132–134, 156–157; rivers and lakes, 13; of South America, 25; of Venezuela, 25, 27, 148–153, *c 151*
natural vegetation, *m 5*, 14–19, *m 18*, *c 179*; in the Atacama Desert, 19; and elevation, *c 17*, 19
New Spain, 46, 47
Nicaragua, *m 15*, *m 18*, 64; language, 64
nickel, 23

O

oil, 23, 148–153; in Ecuador, 27; in Latin America, 56; in Mexico, 27; prices, 56; in Veneuezla, 25, 27, 148–153, *c 151*
Orinoco River, 13

P

Pachacuti, 39–40
Pacific Ocean, 39, 96
pampas, 12, *p 12*, 74
Panama, *m 15*, *m 18*, 53, *m 82*, 96–101; Country Profile of, 97; language of, 64; Panama Canal in, 96–101, *m 98*; revolt in, 99; and United States, 99, 101
Panama Canal, 96–101, *m 98*; Canal Zone, 101; change of ownership of, 101; lab activity shop, 104–105; locks, 96–97; malaria, 99, 100–101; Panama Canal Company, 100; problems in building, 98–101; rights to build canal, 98–99, 101; United States rights to canal, 99, 101
Panama Canal Company, 100
Paraguay, *m 15*, *m 18*, *p 25*, *m 128*; climate of, *m 15*, 17
Paraguay River, 13
Paraná River, 13; hydroelectric power of, *p 25*
Patagonia, 17
Peru, 13, *m 15*, *m 18*, 26, 39, 40, 46, 73, 74, 77, *m 128*, 135–139; altiplano in, 135, 137–138; ancestry of, 137; Aymara in, 135, 138, 139; change in, 139; climate of, 136–137; coastal plain in, 136; Country Profile of, 136; descendants of Incas in, 42; geographic regions of, 136–137; montaña in, 137; Native Americans in, 47, 137, 139; people of, 137; Quechua in, 42, 137–138, 139; rural areas in, 138; sierra in, 136; tundra in, 138; urbanization in, 139
pesticide, 147; and Chile's crops, 147
photosynthesis, 133
Pizarro, Francisco, 45–46, 137; Lima, Peru, 137
plateau, 11
plaza, 85
population: growth in Latin America, 59; in the United States and Mexico, *c 65*
Port-au-Prince, Haiti, 113, 116
Portugal, 43–44, 54, 74; empire, *m 46*
Portuguese language, 10, 44, 74
Prince Ferdinand, 52–53
privatization, 152
project possibilities, 160–161
Puerto Rico, 11, *m 15*, *m 18*, *m 106*, 120–125; ancestry of, 122; and becoming a state, 124–125; cities in, 123; citizens, 121; Condado, 123; constitution of, 123; Country Profile of, 121; culture in, 122; farming in, 123; independence of, 125; population of, *c 122*, 123; Spanglish, 122; status of, 121; sugar cane in, 123; and United States, 121, 122, 124–125

Q

Quechua: language, 42, 74; people, 42, 74, 137–138, 139
Quiche language, 89
quipu, 41, *p 41*
Quito, Ecuador, 40

R

rain forest, 12, 129–134; climate of the, 16, 19; dangers to the, 133–134; farming in the, 58–59, 134; gold mining in the, 134; laws to protect the, 134; importance to Brazil's economy, 132; interdisciplinary activity shop, 156–157; Native Americans in the, 59; natural vegetation in the, 19; oxygen in the, 132; pollution in the, 134; resources of the, 132, 133; smuggling in the, 134; water, 133; worldwide impact, 132
read actively, vii–ix
religion: in the Caribbean, 70, 72; in Mexico and Central America, 64–65; in South America, 73
revolution, 50; in Haiti, 50, 113
Rio de Janeiro, Brazil, 129, 131
Río de la Plata system, 13
rivers and lakes, 12; Amazon River, 13, *p 13*; Lake Maracaibo, 13; Lake Titicaca, 13; Orinoco River, 13; Paraguay River, 13; Paraná River, 13, *p 25*; Río de la Plata system, 13; Uruguay River, 13
rural, 59

S

Saint-Domingue, 50
Salvador, Brazil: heritage of, 130; enslavement of Africans in, 130–131
San Juan, Puerto Rico, 123
San Martín, José de, 53–54
Santiago, Chile, 142, 144–145
São Paulo, Brazil, 74
sierra, 136
slavery: in Brazil, 74, 130–131; in the Caribbean, 69; in Haiti, 50, 113–114
Social Studies Skills Activities: facts and opinions, 78–79; isolines, 140–141; locating information, 118–119; previewing, 94–95; regional maps, 20–21; time line, 48–49
soil, 12, 23, 25, 58
Sonoran Desert, 14, *p 14*
South America, 9, *m 10*, 12, *p 12*, *m 24*, 63, 69, 73–77, 128–153, *m 128*; ancestry of, 73; Andes, 8, *p 8*, 9, 12, 14, 39, 73, 74, 143–144, 145; climate of, 17; colonization of, 73; culture in, 73–77; export crops of, 75; farming in, 12, 17, 25, 75–76; independence in, 52–54, *m 52*; landforms of, 9, 12; language of, 73; Native Americans in, 73; natural resources of, *m 24*, 25; population growth in, 77; religion in, 73; urbanization in, 75, 77; women in, 77
Soviet Union: and Cuba, 109, 111; government in, 111; and United States, 109
Spain, 43–47, 52–54, 73
Spanish, 40, 92; in Chile, 144; colonies, 108; colonization, 46–47, 73; culture, 123, 125; empire, 46, *m 46*; explorers/conquistadors, 42–47, *m 44*, 137; government, 46, 51; influences in Chile, 144; influences in Peru, 137; influences in Puerto Rico, 122; language, 10, 64, 70, 73, 125, 148; missionaries, 64; social classes, 46–47
Spanish-American War, 108
squatter, 84
strike, 93
subsistence farming, 75
sugar: plantations, 69; production, 107, 108
sugar cane, *p 16*, 114, 123
Suriname, *m 15*, *m 18*, *m 128*

T

tables: foreign debt, 56
Tenochtitlán, 37, 38. *See also* Mexico City
Tikal, 36
Topa Inca, 40
trade: in Cuba, 108–109; in Latin America, 57
treaty, 44
Treaty of Tordesillas, 44
tributary, 13
Trinidad: Carnival in, 72; economy of, 27; oil in, 27
Tobago, 72
Trujillo, Peru, 136
tundra, 138

U

United States, 128, 129; and Chile, 147; and Cuba, 107, 108–109, 111; culture, 123; and Haiti, 113, 116–117; and Mexico, 66; and Panama, 99, 101; population growth in, *c 65*; and Puerto Rico, 121, 122, 124–125; and the Soviet Union, 109; Spanish-American War, 108
urban, 59; versus rural, *c 83*
urbanization: in Brazil, 131; in Central America, 66–67; in Latin America, 59; in Mexico, 66, 67, 83–88; in Peru, 139; in South America, 75, 77; in Venezuela, 150
Uruguay, 12, *m 15*, *m 18*, 74, 75, *m 128*; climate of, *m 15*, 17, 19; farming in, 75; natural vegetation of, *m 18*, 19
Uruguay River, 13

V

Valley of Mexico, 36
Venezuela, 12, 52, 53, 74, *m 128*, 148–153; agriculture in, 150; barrios in, 77; cities in, 150; Country Profile of, 149; culture in, 150; diversification in, 152; economy of, 27, 148–149, 150, 152–153; employment in, 148–149, 150; government of, 148, 152; Lake Maracaibo, 149, 151; language of, 148; migration of people in, 148–149; oil in, 25, 27, 148–153; oil imported in, *c 151*; privatization in, 152; standard of living in, 150; unemployment in, 150; urbanization in, 150

Western Hemisphere, 9, 96
West Indies, 69. *See also* Caribbean
wheat, 25
women, 77

Yanomamo, 132
Yucatán: Mexico, *p 55*; Peninsula, *m 4*, *m 34*, *m 44*

Acknowledgments

Program Development, Design, Illustration, and Production
Proof Positive/Farrowlyne Associates, Inc.

Cover Design
Olena Serbyn and Bruce Bond

Cover Photo
Jon Chomitz

Maps
GeoSystems Global Corp.

Text
30, "Where the Flame Trees Bloom," by Alma Flor Ada. Text © 1994 Alma Flor Ada. Reprinted with the permission of Atheneum Books for Young Readers, an imprint of Simon & Schuster Children's Publishing Division. 110, Excerpt from "Finding My Father," by Lydia Martin, *The Miami Herald,* June 18, 1995. Reprinted with permission of *The Miami Herald.* 158, Poem LXXII (Question Book) by Pablo Neruda. Spanish original reprinted from *Libros de las Preguntas,* by Pablo Neruda. © Pablo Neruda and Fundación Pablo Neruda, 1974. English translation from *Late and Posthumous Poems 1968–1974,* by Pablo Neruda, translated by Ben Belitt. © 1988 by Ben Belitt. Used by permission of Grove/Atlantic, Inc.

Photos
1 TL, TR, © Chip & Rosa María de la Cueva Peterson, 1B, © Mark Lewis/Tony Stone Images, 5, © Mark Thayer, Boston, 7, © Photri, 8, 11, © Chip & Rosa María de la Cueva Peterson, 12, © Bryan Parsley/Tony Stone Images, 13, © Will & Deni McIntyre/Tony Stone Images, 14, © Robert Frerck/Odyssey Productions, 15, © William J. Hebert/Tony Stone Images, 16, © Martin Rogers/Tony Stone Images, 19, © Wolfgang Kaehler/Wolfgang Kaehler Photography, 22, © Chip & Rosa María de la Cueva Peterson, 23, 25, © Robert Frerck/Odyssey Productions, 26 L, © Erik Svenson/Tony Stone Images, 26 R, © Chip & Rosa María de la Cueva Peterson, 31, © Photri, 32, 35, © Chip & Rosa María de la Cueva Peterson, 36 T, BL, BR, © Robert Frerck/Odyssey Productions, 38 L, © Chip & Rosa María de la Cueva Peterson, 38 R, © Robert Frerck/Odyssey Productions, 39, © Chip & Rosa María de la Cueva Peterson, 40, © Ed Simpson/Tony Stone Images, 41, © Robert Frerck/Odyssey Productions, 42, © Wolfgang Kaehler/Wolfgang Kaehler Photography, 43, © Daniel Aubry/Odyssey Productions, 45, © Stock Montage, 49, © David Young-Wolff/PhotoEdit, 50, © North Wind Picture Archives, 51, © Robert Frerck/Odyssey Productions, 53, © Chip & Rosa María de la Cueva Peterson, 55, © Robert Frerck/Odyssey Productions, 57, © Mark Segal/Tony Stone Images, 58, © Elizabeth Harris/Tony Stone Images, 59, © Chip & Rosa María de la Cueva Peterson, 62, © Robert Frerck/Odyssey Productions, 64, © Sheryl McNee/Tony Stone Images, 66 L, © Robert E. Daemmrich/Tony Stone Images, 66 R, © Tom Benoit/Tony Stone Images, 68, © Jason Laure'/Laure' Communications, 70, © SuperStock International, 71 L, © Corbis-Bettmann, 71 R, © Photri, 72, © Doug Armand/Tony Stone Images, 73, © Alex Irvin/Alex Irvin Photography, 74, © Ed Simpson/Tony Stone Images, 75, Untitled, by Yhaninc Puelles Enriquez, age 12, Peru. Courtesy of the International Children's Art Museum, 85, © Demetrio Carrasco/Tony Stone Images, 87, © David R. Frazier/Tony Stone Images, 88, 89, © Robert Frerck/Odyssey Productions, 91 L, © James Nelson/Tony Stone Images, 91 R, © James Strachan/Tony Stone Images, 92, © Chip & Rosa María de la Cueva Peterson, 94–95, © David Young-Wolff/PhotoEdit, 99, © Chip & Rosa María de la Cueva Peterson, 100 L, R, © Odyssey Productions, 107, © Shepard Sherbell/SABA Press Photos, 109, © Corbis-Bettmann, 110, © Alyx Kellington/D.D. Bryant Stock Photo, 111, © Miami Herald/Miami Herald Publishing Co., 112, © Mary Altier/Mary Altier Photography, 113, 115 L, R, © Corbis-Bettman, 116, Untitled, by Cange Walthe, age 12, Haiti. Courtesy of the International Children's Art Museum, 117, © Corbis-Bettman, 120, © Benno Friedman, 123, © Lawrence Migdale/Tony Stone Images, 124 L, © Robert Frerck/Odyssey Productions, 124 R, © Wolfgang Kaehler/Wolfgang Kaehler Photography, 125, © Suzanne L. Murphy/D.D. Bryant Stock Photo, 129, © Jacques Jangoux/Tony Stone Images, 131, © Sylvain Grandadam/Tony Stone Images, 132, © Ary Diesendruck/Tony Stone Images, 135, © Wolfgang Kaehler/Wolfgang Kaehler Photography, 137, © D.E. Cox/Tony Stone Images, 138 L, R, © David Mangurian/David Mangurian Photography, 139, © Robert Frerck/Odyssey Productions, 140, © David Young-Wolff/PhotoEdit, 142, © Photography by S.R.H. Spicer, Vermillion, South Dakota, U.S.A., 144 L, © Rhonda Klevansky/Tony Stone Images, 144 R, © Robert Frerck/Odyssey Productions, 145, © Chip & Rosa María de la Cueva Peterson, 146, © Charles Philip/Photri, 148, © Photri, 150, © Chip & Rosa María de la Cueva Peterson, 152, © Jacques Jangoux/Tony Stone Images, 153, © Julie Marcotte/Tony Stone Images, 156, © David Young-Wolff/PhotoEdit, 159 L, R, © Francois Gohier/Francois Gohier Pictures, 160, 163, © Mark Thayer, Boston, 164 I, © Steve Leonard/Tony Stone Images, 164 B, © Robert Frerck/Odyssey Productions, 165 T, © Wolfgang Kaehler/Wolfgang Kaehler Photography, 165 BL, © John Elk/Tony Stone Images, 165 R, © Will & Deni McIntyre/Tony Stone Images, 175, © G. Brad Lewis/Tony Stone Images, 177, © Nigel Press/Tony Stone Images, 204 T, © A & L Sinibaldi/Tony Stone Images, 204 B, © John Beatty/Tony Stone Images, 205 T, © Hans Strand/Tony Stone Images, 205 BL, © Spencer Swanger/Tom Stack & Associates, 205 BR, © Paul Chesley/Tony Stone Images.

Artists for Artists

THE Allan Stone Gallery, on Eighty-sixth Street right around the corner from Madison Avenue, has just been the scene of what may prove to be an epochal new development in foundation-founding. More than seventy of our leading artists and sculptors, including such supernovae as Willem de Kooning, Jack Tworkov, Larry Rivers, and Mark Rothko, and a whole galaxy of the younger New Realist, or Pop, artists, such as Robert Rauschenberg, Jasper Johns, James Rosenquist, and Andy Warhol, donated one or two of their works for a week's show that opened there February 25th and whose proceeds went into a fund to finance New York recitals and concerts by avant-garde musicians, dancers, and other needy practitioners of the performing arts. The show is over now, but the unsold pictures can still be seen (on request), are owned by the fund, and are for sale. The fund, which goes under the name of the Foundation for Contemporary Performance Arts, may stand as a historic watershed in the flow of money to artists, for it was not so long ago that many of the donors represented at the gallery were themselves needy applicants for grants from the Guggenheim and other old-style, or pre-art-boom, foundations. At the somewhat seismic opening, we were told that Jasper Johns was the prime mover and organizer of the exhibition, and, accordingly, we wasted no time in calling on this highly influential young painter of targets, numbers, flags, and other New Realist talismans. We found him in his studio, which is, significantly, in a lower-Manhattan loft just a grant-in-aid's throw from Wall Street.

Mr. Johns, who proved to be courteous and poised, sat us down facing a large red-and-blue unfinished canvas. How, we asked him, had he managed to turn so many artists into patrons? "It started last August," he said, perching on a stool. "A group of us began to think about raising some money so that Merce Cunningham, the dancer, could have a New York recital. Merce hasn't appeared in New York in two or three years. Most dancers in his position hardly ever appear in New York, or they appear one night a year in some obscure hall, because there is simply no provision here for their kind of performance. Broadway is geared to the long run, and a limited engagement loses too much money. Anyway, the four people in the original group—John Cage, the composer; Lewis Lloyd, a young producer; Alfred Geller, a lawyer; and myself—looked into it and found that it would cost over thirty thousand dollars to finance a week on Broadway for Merce and his company. We also found that we couldn't expect to recover more than half of that at the box office. Impossible, obviously. Then we got the idea of setting up a foundation for short-run performances of this sort by Merce and others, and asking artists to donate their work to it. A lot of us have known Merce and other performers in the fields of music, the dance, and the theatre for years, and it just happens that the economic situation has improved for some of us lately but not for them, mainly because they have no product for sale. Elaine de Kooning, Bill's wife, and David Hayes, who's with the Guggenheim Museum, came in with us at this point, and we set up a foundation, with ourselves as directors. We all sat down then and drew up a list of the painters who we thought should be represented, and sent each of them a telegram explaining the idea briefly and inviting them to a party at the Allan Stone Gallery to discuss it further. Allan had offered us his gallery and his time, and offered to take no commission on anything sold from the show. Most of the people we asked came through magnificently, I must say."

Had it really been that easy?

Not altogether, said Johns, and went on to admit that the last two months had been an administrative hell. "A lot of artists offered us a choice of works, and that meant going around to everybody's studio at least once to make the selection," he said. "People promised us things and then forgot, or they were out of town when we wanted to check, and we didn't really know until the last minute what we were going to get. When *Art News* and a new magazine called *Art Voices* wanted to do pieces on the show, we had to dash out and take pictures of promised works with one of those Polaroid cameras—you know, the kind that develops the film in ten seconds—and even then their articles listed contributors who didn't contribute. We were much too busy to do anything about publicity—there were no newspapers anyway—and I had a feeling nobody would show up for the opening, which was on a Monday night. We planned to get the announcements out on the Wednesday before, so that people would get them on Saturday—Friday was Washington's Birthday—but the addressing machine broke down and we didn't get some of them *out* until Saturday. I guess the word got around, though. Allan Stone talked to everybody about the show."

With the exception of Richard Lippold's delicate wire "Variations Within a Sphere," which Lippold himself came in to hang, Johns installed every painting and sculpture in the show. The job took him all of Saturday night, all day Sunday, and most of Monday. Pictures kept turning up until the last moment. "Jim Rosenquist's large canvas came in on Monday afternoon, wet," he said. Elaine de Kooning, whose latest commission is a portrait of John F. Kennedy, was represented by an impressive portrait of Merce Cunningham, but her famous husband had nothing there on opening night. "He gave us two pictures, but we didn't get them in time," Johns said, a trifle ruefully.

To judge by the packed opening, in the course of which seven works of art were either sold or reserved, the Foundation for Contemporary Performance Arts is now well launched. Tentative plans include an initial grant for a Merce Cunningham recital on Broadway sometime in April, provided a theatre can be found. ("He needs a big stage and not too big an audience," Johns explained.) And requests have begun to pour in from other grant-seekers. "The main problem is still money, of course," Johns said, sounding more and more like a foundation executive. "We have no way of knowing at this point how much we'll make, but there's certainly going to be no problem in giving it away."

•

This page: Calvin Tomkins, "Artists for Artists," from "The Talk of the Town," *The New Yorker*, March 9, 1963. Opposite page: Merce Cunningham and John Cage, c. 1968. Courtesy John Cage Trust.

Voice: Fred W. McDarrah

MORTON FELDMAN, left, and EARLE BROWN in rehearsal.

Two Composers

Feldman: 'Sound the Hero'; Brown: 'Images in Space'

by Jill Johnston

The concert of music by Earle Brown and Morton Feldman to be given in Town Hall this Friday, October 11, will be the first time the two composers will have had

by the
free cir
space.
In his
set of co
ers whic
a field
material
of the n
cians in
details,
terials
Brown s
the more
making
king con
a group
patient
sitions w
same. In
performe
they say
composit
the fre
through
ment of
cians, h
sense o
think a
set of re
of art is
best solu
lutions o
is is inv

This page, clockwise from top left: Article on "Feldman/Brown," concert organized and sponsored by the FCPA, *The Village Voice*, October 10, 1963. Meredith Monk, 1969 grantee, *Juice*, FCPA-supported performance, Solomon R. Guggenheim Museum, New York, 1969. Performer: Blondell Cummings. Philip Glass, 1970 grantee, page from musical score of *Music in Twelve Parts*, supported by the FCPA, 1971–74. Paper Bag Players, 1963 grantee, *Scraps*, performance, venue unknown, 1963. Performers: Marni Mahaffay, Betty Osgood, and Judith Martin. Photo: John Wulf. Merce Cunningham and Dance Company, lecture-demonstration at Ballets Modernes de Paris, June 8, 1964. Performers: Viola Farber, Carolyn Brown, Shareen Blair, Sandra Neels, Barbara Dilley, and Deborah Hay. Opposite page: Yvonne Rainer, 1970 grantee, *Continuous Project—Altered Daily*, FCPA-supported performance, Whitney Museum of American Art, New York, April 5, 1971. Performers: Yvonne Rainer, 1985 grantee Douglas Dunn, and 1972 grantee Steve Paxton (background). Photo: James Klosty.

Sept. 6, 1971

Dear Jasper, Carolyn, and David

The winter of 71 is over and I am looking forward to joy and dancing in 72.

Now is the time to queque up in a serious way for larger sums of money. I do not know whether you're foundation requires a formal application so going a step further she told them about herself...just call me an aging unknown. Little publicity and powerful love is what I've got. I can produce two or three big guys who will tell you "give that girl anything she asks for". Aunt Lena will tell you. Alex Hay...

Alright I'll get serious again. Listen...I got ideas for dances you wouldn't believe. You know that clock on the Pan Am building? heh heh. Well there isn't a clock on the Pan Am building.

Actually I can't dance at all but like most cripples I got heart and heart is interested in 3 thou in 72. That's our motto gang. 3 thou for Trisha in 72. You can do it I know you can. And I'll throw in a salmon bake to square it with you. Bribe? I know. Out and out bribe. Well if you had a 6 year old who discovered that saliva after eating blackberries makes good bubbles-lavendar yet-you'ed get into bribing too.

Love, you know this
letter is with love

Trisha Brown

Trisha Brown

Opposite page: Request for funds from Trisha Brown, September 6, 1971. This page, clockwise from top left: Trisha Brown, 1971 grantee, *Accumulation,* FCPA-supported work, performance, L'Attico Gallery, Rome, c. June 1972. Photo © 1972 Babette Mangolte. All rights reserved. Steve Reich and Musicians, 1971 grantee, *Drumming*, FCPA-supported work, performance, New York University, 1973. Photo: Gianfranco Gorgoni. Anne Waldman, 2001 grantee, with Steven Taylor, reading at FCPA grantee the Poetry Project, St. Mark's Church, New York, 1988. Photo: Vivian Selbo. Eiko & Koma, 1983 grantee, *Grain*, FCPA-supported performance, 1983. Photo: David Fullard. Bill T. Jones, 1981 grantee, and Arnie Zane, c. 1980–82. Photo: Lois Greenfield.

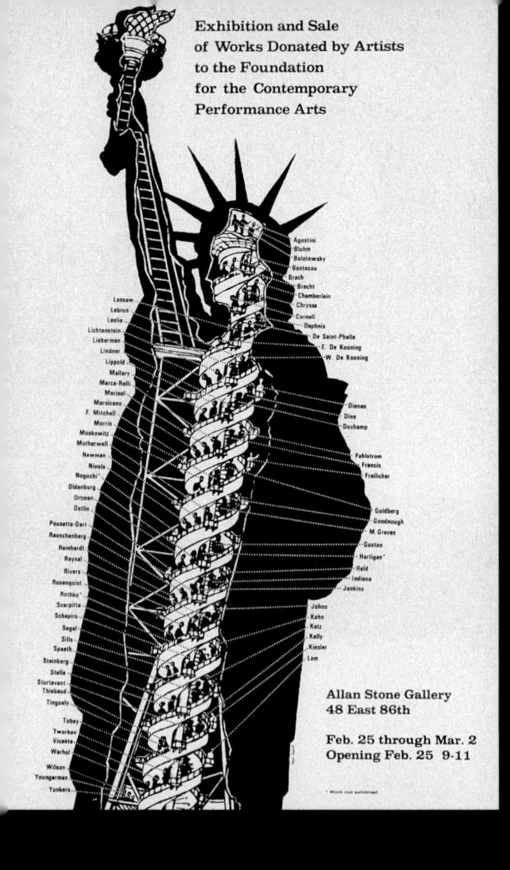

Exhibition and Sale
of Works Donated by Artists
to the Foundation
for the Contemporary
Performance Arts
Allan Stone Gallery
48 East 86th
Feb. 25 through Mar. 2
Opening Feb. 25 9-11

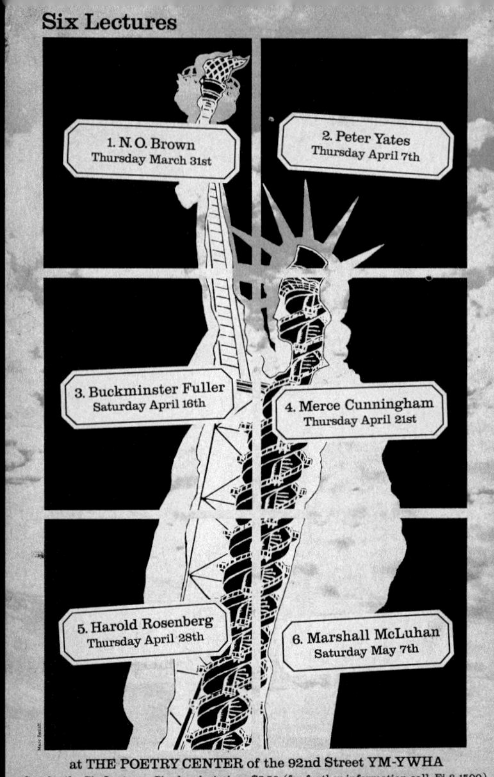

Six Lectures
1. N.O. Brown
Thursday March 31st
2. Peter Yates
Thursday April 7th
3. Buckminster Fuller
Saturday April 16th
4. Merce Cunningham
Thursday April 21st
5. Harold Rosenberg
Thursday April 28th
6. Marshall McLuhan
Saturday May 7th
at THE POETRY CENTER of the 92nd Street YM-YWHA
$12. for the Six Lectures. Single admissions $2.50 (for further information call Fi 8-1500)
Benefit: Foundation for Contemporary Performance Arts

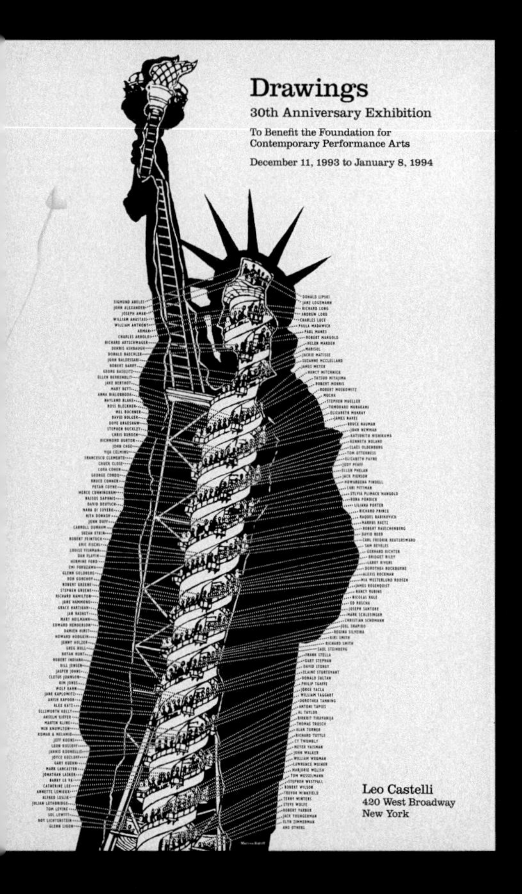

Drawings
30th Anniversary Exhibition
To Benefit the Foundation for
Contemporary Performance Arts
December 11, 1993 to January 8, 1994
Leo Castelli
420 West Broadway
New York

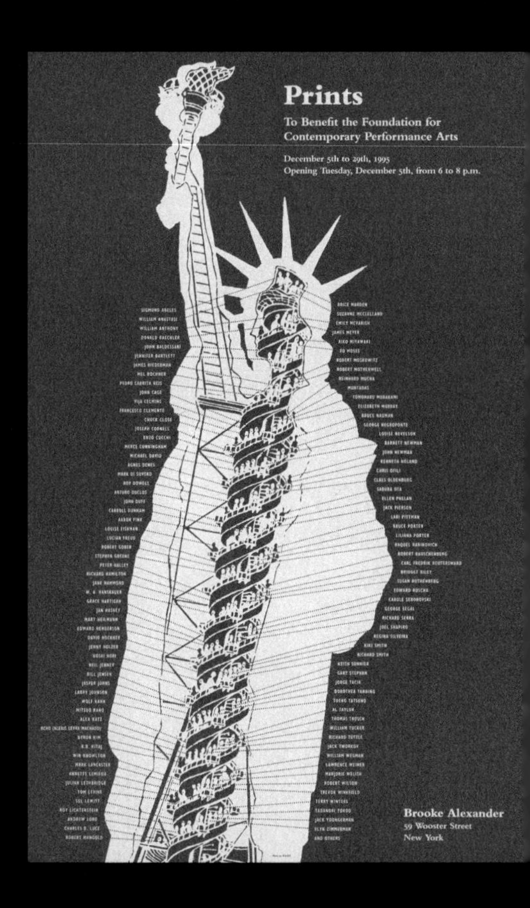

Prints
To Benefit the Foundation for
Contemporary Performance Arts
December 5th to 29th, 1995
Opening Tuesday, December 5th, from 6 to 8 p.m.
Brooke Alexander
59 Wooster Street
New York

Clockwise from top left: Exhibition announcement, inaugural FCPA benefit, 1963. Promotional poster, "Six Lectures," 1966. Exhibition announcement, "Prints" benefit, 1995. Exhibition announcement, "Drawings" benefit, 1993. All designed by Marcus Ratliff.

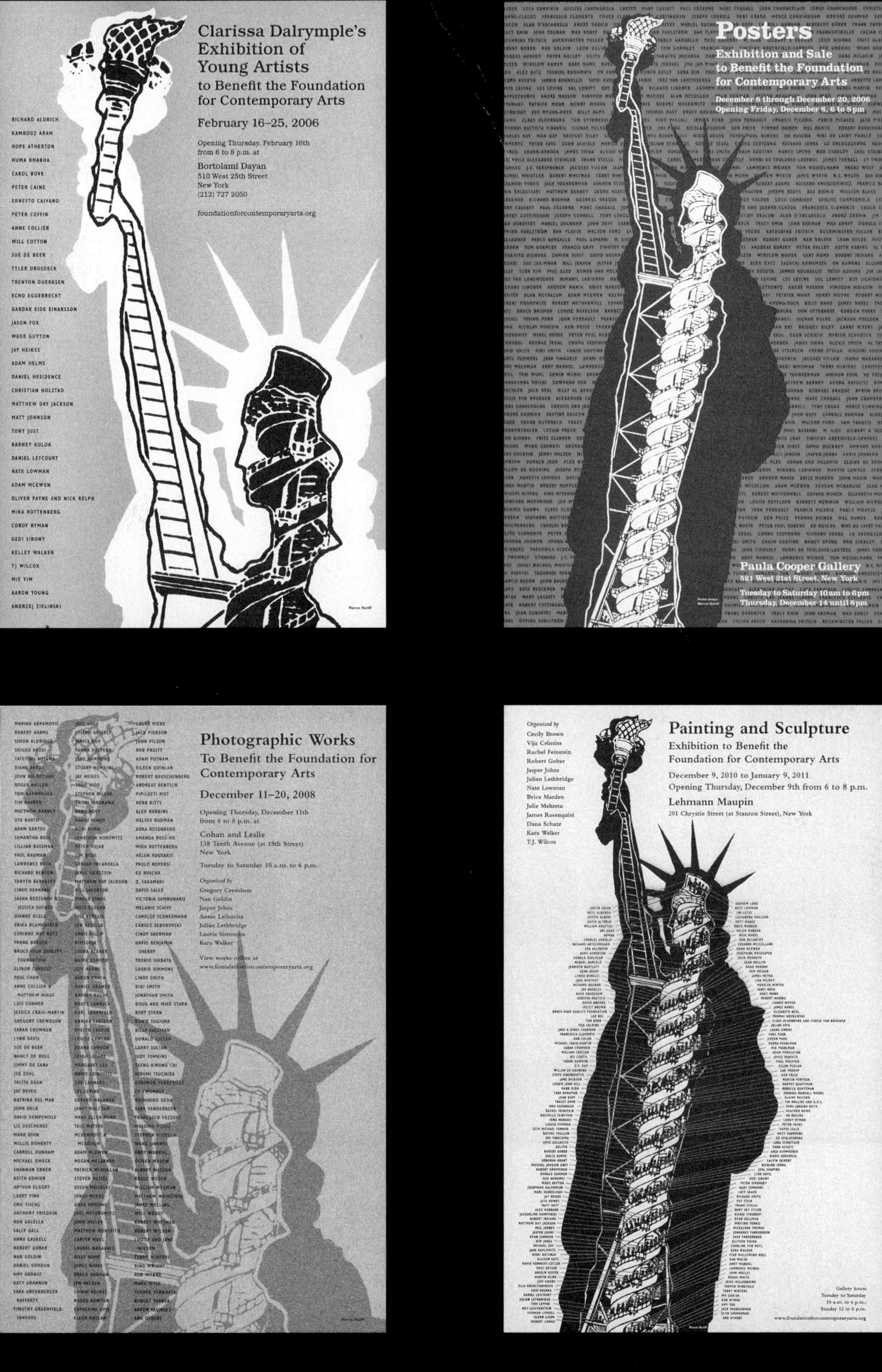

Clockwise from top left: Exhibition announcement, "Clarissa Dalrymple's Exhibition of Young Artists" benefit, 2006. Exhibition announcement, "Posters," benefit, 2006. Exhibition announcement, "Painting and Sculpture" benefit, 2010. Exhibition announcement, "Photographic Works" benefit, 2008. All designed by Marcus Ratliff.

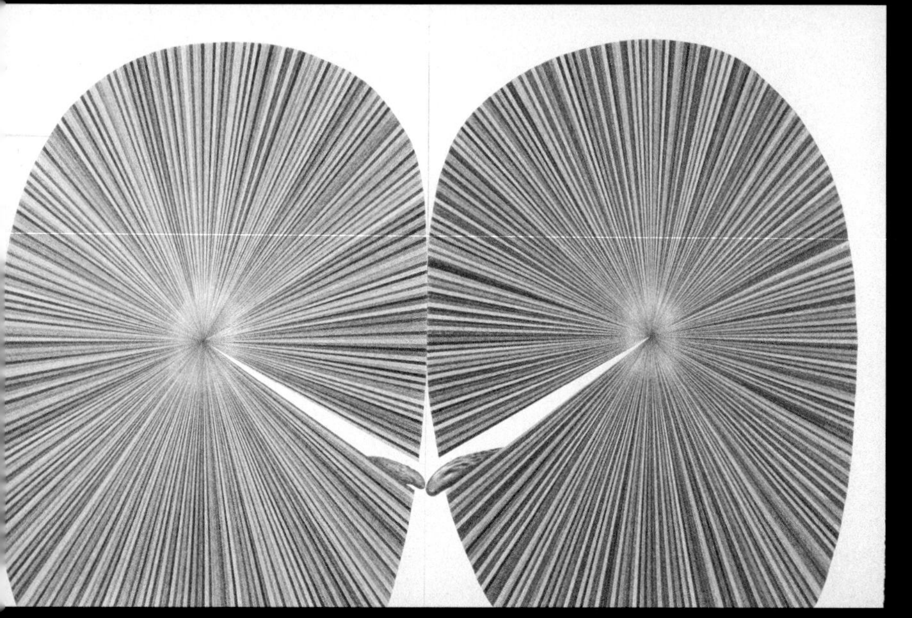

This page, clockwise from top left: chameckilerner, 1998 grantee, *I Mutantes Seras*, FCPA-supported performance, Dance Theater Workshop, New York, 1999. Photo: Anja Hitzenberger. Jon Kessler, 2000 grantee, *Global Village Idiot,* installation view, Deitch Projects, New York, 2004. Courtesy the artist. Photo: Tom Powel Imaging. Zoe Beloff, 1997 grantee, still from *Where Where There There Where*, FCPA-supported CD-ROM, collaboration with FCPA grantee The Wooster Group, 1997. David Dupuis, 1998 grantee, *The Kiss*, 2000, graphite, color pencil on paper, 50" x 76". Courtesy Derek Eller Gallery, New York. Opposite page: Riverbed Media, 1998 grantee, FCPA-supported digital projections for Merce Cunningham's *Biped*, 1999. Photo: Stephanie Berger.

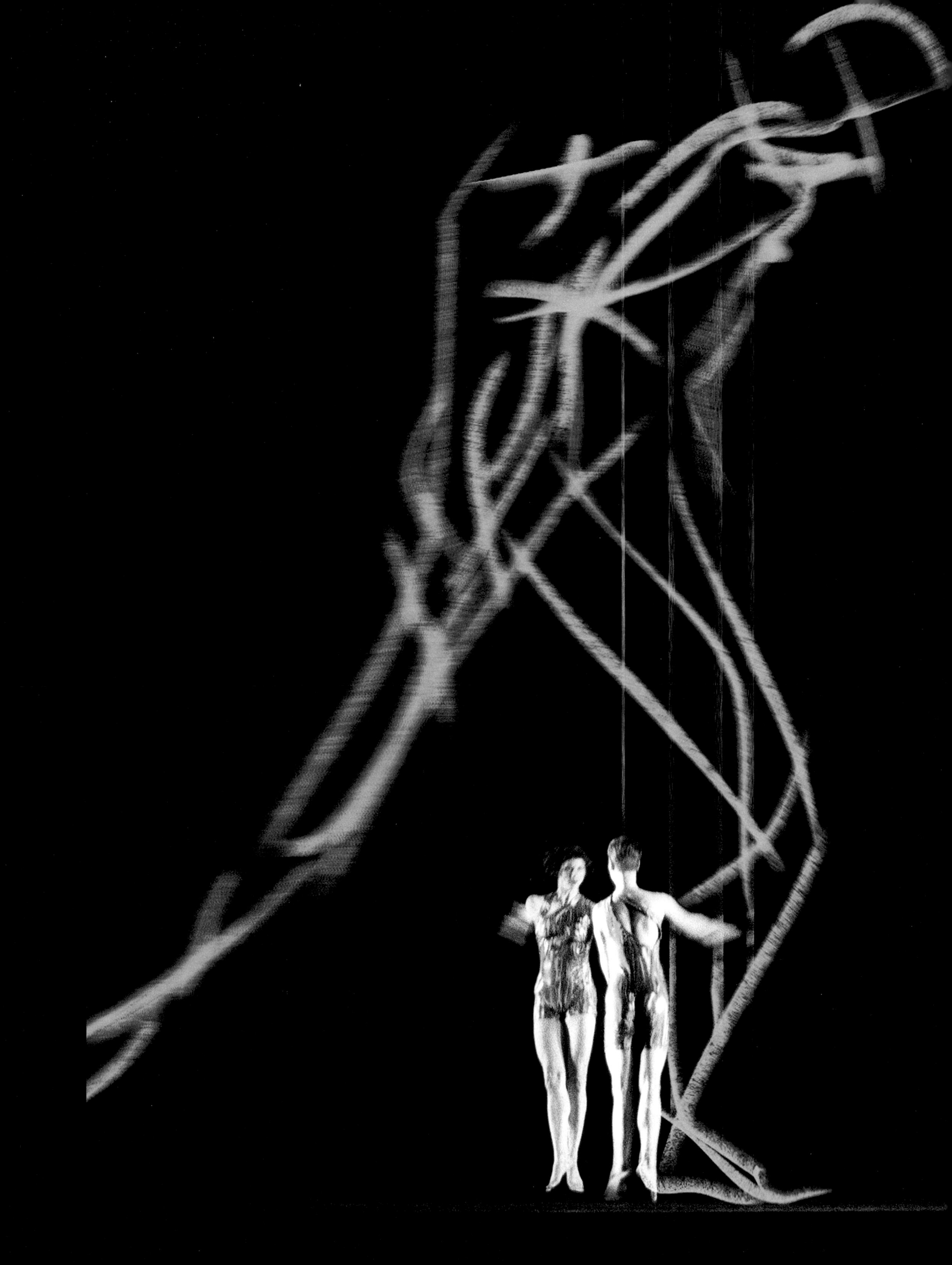

Clockwise from top left: Wang Jianwei, 2008 grantee, *Welcome to the Desert of Real*, FCA-supported performance, Kaserne Basel, Switzerland, 2010. Pan Pan Theatre, 2007 grantee, *The Crumb Trail*, FCA-supported performance, Project Arts Centre, Dublin, 2008. Photo: Ros Kavanagh. Alix Pearlstein, 2011 grantee, production still from *The Drawing Lesson*, FCA-supported single-channel HD video, 2012. Photo: Boru O'Brien O'Connell. Caden Manson/Big Art Group, 2001 grantee, *Flicker*, FCPA-supported performance, Festival d'Automne, Paris, 2002. Photo: Linsey Bostwick. Raha Raissnia, 2011 grantee, *Untitled,* 2011, sumi ink, crayon, and collage on paper, 14" x 17". Courtesy Miguel Abreu Gallery, New York.

PHOTO: PAULA COURT

Clockwise from top: Christopher Williams, 2006 grantee, *Golden Legend*, FCA-supported performance, Dance Theater Workshop, New York, 2009. Performer: Aaron Mattocks. Ohad Meromi, 2008 grantee, *Who Owns the World?*, installation view, FCA-supported work, Harris Lieberman, New York, 2008. Courtesy the artist and Harris Lieberman. Nature Theater of Oklahoma, 2010 grantee, *Life and Times—Episode 2*, FCA-supported work, performance, Burgtheater Wien, Vienna, 2012. Photo: Anna Stöcher/Burgtheater Wien.

1, 2, 3

4

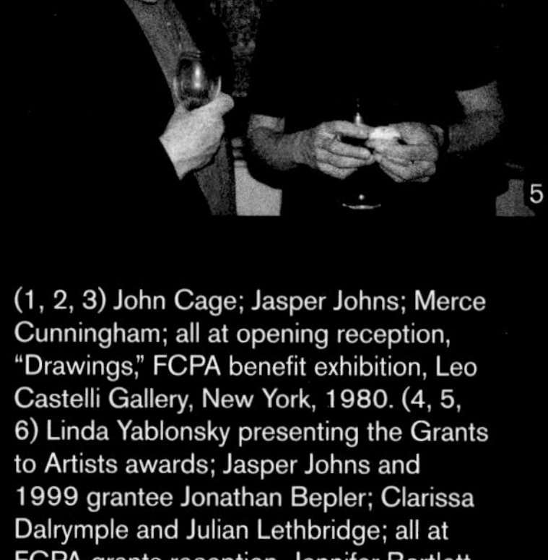
5

(1, 2, 3) John Cage; Jasper Johns; Merce Cunningham; all at opening reception, "Drawings," FCPA benefit exhibition, Leo Castelli Gallery, New York, 1980. (4, 5, 6) Linda Yablonsky presenting the Grants to Artists awards; Jasper Johns and 1999 grantee Jonathan Bepler; Clarissa Dalrymple and Julian Lethbridge; all at FCPA grants reception, Jennifer Bartlett Studio, New York, 2001. (7, 8, 9) Lisa Boudreau, 2001 grantee Mikel Rouse, and 1993 grantee John Jesurun; Elizabeth Murray and Julian Lethbridge; Merce Cunningham and 2000 grantee Molissa Fenley; all at FCPA grants reception, Jennifer Bartlett Studio, New York, 2002.

10

11

12

13

(17) Kara Walker, FCA Young Friends gallery talk, Sikkema Jenkins, New York, 2009. (18, 19, 20, 21) Grantees and guests; Scott Rothkopf, Terry Winters, and Trevor Carlson; 2003 grantee Kate Valk performing; Morton Subotnick, Stacy Tenenbaum Stark, and 1994 grantee David Berhman; all at FCA grants reception, Robert Rauschenberg Studio, New York, 2010. (22, 23, 24, 25) Guests; T.J. Wilcox and Mary Simpson; Jasper Johns and Vija Celmins; John Currin and Rachel Feinstein; all at opening reception, "Painting and Sculpture," FCA benefit exhibition, Lehmann Maupin, New York, 2010. (26) 2000 grantee Julie Mehretu, FCA Young Friends talk, Goldman Sachs, New York, 2011.

18 19 20 21

17

27 28 29

(10, 11, 12) Marian Seldes and Edward Albee; Jennifer Bartlett and 2004 grantee Karole Armitage; Hope Atherton and Adam McEwen; all at FCA benefit reading of *Edward Albee's Occupant*, Diane Von Furstenberg Studio, New York, 2005. (13) Jasper Johns, John Delk, and Julian Lethbridge, installation of "Posters," FCA benefit exhibition, Paula Cooper Gallery, New York, 2006. (14, 15) Jasper Johns and Agnes Gund; guests; all at opening reception, "Photographic Works," FCA benefit exhibition, Cohan and Leslie, New York, 2008. Photo (14): PatrickMcMullan.com. (16) 1999 grantee Stephen Petronio's company performing, FCA grants reception, Brooke Alexander, New York, 2009.

(27, 28, 29) 2009 grantee Elevator Repair Service performing; Nancy Dalva presenting the Grants to Artists awards; 2006 grantee Jonah Bokaer performing; all at FCA grants reception, Merce Cunningham Studio, New York, 2011. (30, 31, 32, 33, 34) David Vaughan, 2012 grantee Pauline Oliveros, Ione, and Lewis Lloyd; Yegor Shevtsov at prepared piano; 2012 and 2008 grantees Ralph Lemon, Kimberly Bartosik, and Beth Gill; 2006 and 2011 grantees Vicky Shick and Jodi Melnick; 2012 grantees Thomas Bradshaw and Rhodri Davies; all at FCA grants reception, Merce Cunningham Studio, New York, 2012.

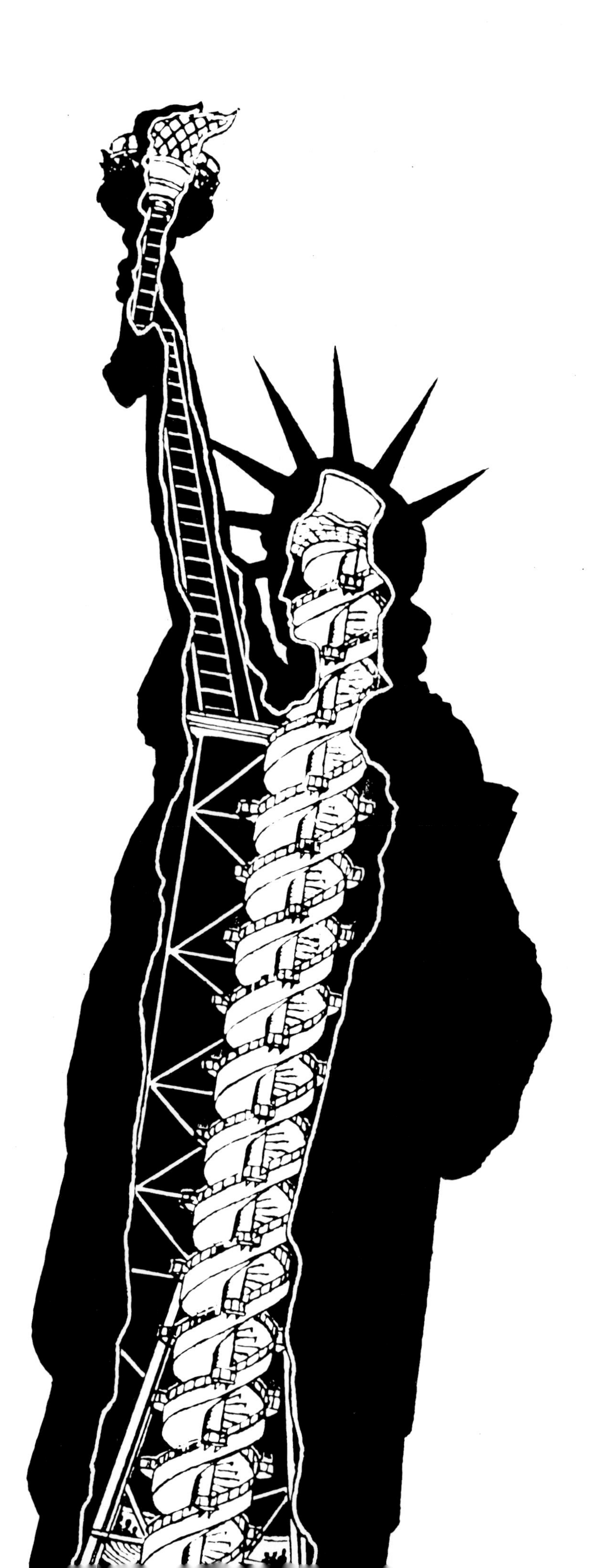

ARTISTS FOR ARTISTS

FIFTY YEARS OF THE FOUNDATION FOR CONTEMPORARY ARTS

ARTISTS FOR ARTISTS: FIFTY YEARS OF THE FOUNDATION FOR CONTEMPORARY ARTS

Published on the occasion of the 50th anniversary of the Foundation for Contemporary Arts

Published by
Foundation for Contemporary Arts
820 Greenwich Street
New York, NY 10014
212.807.7077
info@contemporary-arts.org

Distributed in part by
Distributed Art Publishers (D.A.P.)
155 Sixth Avenue
New York, NY 10013
800.338.2665

Publication team
Editor: Eric Banks
Executive Director, Foundation for Contemporary Arts: Stacy Tenenbaum Stark
Designer: Joseph Logan, assisted by Rachel Hudson
Researcher: Bridget McCarthy
Assistant: Roxanne Smith

This book is typeset in Bembo and Akzidenz-Grotesk and is printed on Galerie Art Volume and Arcoprint Milk.
Separations and printing by Trifolio, Italy

Library of Congress Catalogue Card Number
2012955359

ISBN
978-0-615-66945-8

Support for *Artists for Artists: Fifty Years of the Foundation for Contemporary Arts* has been provided by the National Endowment for the Arts and by Marie-Josée and Henry Kravis.

Inside cover jacket: Merce Cunningham, 1964 grantee, *Canfield,* performance at Brooklyn Academy of Music, New York, 1970. Photo: James Klosty.
Cover illustration and frontispiece (page 18): design by Marcus Ratliff.

TABLE OF CONTENTS

Foreword 22
Stacy Tenenbaum Stark

Introduction 25
Eric Banks

PART I, 1963–1992

Founding the FCPA: An Oral History 29
Carolyn Brown, Jill Jakes, Jasper Johns, and Lewis Lloyd

The Foundation for Contemporary Performance Arts and a New Economy for Experimentation 47
Eva Díaz

A United Front: John Cage and the Foundation's First Decade 61
Rebecca Y. Kim

Technical Difficulties: The FCPA, Experiments in Art and Technology, and "9 Evenings" 83
Julie Martin

"Six Lectures" at the 92nd Street Y

Introduction 93
Irving Sandler

Norman O. Brown 98
Peter Yates 108
R. Buckminster Fuller 114
Merce Cunningham 122
Harold Rosenberg 124
Marshall McLuhan 129

PART II, 1993–2013

A Bigger Boat: The Foundation Since 1993 139
Nancy Dalva

Selected Grants to Artists, 1993–2012 144
Eric Banks, Mark Beasley, and Debra Singer

Chronology 163
Stacy Tenenbaum Stark

Appendix 193

Foreword

IN THE EARLY 1960s, a time of invention and energetic collaboration in the visual and performance arts, expectations for the funding of experimental work in dance, music, and theater were limited. Lacking other avenues, Jasper Johns, John Cage, Robert Rauschenberg, and other painters and sculptors joined to raise money for a season on Broadway for Merce Cunningham and soon realized that they had discovered a way to encourage, sponsor, and promote the work of others in their community. *Artists for Artists: Fifty Years of the Foundation for Contemporary Arts* documents and celebrates the first 50 years of the Foundation's activities.

Originally called the Foundation for Contemporary Performance Arts, the Foundation remains the only organization of its kind to come into being solely through the efforts of artists. In 1963, on the occasion of its first benefit exhibition, critic Calvin Tomkins described the enterprise as "an epochal new development in foundation-founding." That first exhibition definitively established the Foundation's roots in the community of artists.

From the start the Foundation supported the fields of dance, music, theater, and performance, later adding poetry and visual arts to its roster. Fifty years on, the Foundation has made nearly 2,000 grants to artists and organizations, amounting to more than $10 million. Almost 1,000 artists have donated their work—some 4,000 individual artworks—to finance these efforts. They count as part of the FCA's ever-growing community as do the 300-plus artists who have served as nominators or grants panelists for the Grants to Artists awards.

For five decades Jasper Johns has quietly led the Foundation, with little fanfare and no desire for recognition of his tireless and generous support. While initially skeptical that the Foundation's jubilee warranted commemorating in the form of a publication, Jasper has nevertheless given his time to this project, answering countless questions to help piece together much of the Foundation's history. This book—really, the Foundation—would not exist without his substantial contributions.

I wish to thank early FCPA directors Lewis Lloyd, Carolyn Brown, and Jill Jakes, who, like Jasper, sat for interviews and whose input on the Foundation's activities in the 1960s and 1970s was invaluable. I am also grateful to current FCA directors Brooke Alexander, Robert Gober, Agnes Gund, Julian Lethbridge, Glenn Ligon, Kara Walker, and T.J. Wilcox for their enthusiastic support.

Many grantees contributed documentation of their FCA-funded work to this book and have thus helped establish an archive for the Foundation. Numerous artists, friends, and associates have contributed their memories of the Foundation, many of which appear in these pages: Edward Albee, Bill Anastasi, Robert Ashley, Jared Bark, Dove Bradshaw, Joseph Byrd, Barbara Castelli, Philip Corner, Barbara Dilley, Frances Fergusson, Michael Findlay, Alanna Heiss, Bob Holman, Mary Judge, Takehisa Kosugi, Petr Kotik, Mark Lancaster, Dorothy Lichtenstein, Alvin Lucier, Claes Oldenburg, Pauline

Oliveros, Yoko Ono, Ron Padgett, Steve Paxton, Yvonne Rainer, Steve Reich, Edwin Schlossberg, Frank Stella, Sarah Taggart, Robert Whitman, Terry Winters, Christian Wolff, and Linda Yablonsky.

Several close colleagues provided critical assistance: John Delk, Lynn Kearcher, and Sarah Taggart at the Jasper Johns Studio; Laura Kuhn, executive director, John Cage Trust; David Vaughan, former Cunningham Dance Foundation archivist; Lynn Wichern, executive director, Merce Cunningham Trust; Gina Guy and Kayla Jenkins, archivist and assistant archivist, Robert Rauschenberg Foundation; and designer Marcus Ratliff. Our gratitude goes to those who have aided us throughout our research, particularly Julie Martin, director, E.A.T.; Elizabeth Frengel and Anne Marie Menta of Yale University Beinecke Rare Book and Manuscript Library; Greg MacAyeal of Northwestern University Music Library; and Margaret Zoller of the Archives of American Art. James Klosty and Barbara Moore provided significant photographic contributions that document the FCA's early history.

Others who provided research support and/or donated rights to photographs and music scores are the Richard Avedon Foundation, John Beckwith, Roberta Bernstein, the Earle Brown Music Foundation, Dan Budnik, Susan Cary, Paula Court, Jessica Craig-Martin, Jade Dellinger, Todd Eberle, Brad Farwell, Sidney Felsen, Sandra Geller, Bill Goldston, Timothy Greenfield-Sanders, John Houck, Alison Knowles, Éditions Alphonse Leduc, Babette Mangolte, Geoffrey Marsh, Dona Ann McAdams, Patrick McMullan, Robert Moran, Ryan Muir, Peter Namuth, Lillian Palmer, Rachel Rosenthal, Fondation Erik Satie, Beatriz Schiller, Michael Sesling, Sony/ATV, the Allan Stone Collection, Marvin Taylor, Calvin Tomkins and Dodie Kazanjian, Alison Smith and Andrea Mihalovic of VAGA, Tom Walker, and Matt Wrbican. The section reproducing the "Six Lectures" texts, which came together after the discovery of audio recordings of four of the lectures, would not have been possible without the cooperation of John Ferry and Jaime Snyder, the Estate of R. Buckminster Fuller; Michael McLuhan and Eric McLuhan; Peter Yates; Patia Yasin; the University of California Press; and Nicholas Pavlik, archivist, 92nd Street Y. Appreciation goes to Scott Rothkopf for his thoughtful recommendations early on. We also thank Todd Bradway of Distributed Art Publishers for his interest in our book.

Making a book is a tremendous undertaking and, in this case, a team effort. I wish to thank my talented collaborators, editor Eric Banks and designer Joseph Logan, and project coordinator Bridget McCarthy. FCA staff and interns Roxanne Smith, Catherine Massey, Mary Simpson, Molly Eckel, Natasha Rosenblatt, Maryam Parhizkar, and Maria Castex are to be thanked for their hard work, as is Joseph's assistant, Rachel Hudson.

Finally, we thank the National Endowment for the Arts and Marie-Josée and Henry Kravis for their generous support.

The Foundation for Contemporary Arts was conceived and has been directed by artists for five decades. The informal and spontaneous nature that characterized the first 30 years of its grant-making, which evolved into a more structured yet still community-supported organization in the next 20, still embodies the organization today, and will continue to do so tomorrow.

—Stacy Tenenbaum Stark, Executive Director

Richard Avedon, *John Cage, musician; Merce Cunningham, choreographer; and Robert Rauschenberg, artist, New York, May 2, 1960.*

Introduction

Eric Banks

PHILIP LARKIN FAMOUSLY CONFERRED on 1963 the phrase *annus mirabilis*. If we fudge the calendar just slightly and consider the twelve months between July 1962 and July 1963, Larkin's characterization applies no less aptly to the arts. Witness just a sample of how many institutions, organizations, and movements without which the next half century would be unthinkable took root over that span. On July 6, 1962, Fred Herko's multimedia program inaugurated the Judson Dance Theater as the epicenter of the experiments in performance to come. Three days later, on the other side of the continent, Andy Warhol's solo show of 22 Campbell's soup cans opened at Ferus Gallery in Los Angeles; a month later, Warhol executed his very first photo-silk-screen painting. In September, up the California coast in San Francisco, *Artforum* published its debut issue. And in Pasadena, Walter Hopps was finalizing his plans for the 1963 retrospective that would salvage Marcel Duchamp from almost unimaginable critical neglect and put him firmly at the heart of the next five decades' most decisive art. All across the American art world, in music, dance, theater, and the visual arts, there seemed to be ferment, a palpable sense of discovery and rediscovery, and excitement about the spirit of experiment and new possibilities for art.

The rapid gestation of the Foundation for Contemporary Performance Arts fits squarely in this same time frame. Almost overnight, the idea of Jasper Johns, John Cage, and Robert Rauschenberg donating works they created or owned to underwrite a proposed Broadway run for Merce Cunningham grew to the much more radical gesture of approaching a who's who of the visual arts to support a range of less remunerative art forms. Their inspired appeal quickly led to the debut benefit exhibition, which was almost single-handedly commandeered by the 32-year-old Johns at the Allan Stone Gallery. What might have been a one-off attempt by three friends to help a fourth became in a few months a model that has proved in retrospect remarkably sustaining, as the recollections by the principals in this volume's oral history of the FCPA's early days demonstrate.

From the perspective of today, when artists are routinely asked to donate works to help underwrite alternative and nonprofit venues, the example of the founders of the FCPA may seem a virtual fait accompli, a case of artists drawing on the resources of the community around them to help buoy the work of others. But a closer look shows just how much the efforts of Johns and Cage in particular helped create this community in the sense we know it now. They and others had found aesthetic inspiration in what was taking place in the wider creative world of performance in the 1950s and early 1960s; in founding the FCPA and mobilizing it as a model of real financial support across media, they in practice solidified a sense of camaraderie and kinship among all artists, making visible unseen disciplinary connections from which, like a kind of artistic co-op, everybody would profit. In the press release to a 1964 concert by Earle Brown and Morton Feldman at Town Hall in New York, commissioned by the Foundation, Johns laid the stress on this beneficial back-and-forth: "If performers are to function with any sense of freedom and if the public is to be able to see such work, some kind of subsidy is necessary. The response of artists to this idea reflects the involvement on levels of ideas and friendship between painters and sculptors and performers in dance, music and theatre."

The tangibility of support, of "ideas" and "friendship" made manifest and material, is a thread that runs through the Foundation's history from the very start, and one that is explored in several of the essays written for this volume. Eva Díaz argues that the experiences of Cage at Black Mountain College prepped him to discover, with Johns, a new model that transferred his evolving collaborative work as a composer to his "creative entrepreneurship" whereby the FCPA could be seen as a sort of artwork in itself. Meanwhile, in surveying the Foundation's numerous benefit performances in its first decade, Rebecca Y. Kim provides a forceful and nuanced reading of the Foundation as a kind of substantiation of Cage's idea of a "united front" of culture. The reflections of Julie Martin and Irving Sandler, both of whom remember firsthand two other events from 1966 that the FCPA either helped along ("9 Evenings") or directly realized ("Six Lectures"), are no less marked by what we might call the spirit of '63: a dogma of collaborative support and do-it-yourself moxie—a gleeful creative activism—that amounted to a flanking maneuver around institutional and funding roadblocks. The FCPA set a precedent in refusing to see the arts as balkanized by medium. Throughout its 50-year history, the Foundation has disrespected boundaries whenever it has run up against them.

This kind of creative interloping is apparent too in the series of profiles that chronicles the Foundation's post-1993 Grants to Artists program. Governed by a blind nomination process, which itself, as Nancy Dalva notes in her essay introducing the section, draws strongly from the artist community at large, the Grants to Artists program is a signal award in recognizing and encouraging the whole gamut of visual and performance-based work (as well as poetry, maybe the most cash poor of all the fields the Foundation supports). There is a division marked in this volume between the pre- and post-1993 phases of the Foundation's 50-year existence, but that distinction is more relative than it may at first appear. In the 20 years since the Foundation's grant-making activities were rebooted to respond both to the needs of artists and to the burgeoning diversity of the art world, and in the almost ten years since it renamed itself the Foundation for Contemporary Arts, a host of activities—most notably, the series of benefit exhibitions held semi-regularly since 1988—hark back to the organization's salad days of the early 1960s, and the particular potlatch spirit of giving in order to receive that has long made the Foundation a model worth emulating and admiring. In honoring that spirit and reflecting on its place in the FCA today, *Artists for Artists* hopes to point to a future where artists will continue to benefit mutually from their fellow practitioners' success, munificence, and goodwill. ◆

I

1963-1992

Bill Giles, Anna Moreska, Robert Rauschenberg, Merce Cunningham, John Cage, and Jasper Johns, Dillon's Bar, New York, 1959.
Photo: Fred W. McDarrah/Premium Archive/Getty Images

Founding the FCPA: An Oral History

Carolyn Brown, Jill Jakes, Jasper Johns, and Lewis Lloyd

The creation of the Foundation for Contemporary Performance Arts in 1963 was the work of several key individuals, among them Jasper Johns, who has remained the Foundation's board chairman and president since that time, and Lewis Lloyd, who served on the board until 1965. Carolyn Brown, a Merce Cunningham dancer and FCPA board member from 1966 to 2001, and Jill Jakes, the FCPA's first board secretary as well as a member of the board until 1971, joined Johns and Lloyd in offering their recollections of the FCPA in the 1960s.

JASPER JOHNS: I met John Cage after a concert at the music publisher C.F. Peters, on 57th Street across from Carnegie Hall. The artist Sari Dienes, who had a large studio on 57th Street, gave a party, and I think I met John there. I met Merce Cunningham after a performance of his dances at the Henry Street Settlement.

CAROLYN BROWN: I had just graduated from college, married Earle Brown, and moved to Denver. In 1951 Merce and John were on a tour. John was playing his *Sonatas and Interludes* and other pieces, and Merce was doing solo concerts. At that time, I was studying and dancing with a former Martha Graham person who knew Merce and invited him to come and teach classes. She gave a couple of parties for them. Earle and I sat at their feet the first night. Merce never had much to say. John had a lot to say, always. He was an extraordinary, visionary person. At the end of that period, Earle and I said, "We have to go to New York." But we didn't have the money to move, so that didn't happen for another year or so.

LEWIS LLOYD: Barbara Dilley, whom I had married in the spring of '61, was very eager to be a member of Merce Cunningham's company. She was a young dancer out of Mount Holyoke and this was her dream, so she was going to that studio all the time. I used to go over to Fourteenth Street and meet Barbara after her classes. I met John at the studio. That summer we were going back and forth to Williamstown and at one point we went to New London, to the American Dance Festival. That was the first time I saw Merce's company.

JOHNS: In 1954 I had helped Bob Rauschenberg a bit with his *Minutiae* set, his first for Merce. We became friends with Merce and John and saw them frequently. In 1955 there was an evening of Cunningham/Cage performances at Clarkstown High School in Rockland County where we met Emile de Antonio. Bob, De, as he was known, and I decided that there should be a concert devoted to John's music in a public place, and John

Robert Rauschenberg and Jasper Johns, Larry Rivers opening, Tibor de Nagy Gallery, New York, December 1, 1958. Photo: Fred W. McDarrah/Premium Archive/Getty Images.

In its 50 years of celebrating the culturally essential creative movements of the arts in twentieth-century America, the Foundation for Contemporary Arts has focused on what truly matters, leaving to lesser endeavors the trendy, the glib, the safe, and the predictable. It is by such distinctions that we are able to comprehend the significance of a nation's breathing self. I am proud to have participated in the adventure.

—Edward Albee

agreed to make a selection, sampling 25 years of his work. We had little money but the three of us each gave $1,000, a lot for us in those days. We formed Impresarios Inc., which financed and produced the retrospective of John's music at Town Hall in New York. I don't remember what the rental fee for the hall was or the other expenses. Somehow everything got covered. In 1960 we also presented Merce Cunningham and Dance Company at the Phoenix Theatre, downtown on Second Avenue. Those were Impresario Inc.'s two ventures.

LLOYD: At the time there was a path from the Yale Dramatic Association into CBS. Sure enough I got a job there the summer after my senior year, in 1960. I was assigned to work on a soap opera, *The Brighter Day*, and a quiz show, *To Tell the Truth*. After several months, I realized selling soap and detergent was not my idea of theater. I started looking for a building I could put a theater in. I ended up looking at this fleabag film house on Third Avenue called the Comet Theater. Through one set of circumstances or another, I took over the building, including four floors above it. So my partner Arthur Conescu and I took it apart and put it back together as the Pocket Theatre.

The Foundation came into being around the attempt to produce a Merce Cunningham and Dance Company season on Broadway in spring 1963.

JOHNS: I doubt that Merce told us [that he wanted a season on Broadway]. My guess is that John told Bob and me of Merce's ambition. Bob and I said, "We'll help. We'll each give a painting to be sold to help cover the loss that a Broadway 'season' would incur." Cage said he had a Richard Lippold

Foundation for Contemporary Performance Arts, Inc.
presents
MERCE CUNNINGHAM
and
DANCE COMPANY
John Cage, Musical Director
1963 SPRING SEASON
At a Broadway Theatre to be Announced
For ticket information write:
Foundation for Contemporary
Performance Arts, Inc.
Suite 605
667 Madison Avenue
New York 22, N.Y.
Tel. TE 2-9450

Advertisement for anticipated Merce Cunningham and Dance Company 1963 Broadway season, funded by FCPA, *Dance News*, March 1963.

sculpture that he would contribute, a work in five parts that he had returned to Richard years before. Now that he needed it, John decided that it was his again. Richard must have gone along with the idea, because he gave it to the cause. We estimated the value of these three works and it seemed a bit more than Merce's season would require. I asked him what we should do with the extra money, perhaps a couple thousand dollars. And Merce said, "Help others, because we're all in the same boat." So I said, "Well, it's not enough, really. Why not invite other artists to join us and give works, and then we'll be able to help others." That's how it started.

LLOYD: I was in awe of Jasper and Bob. At Yale, my art history professor, Vincent Scully, had lectured about modern American art, and I had heard Jasper's and Bob's names for the first time.

BROWN: John had originally asked another person, Carmen Capalbo, to produce the Broadway concert, and he had turned it down. So Lew said, "Wow, Broadway. OK, I'll do it then."

LLOYD: In fall 1962, John walked into the lobby and looked around at the theater, which was virtually complete at that point. He said, "I like this little theater and maybe we can put together some music concerts for next summer." It was very vague.

JOHNS: I can't think of any organized efforts at that time that operated to support artists. A few individuals, friends of particular artists, would help them. And I imagine performing artists of various sorts approached benefactors, friends that they thought had means to help and asked them to do so. But I know of no organized effort.

POCKET THEATRE

Exterior of the Pocket Theatre, 100 Third Avenue, New York, c. 1963. Photo courtesy Lewis Lloyd.

LLOYD: My attorney, Alfred Geller, and I were trying to organize a mechanism for the Broadway season for Merce. Then somehow we realized, wait a minute, when Martha Graham performs on Broadway, it is always supported by the Bethsabée de Rothschild Foundation. So why are we bothering with a commercial partnership, which is only going to get rolled up anyway?

BROWN: In terms of support, there were individual patrons. Merce had Paul Williams for the [1953] Theatre de Lys season, and he also supported Cage's tape music. The Guggenheim Foundation was also there for a long, long time—they gave a grant to John, and eventually Earle got one—but sometimes it was for just typical conventional composing.

LLOYD: I give John a lot of credit in coming up with the way to put this together. Alfred and I were basically the mechanics, trying to figure out a way to accomplish the goals, which was to get Merce's work produced, but also to benefit the donors.

JOHNS: We were going to call it the "Foundation for Contemporary Performing Arts" but John said, "The arts do not perform."

LLOYD: Our board meetings were very simple and very quick. John knew what he wanted to accomplish, and if Jasper had a particular idea, we would talk about it for about 30 seconds, and that was it. Alfred and I were doing the legal and logistical organization. Once I said to John, "Well, who am I in this whole picture?" He said, "Oh yes, do they need somebody to call themselves secretary, or incorporator? Because you can do that."

JILL JAKES: I don't think I was asked to be involved through Jasper or John—I think Lew had heard of me because I had worked as a production assistant off-Broadway and in movies.

The Foundation began to make plans to hold a first benefit exhibition in February 1963.

LLOYD: The discussion about how to raise the money for the Foundation was so informal, and it was all between John and Jasper and Bob. I think it then got around by word of mouth.

JOHNS: In order to explain to artists what we had in mind, we invited them to come to the Allan Stone Gallery for a cocktail party. We sat down and drew up a list of painters who we thought should be represented and sent each of them a telegram invitation, thinking we were being very smart. A lot of artists showed up and it was a nice occasion. Alfred and I spoke. We explained our intention to establish a foundation and asked them to contribute works for a benefit show. The response was enthusiastic. Artists, particularly then, their work hadn't been turned into commodity the way it has more recently. They were not accustomed to being asked to give things for purposes. Many people who were there said they would help and some did not. We began to plan an exhibition. Allan offered us his gallery and his time and offered to take no commission on anything sold at the show.

LLOYD: It dawned on us that, well, if we are going to ask artists to donate paintings, we wanted them to have a tax advantage. So Jasper proposed it.

JAKES: I was put in an empty room with a desk, a typewriter, and a telephone. It was so impoverished. I guess I was paid something. It was so unconventional; it was improvised, as it should have been under the circumstances. The whole enterprise was out there on the edge. Down to what's usually the most mundane aspect it was equally improvised. Maybe Alfred Geller contributed the room?

JOHNS: I think we all knew Allan Stone, but [FCPA board member] Elaine de Kooning was friendly with him. She must have been the one who asked him to help.

JAKES: I think I went every regular workday to that room. But I was always late, and there was no one to supervise me. The initial letter I sent out to various artists to ask if they would make contributions—I remember I misspelled "sculptor" as "sculpter."

In 1963, I designed the Statue of Liberty poster for the Foundation's first benefit exhibition. It became an iconic image for the Foundation. At the time, I was working in the art department at *Fortune*. I remember having lunch with Jasper at La Fonda del Sol to talk about the exhibition, but I also remember discussing the possibility of eventually leaving my job and going out on my own. In that moment, it was the most unthinkable thought, but after that conversation with Jasper, the idea stuck with me. He was one of my idols, and when somebody of that stature puts a bug in your ear, you never forget. Five years later, I did leave and start my own studio. I made a very successful career in graphic design working for galleries, museums, foundations, and art-book publishers. Lunch with Jasper was only 50 years ago. I don't remember if we split it or who picked up the check.

—Marcus Ratliff

Jill Jakes with 1965 grantee Max Neuhaus, New York, c. 1963-65. Photo courtesy Jill Jakes.

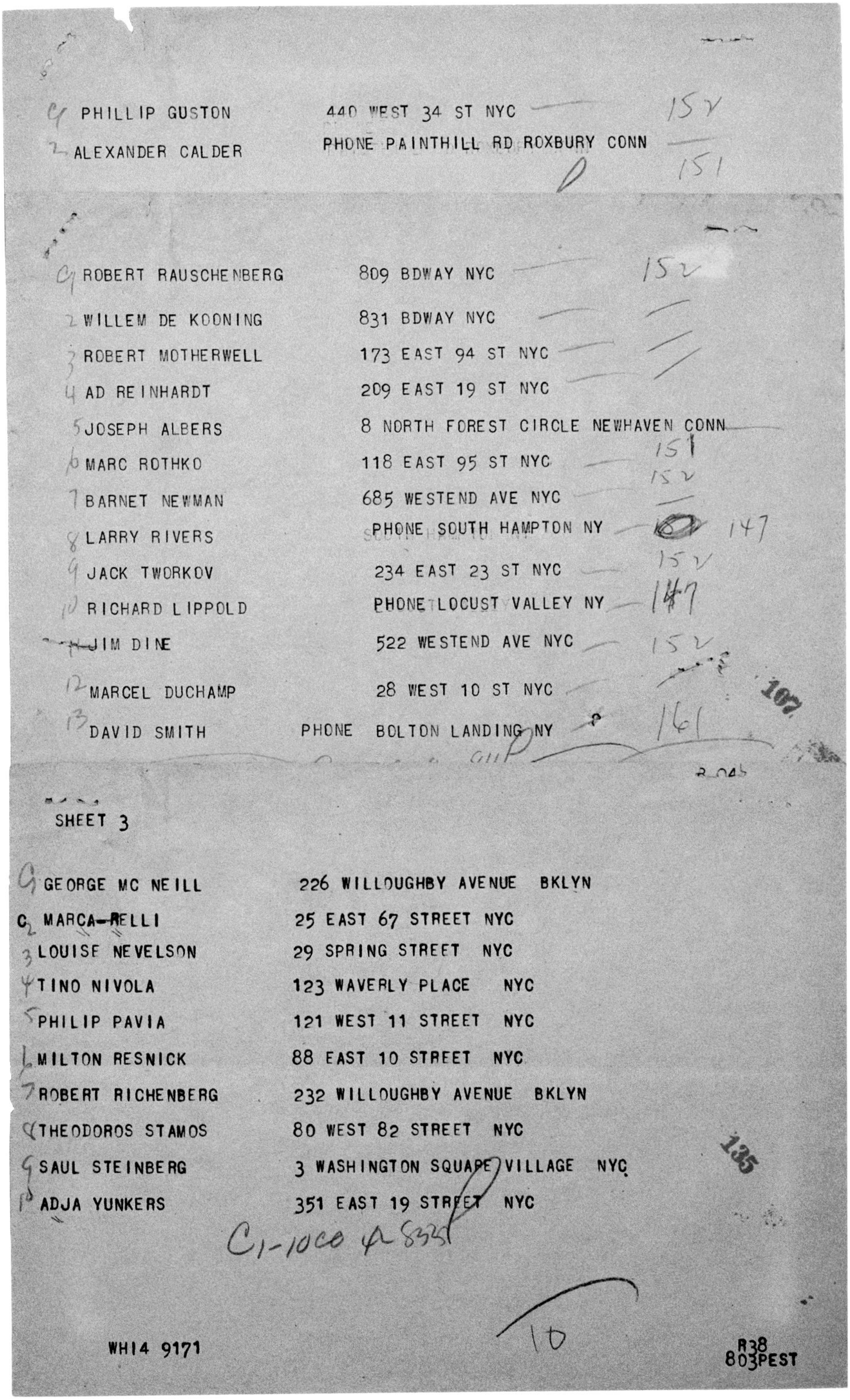

PHILLIP GUSTON 440 WEST 34 ST NYC
ALEXANDER CALDER PHONE PAINTHILL RD ROXBURY CONN

ROBERT RAUSCHENBERG 809 BDWAY NYC
WILLEM DE KOONING 831 BDWAY NYC
ROBERT MOTHERWELL 173 EAST 94 ST NYC
AD REINHARDT 209 EAST 19 ST NYC
JOSEPH ALBERS 8 NORTH FOREST CIRCLE NEWHAVEN CONN
MARC ROTHKO 118 EAST 95 ST NYC
BARNET NEWMAN 685 WESTEND AVE NYC
LARRY RIVERS PHONE SOUTH HAMPTON NY
JACK TWORKOV 234 EAST 23 ST NYC
RICHARD LIPPOLD PHONE LOCUST VALLEY NY
JIM DINE 522 WESTEND AVE NYC
MARCEL DUCHAMP 28 WEST 10 ST NYC
DAVID SMITH PHONE BOLTON LANDING NY

SHEET 3

GEORGE MC NEILL 226 WILLOUGHBY AVENUE BKLYN
MARCA-RELLI 25 EAST 67 STREET NYC
LOUISE NEVELSON 29 SPRING STREET NYC
TINO NIVOLA 123 WAVERLY PLACE NYC
PHILIP PAVIA 121 WEST 11 STREET NYC
MILTON RESNICK 88 EAST 10 STREET NYC
ROBERT RICHENBERG 232 WILLOUGHBY AVENUE BKLYN
THEODOROS STAMOS 80 WEST 82 STREET NYC
SAUL STEINBERG 3 WASHINGTON SQUARE VILLAGE NYC
ADJA YUNKERS 351 EAST 19 STREET NYC

WH14 9171 R38 803PEST

Detail of Western Union telegram, partial list of artists who received telegram invitations from FCPA to a party at Allan Stone Gallery to announce the formation of the Foundation, November 26, 1962.

FEBRUARY 12, 1963

FOUNDATION FOR CONTEMPORARY PERFORMANCE ARTS, INC.
SUITE 309, 30 EAST 60 TH STREET, NEW YORK 22, NY.

DEAR JASPER JOHNS, DIRECTOR:
RECEIVED YOUR SELF-EXPLANATORY INFORMATION LETTER AND FOUNDATION RECEIPTS. RETAINED ONE COPY FOR MY FILE. ANY QUESTIONS I MAY HAVE MAY BE DIRECTED TO THE DIRECTORS OF THE FOUNDATION OR ALFRED GELLER, ATTORNEY AT LAW?
MY QUESTION IS THIS. THIS REALLY A GOOD IDEA EXCEPT MAYBE FOR ONE OR TWO FELLOWS WE KNOW? SOMETHING WRONG SOMEWHERE AN ARTIST CAN'T GET WHAT HE NEEDS TO LIVE AND WORK? THIS FIX UP ANYTHING EXCEPT MAYBE FOR NOW, ONE OR TWO FELLOWS?
FELLOW COMES UP TO ME AT THE WHITNEY, T. HESS, SAYS SOMEBODY BOUGHT THAT PAINTING, STATE DEPARTMENT LADY, LENDS ART ALL OVER, TO EMBASSIES. REGULAR HOTCAKE THAT OIL ON CANVAS, 22 X 22, HEY? FIRST TIME MY PAINTING HELPED ANYBODY. GLAD TO HELP MERCE CUNNINGHAM. BUT NOBODY ELSE THIS WAY.
YOU WANT A FOUNDATION, ARTISTS HELP ARTISTS, YOU GET US ARTISTS A REAL UNION, NON-COMPANY-UNION, SOCIAL-SECURITY-NUMBERS, GET GOVERNMENT TO TAX, DEDUCT, GARNISH, TAKE EACH ARTIST ACCORDING TO HIS ANNUAL-INCOME, EVERY-YEAR, GIVE EACH ACCORDING TO HIS NEED. CHRISTIAN-BUDDHIST EQUALITY. NO FREE ENTERPRISE.
MY QUESTION IS THIS. HOW MUCH DID YOU GET FOR THAT SMALL PAINTING? MAYBE I SHOULD HAVE GIVEN YOU A BIGGER ONE? WHAT MARKET-QUOTED IT?
WHAT SHALL WE DO ABOUT POOR PAINTERS, FELLOWS NOT IN HIGH BRACKETS, DON'T HAVE HOTCAKES, LIKE YOU AND ME?

SINCERELY,
AD R.

Sept 10, 1963

Dear John Cage –
This is a contribution for your foundation.

Mark Rothko

Left: Letter from Ad Reinhardt to Jasper Johns, February 12, 1963. Right: Letter from Mark Rothko to John Cage, September 10, 1963.

JOHNS: I think we did [the publicity] ourselves. I know that I worked at it and I imagine that others did. I remember going to see someone at *Art News* to ask if they would do something. Anyone we knew, we approached for help.

LLOYD: Jill and I were sending Art Cart, the shipping company, all over town to collect paintings from Jasper, Bob, Willem de Kooning, Marcel Duchamp, and others, and dealing with Allan Stone and his assistant. I remember being overwhelmed at the scale of who was contributing. To see it all together in one place was unbelievable.

JAKES: I helped get the art to the gallery. I can recall the layout of the gallery with the pictures on the walls. I don't remember much about the opening except that it was a success.

LLOYD: Jasper's *Map* was in the show. I hadn't seen anything by him before, and I teared up when I saw it. I had never had such a reaction to a work of art before. To this day, I can see it clearly as it was hung in the show. I

There was a sense from the very beginning that what was being assembled by the Foundation for Contemporary Performance Arts was very important, very new, and completely interesting. The audience and the artists and the scientists and the engineers all seemed to be experimenting and being encouraged to experiment to make life more interesting. My memories of the lectures, the evenings, the shows were so filled with focus and intensity and laughter that it almost seems as if they never happened. Gratefully, they did—and do—which is astonishing especially since the Foundation has been generating great experiences for so long.
—Edwin Schlossberg

recently spoke to Carolyn about it, to make sure that it was as I remembered it. It was. The impact of his art coming on top of such a good working relationship as we'd had with him just made my feelings for him and his art even more profound.

JOHNS: The exhibition was lively and a good many of the works were sold. It was a real expression of community feeling and of the possibility of helping someone in it.

LLOYD: Jasper was this calm, organized, pleasant guy, only eight years older than I was. He knew all the painters in the art world. And as far as I could tell, they all liked him. I guess I had a clichéd image of the modern artist, a tortured soul out of the Van Gogh school of personalities. Yet there was Jasper, very business-like and accessible.

JOHNS: After the benefit, all the works were stored in my basement, first in my apartment on 106th Street, then in the basement on East Houston Street, and later in the basement on 63rd Street.

LLOYD: Though he was one of the initiators and donated an important work, Bob was not interested in being on the FCPA board. He just was not the most systematic guy, and you can tell that in the difference between his work and Jasper's. I remember just before we were to leave on the Cunningham world tour, the company had never assembled all their scenery, props, and costumes in one place. There were eighteen dances in the repertory and Merce wanted to tour them all—which is insane in itself. Usually you might take five. I went to Bob's loft, looked at this stuff, and thought, Well, we do not have containers for it. I ran around frantically buying containers—and the stuff just kept showing up, from who knows where. Finally, the day we had to leave, Bob was still wandering around in his studio. He really lacked what I'd call a systematic approach.

JOHNS: I suppose that I was the instigator of these events and that I was more interested in their success. It became a habit.

After the funds had been raised for the Cunningham Broadway appearance, a three-month-long printers union strike shut down New York's newspapers. Without advertising, theaters were also adversely affected, and eventually the planned 1963 concert had to be canceled. Cunningham instead decided to take the company on a world tour in 1964. The FCPA provided almost $34,000 in grants to the Cunningham Dance Foundation in 1964—the equivalent of $250,000 in 2013 dollars.

LLOYD: I said to Merce many times that the newspaper strike was the luckiest thing that ever happened, because if we had gone on to that Broadway season, we would have been whacked by the critics. Nobody would have come, and it would have been a huge financial hit for the Foundation, without much to show for it, whereas in that time-honored fashion, we went to Europe, we were praised, and we came back a success.

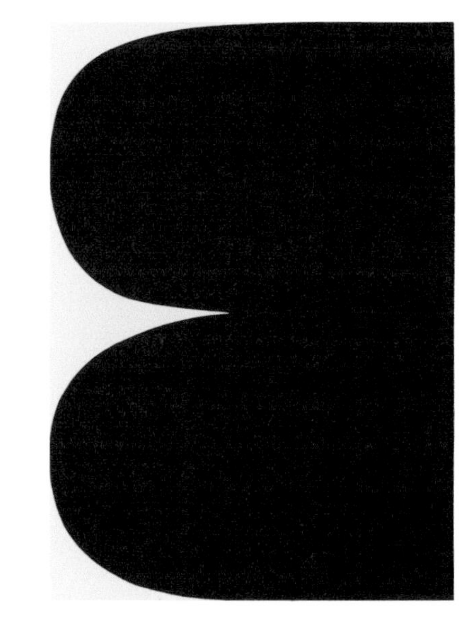

A selection of artworks donated to FCPA's first benefit exhibition at Allan Stone Gallery, February 1963. Clockwise from top: Jasper Johns, *Map*, 1962, encaustic and collage on canvas, 60" x 93". Ellsworth Kelly, *Red White*, 1963, acrylic on canvas, 36" x 26". Andy Warhol, *Merce*, 1963, silk-screen ink and black spray paint on linen, 82" x 81 ½".

A selection of artworks donated to FCPA's first benefit exhibition at Allan Stone Gallery, February 1963. Clockwise from top left: Elaine de Kooning, *Portrait of Merce*, 1963, oil on canvas, 96" x 48". Robert Rauschenberg, *Overcast II,* 1962, oil and silk-screen ink on canvas, 95" x 72". Richard Lippold, *Five Variations within a Sphere (for John Cage)* (detail), 1947, brass, silver, stainless steel, and copper wire, 6 ½" x 6" diameter, 8" x 9" diameter, 3" x 3" diameter, 12" x 10.5" diameter, and 6" x 5" diameter. Roy Lichtenstein, *Flatten—Sand Fleas!* 1962, oil and Magna on canvas, 34 ½" x 44 ½".

BROWN: The strike was what postponed it, but what actually derailed it were three things. Merce was very particular about the size of [the stage], so it had to be limited to those choices. Then John and David Tudor had a tour that was going to take them to Europe at the same time. But the biggest reason that it was canceled was that Merce lost two of his four women dancers. To get the company back in the shape we had been in was impossible, really.

LLOYD: Originally there were going to be two tours in 1964, one in Europe and one in India and Japan, and then it began to grow in scale. As the two parts came together, I went to Air France, since our first date was in France. At the time, it was a tightly regulated system for booking group air tickets, and you had to have a fixed itinerary and passenger list. I was not experienced enough to realize that if expedient, en route engagements came up, we would take them, and go to Poland, or as it turned out, to Finland. And, of course, unexpected things happen—one of the dancers, Shareen Blair, got married in London, and the composition of the company changed. At that point in the trip, Air France said we could no longer have a group discount, and that we had to start paying for single passenger tickets. That was a big problem. As I said to Carolyn, "We had no business not knowing what we did not know."

BROWN: The world tour was a monumentally important thing for the Cunningham company. In London, we had a week at Sadler's Wells and caused a sensation. Our impresario said, "We'll move you to the West End," which is like the Broadway of London. The audience was really involved, and theater people came. The Royal Ballet people came. Choreographers came. That was the moment when the Cunningham company took off. Clive Barnes was the dance and theater critic for several papers in London

The Foundation has always been about artists giving, showing, performing their work in order to help other artists, and it started at a time when such resources were rare. (The National Endowment for the Arts did not exist until 1965.) That the Foundation for Contemporary Arts is 50 years old and still at it is a cause for celebration.

—Mark Lancaster

Carolyn Brown and John Cage, airport bus in Paris, c. July–August 1970. Photo: James Klosty.

Unidentified guide, John Cage, Steve Paxton, Lewis Lloyd, and Barbara Dilley, Merce Cunningham and Dance Company World Tour, India, October 1964. Photo courtesy Carolyn Brown.

at the time and was sending reviews to New York. So we got more press coverage in New York than when we were performing here.

LLOYD: When we were planning the tour, I was sure we did not have enough money to cover what it would cost. By the end of May 1964 I was frantic. I talked to Bob about this in his loft, and I remember him taking *Round Sum* [1964] and saying something to the effect of, "Well, I'll just sell another painting."

BROWN: We had never worked so hard in our lives. We'd never had to dance night after night after night, matinee and evening. I knew from [Merce's then-administrator] David Vaughan that Jasper was desperately trying to raise more money for the company. But I don't think the dancers were thinking about it at all. They were just trying to stay un-hurt.

LLOYD: We had a very bad experience in Venice in June where we performed at La Fenice opera house. It had been arranged by Alan Solomon, the director of the American Pavilion at the Biennale that year. He assured us, before we left New York, that the proceeds would be $3,000, a gigantic amount of money for us. Well, the management at La Fenice did a little

"Hollywood accounting." There were no net proceeds, it was zero. This was the second week of the tour, and the whole thing of course had already been set up. I was frantic. I remember throwing a bottle of Coca-Cola against the back wall of the stage, where it exploded in a million pieces. That caught everybody's attention. And Bob said, "OK, OK, I can work this out. I can lend you the $3,000." Carolyn points out in [her memoir] *Chance and Circumstance* that that was the money from the Biennale prize that he had just won.

I was able to repay Bob $1,000 later in the tour, but I don't think he expected to get a dime back. He and John and Merce had had a terrible falling-out. Anyway, I told him that I had been able to pull some of the money together. And I think he probably said, "Well, you can just have the rest as a gift."

Carolyn Brown, Alex Hay, and Deborah Hay, Orly Airport, Paris, Merce Cunningham and Dance Company World Tour, June 1964. Pictured in background: Ileana and Michael Sonnabend, Robert Rauschenberg, Merce Cunningham, John Cage, and others. Photo: attributed to Steve Paxton. Courtesy Robert Rauschenberg Foundation Archives.

The FCPA had issued its first grants in April 1963, shortly after the first benefit exhibition, beginning a 50-year tradition as a supporter of dance, music, theater, and later poetry and the visual arts, as well as the organizations that help nurture them.

JOHNS: I'm not sure when we started to get requests for grants. My memory is that we spontaneously generated the names of people who should receive help from us, because we were familiar with people that we thought were interesting, whose work was interesting. And everybody needed help at that time. Then word gets out. There were grants to Earle Brown and Morton Feldman and we produced the concert of their music at Town Hall. We also made grants to the Judson Memorial Church, the dancer Merle Marsicano, and the Paper Bag Players.

LLOYD: I think the Paper Bag Players came through me. Knowing [former Cunningham dancer] Remy Charlip and Judith Martin, I produced the Paper Bag Players at my theater. Merle Marsicano, I saw one or two concerts of her work. Her husband was the artist Nicholas Marcisano, and she was very much admired by the downtown art world and performed in the same places Merce did.

JAKES: The hallmark of the Foundation, because it was so modestly funded, was that we wanted to give grants to people for whom a little bit of money would make a big difference. It was typically artists who were very avant-garde, who weren't in any way commercially established. In terms of what artistic merit warranted a grant, it was just the opinion of the group.

Beginning in June 1963 with "The Pocket Follies," at Lloyd's Pocket Theatre, the Foundation produced a number of benefits, including a marathon performance of Erik Satie's Vexations. *Other events included a Town Hall concert of the music of Morton Feldman and Earle Brown and a 1966 series of talks, "Six Lectures."*

JOHNS: I think John saw the Foundation as a resource that could be used to promote ideas with which he was sympathetic.

LLOYD: John was a very paradoxical character. He had incredible will. I will

Paper Bag Players, flyer announcing FCPA-supported performances at the Henry Street Settlement Playhouse, New York, 1963.

When I was composing and rehearsing *Drumming* back in 1970, I barely had the money to buy the drums. Then there was the question of three marimbas… I picked up my mail one day and there was a check from the Foundation for Contemporary Performance Arts! Out of the blue there was enough money for the marimbas, with some to spare. It was especially satisfying because I knew this was a foundation supported by great artists like Jasper Johns, so it meant a good deal more than government or corporate support. I find it remarkable that the Foundation for Contemporary Arts is still flourishing. Long may it continue!

—Steve Reich

not say he had ambition, because that is not an appropriate term for him philosophically or personally, because he had no interest in self-aggrandizement or accumulation of fame or any of that. What was interesting to him was to do his work and be involved with other like-minded artists who were doing their work.

John didn't like Jimmy Waring's work [the organizer of the first FCPA benefit performance, "The Pocket Follies"]. He thought it was much too fey and whimsical, and you can tell that from looking at the "Pocket Follies" program. Jimmy was a choreographer and a very well-loved teacher, and he was fascinated by this idea of artists helping artists. And from John's perspective, if somebody could raise $500 for the Foundation, that was great. It did not mean he had to go to the show.

BROWN: I think a lot of the "Pocket Follies" pieces were made for the occasion, so they were short works. Some of them were hilarious, wonderful, funny. Trisha Brown did a piece in which she just kept falling down, over and over. I was backstage, because I was going to go on for this idiotic finale. I think some of it never even had a proper dress rehearsal.

LLOYD: Even if it was a bit fey, there were some remarkable artists in "Pocket Follies." Ruth Sobotka was a lovely dancer from the New York City Ballet and a friend of David Vaughan's and Jimmy's. She was married to Stanley Kubrick at the time. And Valda Setterfield. The English actress Christine Pickles was in it, and Remy.

★ ★ ★

LLOYD: John had been thinking about *Vexations* for a long time and was looking for a way to get it produced. When he told me about it, I thought it was a great idea. It was less about fund-raising than about presenting this remarkable piece of music. Because that was John's goal, to get Satie's work out.

JOHNS: Satie was a particular interest of John's. And this endurance thing was the kind of thing that John enjoyed. It was very long.

BROWN: I was at *Vexations* at the beginning, and I came back the next morning. The audience fluctuated, though maybe that is hearsay. Sometimes there were two people there.

JAKES: John had all the different pianists lined up. The theater was dark and the piece was going on and on. One pianist would be playing and the other would sit down next to him and seamlessly take over. It was just brilliant.

JOHNS: I arrived late. For some reason, I remember that I was wearing a tuxedo, so I must have attended an opening [possibly Hans Hofmann at the Museum of Modern Art] before going to the Pocket. It seems unreal, but I do remember riding a bicycle—maybe I took a break from the performance and borrowed it to ride around the block.

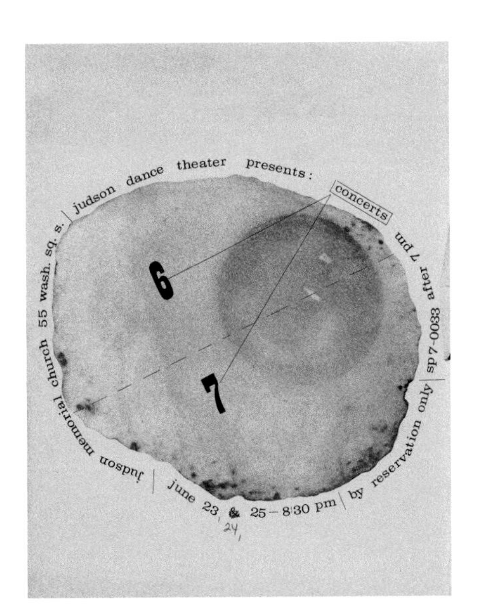

Judson Dance Theater, flyer for *Concerts #6 and #7*, FCPA-supported performances, Judson Memorial Church, New York, June 23–25, 1963.

LLOYD: There was probably more press than paying patrons. The *Times* did something remarkable. I mean, who knew back in 1963 that *The New York Times* had a sense of humor? To send a relay team of critics to this little off-Broadway theater to hear an obscure piece by Erik Satie? It was a mini-media event for its time.

BROWN: The press worldwide were calling and recording. It made a huge, huge impact at the time, which I'm sure delighted John. But he didn't think of it as a joke. Most people thought of it as a joke. It was not a joke to him.

LLOYD: John had this idea that there would be refunds of a nickel for each twenty minutes that you stayed, so that, he said, "One will learn that the more art you consume, the less it costs." That's why we used the time clock. I went up to the Garment District and found a place that rented time clocks. And then of course we got a stack of time cards, too. The time card is what we sold at the box office window. You punched in, then when you got tired of listening, you punched out and handed the card to Arthur [Conescu], who was in the box office, and he calculated the amount of time and gave you your refund. I remember that there was a review in the communist newspaper which complained that the device that the theater owners used to gouge the customers was this monotonous music, which so confused them that they would forget to clock out at the box office, and thus the capitalist theater owners would keep all the extra money. That one was worth reading.

★ ★ ★

In December 1994 Leo was not able to attend the Foundation's award celebration; Jasper thought the event would be of interest to me. It was hosted at the Drawing Center. I remember Susan Sontag reading to a small audience from her book *The Volcano Lover*. I had not been in New York for long and knew very few people at the reception, but I was left with the feeling that we were united by passion and interests. Through the years this impression was confirmed again and again. As the Foundation has continued to grow, in this way it has remained unchanged.

—Barbara Castelli

Review of *Vexations* performance, *The New York Times*, September 11, 1963.

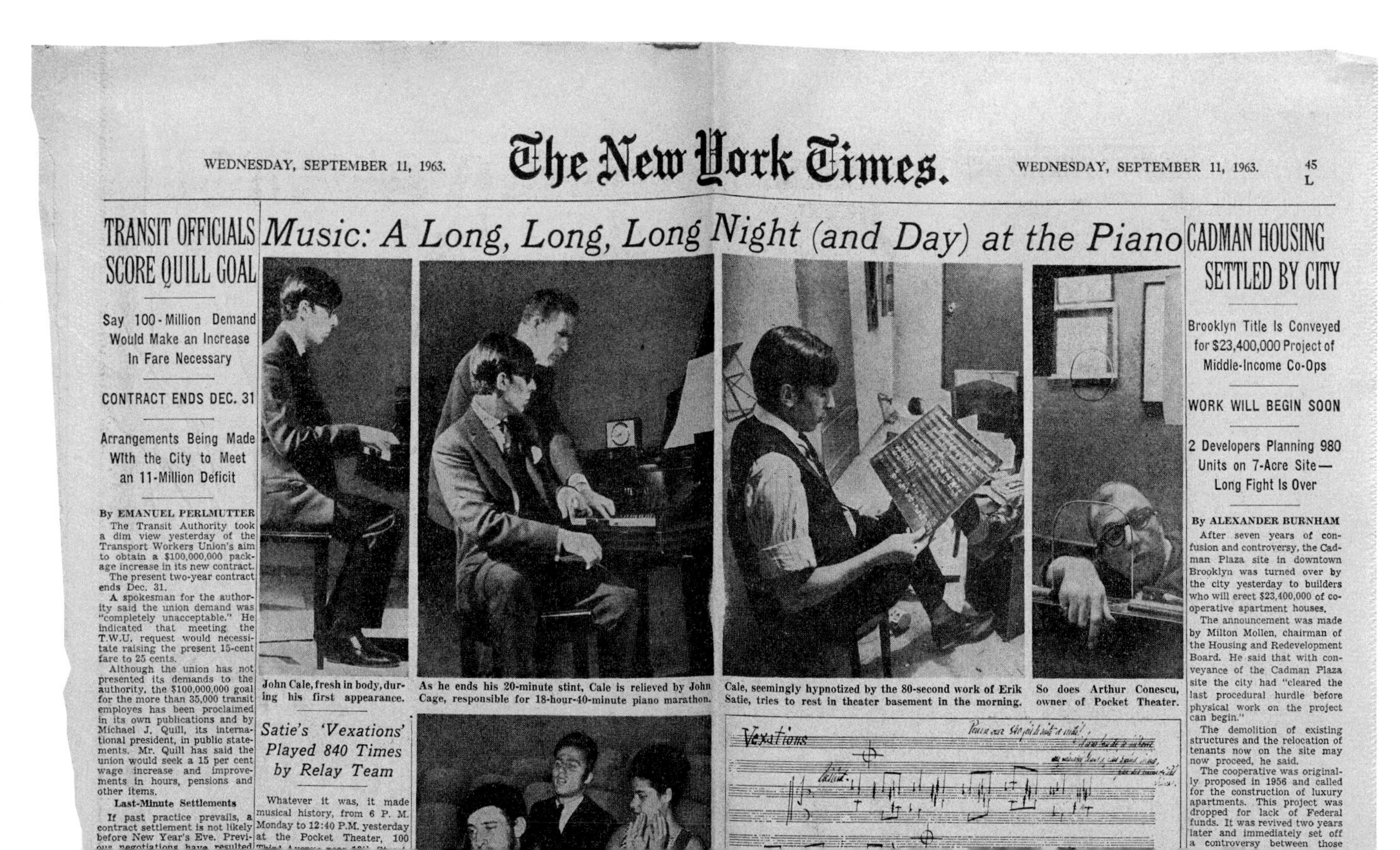

WEDNESDAY, SEPTEMBER 11, 1963. The New York Times. WEDNESDAY, SEPTEMBER 11, 1963. 45 L

TRANSIT OFFICIALS SCORE QUILL GOAL

Say 100-Million Demand Would Make an Increase In Fare Necessary

CONTRACT ENDS DEC. 31

Arrangements Being Made With the City to Meet an 11-Million Deficit

By EMANUEL PERLMUTTER

The Transit Authority took a dim view yesterday of the Transport Workers Union's aim to obtain a $100,000,000 package increase in its new contract.

The present two-year contract ends Dec. 31.

A spokesman for the authority said the union demand was "completely unacceptable." He indicated that meeting the T.W.U. request would necessitate raising the present 15-cent fare to 25 cents.

Although the union has not presented its demands to the authority, the $100,000,000 goal for the more than 35,000 transit employes has been proclaimed in its own publications and by Michael J. Quill, its international president, in public statements. Mr. Quill has said the union would seek a 15 per cent wage increase and improvements in hours, pensions and other items.

Last-Minute Settlements

If past practice prevails, a contract settlement is not likely before New Year's Eve. Previous negotiations have resulted

Music: A Long, Long, Long Night (and Day) at the Piano

John Cale, fresh in body, during his first appearance.

As he ends his 20-minute stint, Cale is relieved by John Cage, responsible for 18-hour-40-minute piano marathon.

Cale, seemingly hypnotized by the 80-second work of Erik Satie, tries to rest in theater basement in the morning.

So does Arthur Conescu, owner of Pocket Theater.

Satie's 'Vexations' Played 840 Times by Relay Team

Whatever it was, it made musical history, from 6 P. M. Monday to 12:40 P.M. yesterday at the Pocket Theater, 100

CADMAN HOUSING SETTLED BY CITY

Brooklyn Title Is Conveyed for $23,400,000 Project of Middle-Income Co-Ops

WORK WILL BEGIN SOON

2 Developers Planning 980 Units on 7-Acre Site—Long Fight Is Over

By ALEXANDER BURNHAM

After seven years of confusion and controversy, the Cadman Plaza site in downtown Brooklyn was turned over by the city yesterday to builders who will erect $23,400,000 of co-operative apartment houses.

The announcement was made by Milton Mollen, chairman of the Housing and Redevelopment Board. He said that with conveyance of the Cadman Plaza site the city had "cleared the last procedural hurdle before physical work on the project can begin."

The demolition of existing structures and the relocation of tenants now on the site may now proceed, he said.

The cooperative was originally proposed in 1956 and called for the construction of luxury apartments. This project was dropped for lack of Federal funds. It was revived two years later and immediately set off a controversy between those

I first learned about the Foundation in 1980, when I was invited to participate in the benefit exhibition being held at the Leo Castelli Gallery. That show included a wide range of artists, spanning various sensibilities and degrees of prominence.

For myself, I had barely exhibited—just a couple of group shows and my first solo exhibition was still two years away. So my inclusion offered the privilege of participation and an immediate membership into a generous community with a shared sense of purpose: artists supporting other artists.

A perfect merger of the artistic and the altruistic.

And as I remember, it was a very beautiful exhibition.

—Terry Winters

Earle Brown and Carolyn Brown, Berkshire Festival, Tanglewood, MA, 1962. Photo: James Klosty.

JAKES: Once the benefit exhibition was over and we had raised that money, the first thing we decided to do (and by "we," I mean the rest of the group, since I had no say) was to put on the concert of Earle Brown's and Morton Feldman's music.

LLOYD: I was responsible for managing "Feldman/Brown" at Town Hall, and I felt badly that I did not get enough publicity for it. But it was like pulling teeth to get the press to pay attention to Morty and Earle.

JAKES: I remember helping with the concert. It was a pretty big deal. We had to get musicians from the union. There was negotiating, and transportation of instruments. And rehearsal space and rehearsals.

LLOYD: The orchestra was good. Arthur Weisberg was the conductor. It was called the Contemporary Chamber Ensemble, I don't think it ever formed again. Alvin Lucier's group from Brandeis, the chamber chorus, was also there.

BROWN: It was thrilling, but what happened in terms of press is that these total morons left at intermission! And all of Morty's music was played before intermission and Earle's after. It was so painful and so hurtful for him.

★ ★ ★

JOHNS: I think that "Six Lectures" was, again, John's idea of what was interesting. He had been promoting Marshall McLuhan's ideas and Norman O. Brown's. And he had known and admired Bucky Fuller for a long time.

BROWN: Peter Yates was very supportive of Merce and John. He wrote a beautiful piece in an architectural magazine about visiting us at a beach.

JOHNS: Yates was probably less familiar to a New York audience. But three of the lectures—Bucky, McLuhan, and Brown—must have been sold out.

BROWN: Bucky's talk was still going at midnight, and he just would not stop.

JOHNS: Bucky had to be coaxed off the stage, because he loved to explain his ideas. He would walk away from the mic as though he had finished, and then come back and talk some more. We had the auditorium until a certain hour, but Bucky continued talking until the people who worked there were very upset.

BROWN: I remember being so impressed with Cunningham's voice—there was recorded voice as well as live voice—and the dance. It was so seamless, so beautifully constructed. The guy who played the piano for our classes used to say dancers are so stupid that they need to have an accompanist. After he heard Merce's talk, he said, "I'm so embarrassed. I'm so humiliated."

Looking back, Johns, Lloyd, Jakes, and Brown comment on the Foundation's 50-year history and its future.

JOHNS: I'm amazed that it's 50 years. When you're working with something all the time—it's just what you're doing. So it's very difficult to see it from a distance.

LLOYD: Because it did not grow out of any organized principles or long-range ideas, I thought that it would stay as a mechanism of artists helping performing artists, but on a rather modest scale.

JAKES: I lived in a world away from it for so long that I'm astonished to learn that the Foundation has had this continuity over the decades. It's thrilling and heartening to know that the original concept had the power and that the core people, of whom Jasper is the only remaining one, had the determination and vision to keep it going.

JOHNS: The informal nature of the earlier years was more amusing and entertaining, more surprising. But it was fitting for that time and I don't think it would be very appropriate now. And, when I think that it's been 50 years, it makes sense to me that it's altered so much. What is exciting about our Foundation is that it's rooted in the community from which art arises, not in the community that uses art. Artists encouraging one another remains an interesting idea.

BROWN: Without Jasper, there would not have been a Foundation. His deeply held belief in Merce's work, and John's, was what started it all. He was, and still is, the driving force behind its continuing existence. From the beginning, it was housed in his studios/homes. He gave considerable time and thought to its activities, taking him away from his own work.

JAKES: Jasper was taciturn and forceful at the same time. It is a tribute to him, the power of his determination, the force of his dedication, to involve other people in keeping it going.

JOHNS: Someone had to take care of it. And I'm the person who did it, by having everything literally where I lived and trying to keep it from disappearing. I suppose I simply fell into the habit of accommodating it.

BROWN: By the time I left the Foundation it seemed on very firm footing and I believed it could go on indefinitely. When the time comes that Jasper no longer wants to be actively involved, he wants it to go on without him.

JOHNS: Of course people from many fields have contributed over the years to the Foundation's program. But artists themselves are primarily responsible for its existence, its growth, and its continuation. And it's the only thing I know that is like that. I hope that younger artists will continue to be aware of this unique thing that artists have made, that they will take pride and pleasure in assisting its ongoing development. ◆

Some of the most gratifying memories I have involving the Foundation are of occasions when I have learned directly from people who received grants of how much the award meant to them. A letter that Ron Padgett wrote to the Foundation made such an impression on me that it has not dimmed in the seventeen years since then. I offer it as a surrogate for the many similar expressions that have affected me since and continue to reinforce my commitment to the Foundation's work.

—Julian Lethbridge

22 December 1996
Dear Board of Directors of the FCPA,

I have been waiting until I felt that I had a chance of writing you a letter that would be as surprising and delightful—OK, as electrifying—as your phone call to me. But I fear that I would have to wait forever! As you know, it is very rare when a poet such as myself gets a call out of the blue notifying him he has been awarded $20,000. That is five or six times the amount I've received for all my books of poetry combined. In the little world of poetry, it is a hefty sum. And in the big world of life, I intend to translate it into travel to parts of the world I've never seen and into extended writing time next summer.

But it isn't just the money. It's also the source. For years I've heard about the good works of the Foundation, both in the admirable way it raises and redistributes art money and in the terrific organizations and individuals it has funded. But when I saw the list of your Board of Directors, I was truly honored. To know that these people feel that my work is worthwhile turns today, the darkest day of the year, into the brightest—a radiant effect that will last a very long time.

Ron Padgett

Jasper Johns and Merce Cunningham, Stony Point, NY, c. mid-1970s. Photo: Yasuo Minagawa.

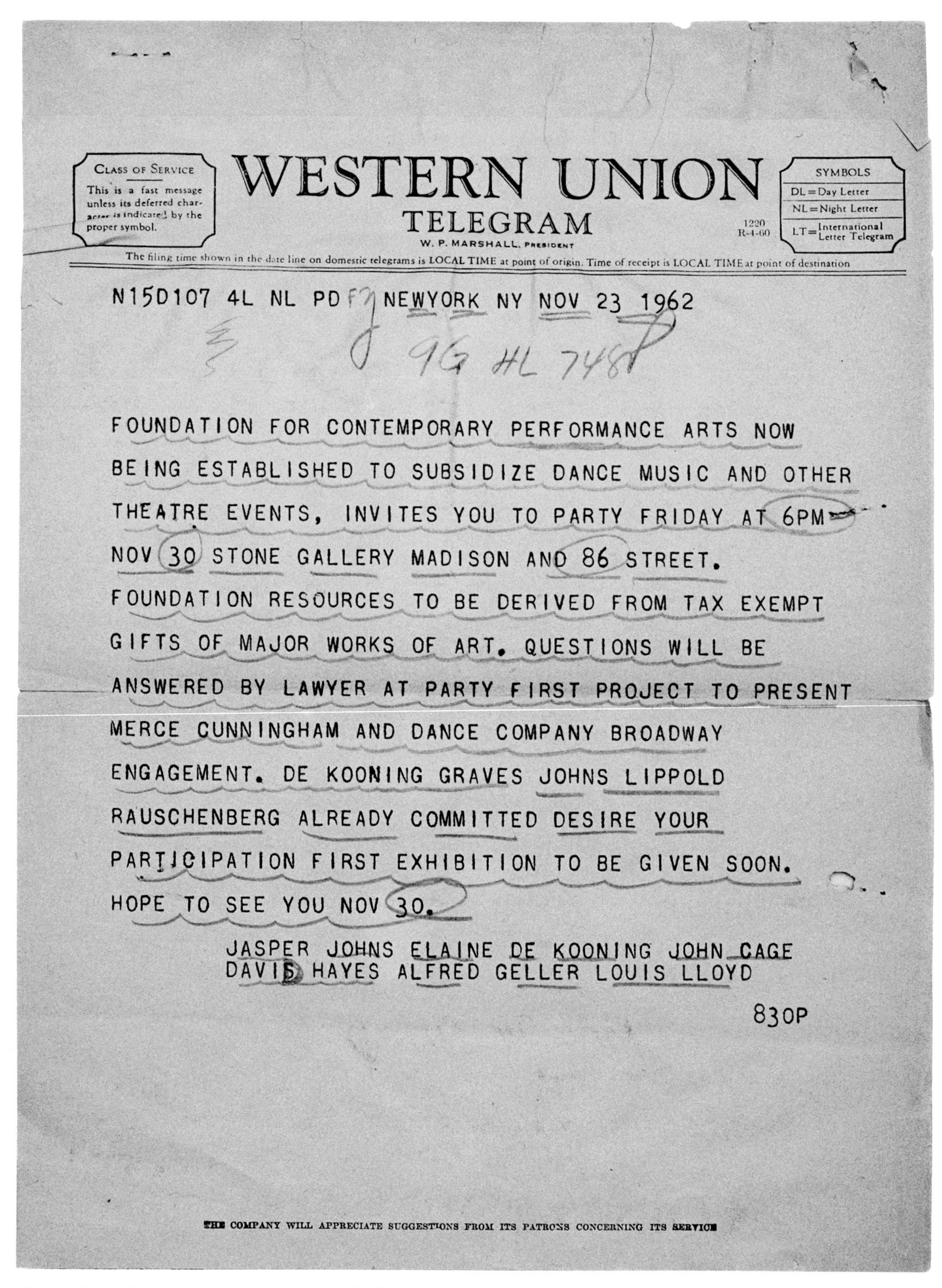

CLASS OF SERVICE
This is a fast message unless its deferred character is indicated by the proper symbol.

WESTERN UNION
TELEGRAM
W. P. MARSHALL, PRESIDENT

SYMBOLS
DL=Day Letter
NL=Night Letter
LT=International Letter Telegram

The filing time shown in the date line on domestic telegrams is LOCAL TIME at point of origin. Time of receipt is LOCAL TIME at point of destination

N15D107 4L NL PD NEWYORK NY NOV 23 1962

FOUNDATION FOR CONTEMPORARY PERFORMANCE ARTS NOW BEING ESTABLISHED TO SUBSIDIZE DANCE MUSIC AND OTHER THEATRE EVENTS, INVITES YOU TO PARTY FRIDAY AT 6PM NOV 30 STONE GALLERY MADISON AND 86 STREET. FOUNDATION RESOURCES TO BE DERIVED FROM TAX EXEMPT GIFTS OF MAJOR WORKS OF ART. QUESTIONS WILL BE ANSWERED BY LAWYER AT PARTY FIRST PROJECT TO PRESENT MERCE CUNNINGHAM AND DANCE COMPANY BROADWAY ENGAGEMENT. DE KOONING GRAVES JOHNS LIPPOLD RAUSCHENBERG ALREADY COMMITTED DESIRE YOUR PARTICIPATION FIRST EXHIBITION TO BE GIVEN SOON. HOPE TO SEE YOU NOV 30.

JASPER JOHNS ELAINE DE KOONING JOHN CAGE
DAVIS HAYES ALFRED GELLER LOUIS LLOYD

830P

THE COMPANY WILL APPRECIATE SUGGESTIONS FROM ITS PATRONS CONCERNING ITS SERVICE

Western Union telegram, announcing formation of FCPA and inviting recipients to a party at Allan Stone Gallery, November 23, 1962.

The Foundation for Contemporary Performance Arts and a New Economy for Experimentation

Eva Díaz

WHEN THE FOUNDATION FOR Contemporary Performance Arts was created 50 years ago as an organization dedicated to intra-artist funding, it was a unique approach to a problem that lingers in the art world five decades later: how to address the uneven pressures exerted by market forces upon various artistic practices and to redistribute economic capital among a wider community of cultural producers. In this day of minimal state and national funding for individual artists' projects and of the atomization of philanthropy in the age of Kickstarter, the Foundation remains an example of arts funding well worth considering—in Merce Cunningham's charter words, "artists helping other artists." So successful, in fact, has been the legacy of the FCPA model—and in its latter-day form, the FCA—that its radical nature at the time of its formation may be less apparent to contemporary observers. The Foundation grew in part out of the efforts of Jasper Johns, Robert Rauschenberg, and filmmaker Emile de Antonio to finance performances by John Cage and Merce Cunningham, under the auspices of Impresarios Inc., when there was little market support for their art. And as I will argue, it emerged in part from the melding of Cage's aesthetics and creative entrepreneurship, an inspired response to economic necessity and desperation. Above all, in organizing what would become the FCA, Johns, Cage, and others were catalyzed by the awareness that the viability of various art practices is too frequently determined by the distortion of the art market's demand for exchangeable commodities. Because of this, fleeting and ephemeral events like dance, theater, and other performance practices often found—and find—themselves with enthusiastic audiences though with never enough check-writing patrons. As Johns later reflected, "What is exciting about our Foundation is that it's rooted in the community from which art arises, not the community that uses art."[1]

1. POVERTY

John Cage was ever the entrepreneur, if you consider acting on the necessity of raising money to make your art entrepreneurial. As early as 1938, when Cage was all of 26 years old, he began writing to colleges and universities throughout the United States proposing to fund an experimental music center, recommending himself as its director. When he met László Moholy-Nagy while working as Merce Cunningham's accompanist at Mills College

1. Mary Judge interview with Jasper Johns, 1999, FCA Archives.

in Oakland, California, Moholy-Nagy was enthusiastic about bringing the music center to the interdisciplinary Institute of Design he had founded in Chicago, but the institute had little money and few assets. As Cage later reflected on the disappointing experience, "I spent two years trying to establish a Center for Experimental Music, in a college or university or with corporate sponsorship. Though I found interest in my work I found no one willing to support it financially."[2]

Though the music center never panned out, one of his pitches, to Black Mountain College in North Carolina, put him on the radar of the faculty. In 1947 he and Cunningham visited the campus, and by the summer of 1948 Cage was invited to teach music composition there, his first gig of the sort.[3] Black Mountain did not pay well, however, and offered only a small stipend and train fare to its rural campus. Cage slept on the hardwood floor.

But Black Mountain was a "galaxy of talent," according to college student Ray Johnson's (somewhat teasing) account.[4] The individuals Cage met there from 1947 to 1953 became lifelong associates and, most important, frequent collaborators: Rauschenberg, R. Buckminster Fuller, M.C. Richards, Elaine and Willem de Kooning, and Cy Twombly, as well as the friends he already knew at the college such as David Tudor and Richard Lippold. In fact, it seems that in Cage's years at Black Mountain he shifted from the desire to found a music center he would lead as director to a much more collaborative sense of creativity as a uniquely generous and cooperative sort of practice.

The culmination of this spirit of collaboration was the first Happening, *Untitled Event* (also known as *Theater Piece No. 1*), which took place in August 1952. Cage and his close interlocutor Tudor formulated ideas for a performance with multiple participants who would carry out discrete activities during various overlapping time segments totaling 45 minutes. Cage proposed that college rector Charles Olson and faculty member Richards read their poetry, student Rauschenberg display his paintings and play records, and Cunningham dance. Tudor was to perform on the piano, and Cage to read from a previously prepared lecture on Zen and the medieval mystic Meister Eckhart. To Cage, the event represented the possibility of events taking place without being causally related; as he claimed, *Untitled Event* expressed "the centricity within each event and its non-dependence on other events," though he had in fact established strict temporal brackets and organized the performance with particular parameters of time, content, and location.[5]

Ever indefatigable, after his experiences at Black Mountain in 1953, Cage proposed another center of sorts, what he termed the "Package Festival," which bundled the elements of interdisciplinarity and simultaneity of *Untitled Event*. Cage's scheme for an itinerant cultural fete, as Cunningham dancer Carolyn Brown noted, was undertaken primarily as a means to provide financial support for the Cunningham troupe of six dancers, two musicians (Cage and Tudor), and a stage manager (in the early years, Rauschenberg). Listed on the large newsprint poster that circulated was a slate of nine possible and combinable events including dance programs, various lectures, and music recitals, as well as a panel discussion; Cage instructed interested parties to "choose your own schedule of events for a 4, 3, 2, or 1 day Festival of the Contemporary Arts." As with the projected music center, the Package Festival attracted inquiries but ultimately no takers. Money

Robert Rauschenberg, Merce Cunningham, John Cage, M. C. Richards, Jasper Johns, and Bob Cato, 1958. Photo: Bob Cato.

2. See John Cage, "Autobiographical Statement," 1990, on the website of the John Cage Trust, http://johncage.org/autobiographical_statement.html.
3. Cage had frequently accompanied Merce Cunningham (in 1947 Cage had visited Black Mountain College as Cunningham's backing musician) as well as other dancers as a pianist, and Cage had also taught music performance at various schools including Mills College and the Institute of Design in Chicago. His attempt to teach a course titled Sound Experiments at ID in 1941–42 was aborted when he realized that all classes were held in a common room. See "Oral History Interview with John Cage," May 2, 1974, Archives of American Art, Smithsonian Institution, available at http://www.aaa.si.edu/collections/interviews/oral-history-interview-john-cage-12442.
4. Ray Johnson, "Norman Solomon's Doberman Interviews Ray Johnson," n.d. (c. 1968) [NC State Archives]. Johnson's often parodic text was sent to historian Martin Duberman in lieu of granting an interview when Duberman was conducting the research on Black Mountain College that resulted in his book *Black Mountain College: An Exploration in Community* (New York: Norton, 1972).
5. Cage quoted in Martin Duberman, "Phone Interview with John Cage," April 26, 1969, 15 [Duberman Papers, NC State Archives]. Further discussion of the Black Mountain College Happening appears in my forthcoming book *The Experimenters: Chance and Design at Black Mountain College* (Chicago: University of Chicago Press, 2013). See also my article "Experiment, Expression, and the Paradox of Black Mountain College" in *Starting at Zero: Black Mountain College, 1933–1957,* ed. Caroline Collier and Michael Harrison (Cambridge, UK: Arnolfini Gallery, Bristol and Kettle's Yard, Cambridge University, 2005).

It was fun. The whole thing started from this generous and loving idea of two visual artists who wanted to help their friends. Jasper Johns and Robert Rauschenberg had just burst onto the scene and Merce Cunningham and John Cage were still struggling avant-garde artists. The impulse was to share—that was the Foundation's humble beginning and I was just implementing their humble idea.

—Jill Jakes

continued to be a problem for Cage, Cunningham, and the Cunningham dance company throughout the 1950s and 1960s.

2. NEW FINANCING

Unsuccessful in attracting institutional funders for his work, Cage was nonetheless able to stage his 1958 Town Hall concert in New York, thanks to the generosity of fellow artists. Through their group Impresarios Inc., Rauschenberg, Johns, and de Antonio each contributed $1,000 to support the programming, and subsequently also produced the 1960 Merce Cunningham and Dance Company performances at the Phoenix Theatre on Second Avenue in New York (the first full program by the company in New York City since its Brooklyn Academy of Music run in 1957), for which Cage conducted an orchestra of fourteen musicians.

The experience of those concerts spurred Cage and Johns to initiate a major innovation in performance-arts funding, the Foundation for Contemporary Performance Arts, or FCPA. In founding the FCPA, Cage, Johns, theater owner Lewis Lloyd, and attorney Alfred Geller pushed Cage's revelation about collaborative creativity and Johns's support for fellow artists further and began to question the existing models of financial support necessary to underwrite any "free" and creative act.

The FCPA originated out of the efforts of Cage, Johns, and Rauschenberg to donate their work or—in Cage's case—that of others to support a proposed 1963 run on Broadway for Merce Cunningham and Dance Company. Realizing the potential of reaching out to other visual artists to fund the nascent Foundation, they decided to organize a benefit exhibition to be held in February 1963 at the Allan Stone Gallery in New York, a show put together and installed at break-neck speed comprising donated works by more than 60 painters and sculptors. In addition to Rauschenberg, Johns, and Elaine de Kooning (as well as her husband, Willem), a multigenerational group of artists contributed work to the debut exhibition, including Lee Bontecou, Marcel Duchamp, Morris Graves, Philip Guston, Alex Katz, Ellsworth Kelly, Roy Lichtenstein, Marisol, Robert Morris, Barnett Newman, Claes Oldenburg, Ad Reinhardt, James Rosenquist, George Segal, Frank Stella, Wayne Thiebaud, and Andy Warhol. In addition to Johns's *Map* (1962), which sold for nearly $15,000, Rauschenberg's oil on canvas screenprint was a big earner; all told, some fifteen works sold during the course of the exhibition, and a sixteenth, a print by Sam Francis, was sold shortly after. The event raised more than $34,000 dollars.

Thus was born an exceptional model—perhaps the first of its kind—of the benefit exhibition, one that has proved robust not just for other arts organizations but for the Foundation itself.[6] The FCPA reprised its 1963 benefit in late 1965 with a monumental three-gallery show of 163 works on paper at Leo Castelli, Tibor de Nagy, and Kornblee and in 1967 in a print show at Kornblee. Together, the two ventures raised more than $28,000. The simultaneous three-gallery 1965 endeavor itself was a mammoth undertaking, with some 159 artists showing works. Johns installed two of the three drawing shows himself (as he would the 1967 benefit and the ten

6. Though galleries such as Wildenstein and Paul Rosenberg held benefit exhibitions for hospitals and children's charities throughout the 1930s and 1940s, the events were ticketed and did not raise money through the sale of artwork. In 1961 the Living Theatre held a benefit auction that helped raise funds for a European tour, with works donated by Johns, de Kooning, and Rauschenberg, among others. According to Johns, the Living Theatre fund-raiser was "not common." Judge interview with Johns, 1999, FCA Archives.

Top: Exterior of Allan Stone Gallery, 48 East 86th Street, New York, 1970s. Bottom: Article on first FCPA benefit exhibition at Allan Stone Gallery, *Art Voices*, February 1963.

art on STAGE

AVANT-GARDE ARTISTS

band together to assist

DANCE, MUSIC, THEATRE

by Roland F. Pease, Jr.

Seventy American painters and sculptors are contributing their works to an exhibition at the Allan Stone Gallery February 25 through March 2 for one purpose: to help the allied creative fields of the dance, music, the theatre—even a poetry reading or Happening.

Among the artists contributing their work are Peter Agostini, Norman Bluhm, Ilya Bolotowsky, Lee Bontecou, Paul Brach, John Chamberlain, Chryssa, Nassos Daphnis, Elaine de Kooning, Sari Dienes, Jim Dine, Marcel Duchamp, Willem de Kooning, Oyvind Fahlstrohm, Sam Francis, Jane Freilicher, Michael Goldberg, Morris Graves, Philip Guston, Grace Hartigan, Al Held, Jasper Johns, Alex Katz, Frederick Kiesler, Ellsworth Kelly, Ibram Lassaw, Rico Lebrun, Al Leslie, Roy Lichtenstein, Richard Lippold, Richard Lindner, Robert Mallary, Marisol, Nicholas Marsicano, Fred Mitchell, Robert Motherwell, Constantino Nivola, Barnett Newman, Isamu Noguchi, Claes Oldenburg, George Ortman, Barbro Ostlihn, Richard Pousette-Dart, Ad Reinhardt, Robert Rauschenberg, Jeanne Reynal, Larry Rivers, James Rosenquist, Mark Rothko, Niki de St. Phalle, Salvatore Scarpitta, Miriam Schapiro, George Segal, Thomas Sills, Frank Stella, Saul Steinberg, Wayne Thiebaud, Jean Tinguely, Jack Tworkov, Esteban Vicente, Andy Warhol, Jane Wilson, Jack Youngerman, Adja Yunkers.

Altruism—regard for, and devotion to, the interest of others—is generally held to be in short supply when speaking of Bohemians who make up the art world. Outsiders consider artists to be self-absorbed to the point of selfishness. Well, it's just not true.

A few months ago a business venture was established to assist the Merce Cunningham dance company present a brief series of performances on Broadway this spring. Someone figured out that if the series played to full houses, the company would lose only some 50 per cent of what operating expenses totalled. Jasper Johns came to the fore and volunteered to give a painting to help Cunningham break even. Then Elaine de Kooning chipped in with a painting. Five other friends of Cunningham came along to say they would contribute a work of art, too, to help cover expenses.

When it was found that the value of these works was in excess of Cunningham's immediate needs, he gallantly suggested that a permanent fund be established that would help performers in allied fields of artistic endeavor, people having the same kind of financial problems he does, by covering the costs of performance.

Thus, the non-profit Foundation for Contemporary Performance Arts was born. Its address is 30 East 60th Street, New York City. Its directors are Mr. Johns and Mrs. de Kooning; John Cage, the composer; David Hayes of the Guggenheim Museum; Lewis Lloyd, theatrical producer; and Alfred Geller, lawyer.

The Foundation welcomes applications for financial assistance and will be happy to consider the merits of any sincere and talented group (or individual) wishing to present a performance, or a series of performances in the dance, music, experimental theatre, a poetry reading, a Happening—anything of a theatrical nature that is interesting and has creative merit.

Many worthwhile artists in these fields need a large theatre to present, properly and effectively, their work. Especially dancers; there is nothing more painful for dancers than an inadequate stage and a cramped house. If they hire a Broadway house, they immediately get involved with the union situation which makes things impossible.

The Foundation is a new kind of "angel" with no strings attached. Its point of view is entirely altruistic and the sole criterion, in judging eligibility, will be Art—if there is quality, there will be assistance forthcoming; if not, not.

Some contemporary American artists today are able to make a living by painting and creating sculpture. This is not true in the fields of dance, music and poetry. Many of the artists contributing to the Foundation's cause have been involved with people in these other professions. Robert Rauschenberg has done the sets and costumes for Cunningham in many past performances, and will create them for this spring season. Noguchi's settings for years have been an integral part of Martha Graham's dance programs. Kiesler, Katz and Kelly also have created works for the dance.

The response from artists has been heartening. The directors initially made a list and sent out telegrams, inviting artists of their choice to the Stone Gallery where the unique proposal was set forth. Many came, and others not in town at the time received letters with an explanation of what was being developed. Works of art that have been contributed are of the first rank—not new necessarily (the Graves' work is dated 1939, the Lippold 1947, for instance) but each piece is given as an act of love and conviction. The prices are standard, set by each artist's gallery. This is not a bargain sale, and Allan Stone is taking no commission on sales. But each purchase will provide the buyer with a double satisfaction: a work of art to love, and a work of art that transcends ownership by contributing to the cause of the arts in America today.

"*Newburyport*," 1962, oil by FRANK STELLA. 30½" by 60½".

"*Untitled*," 1949, oil by RICHARD LINDNER. 9" by 12".

"*Funeral Heart*" by CLAES OLDENBURG.

"*Untitled*," 1962, by RICHARD POUSETTE-DART. 24" by 30".

"*Star*" by GEORGE ORTMAN. 48" by 48".

"*In The Moon Light*," 1939 tempera on paper, by MORRIS GRAVES.

"*Boite-en-valise*" by MARCEL DUCHAMP.

"*Overcast I*," 1962 oil by ROBERT RAUSCHENBERG. 97½" by 72".

"*Sphinx*," 1960 canvas relief by SALVATORE SCARPITTA. 18" by 22".

It was just before the Christmas holidays and Roy and I were spending Saturday as we usually did, going to galleries to see the latest art exhibitions. What we came upon at the Kornblee Gallery and the Castelli Gallery were walls filled salon style with work by contemporary artists, donated by the artists as usual, to raise money for the Foundation. I recall that everything had a price tag of under $400. We acquired a mini-art collection that day . . . two Warhol drawings, a Twombly, a Christo, a Scarpitta; too bad we only had a few hundred dollars to spare! Roy had donated a drawing too, which was hung at Tibor de Nagy.

—Dorothy Lichtenstein

exhibitions the Foundation would hold after 1980). The 1969 change to the U.S. tax code, which barred artists from taking deductions on work donated to public causes, perhaps accounts for the fact that the 1967 exhibition would be the final one held by the Foundation until 1980.

Yet for all the benefit exhibition's success, it bears remembering that it was a unique model for its time. Other sources of funding that might be taken for granted today simply did not exist. The National Endowment for the Arts would not be established until 1965; the New York State Council on the Arts, which began in 1961, only funded arts organizations, not individuals; and the New York Foundation for the Arts, which does fund individual artists, was founded much later, in 1971. From the moment of its inception in 1925 the John Simon Guggenheim Memorial Foundation proved the exception in giving grants to individuals, though of course its wealth derived from the family's mining interests, not aid provided by artists. The same was true for the Ford Foundation (whose arts grants were established in 1959) and the Rockefeller Foundation (which made grants beginning in the 1930s), and neither focused exclusively on the arts.

Since a number of the FCPA's founding members and early donors had histories of collaboration in performance-based actions beyond the Black Mountain events of the previous decade, it is not surprising that some of the earliest grants the Foundation made went to dancers, composers, and choreographers who came out of the Cage/Cunningham circle, just as the original donations were drawn, in Johns's words from a "network of friends who asked other friends."[7] When the 1963 Cunningham run on Broadway fell through, a victim of the longest newspaper strike in New York history, the Foundation gave its first round of grants to composer Earle Brown (then married to Cunningham dancer Carolyn Brown) and composer Morton Feldman, followed quickly by Judson Memorial Church, where many dances of the so-called Judson Dance Theater group were held (staged by those trained by or associated with Cunningham such as Trisha Brown, Lucinda

Installation view, "Drawings," FCPA's second benefit exhibition, Leo Castelli Gallery, New York, December 1965. Photo: Rudy Burckhardt. Leo Castelli Gallery records, Archives of American Art, Smithsonian Institution.

7. Judge interview with Johns, 1999, FCA Archives. Johns and Rauschenberg had at various times individually acted as visual director of the Cunningham dance company, designing its costumes, lighting schemes, props, and stage sets. In both these artists' cases, their interests in time-based performance were expressed in the ways their own paintings encouraged viewer participation and incorporated a sense of the duration a work required in its composition and reception. Johns's *Target with Plaster Casts* (1955) and *Device Circle* (1959), for example, included dynamic and movable portions that were hinged or that pivoted. In the former work, casts of actual body parts that had "performed" stillness in the composition of the work's components were a key element of the completed work. Rauschenberg's *White Paintings* (1951), according to a text Cage published about them, were "airports for lights, shadows and particles," and thereby functioned as screens for dynamic activities happening around them (Cage, "On Robert Rauschenberg, Artist, and His Work," *Silence* [Middletown, CT: Wesleyan University Press, 1961], 102). The fascination with activating or encouraging imagined movement on the part of the painting's beholder was, in a fashion, similar to the identification a dance performance promotes: a kind of empathetic experience of physical exertion by the audience (always tempered, in the case of dance, by the spectators' awe of the athleticism performed by the lithe bodies onstage). In this sense, working in dance seems to have activated Johns's and Rauschenberg's awareness of how a play of time and space could be depicted in painting.

PHOTO: PETER MOORE

Judson Dance Theater, *Concert of Dance #13*, FCPA-supported collaborative performance, Judson Memorial Church, New York, November 20, 1963. Pictured: one of the set's elements by artist Charles Ross.

Childs, Deborah Hay, Fred Herko, Meredith Monk, Steve Paxton, Yvonne Rainer, and James Waring). Other grantees of the FCPA's first two years included the Paper Bag Players, cofounded by Cunningham dancer Remy Charlip, and dancer-choreographer Merle Marsicano. In subsequent grants throughout the 1960s and early 1970s, the circle of support expanded to encompass the Bread and Puppet Theater, Dance Theater Workshop, and composers and musicians Cornelius Cardew, Kurt Schwertsik, Max Neuhaus, and La Monte Young, as well as choreographers including Brown, Childs, Monk, Paxton, Rainer, and Midi Garth. The FCPA's grant-giving strategy had the particular effect of supporting artists at the formative stages of their careers—a move that would have a lasting influence on the constitution of the performance avant-garde of New York City. The most significant amount of FCPA funding would involve Cunningham's company itself: the 1964 world tour, for which the Foundation contributed some $34,000 in 1964 alone at a time when the company was still at a loss for revenue and even faced hurdles in garnering support from the U.S. Department of State.[8]

In addition to the benefit exhibitions, in its early years the FCPA organized several public events that reflected in particular Cage's presence on the board of directors. There were three nights of performances that the Pocket Theatre in New York staged from June through August 1963 (including a marathon, nearly nineteen-hour performance of composer Erik Satie's score *Vexations*), an evening of Feldman's and Brown's music at

8. On the tour and State Department funding, see Seth McCormick, "Fête in Venice," *Art Journal* 70, no. 4 (Winter 2011): 113–16. The FCPA played an important role as well in the funding apparatus of the Experiments in Art and Technology's "9 Evenings" event in New York in October 1966, serving as fiscal sponsor. Under such an arrangement, a novelty in 1966 but now commonplace, an organization or performance group without tax-exempt foundation status (in this case, E.A.T.) works through an umbrella plan in which donations are made to one organization that in turn grants out the money to the unincorporated group. The donors receive a tax deduction, and the recipients get the benefits of avoiding legal and administrative costs attached to incorporating.

Awarding the grants was a joy because we knew how much some small monetary assistance would mean to these artists in doing their work, as well as being a confirmation of their worth made by established artists. Best of all were the times we awarded grants to people who hadn't applied but who one or the other of us knew were in need. My favorites: Grete Sultan, an extraordinary pianist who had escaped from Nazi Germany during World War II, and Edwin Denby, the dance critic, poet, and writer. In Grete's case, John Cage knew she would greatly benefit from a grant. A few years later, when I visited Edwin, then 72, and realized that he was living in very straitened circumstances, I suggested he be given a grant. The directors' response to both was overwhelmingly unanimous. The grants were made, much to the recipients' surprise and our delight.

—Carolyn Brown

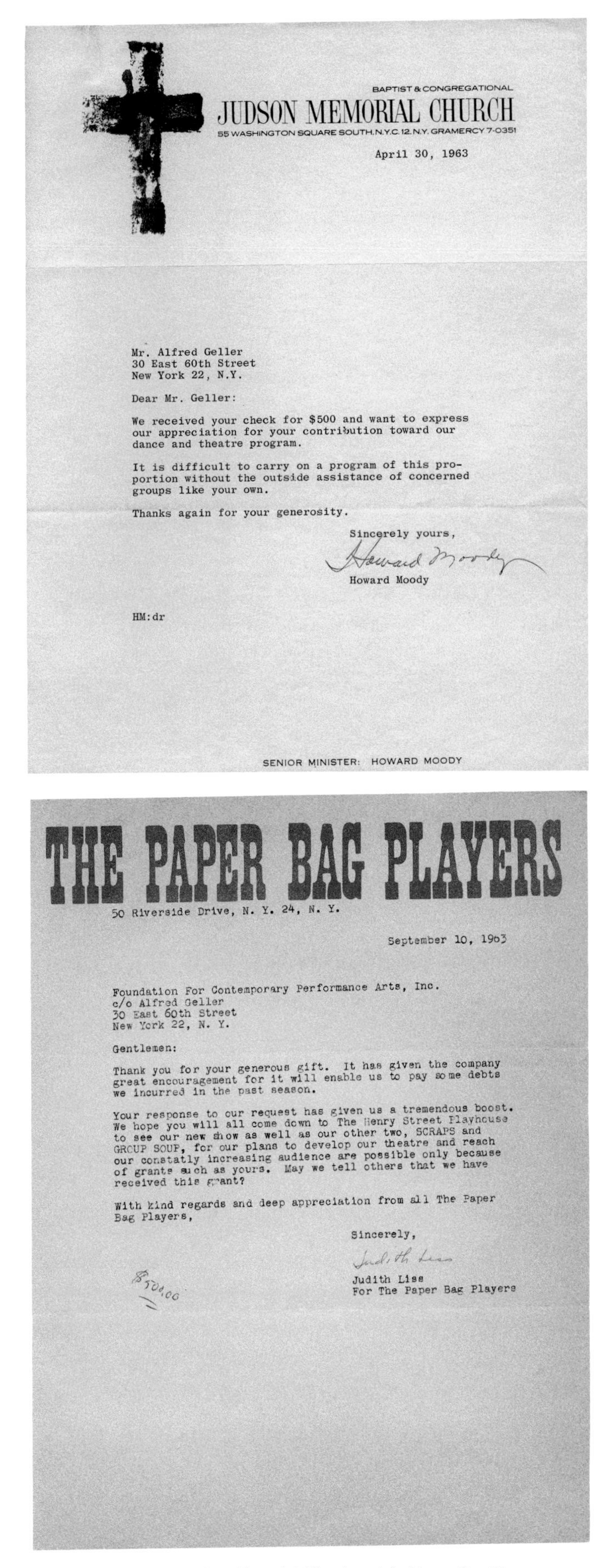

BAPTIST & CONGREGATIONAL
JUDSON MEMORIAL CHURCH
55 WASHINGTON SQUARE SOUTH. N.Y.C. 12. N.Y. GRAMERCY 7-0351

April 30, 1963

Mr. Alfred Geller
30 East 60th Street
New York 22, N.Y.

Dear Mr. Geller:

We received your check for $500 and want to express our appreciation for your contribution toward our dance and theatre program.

It is difficult to carry on a program of this proportion without the outside assistance of concerned groups like your own.

Thanks again for your generosity.

Sincerely yours,

Howard Moody

Howard Moody

HM:dr

SENIOR MINISTER: HOWARD MOODY

THE PAPER BAG PLAYERS
50 Riverside Drive, N. Y. 24, N. Y.

September 10, 1963

Foundation For Contemporary Performance Arts, Inc.
c/o Alfred Geller
30 East 60th Street
New York 22, N. Y.

Gentlemen:

Thank you for your generous gift. It has given the company great encouragement for it will enable us to pay some debts we incurred in the past season.

Your response to our request has given us a tremendous boost. We hope you will all come down to The Henry Street Playhouse to see our new show as well as our other two, SCRAPS and GROUP SOUP, for our plans to develop our theatre and reach our constatly increasing audience are possible only because of grants such as yours. May we tell others that we have received this grant?

With kind regards and deep appreciation from all The Paper Bag Players,

Sincerely,

Judith Liss

Judith Liss
For The Paper Bag Players

$500.00

Thank you letters from Judson Memorial Church and the Paper Bag Players, following receipt of FCPA grants, 1963.

John Cage, Merce Cunningham, and Robert Rauschenberg outside Sadler's Wells theater, London, late July–early August 1964. Photo: Douglas H. Jeffrey. © V&A Department of Theatre & Performance.

Town Hall in October 1963 featuring works commissioned by the FCPA, a benefit performance of Cage's *Variations IV* in January 1965, and a series of "Six Lectures" in March through May 1966 at the 92nd Street YMHA by Cunningham, Norman O. Brown, Peter Yates, R. Buckminster Fuller, Harold Rosenberg, and Marshall McLuhan.[9] Other than "Six Lectures," which raised nearly $5,000, the smaller benefits often raised only a few hundred dollars at most per evening—though fund-raising was a secondary concern in putting on such events. It was (and continues to be) the income raised by artwork sales that allowed the FCPA to stage these performance events and make cash awards to artists.

3. THE GAVEL FALLS?

The founders of the FCPA were able to extend the notion of participation and collaboration from the creative realm into the economic. Arts patronage is a funny thing. As Johns recognized, the people who make art are nearly always less affluent than the people who buy it, and artists who make saleable work are nearly always financially better off than those who do not. Visual artists and performing artists face entirely different pressures when it comes to private support. To paraphrase contemporary artist Andrea Fraser, collectors collect artists, in addition to their work. In contrast, performance events are by their very nature ephemeral and difficult to convert to exchange value; performers are difficult to "collect." Take, for example, Merce Cunningham's "Country Happening," performed on June 3, 1967, at the Glass House on the Philip Johnson estate in tony New Canaan, Connecticut (the eighth wealthiest city in the United States according to a recent study).[10] The event, organized by Mr. and Mrs. John de Menil with Johnson, was billed as a benefit for the Merce Cunningham and Dance Company, with performances by Cage and the Velvet Underground. "For $75 a ticket," the *Bridgeport Post* wrote, "guests will see an hour-long performance by the dance company and hear the premiere of a score by John Cage, electronic composer. . . . Dinner will be served and guests will help themselves to wine from barrels scattered in the gardens." Archival film from the evening shows white-jacketed waiters serving champagne and cocktails to some 400 wealthy-looking patrons across a rolling lawn. The Cunningham company performed for an hour on a raised platform stage at center, took a bow, piled into a white station wagon, and hastily drove off.[11] According to Carolyn Brown, the fast exit was the culmination of an evening of poor treatment: among other things, the music was deafening. "Once in the car, our pent-up fury erupted like a hornet's nest run over by a lawn mower. I'd rarely seen Merce so demonstrably angry and distraught. . . . But the benefit did what it set out to do: it wiped out the Cunningham Foundation's debts. Not only were we no longer in the red, we were actually just a little in the black."[12]

Indeed, benefits often require many sacrifices on the part of performers invited to entertain at the party (including being paid little or nothing to do so), and sometimes these parties seem to cost nearly as much as what they take in. There are back-end costs—staff, overhead, printed invitations, and anything else that might not be donated, like food, drinks, entertainment,

9. Transcripts of these lectures are reprinted in this volume.
10. Assessed according to median family income, *CNN Money*, "Top Earning Towns," 2011, http://money.cnn.com/galleries/2011/moneymag/1108/gallery.best_places_top_earning_towns.moneymag/8.html.
11. *Women's Wear Daily* published a brief article on the event, and *Vogue* ran a spread, with photos showing fashionable guests dancing "to the frantic sounds of the Velvet Underground." See Richie Unterberger, "The Twelve Strangest Velvet Underground Concerts Ever Given," http://www.richieunterberger.com/vucon.html.
12. Carolyn Brown, *Chance and Circumstance: Twenty Years with Cage and Cunningham* (New York: Knopf, 2007), 492–93.

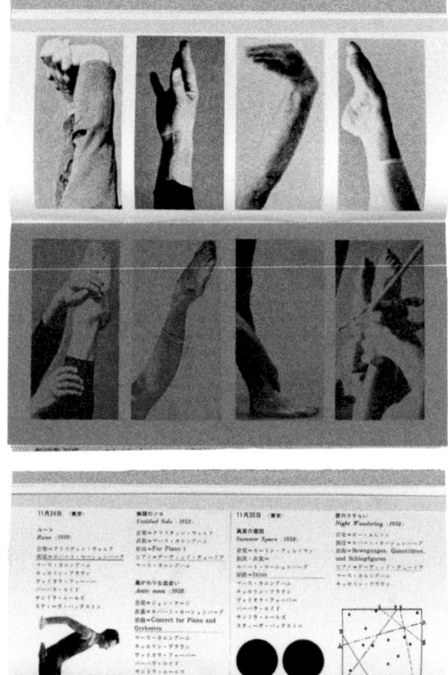

Photographs and ephemera from FCPA-supported Merce Cunningham and Dance Company 1964 World Tour. Clockwise from top left: Company members boarding tour bus, location and date unknown. Pictured: Barbara Dilley holding son Benjamin Lloyd, Robert Rauschenberg, David Vaughan, and Merce Cunningham. Photo: attributed to Steve Paxton. Courtesy Robert Rauschenberg Foundation Archives. On the tour bus, date and location unknown. Pictured: Deborah Hay, John Cage, Merce Cunningham, and David Vaughan, Photo: attributed to Steve Paxton. Courtesy Robert Rauschenberg Foundation Archives. David Vaughan, David Tudor, Carolyn Brown, and unidentified guide, Japan, November 1964. *Septet* rehearsal, Sadler's Wells theater, London, July 1964. Pictured: Shareen Blair, Carolyn Brown, Merce Cunningham, Viola Farber. Photo: Douglas H. Jeffrey. Japanese program, Sogetsu Art Center, Tokyo, November 1964.

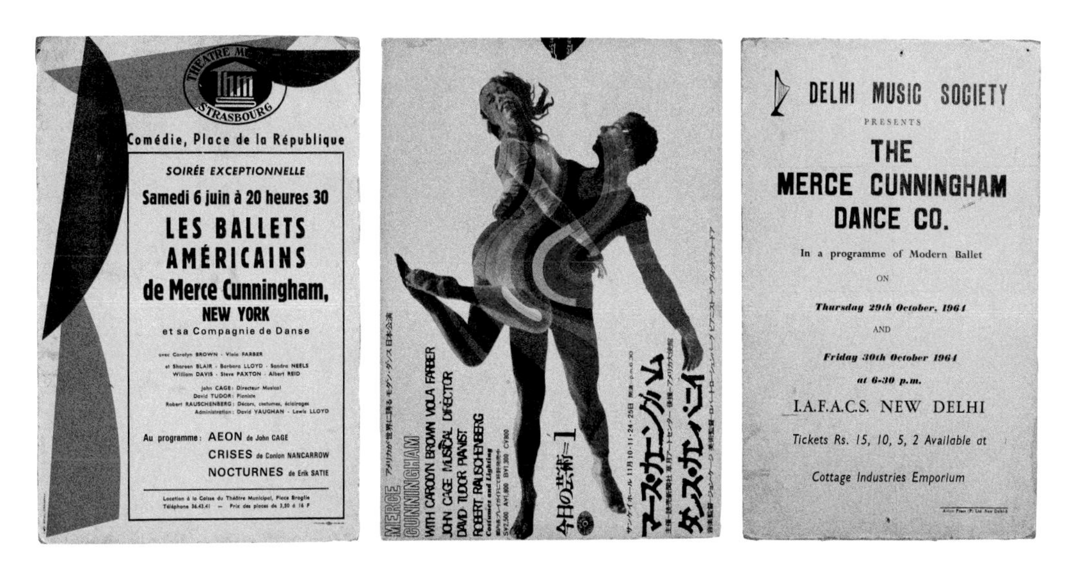

Clockwise from top left: Promotional posters, France, Japan, and India. *Septet* rehearsal, Sadler's Wells theater, London, July 1964. Pictured: Merce Cunningham (rear), Viola Farber, Steve Paxton (front) Photo: Douglas H. Jeffrey. Pre-tour rehearsal at the Cunningham Studio, New York, 1964. Seated: Barbara Dilley, John Cage, Sandra Neels, Shareen Blair, and Robert Rauschenberg; in mirror, standing: Merce Cunningham, Carolyn Brown, Steve Paxton, William Davis, and Viola Farber. Photo: Robert Rauschenberg. Courtesy Robert Rauschenberg Foundation Archives. Lewis Lloyd, Merce Cunningham, John Cage, and Viola Farber, India, October 1964. John Cage in front of Taj Mahal, India, October 1964.

David Tudor, Mark Nelson, John Cage, and Gordon Mumma, *Event #5*, benefit performance for Cunningham Dance Foundation, Philip Johnson's Glass House, New Canaan, CT, June 3, 1967. Photo: Dan Budnik.

and decor. Almost every arts organization has a development and fund-raising office of a size equal to or greater than the "creative" departments. Truth is, almost everyone in the arts—from John Cage to your local nonprofit arts organization—spends much of their time making rent, and benefits are a major way to do that.

So when visual artists do have successful careers, at least a few cultural producers can relax about the money hustle. But intra-artist philanthropy is a difficult path, and money tends to warp perspectives. As artist Robert Longo reflected, what happened to his generation can serve as a cautionary tale: "As things evolved in the 1980s, money flowed. . . . Generosity between artists and the aesthetic dialogue ended. Instead, drugs, sex, and business were the subject matter during the late nights at the Odeon, where we went instead of the rock clubs and the movie theaters."[13] It is interesting that Longo mentions a trendy expensive restaurant as the "end up" of choice rather than the cultural events he and his fellow artists once attended. In contrast, as Carolyn Brown recounts, in the 1950s and 1960s most of the audience for performance events was composed of visual artists, and many art gallery openings were populated by dancers and musicians.

In using John Cage's experience at Black Mountain and the subsequent founding of FCPA to consider the changing economics of art production, I

13. Quoted in Richard Hertz, *Jack Goldstein and the CalArts Mafia* (Ojai, CA: Minneola Press, 2003), 173–74.

These days we are all used to hearing about this or that multimillion-dollar international business underwriting one arty event after another, from a major museum retrospective on West 53rd Street to an avant-garde opera at BAM. But for a long time now, there has been thriving quietly a more modest and disinterested grassroots support system that is not only for the arts but comes from the heart of the arts, namely, the Foundation for Contemporary Performance Arts. It is no secret that the prominent artists of our time make far more money than do their friends who struggle with, say, minimal poetry or aleatory music; and it should be equally common knowledge that there has long existed a community feeling among them, in which names like John Cage, Merce Cunningham, James Schuyler, and Philip Glass are talked about in the same breath as Jasper Johns, Donald Judd, Alex Katz, and David Salle. As much to the point, since the days of Futurism and Dada, of Cocteau, Stravinsky, and Picasso, many of the best visual artists of our time have often joined forces with their colleagues in dance, poetry, theater, and music in order to blur old boundaries among the arts and to open new vistas. There are, of course, philanthropic organizations galore to help the artistically gifted and financially needy; but the Foundation for Contemporary Performance Arts is special. Its funding comes largely from the source, from art donated by artists who know what goes on outside their own walls and would like their works to be swiftly transformed through sales into funds that can help their less fortunate peers whose stock-market graphs don't make headlines in the daily newspaper. As the saying goes, charity begins at home; and we are lucky that so many of our best visual artists have opened the doors of their hearts and studios to embrace so many less well-heeled territories—dance, poetry, music, theater in every imaginable combination—where things other than pockets are enriched.

—Robert Rosenblum (1988)

have touched on examples from the 1930s, 1940s, and 1950s to bring us to the model of collaborative financing begun by the FCPA and continued by the FCA. This model was ahead of its time, yet at the founding of the FCPA in 1963 it was of course not apparent how drastically the contemporary art market would change. Consider the following watershed event, which previewed just how the market would evolve, an example that coincidentally involves many of the major players in the FCPA's 1963–65 events.

In 1973 art collectors Ethel and Robert Scull sold 50 works from their collection at a highly publicized auction at Sotheby Parke Bernet in New York. The flamboyant Sculls, proprietors of the so-called Scull's Angels fleet of taxis, had been collecting contemporary art since 1954 and had acquired a substantial group of important Dada, Neo-Dada, AbEx, and Pop works. (In fact, they had bought Duchamp's *Box in a Valise* for $750 at the first FCPA exhibition in 1963.) At the 1973 auction of their collection, Rauschenberg's *Thaw* (1958), which Robert Scull had purchased for $900 out of the studio, went for $85,000; a Twombly, purchased for $750, sold for $40,000; and Johns's *Double White Map* (1965), bought for $10,500, fetched a then-astronomical $240,000. Works by Willem de Kooning, Newman, John Chamberlain, Warhol, and Oldenburg also earned exorbitant returns.[14]

When the final gavel fell, the auction netted an unprecedented $2.24 million. Footage from E.J. Vaughn and John Schott's remarkable vérité film about the auction, *America's Pop Collector: Robert C. Scull—Contemporary Art at Auction*, depicts the carnivalesque lead-up to the auction and its aftermath. At the auction's end, the film captures a quite tipsy Rauschenberg confronting Scull. Shoving Scull, Rauschenberg spits out a furious accusation, exposing the core of the speculative contemporary art market Scull had "worked" so well: "I've been working my ass off just for you to make that profit!"[15]

Indeed, the Sculls' auction of Rauschenberg's *Thaw* represented a 9,344 percent return on investment. Put another way, if the Resale Royalty Act, passed in California in the wake of the Scull sale, had been in effect in 1973, the Sculls would still have earned an 8,872 percent profit and Rauschenberg would have received a $4,250 royalty from the $85,000 Sotheby's sale to do with what he pleased—like donate it to the Cunningham dance company, for example. Of course, the Sculls could have done the same with their $84,100 profit.

The point is, they didn't. It was Rauschenberg, Johns, and other visual artists of their generation who did. And the model they developed—and that artists of every stripe continue to embrace and to benefit by—meant that less saleable artists do not have to depend entirely on the market or collectors to provide funding for their work. ◆

14. Although most of the works' final prices exceeded estimates, it should be noted that the Oldenburg boxed sculpture *Street Ray Guns* (1959–60), sold for less than its estimate, as did John Chamberlain's *Zaar* (1959).
15. In response to Rauschenberg's attack, Scull averred, "It works for you too, Bob. Now I hope you'll get even bigger prices."

A United Front: John Cage and the Foundation's First Decade

Rebecca Y. Kim

WHEN JOHN CAGE AND JASPER JOHNS established the Foundation for Contemporary Performance Arts in 1963, they called attention to a united front that had been in place for some time among the New York avant-garde. For Cage especially the support of artists had been crucial to his narrative as a composer. De Kooning, Lippold, Motherwell, Kline, Duchamp, Tworkov, de Antonio, Rauschenberg, Johns—they had attended and supported Cage's concerts of experimental music when few in the music world did, and their interests across the arts influenced his historically unprecedented conception of sound. "What is the purpose of writing music?" Cage asked in 1957: "an affirmation of life . . . a way of waking up to the very life we're living, which is so excellent once one gets one's mind and one's desires out of its way and lets it act of its own accord."[1] After three decades of writing music, Cage in 1963 had arrived at an auspicious moment in his career, at last with a publisher for his music and invitations to present his work in Europe and Asia; there was even fan mail after his prose was published in *Silence*. As international recognition grew, however, his efforts to promote the work of his colleagues, particularly Morton Feldman, Earle Brown, Christian Wolff, and Merce Cunningham, continued unabated and became his focus during the Foundation's first year, to the neglect of his own compositional output, which during 1963 consisted of only one new work. "I was too busy writing letters!" he told Gordon Mumma.[2] In revisiting Cage's role during the Foundation's first decade, it is evident he seldom lost sight of his own past while advocating the work of others and understood that support received from within the arts community was far more valuable than any outside patronage. If the Foundation provided performers the opportunity to present new work to a New York audience, Cage believed with firm optimism that such events, particularly in the field of music, also meant "an opportunity for the New York audience to present a united front for music of its own time and place."[3]

The avant-garde on Broadway was the most audacious expression of this hypothesis, and Cage headed the Foundation's first order of business to sponsor Merce Cunningham and Dance Company in a one-week Broadway engagement during March 1963 featuring music by Feldman, Brown, Wolff, and Cage himself with an orchestra of twenty musicians that he would conduct.[4] Cunningham and his colleagues had been embraced downtown but their marquee appeal with the general public was largely untested. Cage and Cunningham had found further success internationally during their 1958 and 1960 European tours with principal dancer Carolyn Brown and pianist David Tudor, but the situation in New York remained largely unchanged as Martha Graham, Agnes de Mille, and George Balanchine took center stage

My gratitude to Lewis Lloyd, Alison Knowles, Lillian Palmer, Robert Moran, Thomas Fichter, Jason Cady, Peggy Monastra, Laura Kuhn, Carolyn Brown, and Christian Wolff for providing important research materials, historical details, and comments on drafts. I am indebted to Gregory MacAyeal and D.J. Hoek of the Music Library at Northwestern University for their phenomenal assistance with the John Cage and Notations Collections. Lastly, a warm thank you to Jasper Johns, Stacy Tenenbaum Stark, Eric Banks, and Bridget McCarthy for their support and dialogue throughout the writing of this essay.

1. John Cage, "Experimental Music" (1957) in *Silence* (Middletown, CT: Wesleyan University Press, 1961), 12.
2. Gordon Mumma, interview with the author, November 13, 2004, Seattle.
3. Quoted in letter from Jill Jakes to Alan Rich, September 29, 1963, FCA Archives.
4. Letter from John Cage to Peter Yates, September 20, 1962, Peter Yates Papers, MSS 0014, Mandeville Special Collections Library, UCSD. In the letter Cage projected $45,000 in art sales to support the one-week engagement, a figure that is at odds with other estimations, which were closer to $30,000. The formal prospectus for the Broadway run listed thirteen works that also included Bo Nilsson, Erik Satie, and Pierre Schaeffer; and two premieres. "Merce Cunningham and Dance Company 1963 Spring Season, Broadway: A Prospectus." Box 10, folder 12, Leo Castelli Archives, Archives of American Art. The investors page included in the prospectus was hypothetical and not officially offered.

John Cage, Stony Point, NY, 1963.
Photo © Hans Namuth.

while Cage and Cunningham waited in the wings for opportunity and visibility within a cultural infrastructure that left little room for experiment. Cage knew from past experience that publicity would be paramount to the success of a Broadway project, and he allocated nearly as much of the budget to advertising as to rehearsal and performance fees for the dancers and musicians combined.[5] By fall 1962, Cage asked theater producer Lewis Lloyd, whose then-wife Barbara was taking classes at the Cunningham studio, to oversee the Broadway project.[6]

A funny thing happened on the way to the theater, however. When the New York printers' union initiated a strike against the newspaper presses on December 8, 1962, it blighted all efforts to publicize the Cunningham company's Broadway debut since daily print ads were the main channel of communication with the public.[7] The company was willing to wait out the strike, but once it ended on March 31, 1963, most Broadway venues faced a backlog of productions and deemed Cunningham's one-week "interim booking" impractical.[8] Thus, in the March 1963 cover story of *Dance Magazine*, "Merce Cunningham Comes to Broadway," the project had been revised to a two-week engagement set for April, though the theater and specific dates remained unconfirmed.[9] After various venue issues and personnel changes, the Broadway project reached an impasse.[10] "Unforeseen situations" were central to Cage's experimental aesthetic, and the coincidence of the Broadway project with the worst newspaper strike in New York history was an uncanny instance of life colliding with art. What one does with the possibilities created by them is what matters, however, and as the Cunningham company would embark on a highly successful world tour the following year, Cage's next project for the Foundation would also make history.

Merce Cunningham, cover of *Dance Magazine*, March 1963.

WAKING UP NEW YORK: *VEXATIONS* AT THE POCKET THEATRE

In late summer 1963, Cage curated a series of benefit concerts at the Pocket Theatre in the East Village. He coproduced the concerts with Lewis Lloyd, who had opened the off-Broadway theater with Arthur Conescu in 1962. James Waring had organized "The Pocket Follies" on June 10, 1963, to benefit the Foundation, and Cage followed up with a benefit series, "New Music at the Pocket Theatre," on three Monday evenings in August and September, the most celebrated of which was the first complete performance of Erik Satie's *Vexations* from 6 PM September 9 to 12:40 PM September 10—a concert of 18 hours and 40 minutes.[11]

The *Vexations* performance had been a long-standing project for Cage, who obtained a photostat of the unpublished 1893 manuscript while researching Satie's music in Paris in 1949. The one-page work requests that four musical phrases be repeated 840 times. In 1951, Cage had approached Cherry Lane Theatre with a twelve-hour performance featuring Tudor, Feldman, and Wolff, but its overnight aspect was like a "crucifix."[12] Cage nearly reached an agreement with Provincetown Playhouse in New York, but residents living above objected to any music being played as they slept, even the hushed dynamics of

5. "Merce Cunningham and Dance Company 1963 Spring Season, Broadway: A Prospectus."
6. Cage had initially approached theater producer Carmen Capalbo, who had recently directed the longest-running musical in New York with the revival of Kurt Weill's *Threepenny Opera* at Theatre de Lys between 1954 and 1961. Lewis Lloyd, interview with the author, June 28, 2012, Lincoln, MA.
7. See A. H. Raskin, "The Strike: A Step-by-Step Account," *The New York Times* (April 1, 1963): 1, 22–24.
8. Lloyd had been in talks with the Shubert Organization theaters for a one-week interim booking. E-mail from Lewis Lloyd to Bridget McCarthy, July 18, 2012.
9. *Dance Magazine* 37, no. 3 (March 1963), 44–45. The two-week budget was estimated to be $80,000, according to the article. On the impact of the newspaper strike see also letter from Jill Jakes to Elaine de Kooning, March 20, 1963, FCA Archives.
10. See Carolyn Brown, *Chance and Circumstance: Twenty Years with Cage and Cunningham* (New York: Knopf, 2007), 352–54; and David Vaughan, *Merce Cunningham: Fifty Years* (New York: Aperture, 1997), 129. Vaughan notes that a news item in the July 1963 issue of *Dance Magazine* announced that Cunningham would appear at the Winter Garden, September 23–30.
11. Five concerts had originally been planned: August 19 and 26 ("Various new composers"), September 2 ("David Tudor plays Japanese composers"), September 9 ("John Cage plays Satie's *Vexations*"), and September 16 ("most popular of preceding repeated"). Undated document on Foundation letterhead, Lewis Lloyd Papers, Beinecke Rare Book and Manuscript Library, Yale Collection of American Literature, Yale University.
12. Letters from John Cage to David Tudor, undated [c. 1951], David Tudor Papers, Box 52, folder 3, Getty Research Institute. Cage also considered approaching the gallery where the 1951 Ninth Street Show had been held.

Foundation for Contemporary
Performance Arts Presents
MERCE
CUNNINGHAM
AND DANCE COMPANY
1963 SPRING SEASON
at a Broadway Theatre to be announced
2 New Works 3 New York Premieres
JOHN CAGE, Musical Director
For ticket information, write
Foundation for Contemporary Performance Arts, Inc.
Suite 605, 667 Madison Avenue
New York 22, N. Y. TE 2-9450

Advertisement, Merce Cunningham and Dance Company's planned Broadway season, *Dance Magazine*, March 1963, paid for by the FCPA.

Vexations—a case in point that Cage's view of music as "a way of waking up" to life was more than mere metaphor.[13]

Accounts of the Pocket Theatre premiere are both history and lore. The complete performance demonstrated that the spirit of Dada had descended on the New York avant-garde, and Cage, who had outlined his affinity with the composer in his 1948 "Defense of Satie" lecture at Black Mountain College, was rumored to be planning an extended version of his meditation on silence *4'33"* (1952) as a follow-up concert, according to *Newsweek*.[14] The night inspired many ideas and associations, not least of which was the impact of *Vexations* on Andy Warhol, whose attendance at the Pocket Theatre has long been debated, as if he had been an apparition.[15] The coverage by journalists was extensive and reported internationally with commentary drifting between the concrete and contemplative, particularly as the hours wore on. Howard Klein, one of the eight *New York Times* critics who covered the concert, found himself in the unforeseen role of pianist following his 7 to 9 AM shift as critic, filling in for Joshua Rifkin, who had slept through the second of his two "Special Mystery Guest Star" appearances. Klein took up the sleep theme in describing his participation in the *Times*: "The hypnotic music provides a point of concentration, which, being of such a fragile, unresolved character, the mind is led deep into oneself. . . . The experience is dreamlike, and the pianist tries to resist waking up."[16] Indeed, once the performance was over, Cage recalled that "the silence was deafening" and that he and others had, in his own sense, woken up: "I wasn't the same after that performance as I was before. The world seemed to have changed. I don't know quite how to say it. A moment of enlightenment came for each one of us, and at different times. . . . After it was over, I drove back to the country and I slept for a long time, something like twelve hours. When I got up, the world looked new, absolutely new."[17]

Satie's instructions for *Vexations* are at once an invitation and a warning: "To play this motif 840 times, it is advisable to prepare oneself beforehand, in deep silence and serious immobility." The score's layout is also unusual as it forces the eye to move back and forth from the lower right of the page, where the cantus firmus "theme" appears, to the first harmonization of the theme above, then back to the theme below, concluded by a second (albeit nearly identical) harmonization above, creating a kind of liturgical call-and-response form. Satie had incorporated repetition within the four phrases themselves, since the theme is twice stated and twice harmonized so that in reality we hear the cantus firmus bass four times the 840 repetitions—3,360 times total!

Cage organized a "relay team" of ten pianists and two stand-by "guest stars," all of whom donated their time for the benefit.[18] Cage had initially planned a performance of twelve hours and ten minutes, but in rehearsal he and the other pianists found it difficult to establish his precalculated tempo and ultimately settled on a slower, more intuitive phrasing—twenty seconds for each of the four phrases so that one cycle was 1'20", each pianist playing fifteen repetitions in twenty minutes for five cycles for a total of 18 hours and 40 minutes, which was a more numerically elegant calculation for performance than Cage's initial estimate of one beat per second. Indeed, *Vexations* tends to hover between musical time and real time and frustrates the counting of time altogether. Satie wrote no bar lines, no meter, and

In those late hours of *Vexations* we got to talking about how Satie might have made the piece: Did he write it first, then decide it should be repeated 840 times? Or did he decide to make a piece that would be repeated many times, then write the notes? We decided it must have been the latter, because the music withstood all those repetitions without driving you crazy.

Also noticeable: at first, when one was offstage and unable to see who was playing, one could tell who the pianist was by their individual manner. After a few hours that was no longer possible. The music had defeated all efforts to individualize expressiveness; it played itself.

—Christian Wolff

13. John Gruen, "18 Hours, Over and Over, Same Music 840 Times" *New York Herald Tribune* (September 10, 1963): 1.

14. "Music Marathon" in *Newsweek* (September 23, 1963): 95.

15. Branden W. Joseph, "The Play of Repetition: Andy Warhol's *Sleep*," *Grey Room* 19 (Spring 2005): 22–53.

16. "Music: A Long, Long, Long Night (and Day) at the Piano," *The New York Times* (September 11, 1963): 48. On Rifkin (misspelled "Rivkin" in the program), see Alex Ross, "Yet More Vexations," May 21, 2007, http://www.therestisnoise.com/2007/05/vexations_updat.html (accessed September 11, 2012).

17. Quoted in Jean Stein, *Edie: An American Biography*, ed. George Plimpton (New York: Knopf, 1982), 235.

18. Gavin Bryars notes that thirteen-year-old Richard David Hames of England may have premiered *Vexations* in 1958 to an audience of at least ten listeners for a school charity concert. Bryars, "*Vexations* and Its Performers" in *Contact* 26 (Spring 1983): 12–20; rpt. *Journal of Experimental Music Studies*, http://www.users.waitrose.com/~chobbs/Bryars.html (accessed August 17, 2012). Cage had brought the *Vexations* score to the attention of the French journal *Contrepoints*, which printed the score in 1949 (volume 6, plate facing page 8); and in 1958 *Art News Annual* printed Cage's photostat of the manuscript alongside his essay on Satie, written while teaching a course on Satie at the New School for Social Research in fall 1957 (volume 27, adjacent to page 77); rpt. (without image) *Silence*, 76–82.

THE POCKET THEATRE PRESENTS

"VEXATIONS"

by

ERIK SATIE

Performed by the Pocket Theatre Piano Relay Team
For the benefit of the Foundation for Contemporary Performance Arts
Monday, September 9, 1963 at 6:00 PM

Players in order of appearance:

6:00-6:20	Viola Farber	3:20-3:40	Christian Wolff
6:20-6:40	Robert Wood	3:40-4:00	Robert Wood
6:40-7:00	MacRae Cook	4:00-4:20	David Tudor
7:00-7:20	John Cale	4:20-4:40	John Cage
7:20-7:40	? Special Mystery Guest Star	4:40-5:00	James Tenney
7:40-8:00	John Cage	5:00-5:20	Viola Farber
8:00-8:20	Christian Wolff	5:20-5:40	Robert Wood
8:20-8:40	David Del Tredici	5:40-6:00	MacRae Cook
8:40-9:00	David Tudor	6:00-6:20	John Cale
9:00-9:20	Philip Corner	6:20-6:40	? Mystery Guest Star
9:20-9:40	James Tenney	6:40-7:00	Philip Corner
9:40-10:00	Viola Farber	7:00-7:20	Christian Wolff
10:00-10:20	Robert Wood	7:20-7:40	David Del Tredici
10:20-10:40	MacRae Cook	7:40-8:00	David Tudor
10:40-11:00	John Cale	8:00-8:20	John Cage
11:00-11:20	? Special Mystery Guest Star	8:20-8:40	James Tenney
11:20-11:40	Philip Corner	8:40-9:00	Viola Farber
11:40-12:00	Christian Wolff	9:00-9:20	Philip Corner
12:00-12:20	David Del Tredici	9:20-9:40	MacRae Cook
12:20-12:40	David Tudor	9:40-10:00	John Cale
12:40-1:00	John Cage	10:00-10:20	? Mystery Guest Star
1:00-1:20	James Tenney	10:20-10:40	Philip Corner
1:20-1:40	Viola Farber	10:40-11:00	Christian Wolff
1:40-2:00	Robert Wood	11:00-11:20	David Del Tredici
2:00-2:20	MacRae Cook	11:20-11:40	David Tudor
2:20-2:40	John Cale	11:40-12:00	John Cage
2:40-3:00	? Special Mystery Guest Star	12:00-12:20	James Tenney
3:00-3:20	Philip Corner	12:20-12:40	David Tudor

HOUSE RULES

Patrons may enter or leave at any time. Price is always $5.00 for first admission.
Punch time clock when entering and leaving. Refunds will be figured for elapsed time thus registered at the rate of 5 ¢ for each twenty minutes, with a 20 ¢ bonus at the end of the program for those who have remained throughout.
Patrons may check their time cards with box office when going out and pick them up when they return later at no additionalcost.

Piano by Steinway

Time clock courtesy of Union Time Recorders

Top left: John Cage's photostat of Erik Satie's musical score for *Vexations*. Top right: David Tudor (left), performing just after 12 AM near the 400th repetition of *Vexations*, John Cage (far right), awaiting turn at piano, and outgoing pianist David Del Tredici (center), keeping count of Tudor's repetitions, "New Music at the Pocket Theatre" FCPA benefit, Pocket Theatre, New York, September 9–10, 1963. Bottom: *Vexations* concert program.

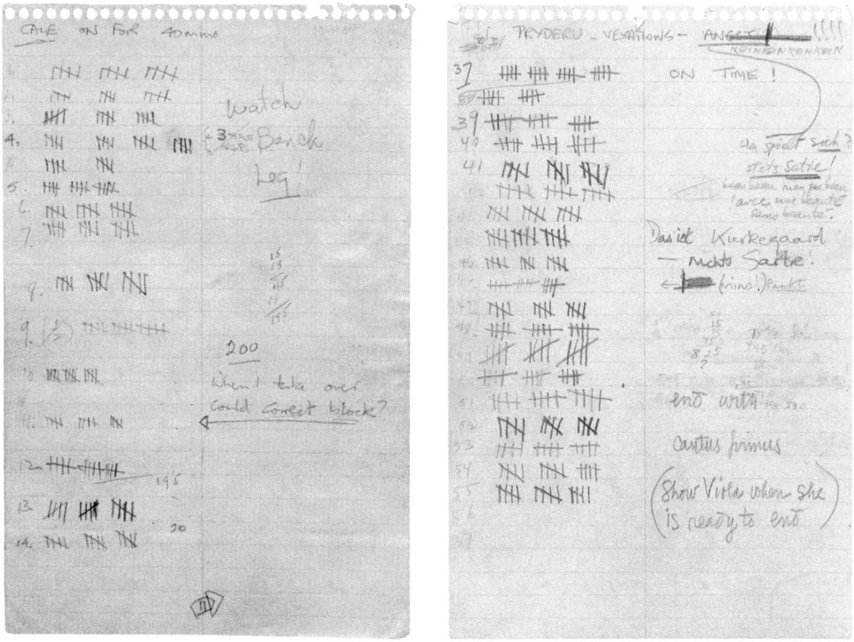

Left: First page of log kept by rotating "registrar" during Pocket Theatre performance of *Vexations*, September 9–10, 1963. Right: Final page of registrar's log.

only a general tempo marking of *Très lent*. He also punctuated the end of each phrase with a half-beat rest, allowing the line to breathe and ultimately humanize a repetition that verges on the mechanical. Otherwise, one might propose that a machine could better execute *Vexations*, in the way that sandbags have enabled the organ keys at the St. Burchardi Church in Halberstadt, Germany, to actualize a performance of Cage's most ambitious all-night work *Organ²/ASLSP* (1987), which began in 2001 and is expected to end in 639 years (the title is, ironically, shorthand for "as slow as possible").[19]

The log sheet maintained by the pianists of *Vexations* provides a fascinating record of how the night progressed.[20] The performers followed a specific system: as each pianist played for twenty minutes, the succeeding pianist sat onstage for the same duration to the rear left of the pianist in a "period of preparation," observing Satie's "deep silence and serious immobility." Once the music was handed off to the succeeding pianist, the outgoing pianist remained onstage for another twenty minutes, taking a seat to the rear right of the performing pianist, to function as "registrar" by counting the repetitions played by his or her successor, indicated with hash marks on the log sheet.[21] With repetition upon repetition, the visual circuitousness of Satie's score, and diminishing fortitude, how did each pianist on the dimly lit stage keep from losing count within the fifteen repetitions? The first page of the log shows at least one error, at the ninth entry, in which the pianist appeared to play a half repetition, then restarted completely. With "Cale on for 40 mins" the pianist in error may have been Philip Corner, in which case James Tenney perhaps leaned over to the registrar David Tudor and wrote, "When I take over could correct block?" More reflective annotations appeared later on: "We are approaching serenity . . . BLISS . . . Oh sleep fitful sleep"; and, written in German, "This is Kierkegaard—not Satie!"

19. Daniel J. Wakin, "John Cage's Long Music Composition in Germany Changes a Note," *The New York Times* (May 6, 2006).
20. Lewis Lloyd Papers, Beinecke Rare Book and Manuscript Library, Yale Collection of American Literature, Yale University.
21. Letter from John Cage to J. Bernlef, December 4, 1965. Reprinted in special issue on Erik Satie, ed. Heinz-Klaus Metzger and Rainer Riehn, *Musik-Konzepte* 11 (1980): 47.

For the *Vexations* performance, John Cage organized a Piano Relay Team. Piano players slept on our couch between rounds. I remember sandwiches all through the night and that soft dawn light slowly filling the avenue in front of the theater as several of us stood on the sidewalk listening to the slow haunting piano sounds coming through the open door.

—Barbara Dilley

Vexations, and Satie in general, has followed me through the years. When John Cage first proposed it to me, my reaction was that this was surely some sort of spoof, but when I saw the score I realized immediately that the title was ironic and the music was in fact deeply meditative, perhaps the most perfect mantra in the history of Western culture. The performance solution, thought up by Cage, was wonderfully appropriate: I think the rotation of pianists tended to support the transcendent, non-ego content of Satie's music, unlike some of the subsequent soloistic or nearly soloistic marathon attempts to perform it.

—Philip Corner

Vexations was a performance exhibit for the eye and ear, and after paying their five dollar admission audience members were free to enter and exit with the aid of a punch clock in the lobby that also ensured patrons of an advertised promise: five cents refunded per twenty minutes attended, with a twenty cent "bonus" for attending all eighteen hours and twenty minutes (a handful of attendees achieved this). Lewis Lloyd recalled that Cage's purpose in offering the refund was "to show the audience that the more art you consume, the less it should cost."[22] *The New York Times* coverage was extraordinary, but its one oversight was to not mention that the purpose of the concert was to benefit the Foundation. It did note, however, an important fail-safe during the 12:45–2 AM shift, which had been the arrival of a number of artists and their friends, 40 strong, who came down to the Pocket Theatre in support of the Foundation after the Hans Hofmann show had let out at the Museum of Modern Art.

MUSIC FROM HERE: "FELDMAN/BROWN" AT TOWN HALL

Bringing the eye into close relation with the ear as if an unstudied object, the poster designed by Marcus Ratliff for the Feldman/Brown concert of October 11, 1963, starkly conveyed the focus of the Foundation's first publicly sponsored event. *Vexations* had been an important prelude, and the New York avant-garde now had the attention of its major critics. Town Hall was an uptown venue located in the Theater District that accommodated an audience of 1,500, and Cage conceived of the concert as a rare and lavish opportunity for Feldman and Brown each to present four works for a large ensemble. Each received commissions for a new work from the Foundation and also support for fees related to more than 29 hours of rehearsal with the 30 musicians of Arthur Weisberg's Contemporary Chamber Ensemble and 18 singers in Alvin Lucier's Brandeis University Chamber Chorus.[23] Jill Johnston noted in her preview for *The Village Voice* that the concert was the first time either composer had major works presented "under the best professional conditions in New York."[24] Indeed, as the title of Brown's commissioned work suggested, this was music *From Here*. Wolff had initially been part of the concert but the already lengthy program and Wolff's graduate studies at Harvard may have factored into the final decision to feature Feldman and Brown alone.[25] That Wolff only recently learned of his inclusion in the initial Town Hall program shows the extent to which Cage often labored quietly in support of his colleagues.[26]

In spite of a strong press turnout at Town Hall, the audience was smaller than expected, with approximately $1,160 in ticket sales reflecting that about a third of the hall was filled.[27] Reviews were mixed. Most critics made efforts to explain the experimental performance practices of variable time and structure in the works of Feldman and Brown, but just as many felt the program was too long and disparate. *The New York Times* was again the most receptive, but Theodore Strongin was not entirely convincing in writing that one of the "great beauties" of their music was that "you can make of it what you want."[28] Leighton Kerner of *The Village Voice* was similarly neutral, particularly about Feldman's commissioned work, *Vertical Thoughts*: "I can't say

22. Lewis Lloyd, correspondence with the author, September 25, 2012.
23. Rehearsal schedule at Carroll Studios, FCA Archives. Weisberg had also conducted Brown's work at Juilliard in April 1963.
24. Jill Johnston, "Feldman: 'Sound the Hero'; Brown: 'Images in Space,'" *The Village Voice* (October 10, 1963): 13.
25. Contract for Town Hall, April 25, 1963, FCA Archives.
26. Christian Wolff, correspondence with the author, September 29, 2012.
27. "Expenditures for Feldman/Brown Concert," FCA Archives.
28. Theodore Strongin, "The Music of Morton Feldman and Earle Brown Is Presented," *The New York Times* (October 12, 1963).

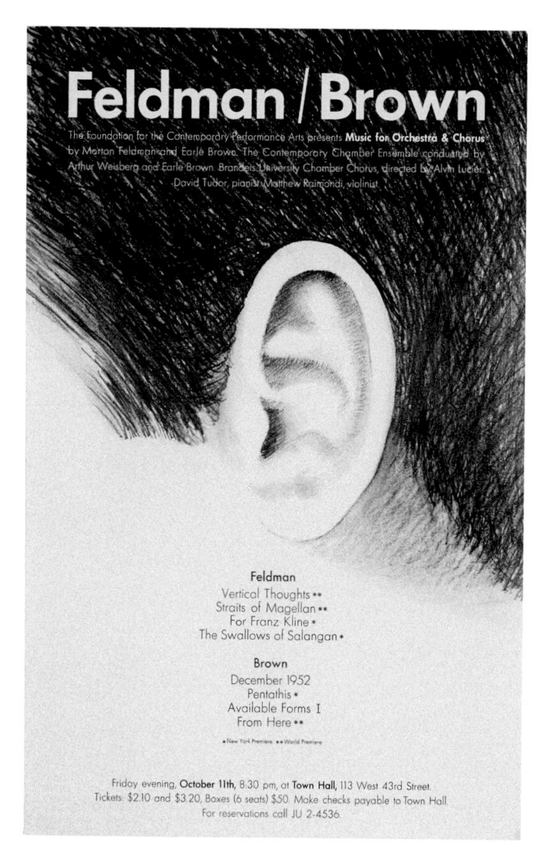

Promotional poster, "Feldman/Brown" concert, 1963. Design by Marcus Ratliff.

In the spring of 1962 I went to a party at David Behrman's apartment in New York. Morton Feldman was there. During a conversation he learned that I was director of the choral program at Brandeis University. He asked if I could bring my chorus down from Massachusetts to participate in a concert in New York in the fall. None of my singers had ever sung music like this before. I said yes anyway. When Earle learned that the Brandeis Chamber Chorus was going to participate in the concert he wrote separate choral parts for a new work of his, *From Here*.

Feldman's piece, *The Swallows of Salangan*, had no notated rhythm, only tones for the players to hold for indeterminate durations. I just gave a downbeat at the beginning, then stood quietly for the duration of the performance. *From Here* had two conductors; Earle Brown handled the instrumental players, I managed the singers. The orchestra consisted of the finest musicians in New York. John Cage and David Tudor played pianos, Paul Price and Max Neuhaus, vibraphones. "Music for Orchestra and Chorus by Morton Feldman and Earle Brown" was performed on October 11, 1963, at Town Hall. It was one of the great events in my life.

—Alvin Lucier

that the listening experience wasn't at times intolerably tedious, but I also can't honestly say that I wouldn't like to hear those wraiths of tone again."[29] The *New York Herald Tribune* was less intrigued, and while it recognized Feldman and Brown as "prophets unhonored in their own land" and noted some in the audience "breathlessly attentive," the composers would "have to get their just critical due from another corner."[30]

The success of the Foundation's Town Hall program was better measured against the profound flaws of the avant-garde program of Cage, Feldman, and Brown presented by Leonard Bernstein and the New York Philharmonic at Lincoln Center, February 6–9, 1964. In fact, less than a week after the Town Hall concert, perhaps in light of the reviews it received, Cage wrote to Bernstein requesting that he reconsider programming a free-form orchestral improvisation to close their half of the two-part program, which had been titled "Music of Chance": "Improvisation is not related to what the three of us are doing. . . . I can only imagine that your plan is a comment on our work. Our music is still little understood and your audiences, for the most part, will be hearing it for the first time. It would seem best if they could do so without being prejudiced."[31] "Your letter astounds me," replied Bernstein, taken aback by Cage's assumption of intentions, but he provided little reassurance as he defended the improvisation and offered only to move it from the end to the start of their program.[32] The flaws in the program were evident in his reasoning: "We are trying to have as comprehensive a look at the aleatory world as is possible in half a subscription program."[33] However, rather than include antecedents

29. Leighton Kerner, "Feldman and Brown," *The Village Voice* (October 17, 1963).
30. Eric Salzman, "With the New Music, Real Time's a Trouble," *New York Herald Tribune* (October 12, 1963). Salzman left the concert before most of Brown's music because of the review's deadline.
31. Letter from John Cage to Leonard Bernstein, October 17, 1963. John Cage Notations Project Correspondence, NUML.
32. Bernstein recorded "Four Improvisations by the Orchestra" with the New York Philharmonic with the durations 0:55, 1:52, 1:32, and 2:22 in 1965. *Leonard Bernstein Conducts the Music of Our Time*, Columbia ML 6133, 1965, LP. The LP also included Feldman's *Out of "Last Pieces."*
33. Letter from Leonard Bernstein to John Cage, October 22, 1963. John Cage Notations Project Correspondence, NUML. Note that Bernstein later made a personal donation to the Cunningham world tour; letter from May 22, 1964, John Cage Correspondence, NUML.

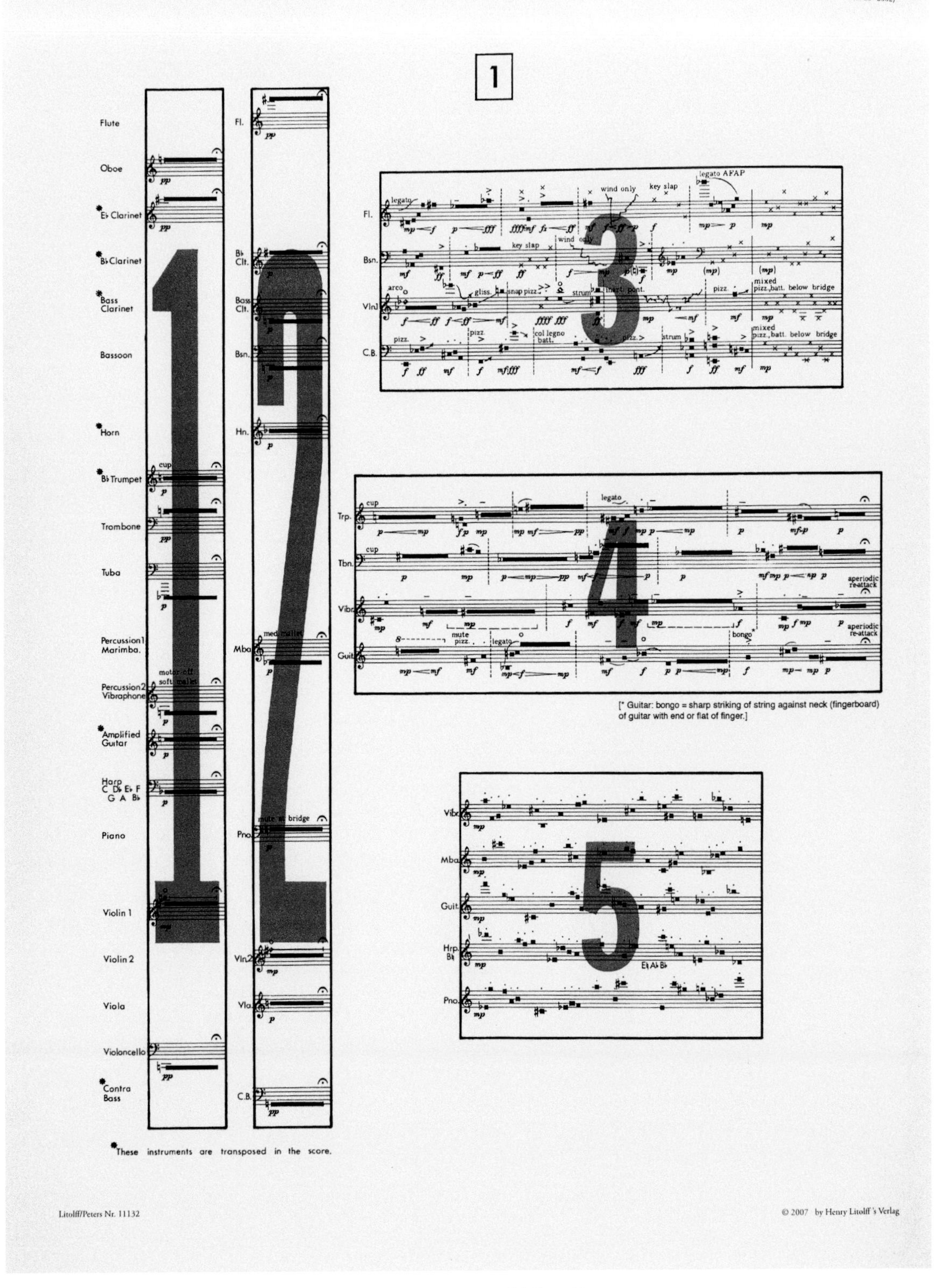

Earle Brown, page from the musical score of *From Here*, commissioned by FCPA,1963.

PHOTO: PETER MOORE

Earle Brown, conducting *From Here*, “Feldman/Brown” concert organized by FCPA, Town Hall, New York, October 11, 1963.

Morton Feldman with John Cage, c.1960s.

germane to the "aleatory world," the first half of the program featured instead standard repertoire that highlighted historical discontinuities, with Vivaldi's "Autumn" concerto from *The Four Seasons* and Tchaikovsky's *Symphony No. 6 "Pathétique"* constituting a concert in and of itself such that the "Music of Chance" program that followed the intermission seemed an afterthought. Critics praised Bernstein for the sensitivity of his introductory remarks, but no words could finesse the triviality of his decision to conduct a few measures from an unannounced twelve-tone work for oboe, clarinet, and bassoon that had been generated by an IBM computer. After the 90-second improvisation by the Philharmonic, Cage, Feldman, and Brown each presented eight minutes of music.[34] It was arguably a mistake to feature Cage's work first, as he had substituted the conductor with a mechanical clock with a rotating arm in the 1961 *Atlas eclipticalis* (played simultaneously with his 1957 piano work *Winter Music*), which elicited vociferous boos and an audience exodus before Feldman's *Out of "Last Pieces"* (1961) and Brown's *Available Forms II* (1962). The critical response was unsurprising. Winthrop Sargeant of *The New Yorker* reviewed the concert after attending an all-Chopin recital by Arthur Rubinstein, and he showed no hesitation in describing the works of Cage, Feldman, and Brown as "trash" that had nothing to do with music, not even "art of the future."[35] While Harold Schonberg of the *Times* noted that the music did at least expose many listeners to the avant-garde for the first time and "[shook] the innocence of many," Sargeant took even Schonberg to task for insinuating that the public had any responsibility to consider such music.[36]

The raison d'être of the Foundation could not have been more strongly affirmed in the aftermath of the Lincoln Center fiasco, demonstrating that no matter what the prestige of the venue or the rarity of the opportunity to reach a public, performances of new music had to be done under the right conditions and with the right people. Controversy had courted Europe's interest in the American avant-garde, but Cage, Feldman, and Brown endeavored to be taken more seriously at home. Jasper Johns therefore noted, "If composers are to function with any sense of freedom" in presenting their music in America, they needed opportunities such as the Town Hall concert, where they would be able themselves to curate and cultivate their programs.[37]

AT THE SAME TIME AND PLACE: CAGE IN CALIFORNIA

The Foundation's benefit concert at the Feigen/Palmer Gallery on January 12, 1965, was a homecoming of sorts for the Los Angeles–born Cage, and featured the composer and David Tudor performing *Variations IV*, which Cage had written in Malibu and premiered at UCLA in July 1963 as the sole new work completed in the Foundation's charter year. Music patron Betty Freeman approached gallery owners Richard Feigen and Herbert Palmer about hosting the concert, and Palmer informed Cage in late 1964: "We have decided that the performance will go 100% for the benefit of the Foundation for Contemporary Performance Arts, Inc. The gallery will undertake to pay for the expenses of the publicity, tickets, mailing, and securing the electronic equipment." Palmer explained that listeners could walk through the four

34. Louis Biancolli, "Composer Booed at Philharmonic," *New World-Telegram and Sun* (February 7, 1964): 26. For a detailed account of the 1964 concert see Benjamin Piekut, "When Orchestras Attack! John Cage Meets the New York Philharmonic" in *Experimentalism Otherwise: The New York Avant-Garde and Its Limits* (Berkeley: University of California Press, 2011), 20–64.
35. Winthrop Sargeant, "First Causes," *The New Yorker* (February 15, 1964): 126.
36. Harold Schonberg, "Music: Last of a Series," *The New York Times* (February 7, 1964).
37. Press release, Feldman/Brown concert, September 15, 1963, FCA Archives. Town Hall had also been host to Cage's first retrospective concert in 1958, which had been produced by Rauschenberg, Johns, and de Antonio under the entity Impresarios Inc. On the European reception of American experimentalism, see Amy C. Beal, *New Music, New Allies: American Experimental Music in West Germany from the Zero Hour to Reunification* (Berkeley: University of California Press, 2006). Brown, for instance, had received many commissions from Europe, but told Jill Johnston in her *Village Voice* preview that Europe did not view his music as "compositions" because they exhibited no fixed relationships or "final best solutions" to musical "problems" but rather as "involvement in process."

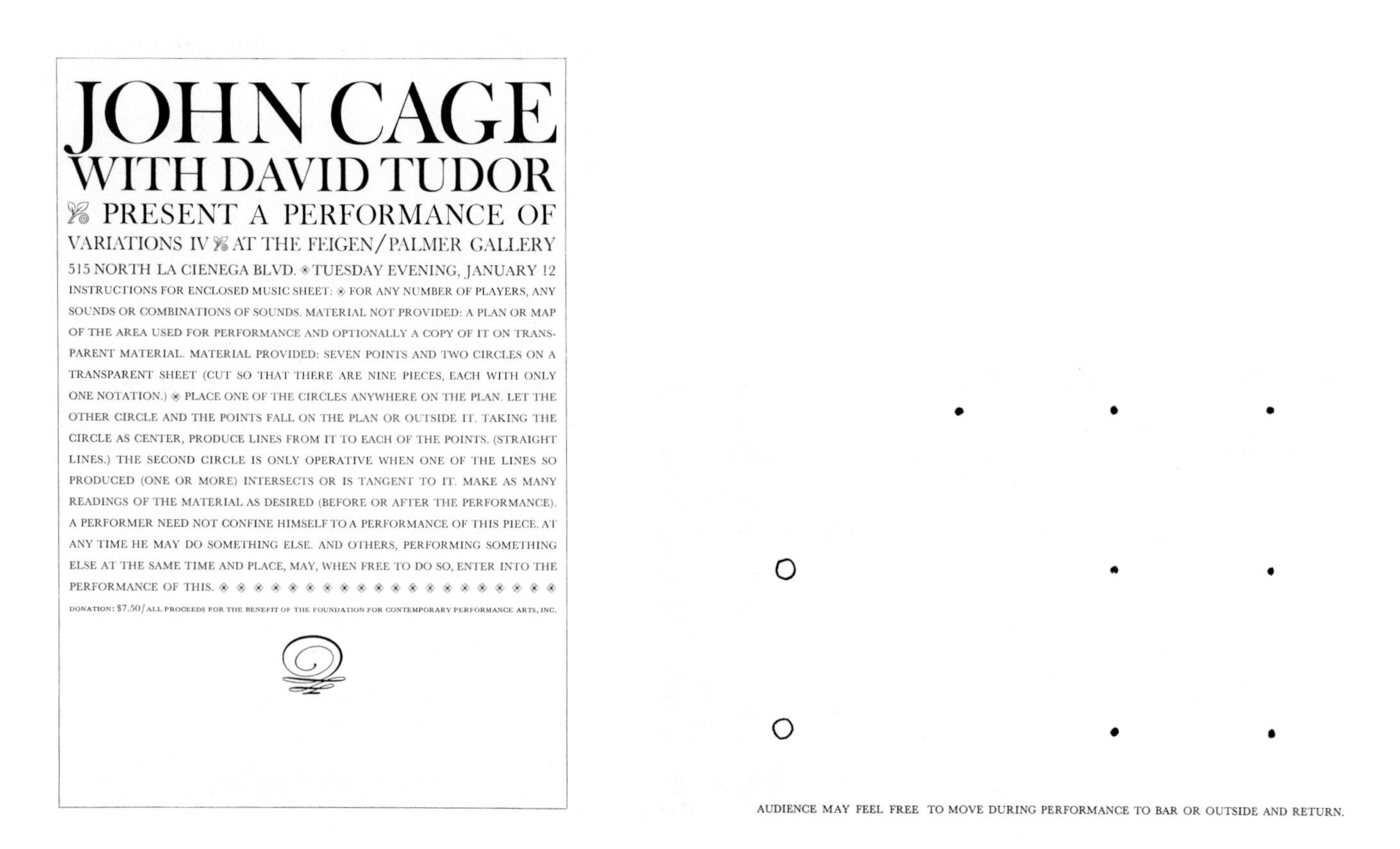

Left: Program for FCPA benefit concert at Feigen/Palmer Gallery, Los Angeles, January 12, 1965. Right: John Cage, musical score for *Variations IV* (1963), insert of Feigen/Palmer Gallery concert program (program not pictured).

rooms of the gallery in a circular fashion with seating limited in the two larger rooms to about 35 people each.[38] The performance would have two seatings at 8 PM and 9:30 PM, and Cage and Tudor played continuously from 7 PM to 1 AM. Palmer recalled a couple hundred guests throughout the night: "People interested in avant-garde music were crazy to come. . . . People were sitting outside on the street. We had filled up the gallery."[39]

Indeed, Cage's view of the Foundation as a support to music of "its own time and place" was captured in the language of *Variations IV*, which invited anyone "at the same time and place" to become part of the performance. Cage included the score of *Variations IV* in the benefit invitation. As a work for "any number of players" and "any sounds," it was sparely notated with nine points (two open and seven closed) on a transparent sheet to be cut into separate segments and scattered randomly over a map of the performance space with the exception of one central point to be placed anywhere. Cage emphasized that the work had everything to do with the space of the performance and "nothing whatsoever about the sounds to be produced."[40] In fact, he went so far as to say that he had "renounced" parametric measurements of dynamics, pitch, time, attack, and timbre that his other *Variations* had required. His interests were now broader: "My notion is that everything we do is productive of sound, that that doing is continuous . . . and what sounds they produce, are questions which I prefer to leave open."[41] The basis for *Variations IV* (and the Cunningham dance with which it was paired, *Field Dances*, which was his first to incorporate indeterminacy by permitting

38. Letter from Herbert Palmer to John Cage, December 2, 1964. John Cage Correspondence, NUML.
39. Herbert Palmer interview with Susan Ehrlich, December 6 and 22, 2004, West Hollywood, CA, Archives of American Art.
40. Letter from John Cage to Edward Downes, March 31, 1965. John Cage Correspondence, NUML.
41. Letter from John Cage to Kenneth Werner, June 7, 1965. John Cage Correspondence, NUML.

I was present at the *Variations IV* performance. Frankly, it was a kind of parody of an art-gallery opening, with the sounds Cage and Tudor were making competing against a group of "arty" people talking even more loudly than usual. It was simply a deadly dull bombardment of noise (spread out with speakers in each of several rooms), and staying the entire time was an act of martyrdom. But here's the thing: experimental music is not supposed to be wonderful every time; in fact, if you are successful even half the time, you probably are not being very experimental. Willingness to fail was one of Cage's great virtues, though he would not ever have used terms like *succeed* or *fail*, because that wasn't the point. His late music was often very dull. He was in my view a saint: by which I mean he was absolutely consistent with his principles, whatever the outcome.

—Joseph Byrd

dancers to control the order and execution of a set of given movements) was Cage's experience at a roadside restaurant overlooking a pond and observing how well the music from the jukebox inside complemented those swimming, diving, and sliding outside. Thus, in *Variations IV* "the sounds would come from 'other' places."[42]

At Feigen/Palmer Gallery, Cage and Tudor performed in two separate rooms according to the pattern of scattered points yielded by their individual score realizations, and among the "instruments" each used to generate sound were a portable phonograph player, a stack of phonograph records, two short-wave radios, two tape machines, a stack of reel-to-reel tapes, a stereo amplifier, and a bullhorn.[43] There were at least four loudspeakers placed within the gallery rooms that channeled their sounds as well as microphones placed above the bar and outside the gallery that further channeled sounds from "other" places. Palmer was an ideal listener: "If you would sit someplace, you would hear one kind of music. If you moved 10 or 15 feet away, you heard some other kind of music. So it was just wild, with all of the different kinds of music going at once. . . . You would never know where anything was coming from."[44]

The performance became one of the first indeterminate works by Cage accessible on recording. Everest Records released excerpts of the live performance in 1966 as two separate "volumes," prompted by Cage's objections to the way "movements" and cheeky titles had been labeled on the first volume: "1st movement: Arrivals (7 PM to 8 PM), 2nd movement: Small Talk (8 PM to 9 PM), 3rd movement: After Three Martinis (9 PM to 10 PM), 4th movement: Departures (10 PM to 11 PM)." Cage expressed anger over the "unfaithful" representation: "You assured me, you will remember, that I would not suffer from your hands the treatment I have received from other companies."[45] Volume 2 therefore comprised excerpts from the final two hours of the performance, labeled simply as "Part I" and "Part II." The performance was a melee of sound "samples" that call out for identification, unlike Cage's earlier works that aimed to distort and transform the familiar: Tchaikovsky's "Dance of the Sugar Plum Fairy" from *The Nutcracker*, Mozart's 40th, the *Dies irae* from Berlioz's *Symphonie fantastique*, the finale of Beethoven's Ninth, a solo accordion, early jazz, talk radio, bagpipes, and much more. While the collage obscured Cage's own musical imprint—its excesses led Eric Salzman to call the performance a "kitchen-sink sonata"—several passages betrayed a distinctly Cagean historical view. The opening of Beethoven's Fifth, for instance, is followed by archival radio announcements of the liberation of Europe from Hitler. Cage had voiced his disdain for Beethoven's music in his 1948 lecture on Satie, based on the conflation of *man* and *sound* as "deadening to the art of music," and claimed that Satie, particularly his use of time over harmonic structure, was the future.[46]

THE MUSIC MANUSCRIPT ARCHIVE AND *NOTATIONS*

A project that Cage began during the Foundation's first year that he brought to partial fruition with the publication of *Notations* in 1969 was a music manuscript collection consisting of original autograph scores donated by

42. Letter from John Cage to Peter Yates, undated letter [1963], Peter Yates Papers, MSS 0014, Mandeville Special Collections Library, UCSD. For the jukebox story see "John Cage's Lecture 'Indeterminacy'" in *Die Reihe* 5 (English Edition), edited by Herbert Eimert and Karlheinz Stockhausen (New York: Theodore Presser, 1961), 115. *Variations IV* was also the second of three works grouped together, of which *Atlas eclipticalis* (1961) was the first and *0'00"* (1962) was the third, based on a theory by Japanese musicologist Hidekazu Yoshida that the three lines of a haiku represent nirvana, samsara, and happening. Program notes by Edward Downes in *John Cage: A Monograph* (New York: Praeger, 1970), 143.
43. Annotations by Cage along the margin of a letter from Betty Freeman to John Cage, October 16, 1964. John Cage Correspondence, NUML. The annotations indicate Cage replied to Palmer 11/14/64. To Edward Downes, he described "a combination of taped material with short wave radios, electronic circuits, cartridges, and alarm devices (horns, etc.)." Letter from John Cage to Edward Downes, March 31, 1965. John Cage Correspondence, NUML. See also the description by Peter Yates, who attended three hours of the event, in *Twentieth Century Music: Its Evolution from the End of the Harmonic Era into the Present Era of Sound* (New York: Pantheon, 1967), 335.
44. Herbert Palmer interview with Susan Ehrlich, December 6 and 22, 2004, West Hollywood, CA, Archives of American Art.
45. Letter from John Cage to Bernard C. Solomon, March 12, 1966. John Cage Correspondence, NUML. The two volumes appear as Everest LPBR 6132 and SDBR 3230; the recordings were digitized and released in 2001 by Legacy 439.
46. John Cage, "Defense of Satie" in *John Cage: A Monograph*, 77–84.

composers of his time. Cage's initial plan had been to hold a benefit exhibition in which the manuscripts would be sold to raise money for the FCPA, in much the same way as the donated artworks. Pages of his own works had successfully sold in 1958 at Stable Gallery, an exhibition held in connection with Cage's retrospective concert at Town Hall produced by Impresarios Inc., and he saw similar potential in the works of his contemporaries that increasingly explored graphic and gestural notations.[47] Cage also viewed the collection as a historical document, and by 1965 sought to include early masters of the avant-garde such as Charles Ives and Anton Webern, and therefore wrote to the widow of his former teacher Arnold Schoenberg that October requesting any manuscript in the composer's original hand: "The entire event would be unthinkable without his being represented."[48] The event to which Cage referred was an exhibition of the manuscripts planned for April 1966 at Stable Gallery, but as the months passed neither the gallery nor Schoenberg's widow came through. By March 1966 it appeared that the newly opened New York Public Library for the Performing Arts at Lincoln Center would host an exhibition of the 54 manuscripts in the next year, and Cage felt confident that his collection was "proceeding beautifully" and mused that he even wanted to include "a Hollywood movie score, showing how a tribe makes music."[49] With "well over 300" manuscripts by December 1966, the collection was nearing completion, but by then Lincoln Center was no longer a possibility and the Museum of Modern Art had declined on the grounds that the collection was "music instead of art."[50]

Earlier in 1966, however, artist-composer and editor Dick Higgins of Something Else Press proposed the idea of creating a "Catalogue" of the Foundation's manuscripts not only as a book of notation for its own sake but also as a kind of exhibition catalogue should the collection be shown.[51] This catalogue was the beginnings of the *Notations* book. Over the next two years, Higgins and wife Alison Knowles, both of whom had known Cage since the late 1950s when he taught Experimental Composition at the New School (they were also inspired to host a performance of *Vexations* in their home after the Pocket Theatre premiere), photographed a representative page of each of the 259 composers to print in the book and compiled an index listing the manuscript's dimensions and additional scores donated to the collective "Archive," which included another approximately 132 manuscripts at the time.[52]

Higgins and Knowles made significant contributions to the progress of the collection, as is evident in its exponential growth from 54 to more than 300 scores between March and December 1966. Higgins contacted Fluxus figurehead George Maciunas, for instance, who intended to contribute a work for the Foundation's cause but only on the condition that his work not be photographed since "only Fluxus should publish Fluxus people."[53] Perhaps building on Cage's idea to include a film score, Higgins also felt it was important to consider the inclusion of the Beatles, Jerome Kern, Cole Porter, George Gershwin, Bob Dylan, Cecil Taylor, the Fugs, Sun Ra, and what Higgins believed, in his own opinion, to be the "best rock-and-roll group in the USA" at the time, Jefferson Airplane.[54] Higgins seems to have been the one responsible for actively pursuing the Beatles manuscripts through Yoko Ono, who had recently met the group and in February

47. Johns recalled Cage's scores on exhibit in the upper level of Stable Gallery and works possibly by Joseph Cornell on the ground level. Johns acquired a page of Cage's *Concert for Piano and Orchestra* (1958), and recalls that Jack Tworkov may have acquired *Water Music* (1952), and Ileana Castelli the movement on Willem de Kooning from *Seven Haiku* (1952). Jasper Johns, correspondence with the author and Stacy Tenenbaum Stark, September 25, 2012.

48. Letter from John Cage to Gertrude Schoenberg, October 30, 1965. John Cage Notations Project Correspondence, NUML. Cage later wrote to Leonard Stein after three unanswered letters to Mrs. Schoenberg and indicated that he had well over 300 manuscripts, as reported to Peter Yates, March 10, 1967, Peter Yates Papers, MSS 0014, Mandeville Special Collections Library, UCSD.

49. John Cage to Peter Yates, March 7, 1966, Peter Yates Papers, MSS 0014, Mandeville Special Collections Library, UCSD.

50. Letter from Thor E. Wood to John Cage, November 7, 1966, Music Division, New York Public Library for the Performing Arts. Letter from John Cage to Peter Yates, December 21, 1966, Peter Yates Papers, MSS 0014, Mandeville Special Collections Library, UCSD.

51. The state of the project is described in part in the formal letter of permission sent to each publisher. Letter from Cage to Walter Hinrichsen (C. F. Peters Corporation), June 8, 1967, FCA Archives.

52. On Cage's influence on younger artists in the late 1950s, see Rebecca Y. Kim, "The Formalization of Indeterminacy in 1958: John Cage and Experimental Composition at the New School" in *John Cage* (October Files No. 12), ed. Julia Robinson (Cambridge, MA: MIT Press, 2011), 141–70.

53. Letter from Dick Higgins to John Cage, September 1, 1966. John Cage Notations Project Correspondence, NUML. There are no works by Maciunas in the manuscript archive, and those by Fluxus artists are amply represented in the *Notations* book.

54. Letter from Dick Higgins to John Cage, January 30 and March 8, 1967. John Cage Notations Project Correspondence, NUML. Higgins was particularly keen on Jefferson Airplane's "Comin' Back to Me" in the March letter.

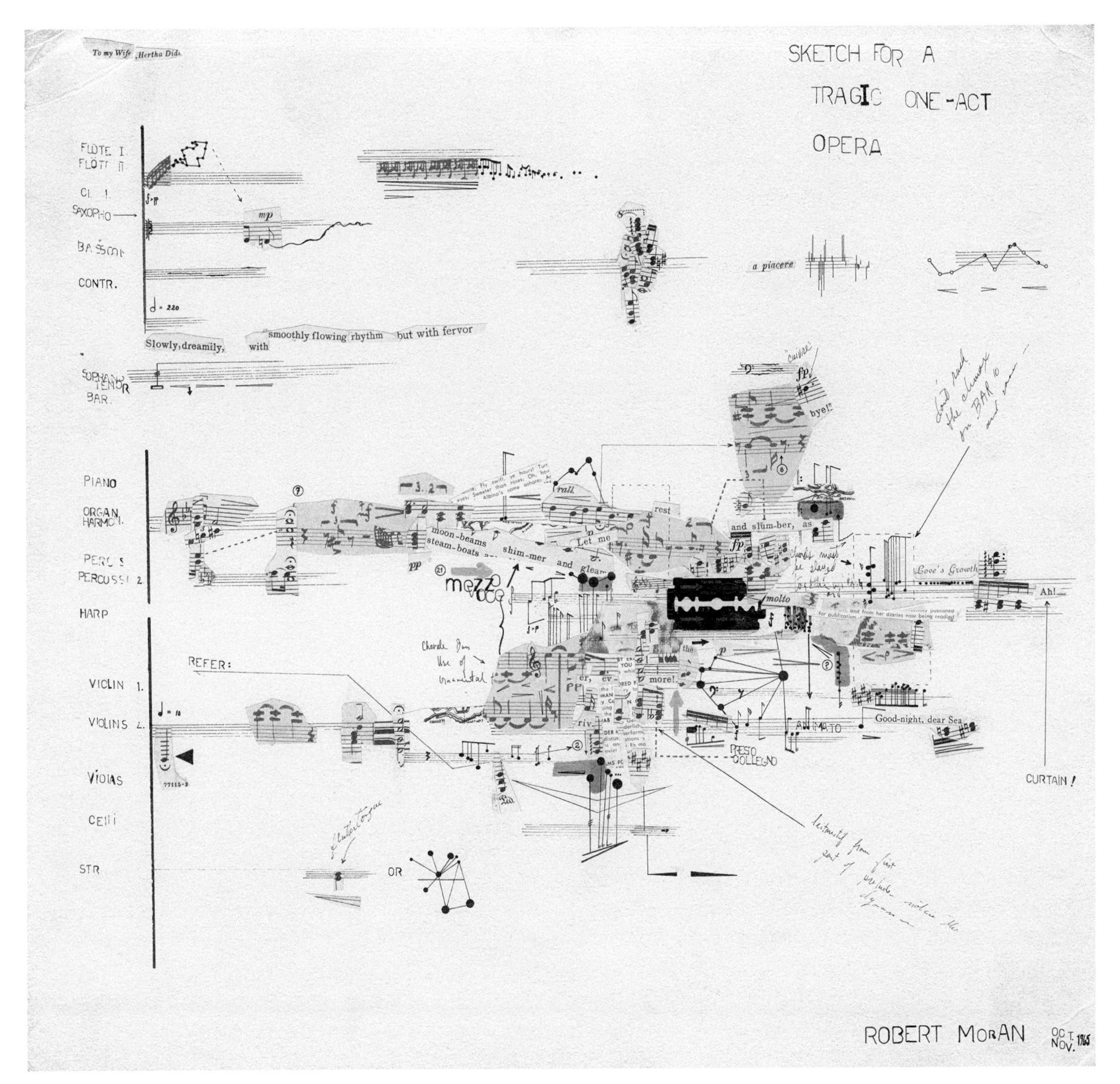

Robert Moran, musical score for *Sketch for a Tragic One-Act Opera*, 1965. John Cage Notations Project Manuscript Scores, Northwestern University Music Library.

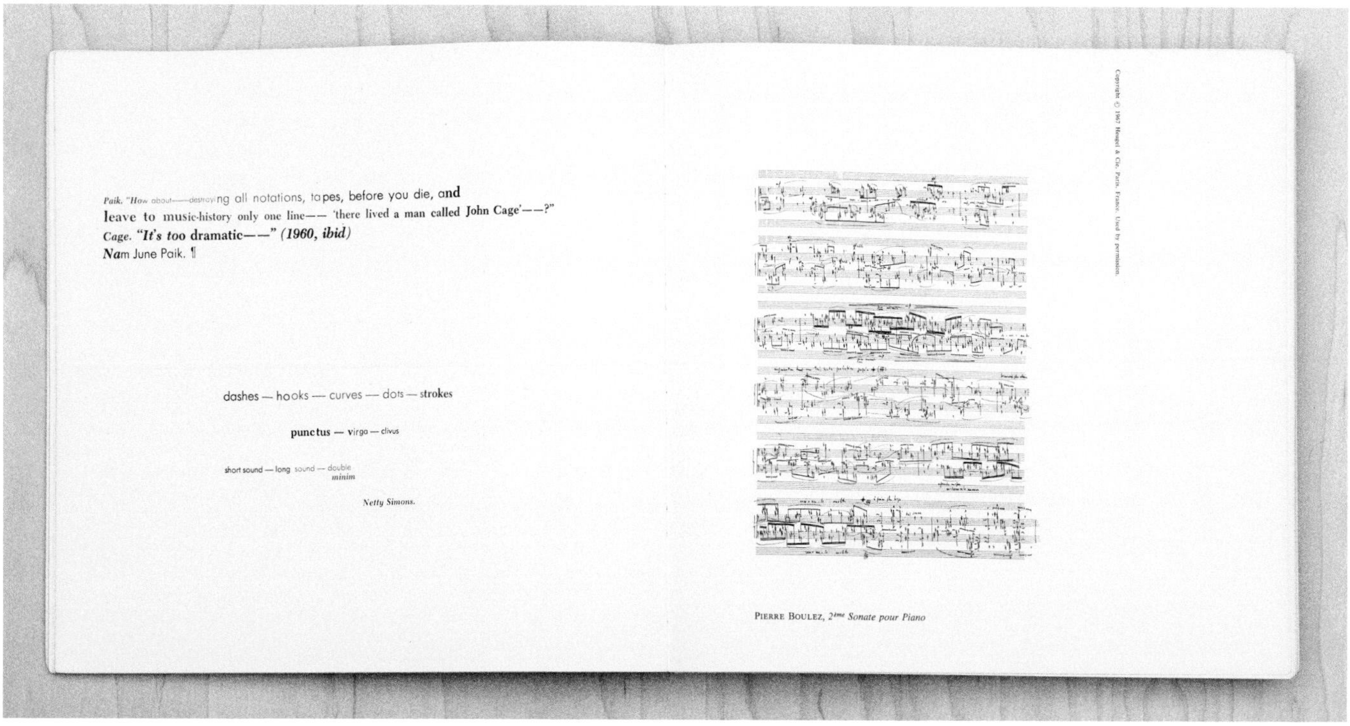

Spread from *Notations* (Something Else Press, 1969). Left side, text selected according to *I Ching;* right side, Pierre Boulez, page from musical score of *Deuxième Sonate pour Piano.*

1967 mailed seven Beatles lyrics manuscripts from London, all of which remain in the collection: "The Word" (1965) and "Eleanor Rigby," "Good Day Sunshine," "I'm Only Sleeping," "Why Did it Die"/"For No One," "Yellow Submarine," and "You Don't Get Me" (1966). A lengthy note from Ono to Cage explains, however, that the names of John Lennon and Paul McCartney written on these works were scribbled by her in haste.[55] Cage wrote in gratitude to the Beatles, but it does not appear that he approached the others on Higgins's list. Cage's feelings about popular music at the time, broadly speaking, might best be conveyed by a note in the minutes to a Foundation board meeting in 1968: "The meeting was adjourned because John Cage left so the rest of us danced to the music of the Rolling Stones."[56]

By fall 1967, Cage decided *Notations* should include a "mosaic text" that would run throughout the book and comprise the statements on notation solicited from each contributor. Originally Higgins had requested a 42-page essay on notation by Cage to publish with the book, but Cage apparently felt that a polyphony of views better represented the collection.[57] "I want the text to have the same many-mindedness that the mss. have!" he wrote on several of the postcards soliciting composer statements.[58] While Cage and Knowles researched statements to include by composers no longer living, they sent the following postcard to all other contributors, with the blank space filled by the number of words requested. That number was derived by chance operations according to the *I Ching*, an ancient Chinese oracle, which yielded a number ranging between 1 and 64:

> For *Notations*, the book which will illustrate your work, a mosaic text is being prepared, for which I would be most grateful if you

55. Letter from Yoko Ono to John Cage, February 28, 1967. John Cage Notations Project Correspondence, NUML.
56. Board meeting minutes, January 5, 1968, FCA Archives.
57. Letter from Dick Higgins to John Cage, December 9, 1966. John Cage Notations Project Correspondence, NUML. Higgins had set an initial deadline for Cage's text at the end of January 1967.
58. Letter from Cage to Alison Knowles, September 12, 1967. John Cage Notations Project Correspondence, NUML.

The *Notations* book was the first publication that we did from the Something Else Press. Not only was it radical but it was the first time almost all of those musicians had been produced in a major publication. John was delighted with the book since it was through his energy and associations that we could produce the document at all. Some of my favorite aspects of this book are that it is in the form of a square and that each of the contributors was able to make a statement about new music. I, as designer of this document, had such a good time using a variety of typefaces and organizational styles.

—Alison Knowles

> would consent to write—as soon as you conveniently can—_____ words on the subject of notation, or on any other subject which seems to you to be relevant. Would you, if you agree to do this, please accompany your text with a statement permitting me to use it free of copyright problems.[59]

The request did not go over well with some, and in sorting through replies at the time, Knowles remarked, "Boy are we waking them up from Frisco to Timbuktu."[60] Harry Partch, for instance, replied indignantly: "if you dare to mention that number 43 you are deliberately misrepresenting me."[61] Cage would spend two months "counting characters" and going through the mosaic "letter by letter, with three operations: 3 kinds of type-face, three sizes, and three weights."[62] This visual effect, as Cage explained in the *Notations* preface, was done "to lessen the difference between text and illustrations." Moreover, a contributor's text, whether about notation or another issue pertaining to the manuscript donated, would not appear on the same page as his or her score but instead on any page in the collection as determined by chance operations. Feldman's text, for instance, begins on Gardner Read's manuscript page ("This is what I mean by 'the medium': that incomprehensible physical fact. Technique . . . ") and concludes 57 pages later split across two pages and in between Wolf Vostell's manuscript image and its caption (" . . . can structure it—but can not make it comprehensible. And the deeper you go into it the clearer it becomes that our technical tools . . . can not any longer even structure it. They seem to me like devices belonging to the Stone Age."). *Notations* was not intended to be read from start to finish, and the lack of page numbers encourages readers to get lost in its contents and interrelationships.

As the book took shape, and still more letter-writing ensued to clear copyright—a reported 1,400 letters—Cage began to feel that the collection should be kept together rather than sold off piece by piece and looked into universities that might acquire the oeuvre.[63] He had already had the collection appraised in September 1967 at $24,915, but it came to little more than the $20,000 he told Yoko Ono he needed to subsidize the *Notations* book, which would not come from FCPA funds.[64] With the photo-positives of each manuscript complete, Cage explored the idea of a new kind of public display, which he presented to Alan Solomon of the Jewish Museum, where Jasper Johns's first solo exhibition had recently been held. Rather than exhibit select manuscript pages, he proposed a multimedia installation in which four slide projectors would show changing manuscript images of the whole collection simultaneously on four walls; in the four corners of the room audiotapes would play the selections of Satie's *Furniture Music* (c. 1918) in the collection (*Carrelage phonique* and *Tapisserie en fer forgé*, each of which are only four measures long and repeated indefinitely as "background music") plus an additional tape with the mosaic text recited by composers.[65] The concept was not unrelated to Cage's own multimedia project *HPSCHD* (1967–69), which included more than 100 projectors for images and more than 200 tapes of sound. While Cage held to the principle of presenting the whole collection indiscriminately and simultaneously as image, sound, and "poetry" rather than as select images, the concept for the Jewish Museum still fell short of

59. Alison Knowles Correspondence File, Undated. John Cage Notations Project Correspondence, NUML.
60. Letter from Alison Knowles to John Cage, Undated. John Cage Notations Project Correspondence, NUML.
61. Letter from Harry Partch to John Cage, October 14, 1967. John Cage Notations Project Correspondence, NUML.
62. Letter from John Cage to Alison Knowles, January 8 and February 18, 1967. John Cage Notations Project Correspondence, NUML.
63. *Camille's Reports #2* of the Something Else Press newsletter indicated in 1968 that "it took over 1400 letters to settle all the rights and permissions questions in John Cage's new *Notations,* ready in December. A very interesting book could be made of all the correspondence!" Camille Gordon was a pseudonym for Dick Higgins.
64. Board meeting minutes, October 11, 1967, FCA Archives. The initial selling price of $45,000 was assigned according to the Board meeting minutes of January 5, 1968, FCA Archives. At the June 9, 1969, board meeting a new price was set between at least $50,000 and $100,000. Letter from Rubin Gorewitz to John Bergman, June 11, 1969, FCA Archives. See also letter from John Cage to Yoko Ono, September 23, 1967. John Cage Notations Project Correspondence, NUML. The Foundation does not have a record of payment to either Cage or Higgins for the *Notations* project. Jasper Johns and Stacy Tenenbaum Stark, correspondence with the author, September 25, 2012.
65. Letter from John Cage to Alan Solomon, September 12, 1967. John Cage Notations Project Correspondence, NUML.

showcasing the collection's range of formats, sizes, colors, and materials that a slideshow could not convey: collage, décollage, cardboard, film, magnetic tape, wood, spray paint, crayon, scrolls, books, and photographs as well as the more conventional vellum and onion skin masters.

A manuscript such as Robert Moran's *Sketch for a Tragic One-Act Opera* (1965) is a different work altogether when viewed closely and in color. The collage was a "visual suggestion" for a future opera project, and the razor blade embedded just off center proposed "a good dose of operatic violence somewhere in the event."[66] The violence presumably occurs between the male and female characters whose faces are sketched on either side of the razor. Alison Knowles's *Blue Ram* (1967) is another work that appears in its entirety in *Notations*, with the pack of six cards used by each of the four performers fully displayed, though it is not reproduced in the vivid colors that contribute to the performer's interpretation.

By the time *Notations* was printed and released in early 1969 as an unpaginated square-shaped text, Cage was still in search of a venue to exhibit the collection.[67] There was steady interest from exhibitors and even potential university buyers, but none of these prospects materialized and the inertia of the situation was not unlike what Cage and the Foundation had faced on Broadway in 1963. Like many projects of the avant-garde, *Notations* was a collection sui generis. Moreover, Cage had articulated the imperative that music be treated not as an object but as a process, and he arguably ran up against this very assertion in planning the exhibition of scores for the Foundation. The static black-and-white images throughout *Notations* are indeed merely notations waiting to be brought to life by the performer, and the "Archive" in its entirety is an oeuvre of manuscripts ready for discovery. Toru Takemitsu's *Notations* statement comes to mind here: " . . . role of notation . . . to change the noun 'music' into the verb 'music.'"

The manuscript collection was many things, which was thematic of Cage's artistic views at the time but which confounded galleries, museums, universities, and, in turn, the capacities of the Foundation. From the time Cage began accumulating a few dozen manuscripts in Stony Point, to the years they occupied an entire floor of the Higgins-Knowles Chelsea walk-up, to the day they were shuttled away in Jasper Johns's yellow Jeep and stored at the Foundation until their temporary deposit at Northwestern University in 1973, the collection had been an orphan of sorts.[68] While Cage may have emphasized the "many-mindedness" of the manuscripts, it was no less a very personal collection that presented Cage's particular view of history (Satie, Webern, Ives, Josef Matthias Hauer, Edgard Varèse), his closest associates in experimental music (Tudor, Wolff, Feldman, Brown), the emergent generation that transgressed boundaries of music, art, and language (George Brecht, Higgins, Knowles, Jackson Mac Low, Nam June Paik), composer-critics who appraised the changing musical scene of his time (Eric Salzman, Charles Hamm, Peggy Glanville-Hicks, Virgil Thomson, Benjamin Boretz) according to Cage's complicated relationship with the music establishment (Bernstein, Otto Luening) and the more sanguine reception he received from those who, for instance, dedicated or addressed their scores to Cage explicitly (Ono, Glanville-Hicks, Sylvano Bussotti, Tomás Marco—a dedication implicit in the *I Ching* hexagram that constituted his manuscript

To John:

My pieces are meant to be spread by word-of-mouth, the gradual change which occurs in the piece by words spreading is also part of the piece, most pieces only have titles or very short instructions. And passing words as to how they were performed previously has become a habit.

My music is performed only to induce a situation in which people can listen to their own mind music. Therefore, maximum silence is required in presenting the pieces. Also, every performance should be considered a rehearsal and unfinished.

There are 15 pieces here. Please select the 9 you like.

9 is a spiritual number which has a meaning of being unfinished.

—Yoko Ono
Letter to John Cage
December 15, 1966

66. Robert Moran, correspondence with the author, October 6, 2012.

67. Alison Knowles, interview with the author, August 8, 2012, New York.

68. Letter from Alison Knowles to John Cage, undated. John Cage Notations Project Correspondence, NUML.

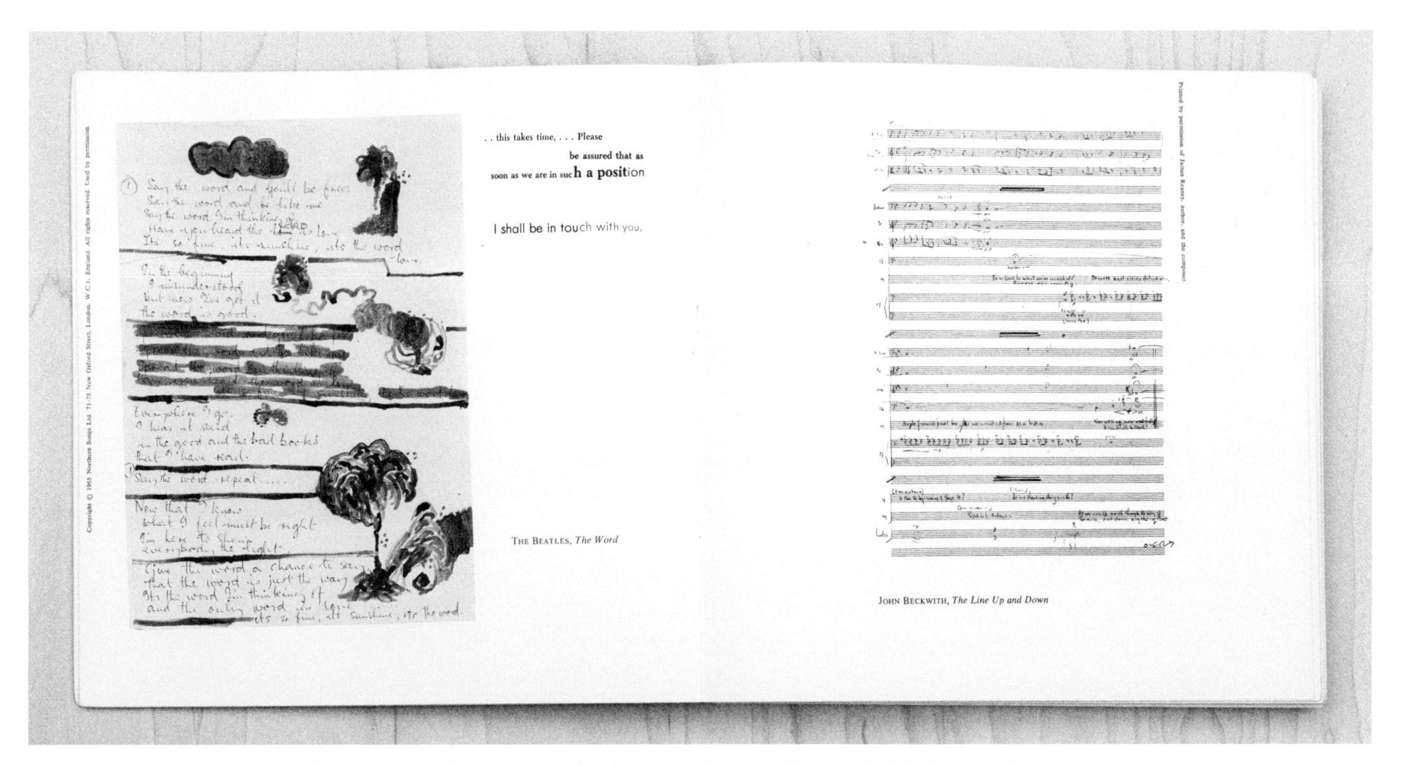

Spread from *Notations* (Something Else Press, 1969). Left side, The Beatles, musical score of "The Word"; right side, John Beckwith, page from musical score of *The Line Up and Down*.

page—and additional dedications listed in the "Archive" by Albert Fine, Horacio Vaggione, Mac Low, and Paik). Cage's early composition teacher Adolph Weiss is included, and there is a particularly strong presence of his mentor Henry Cowell in the collection. Cowell's passing in 1965 during the book's compilation is referenced by New School colleague Frank Wigglesworth's manuscript *To the Memory of Henry Cowell*, and his importance to new music marked by Carl Ruggles's page featuring a layout for Cowell's publication series *New Music*, which brought to print dozens of new works. For Cowell's own page, Cage chose for sentimental reasons, perhaps, to feature the incidental music Cowell had written in 1939 for Cocteau's *Les mariés de la Tour Eiffel*, parts of which Cage had also composed along with George McKay, whose manuscript in *Notations* comes also from this joint composition. Referring to the text as a "mosaic" was arguably another homage to Cowell, who had experimented with mobility of form in his 1935 *Mosaic Quartet*.

A significant inclusion is Pierre Boulez's *Deuxième Sonate* (1948), which had enormous impact on Cage and his colleagues as notation and as sound. Cage in particular described himself as "trembling" before it in admiration: "The day I show you my new works, I shall be full of dread."[69] Cage's own contribution to *Notations* is meaningful in this context, as he chose to include *Music of Changes* (1951), which indeed became one of the "new works" he was justified in hesitating to show Boulez as it created a rift in their friendship because of its chance-based methods. Cage's choice of manuscript was also surprising for its traditional notation and fixity of performance. He instead featured Tudor's performance score of his magnum

69. John Cage letter to Pierre Boulez, before April 1950 and December 18, 1950, *The Boulez-Cage Correspondence*, ed. Jean-Jacques Nattiez and trans. Robert Samuels (New York: Cambridge University Press, 1993), 56, 78. Boulez's Second Sonata was premiered by Tudor in New York on December 17, 1950, and introduced Cage and his colleagues to Antonin Artaud's essays in *The Theatre and Its Double* (1938). While only the second and third movement of Boulez's score belongs to the manuscript collection, this is by far more substantive than the manuscripts by Webern (a transcription of a work by Bach) and Ives (blank staff paper with the following note handwritten along the bottom: "return to C E Ives Redding Conn").

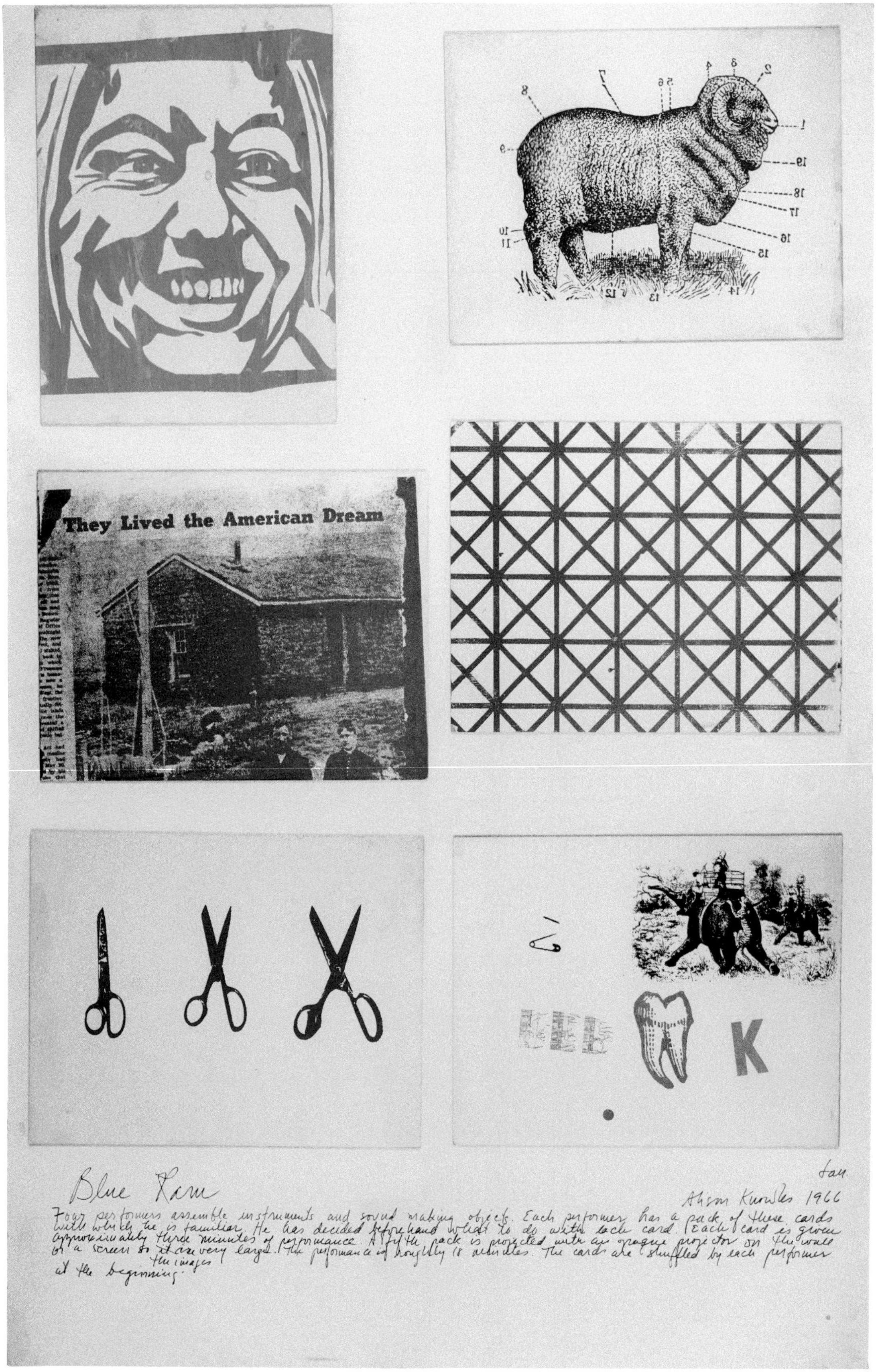

Alison Knowles, musical score of *Blue Ram* (six pages), 1967. John Cage Notations Project Manuscript Scores, Northwestern University Music Library.

I received an invitation from Alison Knowles to submit a score page for John Cage's *Notations*. I was surprised and delighted to do so. I was even more surprised when I received my copy of *Notations* at the range of styles represented so very democratically. Every kind of composer was welcomed as the community of composers. This kind of presentation was new, inspirational, and very educational.

—Pauline Oliveros

opus in notation, *Concert for Piano and Orchestra*, which he had premiered in the 1958 Town Hall concert produced by Impresarios Inc. and which Cage later deposited in the manuscript collection. Another footnote to the Foundation's history is Henri Sauguet, the figure who first showed Cage the *Vexations* manuscript in Paris during 1949 and donated his own work to the manuscript collection nearly three decades later.

The collection continued to grow even after the publication of *Notations*, particularly with the donation of two works by Duchamp around 1971, the date of which may explain the absence of such an influential source for Cage in *Notations*.[70] Beginning in 1966, he and Duchamp had met regularly in New York to play chess, at first once or twice a week.[71] Duchamp's death intersected with the printing of *Notations* in late 1968, and the omission of his manuscript may have been another form of Cage "not wanting to say anything about Marcel," the title for his 1969 commemorative work. Perhaps Cage deliberately left three pages blank in *Notations* to reference contributors not represented in the collection or as specific standing invitations for composers such as Schoenberg and Berg, whose manuscripts he pursued without success.

While few composers could have assembled as diverse a collection of manuscripts as Cage did, finding a home for the past century's music was a project that ultimately outlived Cage, though he remained hopeful of locating a supporting institution as late as 1985 and made plans for some of the manuscripts to travel posthumously with his *Rolywholyover: A Circus* in 1993, an exhibit that also defied classification.[72] Select manuscripts were loaned and exhibited in numerous cities throughout the world, but the music manuscript collection never sold and was officially taken off the market in 1999 when the Foundation formally donated it to the Music Library of Northwestern University, complementing Cage's personal archive of letters and ephemera he had bequeathed there.[73]

Cage's work with the Foundation enabled him to continue doing what he had been doing as a composer, performer, publicist, fund-raiser, conductor, editor, curator, and colleague, and to continue his work with characteristic rigor and vision. When the topic of planning new special events for the Foundation arose at a board meeting after the long-labored completion of *Notations* and Cage raised the possibility of a six-hour program he could do of spoken text and music, it was noted that some felt the Foundation "should not produce anything requiring great organization." Yet, by the end of the meeting, the minutes note, "Everyone was enthused by Cage's idea" and Cage brought up St. Mark's Church, Carolyn Brown suggested the Guggenheim, and Jasper Johns offered to approach Ivan Karp. It would be "in May or late April, on a Sunday". . . .[74]

The projects Cage curated during the 1960s are noteworthy for their collaborative, ambitious, and inclusive spirit, but in recalling his work with Cage during the Foundation's first year at the Pocket Theatre, Lewis Lloyd has emphasized: "He was interested mainly in having a civilized setting, a lovely setting, which our little theater was, with a nice piano if you needed it, so that the artists could be respected for their work."[75] ◆

70. Cage received a manuscript worth $15,000 (donor unidentified) and another manuscript from Mrs. Duchamp worth $10,000 according to the minutes of a board meeting, November 30, 1971, FCA Archives.
71. John Cage, *A Year from Monday* (Middletown, CT: Wesleyan University Press, 1967), 70.
72. Significant collections of unorthodox scores around this time included *An Anthology of Chance Operations* published by Jackson Mac Low and La Monte Young in 1963, and the periodical *Source: Music of the Avant-Garde*, published by the University of California at Davis, 1967–73.
73. During the three decades that the collection was housed at Northwestern, Cage made ample efforts to help the university raise funds to acquire the collection. In reviewing the history of the collection, John Cage Trust director Laura Kuhn indeed saw Cage's "many, many fundraising letters." Letter from Laura Kuhn to Jasper Johns, September 26, 1997, FCA Archives.
74. Board meeting minutes, December 20, 1969, FCA Archives.
75. Lewis Lloyd, interview with the author, Lincoln, MA, June 28, 2012.

Promotional poster, "9 Evenings: Theatre & Engineering," 1966. Design by Robert Rauschenberg.

Technical Difficulties: The FCPA, Experiments in Art and Technology, and "9 Evenings"

Julie Martin

THE FOUNDATION for Contemporary Performance Arts played an important role in the 1966 performance series "9 Evenings: Theatre & Engineering," in which ten New York artists, composers, and choreographers worked for nine months with engineers from Bell Telephone Laboratories to make works that incorporated the new technology and presented their performances over nine nights at the 69th Regiment Armory in New York. However, the exact details of the relationship between FCPA and the newly formed foundation, Experiments in Art and Technology (E.A.T.), have been difficult to unravel. In his writings, Billy Klüver, a Bell Labs engineer who spearheaded E.A.T., recounted that the FCA, then called FCPA, supported the "9 Evenings" project by allowing donors to make contributions to the FCPA, a tax-exempt foundation, that were then used to pay the expenses of the project. In contemporary parlance, the FCPA was the fiscal sponsor of "9 Evenings." This had been somewhat obliquely acknowledged on the title page of the "9 Evenings" program, which read: "Presented under the auspices of The Foundation for Contemporary Performance Arts, Inc. in cooperation with Experiments in Art and Technology, Inc."

Below this were the donors to "9 Evenings," which included many of the leading collectors and supporters of contemporary art at the time: Lester Avnet, Mr. and Mrs. Victor Ganz, Mr. and Mrs. John de Menil, Vera List, Harry Abrams, Philip Johnson, and Virginia Dwan, among others.

As I began to look at more and more documents in the archives of the FCA and also in the daybooks that Klüver kept to try to determine the specifics of the FCPA's role in "9 Evenings," I realized they told the story of a nearly 50-year-long relationship among Klüver, E.A.T., and the Foundation.

Klüver had been voted onto the FCPA board of directors at the September 28, 1965, meeting, but his involvement with the arts started in the early 1960s, when he began to work with artists including Jean Tinguely, Robert Rauschenberg, and Andy Warhol to help them realize works that incorporated new technology. Beginning in 1962 and continuing on and off through 1965, he worked with Jasper Johns on neon letters to be attached to paintings—a red "R" for *Field Painting* (1963–64) and a blue "A" for *Zone* (1966)—a project made technically challenging because Johns wanted no wires connecting the paintings to the wall. Klüver and his colleagues at Bell Labs also worked with John Cage on his 1965 piece *Variations V* for Merce Cunningham, developing a photoelectric system for dancers to trigger sounds.

Klüver wanted to broaden the participation of engineers working with artists and decided in the summer of 1965 to write a book, *Engineering in*

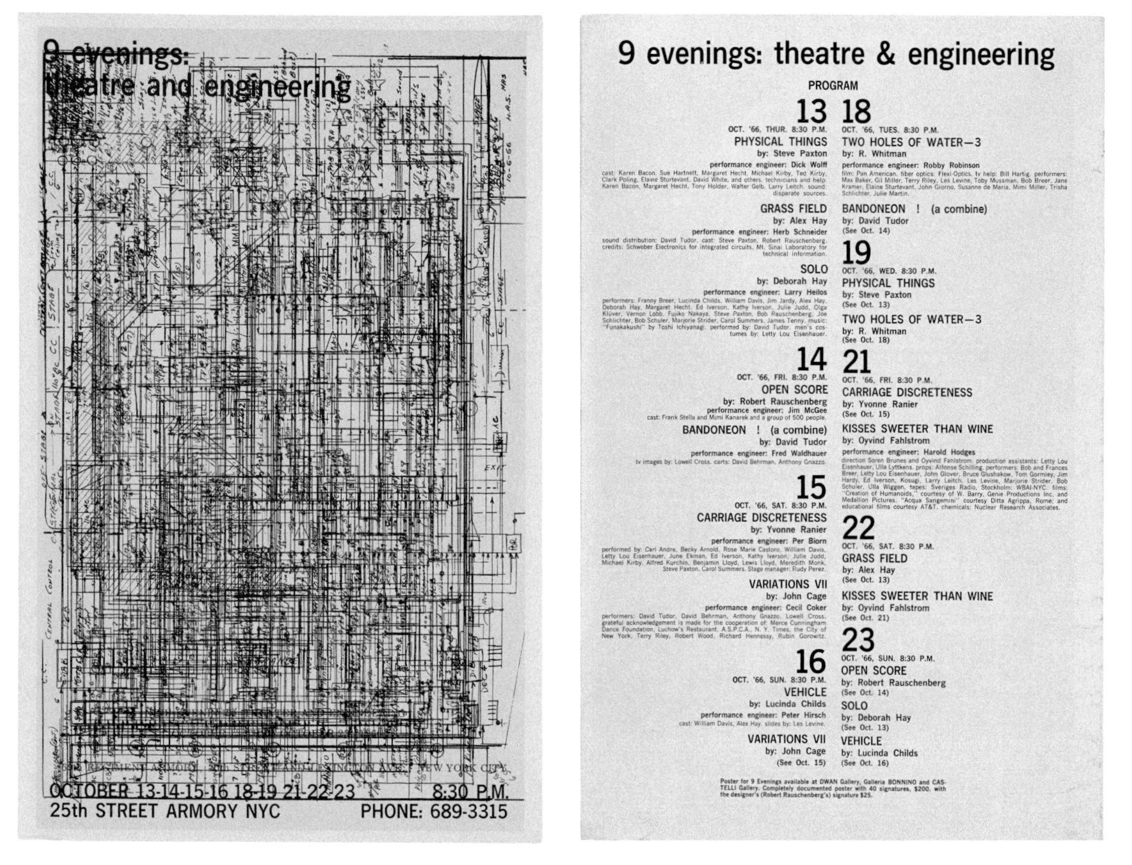

9 evenings: theatre & engineering

PROGRAM

13
OCT. '66, THUR. 8:30 P.M.
PHYSICAL THINGS
by: Steve Paxton
performance engineer: Dick Wolff
cast: Karen Bacon, Sue Hartnett, Margaret Hecht, Michael Kirby, Ted Kirby, Clark Poling, Elaine Sturtevant, David White, and others. technicians and help: Karen Bacon, Margaret Hecht, Tony Holder, Walter Gelb, Larry Leitch. sound: disparate sources.

GRASS FIELD
by: Alex Hay
performance engineer: Herb Schneider
sound distribution: David Tudor. cast: Steve Paxton, Robert Rauschenberg. credits: Schweber Electronics for integrated circuits, Mt. Sinai Laboratory for technical information.

SOLO
by: Deborah Hay
performance engineer: Larry Heilos
performers: Franny Breer, Lucinda Childs, William Davis, Jim Jardy, Alex Hay, Deborah Hay, Margaret Hecht, Ed Iverson, Kathy Iverson, Julie Judd, Olga Klüver, Vernon Lobb, Fujiko Nakaya, Steve Paxton, Bob Rauschenberg, Joe Schlichter, Bob Schuler, Marjorie Strider, Carol Summers, James Tenny. music: "Funakakushi" by Toshi Ichiyanagi. performed by: David Tudor. men's costumes by: Letty Lou Eisenhauer.

14
OCT. '66, FRI. 8:30 P.M.
OPEN SCORE
by: Robert Rauschenberg
performance engineer: Jim McGee
cast: Frank Stella and Mimi Kanarek and a group of 500 people.

BANDONEON ! (a combine)
by: David Tudor
performance engineer: Fred Waldhauer
tv images by: Lowell Cross. carts: David Behrman, Anthony Gnazzo.

15
OCT. '66, SAT. 8:30 P.M.
CARRIAGE DISCRETENESS
by: Yvonne Ranier
performance engineer: Per Biorn
performed by: Carl Andre, Becky Arnold, Rose Marie Castoro, William Davis, Letty Lou Eisenhauer, June Ekman, Ed Iverson, Kathy Iverson, Julie Judd, Michael Kirby, Alfred Kurchin, Benjamin Lloyd, Lewis Lloyd, Meredith Monk, Steve Paxton, Carol Summers. Stage manager: Rudy Perez.

VARIATIONS VII
by: John Cage
performance engineer: Cecil Coker
performers: David Tudor, David Behrman, Anthony Gnazzo, Lowell Cross. grateful acknowledgement is made for the cooperation of: Merce Cunningham Dance Foundation, Luchow's Restaurant, A.S.P.C.A., N. Y. Times, the City of New York, Terry Riley, Robert Wood, Richard Hennessy, Rubin Gorowitz.

16
OCT. '66, SUN. 8:30 P.M.
VEHICLE
by: Lucinda Childs
performance engineer: Peter Hirsch
cast: William Davis, Alex Hay. slides by: Les Levine.

VARIATIONS VII
by: John Cage
(See Oct. 15)

18
OCT. '66, TUES. 8:30 P.M.
TWO HOLES OF WATER—3
by: R. Whitman
performance engineer: Robby Robinson
film: Pan American. fiber optics: Flexi-Optics. tv help: Bill Hartig. performers: Max Baker, Gil Miller, Terry Riley, Les Levine, Toby Mussman, Bob Breer, Jane Kramer, Elaine Sturtevant, John Giorno, Susanne de Maria, Mimi Miller, Trisha Schlichter, Julie Martin.

BANDONEON ! (a combine)
by: David Tudor
(See Oct. 14)

19
OCT. '66, WED. 8:30 P.M.
PHYSICAL THINGS
by: Steve Paxton
(See Oct. 13)

TWO HOLES OF WATER—3
by: R. Whitman
(See Oct. 18)

21
OCT. '66, FRI. 8:30 P.M.
CARRIAGE DISCRETENESS
by: Yvonne Ranier
(See Oct. 15)

KISSES SWEETER THAN WINE
by: Oyvind Fahlstrom
performance engineer: Harold Hodges
direction Soren Brunes and Oyvind Fahlstrom. production assistants: Letty Lou Eisenhauer, Ulla Lyttkens. props: Alfonse Schilling. performers: Bob and Frances Breer, Letty Lou Eisenhauer, John Glover, Bruce Glushakow, Tom Gormley, Jim Hardy, Ed Iverson, Kosugi, Larry Leitch, Les Levine, Marjorie Strider, Bob Schuler, Ulla Wiggen. tapes: Sveriges Radio, Stockholm; WBAI-NYC. films: "Creation of Humanoids," courtesy of W. Barry, Genie Productions Inc. and Medallion Pictures. "Acqua Sangemini" courtesy Ditta Agrippa, Rome; and educational films courtesy AT&T. chemicals: Nuclear Research Associates.

22
OCT. '66, SAT. 8:30 P.M.
GRASS FIELD
by: Alex Hay
(See Oct. 13)

KISSES SWEETER THAN WINE
by: Oyvind Fahlstrom
(See Oct. 21)

23
OCT. '66, SUN. 8:30 P.M.
OPEN SCORE
by: Robert Rauschenberg
(See Oct. 14)

SOLO
by: Deborah Hay
(See Oct. 13)

VEHICLE
by: Lucinda Childs
(See Oct. 16)

Poster for 9 Evenings available at DWAN Gallery, Galleria BONNINO and CASTELLI Gallery. Completely documented poster with 40 signatures, $200. with the designer's (Robert Rauschenberg's) signature $25.

Program, "9 Evenings: Theatre & Engineering," 1966: left, cover; right, schedule of performances. Design by Pontus Hultén.

Art, that would stimulate interest among engineers and scientists. However, he soon felt that a much greater effort would be needed and the impetus would have to come from something more concrete than a book. And that impetus came from his native Sweden.

Knut Wiggen, chairman of Fylkingen, the contemporary music society in Stockholm, met with Klüver in New York on November 17, 1965, and asked him to organize a group of American artists to participate in a festival of art and technology that Fylkingen was planning to hold in the Swedish capital the next year. Klüver took Wiggen to meet with Rauschenberg, and they agreed to participate. Klüver and Rauschenberg in turn invited nine artist friends to join them: John Cage, Lucinda Childs, Alex Hay, Deborah Hay, Öyvind Fahlström, Steve Paxton, Yvonne Rainer, David Tudor, and Robert Whitman; and Klüver recruited 26 engineers from Bell Labs to work on the project.

Soon after, Fylkingen announced that the Stockholm Festival for Art and Technology—Visions of the Present would take place September 18–25, 1966. Wiggen conceived of the festival as a means to present modern technology to artists, art to the technically oriented, and both to the general audience. In addition to artists' performances and an exhibition at the National Museum of Science and Technology in Stockholm, philosophers, scientists, and other theorists, including Marshall McLuhan, R. Buckminster Fuller, and J.R. Pierce, director of the Bell Labs Communication Research Division,

I arrived in New York in 1966, just before "9 Evenings" at the Armory. I was so broke, I thought I couldn't afford to go. I read all about it afterward. From then on I missed a lot less.

—Jared Bark

were invited to participate through lectures, demonstrations, and symposia.

The American group of artists and engineers met for the first time on January 14, 1966. As Klüver noted:

> At the first artist-engineer meeting, I told the artists to ask for anything they wanted and the engineers responded with suggestions on how to accomplish their ideas. These meetings lasted through March, and we collected more than seventy artists' requests. The engineers went to work. As time went on one engineer was assigned to each artist depending on what the technical requirements of the artist's project were and what the engineer's specialty was. By the end of February some of the engineers were working on the design of equipment and a system using wireless FM transmission that could be used by all the artists.

For the American group, the impulse was to get to work. Their attitude was expressed by Rauschenberg at a March 3 meeting: "I like our organic collaboration with technical facilities where technique and aesthetics are both being experimented with rather than our having a set esthetic to implement with technology." Through the process of collaboration, new work would be created and new relationships established. Klüver believed that the engineers and scientists would benefit from this relationship as much as the artists. Both the Swedish and the American groups were equally positive about the benefits of the artist-engineer collaboration for society as a whole, but neither the artists nor the engineers in the American group had any interest in theorizing about the meaning of the work or the future of art and technology in society.

Klüver foresaw that there would be problems if the Swedish sponsors did not regard the American group as made up equally of artists and engineers. Although some money for the project was promised from Sweden, he began to raise funds himself to ensure the independence of the American group. He met on March 5 with Walter Gutman, a stockbroker, artist, filmmaker, art collector, and longtime supporter of downtown dancers, to invite him to be the lead American sponsor. Gutman agreed and promptly approached Seymour Schweber, president of Schweber Electronics Corporation, who became not only a sponsor but also an adviser and technical consultant. Klüver continued to approach possible donors to the project.

At first glance the Foundation documents seemed to show that the FCPA was a direct sponsor of the festival. The minutes of the board meeting of April 26, 1966, record that Klüver asked the board to "authorize a grant of $1,500 to an American group of performing artists who had been invited to participate in the Stockholm Festival for Art and Technology to assist in defraying the costs of participation." The board agreed. However, supporting documents and a study of the bank statements of the Foundation revealed that before the money was disbursed, contributions came into the Foundation in the amount of $1,500 from people Klüver knew and had worked with on several exhibitions. And this remained true over the next few months: funds were deposited, and checks for the same amounts were written to the Stockholm Festival.

Group portrait of many of the "9 Evenings" participating artists and engineers outside the 69th Regiment Armory, New York, October 8, 1966.

PHOTO: PETER MOORE

David Tudor performed his *Bandoneon! (a combine)* at "9 Evenings." He brought the *bandoneon* to operate the electronic system, combining sound and visual elements. Radio-controlled carts of loudspeakers were moving around on the huge floor of the Armory according to the sound signals the instrument made, as were the lights and video projections.

The *bandoneon* was Tudor's favorite instrument. He loved the music, but in this performance, he never produced the original sound of the instrument. The sounds became complex through the electronic system. The musical performance was a way to realize a compound realm of creativity.

—Takehisa Kosugi

David Tudor, *Bandoneon! (a combine)*, performance, "9 Evenings," 69th Regiment Armory, New York, October 18, 1966.

PHOTO: PETER MOORE

Billy Klüver, overlooking rehearsal of Robert Whitman's *Two Holes of Water—3*, performance, "9 Evenings," 69th Regiment Armory, New York, October 18, 1966.

The differences between the American and Swedish groups became evident during a trip Wiggen made to New York in May, when entries in Klüver's daybook indicate "May 3 See Knut at Chelsea / Have dinner Not clear up" and the next day "See Knut at Öyvind's more arguments." However, some agreement on language seemed to have been reached at a meeting with Wiggen at Robert Whitman's loft with some of the artists and the group's lawyer, Franklin Königsberg: "Lunch at Simone's with Knut, Königsberg, Rauschenberg, Paxton, Whitman, text set." The two groups were able to sign a letter of agreement.

It was at this point in my research that I remembered that Klüver had asked Harriet DeLong in the mid-1970s to compile documents in the E.A.T. archives for a book on "9 Evenings." In her unpublished first chapter, "Origin," she wrote:

> The agreement between the American group and Fylkingen which was signed by each party in the middle of May did not recognize or resolve their differences. The arrangements provided that Fylkingen would make available to the Americans $10,000 for their expenses for technical equipment, of which $3,000 had

I went to at least one "evening," involving Alex Hay. I recall a gymnasium atmosphere; we sat on bleachers. What struck me was that the ubiquitous laboratory equipment and technicians were as prominent as the artists/performers. I was more impressed with the general setup than perhaps the particular work I was seeing—what seemed radical was the "where" and "how" rather than the "what." It was well attended but perhaps not packed, and while most of the audience was quietly attentive, the feeling was much more casual than that of a standard theatrical performance. In 1964 I sat through part of the first showing of Andy Warhol's film *Empire* and the experience was similar. It was new and exciting, but that is what I had come to New York to be part of.

—Michael Findlay

> been received and the balance to be paid by the first week in July. The American artists would receive a salary of $400, their living expenses while in Stockholm, and some would receive round-trip air transportation. Other points in the agreement touched on expenses and air transportation for some of the American engineers, the television rights and disposition of material and equipment after the festival.

These differences became more pronounced as the months wore on. In particular, the Swedish organizers did not value the participation of the engineers, whom the Americans saw as equal partners. Misunderstandings grew, and by the end of June communications were marked by anger and mistrust. Finally the American group asked Königsberg to go to Sweden to negotiate an agreement with Fylkingen. DeLong's account continues:

> After long and intense negotiations with the sponsors, [Königsberg] sent back a joint communiqué of 33 points on July 10 which he and Knut Wiggen had worked out. His letter concluded, "Go ahead. All is okay." Encouraged by this, Klüver met with the engineers to make the final push, and they set August 8 as the deadline to complete their projects. Klüver and Rauschenberg continued their efforts to mobilize support from industry and private sponsors.
>
> But on July 18, Simone Forti received a letter from Wiggen saying he did not have the authority to accept the 33 points and that Fylkingen would meet and make a decision on July 20. . . . Refusing to believe that their contribution to the Festival might not be realized, the Americans spent the next ten days frantically attempting to re-establish communications and at the same time, continued with preparations. . . . Word came on July 25 from Wiggen that a new proposal to the group was in the mail, but it was never received. Rather, Wiggen had decided to deal with each artist separately and sent individual contracts. Königsberg advised the group to call it off.

A number of the artists and engineers met again at Rauschenberg's loft and decided that they were involved in a process that was too important to be dropped. In Klüver's words, "they weren't quite sure what, except that it was good." Forti suggested the 69th Regiment Armory as a venue, and Schweber found that it was available in October. The risks were high, but by July 30 plans were under way to mount the performances in New York during Columbus Day week and to call it "9 Evenings: Theatre & Engineering." They had two-and-a-half months to prepare.

⋆ ⋆ ⋆

Once the decision had been made to hold the performances in New York, things got hectic as the group of artists and engineers began final preparations for the performances at the Armory. Klüver had resigned from the board of the FCPA on July 1, probably just as the work for the performances was escalating and plans were being made to establish a new foundation to carry on the work being begun by the upcoming "9 Evenings."

Experiments in Art and Technology was incorporated September 26, 1966. A letter of agreement between E.A.T. and the FCPA was drawn up by Königsberg on September 28, in which the FCPA would "conduct the production of the above programs" and "enter into the necessary leases with the Armory and the FCC for FM radio licenses," while E.A.T. would be "retained to operate and administer the above project." A bank account would be opened in the name of "9 Evenings: Theatre and Engineering." The allocation of funds from the Foundation to the project was limited to money the Foundation had already received or would receive from donors and ticket sales until the end of the performances. The attached proposed budget estimated the cost of the performances at $76,000. Rauschenberg submitted an accompanying letter agreeing to cover any "net deficit" if costs exceeded the amount taken in. (There is no indication that this agreement was ever signed by FCPA or E.A.T., but perhaps a signed copy was kept in the lawyers' offices.) The bank account was opened, and all transactions from September 30 on went through this account.

The group moved into the 69th Regiment Armory on October 8, and they had five days to turn the Armory into a performance space, with bleacher seating for 1,500. They installed theatrical lighting, speakers, and miles of audio cable, rigged and attached objects to the ceiling, finalized the technical systems for the performances, and scheduled rehearsals. Performances began October 13 and ran until October 23 to an audience of roughly 10,000 viewers over the full nine nights. When the performances were over, activity in the "9 Evenings" bank account stopped, and it was closed in May 1967, with a remaining $29.08 being transferred back to the Foundation.

An accountant's report to the board of E.A.T. on March 7, 1967, that I recently found in the archives of the Robert Rauschenberg Foundation, set the total expenditures for the "9 Evenings" at $161,547, with total moneys raised of $132,411 and a deficit of $29,136, as well as a number of loans outstanding. Among the loans payable was one to the FCPA for $3,250. At the board meeting of the FCPA on October 11, 1967, it was reported that "E.A.T. owes the Foundation $4,050." The board agreed that they would "try to be re-imbursed, but if this was not possible, the money would be donated to E.A.T." The entry ends with the sentence: "They have informed us that they intend to pay." There is no indication that E.A.T. ever repaid this money.

I felt badly when I read this. Then I remembered that in 2006, I had donated a number of E.A.T. posters, including the one for "9 Evenings," to the "Posters" benefit exhibition the FCA was holding, and I had recently agreed to donate more posters for the next sale. So not only had E.A.T. supported current activities of the Foundation; inadvertently, it had begun to pay back its 40-year-old debt, and the relationship continues. ◆

In *Open Score*, the technology, which was the running theme of "9 Evenings," didn't work. The Armory was a place where one could play tennis on the wood floors. I rallied with Mimi Kanarek, a pro from the club where I played tennis. I had wanted someone who could hit the ball to me so I wouldn't miss. The racquets were wired for sound. The idea was that when the ball made contact with the racquet, the sound of the ball would be picked up by microphones, transmitted to a radio receiver, then to speakers. Each amplified stroke would turn out a light in the Armory. We hit until we were playing in darkness. That was it. The audience could hear the sound of the tennis ball, but it didn't transmit to turn off the lights as planned, so the engineers had to turn each light switch off manually as they heard the ball being hit.

—Frank Stella

As a participant in this series, I shared two evenings with John Cage. The preparations were arduous and frustrating, the events publicized as one of the wonders of the world. On the first night the program didn't work; nothing seemed to be happening, and the audience began to rhythmically clap in frustration. Later that night I landed in the emergency ward at St. Vincent's Hospital with the first of a series of life-threatening intestinal blockages. I saw rehearsals of some of the other events. They were all very minimal and could not possibly live up to the expectations. But I have no regrets about being part of "9 Evenings." It was unbelievably ambitious, a noble failure in the spirit of historical in-your-face avant-garde challenges.

—Yvonne Rainer

Above: Robert Rauschenberg, *Open Score*, performance, "9 Evenings," 69th Regiment Armory, New York, October 23, 1966. Performers: Frank Stella and Mimi Kanarek. Below, left to right: Yvonne Rainer, rehearsal for *Carriage Discreteness*, performance, "9 Evenings," 69th Regiment Armory, New York, October 10, 1966. Simone Forti and unidentified woman, attaching plugs to audio wires for "9 Evenings" performances, 69th Regiment Armory, New York, October 12, 1966. John Cage, *Variations VII*, performance, "9 Evenings," 69th Regiment Armory, New York, October 15, 1966.

PHOTOS: PETER MOORE

PHOTO: PETER MOORE

Marshall McLuhan, speaking at "Six Lectures," 92nd Street YMHA, New York, May 7, 1966.

"Six Lectures" at the 92nd Street Y

Irving Sandler

LOOKING BACK AT THE ART WORLD IN 1966, I recall two events that impressed me strongly. One was "9 Evenings: Theatre & Engineering," organized by Experiments in Art and Technology (E.A.T.) at the 69th Regiment Armory on 26th Street in New York (the site of the Armory Show of 1913). The other was a series of six lectures at the YMHA given by Norman O. Brown, Merce Cunningham, R. Buckminster Fuller, Marshall McLuhan, Harold Rosenberg, and Peter Yates. The lecture series was well attended, often standing room only, as the speakers were well known in the art world.

What connected these events was the role of the Foundation for Contemporary Performance Arts, which sponsored "Six Lectures" and was the financial sponsor of "9 Evenings," and particularly the role of John Cage. In the case of the six speakers, it was probably Cage who chose them since their thinking (with the exception of Rosenberg's) was closely related to his. Their names appeared repeatedly in Cage's interviews and essays. In 1966, for example, he had written that he was "studying with Brown, McLuhan, Fuller and Marcel Duchamp."[1] Actually, Cage should have delivered one of the lectures himself, and I did spot him in the audience.

I was already aware of Cage's outlook. He had spoken at The Club, the hangout of the artists of the New York School, whose programs I arranged in the late 1950s. And I had interviewed him at length in 1966. But his artistic stance then had been eclipsed by Rosenberg's angst-ridden Existentialism and Clement Greenberg's art-as-art formalism. Nevertheless, as the 1960s progressed, Cage's aesthetic increasingly overshadowed theirs. Although Cage is recognized as a major composer of avant-garde music, he is also arguably the most influential art theorist of the second half of the twentieth century.

Cage believed that art should provide a "way of waking up to the very life we're living, which is so excellent once one gets one's mind and one's desires out of its way and lets it act of its own accord." He called for art to break down the barriers between art and life. The purpose of art, as he conceived of it, was to open up one's eyes to just see what there was to see and one's ears to the activity of sounds.[2] In his view, every (ready-made) sound is music, and any material, form, and color is art. Cage advocated an optimistic art-as-life aesthetic. Rejecting Rosenberg's views, he said, "I prefer laughter to tears [of Abstract Expressionism]."

Cage's music and his aesthetics were often rejected as a nihilistic subversion of Western music, but they were actually a visionary attempt to open music to new possibilities. In the visual arts, Jasper Johns and Robert Rauschenberg, championed by Cage, used everyday subjects and materials. Cage also supported performance art because he believed that it was more

1. John Cage, "Foreword," *A Year From Monday* (Middletown, CT: Wesleyan University Press, 1967), x.
2. John Cage, *Silence: Lectures and Writings* (Cambridge, MA: MIT Press, 1967), 10.

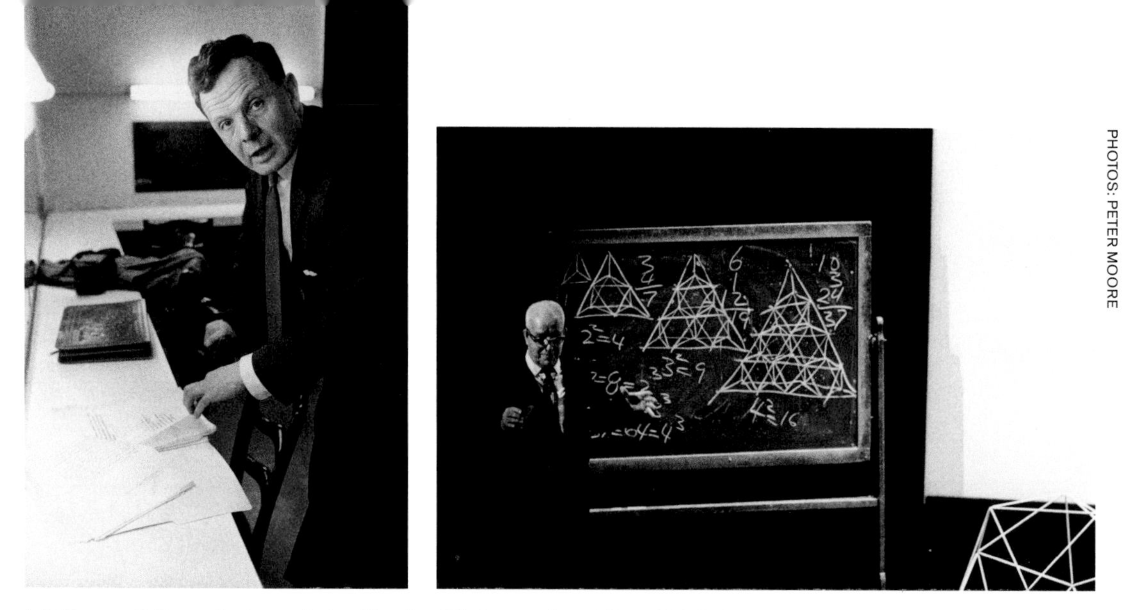

PHOTOS: PETER MOORE

Left: Norman O. Brown, backstage before his talk at "Six Lectures," 92nd Street YMHA, New York, March 31, 1966. Right: R. Buckminster Fuller, speaking at "Six Lectures," 92nd Street YMHA, New York, April 16, 1966.

lifelike than the visual arts. In 1952, he staged the first Happening at Black Mountain College in North Carolina, which inspired the theatrical events of Allan Kaprow and Claes Oldenburg as well as the Fluxus performances of Nam June Paik, along with those of many others. Cage sought to expand music (and all the arts), to the point where he hoped the audience could be enlisted in the act of creation (anticipating what today we term relational aesthetics or participatory art).

Stretching the limits of music was the theme of Yates's talk at the Y. It was highly technical, and his detailed use of musical terminology was difficult for an amateur like me to follow fully. But the message was clear. Modern composers had broadened the range of music to use chance and to embrace any sound, including not only dissonance and discord but "noise" and "silence." He predicted that the next stage of music would be based on computer technology and would merge music with theater, dance, and audience participation. Yates also sought to broaden the range of Western music by incorporating so-called primitive, Asian, and other regional modes. His reach was global. He demonstrated his ideas by playing tapes of diverse kinds of music, much of it new to me, and all of it an exciting earful.

Like Yates's introduction of actual music into his talk, Cunningham, Cage's close collaborator, included dance. His presentation was essentially a performance, and it made Cage's aesthetic eminently watchable. Just as Cage had amplified music to encompass any and every sound, Cunningham's dance extended the range of movements to include ordinary walking, falling, and running.

Cage believed that we were entering a new world order. He derived this vision from Fuller. Fuller's lecture was a rousing performance. It was very long—an average Fuller lecture lasted from four to eight hours—but no one I saw in the audience nodded off. He began with a presentation of his "World Game," in which he plotted in considerable detail the resources of the world and showed that they were manifestly interrelated. He then presented his comprehensive plan to solve the problems of the world by

Tickets for talks by Norman O. Brown and Marshall McLuhan, "Six Lectures," 1966.

PHOTOS: PETER MOORE

Left: Merce Cunningham, at "Six Lectures," 92nd Street YMHA, New York, April 21, 1966. Right: Peter Yates, speaking at "Six Lectures," 92nd Street YMHA, New York, April 7, 1966.

distributing its resources to all of humanity. He hoped that his recommendations would reach the peoples of the world via new technologies. Their recognition of the validity of Fuller's proposals would move them to force political changes through voluntary cooperation.

McLuhan's lecture was prescient. He maintained that global society was undergoing a pervasive socio-physiological transformation created by electronic technology, which had replaced the print medium as the primary source of sense perceptions. As the outcome of this change of medium, the human nervous system had been exteriorized.

Brown had written *Life Against Death: The Psychoanalytic Meaning of History* (1959), which was required countercultural reading at the time. In it he declared that individuals and society were in the throes of repression and the only way to emancipation was the affirmation of life. Brown's follow-up book, *Love's Body*, had not yet been published when he spoke, and he read sections of it.[3] From what I was able to gather, it was a psychological, philosophical, mystical, and poetic attack on the repression of sexuality in Western society and culture and the need for the erotic liberation of the entire human body.

I was surprised that Rosenberg was invited to speak, except that he was a long-time friend of Cage's, going back to 1947, when they both were editors of *Possibilities*. Of the six lecturers, he was the odd man out, but in keeping with one of the themes of the series, his topic was "Art and the Media." Rosenberg connected the mass media with Pop art and the museum practices and art criticism that favored it, but he deplored them all. Rather than try to bridge the media and art, he made a plea for elitist art-as-art. Hence he updated an old view in intellectual circles that held that there was no common ground between "low" and "high" art. He concluded with a demand for the subversion of the media.

How to sum up the six lectures? With a quote from Cage: "I'm all for multiplicity, unfocused attention, decentralization, and so I would be on the side of individual anarchy with minimal government."[4] ◆

3. Brown read from chapters "Food," "Fire," and "Fraction."

4. Quoted in Marjorie Perloff, "Difference and Discipline: The Cage/Cunningham Aesthetic Revisited," in "Conversation with John Cage," in *John Cage: An Anthology*, ed. Richard Kostelanestz (New York: Da Capo, 1970), 8

Pages from FCPA "Six Lectures" mailer brochure, 1966. Design by Marcus Ratliff.

Six Lectures

March–May 1966

The benefit series "Six Lectures" took place over six evenings at the Poetry Center of the 92nd Street YMHA, 1395 Lexington Avenue, New York.

1. Norman O. Brown (March 31) 98

2. Peter Yates (April 7) 108

3. R. Buckminster Fuller (April 16) 114

4. Merce Cunningham (April 21) 122

5. Harold Rosenberg (April 28) 124

6. Marshall McLuhan (May 7) 129

1 Norman O. Brown

In his contribution to "Six Lectures," classicist Norman O. Brown (1913–2002) read three chapters from his forthcoming, highly aphoristic book Love's Body *(1967). The texts reproduced here, comprising those sections ("Food," "Fire," and "Fraction"), are from the subsequent published version of the book.*

FOOD

There is only one psyche, in relation to which all conflict is endopsychic, all war intestine. The external enemy is (part of) ourselves, projected; our own badness, banished. The only defense against an internal danger is to make it an external danger: then we can fight it; and are ready to fight it, since we have succeeded in deceiving ourselves into thinking it is no longer us.

Murder is misdirected suicide, to destroy part of oneself; murder is suicide with mistaken identity. And suicide is also a case of mistaken identity, an attack on the (introjected) other.

A case of mistaken identity, an accident, at the crossroads; the stranger is the father. *Pater semper incertus*; his identity is established by killing him. "Passing strangers were regarded as manifestations of the corn-spirit escaping from the cut or threshed corn, and as such were seized and slain."

Frazer, *The Golden Bough*, 439.
Cf. Brophy, *Black Ship to Hell*, 97.

An "accident." There is no death from natural causes; if a man is killed they do not blame the real murderer. "He had to die you see," they say, and set out in search of a fictitious person, naturally a member of a foreign tribe, whom they regard as the real cause of death. The real cause of all death is the father (*Der Erlkönig*); the member of a foreign tribe is the culprit, scapegoat, or father.

Cf. Roheim, *Animism*, 62; *Psychoanalysis and Anthropology*, 136.

Killing is always inside the family (Oedipal). In the wisdom of primitive war, enemy blood is kindred blood; blood becomes kindred blood by being shed. Whatever is killed becomes the father. Head hunting. An enemy must be killed for a boy to grow up; a head must fall. The boy kills his father in the person of an enemy. And then the slain enemy becomes his guardian spirit: the enemy head (super-ego) presides over the house; love your enemy. "We tend to identify ourselves with whatever we kill—and then reactively to venerate our victims." Or an enemy is killed to provide spirit for a son: the enemy is reincarnated in the son. The pile of skulls that represents the chief's *mana* are those of enemies, ancestors. The super-ego is our god, enemy; and suicide (or any self-defeat) is our obedience and revenge.

Roheim, *War, Crime and the Covenant*, 57.
Cf. Turney-High, *Primitive War*, 199, 222–226.

We identify with what we kill. The hidden truth which makes peace: the identity of the killer and the victim.

Whatever is killed becomes the father. All killing is ritual killing; totemic sacrifice; Holy Communion. We drink the blood of our enemies.

Cf. Turney-High, *Primitive War*, 87, 152, 156, 158, 191–192.

Genocide, holocaust. "The practice of devoting a recalcitrant foe to destruction as a kind of gigantic holocaust to the national deity was apparently universal among the early Semites." Of the cities of these people, which the Lord thy God doth give thee for an inheritance, thou shalt save alive nothing that breatheth.

Albright, *From the Stone Age to Christianity*, 230. Deuteronomy XX, 16.

Hostilities: our enemy our host, who feeds us; to kill is to eat. Our enemy our host, *hostia*, our Eucharistic meal.

All killing is sacrificial; and all sacrifice is eating. Killing is eating. "Dainties that would be hot and fresh, taken from the field of battle," to feed the sun, in Mexico; "delightful food of the warrior, the well fed Warrior's flesh of him who is slain in War" (Blake).

Séjourné, *Burning Water*, 32. Blake, *Jerusalem*, pl. 68, ll. 34–35.
Cf. Balint, "Die mexikanische Kriegshieroglyphe," 414–415.

The killing is cannibalistic, to incorporate the enemy. The brothers overcame the father, and all partook of his body. "This cannibalism need not shock us, it survived into far later times. The essential point is, however, that we attribute to these primeval people the same feelings and emotions that we have elucidated in the primitives of our own times, our children, by psychoanalytic research. That is to say: they not merely hated and feared their father, but also honored him as an example to follow; in fact, each son wanted to place himself in his father's position. The cannibalistic act thus becomes comprehensible as an attempt to assure one's identification with the father by incorporating a part of him." Head hunting, ending in super-ego formation: the installation of the murdered man in our house as guardian spirit.

Freud, *Moses and Monotheism*, 131–132.
Cf. Fenichel, "Introjection and Castration Complex," 56.

Identification, introjection, incorporation, is eating. The oldest and truest language is that of the mouth: the oral basis of the ego. Even in seeing there is an active process of introjection: perception is a partaking of what is perceived (Fenichel); we become what we behold (Blake).

Cf. Isaacs, "The Nature and Function of Phantasy," 104–106, 109. Fenichel, "Scoptophilic Instinct and Identification," 379–381. Roheim, *Magic and Schizophrenia*, 224–225. Freud, "Negation," 183.

The question what is a body, is the question what is it to eat: Take, eat; this is my body.

Our body is an incorporated body; we are what we eat (*man ist was er isst*). We are father (mother) eaten. The species is cannibalistic. *Erst kommt das Fressen.* "I am Saturn who devoured his children because it was foretold that otherwise they would devour him. To eat or be eaten—that is the question." But who is my father; and who is my mother? Is it the Blessed Virgin, the Air we breathe, the world-mothering air—

This needful, never spent,
And nursing element;
My more than meat and drink,
My meal at every wink—

From the point of view of *prana,* breath, there exists nothing which is not food. "He who meditates on the Universal Self as the measure of the span from earth to heaven, and as identical with the self, eats food in all the world, in all beings, in all selves."

Strindberg quoted in Lidz, "Strindberg's Creativity and Schizophrenia," 403.
Hopkins, "The Blessed Virgin Compared to the Air We Breathe." *Chandogya Upanishad*, V, ii, 1; V, xviii, 1.
Cf. Roheim, "Das Selbst," 12.

The testimony of schizophrenia: *they eat and are eaten.* Schizophrenia is "food trouble"; schizophrenia says, "Hunger, that is the soul"; "There is only one story—that somebody was starved. But not really—only inside, in my stomach." Prisoners of starvation. "The whole trouble started with a party. People were dreaming that they were hungry, but hungry inside; they were not understood and the police broke it up."

Roheim, *Magic and Schizophrenia*, 104, 115, 126, 127, 129.

"Food trouble." "Somebody was starved. But not really—only inside." What is it to eat; what is the real food. I have meat to eat that ye know not of; for my flesh is meat indeed, and my blood is blood indeed.

John IV, 32; VI, 55.

Hung up between seeing and eating, as in schizophrenia, which makes the patient see pictures of people eating—"the doctors built it to see who was putting his head inside me and eating my food." Paradise regained is Eucharist: taste and see. "The great sorrow in human life, which begins in childhood and continues until death, is that seeing and eating are two different operations. Eternal beatitude (myth of the *Phaedrus*) is a state where to see is to eat." "What is seen is not real, is only an image. What is eaten is destroyed, is not real either. Original sin produced this separation in us."

Roheim, *Magic and Schizophrenia*, 110, 165. Weil, *Cahiers* III, 338–339; *La Pesanteur et la grâce*, 117.

Eating is the form of the fall. The woman gave me and I did eat. Eating is the form of sex. Copulation is oral copulation; when the Aranda ask each other, "Have you eaten?" they mean, "Have you had intercourse?" The schizophrenic girl refused to eat; the case of Simone Weil. Eating is the form of war. Human blood is the life and delightful food of the warrior. Eating is the form of redemption. Except ye eat the flesh of the Son of man, and drink his blood, ye have no life in you. We must eat again of the tree of knowledge, in order to fall into innocence.

Cf. Roheim, *Animism*, 48; *Gates of the Dream*, 96. Storch, *Primitive Archaic Forms*, 17, 75. Richard, *Mallarmé*, 142, 167. Kleist, "Über das Marionettentheater."

Communion; oral copulation. *Ist nicht die Umarmung etwas dem Abendmahl ähnliches?* Eucharist is marriage feast; the union of the bridegroom and the bride. He gives himself to his bride with the bread. Eat your fill, lovers; drink, sweethearts, and drink deep. The two become one flesh, incorporate each other, by eating. The transubstantiation is the unification; is in the eating.

Novalis in Rehm, *Orpheus, Der Dichter und die Toten*, 133.
Cf. Williams, *Radical Reformation*, 308. Daniélou, *Lord of History*, 230–231.

The transubstantiation is in the eating: "Just as, in His days on earth, bread and wine taken by Him as food were metabolized into His flesh and blood at digestion." By eating we become his body; eating makes it so. *Manducando Christi corpus fiunt Christi corpus.*

Lubac, *Corpus Mysticum*, 97.

Transubstantiation—the whole problem of symbolism. Metaphor is really metamorphosis; and the primal form of the sentence is *Tat tvam assi*, Thou art That; or, of bread and wine, *hoc est corpus meum*, this is my body.

Communion. The individual (personal, historical) body; the eucharistic body; the corporate (mystical) body. To see these three as one body.

Communion. The unification is in the eating. We are one body because we are all partakers of that one bread. We become one body as we become his body, that is to say bread. We being many are one bread. "They are nourished by one another."

Cf. I Corinthians X, 17. *Bhagavad Gita*, III, 11-12. Lubac, *Corpus Mysticum*, 79-80.

The true human sacrifice is unification: *hoc est sacrificium Christianorum, ut multi unum corpus sint in Christo.* It is only as we are eaten that we are unified by incorporation into his body.

Lubac, *Corpus Mysticum*, 279, 289.

To be human is to be eaten, to be sacrificed. "The Prajapati, in the beginning, created men together with sacrifice, and said: 'By this shall you multiply. Let this be the Cow of Plenty and yield unto you the milk of your desires.' "

Bhagavad Gita, III, 10.

This world as sacrifice; this world as food; to be is to eat and to be eaten. The sacrifice is the eating, the crucifixion is the supper. "We are fed by the cross of the Lord, since we eat his body."

Lubac, *Corpus Mysticum*, 74–76.
Cf. *Bhagavad Gita*, III, 14.

The real body. To be real, it must be bodily; and to be a body is to be eaten. The humiliation in incarnation: to become bread. To be eaten: to be consumed by sorrow, sickness, and death.

Cf. Weil, *La Pesanteur et la grâce*, 38, 41.

We become one as we become the (sacrificial) food. The sacrifice is the mystical body; which is not offered on behalf of martyrs, since they are themselves that sacrificial body. In the unified body there is no vicarious (representative) sacrifice. The unified body feeds on itself: *ut solum corpus Christi ipsius carne reficiatur.* He gives us his body to eat, so that we might be assimilated into his body. The offering of ourselves must be of him in us to him, that is to say, our union.

Cf. Lubac, *Corpus Mysticum*, 34, 40, 53, 94-95.

This world as food feeds on itself. The mystical body feeds on itself. Autophagy. The supper as self-sacrifice: *semetipsum in cena apostolorum immolavit.* The supper as autophagy: *se cibat ipse cibus; ut nos qui sumus corpus Christi sumamus corpus Christi.*

Lubac, *Corpus Mysticum* 84, 96–97.

Autophagy. The identity of the eater and what he eats; but in a reversal of the naturalistic view: the eater is changed into what he eats. We become his body, and his body is food. We become his body by becoming food. By being eaten we become food. *Cum pascit pascitur, et cum pascitur pascit.* The dualism is overcome. When every action is sacrifice, then Brahman is the sacrificial act, and Brahman the thing sacrificed; and it is Brahman who does the sacrificing, in the fire which is Brahman.

Cf. Lubac, *Corpus Mysticum*, 200–202, 279, 289–290. *Bhagavad Gita*, IV, 23–24.

The true sacrifice is human sacrifice. Animal sacrifice is a false substitute, a pale imitation, a shadow. Abraham departs from human sacrifice, and Christ returns to it. From the shadow of substitutes to the reality of the human body: *de umbra transfertur ad corpus*. Present your bodies, a living sacrifice. The return of the projections. "Man contained in his limbs all Animals, and they were separated from him by cruel Sacrifices." As in schizophrenia: "Some patients declare that elephants and other beasts live in their bodies."

Blake, *Jerusalem*, pl. 27. Roheim, *Magic and Schizophrenia*, 102.
Cf. Freud, *Totem and Taboo*, ch. IV, section 6.

The true sacrifice is in one body. "The slave [captive] represents the master's [victor's] body offered to the god, the former being merely a symbol for the latter." The Place of Holy Sacrifice where Friends Die for each other, will become the Place of Murder & Unforgiving, Never-awaking Sacrifice of Enemies. "Mahomet slew, Jesus Christ caused his own to be slain." But mostly Mahomet slays. Overcoming the dualism of self and other: the identity of the sacrificer, the victim, and the god. *Ipse offerens, ipse et oblatio*.

Séjourné, *Burning Water*, 155. Blake, *Jerusalem*, pl. 48, ll. 55-57. Pascal, *Pensées*, no. 598. Augustine, *De Civitate Dei*, X, 21.
Cf. Hubert and Mauss, *Sacrifice*, 42, 101.

The identity of the sacrificer and the victim: the sacrifice of identity. The last cruel sacrifice is sacrifice of the separateness or the self; self-sacrifice, self-slaughter, self-annihilation. The last cruel sacrifice is the crucifixion of the self.

The identity of the sacrificer, the victim, and the god: no more sacrifice. The unified body feeds on itself. From crucifixion to eating. The Last Supper is the New Testament: "my blood of the new testament." His crucifixion, the last of the old sacrifices; our Eucharist, the first of the new. The supper is the last thing, not the cross: eschatology is eating; the marriage feast of the Lamb.

From crucifixion to eucharist; from the blood to the bloodless sacrifice; from sacrifice to feeding. The solution to the problem of war. Bread and wine, this is my body. *Hoc in carne nihil carnale nihilque cruentum*. And Melchizedek, King of Salem, which means Peace, brought forth bread and wine.

Cf. Lubac, *Corpus Mysticum*, 160-161. Genesis XIV, 18.

"My whole Christianity is a taste for *signs* and for the elements of water, bread, wine." His body is to be found in bread; *caro sub forma panis operta*. Our daily bread; a daily incarnation. It is always his body that we eat. He dies daily. The reality of body is in bread, eaten. The real presence; bread worship. Dionysus, worship of the wine. Corporeal presence in or under or with the bread and wine. In any meal. Revelations III, 20: Behold, I stand at the door and knock: if any man hear my voice, and open the door, I will come in to him, and will sup with him, and he with me.

Hamann in Smith, *J. G. Hamann*, 69.
Cf. Lubac, *Corpus Mysticum*, 69, 71, 178, 186, 236.

Real presence; in the present. If he is not present in the food, he is not present at all. In the real eating: his body is sensually present, handled, broken, chewed.

Cf. Lubac, *Corpus Mysticum*, 167.

Incarnation is impanation, invination, immolation. "Every householder commits inevitably the five-fold sin of killing, which results from (1) the pestle and mortar, (2) the grinding-stone, (3) the oven, (4) the water-jar, and (5) the broom. He is absolved from these sins by the performance of the five obligatory sacrifices." There is no way to avoid murder; except by ritual murder.

Bhagavad Gita, III, 13 (and Nikhilananda commentary).

Impanation, invination, unification: out of many grains one bread: out of many grapes one wine. The secret of unification is in bread and wine. In Blake, "the wine-press and the mill may represent not only the disintegration of form, but the reuniting of all nature into the body and blood of a universal Man . . . the great communion feast in which human life is reintegrated into its real form."

Frye, *Fearful Symmetry*, 290.

From crucifixion to eating; from the bloody to the bloodless sacrifice; from the old to the new; from the letter to the spirit. Idols require human sacrifice, literally; Moloch. Abstain from things offered to idols, and from blood. The problem of war is the problem of idolatry, or literalism. The crude materialism of physical conquest: *wie schwer der andere wirklich* einzuverleiben *ist.* Therefore the opposite of war, the true war, is poetry. "Art Degraded, Imagination Denied, War Governed the Nations." "Rouse up, O Young Men of the New Age: set your foreheads against the ignorant Hirelings! For we have Hirelings in the Camp, the Court and the University, who would, if they could, for ever depress Mental and prolong Corporeal War."

Blake, *Milton*, Preface; *Laocoön*, 775. Nietzsche, *Aus dem Nachlass*, 421. Cf. Acts XV, 29; XXI, 25.

From the bloody to the bloodless sacrifice: from the literal to the spiritual body. Real presence, in a bloodless sacrifice; not sublimation, but transubstantiation of the body. *Corpus non corporaliter.* The solution to the problem of war in the Eucharist, with transubstantiation. *Hoc in carne nihil cruentum.*

Lubac, *Corpus Mysticum*, 160–161.

Communion. The spiritual body a mystical body. The union is not a sociological fact, is not a fact of ecclesiastical or temporal power, is not a fact of this world of power politics, is not a fact according to the reality-principle. The union is not given but made, in the Eucharist, in the eating. The unity is not an analogy of the natural (organic) body given, but is made by the transubstantiation.

Cf. Lubac, *Corpus Mysticum*, 103, 129–131, 145, 209.

The transubstantiation of the Eucharist is the transfiguration of the resurrection. *Mutatio carnis in spiritum*: it is raised a spiritual body. A spiritual body, a body which is not in Simple Location; *corpus non corporaliter*. The paradoxes of action at a distance: the ubiquity of Christ's glorified body; Christ is able to project the life-giving power of his glorified body without spatial limitation.

Cf. Lubac, *Corpus Mysticum*, 153–154.

The true sacrifice is total, a making holy of the whole; the false sacrifice sacrifices a part, *pars pro toto*; a part cut off, bitten off, *the* part; castration. Partial incorporation is castration; the part eaten, when the eating is partial, is always a penis. Castration is mitigated (symbolic) cannibalism; the original aim is to eat, and to eat all.

Cf. Fenichel, "Trophy and Triumph," 144, 150–153, 159, 161; "Respiratory Introjection," 223. Roheim, *Gates of the Dream*, 96. Lewin, "Body as Phallus," 33.

Partial incorporation or total incorporation; eating a penis and eating a body. Partial incorporation is eating of a representative (symbolic) part, which is only partially (symbolically) eaten; as possession is mitigated (symbolic) eating. The part partially eaten remains a separate part, undigested; the original ownership is not obliterated: it is a part "borrowed," i.e., stolen: private property is theft. "The incorporated object retains its separate existence, rages inside her against the sinful eater, becomes her super-ego." The attempt "to assure one's identification with the father by incorporating a part of him" is not enough. The conflict of ambivalence is not resolved. "The phantasy of oral incorporation of the penis was an attempt to eliminate the hated penis from the world. This attempt, however, failed, since the introjected penis continued to threaten her from the inside."

Fenichel, "Introjection and Castration Complex," 56, 58; cf. "Trophy and Triumph," 144. Freud, *Moses and Monotheism*, 132.

Partial incorporation, or total incorporation, integration. "It is possible that we have in the relation between body-images two different types, the one completely integrating his own body-image with the body-image of others, and the other having the various parts of the body-image not integrated into a whole. . . . Summation and integration." Participation (playing a part) or fusion. *L'Apocalypse, c'est-à-dire la dissolution de la série dans le groupe en fusion.*

Schilder, *Image of the Human Body*, 237. Sartre, *Critique de la raison dialectique*, 391.

FIRE

The choice is between partial incorporation and total incorporation (integration). Participation (playing a part) or fusion. Total incorporation, or fusion, is combustion in fire. "The way he behaved could also be described by saying that he kept me inside of him. . . . Yet I did not feel that these ways of talking about what happened were entirely adequate; for all of them take for granted the idea of a clear boundary; if I am felt to be inside him then he has a boundary, and the same if a bit of him is felt to be projected into me. But there was much material in this analysis to do with burning, boiling down, and melting, which seemed to me to express the idea of the obliteration of boundaries."

Milner, "The Role of Illusion in Symbol Formation," 94.

Set fire to the sacrifice. The sacrificial fire, the sacrificial food; the food is fuel. All things are food, are fire. The real prayer is to see this world go up in flames.

Cf. Evdokimov, *La Femme et le salut du monde*, 240. *Chandogya Upanishad* V, iv, 1.

The true sacrifice is total, holocaust. *Consummatum est.* The one is united with the all, in a consuming fire.

To bring this world to an end, in a final conflagration, or explosion, bursting the boundaries. "If the whole of mankind were once more integrated into a single spiritual body, the universe as we see it would burst." Satori is explosion: "The balloon bursts, every limitation disappears: the one is united with the all." "To accumulate in the invisible the charge of energy which will one day blow up in him all the cave of phantoms."

Frye, *Fearful Symmetry*, 44; cf. Blake, *Night* IX, 230. Benoit, *Supreme Doctrine*, 111, 104. Cf. Meerloo, *That Difficult Peace*, 23, 28, 107, 131, 187.

The final conflagration; or apocalypse. The unity of life and death as fire. "That Nature is a Heraclitean Fire and of the comfort of the Resurrection."

Das Lebend'ge will ich preisen
Das nach Flammentod sich sehnet.

Hopkins, *Poems.* Goethe, "Selige Sehnsucht," *West-Östlicher Divan.*

To heal, to cauterize. Therapy as apocalypse, conflagration; error burned up. Not catharsis but cruelty. "He would make what he called furnaces, with a very careful choice of what ingredients should make the fire. . . . And often there had to be a sacrifice, a lead soldier had to be added to the fire, and this figure was spoken of either as the victim or the sacrifice. . . . The fire seemed to be here not only a destructive fire, but also the fire of Eros; and not only the figurative expression of his own passionate bodily feelings, not only the phantasy representative of the wish for passionate union with the external world, but also a way of representing the inner fire of concentration."

Milner, "The Role of Illusion in Symbol Formation," 96.
Cf. Artaud, *The Theater and Its Double*, ch. I. "Plague."

The fire next time. The revolution, or second coming; he will baptize you with the Holy Spirit and with fire.

Luke III, 16.

A fiery consummation. Not suspense, but end-pleasure; not partial sacrifice (castration), but total holocaust. It is as fire that sex and war and eating and sacrifice are one. "Woman, very, O Gautama, is a sacrificial fire. In this case the sexual organ is the fuel: when one invites, the smoke; the vulva, the flame; when one inserts, the coals; the sexual pleasure, the sparks. In this fire the gods offer semen. From this oblation arises the fetus." Sex and war and the Last Judgment—"the Loins, the place of the Last Judgement." The word consummation refers both to the burning world and the sacred marriage.

Chandogya Upanishad, V, viii, 1-2. Blake, *Jerusalem*, pl. 30, l. 38.
Cf. Frye, *Fearful Symmetry*, 196. A. Balint, "Die mexikanische Kriegshieroglyphe." Reik, *Masochism in Modern Man*, 51, 59–64.

Learn to love the fire. The alchemical fire of transmutation: *Wolle die Wandlung. O sei für die Flamme begeistert.* To be content in the purgatorial fire. The fires of hell: "Walking among the fires of hell, delighting in the enjoyment of Genius, which to Angels look like torment and insanity." The apocalyptic fire: "Meditate on the make-believe world as burning to ashes, and become *being above human.*"

Blake, *Marriage of Heaven and Hell*, pls. 6–7. Reps, *Zen, Flesh, Zen, Bones*, 165.
Rilke, *Sonnets to Orpheus*, II, xii.
Cf. Dante, *Inferno* I, 118–120.

Love is all fire; and so heaven and hell are the same place. As in Augustine, the torments of the damned are part of the felicity of the redeemed. Two cities; which are one city. Eden is a fiery city; just like hell.

Cf. Augustine, *De Civitate Dei*, XXII, 30.

The truth concealed from the priest and revealed to the warrior: that this world always was and is and shall be ever-living fire. Revealed to the lover, too: every lover is a warrior; love is all fire.

Chandogya Upanishad, V, iii 7. Heraclitus, frg. 29.

The resolution of the antinomy between liberation and repression: fire. "Some allow the senses to wander unchecked, and try to see the Brahman everywhere; for theses sense-objects are the offering and sense-enjoyment the sacrificial fire." To be aflame at every point. To be alive is to be burning.

Bhagavad Gita, IV, 27.
Cf. Voznesensky in Blum, "The Artist in Russia," 72.

Fire is freedom. Spontaneous combustion. Spontaneity is ardor.

Violent eruption, vulcanism; the patient becomes violent, as he wakes up. The madness of the millennia breaks out: madness is, Dionysus is, violence.

Love is violence. The kingdom of heaven suffereth violence, from hot love and living hope.

Sartre, *Critique de la raison dialectique*, 428, 439, 455. Dante, *Il Paradiso*, XX, 94.
Matthew XI, 12.

Birth is bursting, the shell burst. The start is violent. The great heroic deed is to be born; to slay the dragon, to kill the mother, to conquer Tiamat. Every child, like Athena, is born fully armed; is a knife that opens the womb.

Cf. Arendt, *Revolution*, 10. Roheim, "The Dragon and the Hero: Part One," 43–53.

Not peace but a sword. Peace lies in finding the true war. The reconciliation of opposites, the making of friendship, takes place on the battlefield. The hieroglyph for war is Atlachinolli, "Burning Water." Burning water; *effusion et ardeur*, efflorescence and hemorrhage; blossoming war. In ancient Mexico, "The symbol of the world thus brought together is a cross."

Séjourné, *Burning Water*, 73.
Cf. *Iliad*, VI, 212-236. Balint, "Die mexikanische Kriegshieroglyphe," 413–428.
Richard, *Mallarmé*, 119, 473, 501.

The identity of peace and war, of Zen and Ken. "The secret of victory without conflict. . . . One must break through to the world where all things are essentially of one body." "In the consciousness that all things are essentially of one body the 'other' can be equated with oneself and oneself with the 'other.' " "Victory without contending—how can this be achieved? . . . It comes the moment the stage is reached when the enemy no longer sees me nor I the enemy, when heaven and earth are yet undivided and light and shade are one, before *In* and *Yo* (Yin and Yang) reveal themselves."

Durckheim, *The Japanese Cult of Tranquility*, 83.

Find the true fire; of which the fires of war are a Satanic parody. Fight fire with fire. The true teachers of peace are those who have the highest power, who can work miracles, who are master of fire. Therefore, the Buddhas are called Jinas, Conquerors.

Cf. AE, *Candle of Vision*, 137–139. Govinda, *Foundations of Tibetan Mysticism*, 279.

In Eden the two Fountains of the River of Life are War and Hunting; perverted here into Fountains of bitter Death and corroding Hell.

Blake, *Milton*, pl. 35, ll. 2–3; *Jerusalem*, pl. 43, ll. 31–32.

War is war perverted. The problem is not the war but the perversion. And the perversion is a repression; war is sex perverted. "War is energy Enslav'd."

Blake, *Night* IX, 152.
Cf. Frye, *Fearful Symmetry*, 262–263.

War is energy Enslav'd. War is what happens to the weak, the impotent; so that they might at least be touched with lowest form of violence; or as the death decreed for those who run away from battle.

> The plain truth is that people want war. They want it anyhow: for itself, and apart from each and every possible consequence. It is the final bouquet of life's fireworks. The born soldier wants it hot and actual. The non-combatant wants it in the background, and always as an open possibility, to feed his imagination. War is human nature at its uttermost. We are here to do our uttermost. It is a sacrament. Society would rot without the mystical blood-payment.

James, "Remarks at the Peace Banquet," 304.

The thing, then, is not to abolish war but to find the true war. Open the hidden Heart in Wars of Mutual Benevolence, Wars of Love.

Blake, *Jerusalem*, pl. 97, l. 14; cf. pl. 43, ll. 40–43.

To find the true war, the true sacrament; to avoid idolatry (Mexican sacrifices, Moloch); it is all a question of symbolism. To see the sacrament of war as a false sacrament is to see the demonic parody, the anti-Christ. To see it is to see through it; to see through it is to burn up the idols. "It is Burnt up the Moment Men cease to behold it."

Blake, *A Vision of the Last Judgement*, 617.

To find the true fire. Semele asked for the full presence of her divine lover, and received the thunderbolt. *Hiroshima mon amour.* Save us from the literal fire. The literal-minded, the idolaters, receive the literal fire. Each man suffers his own fire.

The real fire, the chariot of fire, the Fiery Chariot of his Contemplative Thought. The real fight, the mental fight; poetry, a sword of lightning, ever unsheathed, that consumes the scabbard that would contain it.

Cf. Blake, *A Vision of the Last Judgement*, 611. Shelley, "Defence of Poetry," 221.

Apocalyptic fire. "Error or Creation will be Burned up, and then, and not till Then, Truth or Eternity will appear. It is Burnt up the Moment Men cease to behold it." "The whole creation will be consumed and appear infinite and holy, whereas it now appears finite and corrupt." If these fires are discovered, no other fires are necessary: in these fires not a hair of their head is singed.

Blake, *Marriage of Heaven and Hell*, pl. 14; *A Vision of the Last Judgement*, 617.

The final judgment, the everlasting bonfire, is here now. Truth is error burned up.

The true body is the body burnt up, the spiritual body. The unity is not organic-natural unity, but the unity of fire. "But first the notion that man has a body distinct from his soul is to be expunged; this I shall do by printing in the infernal method, by corrosives, which in Hell are salutary and medicinal, melting apparent surfaces away, and displaying the infinite which was hid." The apocalyptic fire burns up the reality of the material world. In the baptism of water we are buried with Christ; in the baptism of fire we are conformed to the body of his glory.

Blake, *Marriage of Heaven and Hell*, pl. 14.
Daniélou, *Origen*, 95.

FRACTION

To eat and to be eaten. The grain must be ground, the wine pressed; the bread must be broken. The true body is a body broken.

> Nothing can be sole or whole
> That has not been rent.

Yeats, "Crazy Jane Talks with the Bishop."
Cf. Dylan Thomas, "This bread I break." Frye, *Fearful Symmetry*, 290.

To be is to be vulnerable. The defense mechanisms, the character-armor, is to protect from life. Frailty alone is human; a broken, a ground-up (contrite) heart.

Cf. Weil, *La Pesanteur et la grâce*, 125.

In the upper sector, the realm of the gods, "whose carefree life, dedicated to aesthetic pleasures, is indicated by dance and music. On account of this one-sided dedication to their own pleasures, they forget the true nature of life, the limitations of their own existence, the sufferings of others, their own transiency. They do not know that they live only in a state of temporary harmony. . . . They live, so to say, on the accumulated capital of past good deeds without adding new values. They are gifted with beauty, longevity and freedom from pain, but just this lack of suffering, of obstacles and exertion, deprives the harmony of their existence of all creative impulses." "Rebirth in heavenly realms is not an aim which Buddhists think worth striving for. . . . It leads to a strengthening of the ego-illusion and to a deeper entanglement in the *sa s ric* world."

Govinda, *Foundations of Tibetan Mysticism*, 238–239.

There is a seal or sepulcher to be broken, a rock to be broke open, to disclose the living water; an eruption. Begin then with a fracture, a cesura, a rent; opening a crack in this fallen world, a shaft of light.

Cf. Richard, *Mallarmé*, 539.

Literal meanings are icons become stone idols; the stone sepulcher, the stone tables of the law. The New Testament remained hidden in the Old, like water in the rock; until the cross of Christ broke the rock open. Iconoclasm, the word like a hammer that breaketh the rock in pieces.

Cf. Luther cited in Hahn, "Luthers Auslegungsgrundsätze," 190n. Jeremiah XXIII, 29.

Open is broken. There is not breakthrough without breakage. A struggle with an angel, which leaves us scarred, or lame. Every dream is a struggle; the possible confronting the real, abruptly.

Man the measure of all things is the microcosmic man; in little all the sphere. Stretch yourself, then, to the breaking point: "*Ehr sey also hoch, dicke, breyt und lang, wye er am kreuz gehangen hat.*" To be so stretched is to be crucified; it is the crucified body that is the measure of all things: *statera facta corporis.*

Müntzer cited in Holl, "Luther and die Schwärmer," 437. Weil, *La Pesanteur et la grâce*, 109.

The crucified body, the crucified mind. The norm is not normality but schizophrenia, the split, broken, crucified mind. "If we throw a crystal to the ground, it breaks, but it does not break haphazard; in accordance with the lines of cleavage it falls into fragments, where limits were already determined by the structure of the crystal, although they were invisible. Psychotics are fissured and splintered structures such as these. We cannot deny them a measure of awe with which madmen were regarded by the people of ancient times." Split the stick and there is Jesus.

Freud, *New Introductory Lectures*, 80. Cage, *Silence*, 70.

Stretch yourself, to the breaking point. It is not true unless it hurts; the evidence is martyrdom. "All truths are bloody truths for me." We do not know the truth because we repress it; and we repress it because it is painful.

Kaufmann, *Nietzsche*, 68.

To the breaking point. Carrying the thought through to the end; crucial experiments, *experimentum crucis*. A witness (martyr) steadfast to the end, tested *in extremis*. Extremism. Truth is not in safety or in the middle. "*Les oeuvres d'art naissent toujours de qui a affronté le danger, de qui est allé jusqu'au bout d'une expérience.*"

Rilke cited in Bachelard, *La Poétique de l'espace*, 198.

Aphorism is exaggeration, or grotesque; in psychoanalysis nothing is true except the exaggerations; and in poetry, "*cet extrémisme est le phénomène même de l'élan poétique.*" Aphorism is exaggeration, extravagant language; the road of excess which leads to the palace of wisdom.

Adorno, *Minima Moralia*, 78. Blake, *Marriage of Heaven and Hell*, pl. 7. Bachelard, *La Poétique de l'espace*, 198.

Exaggeration or extravagance; not to count the cost. Go for broke. Aphorism is recklessness; it goes too far. Intellect is courage; the courage to risk its own life; to play with madness. "*Poètes, voici la loi mystérieuse: Aller au delà. Aller au delà, extravaguez, soit, comme Homère, comme Ezéchiel, comme Pindare, comme Salomon, comme Archilogue, comme Horace, comme Saint-Paul, comme Saint-Jean, comme Saint-Jérôme, comme Tertullien, comme Pétrarque, comme Alighieri, comme Ossian, comme Cervantes, comme Rabelais, comme Shakespeare, comme Milton, comme Mathurin Régnier, comme Agrippa d'Aubigné, comme Molière, comme Voltaire. Extravaguez avec ces doctes, extravaguez avec ces justes, extravaguez avec ces sages. Quos vult AUGERE Jupiter dementat.*" Aphorism, the form of the mad truth, the Dionysian form.

Hugo, "Promontorium Somnii," 309.

Only the exaggerations are true. *Credo quia absurdum*; as in parables or poetry. Aphoristic form is suicide, or self-sacrifice; for truth must die. Intellect is sacrifice of intellect, or fire; which burns up as it gives light.

Cf. *Bhagavad Gita*, IV, 19.

Broken flesh, broken mind, broken speech. Truth, a broken body: fragments, or aphorisms; as opposed to systematic form or methods: "Aphorisms, representing a knowledge broken, do invite men to inquire farther; whereas Methods, carrying the show of a total, do secure men, as if they were at farthest."

Bacon in McLuhan, *Gutenberg Galaxy*, 102–103.

Systematic form attempts to evade the necessity of death in the life of the mind as of the body; it has immortal longings on it, and so it remains dead. *Ducunt volentem fata, nolentem trahunt.* The rigor is *rigor mortis*; systems are wooden crosses. Procrustean beds on which the living mind is pinned. Aphorism is the form of death and resurrection: "the form of eternity."

Kaufmann, *Nietzsche*, 66.

Aphorism, or symbolism, as in *Finnegans Wake*: "A mode of broken or syncopated manipulation to permit *inclusive* or simultaneous perception of a total or diversified field. Such, indeed is symbolism by definition—a collocation, a *parataxis* . . . without a point of view or lineal connection or sequential order." Symbolism, or grotesque: "A fine grotesque is the expression, in a moment, by a series of symbols thrown together in bold and fearless connection, of truths which it would have taken a long time to express in any verbal way, and of which the connection is left for the beholder to work out for himself; the gaps, left or overleapt by the haste of the imagination, forming the grotesque character."

McLuhan quoting Ruskin, *Gutenberg Galaxy*, 266–267.

Systematic form; generalities. All knowledge is particular, goes into the natural man in bits, a scrap here, a scrap there. Food is taken in bites. Bread broken to feed five thousand.

Cf. Blake in Frye, *Fearful Symmetry*, 15. Pound, *Kulchur*, 98–99.

Broken form. Against beauty as such. No form nor comeliness. Abrupt; uneven; inconsistent. By Ciceronian standards, *mutila quaedam et hiantia*.

Isaiah LIII, 2. Cicero, *Orator*, 32.

"A new heroic era has opened," Mandelstam wrote in 1921, "in the life of the word. The word is flesh and bread. It shares the fate of bread and flesh: suffering."

Fanger, "The Prose of Osip Mandelstam," 47.

Beyond atomism. Fragmentation unto dust, and the word becomes seminal again. The sower soweth the word. Dionysus broken and scattered is seed scattered. But if it die it bringeth forth much fruit. The body is made whole by being broken.

John XII, 24.

Sanskrit *bindu:* "This word, which has many meanings, like 'point, dot, zero, drop, germ, seed, semen,' . . . It is the point from which inner and outer space have their origin and in which they become *one* again." The thought, poem, is a cell or seed; a germ of living thought: growing from nothing to ripeness. Instead of the dead wood of systems, the tree of life; ramifications; branched thoughts new-grown with pleasant pain.

Govinda, *Foundations of Tibetan Mysticism*, 116.

Broken speech; speech broken by silence. To let the silence in is symbolism. "In symbol there is concealment and yet revelation: here therefore, by Silence and by Speech acting together, comes a double significance."

Carlyle, *Sartor Resartus*, Book III, ch. III, "Symbols."

2 Peter Yates

Composer and writer Peter Yates (1909–76) contributed a talk featuring several musical samples of three- to four-minutes duration. Where possible, the musical examples he provided, which spanned ethnomusicology, historical tuning and notational practices, and approaches to dissonance and noise, are identified in the text in brackets.

My friends here have been so good to me during this past week, I hope tonight to be able to repay some part of this pleasure. This is a simple theatrical performance lecture. I started giving it in 1959 as four lectures, then as I learned more about the material, I cut it into two lectures, and sometimes two successive lectures in one evening. Now, I have written two books about the subject and feel confident that I can reduce it to a single lecture.

The lecture involves audience participation because you will have to do most of the explaining for yourselves while listening to a concert of examples. The examples, if you really hear them, will tell you more than my explaining. The lecture is not meant to be difficult, but the subject is.

We begin with an example of primitive music, "Lady Carey's Dompe," composed in an improvising tradition, like that of early jazz, at or around the court of Henry VIII of England. It is one of the examples from the four-and-a-half-hour history of tuning, spoken and recorded on tape by my late friend, Wesley Kuhnley, a student of historical keyboard performance practice. He designed and built the harpsichords we hear him play and learned to tune them in the historic manner from the instrument, thus reconstituting the music in its original harmony and sound, which has much to do with the correct way of playing it.

"Lady Carey's Dompe," played in the acoustically correct tuning, which underlies all Western musical theory, just intonation.

[*plays "My Lady Carey's Dompe"*]

Here is, for contrast, an example of music in the ancient Chinese tradition, which the Koreans called Confucian music, for a 3,000-year-old orchestra using stone chimes, pots, flutes, and a wooden tiger. The last sound you hear is the scratching of the wooden tiger's serrated back. This is a highly cultivated ceremonial music.

[*plays Confucian music*]

A primitive music is one that exists in terms of its own time and culture and ends when these change. Our music of the harmonic era, the three centuries between 1600 and 1900, which we perform in equal temperament, the music most of us grew up with and take for granted, is on the way to becoming a primitive music.

Now, I should like to play music of an African tribe, which the women perform standing up to their waists in water, slapping the water with their hands.

Moderator: I'm sorry, I do not have an example of that music.

I too am sorry. In that case, I shall play an example of medieval music, performed first in the correct tuning, which is called Pythagorean, with acoustically correct fifth, and immediately afterward, the same fragment in equal temperament, the tuning we use today.

[*plays medieval music*]

This example shows the acoustical superiority of the correct fifth, the first example, and that the narrow, acoustically incorrect fifth of equal temperament, the second example, causes a succession of seemingly false relationships. The difference between the two tunings of the fifth is about one in 300, proving the aesthetic importance of slight microtonal difference.

The narrow degree of false relationship in equal temperament is what we call "consonance." It is one degree in the color chart of sound, between the pure sonority of just intonation and the clashing brilliance of discord. When we understand this, we shall not think ourselves so brave because we write in a more extreme discord than our grandfathers used. Never look down on your ancestors; they may have been more skillful than you.

The only just, or acoustically correct, interval in equal temperament is the octave. I believe that George Tremblay in Los Angeles was the first serial composer to enrich the patterns of dissonant discordant serial music by the deliberate introduction of octaves in his symphony, written in 1949. The symphony has been performed once at Hamburg.

[*plays George Tremblay's* Symphony in One Movement *(1949)*]

We are habituated to a music of twelve notes. We include in performing it a great quantity of microtonal differences that the composer cannot indicate or control by our notation. You cannot find microtones on a piano keyboard; they are in the cracks between the keys, but they play a large part in the world's music. Here is ancient court music from Japan, in origin contemporary with Charlemagne, played by the court orchestra of the University of California, Los Angeles. The sound consists of notated tones embellished with microtones, according to a strict tradition.

[*plays court music of Japan*]

Acoustically correct sound is called "just intonation," the tones in accordance with the overtone series. I am giving the minimum of explanation. It's more important that you hear the music. The polyphonic music of the fifteenth and sixteenth centuries was sung in just intonation. Enharmonic notes in just intonation were recognized as mutable notes, which the performers learned to sing sharp or flat as necessary to avoid a dissonance. Because it involves higher overtones, just intonation is more sonorous than equal temperament.

Just intonation is being revived today for the same reason that our ears welcome the relatively consonant music of Vivaldi as an offset to the dissonant tradition of Germanic music from J.S. Bach to Brahms. Listen to this "Strict Song" by Lou Harrison. The voice is singing just intonation; the pianos and harps tune to a twelve-note just temperament.

[*plays selection from Lou Harrison's* Strict Songs *(1955)*]

Theorists and composers since Hermann von Helmholtz and Ferruccio Busoni have been experimenting with other scales of just intonation, among them the nineteen-tone just temperament of Joseph Yasser, the 31-tone just temperament of Adriaan Fokker in the Netherlands, and the 43-tone just intonation of Harry Partch.

M: The sonata by Henk Badings for two violins in 31-tone just temperament is very beautiful. I regret we have been unable to obtain a tape of it.

The Indians tuned the vina and sitar in a 22-note just intonation but do not use all the notes in any one composition, adding to the melody only those tones that are needed to give a correct leading note.

Here is microtonal just intonation in a scale of 43 tones in the octave, 43 instead of our twelve: *U.S. Highball*, a conversation of hobos in a freight car, riding east from San Francisco, composed by Harry Partch. Observe the great variety of melodic inflection and melisma, not only sung and chanted, but spoken to exact pitches. Hear the abundant sonority in both consonant and dissonant relationships. All the instruments were designed and built by the composer or adapted by him to play his music.

[*plays Harry Partch's* U.S. Highball: A Musical Account of Slim's Transcontinental Hobo Trip *(1955)*]

If you combine just intonation with microtones, the microtones emphasize the smaller interval high overtones, at once enriching and coloring the sonority. This is *Nova Odo* by Lou Harrison in twelve-note just temperament, recorded in Korea by the Seoul Philharmonic Orchestra and Chorus with a microtonal obbligato played by a group of Korean oboes called *p'iri*. The text, sung in the international language Esperanto, is about atomic testing.

[*plays Lou Harrison's* Nova Odo *(1961–63)*]

Twelve-tone just intonation is good only in a single key, unless one avoids or adjusts the mutable tones. Harrison combines techniques of the polyphonic period and the tone row to write complex counterpoint, often with a melody in all four positions of the row.

Meantone, the principal tuning of European music between 1600 and 1800, is good in eight or more keys, depending on whether you tune the enharmonic notes sharp or flat. In the old style of tuning you start from C, and the last note of the tuning cycle is tuned either G-sharp or A-flat, depending on whether you wish to play in three sharps or three flats. The same method can be extended to include more sharps or flats, but only by increasing the risk of unwanted discords, which musicians of the seventeenth and eighteenth centuries called "the wolf." Discords, in their opinion, howled like wolves—and they still do—but we're used to them. Few of us have ever heard a wolf howl, and few of us today consciously distinguish between dissonance and discord.

In meantone, the major third was tuned acoustically correct, and the fifth as narrow as the ear can bear. The intervals are unequal, and each key gives a different harmonic coloring. Modulation changes both the harmony and key coloration, and each key color had, in meantone, its own emotional significance or affect. In the equal temperament we use today, all intervals are equal, the major third is tuned discordantly sharp for brilliance, and the fifth is very slightly flat. Yet we play meantone music in equal temperament as if there were no difference. We think notes instead of sound. Here is a sarabande from the *Eighth Order* by Couperin, played by Wesley Kuhnley in meantone. Notice the resonant clangor caused by the clashing of acoustically correct major thirds and very discordant fifths.

M: He doesn't expect you to remember everything he's saying, just listen to the music, get your ears full of it.

[*plays François Couperin's* Pièces de clavecin, Eighth Order *in B minor, Sarabande "L'Unique" (1717)*]

With meantone tuning, a distinction between dissonance and discord could be used for dramatic effect. The effect was not an emotional meaning attached to music by a program note, it was an aesthetic consequence of a complete microtonal difference in sound.

Today, we try to produce similar emotional affects by other means. Now, in Kuhnau's "Battle Between David and Goliath," played in meantone, we hear the stone flung, then as the giant falls and dies the dissonance becomes discord.

[*plays Johann Kuhnau's Biblical Sonata no. 1 ("The Battle Between David and Goliath") (1700)*]

J.S. Bach wrote his Toccata in F-sharp minor as a test piece in sound, presumably for his students. If they played it in normal meantone, the wolves howled like this.

[*plays J.S. Bach's Toccata in F-sharp minor (1712)*]

If anybody ever tells you there is not such a thing as discord, now you know the difference. Historically informed listeners will claim that Bach meant this music to be played in well-tempered tuning. They believe that well-tempered is the same as equal temperament, as one reads in all the music history books. This is incorrect. Well-tempered is a distinct tuning of unequal intervals, retaining some of the modulatory coloring of meantone, but allowing performance in all keys without retuning. Mozart, and Beethoven in his earlier years, tuned his keyboard well-tempered. You'll have to take my word for it.

You see, the trouble is that we have wonderful classical music, about which we know everything but the sound. We don't know how it was tuned, unless you explore it like this. We don't know what the tuning did to the harmony, unless you explore it like this. And therefore, whenever we play it, we play it wrong.

In January of this year, Margaret Fabrizio performed Bach's *Art of Fugue* in San Francisco on a well-tempered harpsichord. The principled critics responding to the sound rhapsodized over the tone coloration and the sense of freedom from the prevailing D minor. They did not know how the instrument was tuned. Now listen to Beethoven's *Prelude Through All the Keys*, opus 39, played by Wesley Kuhnley on a well-tempered piano. To prevent outphasing and clarify the tuning, one string of each note has been damped with felt.

[*plays Ludwig van Beethoven's* Two Preludes Through All Major Keys, *op. 39 (1789)*]

See, the musicological explanation for that is that Beethoven must've written it when he was very young, and it was an exercise, because that's the only way you can explain his going to all that trouble. It didn't occur to anybody that he might've written it for an aesthetic reason.

Returning to Bach's F-sharp minor Toccata, the solution is not well-tempered tuning, but a special tuning in meantone, designed to bring out the particular coloring that Bach intended. Such a special keyboard tuning in meantone was called an accord. In the entire toccata, there is no C-natural. Mr. Kuhnley, therefore, tuned a sharp meantone from C in the old style until he reached G-sharp. The next acoustically correct major third would be G-sharp/B-sharp. So he retuned C-natural to B-sharp, added an F-double sharp on one set of strings, and a G on the other set of strings, giving him all the notes he needed. And this is what happens: the succession of microtonally distinct colorations as subtle as any we can produce today by instrumental or electronic means. Let me make it clear, this is done by the tuning, it's not done by pulling stops in ways. It's all on one registration. With each of the dozen or so modulations, the harmonic color of the music changes.

[*plays Bach's Toccata in F-sharp minor*]

Arnold Schoenberg told me that Mahler had remarked to him on the great loss to music when we changed from meantone to equal temperament; that gives you some idea of it. The reason I'm taking you on this long journey is not to explain how these things happen, but to let you hear some of the things that have happened in music that are not all correctly recorded in our history and theory books. We are so accustomed to hearing all our European musical classics performed in the one relatively colorless tuning of equal temperament, we need to discover how much we have lost. Then we shall understand why composers have been trying by various means to put back into music what has been hidden from us. And for the same reasons, we have been turning to oriental music and primitive music. Equal temperament solves or escapes the central problem of tuning, what is called the "Pythagorean Comma," by dividing the octave into mathematically equal intervals, all equally discordant. In equal temperament, all keys sound the same. Only one interval, the octave, remains acoustically correct.

What a composer does with the octave is therefore of great importance. Brahms used it merely to outline the chords. Bruckner used multiple octaves to increase sonority. You have heard how George Tremblay used them in his symphony, mingling serial discord with just intonation. Modern harmonic theory, which all schools teach, is based partly on the simple arithmetical relationships of unequal concordant intervals in just intonation, which went out of use around 1600, partly on the modulatory coloring of the unequal intervals in meantone, which went out of use around 150 years ago, and partly on rationalizations of these conflicting systems, in terms of the tuning we use today, equal temperament. Harmonic theory, as we know it, is made up of three mutually exclusive sound systems, which are taught as if the three were one.

M: What you're really saying is, that we don't hear the music of Josquin, or [William] Byrd, or Palestrina, the way their music really sounded, or the music of Couperin, or Handel, or Bach, or Mozart, or some of Beethoven, the way it really sounded, right?

That's right.

M: So that if we've lost the way their music really sounded, why should we shed crocodile tears over what may be happening to music at the present time?

Well, perhaps what I'm trying to say is—

M: When the meantone coloring had all gone out of music in equal temperament, what took its place?

Well, first, more elaborate orchestration. Then, the *acciaccatura*, the little ornamental note that didn't fit in the harmony but was added for brilliance, was domesticated into the harmony by Chopin. Then Liszt and Wagner decided that the old thoroughbass relationship was no longer necessary and started shifting the bass around. They increased the chromatic element of harmony and developed a system of changing tone centers.

Chromatic harmony substitutes the brilliance of increasingly dissonant relationships for the coloring of meantone and the acoustical sonority of just intonation. Chromatic harmony swallowed up key relationship. Dissonance lost dramatic relativity because all music was now heavily dissonant. Therefore, enharmonic change ceased to signify. That is where music had arrived at the start of the twentieth century, the end of the harmonic era.

Debussy exposed a theoretical impasse by dispensing with the traditional harmonic formulas and rationalizations. Schoenberg resolved it by showing that since only the chromatic relationships remained valid in practice, a new single key of the twelve tones should be accepted, and a new twelve-tone method of musical grammar should be derived from it.

Schoenberg's twelve tones, however, are no longer the key-related notes of previous musical theory. In Schoenberg's idea, C-sharp is nothing else than the exactly measured step between D and C without any relationship to harmonic questions. Schoenberg called this new acoustical freedom the emancipation of the dissonance. But since these exactly measured steps are to be thought of only as a gamut of equal-tempered sounds, there is no reason why other gamuts of tones, sounds, noises, or even actions should not be substituted for them.

Two American composers, both of whom studied with Schoenberg, Harrison and John Cage, have extended this theory along contrary paths. Harrison said, "When Schoenberg had reduced all harmony to a single key of the twelve notes, he should've gone farther, and retuned the intervals to their exact acoustical relationships in just intonation." And that is one thing that Harrison has done, as you've heard.

Joseph Yasser, advocating his own scale of nineteen-tone just temperament, made a similar proposal in a letter to Schoenberg. Schoenberg replied, "To be musical means to have an ear in the musical sense, not in the natural sense. A musical ear must have assimilated the tempered scale, and the singer who produces natural pitches is unmusical."

Cage said to me, I believe it was in 1947, "When Schoenberg had emancipated the dissonance, he should've gone farther and emancipated music from its notes." At that time, Cage had already composed for the prepared piano, creating exactly measured artificial tones, which sounded instead of the notated tones. Like this.

[*plays John Cage,* Sonatas and Interludes *(1946–48)*]

Schoenberg's opponents contended that he was destroying music. Schoenberg himself, and his friend Anton Webern, while insisting on the necessity of their actions, also saw the prospect gloomily. Webern has put vividly into words the tense awareness of their experience.

[*plays recording of Anton Webern speaking*]

Anton Webern: It was a hard struggle. Inhibitions of the most terrifying kind had to be overcome. There was an anxious questioning: is that really possible? As if the light had given out—that's how it struck us.

Charles Ives, born a month after Schoenberg, had been educated by his father, a pragmatic experimental Yankee bandmaster, to feel neither the obligation nor the loss. Ives was more concerned with the character of his music than with theoretical explanations. Ives anticipated the emancipation of the dissonance. He did this from boyhood because it was his natural language.

He broke the rules against successive consonance so that it may be said that he emancipated the consonance, a change we do not yet fully appreciate. Ives wrote music containing microtones, incompatible rhythms, and noise. He welcomed what would later be called indeterminacy, and deliberately composed what some would call mistakes. Ives wrote a memo to his copyist.

[*plays recording of Charles Ives speaking*]

Charles Ives: Mr. Price, please don't try to make things nice. All the wrong notes are right.

That is where music is now going. I shall cease talking and let you relax.

M: During the intermission, you will be hearing in the background comfortable domestic vibrations of electronic music, "Lifetime," by Bill Maginnis of the San Francisco Tape Music Center.

[*Intermission*]

During this half of the lecture, I shall speak about the field of sound. Music is composed of sound and silence. Silence is the absence of sound in which sound occurs. In musical tradition, it is the absence of musical sound.

When we hear John Cage's so-called Silent Sonata, we are usually more concerned by the lack of music that we do not hear than by the incidental sounds that occur in its absence. The general habit of sound in music is to draw together the audience, as well as the composition. In Cage's *Concert for Piano and Orchestra*, the sounds seem to repel one another and to define increasing expanse. The audience, having no requirement to listen, can relax in a similar expansiveness. Nothing needs to be followed, to be understood, to be held in memory, awaiting its recurrence. Nothing needs to be explained.

[*plays John Cage's* Concert for Piano and Orchestra *(1958)*]

M: When you listen to it expansively, it is very beautiful.

I shall describe by a simple diagram the dimensions of sound. These include every possibility of sound there is. Let's first visualize the field of sound as a four-sided two-dimensional plane. Here, along the front edge of the platform, is the variable frequency curve, or sine curve, of fundamental pitches without overtones, a linear continuity from the lowest to the highest audible sound. Cage was the first composer to make use of it, when in 1939 he composed his *Imaginary Landscape No. 1*. The sine curve of fundamental pitches was obtained from a record made to test telephone lines. The composition was composed directly on a phonograph record.

[*plays John Cage's* Imaginary Landscape No. 1 *(1939)*]

It might be a good idea to do without the slides while I'm demonstrating the dimensions of sound out here; otherwise we might get our dimensions mixed up. Up above, along the presidium, is white sound. The undifferentiated tonal spectrum, resembling white light.

M: This is white sound.

[*plays white sound*]

M: From white sound, one can filter, by electronic means, any combination of overtones. The combining of fundamental pitches with overtones is the field of timbre.

[*plays combination of overtones*]

Thank you. But we know that timbre includes other characteristics, which we call putting all together the "sound envelope"; I'll get back to that in a minute. Over here on my right, to your left, going up the wall is just intonation. We have already heard examples. In actuality, the variable frequency curve down here and just intonation here cover the same tonal ground, but the frequency curve is a continuous band, whereas just intonation is a series of acoustically related points or notable tones derived from the overtone series along the same curve.

Over here, to my left, is noise: the totally random or inchoate mingling of sounds. Again, noise covers the same ground as white sound up there, except that noise is randomly differentiated. Here is an example of randomly differentiated noise. It is the theme or subject of a set of electronic variations composed by Robert Ashley, called *The Fourth Of July*.

[*plays Robert Ashley's* The Fourth of July *(1960)*]

Between just intonation and noise is the field of temperament, the deviating of tones from an acoustically correct relationship toward discord and noise. The five principal divisions of the field of temperament are: just intonation, or concord; acoustically correct intervallic relationship; consonance, where the relations are slightly incorrect; going on into dissonance, where the relationships recede further from acoustical correctness; and so into discord, where the acoustical relationship is rejected in favor of arbitrarily derived sounds and noise that cannot be indicated by notes.

The music of the fifteenth and sixteenth centuries, the polyphonic era, was composed to be performed in just intonation. The music of the harmonic era, 1600 to 1900, was composed around the dramatic and emotional distinction between consonance and dissonance.

Schoenberg described the emancipated dissonance as an extension of consonance. The twelve-tone serialists followed Webern into the area of dissonance-discord. The consequence is that much post-serialist music, however articulate in design, departs from the acoustical relationships of tonality in favor of the relatively inchoate differences of discord.

The effect of discord is to release the old meantone "wolf" and let him howl, with carefully differentiated wails. And there has been a tendency to redress the loss of consonant sound by including in the ensemble a few instruments of very sweet timbre, like the vibraphone. Here, for a well-made example, is *Hodograph I* by Earle Brown.

[*plays Earle Brown's* Hodograph I *(1959)*]

M: Sounds like pretty good music to me.

I think so myself. Carl Ruggles, in isolation, explored the same sound area, dissonance-discord, using a different method, but he kept a much firmer base in dissonance. Forty years ago, Ruggles began composing his major work for orchestra, *Sun-treader*. It was first performed in the United States at a festival last January, honoring the composer's 90th birthday. It has also been recorded.

M: Thirty-four years seems like a long time to wait for a first performance.

[*plays Carl Ruggles's* Sun-treader *(1931)*]

The Fourth Symphony by Charles Ives waited just less than a half century for its first complete performance. Even now, these two symphonies, by Ives and Ruggles, tell more about the future of music than about its past. Ives was the first composer to bring together in composing the entire field of sound: just intonation and the octaves, which are embedded throughout his larger music; simple consonance and triads often curiously disposed; dissonance and tone rows extending deep into discord; freely assembled vertical harmonic relationships of independently moving melodies; modern isorhythm; and noise.

The final movement of Ives's Fourth Symphony opens with noise, percussion, then gradually reaches out to include the entire field of sound. Listen.

[*plays Charles Ives's Symphony no. 4 (1910–16)*]

The third dimension of sound consists, in the words of Gerald Strang, as "any number of perpendicular relationships erected at any points upon the two-dimensional field of sound, which qualify the nature and dimensions of the individual sounds." Here, at each point, the third dimension of sound, which includes duration, amplitude, attack, decay, crescendo, and diminuendo, intersects with temperament and timbre, to form what composers of electronic music call the "sound envelope."

Understanding this, we can consider with less superstitious fear the advent of the electronic computer as a composing instrument. In the same way that medieval and Renaissance music had at its center the human voice, and music of the harmonic era had as its center the keyboard instruments—organ, harpsichord, piano—the new era of sound will have at its center the computer. A composer using a computer can indicate precisely at every point the exact characteristics of the sound envelope that each moment of his music requires. He can bind these points together in any degree of rhythmic complexity he wishes.

But it is still a machine and does not know any more than a piano knows that it is creating music. And I might say that this music consists of a series of small experiments end to end; it is not intended to be competing with the masters at this point. For that matter, our ears are still incapable of distinguishing the microtonal and microrhythmic subtleties of a composition of this sort.

The fourth dimension of sound—drama, dance, play, theatrical action, and audience participation—though as ancient as the use of sound for any musical ritualistic or dramatic purpose, has to do with the nature of the sound as a means of group relationship and not with its nature or quality as a sound. To put it very simply, in the fourth dimension of sound, an action takes the place of a note. When in ceremony, or in church, we sit, stand, kneel, sing, give responses, we are in the theatrical, the ritualistic, the celebrative dimension of art. It has been, for all peoples at all times, the most necessary dimension. Music, dance, drama, liturgy, rhetoric, representation emerged from it as separate arts. This composite lecture has been an example of the fourth dimension of sound. [*long pause*]

[*film plays*]

This is *Mary's Day Out* in the Immaculate Heart College campus in Los Angeles. [*long pause*]

[*applause*]

In the film, you see, are all the elements that enter into the fourth dimension of sound, and here we see them isolated entirely from sound. Every sound exists in relationship to other sound and silence. The relationship may be exact or indeterminate. To understand the morphology of a sound, we need to grasp, in some degree, its coordinate relationships within the entire field of sound, its temperament, its timbre, the "sound envelope," and the ritualistic, dramatic, playful, or celebrative intent. Just intonation is the one fixed acoustically correct dimension of the field of sound that is capable of setting all other dimensions in a more exact audible relationship. Just intonation is also the most complete form of tonality. Here is a composition in total just intonation, our last example, by La Monte Young. I am permitted to call it, in short form, "A Dream Tortoise," but a longer form of the title, which is itself a part of the composition, is *The Obsidian Ocelot, The Sawmill, And The Blue Sawtooth High-Tension Line Stepdown Transformer Refracting The Legend Of The Dream Of The Tortoise, Traversing The 189-98 Lost Ancestral Lake Region, Illuminating Quotients From The Black Tiger Tapestries Of The Drone Of The Holy Numbers*. And it is performed by La Monte Young, voice; Marian Zazeela, voice; Tony Conrad, violin; and John Cale, three-string drone and voice.

[*plays La Monte Young's "A Dream Tortoise"*]

I might silently talk a great deal about performance standards. The performance standards required to produce that sound are far beyond what are required for most other music. It requires a rigor that very few of us can discipline ourselves to maintain.

So as a final statement, I would say that even in computer music tonality will not be done away with. Indeed, it will become more necessary and, as the last examples have illustrated, will be more subtly divided and refined than it has ever been.

Thank you all very much for your very good attention.

3 R. Buckminster Fuller

The polymathic futurist R. Buckminster Fuller (1895-1993) spoke for more than three hours at "Six Lectures." In his ranging lecture, excerpts of which are presented here, he challenged the audience with a big picture of global trends and the accelerating evolution of humanity's relationship to "spaceship earth."

I've just come from a two-month visit at San Jose State College in California. While I was there, I was asked not only to speak to the college but to meet with people in the community. When I spoke to the chamber of commerce and the Rotary Club, I pointed out to them that one of the great limitations of humanity relates to what I call the motion spectrum. You probably realize that as of World War I, when we started using radio heavily, we got into electronics in a very big way. By 1930, the Westinghouse Company published their first chart of what they call the electromagnetic spectrum. They found that this is where the radiation from this particular element is emitting its particular frequencies, and over here would be ultraviolet radiation. Here would be X-rays, and so forth. And here was a very tiny area of red, orange, yellow, green, blue, violet where humanity had the tuning capability to receive and understand those waves.

This is the first awareness society had that reality extended into all the invisible ranges and that we simply had a very limited tuning set. We could see only a little part of the great show, of the great reality. I discovered then that not only do we have this very limited spectrum range of tuning, we also have our afterimages and memory, and they give us a report of changes of pattern. It is our awareness of changes of pattern that we call motion. Humanity has a very limited motion spectrum. It can't even see the hands of the clock moving. It remembers the hands were there and it credits their move to here. It can't see the atoms in motion. It can't see the stars in motion, though they move as much as a million miles in a day. So we really see very little. We don't see the trees growing. We remember what it was like yesterday and then we see the bud is coming out. We tend not to see things that are happening to us, the great trends of world society.

At any rate, I pointed out to the people in California that there are two great chapters of mankind taking place. The first chapter: because man consists primarily of water, and needs a great deal of it to live, we have him living near the water. I'm going to assume that for hundreds of thousands of years, before written history, men probably lived on rafts at the water's edge or on rivers, bays, and so forth, because the most plentiful food they could get was fish. You liked to be on a raft because it got you offshore where you're safe from wild animals. Of course rafts rotted out very quickly, so we wouldn't have any record of that.

There will be floods, and the rafts will get loose and drift downstream. They get blown out to sea. The predominant winds of the Earth are from West to East, so we have people getting blown across the Pacific from the Orient to the Americas and across from the Americas to Europe and Africa.

Man discovered that if you have a raft with a branch and leaves on it, and wind is blowing on it this way, the log will not go downwind. It'll move in the direction of least resistance. So rafts were not just blowing leeward but were actually drifting and building up some momentum. They found they could stick another tapered, flattened, broad log down and they could steer the raft. They could actually take advantage of wind. Finally they learned, as with a skate, that you could use the low pressure occurring on the lee side of a sail to pull you forward. And they began to sail into the wind.

So the second chapter of humanity is when man started to counter the forces operating on him. Instead of assuming that a great god automatically exercises his wisdom and will, they suddenly began to work against the various forces. This begins in the South Seas and works eastward, westward, where people from this point on are able to follow the sun. They've identified the sun with a metabolic regeneration and feel they must go westward.

So we have people crossing the Asian continent overland and going by water across the Indian Ocean. As they cross the great Asian continent, they get tied up. They're following their sheep one way or another. They find a way of surviving in a little local area and getting on all right. They begin to inbreed, and the chieftain will breed with his own family. We get such extraordinary hybridism that, for instance, in Russia today, there are still 147 nations that are distinguished by their physical characteristics, which you develop by inbreeding.

But as they move farther westward, the very shape of Europe funnels them into crossbreeding. There was great inbreeding as they moved across Africa from the Indian Ocean, and enormous inbreeding until they are pooled on the Western shores. But there was not that funnel action in Africa to force any crossbreeding.

Now we then have these westbound men jumping the

Atlantic and coming to the Americas. And there, they find the drifted people of the first chapter, who by this time are extraordinarily crossbred with one another. It's pretty interesting that in Mexico today you can see every shape of face, every known physiognomy, and every shade of color. There was no color distinction whatsoever. This is a very highly crossbred phase of the Eastern man. And now we have the westbound.

We get to the Americas and ten, twelve generations later, we're in California, very much more crossbred. And these are the people I was talking to for the last two months. I pointed out that they'd gone as far west as they could because they're up against the Pacific. Therefore, they were pooled there and were staying a little longer than people on the rest of the continent. Furthermore, now man has much greater longevity, so there are many more people retiring to California. Therefore, the pattern in California was probably much steadier than the rest of the United States.

San Jose is right in the middle of the West Coast. It would be the most typical kind of area where you could find the most standard conditions of this crossbreeding man. So I said to the chamber of commerce, "Would all those who were born in San Jose please put up their hands?" It was less than 15 percent. Finally I asked, "How many of you have not been here for ten years?" And we got 60 percent of the hands. So I said, "Please look around, because I'm sure that each one of you thought you were the last one to come, that everybody else here was old San Jose-ian. And you're all Johnny-come-lately."

Now this is the case in San Jose. I've tried these kinds of questions in Kansas City and other places. And the pattern always comes out every time to be somewhere about the same. We just aren't aware of it. We organized ourselves for all these years on a geographic basis. You didn't have any way of getting out of the local community. So you thought that way, and you had representatives in terms of where you were born and brought up. This means that if you're moving through town, then you're not going to have any permanent relationship with the political machine. In the last presidential election, somewhere between 20 and 30 million weren't able to vote because they hadn't been in town long enough to qualify. Within two more elections, we won't be able to have a presidential election.

This is the way things go because of our lack of a motion spectrum. Man is not at fault here. But he is going through a very extraordinary evolution where he has to depend on his instrumental readings and his basic counts and learn to look at curves and charts. Society is not yet very literate at looking at curves and charts. So this is going to be a surprise to world society. For us, order means representative government, but we're going to have to have another kind of identification.

When we organized our representative government in the United States, people had for three or four generations been quite well-localized. They picked somebody they knew very well to represent them. The amount of time we gave our representative to hold office was predicated on the fact that they had to go by foot and horse to Washington. They would stop in each town as they went along. They talked to everybody about the problems. And while they were in Washington, they would talk about what they knew about each one of their problems and they would return. But we must realize what the relative velocity of communication was, so that when our representatives came back, they knew just what everybody thought. We had a one-to-one correspondence between the rate at which we receive information and the rate at which we reacted. We had a very effective representative government.

What happened is a whole chain of accelerations in the rate at which man is informed of events, and no acceleration at all in the way in which he can express himself. That is, Lincoln was the first head of state to be wired by telegraph. From this point on, we had news moving around very rapidly and being broadcast to the people. But we're only able to express ourselves about it approximately every four years, and now with less opportunity than before. By the time we come to vote, we don't actually know any of the people put up for election.

This is anything but good representative government. So at the moment, our society is in a great predicament. This is part of what young people are sensing, that we are not being able to express ourselves adequately. That is why we have so much sampling of people. We do have representatives who'd like to know how to represent the people, and they'd like to know how they're reacting, so they have samplings and samplings. We don't have any direct response. We're not geared to our own times, with our own potential. I think it would make a very great difference if every one of us had an electronic means where we had our own ultra high frequency tuning device, and each of us were able to express ourselves several times a day on any and every question. Like a great pari-mutuel machine, you'd have the public attitude on point after point. You would have no face-losing by representatives because this is what the public wants. He could find he's made a mistake and could ask the public and reverse his position, just as you see a great flight of birds able to wheel around if it's going in the wrong direction.

I think these things are imminent, and we hope that they will begin to occur. Because I think that everything that's going on around the world today in relation to man is a very large educational process. We, all of us, intuitively abhor the elite, just picking out a few who might lead. We realize all of man must be able to enjoy the whole Earth. He must enjoy all the history we begin to uncover of all men before us, and enjoy our beginning to sweep out a little larger part of the universe.

We have developed extraordinary industrialization. Industrialization can be looked at in different ways. It can be in terms of an individual exploiting local needs using the inventions that have come his way, having the energy and power to fasten onto the machinery. It can be looked at as smoky, and it can be looked at as exploitation. But I find it has something much bigger about it.

All tools are inventions that externalize originally integral functions. It's quite easy to understand the earliest tools as, for instance, man coming to water that is potable. He's very thirsty because he's been off berry picking. He learns to cup his hands like this. But if he's going to carry his water from the oasis, how is he going to pick berries? Among the very earliest artifacts, we have him making a container, a controlled environment. So he in fact takes a pair of hands that he can hang on his back, holding the water while these other hands are free. These are always externalized capabilities. Now once he's developed that cup, he can do some things. For instance, it can take much more heat than his hands will, hold much more acid than his hands could take. In other words, once we have the invention externalized, we begin to increase its capabilities. But it's not a new function. We often make the mistake in not seeing how it's related to ourselves due to the fact that it's now extended a range of capabilities.

All industrialization represents an externalization of originally integral functions, to such an extent we can say that the total industrialization of today is an externalization of approximately all our original internal, organic, and metabolic regenerating capability. These all have to be integrated. The tools begin to be so complex and so large in their complete undertaking that in order to justify them, we have to have very large numbers of consumers. In order to find the most consumers, you automatically go to the whole world. World industrialization is inherently world-seeking. It takes resources from all the Earth, all the knowledge, all the experience of all men in all history, and integrates it into this extraordinary complex network of power-driven levers to do much more work than man could do with his own muscles.

Now in this world, in order to be able to handle the great leverages and the great heats, we have to use metals in a very large way. We can say that during this whole century, the amount of metal per human being on Earth has been continually decreasing, really very swiftly. Yet there's something else that is quite phenomenal. During the same period, in the last two-thirds of a century, up to 1966, we've gone from less than 1 percent of humanity to 40 percent of humanity enjoying a standard of living superior to that of any sovereign in all of history. We've gone from a longevity expectancy of 42 when I was born up to an expectancy of 70, approximately doubling the longevity during that same period. Something extraordinary is going on here because we are now taking care of 40 percent as against less than 1 percent in 66 years, and despite the fact that we've been continually decreasing metals.

You can't explain it by saying we've found more resources, so let's look for another explanation. Since the last ice age, three-quarters of the Earth has been covered by water. And since that time, 99.95 percent of humanity has lived on dry land, which means they've had to live on something less than a quarter of the Earth's surface. Well, of that quarter of dry land, only about one- third of it was promising in its support of man. So man has been living on approximately 8 percent of the total surface of the Earth.

There are men who went fishing in the water, but there were some who built boats capable of handling the deep sea. They discovered that the waters went all around the Earth. They found the resources of the Earth very different if they went from one place to another. They also found the people extraordinarily localized. They weren't just in one little postage-stamp area of 8.5 percent of the Earth. That 8.5 percent was sprinkled out, so the people were very remote from one another, and in such small numbers, they were unaware of the rest of humanity.

The people who went to sea discovered where all the resources and human beings were. They found main sea lanes and began to fight over them and became the great pirates. They realized they could run the whole world. They could bring miraculous things to people, who would pay great prices for these things. These miraculous things complemented what they had at home, things that had not been useful before but suddenly were.

Meanwhile the people who are on the land found marauders coming from all around. So the local organization of the strong men said, "All right. I like to fight, and I've got some of my friends here who like to fight. We'll give you protection. You grow the food and you feed us. We'll build a big wall, and when the marauders come round, you all can get inside the wall, which will keep you safe."

So we have people on the land thinking of security in terms of the higher, the wider, the heavier the wall, the more secure they felt. The people on the sea find it a very dangerous venture. In order to be able to keep afloat, to be able to exploit storms, and to beat out the other pirates to get to the most important place in the quickest time, you had to have very high capabilities. So you had to find a ratio of the whole thing to what floated. And thus we had the law of displacement. You could not put more weight in that ship than so much and therefore you say: How much is going to go into cannons? How much is going to go into the hold to give me enough booty to make the whole thing worthwhile?

So you build your ship completely on an offensive basis. You don't build it on the basis of defending yourself, as with stone and great walls. You do exactly the opposite, make it very, very light. So through the great periods of history, we have man on the land thinking about security in the wider, the heavier, the more secure sense, to use the expression, as secure as the Rock of Gibraltar. This finds its great epitome in the Maginot Line. But the tank was simply the submarine running up on the land. The airplane was simply the battleship in the sky. It handled everything offensively, and it did so in terms of very high performance per pound of hardware. So we suddenly had that supreme hardware running right over the Maginot Line. Finally you have the comparison. You have contact. And you know who has the greatest hardware, who has the greatest hitting power. Entirely different kind of technology.

Now in developing the great technology of the sea, we have science being employed by the great pirates in a prodigious manner to find out how to do more with less. We finally carry this into the air so it covers 100 percent of the Earth instead of just three-quarters. And in order to have the airplanes stay in the sky, they had to move forward, at enormous velocity, to build low pressure over the wings so they can have lift. In order to do that, they had to have a very heavy engine and a lot of fuel. The first airplane can have just a little additional lift to carry one aviator for a few minutes and a few miles.

That's only half a century ago. In the meantime, the great nations of the Earth put up two and a half trillion dollars to develop this hitting power of the air, to cover the greatest distance in the shortest time, with the greatest accuracy and less effort. It's that technology that suddenly brings us to the point where we'll soon have a 700-passenger ship that is able to go at sonic speed. We also have planes on board that will take you up to 2,000 miles an hour, that will take you any place on Earth in two hours with as many as 500 passengers on board.

This is how much more we've been doing with less, despite the fact that the local thoughts are in terms of security, that you think you live and stay where you are, and that you build yourself great local security, and you do more with more to make you powerful. In the meantime, this doing more with less in the great weaponry has had its fallout. Those contractors whose contract had suddenly run out because somebody else had developed a better weapon looked around in the domestic economies for some outlet. And they found, for instance, the dynamos that were developed completely for the battleship. We had our blast furnaces making steel for 50 years for battleships before we put a piece of steel in a building. So the dynamos came off the battleship. Refrigeration came off the battleship. Air-conditioning came off the battleship.

This is then the fallout from weaponry. Suddenly you didn't need an icehouse because you just turn the button and there's refrigeration. Gradually the tools began to do away with very large buildings. You didn't have a lot of rooms for servants, houses got smaller and smaller with more and more machinery in them. And we continually use more and more energy to give us the preferred conditions that improve the number of days that we can count on living.

If you look at the curve showing improved standards of living, by 2000 AD we will come to a condition where 100 percent of humanity will be physically and metabolically successful, economically successful, living obviously a very much higher standard of living than we can even dream of today. They will be completely "world men," not operating at all in the terms of the geographic identifications we have today.

Now there are some very important things to be observed. First, I come back to political organization. You have the two great world political systems, with each one saying its system is the best to make the world work, and both developing enormous hitting capability. They both assume in the end there will be a war. There's not enough for either side.

Then suddenly we have Khrushchev and Eisenhower going to meet because both sides realized that political influence was of a very negative nature. They said it would be a good thing if we could at least look into the possible beneficial uses of this great amount of atomic energy. So they agreed to go to Geneva and allow the scientists to talk through the curtains and compare notes and see what might be useful to society. Both of them then might be able to boast what their side could do to benefit man.

The scientists came together by coincidence with a meeting of the food and agriculture organization of the United Nations. So at Geneva it became very evident that the amounts of energy available would make possible the quick freezing of foods anywhere in the fields. No food should ever rot. The energy available could go into all the preferential chemistries that would be able to accelerate the production of food. Scientists were able to see for the first time in history that Malthus was wrong and that there could now be enough to go around for everybody. But it could not possibly be realized in view of the political barriers.

At any rate, it has only been twelve years since humanity has known scientifically that there can be enough to go around. This is big news. And the number of people who read about that around the world were probably less than 1 percent of humanity. So this is not yet the popular way of looking at things, and it's one of the things you have to call young people's attention to, that we now could make the world work.

But in order to make the world work, we have to do what has been going on so far, that is, doing more with less. The total amount of metal that I've spoken about is now occupied in machinery and structures that are operating at full capacity. If you had full production, it would still only take care of 44 percent. It wouldn't take care of even half of humanity. But the curve that's been improving things has been one of a change in technology. It's a design change. For an example, I'll just give you Telstar, which with less than a ton of material provides a transoceanic communication capability superior to that which had been arrived at previously by 75,000 tons of copper. That is a 75,000-fold difference, typical of the upping of performance at a very high acceleration. But you don't do it just by trying to make a better set of copper wires. You actually go in for entirely new technique.

So what I'm able to say to students is that if they would like to have the world work and give up war, the way they do it is to bring about enough for everybody. With the kind of war effort that we talk about, of building this higher technology in weaponry, it takes 22.5 years longer for these inventions to come out of the weaponry and fall into the home economy than it would take if you directly redesigned the world's resources. So this could be shortened. Instead of having to wait until the year 2000, it could be actually arrived at in a decade. If you only have to wait ten years, there is very much less chance that we're going to blow ourselves off the Earth.

As best I can, I'm putting before you what seems to me to be the great challenge. I find young people responding all around the world, and I do travel all around the world. Incidentally, I have people say to me all the time, "Where do you live?" I say, "A little spaceship called Earth."

I'm going to call your attention to the spaceship idea. I hear lots of people say, "I wonder what it'd be like to be on a spaceship." And the answer is to them is, that's all you've ever been on. You just have not caught on that you're on a spaceship. We have to realize that this whole thing was so beautifully designed that we've been utterly ignorant of the means of our success, that we've been on this spaceship for two million years. I like the students to realize how vain man is. We boast a great deal about all the things we've done. But I don't find that any of humanity really knows anything. You've always been automated. You don't, any of you, know what you're doing with your supper right now, and you're not charging off a certain amount of energies to push special hairs out through your head. None of you even know why you have hair. You're complete. It's all automated. Automation is not even mildly new!

We're coming to a whole new chapter three of humanity. You feel it quite strongly in California, where we have this westbound man, coming to the Coast. And he's about to take off to become a world man, not only a world man, but a universe man. He's going to penetrate the skies in a very large way. He's going to the bottom of the ocean. He's going to begin to occupy an enormous part of the universe he has not occupied up to now.

I'm now going to change what we are talking about because I'm quite confident that the only way that humanity is really going to survive and be responsible is by understanding whether humanity even has a function in the universe. I started playing a game with myself many years ago in which I would ask myself little larger questions, just as you lift a little greater weight each day and build up your muscles. I felt that I could build up my answering capability if I gave myself bigger and bigger questions. And I finally came to the biggest question I could think of: "What do you mean by universe?"

I had a rule for playing this game. I must answer my questions out of my own experience. I mustn't answer any question in terms of what I've been told to believe. So my game playing always had to be answered by what I considered reliably reported experiences, primarily by myself. Now the answer I finally came to of what I mean by universe was "the aggregate of all humanity's consciously apprehended and communicated experiences." The communication could be to yourself or to others. Now you may say, "That doesn't sound very familiar to me." It isn't, because I'm the one who found that answer.

Now when scientists working under the enormous patronage of the great pirates developed the laws of thermodynamics, this related to the fact that pirates now could have steam to drive their ships instead of waiting for the wind. And the famous second law of thermodynamics related to the fact that experiments showed that local systems always lose energy. This is called entropy.

It had been thought that energies escape right out of the universe. Even as I went to Harvard in 1913, before World War I, scholars still thought in Newtonian terms that the universe is losing its energy, therefore it would eventually run down, that the Earth would finally stop spinning. Newton's first law of motion says, a body persists in a state of rest or in a line of motion except as affected by other bodies. The norm is at rest. And the universe was going to come to rest.

At the beginning of the century scientists began to make experiments regarding entropy, and they found that when energy escaped from any system, as it always did, it could only escape by joining that system. Therefore, they found the energies were always 100 percent accountable, that they were not going out of the universe at all. They announced an entirely new law of energy, the law of the conservation of energy, which says no energy can be created and no energy can be lost. That is the observational experience.

Now once you discover that, you have to have an entirely new way of looking at things. Einstein came into that world. He predicated his thinking also on the very immediate discovery that light had a speed. Up to this time, man thinks sight is instantaneous. We still think "instant universe." Newton thought in terms of an instant universe with instant reaction to everything upon everything else in the universe. Einstein saw that there was a speed of light, which we then found characterized other radiation.

So we have now an entirely new norm, a norm of a universe in constant transformation, with no energy ever getting lost. Now in these terms, more experiments have been made. And we've come to a point where we find that every one of the smallest energy components has a complementary opposite. The opposites frequently are not mirror images, but they have the opposite fundamental characteristic, as for instance, they have positive weights and negative weights. And we come to a condition where the average of all the weights is zero, which informs us that we are in an age of the very extraordinary realization that we're dealing in a universe of pure principle, intellectual principle.

The mathematicians speak about entropy as a law of increase of the random element, an increasing disorderliness of the distribution of the radiation, and so forth. This was fortified by the astronomers' observation, the red shift that led them to pronounce an apparently expanding universe. Entropy brings about more and more randomness and diffusion of energies. Because we find then the energies can't be lost and can't be created, the total amount of energy is finite.

Now in seeking some kind of answer to whether man has a function in the universe, I began then to look at the total physical universe in terms of the physicists' expanding universe and an increasing disorderliness of the physical universe, even though it was finite. Apparently all experiment shows that every fundamental patterning has its opposite, whether it's in very small components or in hierarchies. Therefore, an expanding and an increasingly disorderly universe must have a counterpart of some kind in a contracting and increasingly orderly aspect of universe. I said, let's look and see if we can find any clue to that.

I'll now for a moment seemingly digress by coming to the most recent experiments we have of neurologists and physiologists. We have the leading neurologists saying in recent years that in effect they've discovered a complete telephone system, with answering services and message-taking services and storing of the messages and memory patterns. In fact, it is a video telephone system, where there are a number of television sets operating and we have memory sets, forecasting sets, and so forth.

But they say it is easier to explain all the data they have regarding the phenomena if they assume a phenomenon of mind as well as a phenomenon of brain. Now I'm going to give you my explanation of what is meant by the brain. First, they point out that over this telephone and video system, there are messages that are picked up. There are conversations that go on that cannot be attributed as feedback of the telephone system itself. That's why they have to have the additional phenomenon of mind.

I'll illustrate the difference between brain and mind.

I'm going to say to you: "I'm going to take a piece of rope." And I'm going to pull on it very, very hard. As I pull it, it contracts in its girth. It's a natural consequence of my pulling it, which if it's contracting its girth, it means it's going into compression. Then when I load a compression member, it might be cigar-shaped, and as I load it, its girth tries to expand, which means the girth goes into tension at 90 degrees. In fact, you'll discover experimentally that tension and compression always and only coexist. They're cofunctions.

I can also then show you something I call a system. A system is a subdivision of the universe. A system is a first subdivision of the universe, and the first subdivision of the universe divides the universe into two parts. All the universe is outside the system and all the universe is inside the system.

Now it is characteristic of systems that as viewed from inside, they are concave, and as viewed from the outside, they are convex. All systems then have convexity and concavity, and convexity and concavity always and only coexist. Convexity converges the radiation and the convexity diffuses the radiation, so that they behave quite differently, but they always and only coexist. Scientists have developed what we use in mathematical science, the theory of functions. And a function does not exist by itself. The word *function* immediately tells you there must be complementary functions. So the theory of functions are these always and only coexisting phenomena, all brought into one very tight classification.

Now Einstein goes still further. He just says one word—*relativity*. Now I've done something with you. In the first place, I said I'd take a piece of rope and I didn't take a piece of rope at all. You've all had so many experiences with pulling things that you're able to immediately accredit my saying, take a piece of rope. And I watch your eyes and I can see you follow through exactly with me.

So what I did was to generalize it. I didn't say it was Manila or cotton or nylon or what its size was. It was a generalization to say, "Take a piece of rope." So this is a first-degree generalization. It was a second-degree generalization when I then found the coexisting qualities, the always and only coexisting qualities. Then there's a third-degree generalization when I came to the theory of functions themselves. It's a fourth-degree generalization when you just say the word *relativity*.

Now you have a little dog who will tug on a stocking or leather belt or anything, who'll play a game with you of pulling. He'll tense and he'll block like this. And he'll use compression with his teeth to hold onto it. He coordinates beautifully with this. But there's nothing in our experience to suggest that a little dog develops a theory of functions. The difference between brain and mind is the ability to generalize, of progressive generalization.

Now I'm looking for a function of man in the universe. I'd like to find some relationship to a physically expanding universe that is becoming more entropic and more disorderly. And I then see man, we're on Earth. It's part of our experience that here is this Earth. And it is a heavenly body, too, our little spaceship here. One of the things we know about it is that it's not radiant, or we'd burn up. We know that it's receiving energy, radiation, all the time from the sun. That radiation doesn't just bounce off the Earth. We begin to impound it here, particularly in the liquid part. It's impounded in the biosphere in the gases, and then impounded very much in the waters. And then we have biological life in the waters that begins to use that radiation.

So we have photosynthesis in the biologicals. We also know from the geophysical that we're receiving around 100,000 tons of stardust daily, which is very much more tonnage than we're sending off in satellite so far. So we are very much in the receiving or collecting part of the universe. There have been suppositions by astronomers that there may be actually black bodies. But the only one we know much about would be our own Earth.

The biologicals are not only inhibiting those energies, not letting them go off, which is antientropic, but they are inhibiting the energies and making beautiful molecular chains, very orderly chains, which are just the antithesis of disorderliness and chaos. Of all the biologicals, none is so antientropic as the human. And it took all the hundreds of thousands of tension experiences we have all had in this one room, or the hundreds of billions of tension experiences all of humanity has had, and we've been able to generalize it down to just saying a piece of rope, or the tension compression always only coexisting.

So I took an enormous number of special cases, and they were resolved into a very beautiful generalization. And then those were resolved into an even higher generalization, the theory of function, and then just into one word, *relativity*. So we've gone exactly in the opposite of an expanding universe, an increasing entropy. And these are those generalizations that give man extraordinary power to organize his part of the universe in an antientropic manner.

I found myself writing in a book in 1949 that man seems to me to be the great antientropy. It's very interesting that Norbert Wiener wrote it in a book the same year. We come at it completely independent, in fact. This brought us together to be friends.

But now, if we are the great antientropy, we could say that everything we're dealing with here is the mind. And by the mind, we're talking about the metaphysical. I will then say to you, it becomes quite clear to me that we have a physically expanding universe becoming increasingly disorderly, and so forth, and we have a metaphysical universe that is continually contracting and increasingly orderly. So I'd say, I find the metaphysical in complete balance with the physical. This is an entirely new way of looking at things.

Einstein, as intellect, writes regarding the physical universe, and he says the physical universe is energy. So he writes *E* on one side of the equation representing the physical universe. On the other side of the equation, it has to be differentiated in terms of the theory of function, so it takes two to explain it, because the human mind will not understand it except in relation to at least two functions, mass and velocity of light.

Now we have an Einstein as intellect writing the equation of the physical universe. He takes measure, the most compact generalization about the physical universe. This is an irreversible condition. It is inconceivable that energy would write what the intellect is. We have the intellect writing what the energy is, and the energy cannot do the other. So I find the metaphysical mildly more powerful than the physical. I'm not afraid that our universe is in some kind of disintegration.

I'd go along very much with the astronomers such as Edmond Hoyle, who's the most articulate on this, or a man such as our own Harlow Shapley. Hoyle assumes that there are hundreds of millions of stars with planets. There are hundreds of millions of planets, just to use a good, big figure, in which there will be human beings. And in terms of this kind of concept, if man is essential to the universe for his metaphysical capabilities, then the universe is going to have to have a lot of humanity. We find the universe continually providing very well so that these balances of patterns carry on. Therefore, with the working assumption that some human beings and some planets will make a mess of it, you're going to have to have plenty of other planets where they won't.

Hoyle makes a great point of the fact that humans on the Earth have already exhausted our fossil fuels. And he said, we've discovered atomic energy just in time to overlap that. But we're going to have to move very fast for the next step; it's going to throw the balance out very, very much of the energy-saving on this planet. This is the way I begin to see things in terms of the imminence of a task of responsibility. Man will have to be extraordinarily comprehensive and responsible from this point on if he's going to retain the functioning of the concentrations of energy of this part of the universe. Instead, he's letting the whole thing get exploded.

4 Merce Cunningham

The "Talk by a Dancer" that Merce Cunningham (1919–2009) contributed to "Six Lectures" is lost to history. No audio versions of the presentation, a hybrid of lecture and performance, apparently exist. In her 2007 memoir Chance and Circumstance, *Carolyn Brown wrote: "Merce's lecture . . . was very beautiful. Very moving. He danced beautifully. Spoke beautifully. His voice 'live' was low, friendly, warm. His voice on tape was clear, direct, objective. The contrast was integral to the whole—what he said, what he did. He spoke plain facts, some poetics, some stories—all about dancing, dances or dancers. Billy Klüver thought it the best lecture so far [because] Merce talked about what he really knows. I asked him, 'Didn't Fuller?' And Billy said 'No!'"*

Carolyn Brown, *Chance and Circumstance: Twenty Years with Cage and Cunningham*, © 2007. Published by Alfred A. Knopf.

PHOTO: PETER MOORE

Merce Cunningham, lecture-demonstration at "Six Lectures," 92nd Street YMHA, New York, April 21, 1966.

5 Harold Rosenberg

Harold Rosenberg (1906–78) was more strongly associated with Abstract Expressionism than the currents of the 1960s. His lecture explored the ramifications of media on art-making and the museum.

It's an odd experience to be sandwiched in as a speaker between Mr. Buckminster Fuller and Mr. Marshall McLuhan. One feels obliged to take on the giganticism of their outlook, even if it means flattening oneself out and becoming as thin as sandwich meat. On this platform, anything less than a global and world-historical topic is bound to seem picayune. Art was therefore probably a subject to be avoided. Current discussion of it tends to be about as cosmic as a history of the toothbrush. So I've added the subject of media. My talk is entitled, "Art and the Media." [*laughter*]

That brings the subject closer to the proper scale. The media, of course, are a world system. And in relation to them, and as a matter of fact, art too becomes worldwide. It functions or tries to function in the orbit of modern communications mechanisms and techniques. Still, it must be confessed that, in regard to a globalist vision, the presence of art in the discussion is essentially a handicap. Unlike philosophies based on technological marvels, art cannot free itself of an inherent narrowness, or you might call it provincialism. I refer to the limitations of a human individual, which is what the artist always turns out to be. And the same thing is true of the spectator. Though art, as part of the media, stretches out to global and world-historical dimensions, it tends to spring back and coil up into the here and now.

Despite anything I can do, this principle of contraction will prevent the universe of art from measuring up to the universe of Mr. Fuller or Mr. McLuhan. One of the achievements of Pop art, perhaps as a movement its major achievement, was to cross over the line that for 100 years has seemed to separate the arts from the so-called media, that is, the art forms of popular entertainment, information, and propaganda, propaganda, of course, including advertising. I say seemed to separate because the division between the arts and the media has been none too firm. Literature, painting, music have been the blood bank of the commercial crafts, while the arts of the street, what Rimbaud called poetic junk, have constituted a flea market out of which artists have fished innumerable novelties. One thinks, too, of artists who have operated on the border between the opus and the cultural commodities, Poe, for instance, or Daumier or Toulouse-Lautrec.

In our century, there have been movements devoted to the deliberate adulteration of traditional art forms, as by pasting newspaper photographs into paintings, working slogans and popular songs into poems, or injecting film sequences into plays. Infiltration between art and the media has been continuous. Pop art, however, carried the process to a new stage. It executed what military jargon has called a reconnaissance in force, which, if my impression of military terminology is correct, means that the position reached in enemy territory will, if possible, be held. Pop art intended to stay pop. In fact, with it, the notion of the media as the enemy no longer applies. The old device of raiding street art for its effect and retreating with the loot to the picture gallery has given way to the idea of moving in as friendly competitor or even collaborator.

The Pop artist is eager to have a place, preferably, of course, a privileged one, in the entertainment business and the communications. Thus he does not hesitate to devote himself to making movies, acting in plays, or organizing public-relations events. At any rate, through Pop and through Op art, too, the close tie between the arts and the media has been brought to the surface. Objects are being produced by both that have the same style, the same look, though their objectives, their reasons for being, are occasionally somewhat different. Also, art increasingly partakes of the identifying characteristics of the media, which are reproduction and mass distribution.

Voluminous castings of metal sculpture began in the nineteenth century, in roughly the same period as the rise of the popular press. Today everyone is aware that reproductions of paintings in catalogues and magazines and on slides play a larger role in art appreciation and art education than the paintings themselves. The same is true of music reproduced on records and tapes. Enterprises keep springing up to expand painting and sculpture into such areas of reproduction as banners, coins, plastic reliefs. None of this is, in itself, new. The difference is largely in volume and in the active collaboration of artists. Twenty years ago, a fabric shop on Union Square was offering *La Grande Jatte*, of Seurat, by the yard and, as the proprietor said, in all colors. [*laughter*] Seurat, however, had not accepted yard goods as a new medium. Last fall the World House showed an artist who had. Today every artist lives under the pressure of—and enjoys—the advantages of changes wrought in the conditions of aesthetic culture and in art itself by the mass media. Quantity, as some of you older audience members may recall, has been transformed into quality.

Unquestionably, the rapid popularization of American abstract art owed much to the attention paid to it in mass circulation news and fashion magazines, to radio and TV interviews, to new active museum programs and traveling art exhibitions, which, let us emphasize, are also organs of the mass communications system. Through these media, the status of art and of the artist has been transformed and, with it, the conditions of the creation of art. For instance, the prestige of Picasso as a celebrity among multitudes ignorant of painting would be impossible without the mass media.

An effect much deeper and more permanent than change of social status has, however, been produced by the media upon art itself. Local, regional, and even national limits have been dissolved by the simultaneous appearance of new artworks and new art styles in capitals around the world. Earlier international styles centered in a few cities. Though influential elsewhere, each style carried the flavor of its site of origin, as in the School of Paris before the war. To grasp the essence of a new mode in art, artists and art appreciators had to transport themselves physically to the creative center and become sojourners there for an indefinite period of time. Obviously, this put a limit upon the extent and rapidity of dissemination of new art. Today's styles are increasingly global in both conception and transmission. They are picked up everywhere at the same instant and are shot back and forth from continent to continent as items of the total communications package. Art has, in a word, entered into the media system. This does not mean that the situation of art has become more complicated or subtle. A global order is not necessarily more complex than a town; indeed, in being abstracted, it is likely to be simpler, perhaps too simple. At the UN headquarters, gentlemen from Zanzibar, Siberia, and Brooklyn have the same taste in martinis and ideas, and their national costumes, the fez, the burnoose, the homburg, seem to have come out of the same wardrobe.

One of the new problems of art is the ease with which the function of art may now be rationalized. Circulation itself, if sufficiently large, is, in the modern state, regarded as a value beyond discussion. Given the similarities between works of art and the products of the media, what is the distinguishing feature of art? What makes one work art, another merely entertainment or information for daily consumption? Apart from the difference in size, what is the real difference between a comic strip Mickey Mouse and a Mickey Mouse painting by Lichtenstein?

The answer is art history. [*laughter*] The Lichtenstein was created with an eye to art history and to the ideas of art historians about twentieth-century developments in the aesthetics of drawing, composition, motif, and color. The sum of it is that Lichtenstein had his eye on the museum, while the original comic-strip draftsman, at least as expert as Lichtenstein in traditional drawing and composition, worked as a member of a trade outside art history and was intent on amusing the kids and their parents.

Today what distinguishes art from the media crafts is the art-historical destiny of the former. The power of defining art is vested in art history, whose physical embodiment is the museum. Malraux conceived the museum as the ultimate destination of art and being admitted into the museum as the ultimate ambition of all modern artists. What is art goes into the museum. What goes into the museum is art. The soup label or the tire advertisement, though it is the product of a skilled craftsman and is designed to move the spectator through form and color, is not art, in that it lacks rapport with art history and exists at a distance from the museum. Its shortcomings, however, were overcome by Pop artists, who brought the label and the ad into harmony with identifiable items of art history. By slightly altering the image as it appeared on the store shelf or the billboard, Pop shifted it into the art gallery and ultimately into the museum, thus qualifying it to meet the contemporary definition of art, with a minimum sacrifice of its original visual and intellectual qualities, if any. [*laughter*] The purity of Pop, if one may use such an expression, lies in its depending as exclusively as possible on its aesthetics of displacement.

The principle of defining art by its art-historical or museum context was, of course, recognized by Duchamp 50 years ago, when he converted spades and window frames into art by the act of signing them. At present, their location in the museum, and in Malraux's museum without walls, that is, in the system of art reproductions that constitutes world art history, is what defines an object as art, as against the media. But this capacity of the museum to determine what is art seems to me to be temporary. For the museum itself is being transformed into a mechanism of communication. Formerly it was a place where objects dug out of the past were reinterred, with appropriate intellectual honors. The museum was synonymous with "the past." The function of its curators or keepers, as they call them in England, was to preserve. It is as the past that a museum becomes absolute in Malraux's scheme, as absolute as the passage of time or as death itself. But this conception of the museum is out of date, and most obviously, perhaps, in America. Today the museum has lost its character of a tomb and has taken on that of an exchange, if not of a promotion agency or a tourist bureau. Its orientation is not toward the past and its slow drifts but toward the future, toward new trends.

If these are not available, it endeavors to create them. Its representatives circulate around the globe in the hope not of excavating history but of making history. And they seek to have a part in history themselves, through their role of making choices in the limitless range of modern art. Museum officials, though still called curators, have no interest in preservation. On the contrary, they do their best to transform works of art into something different than they are in order to gear them into operation with the new. Masterpieces of all ages are put into competition for public attention by presenting them as news items. Exhibition rooms have traded the atmosphere of the cloister for that of the midway or fairground. In sum, today's museum is an active agency. It is not a final resting place but a testing ground for novelties capable of intriguing the museum's ever-growing public.

In its vocabulary, "museum" means new to the newcomer. Everything is new: Egyptian statuary, Minoan figurines, Romanesque panels, Russian icons. The museum today is the place where all history becomes contemporary, in being made accessible to the media-trained mass. The *Mona Lisa* or Michelangelo's *Pietà* is put before millions as a starred item of our "art heritage today," with the Florentines providing the brand of historical pageantry, popularized by the Sunday supplements. In the media, time blends with space as a tourist attraction. History is what you find when the ship docks or the plane lands. History is a place to go. "Give us a few hours," says a current Pan Am ad, "we can take you back 2,000 years [*laughter*], back to Rome, when Rome meant Caesar." Since the museum has thus become a cog in the global system of the new, it cannot indefinitely continue to authenticate art on the basis of its continuity with the past. Critical references to tradition become increasingly ideological, that is, contrived for the purpose of affecting decisions and actions in the present. As a mechanism of communication dedicated to audience building, the museum is engaged in synchronizing art production and distribution with the rhythm of the cultural commodity market and its insatiable demand for "revolutionary" innovations. Thus the pace of its reputation building becomes more and more identical with that of Hollywood and Broadway.

Once the stronghold of the principle of conservation, the museum has become instead the major source of instant accreditation of works, styles, attitudes, and personalities. Let me give you one example. An announcement from a New York art gallery of the opening of an exhibition of sculpture presents a summary of the artist's professional career. The announcement says, "In 1963 he was included in a group show in a commercial gallery. In 1964 he had a one-man show in the same gallery. In 1965 he became a world figure [*laughter*]. Nine leading galleries and museums in the United States, Canada, and Europe exhibited his work, under a variety of 'new direction' themes, and he was selected to represent the United States at the Biennial of São Paolo." Among the discoverers of the overpowering significance of this three-year-old talent [*laughter*] were the Institute of Contemporary Art of the University of Pennsylvania, the Kane Memorial Exhibition of Brown University, the Moderna Museet of Stockholm, and the Art Institute of Chicago. This year he will be discovered again, by, among others, the Jewish Museum.

Such a concurrence of judgment regarding a new star is more typical of show business than of art criticism. We used to think of art criticism as being a kind of situation in which nobody ever agreed with anybody else. But this is all a matter of the past, obviously. A parallel to this accreditation appeared recently in a feature story in the *Chicago Tribune*, under the title, "Bye-Bye Bogey: Sunset Strip Goes Hip." The story told how cement signatures of former Hollywood stars, like Cagney, Bogart, Joan Crawford, and W.C. Fields, had been chopped out of the wall outside the old Earl Carroll's restaurant on Sunset Boulevard, this restaurant being apparently a species of museum, and had been replaced by such new talents as Bo Diddley, Ike and Tina Turner [*laughter*], and several others, performers who are about as well known to their own specialized public as the young sculptor sponsored by the museums that I mentioned.

Once the museum has gone completely hip, the only identifiable difference between art and the media will be the size of the mass to which art appeals. At present art is still a medium for a relatively small mass, though one capable of expanding indefinitely, as has happened with guitar playing and folk dancing. In maintaining the size of this mass and steadily augmenting it, promotion becomes a vital center of aesthetic discourse. It pours forth in a continuous stream of catalogues, releases, human-interest stories, interviews, picture biographies, statements by the artists. In this context, the function of criticism, where it is not itself promotion in disguise, is to lend variety to the monotonous chant of the builders and disseminators of reputations. In practice, criticism can have no more effect upon art as a medium than it has on TV or the movies.

Neither by the museum nor by criticism can art be kept separate from the media. Not only does art keep approaching the media by way of pace, promotion, and other similarities, the media, for their part, take on the features of art. I see, for example, a promising future for media museums, which should be able, without too much effort, to establish a roster of heroes comparable to those of painting and sculpture or of inventions, in science. Still photos and movies are already recognized by the Metropolitan Museum of Art, the Museum of Modern Art, and most other art institutions as fine arts. It seems inevitable that comic books, billboards, pulp magazines, and radio tapes should soon be accorded aesthetic reappraisal. There has already been a TV series at the Museum of Modern Art. Such apparently knotty problems as whether Lichtensteins are to be assigned to the painting section or hung among the comic books may, under conditions of aesthetic desegregation, simply cease to exist.

From the side of media creation, too, a drive has been developing to overleap the distance that separates commercial art from museum art. Art Gallery 1150—that's the address on the Avenue of the Americas, and the title itself is taken from the old Stieglitz numbered gallery—was established in New York last month to present "a continuing exhibition of outstanding fine art by distinguished art directors and artists of business and industry. Growing evidence shows," says the announcement, "that the only distinction between a purely 'fine artist' and a commercial artist with fine art talent is one of *semantics.* The handicap of the commercial artist," asserts 1150, which is sponsored as "a professional and cultural service," by Monogram Inc., "is simply that, since he," the commercial artist, "paints to earn a living, he has less time to spend on his fine art than other artists and so he falls behind, in volume, the artist who devotes himself entirely to fulfilling gallery demands [*laughter*] for his one particular style or technique." By an amusing turning of the tables, the "gallery artist" is here presented as a specialized craftsman, as a kind of commercial artist, as against the commercial artist, who at least is free on Sundays [*laughter*].

The rejection or refusal to see any difference, except one of presentation, between works of art and the products of the media is raised to the philosophical level by our colleague Marshall McLuhan in his book *Understanding Media.* To McLuhan, the arts are media. The book or the canvas is simply a tool of communication that has been rendered obsolete by the new electronic media that first appeared in the last century with the telegraph and has now attained Comsat. Put another way, it might be said that yesterday's medium is today's art. Or you might say the arts are lagging media [*laughter*]. The book looks backward—as well as around it. TV encompasses the book and marches straight ahead.

McLuhan sees some virtue in the lagging of the brain, that is, of the artist, that prompts it to go on writing novels. Reading helps people, as he says, program their senses at a gradual trot, instead of risking being knocked off balance by the wild gallop of unrestrained electronics. Yet to McLuhan, the medium, in his justly famous phrase, is the message. That is, whatever a book does to the reader, it does as a book, not as a good book or as a work of art. Moreover, the book, good and bad, like the painting, the play, or live music, is destined to be devoured by the new total media, which are transforming our senses of sight, sound, and touch, as well as our nervous system itself.

In the ideas of McLuhan, the encompassing of the arts by the media is carried to its logical conclusion in the metamorphosis of the spectator. We don't have to worry about artists anymore, since there won't be anyone to look at or listen to or read their art. The horns are growing and we are finding them desirable. Better a rhinoceros than a nearsighted owl. In time, even if paintings and books remain, there will be no one capable of perusing them except in the new form given them by the later technologies.

It is sometimes argued that the public life of art is of secondary significance, is not the essential transaction of art, that which takes place between the artist and the individual, who attends to or acquires his work out of love for it. This matter of privacy would seem to provide the fundamental distinction between art and the media. The artist works to satisfy a human being, himself perhaps first of all. The media man works to meet the needs of a system. The first deals with a person, the second with the representatives of a facility. Of course, if McLuhan is right, the distinction between private and public, persons and facilities, is in the process of being wiped out by the formation of a new, electronically fused global village, in which people not only are facilities but even resemble them physically.

I will however assume arbitrarily that individuals will continue to persist for some indefinite period to come. Consequently, there will continue to be, if not an actual distinction between art and media products, at least a desire that such a distinction should exist. The archetypal creation of the media is the package, whether it contains corn flakes, a 240-horsepower motor, or a retrospective exhibition of the paintings of Jackson Pollock. The virtues of the package and its contents are economy and reliability in production, convenience in delivery, speed in assimilation. Art generally has none of these qualities. Indeed it has, at times, tended to emphasize antithetical ones. Art production is wasteful, the completion of the work is not to be depended on, it communicates itself with difficulty, and to absorb it takes time. In short, the production and consumption of art occur under the handicaps of a human organism, rather than with the advantages of more efficient mechanisms. Assuming the survival of individuals, art might continue to be produced in a media-dominated world as an aspect of the natural irreconcilability of the human being and the machine. In short, art belongs to the realm of freedom and is defined by its mode of execution.

Perhaps, then, it would be best to forget about art and pay attention only to the quality of our intellectual acts. There would, of course, be no question of art winning a victory over the media but only of resistance. Resistance to the media for the sake of a certain quality of intellectual action can take two forms: one, the vow of inattention; two, critical subversion. The vow of inattention is a traditional romantic defense, inaugurated upon the first assault of the newspaper and the gibberish of advertising. Its strategy has been simply to refrain, through self-imposed discipline, from reading the papers or looking at advertisements. For example, in a collection of writings on popular culture, Edmund Wilson wrote that he had nothing to say about detective stories, because he thought they stank and therefore refused to read them. This is an example of resolute inattentiveness [*laughter*]. To enable it to operate with a maximum of effectiveness, one should spend as much time as possible away from the centers of civilization, let's say in the country—and not in East Hampton either [*laughter*].

In sum, the principle applied is to refuse to collaborate in ruining one's own mind through absorbing messages, visual or verbal, from sources not designated by oneself and at moments when one has not chosen to receive them. One fights the system of communications by controlling what the electronics people call the *input* of the senses. This species of resistance is based on the assumption that patches of the green earth and a real moon still subsist behind the communications grid. For myself, I find this *Walden*-sian hypothesis highly questionable. All indications point to the likelihood that nature has been totally enmeshed in the products of the human mind and that the dream of a quiet pond is the effect of an artifice that is likely to lead to an actual artifice advertised in the Sunday travel section. Also, to observe the vow of inattention would involve excluding art, too, which one encounters today largely through the media. In sum, the resistance to the media through closing one's senses to them could succeed only under conditions of an extreme primitivism long since out of reach.

We are thrown back, then, upon the second form of resistance, critical subversion. The essence of the media is intentionality. They want to do things to the spectator, first of all to enlist him. Each medium seeks to build its own hard core of insiders, people who will respond automatically to esoteric associations of ideas. There are TV comedy programs that are funny only to faithful watchers of TV, just as there are paintings that are moving only to loyal frequenters of certain art galleries. Critical subversion operates through tearing open the media package and treating its contents as mere fact. One example of this has been collage. A painter cuts a smile out of a toothpaste ad and pastes it into his painting. Or he sticks a TV set into the painting, although this is risky. If the TV set works, it may run off with the painting. Isolated from their context by an act of the mind, the components of the media return to the state of primitive matter. The media turn art into media. Art retaliates by turning the media into art or into a mockery of the media.

To acquire the habit of disintegrating the intellectual packages provided by the media, including the arts as media, requires practice in critical self-dissociation. The first step is the absolute refusal to be an insider. It is essential to be capable of the wrong responses, to fail to admire the best poet of the day, to be bored by the most vanguard composer, to be left blank by the newest painter, and, to make matters worse, to be stirred by a nineteenth-century opera. Critical subversion cannot stop short of subverting even the fear of being square. The mixture of art and media constitutes our environment. It is contemporary nature. Like natural nature, it tends to induce a passive receptivity, a state of being half asleep. On the other hand, the most active element in nature is the human mind. Hence, critical subversion is prepared to admire as art anything that subverts the media world by stowing up the maximum of intellectual action.

Nature has never been favorably disposed to individuals. And the universe of the media is no different in this respect. To survive in the prairies or jungles of the communications world requires the same perpetual wariness as in jungles generally. It seems likely that, in the presence of the media, criticism has become a more indispensable faculty of the mind than it ever has been before. As Kenneth Burke used to say, we live in an age when folk criticism, for example, "Oh, yeah?" has replaced folklore. With the critical sensibility built into all planes of intellectual response, the old war between mind and nature can go happily on in the world of the media.

6 Marshall McLuhan

Media theorist Marshall McLuhan (1911–80) presented a casual but incisive hour-long talk to "Six Lectures" that touched on a number of his key themes, many of which he would explore the following year in his The Medium Is the Massage: An Inventory of Effects.

Good evening, ladies and gentlemen. I'm very happy to dispense with being introduced. I have been introduced quite recently as Canada's revenge on the United States, from the land of the DEW Line, the early warning system. I can bring you a special world of jokes that you may not have encountered, namely, the grievance joke associated with French Canada. I think it was Steve Allen who said that the funnyman is a man with a grievance, and if you look around at the joke world from that point of view it's sometimes rather instructive.

In Canada we have jokes such as the one about the mouse being pursued by the cat and finally hiding under the floor, and all is quiet until suddenly there's a kind of a "bow-wow," "arf-arf" sound, and the mouse figures, "Ah, house dog has come, scared cat away," and up comes the mouse and the cat grabs it. As the cat chews the mouse down, it says, "You know, it pays to be bilingual."

I think it is rather amusing to watch the joke as a sign of grievance. And in the same way slang can be an indicator of a subtle change of sensibility, shifting patterns of perception, and if our youngsters were encouraged to pay the utmost attention and respect to slang from this point of view, it might clarify some of the problems they have. Isn't it strange that no matter how complicated slang is, no child ever made a mistake in slang, and that goes even for the word *cool*.

I once presented one of my children with a strange object. It was actually a yearbook from Rice University. It was about six-by-six inches square, just cards taped together, and it had the little stories and poems of the year. When our thirteen-year-old saw this he said, "Dad, that's real cool." He was using the term quite correctly, but many people have difficulty with that term, especially when I use it. Actually, I merely draw it from the world of slang, in which it means involved and detached at the same time, like a surgeon operating.

Cool means identification with the creative process. When a person is both involved and detached, he has to identify with the creative process. You can read a great deal about the concept *cool* in Mr. Eliot's *Four Quartets*. It's a somewhat oriental concept; Western man tends to be either involved or detached but not both at once. So this is a new development in our society. It is a complicated idea, and it is a profoundly creative idea.

One of the strange changes that is taking place in our world, and John Cage gave me a curious example of what it meant to him, is that we're moving out of the world of the planned or the specialist, out of the world of the fragmented person, into the world of the hunter, the unified person. This is the meaning of James Bond, it's the meaning of the sleuth, the meaning of the obsession with crime in our world, because the criminal and criminologist alike are both hunters. They belong to the old Paleolithic world and are really a new type of human being in our midst: the person who explores the total human environment, the way the old hunter and food gatherer used to explore his entire environment as a unified field. Man the planter, man the basket weaver, the pot maker, and so on, came in after Paleolithic man, and we've had thousands of years of the planter.

When I mentioned this to Cage, he said, "That's very interesting. I spend my life hunting mushrooms. I am not the least bit interested in cultivating them." This is a curious illustration of the difference between the two. The hunter is not concerned with classification or specialism or the processes of cultivation, only with discovery. So, there are some rather exciting things afoot.

For example, if one wanted to talk about the future of work in our world, we know that it has very little to do with jobs as they're presently understood. It has much to do with discovery, much to do with knowing, much to do with involvement in processes, so much so that the future of work is plainly knowing. There was a time when the job of royalty, the prince, was not to learn any special skill but simply to grow up.

Jacques Ellul, the author of *Propaganda*, points out that in our twentieth-century world, the child is the hardest working in human history. Our children, in a twentieth-century information environment, have to process more data than in any previous culture of the world. From early infancy, they are engaged in extraordinarily hard work, and that work is mainly just growing up, because to grow up in a modern electronic environment is a fantastically complex and difficult job. It's also a job that threatens to deprive people of identity and the personal concept, because one of the peculiarities of an electronic environment is that people become so profoundly involved with one another that they lose that sense of private identity. This is one of the peculiar cruxes of our time, that people precisely become profoundly involved with one another in an all-at-once, simultaneous field of happenings and then begin to lose their sense of private identity, because identity used to be connected with simple classification, fragmentation, and noninvolvement. In a world of profound involvement, identity seems to evaporate.

The future of work as knowing, the future of identity as involvement, brings one around to a kind of idea of roles instead of jobs. A mother doesn't have a job, she has 60 jobs, and that's a role. A top exec doesn't have a job, he has many jobs simultaneously, that is a role. I think this is happening to all of us in varying degrees. The very speeded-up world we live in guarantees that we can all have a highly integrated existence that really points in the direction of role playing rather than of job holding.

I was talking to a group of managers one time and I thought I'd just try it out on them. It seemed to me plausible to suggest to them that the real future of old age in business is discovery. Now they were quite struck by this—it seemed to make profound sense. Most of them were over 40. The point about old age as a period of discovery contradicts the merely chronological approach to things, but the older man in business is the man who knows the field and is in a much better position to be a discoverer than some younger man who is merely job holding.

In case I forget, there's another basic theme associated with this computer threat to job holding. Come into my parlor said the computer to the specialist. Anybody who wants to be taken over by a computer, just specialize. But one of the hopeful things about the computer is this, that as a retrieval system, the instantaneous speed of retrieval by computer offers a tremendous future of discovery, because a retrieval system of very high-speed brushes so many facets of knowledge together that they reveal structures, they reveal forms, they reveal the life of forms, they reveal knowledge and all sorts of new patterns. So it is typical of our time, or any other time perhaps, that they should tackle this new form of technology and put it on the old job-classified data.

What we're doing with the computer up until now is merely giving it to the librarians and to the cataloguers. In other words, let the new form do the old work. But the possibility of retrieval as a form of discovery is something we all know from our own memories. When we recall something, we tend to make discoveries. We certainly tend to make changes in the pattern of the thing we know.

Finnegans Wake is a book built entirely on this retrieval system and "casting his perils before swains." Joyce regarded language as the biggest storage system of human knowledge and perception anywhere, and his own use of that vast store of human perception was to retrieve from it in a pattern that made discovery natural. Though he might have been more humble, there's no police like Sherlock Holmes. That's retrieval. The pun as a form of retrieval brushes various layers and contexts together and creates a new discovery pattern. So the computer offers many advantages besides just the threat to wipe out jobs and provide leisure.

Now the future under electric conditions suggests perhaps an approach to various other things, which I might mention while on that theme. Since the planet has its new environment of satellites and information, electronic information, the planet is rapidly becoming an old nose cone, a work of art. Like the Model T, like old silents on TV, the planet is now becoming a content of our own man-made environment, and the future of the planet as work of art, as carefully prepared archaeological exhibit, is really quite amusing. The future work of mankind will be mainly raking and tidying and clipping the whole planet, putting it in shape, reconstructing it pretty much the way it was when the pilgrims landed.

I'm using this merely as an illustration of a basic theme that anything becomes a work of art as soon as it is surrounded by a new environment. Give any form at all a new environment and it acquires art status. In other words, it becomes visible, because this is the peculiar character part. It creates attention, it creates perception. And the role of the artist as a creator of perceptual models and perceptual means is perhaps misunderstood by those who think of art as primarily a blood bank of stored human values.

In our time, there are a great many unhappy people who see the art treasures of the past being polluted by a corrupt new vulgar environment. It never occurs to them that perhaps their job is the penetration and exploration of these new environments and that the mere accumulation of past human experience in blood banks called art does not really contribute very much toward the perception of our current environment.

A great many are confused and unhappy because they sense that all the great values of the past are being polluted and corrupted by a vulgar mass entertainment. In that regard, let's pause a moment on the future of the book.

The printed book created what we call the public. With the coming of electric circuitry, you have what is called the mass. It's a time factor. The book created the public because the book, as a printed form, made possible a very large body of people, but not simultaneously. The peculiar dimension of the mass audience is that it's all at once, it's a Happening, like the telegraph, like the daily paper.

The daily paper is a good example of a Happening, because everything that's in it happens at the same moment. The dateline is the only organizing principle in a newspaper. There is no connection between the items otherwise, and if you take away the dateline from any newspaper, you have a quite handsome surrealist poem. It becomes much more enjoyable as you pull the dateline off. The dateline presents a plausible pretext of rationality, meaning, connection, which is not really very deeply related to the newspaper. The sort of constellation of events that is incorporated on any page of a newspaper is a kind of environmental image for which many people find it natural to identify empathically, and the paper as a happening is very much in this dimension of the all at once. The editorial page, by contrast, represents a point of view, a fixed, arrested position with regard to the happening. The editorial is very closely related to the book as a form.

The book, the printed book, rather, as a form, created the public, and Montaigne, upon recognizing the existence of this new entity, this new environment called the public, said, "I owe *la public* a complete portrait of myself." It was a matter of immediate response on the part of writers that their task would from now on be the etiolation, the evolving of a self-portrait, an image. There was no such impulse or response in the Middle Ages or in the ancient world. It was with the coming of the printed book that people suddenly felt the need to reflect, to bounce their image off this public as a form of self-expression and self-portraiture. Self-portraiture was a very special response to the printed word and was never felt as a need or a response for the manuscript form of culture.

Now, Xerox has brought a kind of revolution into the publishing world that is only slowly being felt. It will be felt more and more. Xerox is the application of electric circuitry to a world that had formerly been merely mechanical and fragmented. Xerox enables, or xerography enables, the reader to become a publisher, and this is an important aspect of all electric circuitry. The audience is increasingly involved in the process. With the public, the audience was detached, observant, but not involved. With circuitry, the reader, the audience, becomes involved in itself and in the process of publishing.

The book, the future of the book, is very much in the order of book as information service. Instead of the book as a fixed package of repeatable and uniform character suited to the market with pricing and so on, the book is increasingly taking on the character of service, an information service, and the book as an information service is tailor made and custom built.

* * *

The strange dynamic or pattern of electric information is to involve the audience increasingly, as part of the workforce, instead of just tossing things to it as consumer or as entertainment. The tendency is to involve the audience as workforce, as with electric toasters, electric razors, electric anything. You do the work.

I'll come back to this perhaps, apropos the future of television or forms like that, in which it will become possible, or is now possible, to brief audiences in prime time on top-level problems in physics, science, whatever, and invite their response to these problems by IBM cards sent out in supermarkets or in magazines. You see, Robert Oppenheimer is fond of saying there are kids playing right here on the sidewalk who could solve some of my toughest problems in physics, they have modes of perception that I lost 40 years ago. Oppenheimer realizes in that remark that most scientific problems are really not concept problems but percept problems, that most scientists are blocked in their perceptions by preconceptions and prepositions.

When you're dealing simultaneously with several million people, it's obvious that somebody in that audience is going to have a perceptual perforation into the problem without any difficulty. Eight scientists working on a problem for 50 years might not get through, but ten million people working on the problem for ten minutes might. Anyway, audience participation can mean many things. In the old quiz shows, the audiences were browned off when they discovered that the shows had been rigged and they'd really been left out. There was nothing dishonest about rigging quiz shows, any more than there is about rigging a movie and making it look different from what a real-life situation might, but it was a misuse of the medium of TV, which calls for participation. The movie world doesn't call for any participation. It's a fantasy world, highly visual, with the audience sitting back from the show.

TV is not like that. TV is a profoundly involving medium, with the audience as environment, the audience as vanishing point, the audience as screen. In the movie, the audience is the camera eye, the audience looks out at the environment. With TV, the audience is the environment, is the screen, is the vanishing point, and this creates a completely different relation to programming. It creates a kind of oriental effect, with reverse perspective. It's no accident that our Western world is taking on many profoundly oriental traits since television, but it's not just television, it's electric circuitry.

The safety car is another peculiar example of electric circuitry afflicting a mechanical object. That is, the consequences of the car are now being felt by the designers of the car, whereas formerly, they merely concerned themselves with the projectile. You hurled it out into the public and you know, let the chips fall where they may. But suddenly, in the age of circuitry, the feedback is coming into the design. Product design now takes on the character of audience participation. But perhaps the safety car is more an example of the effect of the space capsule.

Bucky Fuller is famous for having pointed out, among many brilliant observations, that the space capsule is the first totally man-made environment. You know the old saying, "You can't take it with you?" In the space capsule, you've got to take it with you. You have to take the planet with you. And so the space capsule is really a kind of complete environment in which all consequences of all maneuvers are anticipated by the built-in design pattern. This sense of the space capsule is applied to the motorcar, is not creating the motorcar as a padded cell, and what more appropriate form of design for the maniac driver? But the motorcar, as a feedback design pattern, turns into a padded cell.

I have a friend who speaks of the motorcar as the "carcophagus." The "carcophagus" is a form of peripatetic vehicle in which the effects of object on the environment are built back into the object, and this is something that is characteristic of electric circuits. The circuit as such is a form that feeds back and feeds us into the circuit. All circuits are do-it-yourself objects. The book on Xerox becomes somewhat like the safety car, the reader becomes publisher and author.

In the ancient days of the scribe, in manuscript cultures, the scribe was both publisher and author, and we are sort of circling to that condition again. With Xerox, the reader of the book can excerpt it and relate it to any other excerpts or any other notions or any other sound tracks and publish it as his own creative effort. Teachers are strongly inclined to make their own books for their own classes, designed specifically for the needs of a particular class. This is another peculiar feature of electric technology; it tends toward decentralized, tailor-made, custom-built servicing.

It's typical of our rearview-mirror orientation that we look at all these new technologies as if they were reflexes of the old technology. For heaven knows how long, people have encountered each new technology by translating it back into the old familiar one. You know all the types of examples of that. The first motorcars were made with buggy-whip holders, and the new automation computer devices are being made as if they were card catalogues. This strange habit of looking backward when moving forward is one that perhaps won't quite bear up, isn't quite consistent with jet speeds and electronic speeds. It may be that we are the first human generation to feel the need for a close look at what's actually happening under our noses, instead of that rearview-mirror look, because the rearview mirror is a very comforting spot. It gives you a sense of remoteness. Like *Bonanza*. The suburban world of our times lives in *Bonanza*-land. This gives it a comfortable sense of distance and security. It's a nineteenth-century image.

When the railway was new in the nineteenth century, people formed an image not of the railway and the new world it was creating, the new cities, but of an Arcadian retreat, a pastoral innocent world, a Jeffersonian paradise. That was their image of the railway. This is a normal human reaction to novelty and innovation. Its inappropriateness as a reaction in no way deters people from this strategy. It's a kind of déjà vu. Every time you encounter the new, you say, "I've been here before and this isn't as new as you might think," and all that. This seems to tie in with the ancient theory of human learning as needfully going from the known to the unknown. I don't think there's too much evidence that this is a basic pattern of human learning. I think there's lots of evidence, though, for the fact that the moment you encounter the unknown, you translate it back into the known. This means that we never encounter the unknown, we encounter only convenient self-deceptions.

The world of electric technology and circuitry, then, as involving the audience as workforce, has extraordinary implications, and you can see while this development is taking place, while the audience is becoming profoundly involved in making a world of entertainment, the "gloom whores" stand around classifying the program and providing program ratings of the most unhappy kind. While the audience is about to take over this vast creative act, the gloom whores stand around reading off audience ratings.

For example, 350 million people each week watch *Bonanza*, in 62 different countries of the world. What could be a gloomier image of the human condition? And so what? Actually, *Bonanza* isn't that bad a show.

There was a little boy in Nairobi a few weeks ago who was found wandering around the city, and on being questioned by the police, he explained he had come from some village and he was an orphan. And they said, "Well, why are you here?" He said, "I'm looking for Mr. Cartwright, I think he can help me." And I'm quite sure he could, too. For countries in Africa or in Indonesia and China, *Bonanza* must have a very strange aspect. It must look like some distant science-fiction image of some remote world to come. That is, for countries that never had a nineteenth century [*laughter*]. And by the way, this also happens to apply to the West Coast. California didn't have a nineteenth century. During the nineteenth century, people were making their way out there as best they could. There were no factories, there were no cities, there was no industrial life, etc., etc.

Now, the result is that not having had a nineteenth century, the West Coast leapfrogged out of the eighteenth into the twentieth with great advantage to itself. That is, if you leapfrog out of one century and over a century or two, you can, upon encountering the new conditions, feel completely uncrippled by the older ones. You can behave in a much more spontaneous and much more resourceful way than people who have been through the whole process. Those who lived through the nineteenth century lived through the most stupefying and fragmenting and systematizing and categorizing century in human history. Therefore, anybody who can leapfrog over the nineteenth century might retain some imaginative life. Those who went through the nineteenth century were maimed and mutilated very horribly, because of this enormous power to fragment and systematize and classify everything that happens.

Canada is in a peculiar position, by the way. Canada never had anything but a nineteenth century. That is, Canada was invented in the nineteenth century and the United States was invented in the eighteenth. Wasn't it Adlai Stevenson who said Columbus went too far? This business of leapfrogging, though, is not without its significant features. In our present time, you'll see there are many countries in the world who are leapfrogging out of 10,000 BC into the twentieth century. Leapfrogging out of prehistory into posthistory, just psychically: what is the consequence of skipping thousands and thousands of years of Western history? No one knows. And so to come back a moment to the strange prodigy of the xerographed book, the tendency to involve audience as actor, as publisher, as writer is a characteristic that applies to an enormous amount of electric technology. It's a sort of prospect that will increasingly bring us into the need for new instruments of handling our problems. One way of putting it is to say, for the first time in human history, there is more information and data outside the classroom than inside. The sheer amount and levels of information outside in the environment far exceed it.

This is not just of very recent origin, it's occurring more and more rapidly and on a much bigger and bigger scale. All the statistics one hears, again intended to panic people, that by the year 1980 there will be more scientists than people—but what would seem to be therefore the future of education in a world in which the proportions of information have been reversed. With this spectacular reversal of this condition, it would seem to be possible that the business of the school has also reversed, that the business at the school is no longer instruction but discovery, and that the business of the teaching establishment is to train perception upon the outer environment, instead of merely stenciling information upon the brainpans of children inside the environment.

Now we have never had an educational system programmed to train perception of the outer world and it will create a considerable trauma or shock to switch into that mode of activity, but it's like the audience in the entertainment world that is ready to go into action on high-level problems. The children in our school system in the present time have very high-level information resources, both in their own makeup and nervous systems and in the world immediately accessible to them, and they can be given the task in teams of researching all sorts of fascinating problems. For example, suppose a group of elementary school children were given the job of trying to find out what was happening to America since color TV. Teams of them could be turned loose in just making inventories of effects observable in clothing, in food, in cars, in designs, in family life, in all sorts of forms, if they merely made inventories. They wouldn't have to use any ideas, they wouldn't have to reach any conclusions. They merely were invited to observe, to make inventories of effects. Small children love this kind of work and are just as able researchers as any team of sociologists in the world, and the accumulation of such inventories can be absolutely necessary and indispensable to the highest operations.

I heard a sociologist today suggest that it was quite impossible to make a direct connection between television and any change whatever. Now this is in a certain sense true. On the other hand, if you make an inventory of all the changes that have taken place in the last twelve, fifteen years, since TV, without any preconceptions, without any theories about what television is or what television does, if one merely made an inventory of all the changes in speech, in politics, in habits of human association, habits of reading, habits of dress and food, and so on, it might become quite evident that there had been a kind of pattern of change. And this would be a scientific report in the usual way, of an induction. No conclusions, just here are the changes that have taken place in the past fifteen years in all these fields since TV.

You could in turn look at the same curve in relation to some other technology. If you wanted to study what the motorcar was, you might find out more from what it did to the environment and the community. In other words, if you notice that the motorcar created road systems and vast servicing industries, you would probably have a better idea of the motorcar than you could have from photographic images of cars in catalogues. The car is what it does to people and what it does to the environment, and so with any other medium as far as I know. A medium creates an environment, an environment is a process. It is not a wrapper, it's an action, and it goes to work on our nervous systems and on our sensory lives, completely altering them.

The content of any technology is inevitably the older technology. The new environment goes around the old environment and turns the old one into an art form. This happened to the Greeks, it happened to the Romans, it happened in the Middle Ages, the Renaissance, and so on, where there's no lack of evidence of this happening. Now at the present time, I mentioned the strange fate of the planet as art form, resulting from the new environment of satellite and electronic information.

One of the biggest revolutions in Western culture occurred when the world of the arts in the eighteenth century began to create deliberately, to create landscapes in environments as a way of controlling mental life. Whether in paint or in poetry, or in landscaping and city building, the eighteenth-century artist created landscapes, what he called "the picturesque," making things look as if they were already framed in pictures. And he found that these landscapes or picturesque situations could be used as a means of controlling the mental life of the observer. The function of Romantic art or picturesque art was to control moods. It was all oriented toward effect.

Earlier, the arts had been more concerned with simply permitting the audience to enjoy the sense of community and festive involvement. Medieval arts, as we are popularly aware, were festive and communal and participative. They were not intended to give any sense of privileged or elite life. It's a little bit like the Balinese who say we have no art, we do everything as well as possible. They think of art as that which applies to the environment. They program the environment. Art for them means dealing with the environment itself as if it were a work of art, and this I think is one of the meanings of Pop art. Pop art is a recognition that the outer environment is itself capable of being processed like art, and this I think is an electronic phenomenon, that only in an age of electronic immediacy and totality could we ever dream of tackling the whole human environment as a work of art. This is happening to us and Pop art is merely a report to the nation, as it were, that this event is taking place and that we can prepare ourselves accordingly.

You know how the elite artist, blood-bank people, are shocked by Pop art, because they try to classify the content of Pop art instead of viewing it as a means of perception. They think of it as a means of classification, as merely a means of ratings, and the idea that it might have a function in just training human perception doesn't seem to get through easily to these people. But let's go back for a moment, to the picturesque artist. Having devised this landscape as a way of controlling the mental life of populations, there came shortly after, in the middle of the nineteenth century, a sudden break in which the artist said, it is the inner life, not the outer landscape, that counts. The Symbolists—the Rimbauds, the Wagners, the Baudelaires—began to examine the inner mental landscape as something that could be programmed as a means of enriching consciousness, of creating an inclusive consciousness. Instead of just creating a mood, as the Romantic artists had done, they began to work on the idea of the total consciousness, and they became intensely interested in the mythic consciousness, in the corporate consciousness of the mythic man.

This was a big moment in the history of art and culture that concerns us, because they discovered that the meaning of the work of art was not as a conveyor or a package but as an exploratory probe into the outer world. You will find this quite unanimously expressed by Flaubert and Baudelaire and others. Flaubert's way of putting it was simply that style is a way of seeing, not a way of expressing something but a way of knowing. I derived all my knowledge of media from people like Flaubert and Rimbaud and Baudelaire. They began to study the materials with which they worked in order to be faithful to style. They deliberately began to study the matters, the materials with which they worked. You find Frank Lloyd Wright and modern architects doing this at the turn of the century. They began to study not what they wanted to express but what means were available for expression. And when they began to study these materials, they quickly discovered that the medium is the massage or message. This was a big breakthrough, because what they discovered was that the function of art is to teach human perception. Conrad's remark that's often quoted, "It is above all that you may see"—not that you may know this or that, but that you may have the means of perceiving.

This idea of training all our resources upon a complex world that needs perception very badly; the idea that the future of the future is the present; the idea that if you examine the present deeply enough, you will find all possible futures: this became a very common idea to the Symbolists and to people around the later nineteenth century.

The strange clash between the old Romantic art of the outer landscape and the new Symbolist art of the inner landscape or of inclusive human consciousness was already a kind of indicator of the condition in which we are today, in which we begin to extend the very means of awareness into the environment, in other words, extending consciousness. The artist—as he makes situations that heighten human awareness—and our new media permit this heightened human awareness to be extended into the total human environment. There's only a short time that we need stay locked in this matrix, and we're going to have some questions, but there are some lessons to be learned from the artist in regard to our own time this way.

A man like Seurat, the painter, was painting TV in 1880. That is, he had a model of perception that had all the technical features of TV: rear projection, minute fragmentation of image into these little pointillist patterns. The TV viewer receives these little spots on himself, they wrap around him, he becomes lord of the flies. They settle on him, literally. The TV viewer is covered with these little dots, these little flies. Now, Seurat knew that and he painted that back in 1880, but he wanted an effect. He was not painting the technology, he was painting the effect he wanted, the effect he wanted from the TV image or this type of pointillism. The effect he wanted was that of total audience participation, involvement of a multi-sensuous kind. Seurat was consciously aiming at not merely visual but total sensuous involvement. He wanted all the senses to be involved in the painting and that's why he used this rear projection.

There's a pleasant story about Malraux taking General de Gaulle around an art gallery recently and pointing out this and that, and de Gaulle was saying, "Ah-ha, what's that one over there?" And Malraux said "a Dufy." "And what's that one?" "That's a Renoir." "Ah," says de Gaulle suddenly. "I know, that cartoon over there, that must be a Rousseau." "No sir, that's a mirror." Rousseau came to mind because he too was a rear projectionist, that is, the light came through the image to the viewer. This light through, or rear projection, creates a much higher degree of involvement than otherwise is possible.

The painters suddenly wanted to involve the audience deeply in their images, with all their senses. Electric technology, both radio and TV, for example, has this power of involving us in all our senses. Many people don't seem to recognize very easily that a cartoon, a mere outline, a mere contour, is a profoundly involving experience that requires participation of all our senses, whereas a photograph is more limited to one sense, the visual, merely. A cartoon, although it seems much simpler, is actually more profound and involving of our sensuous lives. Well, the painters knew this. I learned this from the later nineteenth-century painters. All this stuff about the media that I talk about, I learned from them. In fact, you will find the great instructors in all media matters are these painters and poets of the later nineteenth century. People like James Joyce and Eliot and others, they spent their lives studying our senses as they go out technologically into the environment, because they realized this had a profound effect on language and on the medium that they were working with as poets.

One of the things that puzzles many people about our world, about advertising, is that there seems to be such a strange disproportion between the effect of the ad and the content. Now, take a Picasso painting such as a man sitting in chair. You see no chair, you see no man, but the painting is designed to convey the effect of sitting in a chair, not the appearance, not what it looks like but what it feels like. In this painting the effect minus the appearances is a means of involvement, and the painters and poets alike sought increasingly the techniques of involvement in our time. Hence, the return, for example, of poetic drama, because the dramatist discovered that if you want to involve the audience in the action of a play, you must not use prose, which merely leaves the talking at each other, to each other, the audience and the actors. You must use poetry, which brings the audience right up onto the stage. It's rather paradoxical to say that poetry is a more involving experience than prose, when in actual fact, most people read prose and very few read poetry, but in terms of effect this is true, and it's the same with the painting.

So now in modern advertising, there's much the same revolution going forward as has been going forward in painting and poetry, and in the world of entertainment, with the audience moving more and more into the act. Modern advertising is more and more a substitute for the product. Because of its rich resources and means of sensuous solicitation, modern advertising can give you the effect of almost anything, without your having to bother about having the thing at all.

[Media theorist] Tony Schwartz is in the audience tonight, bless him. He is an expert in this very department. In terms of auditory magic, the power of giving effect without *thing* is entirely within his domain. But you see, the advertisers have been puzzled for a long time in their surveys to discover that people don't really read ads until they own the thing [*laughter*]. If you own that icebox or that car, then you notice the ads very much, because this is how you get your satisfaction.

The ad world then becomes an enormous area of information service, part of the service industries, enabling you to substitute the effect for the thing, just like Picasso. This is called nonobjective abstract art, now you see it, now you don't, and so on. But the artists usually go through these maneuvers 50 or more years before the engineers get around to them, and so the advantage of knowing art is orientation in a complex world. It gives you a 50-year breathing space before the thing hits, and that has a considerable advantage.

One of the peculiar results of this profound involvement through circuitry, as compared with the old detachment of literacy and visual culture, has been the increasing orientalization of the Western world. Even as we lavish our nineteenth-century technology on the East, we are doing to ourselves the exact opposite. We are orientalizing ourselves by going inward. And it's very easy to see them going westward and very difficult to see ourselves going inward, because it is so environmental with us that it becomes almost imperceptible. You can, however, if you do inventory, discover the amazing rise of oriental values in the arts and in all sorts of produce and all sorts of habits, and I'm sure that they could, by conducting similar inventories, find that the West made considerable inroads into their world.

For the kind of change that is going on in our own midst, we're doing this to ourselves, nobody is doing it to us. We are orientalizing ourselves while Westernizing the East, and seemingly taking much credit for the Westernizing and not even noticing what we're doing to ourselves. You see how many people find it desirable to saddle me with moral judgments and the need for value judgments, you can see that it would be impertinent and somewhat fatuous to approve or disapprove of anything that concerned the life of nations and many, many millions of people simultaneously. It would be very much like the position of Margaret Fuller, one of Bucky's relatives, by the way, who said back in, what, 1850, "I accept the universe." And it was Emerson, I think, who said, "she'd better."

2

1993–2013

5
6
7
3

A Bigger Boat: The Foundation Since 1993

Nancy Dalva

FOR SEVERAL DECADES AFTER THE CREATION of the Foundation for Contemporary Performance Arts, the board of directors functioned as a benevolent but very loosely organized cohort with no staff. By 1993, with the increasing scope of their task as grant makers, the board took several steps that established the Foundation as it exists today. Hiring Mary Judge, a former program officer from the John Simon Guggenheim Memorial Foundation, it launched a significant expansion of the FCPA's grant making by creating formal programs to support both individual artists and organizations and expand the range of disciplines supported.

For some thirty years the Foundation had supported only the more ephemeral arts. Now the board for the first time awarded six Grants to Artists—$25,000 no-strings-attached grants across the fields of dance, music/sound, performance art/theater, poetry, and the visual arts. Eventually, as many as fourteen artists would receive awards each year from a larger pool of invited nominations. Grants to Artists marked the beginning of assisting painters, sculptors, photographers, poets, filmmakers, and those working in what is now simply called "performance." That boat of Merce Cunningham's—"Help others," he had said in 1962, "We're all in the same boat"—was turning into an ark. In the pages that follow, we highlight some of the recipients of the Foundation's annual grants and the difference the support made in their careers.

Since its inception, the Foundation has consistently supported work of an innovative nature, with as few exactions on the artist as possible. Through Grants to Artists, the Foundation performs its mission by a kind of stealth. There are no applications, none of the tedious paperwork and grant writing that so distract from the making of actual work, and hence no rejections or disappointments.

It all starts with the nominators. For nominators, the request to participate—like the grants themselves—comes as a surprise. The process is confidential: they may not indicate to the artists that they are nominators, and they learn the outcome of the selection committee's deliberations only after the recipients do. Once nominators submit their letters, their part in the process is done—unless, and until, they find out that their nominee has received a grant. Then, they float on air. Instigating a successful Grant to Artists is every bit as meaningful as getting one.

Some of the most articulate criticism extant is in the nominating letters that introduce each artist's portfolio. These documents are models of descriptive generosity, fiercely and wonderfully partisan and passionate. The quiet participation of artists nominating fellow artists is one of the underpinnings of the Foundation, and indeed its founding premise.

Douglas Henderson, 2007 grantee, *Music for 100 Carpenters*, FCA-supported performance/installation, The Boiler, Brooklyn, 2009. Photo: David A. Henderson.

Not only do artists donate art; they donate time, expertise, and what we might call moral support. It is probably not giving away any secret to say that from time to time, past grantees are asked to step into the nominator role. Their participation is ideal, because they know better than anyone else what it means to get a call out of the blue awarding you money you were not expecting for art you had only hoped to make or had already begun and were not sure of completing.

In the early years, nominators had been responsible not only for proposing grantees but also for gathering supporting materials—an ever more complex mélange of slides, catalogues, videotapes, and such. The board then sifted through boxes filled with items, selecting images, cuing tape, and so forth. Today, these roles have been streamlined and brought in-house, with a small staff taking care of the assembly of portfolios and work samples. Another change has been to have a greater number of nominators, each of whom makes just a single nomination rather than three. Limiting nominators to a single selection makes each nomination that much more emphatic. Conversely, the broadening of the pool of nominators makes the Foundation's field of vision even greater.

My first meeting of the Foundation for Contemporary Performance Arts was December 4, 1985, at Jasper Johns's Houston Street studio. Right away I felt honored to be working with the board. Being on the Lower East Side at that time was exciting, as I met artists and attended performances whenever possible. A little over a year later we moved to Jasper's house on East 63rd Street, where my position as board secretary became more business oriented. Since the Foundation responsibilities became more demanding, an executive director was hired in 1993 to run it, but I remained secretary and was grateful for opportunities to see what artists were doing at meeting presentations.

It is remarkable and wonderful what the now FCA has done and continues to do for experimenting artists, and I am happy to have been part of the process for 25 years.

—Sarah Taggart

THE BOARD OVER TIME comprised visual artists; a composer; and, from 1966 until 2001, figures from the dance world: Carolyn Brown and Viola Farber, who had both been longtime and significant members of Merce Cunningham and Dance Company. After the dancers were no longer on the board, the directors also acquired a kind of sidecar, if you will, of advisers from the various fields represented in the Grants to Artists. Whether scholars or practitioners, they serve as advocates and guides during the annual selection process. These advisers are invited to cast votes along with the board, an ardent, interesting, and occasionally contentious process.

The annual deliberations of the board to award the Grants to Artists each November are illustrative themselves of the Foundation's overarching philosophy. The briefing binder has grown over the years to the size of an old-fashioned New York City telephone book. It is a kind of three-ring circus, the binder, containing all the print materials that support the audio and visual materials reviewed by the committee as a group. Joined by these few field-specific advisers, and all having examined in detail the nominators' letters and hundreds of pages of supporting materials, the directors spend two days of meetings looking at videos, slides, computer-generated visual material, listening to music, and talking and talking about all of it. The focus is always on working artists, often at a turning point or stepping-up moment in their careers, and yet, the grants indicate that innovation is not unique to any time of life.

Surprisingly to newcomers at the table, the final selection happens only after every applicant in every field has been considered (and often reconsidered), and everyone votes in every field. This collective involvement enlarges the possibilities of the process. Somehow, after hours of respectful consideration, and arguing and deliberating, a sense of the nominees emerges. Sometimes there is a consensus, sometimes not, and the voting sorts things out. There are no quotas for each area or field. Always,

I started in 1993 in the basement of Jasper's house on East 63rd Street, sharing an office with Sarah Taggart. We sat on hard wooden chairs. Often we'd be called up to the kitchen for lunch and climb the two flights of stairs for the most delicious grilled cheese sandwiches, or whatever Jasper had decided to prepare. We'd talk over something in the board minutes, about the exhibition poster from the first benefit show (did he remember the designer?), or cover details about the benefit drawing show at Leo Castelli in planning. There were no print materials. The first task, though, was to restructure the grant program. I created an informational brochure, reconstructing FCPA's history and announcing new grant-making procedures: significant-sized grants to artists awarded by nomination; smaller grants to organizations; "emergency" grants as needed. All of this to be done with minimal administration costs. It took three moves to get to the office on Greenwich and Jane. The Meat-Packing District was still offensively fragrant.

—Mary A. Judge

It has been a truly wonderful experience serving on the FCA board. I am continuously impressed by the caliber of artist-driven support and how the organization has been able to navigate transitions, especially after the death of Elizabeth Murray. We are so lucky to have artist directors like Robert Gober, Julian Lethbridge, Glenn Ligon, Kara Walker, and T.J. Wilcox. The FCA attracts so many influential, groundbreaking, and philanthropic artists who donate works and lend their support. Jasper created the FCA in this spirit of community and artists helping artists, and the model has proved to be so successful because there are so many parallels across the creative disciplines and artists want to support artistic innovation, however it is expressed.

—Agnes Gund

I had a great time announcing the Foundation's annual awards over the eight years I hosted those evenings. Most were in Jennifer Bartlett's studio in the Village, which meant that I didn't have lighting or a microphone. What I had was a captive audience that scared me. Much of it was composed of artists, poets, writers, composers, and choreographers I admired. But the evening I remember best was when the entertainment was Merce Cunningham. He was quite frail but when he sat down with David Vaughan to read a story by John Cage, his gentle voice seemed to boom and his phrasing mirrored the movements of his own dancing. It was a touching, funny, whimsical, and completely heartrending experience and I will never forget it.

—Linda Yablonsky

afterward, there is a collective sense of achievement and a sense of things set in motion. Soon, the grantees will be called.

Let me take you behind the scenes of two such moments, as they might happen—both in dance, a field the Foundation has been associated with from the start. First, imagine a choreographer—long distinguished in her field, highly accomplished and original, continually evolving, and forever working without the net of her own foundation or board. On this day, as ever, she wonders where she is going to find the studio space to rehearse her next work and the money to pay for it. The phone rings. It is the director of the Foundation for Contemporary Arts with news of a grant. Next, conjure a young dancer-choreographer, out on the road with the company with which he performs, standing in a crowded room filled with the buzz of a party celebrating the work of a master whose work he esteems. How will he get from here to there? His cell phone rings. He answers, and from halfway across the country, the Foundation director tells him he is a recipient of a grant to continue the work in which he has shown so much promise, intelligence, and initiative.

Neither artist knew these calls might be coming. The moment is in every way significant. The money is real and enlarges their possibilities. And the validation they feel in being selected by this organization is also real, and it is lasting.

But interestingly enough, the cash, deeply appreciated though it is, turns out not to be the salient feature cited by grantee after grantee. What matters even more is the recognition from the organization and the knowledge that their work has been seen and valued by their peers. Further, the imprimatur of the Foundation for Contemporary Arts is not only confirmatory and stimulating; it is also practical. It enhances the artist's curriculum vitae, and hence the inevitable applications to other funders.

There is an announcement ceremony each year for the new grantees, with many former recipients filling the room and some even taking the stage after the awards are presented. One recent year, a choreographer came back to perform, and during the conversation afterward met a composer who was a new grantee. Two years later, they collaborated on a new work. It was, said the choreographer of their serendipitous meeting, "in every way fortuitous."

A sense of genuine accomplishment is felt by everyone at the Foundation: the board, the staff, the panelists, the nominators—even the donating artists. Their mission is ongoing.

THE INCREASINGLY COMPLEX VARIETY of artists recognized by the Foundation after 1993 was formally acknowledged in 2004, when the Foundation for Contemporary Performance Arts became, simply, the Foundation for Contemporary Arts. Not only did this name change reflect an enlarged purpose, but it also signaled the growing mutability among and between the arts, the addition to the mix of new technologies and the myriad artists drawn to them from across disciplinary lines. Who's to say that painting isn't a kind of performance, that music doesn't have color, that choreography isn't visual? Yet the original mission persists, as does the original vision. However expansive and elastic the mandate has proved, the common theme that runs through the work of all the recipients is passion, originality, persistence, curiosity, and individuality allied with an openness of intellect.

In addition to the Grants to Artists, the Foundation provides Grants to Organizations, made by annual application to a few dozen presenting and supporting organizations, and a growing number of Emergency Grants. In reality "opportunity grants," this ingenious program enables artists to apply year-round for last-minute assistance to complete projects under way or to take advantage of unexpected opportunities to present their work to the public. As modest as $100 and as much as $2,500, Emergency Grants defray the unforeseen costs of a plethora of practical needs, from supplies, airfare, and equipment rental to performers' fees and beyond. While the budget for Emergency Grants is much smaller than that of Grants to Artists, an Emergency Grant is often the first that an emerging artist might receive, and it can have a legitimizing effect. In another example of the community's generosity to the FCA, a panel of visual artists volunteer their time at monthly Emergency Grants meetings to review applications and determine grants.

A new award made by the FCA for the first time in 2013 exemplifies yet another side of the generosity of spirit within the Foundation's community of artists. The first-ever Robert Rauschenberg Award, named in memory of one of FCPA's instigating artists, was established this year through an endowment from the Robert Rauschenberg Foundation. Like the Grants to Artists, it is an unrestricted $25,000, by-nomination grant, intended to honor Rauschenberg's legacy of innovation, risk-taking, and experimentation. Nonspecific as to discipline, it is also a nod to his collaborations with performing artists and never-ending support of younger visual artists. The recipient is to be selected from the larger pool of Grants to Artists nominees each year by the FCA. In a beautiful and fitting coincidence, the inaugural 2013 Rauschenberg Award recipient is Trisha Brown, who just happened to be nominated for a Grant to Artists—this of all years. The Robert Rauschenberg Award is the first endowed grant for the FCA, and one hopes there will be more in the future.

Finally, there is the $50,000 biannual John Cage Award, first granted in 1992, the year of Cage's death. It too operates through a nomination process. The first recipient was David Tudor. The most recent, in 2012, was Pauline Oliveros. Concerning her work practice, she wrote in a recent personal statement: "Through listening inclusively as well as exclusively in balance, I hope to expand the range of my consciousness in music and in life."

There it is—that gnomic guru factor, so very Cagean, and so reflective of the processes leading to these awards each year. Art offers us propositions not only about its own function and nature but about the nature of life, and how to go through it. What better guides for the twenty-first century? The Foundation makes it possible for artists to keep proposing. ◆

I was first involved with the Foundation for Contemporary Arts as a member of an Emergency Grants panel. We awarded many grants, most often for artists producing new work, but one in particular, of a different nature, has remained with me.

An elderly female artist had submitted a grant application, in which she described her decades working with photography. This work had occasionally found an audience, but she had never been broadly collected and was accustomed to living quite modestly. She described her dilemma; unexpected health care costs had consumed more of her budget than she was able to afford and now her decades of film negatives were at risk. She was at the point of being evicted from the storage facility that contained her work and was physically and financially unable to transport her negatives to another location. She asked if we, by granting her $1,000 to catch up with her past-due rent, would save her life's work.

She had specifically applied to the FCA because she knew it was the only organization that offers grants of this type so speedily. The Emergency Grants panel meets monthly, so it is possible to receive a stipend within several weeks from the time of application. Her situation required just this sort of immediate aid. The Emergency Grants panel was delighted to be able to help and I left the Foundation's offices that afternoon convinced it offers a unique and essential resource to the diverse art-making community.

—T.J. Wilcox

Selection committee deliberations are always engaging. For two days, really talented, really smart, and sometimes strongly opinionated people in each field present nominees for grants to committee members who are often equally strongly opinionated. We debate, we learn, we come to conclusions. And, most frequently, we end up with more people deserving grants than we have grants to give. This is always a sober moment, followed often by the hope and then the possibility that we might just be able to stretch a bit further and offer one or two more grants. Everyone relaxes, smiles, sees their favorite nominee safely granted, and we go home smiling.

—Frances Fergusson

Vicky Shick, 2006 grantee, *Plum House*, FCA-supported performance, Dance Theater Workshop, New York, 2007. Performers: Vicky Shick and Jodi Melnick, 2011 grantee. Photo: Yi-Chun Wu.

Selected Grants to Artists, 1993–2012

Compiled by Eric Banks, Mark Beasley, and Debra Singer

Zeena Parkins, *Regeneration* (collaboration with Daria Martin), performance, Tate Modern, London, 2006. Photo: Sheila Burnett. Courtesy Maureen Paley, London.

Zeena Parkins, 1997

Prior to receiving her Grant to Artists in 1997, composer and harpist Zeena Parkins was "living on Ludlow in the Lower East Side of Manhattan, within a strong artist community, playing lots of concerts, and of course struggling to pay bills and invent clever ways to earn money." The impact of the award, she recalls, was much greater however than the freedom it gave her from practical concerns. "It is the acknowledgment and unmitigated support from my peers that really was profoundly moving for me. This gave me a special kind of extra energy and force. I think I was particularly impressed that the panel included artists from many different disciplines, not only composers and musicians."

The grant helped Parkins realize a specific work, *Pan-Acousticon*, released on John Zorn's Tzadik label in 1999 and the result of three years of labor. Scored for violin, cellos, electric guitar, percussion, daxaphone, electric harp, piano, accordion, and sampler, *Pan-Acousticon* is a piece Parkins describes as concerning "language, hearing, radiance, loss, and the desire for connectivity." Thanks to her FCA grant, Parkins was able to travel to Germany to research on-site the thieves' cant called Rotwelsch—a lexical component of her earlier work *Mouth=Maul=Betrayer* that she further developed in *Pan-Acousticon*.

Parkins's current work includes the project *Spellbeamed, Fixexploded, Fixabolished*, which she performed in September 2012 at Roulette in New York with the Ne(x)tworks Ensemble and JACK Quartet. A frequent collaborator with visual artists and other musicians, including Björk and Yoko Ono, Parkins has worked as well with numerous fellow FCA Grants to Artists recipients, including composers Ikue Mori, Jim O'Rourke, Elliott Sharp, Douglas Henderson, and Pauline Oliveros, and choreographers DD Dorvillier, Neil Greenberg, Jennifer Monson, and John Jasperse. Her work has received three "Bessies" (the New York Dance and Performance Awards) as well as a 2004 award from the British Academy of Film and Television Arts.
—Mark Beasley

Julie Mehretu, 2000

Best known for her intricate abstract drawings and paintings, Julie Mehretu recalls receiving her Grant to Artists at a pivotal moment: "The grant came at a time when I had rented a bigger space, so I could make new paintings that were larger than anything I had done before. I was broke from the renovations and needed to come up with money that day so the contractor could finish—otherwise, I would be without a studio and a home. I opened the envelope with the check inside that same afternoon. It was unbelievable. It came at a critical time because I was preparing for my first solo museum exhibition, at the Walker Art Center, which turned out to be a very significant exhibition for my work."

The work that Mehretu generated for her traveling 2003 Walker show became what she considered a breakthrough cycle of paintings. The expansive compositions marked a new stage where the artist figured out, as she explains, how "to bring the city into the paintings" and refined what would become her signature visual vocabulary—diaphanous layers of finely drawn, whorling lines intermixed with schematic architectural fragments, geometric shards of color, and gestural brushwork. Moreover, she explained, it was the first time she was able to create a group of paintings in conversation with one another—in no small part made possible by her larger studio space, where she could actually *see* them next to one another, as they were being developed.

Since her early FCA recognition, Mehretu has gone on to international prominence. Her work is in myriad museum collections, and in addition to participating in numerous group exhibitions, she has had solo exhibitions at the Detroit Institute of Arts; the Louisiana Museum of Modern Art in Denmark; the Deutsche Guggenheim Museum, Berlin; the Solomon R. Guggenheim Museum, New York; and the Saint Louis Art Museum, among other institutions. She received a MacArthur Foundation "genius award" in 2005. —Debra Singer

Julie Mehretu, *Looking Back to a Bright New Future*, 2003, ink and acrylic on canvas, 95" x 119". Courtesy the artist and Marian Goodman Gallery, New York.

Ikue Mori, 2006

"The grant helped me tremendously, both financially and mentally," drummer and composer Ikue Mori says of her 2006 Grant to Artists. "It pushed me forward to produce the projects I was working on and allowed me to take time off from touring so that I could concentrate and focus." When Mori received the grant, she had embarked on a pair of new projects: an animation, titled *Kibyoshi*, that featured historic Japanese illustrations, and a new music piece using sixteen speakers for Issue Project Room. The FCA grant allowed her to "travel to Japan to film new footage, locate props, and produce a DVD of the work." The effect was salutary: *Kibyoshi* has been described as her most accomplished work to date, drawing on the rich literature of Japanese *kibyōshi*, satirical comics that critically engage with contemporary society and focus on literature, political affairs, and current events. Her *Kibyoshi* animations continue to travel in the US, Europe, and Japan.

A founding member of the No Wave band DNA, a group that helped change the approach to and sound of contemporary rock music, the Tokyo-born Mori has since developed her signature drum style and entered into frequent improvisational and collaborative work with fellow musical pioneers Bill Frisell, Fred Frith, Anthony Coleman, fellow FCA grantee Zeena Parkins, and John Zorn, with whom she continues to collaborate. Mori has received commissions from numerous venues and organizations, including The Kitchen, Roulette/Mary Flagler Cary Charitable Trust, RELÂCHE, and the Montalvo Arts Center. In 2008 she was commissioned by the Tate Modern to create recordings to accompany Maya Deren's silent films. —MB

Ikue Mori, *Kibyoshi*, performance, Unlimited Festival, Wels, Austria, 2010.

Alex Bag, 1995

Grants to Artists recipient Alex Bag describes herself as a "writer who primarily uses video. Everything clicked when I found a video camera, I was always writing and never really had a home for it; video allowed me to make the writing visual." A pioneer of video-performance art in works like *Fall '95*, she deploys a personal cast of characters and a simple, direct performance in order to satirize twin figures—the art student and the art star—in the 1990s. Mixing high and low cultural referents with TV talk shows, commercial advertising, and documentary-style formats, her early work lampoons market forces and the demands made on the artist to "perform."

Before receiving the grant in 1995, Bag had been producing her work with little or no budget. "My camera was borrowed, and my work piecemealed. It was very post-undergrad, working alone and cobbling things together." She immediately made two important purchases, a Hi8 camera and an editing VCR. "I worked on a public access television show at that point, and having the VCR really helped to produce a more professional-looking show." Having the equipment was key to making her signature work of the period, including *The Artist's Mind* (1996) and *Harriet Craig* (1998).

"The grant was the safety net I'd not had before. It's great to have money to realize something you want to give birth to: money for a studio, equipment you need, a break from your full-time job at the beginning of or at any point in your career." Bag has exhibited at the Museum of Modern Art, the Tate Gallery, and the Whitney Museum of American Art, and was the subject of a 2011 retrospective at the Migros Museum für Gegenwartskunst, Zurich. —MB

Alex Bag, production still from *Fancy Pantz*, video, 1997. Courtesy the artist and Team Gallery, New York.

Rae Armantrout, 2007

Many FCA grant recipients relate how momentous the Grant to Artists was, but it is difficult to overstate the particular timeliness of the 2007 grant to poet Rae Armantrout. "I had been diagnosed with cancer in June 2006," she recalls, "and it was a kind of cancer that has a poor prognosis. At the time, when I was thinking that my life might not be long, it was extra great to get that validation for the work I had done."

Armantrout was about to embark on "Dark Matter," a thematically conjoined sequence of poems that would constitute one-half of her Pulitzer Prize–winning volume *Versed* (Wesleyan University Press, 2009). Written in the wake of her illness, "Dark Matter" threads a perspicacious encounter with phenomena invisible and unknowable yet ineffably present (in the poem that gives the section its title, she writes, "Who am I / to experience a burst / of star formation? // I know this— // after the first rush / of enthusiasm // any idea / recedes and dims"). Given the critical attention the book subsequently enjoyed—in addition to a Pulitzer, it received the 2009 National Book Critics Circle Award for Poetry and was a National Book Award finalist—it is all the more surprising that Armantout's FCA grant was the first national, high-profile honor that she had received. "I definitely remember the phone call. It was completely out of the blue. I learned later that the FCA had also awarded grants to writers I know and respect greatly, like Nathaniel Mackey. But it came as a complete surprise."

The grant allowed Armantrout a sabbatical and travel to Rome, Naples, and Capri, experiences that pepper the terse lines of "Dark Matter." Closer to home, she was able to buy a car, no minor consideration in Southern California, where she has taught for the past three decades at the University of California, San Diego. A recipient of a Guggenheim Foundation Fellowship in 2007, she has been included in numerous anthologies, including *The Oxford Book of American Poetry*. Her twelfth collection of poetry, *Just Saying*, was recently published by Wesleyan University Press. —Eric Banks

SIMPLE
for Aaron Korkegian

Complex systems can arise
from simple rules.

It's not
that we want to survive,
it's that we've been drugged
and made to act
as if we do

while all the while
the sea breaks
and rolls, painlessly, under.

If we're not copying it,
we're lonely.

Is this the knowledge
that demands to be
passed down?

Time is made from swatches
of heaven and hell.

If we're not killing it,
we're hungry.

—Rae Armantrout

John Jesurun, *Philoktetes*, performance, Soho Rep, New York, 2007.

PHOTO: PAULA COURT

John Jesurun, 1993

When playwright, director, and designer John Jesurun received his 1993 Grant to Artists, he was already well known for his experimental theater performances integrating language, film, video, and set design. "It helped me turn a corner in my more mature work by freeing me up for the first time to pick-and-choose projects, and allowed me—after so many years of making a lot of work quickly and efficiently—to slow down, consider things more, and make choices in a quieter way."

Such a "slowing down," though, still resulted in an incredibly productive year, in which Jesurun created four new plays, the most significant of which was *Philoktetes*. Commissioned in 1993 by the late, great Wooster Group actor Ron Vawter, *Philoktetes* was a highly reimagined version of the Trojan War myth in which Odysseus and Neoptolumus abandon their fellow warrior, the archer Philoktetes, on a desert island because of his foul-smelling snake-bite wound—only to discover later that they have to return to retrieve his magic bow. In Jesurun's hands, the play ends up serving as a parable about masculinity, loyalty, love, and disease. "It was the middle of the hallmark years of the AIDS crisis, and Ron asked me to write this for him. It was when he really was at a spot where art, real life, and death converge. I was writing this play as quickly as possible. It was a race with Ron's mortality." Indeed, after just one performance of the work in 1994 at Brussels's Kaaitheater, Vawter became too sick to perform, the show closed, and Vawter died a few weeks later. The show, though, has since had many lives around the world, receiving its New York premiere in 2007, at Soho Rep, to great acclaim.

After working for six years in the television industry, Jesurun began his theatrical career in 1982. Since then, he has written, directed, and designed over twenty-five works, and his company has toured extensively in Europe and the United States. He was subsequently also the recipient of numerous grants and awards, including a Guggenheim Foundation Fellowship and a MacArthur Foundation "genius award." —DS

Ryan McNamara, *Untitled (Bricks)*, 2012, canvas, backdrop, performance stills, glue, 119" x 88". Courtesy the artist and Elizabeth Dee Gallery, New York.

Ryan McNamara, 2011

Ryan McNamara has become something of a cause célèbre in the New York performance world over the past few years; having emerged relatively recently, he has in his own words "overthrown the Whitney Biennial with the Whitney Houston Biennial; stank up the Dia building with man smell; forced people to eat my debit card; and learned from a Texan stripper how to disconnect my ass from the rest of my body." The last would refer to *Make Ryan a Dancer* (2010), comprising 104 grueling days of public dance classes inside and outside MoMA PS1 during "Greater New York" and for many critics the key work of the exhibition.

For McNamara, how to transport the museum- and performance-space gestures into a different space—the gallery—was a question the Grant to Artists he received in 2011 permitted him to ponder. The award allowed for "uninterrupted mind space in which to contemplate how my practice could fit within the structure of a gallery exhibition, acting as a bridge for me, giving me the time and space to develop a practice that is self-sustaining." If punk celebrated the amateur musician, then McNamara celebrates the amateur performer, or as he puts it, "I'm continuing my investigation of the boundaries between audience, collaborator, and maker in various venues." Those interrogated boundaries were very much in evidence in the work that resulted, *Still* (2012), his show at the Elizabeth Dee gallery in New York in which the audience became at once the performers-by-proxy and the photographic subjects that made up the actual exhibition. For McNamara, "the generosity of founder Jasper Johns and all the FCA donors not only provided me the freedom to push my practice further, but also gives me a sense of validation that comes from respected members of my field believing in me."

McNamara's performances and what he terms *situations* have been seen in a host of American and international museums and venues, including the Museum of Modern Art, the Whitney Museum of American Art, the Watermill Center, and Performa 09. His work is also included in the permanent collection of the Museum of Modern Art.

—MB

Paul Chan, 2006

"It was a moment of realizing what I had done with my earlier work was completed and over. It was time to start imagining my previous strengths as weaknesses and time to start anew." Visual artist Paul Chan had decided to make a break with what had become signature elements of his vividly colored, darkly chilling, cartoon animations when he received his Grant to Artists. Although using the same computer software, he "betrayed" his earlier work by draining his digital animations of their color and abandoning his precisely rendered, character-based scenes and custom-made screens in favor of more abstract, silhouetted shapes designed to be projected directly onto corners, walls, and the floor. "I had just completed the first work in this new vein—which later became '*1st ~~Light~~*'—and was starting to imagine them as a series. The grant gave me time to work and to live." Chan's FCA award helped him make the *2nd* and *3rd ~~Light~~* video installations. Ultimately, the series grew to be *The 7 ~~Lights~~*, arguably the artist's most significant body of work to date.

Chan also used his grant money to purchase audio-recording equipment to carry out a special Web project, "My Own Private Alexandria": "Audiobooks were really popular at the time, so I decided to create something similar out of texts that I loved or was confounded by. After all, who is going to make an audiobook of an essay by Susan Sontag or a Georges Bataille text? So I spoke my favorite texts into an audio recorder and posted these recordings as audio files on my Web site where anyone could listen to them."

Besides shows of *The 7 ~~Lights~~* at the New Museum and the Serpentine Gallery, Chan has had solo exhibitions at the Renaissance Society, Chicago; Stedelijk Museum, Amsterdam; Portikus, Frankfurt; the Hammer Museum, Los Angeles; and the Institute of Contemporary Art, Boston, among other venues. His work is included in many major museum collections, including the Museum of Modern Art and the Whitney Museum of American Art. —DS

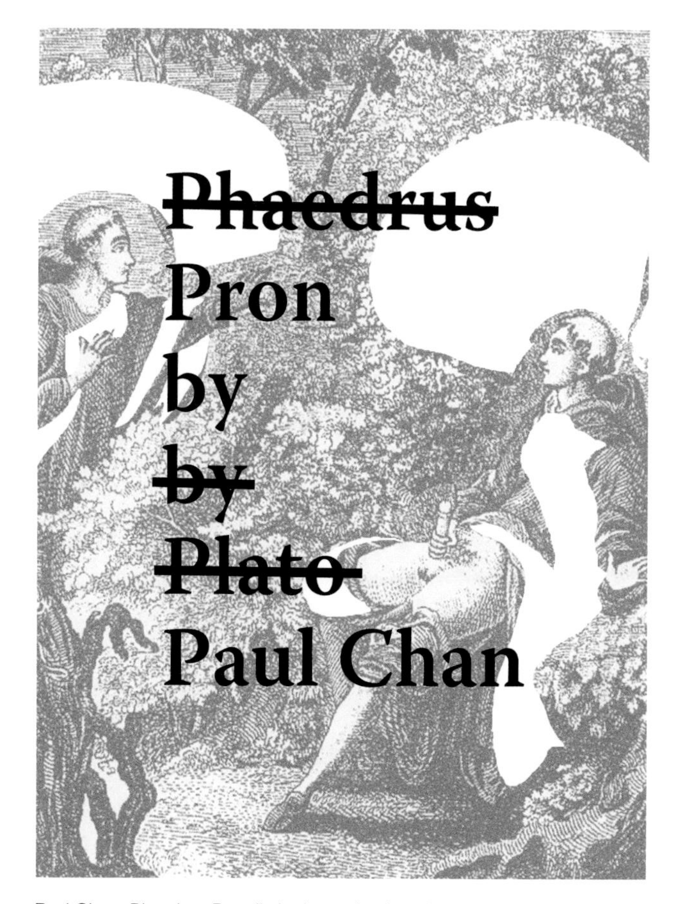

Paul Chan, *~~Phaedrus~~ Pron*, limited paperback and unlimited e-book, 424 pages, 2010. Courtesy the artist.

Miguel Gutierrez, *HEAVENS WHAT HAVE I DONE*, performance, Center for Performance Research, Brooklyn, 2010. Photo: Ian Douglas.

Miguel Gutierrez, 2010

"I know that many of my worthy colleagues in dance are trapped in a cycle of low expectations and the poverty-cum-volunteer economy of the dance world," says the choreographer and performer Miguel Gutierrez. "A grant like the FCA award is instrumental in helping recalibrate an artist's sense of self-worth and usefulness." The Grants to Artists award that Gutierrez received in 2010 allowed him to address urgent financial needs. "I paid off a large credit card bill that was completely crippling me. This was extraordinary. With the remainder of the grant I was relieved from having to be in a constant state of anxiety about my financial health. I literally breathed easier that year."

The FCA grant not only rebooted his relationship to credit cards but resulted in a new work, *HEAVENS WHAT HAVE I DONE*. Originally intended as a one-off performance, it "blossomed into one of the most successful pieces I've made in the past few years." *HEAVENS WHAT HAVE I DONE* has successfully toured throughout North and South America, Australia, and Europe since 2010. Describing his work as a form of hyperemotional honesty that "recalls the history of process-focused experimental dance while drawing on far-reaching influences," Gutierrez has drawn on a number of sources—from noise music and the spectacles of Las Vegas and Broadway to social and religious ritual and club and queer culture—to explore exuberant and ecstatic display.

"Each project involves a mix of ongoing and new collaborators, on both the performance and design side of the piece. In addition I also write poetry, short essays, and songs, some of which end up in my pieces." Gutierrez's work has been performed at venues across the United States and Europe, including Dance Theater Workshop; The Kitchen; DiverseWorks in Houston; and ImPulsTanz, Vienna; and Springdance in Utrecht. His most recent large-scale work, *And lose the name of action*, was commissioned by the Walker Art Center, the Maggie Allesee National Center for Choreography at Florida State University, and the Brooklyn Academy of Music in New York, and made its world premiere at the Walker in late 2012.
—MB

Sarah Michelson, 2008

"Is it possible to make a dance using traditional forms that is also contemporary?" This was a question choreographer Sarah Michelson posed for herself when she was developing her work *Dover Beach* and received news about her Grant to Artists. "The grant was absolutely crucial. It was how I managed to complete *Dover Beach*, which I created in Cardiff, Wales, with three eleven-year-old ballet students in the lead roles. I could otherwise never have afforded to travel there for each school holiday, for a year and half, to work with those girls."

Dover Beach marked a significant departure for Michelson. For the first time, she did not perform in her own work or collaborate with her regular group of performers. These changes allowed her to explore new themes. For instance, rather than draw on popular contemporary dance styles, as she had in her earlier work, Michelson mined more historical material. *Dover Beach* was built around deconstructing elements of late-nineteenth-century narrative ballet as well as Romantic notions of "Britishness." She found the new terrain especially rewarding: "The freedom of the grant meant that I could make a work that I loved, without any pressure of a result, and otherwise would not have made." Critically acknowledged as a milestone in the trajectory of Michelson's career, *Dover Beach* was presented at Chapter Arts Centre in Cardiff (2008) and The Kitchen in New York (2009).

Michelson has received commissions from several international institutions, including the Brooklyn Academy of Music, The Kitchen, P.S. 122, and the Whitney Museum of American Art, all in New York, as well as the Hebbel Theater, Berlin; the Walker Art Center, Minneapolis; On the Boards, Seattle; and the Lyon Opera Ballet, France. She has been the recipient of the Doris Duke Performing Artist Award, a Guggenheim Foundation Fellowship, an Alpert Award, and three New York Dance and Performance "Bessie" Awards. —DS

Sarah Michelson, *Dover Beach*, performance, The Kitchen, New York, 2009.

PHOTO: PAULA COURT

Young Jean Lee, *Songs of the Dragons Flying to Heaven*, performance, HERE Arts Center, New York, 2006. Photo: Carl Skutsch.

Young Jean Lee, 2006

In recent years, Young Jean Lee has been hailed as one of the best and most adventurous experimental playwrights of her generation. However, when she received her Grant to Artists in 2006, she was little known. As Lee recalls, "It was such a shock. It was the first recognition of anything that I ever got, and it changed my life. It marked me as an artist to pay attention to because of the other recipients who had won it in the past."

At that moment, Lee was in the middle of working on what would become her "breakout" play, *Songs of the Dragons Flying to Heaven*, which premiered at HERE Arts Center in New York that year. "I was writing at home, living in a squalid group apartment with roommates who had animals that I was allergic to and black mold growing in the bathroom. That phone call changed everything. I used all of the grant money for a down payment on an apartment. I could finally live and work, in peace and quiet, which made an immeasurable difference to my life."

A brazen satire of ethnic stereotypes and, as its subtitle declaims, "a show about white people in love," *Songs of the Dragons Flying to Heaven* enjoyed an incredibly successful run. Touring more than sixteen cities in the United States and abroad, it enabled Lee to quit her day job and focus on writing and directing full time.

Since then, Lee has continued to create a body of smart and funny works for the stage tackling difficult questions about cultural, racial, and gendered identities. She is the recipient of two Obie Awards, a 2010 Arts and Letters Award in Literature from the American Academy of Arts and Letters, a 2011 Guggenheim Foundation Fellowship, and an inaugural 2012 Doris Duke Performing Artist Award. She is currently under commission from Plan B Entertainment/Paramount Pictures, Lincoln Center Theater, Playwrights Horizons, and the Oregon Shakespeare Festival. —DS

Richard Maxwell, 2000

"I was at home in Greenpoint and got a phone call about a $25,000 award. My first thought," says playwright and director Richard Maxwell, "was that someone was getting me back. It was during a period when I was making a lot of prank calls." But the veracity of the call turned out to be enormously welcome. "I had just founded my own 501(c)(3), the New York City Players, in 1999 and had new administrative costs to contend with. We moved into an office where we had to pay rent and had started working with a managing director and producer who also needed to be paid. The timing of the award was ideal in helping manage the costs."

The transition involved with creating his own nonprofit organization was an important shift for Maxwell and his work. "With experimental theater, there is so much self-producing and coproducing that being on my own was not commercially viable. This route really made sense so we could apply for our own grants and raise money directly. Also, having an office—an actual place away from home where I could work—turned out to be very helpful to me."

Since the late 1990s, Maxwell has written and directed more than 28 plays, which have been performed in more than 20 countries. He has received numerous grants and awards, including an inaugural 2012 Doris Duke Performing Artist Award and two Obie Awards, for either writing or directing, as well as grants from the Guggenheim Memorial Foundation, Andrew W. Mellon Foundation, and the Lila Acheson Wallace Theater Fund, among others. His plays have been commissioned by Festival d'Automne, Paris; Project Arts Centre, Dublin; the Barbican Centre, London; the Wexner Center, Columbus; the Walker Art Center, Minneapolis; as well as P.S. 122, The Kitchen, and Soho Rep in New York. —DS

Richard Maxwell, *Boxing 2000*, performance, Present Company Theatorium, New York, 2000. Performers: Jim Fletcher, Lakpa Bhutia, and Robert Torres. Photo: New York City Players.

David Grubbs, 2006

Composer and musician David Grubbs recalls his Grant to Artists as "marvelously well-timed": "I had been doing music full time and touring constantly, playing concerts to make a living and never said no to an opportunity. But, that grant allowed me to travel less and stay close to home, which was what I really wanted to do because my son was just a year old."

It was also, he says, "incredibly welcome encouragement" to focus more on his experimental projects that might have less popular appeal. The project on which he was able to embark was "Souls of the Labadie Tract," a second collaboration with poet Susan Howe, based on her manuscript of the same name that was inspired by the story of the late-seventeenth-century Utopian sect the Labadists. The results were a lyrical and harrowing marriage of text and sound, with Howe reciting her manuscript and Grubbs on synthesizer and the *khaen*, a Laotian mouth organ, for both a CD recording (Blue Chopsticks, 2007) and live performances at numerous venues, including The Kitchen; the Walker Art Center, Minneapolis; and London's Southbank Centre.

Over his two-decade career as both an inventive experimental rock performer and new-music composer, Grubbs has released eleven solo albums and appeared on more than 150 commercially released recordings. A founding member of the groups Gastr del Sol, Bastro, and Squirrel Bait who has frequently performed with the Red Crayola, Grubbs has also created cross-disciplinary works with many visual artists, including Anthony McCall, Angela Bulloch, and Stephen Prina. In addition to performing at music venues all over the globe, he has also presented his work at the Solomon R. Guggenheim Museum, the Museum of Modern Art, the Tate Modern, and the Centre Pompidou. He is currently completing a book, *Records Ruin the Landscape: John Cage, the Sixties, and Sound Recording*, for Duke University Press. —DS

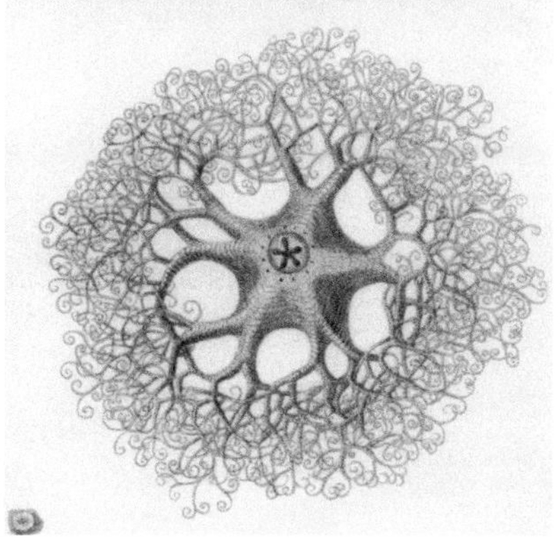

David Grubbs, CD cover image, *Souls of the Labadie Tract* (Blue Chopsticks), 2007.

Elizabeth Streb, *FLY*, performance by STREB, Joyce Theater, New York, 1997.

Elizabeth Streb, 1996

In 1996, when choreographer Elizabeth Streb received a Grant to Artists, she was already known for her physically demanding performances intermixing dance with elements of gymnastics and circus acrobatics. Still, she felt there was still much territory left to explore: "I wanted to fly," she says.

Indeed, her FCA-funded work attempted such a proposition. Appropriately titled *FLY*, the dance involved attaching a performer to an intricate system of counterweights that rendered the body almost weightless. In order to "fly," Streb explains, "it was necessary to rob the floor of its overruling quality—to create a situation where the floor has lost its hegemony."

Premiering at the Joyce Theater in 1997 (the same year Streb received a MacArthur Foundation "genius award"), *FLY* marked the first time in which the Streb company used its "hardware action gizmos" attachments, like the air float, that enable the performers to move in extreme and unconventional ways. As Streb reflects, "new moves become possible when the body is released from vertical constraints, and the audience is released, too, from its normal orientation to the dancers."

Streb, who also received FCA grants in 1981, 1985, 1988, and 1990, founded her own company in 1985. In 2003 she established S.L.A.M. (the STREB Lab for Action Mechanics) in Brooklyn, whose garage doors are regularly open to the public. Besides performances there, her company continues to appear worldwide. Although she had already received notable recognition for her work prior to her Grant to Artists—such as a Guggenheim Foundation Fellowship in 1987—Streb recalls the FCA award as "an enormous honor." "You are nominated by your peers and don't apply, and the legacy of whom you are associated with is so special."—DS

Tere O'Connor, 2001

"Perhaps the most memorable thing about receiving the award," recollects choreographer Tere O'Connor, "was attending the reception for the artists. It was incredible to meet the people that were there—the artists associated with the FCA and the other recipients—and to see all of this history of New York art in one room and feel a connection to this group of artists. Receiving this award was also an acknowledgment of understanding dance in a broader art context, which was inspiring and an overall vote of confidence that validated my own path that was moving both toward, and away from, dance."

The Grant to Artists was also extremely instrumental for O'Connor on a practical level. "I had a goal of raising the dancers' salaries," he says, "and this grant helped me to do that, which was enormously gratifying." At the time, O'Connor was working with an entirely new group of dancers, and it was an important crossover time: "I was working on a dance called *Winterbelly* in which I was trying to let go of text and storied elements that had been central to my last body of work and move back into abstraction. For this piece, I also started dancing again, after having stayed out of my work for a while." *Winterbelly* turned out to have a lengthy touring life: it premiered at Danspace Project in 2001 and then toured to the Yerba Buena Center for the Arts, San Francisco; the Walker Art Center, Minneapolis; and the Wexner Center, Columbus; among other venues.

O'Connor has created more than 35 works for his company, which has performed throughout the U.S., Canada, Europe, and South America. He was a 2009 United States Artist Rockefeller Fellow and has received a Guggenheim Foundation Fellowship, a Creative Capital award, and three New York Dance and Performance "Bessie" Awards for his work. An active dance educator, O'Connor has taught seminars at many prominent dance festivals and universities, and he is currently a professor at the University of Illinois at Urbana-Champaign. —DS

Top: Tere O'Connor, *The World is A Missing Girl*, performance, Dance Theater Workshop, New York, 2001. Photo: Paul Taylor. Bottom: Tere O'Connor, *Winter Belly*, performance, Danspace Project, New York, 2001. Photo: *Houston Chronicle*.

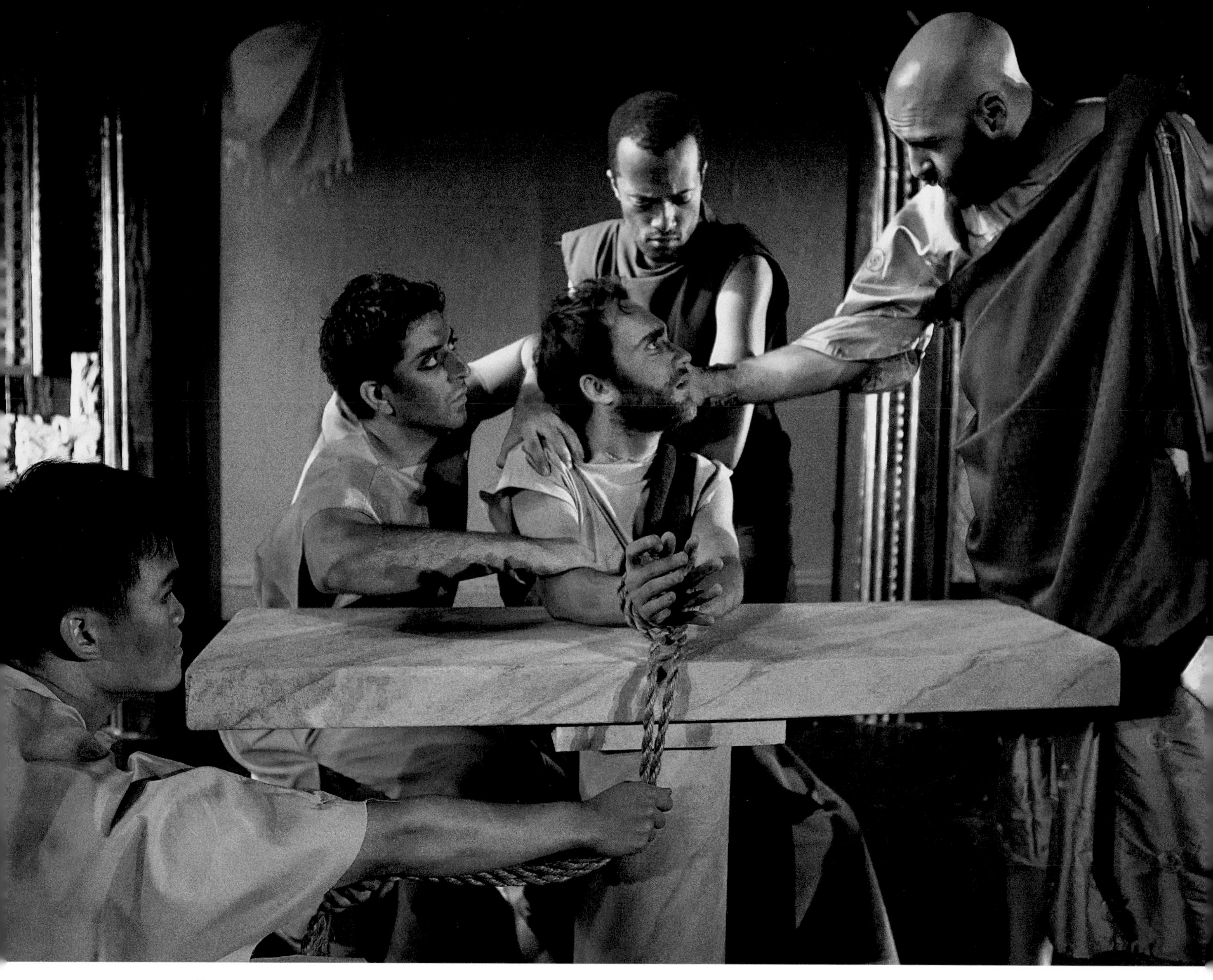

Thomas Bradshaw, *Job*, performance, Flea Theater, New York, 2012. Photo: Hunter Canning.

Thomas Bradshaw, 2012

"I've hoped for an FCA grant for years: some of my favorite theater artists won this grant before me," playwright Thomas Bradshaw says about the Grant to Artists he received in 2012. "I'm honored to have joined their ranks." A veteran of the off-Broadway circuit, Bradshaw writes provocatively about race, class, sex, violence, and religion in a way, critics note, that provides a much-needed shot in the arm to alternative theater. The FCA grant allowed him above all freedom from "obsessing about money all the time. That is one of the greatest gifts." As with many who receive a Grant to Artists, Bradshaw described himself as "in a precarious financial situation. The grant allowed me the freedom to do the work that I wanted to do. In other words, I didn't have to take work that I didn't find to be artistically fulfilling, just for the money."

Bradshaw, who teaches at Northwestern University, had previously received a 2009 Guggenheim Foundation Fellowship and a 2010 Prince Prize. With the FCA award, he was able to travel back and forth more frequently from Chicago to New York, where his play *Job*, an adaptation of the Book of Job, made its premiere last September at the Flea Theater. He is working on other new projects as well. "The artists that receive FCA awards don't tend to make commercial art," he says, "and it's even more important for this reason. This grant gives artists the freedom to relentlessly pursue their passion." Bradshaw's plays have been produced at regional theaters in New York as well as in Europe. He has received commissions from Soho Theatre in London, the Goodman Theatre in Chicago, Soho Rep, Partial Comfort Productions, and the Flea Theater in New York, and Theater Bielefeld in Germany. —MB

Elevator Repair Service, *The Select (The Sun Also Rises)*, performance, New York Theatre Workshop, New York, 2011. Performers, left to right: Matt Tierney, Lucy Taylor, Pete Simpson, Frank Boyd, and Susie Sokol. Photo: Rob Strong.

Elevator Repair Service, 2009

"Although we had already been making work for more than fifteen years," remembers John Collins, the founder and artistic director of the theater company Elevator Repair Service (ERS), "we had hardly received any formal recognition, so it was really meaningful to receive an FCA grant. It is such a serious and widely recognized accolade and also a great vote of confidence about where we might be going."

The happenstance of the award turned out to be "very well timed," Collins recalled, as ERS was about to begin an intensive rehearsal period for *The Select*. "Because the group creates work collaboratively, our process involves an extended period of development. The grant really helped to cover these rehearsal expenses as we geared up to complete the production." A theater work based on Hemingway's *The Sun Also Rises, The Select* premiered in Edinburgh in 2010, and then toured Europe and was presented at New York Theatre Workshop in 2011. *The Select* was notably the third and final installment of the "great novels" trilogy, staged readings appropriated verbatim from significant works of literature, that the company had staged, and its success secured a place for ERS's experimental work at prominent off-Broadway venues. Of the three, *The Select*, Collins explained, "was the only one that was truly an adaptation and a foray into a conventional theatrical form—which was, oddly, extremely new and risk-taking territory for us."

Founded in 1991, ERS is one of New York's most highly acclaimed experimental theater companies, focused on exploring and challenging the fundamentals of live performance. To date, they have created sixteen full-length productions, many of which have toured both nationally and internationally. The company has performed in New York at the Public Theater, New York Theatre Workshop, P.S. 122, the Performing Garage, and Soho Rep, and ERS performances have been presented in more than a dozen cities in the US and abroad. ERS has received numerous awards, including the Theatre Communications Group's Peter Zeisler Memorial Award for Outstanding Achievement; Lucille Lortel Awards for Alternative Theatrical Experience and Best Director; and an Obie Award for Sustained Excellence.
—DS

David Lang, 2002

When composer David Lang received his Grant to Artists, he was tackling what he called a "crazy idea" to write new music to the lyrics of the first Velvet Underground album. The album had obsessed him since his youth. "It changed my idea of what music was capable of," he recalls. "The record was terrifying—portraying a life of crime, danger, sex, and drugs—but it was the texts that I was scared of. They were so direct. I wanted to work with them to make new arrangements that could be compelling in a different context."

The FCA award, Lang said, was the only way he could have realized the work. "My life as a freelance composer means that I primarily work on commission. This Lou Reed project was different. It was what I wanted to do—not something someone asked me to do." The grant "was like commissioning money, but this time I got to decide what the project was going to be."

Since its 2002 debut with the Bang on a Can All-Stars, "Songs for Lou Reed" has undergone numerous incarnations. Five of the songs made up the score for *Amelia*, a work by Édouard Lock's dance ensemble La La La Human Steps that premiered at the Prague State Opera (2002), while the hauntingly spare version of Reed's *Heroin* evolved into an independent music-and-film project, with a commissioned video by artist Doug Aitken. Always experimenting with how to take classical music "to places where it does not normally go," Lang creates difficult-to-categorize compositions, ranging from orchestral, chamber, and solo works to large-scale operas. A cofounder and co-artistic director of the Bang on a Can ensemble, Lang has subsequently received numerous awards, including a 2008 Pulitzer Prize for Music and a 2010 Grammy Award. His work has been performed by the New York Philharmonic, the Boston Symphony, the Munich Chamber Orchestra, and the Kronos Quartet; and at such venues as the Brooklyn Academy of Music, Carnegie Hall, the Kennedy Center, and Lincoln Center. —DS

La La La Human Steps, *Amelia*, performance, 2002, music by David Lang (score: "Songs for Lou Reed"). Choreography and photo: Édouard Lock.

Neil Greenberg, *Part Three (Luck)*, performance, 92nd Street Y Harkness Dance Project at Playhouse 91, New York, 1998. Performer: Justine Lynch. Photo: Tom Brazil.

Neil Greenberg, 1997

"It was a total vote of confidence that came at an intense and confusing time," remembers choreographer Neil Greenberg about receiving his Grant to Artists: "I received the news right after my own first hospitalization due to an HIV-related illness, but it was also a moment when my artistic profile was looking up and when new medicines were available too. I was finishing one thread and trying out something new—both on the work front and on the health front."

With his grant, Greenberg was able to complete the final section of an extended trilogy of diaristic dances about love, friendship, illness, and loss in the time of AIDS. In these dances, Greenberg was experimenting with combining dance and projected written texts whereby "the dance is not a representation of the texts, but where the two run parallel to one another, so that it is up to the audience to interpret possible relationships." *Part Three* was performed at the 92nd Street Y Harkness Dance Center in 1998.

The grant also allowed Greenberg to begin investigating some new ideas about "dance noir" that looked at suspense films as points of departure. "I was interested in how with suspense films, for instance, information is parceled out a little bit at a time and wanted to figure out how to do that in dance terms. I was interested, though, not in narrative information, but in dance information, and how different lines of investigation feed into one another to construct meaning." The first in this new series was *This is What Happened*, which premiered in 1999 at P.S. 122. —DS

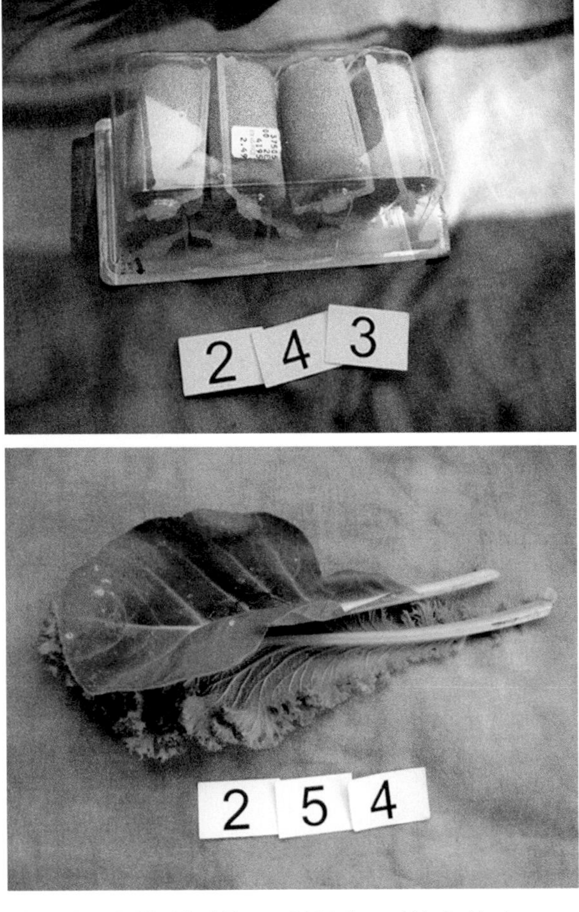

William Pope.L, *The Black Factory*, 2005, donated black objects # 0243 and # 0254. Courtesy the artist and Mitchell-Innes & Nash, New York. Photos: BF Crew.

William Pope.L, 2002

When William Pope.L received a Grant to Artists from the FCA in 2002, it came at a challenging time for the artist. His provocative and arduous performance-based art—which audaciously plumbs the nexus of race, authenticity, and the American-style free market—was self-funded and smaller in scale than he might have hoped, and it was also controversial enough that the grant the NEA had voted to award him in 2001 had been subsequently rescinded by the agency's director. The FCA grant was thus a show of support at a trying time, and it allowed him to work on the larger-scale projects that had been exceedingly difficult to realize.

The result of the 2002 grant was Pope.L's *The Black Factory*, an ambitious project in which a six-ton, 22-foot-long truck traveled from state to state making three tours over as many years, welcoming "visitors to bring us the cultural material that references blackness." Fitted out with a gift shop, a Web kiosk, an archive of "black objects," a sound system, and a "pulverization workshop," the roving installation made literal the artist's entrepreneurial description of a major aspect of *The Black Factory*: "By collecting and recycling (taking old ideas and objects and grinding them up to make new ideas and products), the BF *sells* the possibility for rethinking what makes Americans different." In practical terms, the grant allowed the project to employ and insure staff and extend its run, and it gave Pope.L the time to think about further extensions to the project—as he says, in retrospect, "the opportunity and permission to question the premises of my practice via undertaking a work that was ethically challenged."

The Black Factory forms a piece with Pope.L's parallel and ongoing *Distributing Martin* project, which the artist describes as "the secret distribution" of Martin Luther King Jr.'s "genetic material to force goodness upon the population," both attempts to shake complacent thinking about race and the preconceptions around "black art." Featured in the 2002 Whitney Biennial, Pope.L is the recipient of numerous honors, including a Guggenheim Foundation Fellowship and a United States Artists fellowship. He is currently on the faculty of the University of Chicago. —MB

Stephen Petronio, 1999

Choreographer Stephen Petronio recalls being at the Yerba Buena Center for the Arts in San Francisco premiering "Part I" of his work *Strange Attractors* when he received the phone call about his FCA award. "It was such incredible news. I had just spent so much money on developing 'Part I'—it was the first time I had commissioned high-level collaborators (Michael Nyman created the music and designer Tanya Sarne, the costumes)—and what I wanted to do most was to make 'Part II.' The grant allowed me to commission new collaborators and expand the work into a full-evening-length suite."

For *Strange Attractors, Part II*, Petronio commissioned a score from composer James Lavelle and a set by sculptor Anish Kapoor. To open the evening, he developed *Prelude*, including music by Placebo, with David Bowie, and costumes by Tara Subkoff/Imitation of Christ. The full-length work premiered at the Joyce Theater in 2000 and went on to Dance Umbrella in London and many other venues throughout Europe and America.

Strange Attractors was, in Petronio's words, "a real departure" in his work, a "transition between my rebel bad-boy days and being a more grown-up chorographer. I was becoming less enchanted with the promiscuity in the earlier work and was shifting away from those thematic interests to more abstract, formal concerns. I wanted to highlight a purer movement language that was distinctly my own."

Since this time, Petronio has continued to create work that fluidly integrates his dynamic choreography with new music, art, and fashion. He has received numerous accolades, including a Guggenheim Foundation Fellowship and an American Choreographer Award, and his company has received commissions by many of the world's leading theaters and festivals.

—DS

Stephen Petronio Company, *Strange Attractors*, performance, Joyce Theater, New York, 2000. Photo: Ellen Crane.

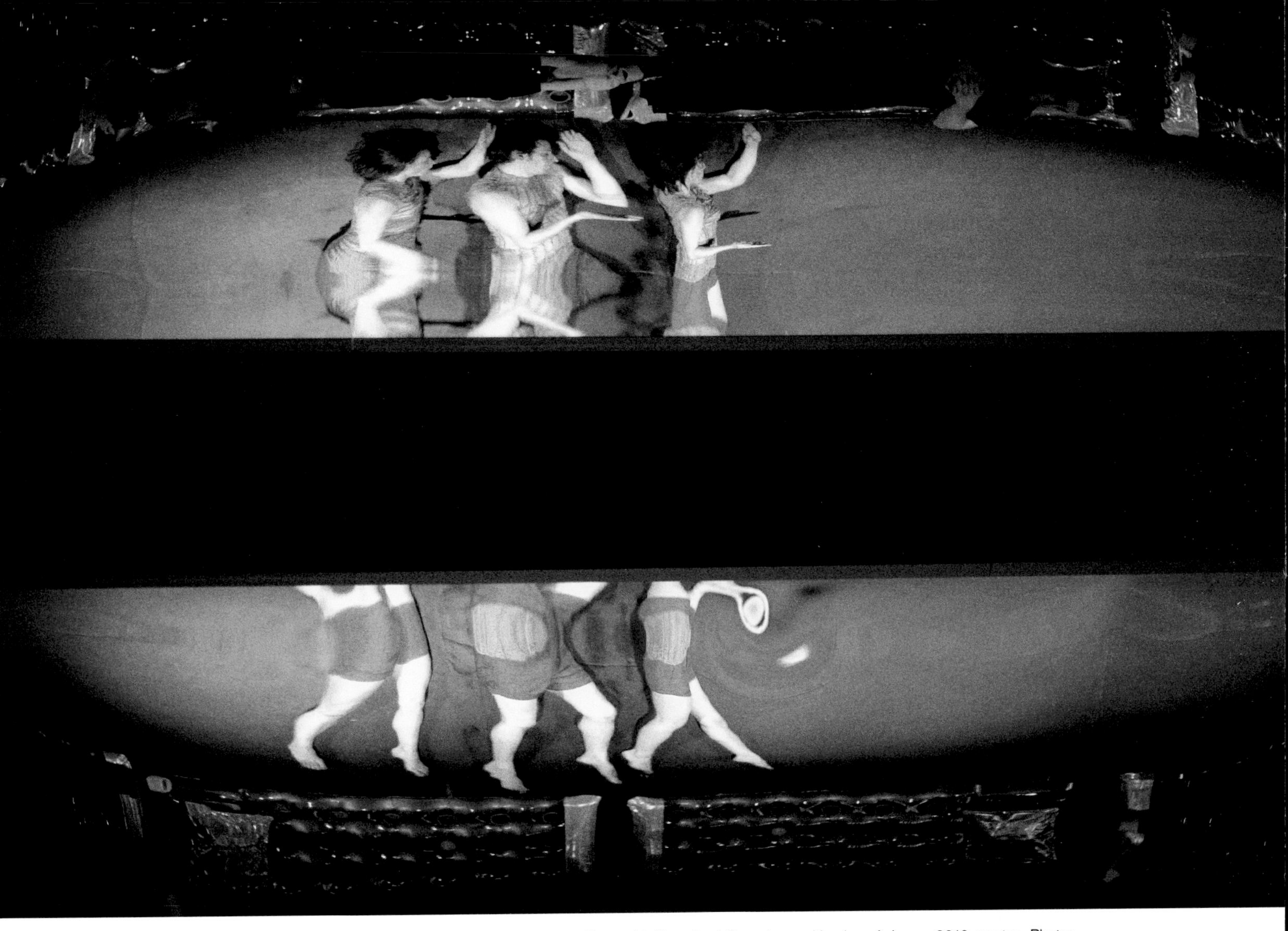

John Jasperse, *Prone*, performance, The Kitchen, New York, 2005. Performers: Eleanor Hullihan, Levi Gonzalez, and Luciana Achugar, 2010 grantee. Photo: Julieta Cervantes.

John Jasperse, 2003

"I wanted to use my practice as a means of discovery or change," says choreographer and dancer John Jasperse. "Sometimes it is really about reminding myself (or others) of things that I or we as a culture have lost touch with—of things that have been forgotten." When Jasperse received his Grant to Artists in 2003, he was drastically shifting his focus and pushing his work into a space of "extreme intimacy with a public." The work that resulted—*Prone*, a 75-minute performance with a score by fellow FCA grantee Zeena Parkins—"was based on an atypical visual perspective of the dancing body with spectators lying on air mattresses dispersed throughout the performing area and dancers performing around and over the audience." It represented a breakthrough in Jasperse's career, a radical alteration in his exploration of dance in the round.

"The funds from the FCA were crucial in giving a time of reflection and exploration for my thought process to grow," Jasperse recalls. "This was especially true of *Prone*, a project that had a maximum of 56 spectators at any one presentation. The project was relatively challenging from an economic perspective. I cannot stress enough how grateful I am for this support and how crucial it is to have funding of this nature that can allow artists to explore new thematic strands in their work."

As artistic director of his New York–based John Jasperse Company, founded in 1985, Jasperse has been at the forefront of choreography for the past two and a half decades. His work has been performed throughout the US and Europe, including such venues as the Venice Biennale, the Brooklyn Academy of Music, the Walker Art Center, Minneapolis, and Tanz im August in Berlin. He has received commissions from the Lyon Opera Ballet, the White Oak Dance Project, and Batsheva Dance Company. In addition to several New York Dance and Performance "Bessie" Awards, Jasperse has received multiple NEA grants, and he was awarded a Guggenheim Foundation Fellowship in 1998. —MB

Patricia Spears Jones, 1996

"I had been toiling in the vineyards of poetry for a while," recalls Patricia Spears Jones of her 1996 Grant to Artists. "I'd begun to think, I'm just not going to be one of those poets who get recognized. Then I get this phone call. I was stunned." Having just left a full-time job at the New Museum in order to devote herself more fully to her writing, Jones found the experience life-changing—it allowed her to take advantage of a residency at the Virginia Center for the Creative Arts, which she estimates she wouldn't have been able to afford without the grant. This led to even greater possibilities.

"After I got the grant, I bought a computer and paid off some debts, which is what every poet does. I was talking to another grant recipient, and I said, 'I have some money left over, and I'm thinking about doing something frivolous, like going to Paris.' And he looked at me sternly and said, 'It is *not* frivolous for a poet to go to Paris!' "

She took the advice and the trip, and the result registers throughout her *Femme du Monde* (Tia Chucha Press, 2006). A collection in which the lure of travel and the anxiety of displacement become dynamic conceits, *Femme du Monde* contains several souvenirs of what Jones describes as "luxuriating in my estrangement" in Paris. In the poem that provides the title to the book, her third, she writes: "Tired and cheered outside my American language, I am / puzzled with the battered glamour of this city / built for electric illuminations, swift flirtations, / as I follow the paths to dead poets shaped in solemn statuary / harboring the austere lawns of the Jardin du Luxembourg."

A poet and playwright whose critical writing has appeared in numerous magazines, including *BOMB Magazine*, *Essence*, and the *Village Voice*, Jones has been the recipient of an NEA Literature Fellowship and the Oscar Williams and Gene Derwood Award from the New York Community Trust as well as grants from the New York Foundation for the Arts and the Goethe-Institut. Her poetry has been widely anthologized, most recently in *Angles of Ascent: A Norton Anthology of Contemporary African American Poetry*. —EB

GHOSTS

He was filled with beauty, so filled he could not stop the shadows
from their walk around his horn, blasting cobwebs in the Fillmore's ceiling.

Somewhere dawn makes up for the night before, but he is floating.
Dead in the water. And yet, my lover tells me, he saw him shimmering.

As did others. It could have been the acid. Or fragmented harmonics.
His reed ancestral. This perilous knowledge. The band went home,

shivering. A girl threw roses in the water. Carnations, daisies. And bright red sashes.
Like ones the Chinese use for funeral banners. A drummer intoned chants

From the Orient. Police wrote up the news. Years later, my lover told me
Friends would hear the whisper, then a tone, full throttle from the wind.

Ghosts on Second Avenue, jazzmen in the falling stars.
If you catch one, your hands will glitter.

—Patricia Spears Jones

Wade Guyton, 2004

In 2004, Wade Guyton was an emerging artist who had just participated in the Whitney Biennial but still lacked a gallery. He was, in his words, "without any financial resources to speak of" to follow through on the idea he wished to pursue. Analogous to how he had been making what he refers to as drawings using his desktop computer, printer, and torn-out pages of old modern art and design books, he wondered: "How could I make painting, if I am not a painter?" A shift in scale and material support would clearly be necessary.

Guyton knew he wanted to use a similar no-hands approach to production, akin to his "inkjet printer drawings," and he had access to a large-scale printer that he shared with the artist Kelley Walker for their collaborative work. However, rather than use faux-canvas material specifically designed for the printer, Guyton wanted to employ a luxurious linen intended for oil painting. But he was "concerned about experimenting freely with such expensive material. The price of inks for the printer alone was prohibitive." With his Grant to Artists award, Guyton was able to purchase a large quantity of both, allowing him to investigate more fully the possibilities of these materials. Some of the very first paintings generated with his new setup became the basis for a show at the Hamburg Kunstverein in 2005—a show he describes as pivotal: "It set me on a course of exploration that still continues today."

Since the time of his Foundation grant, Guyton's career has swiftly taken off. He has been included in many significant group exhibitions and international biennials, and in October 2012, Guyton received his first midcareer survey at the Whitney Museum of American Art. —DS

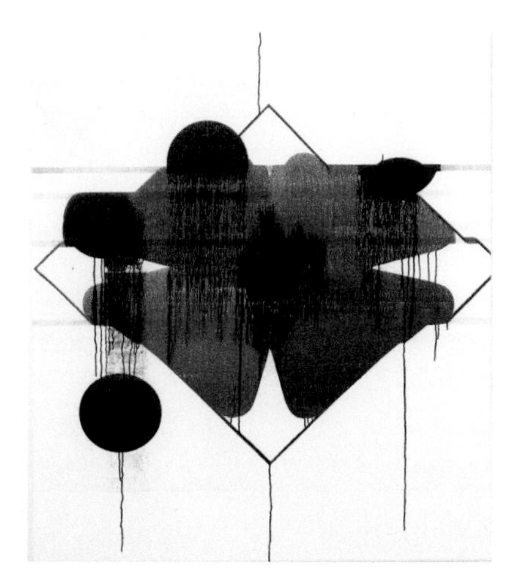

Wade Guyton, *Untitled*, 2005, Epson UltraChrome inkjet on linen, 39 ⅓" x 35". Courtesy the artist and Petzel Gallery, New York.

Timothy Greenfield-Sanders, *Cage, Cunningham, Johns Version 2*, silver gelatin print, 1989.

Chronology

Stacy Tenenbaum Stark
with contributions by Susan Rosenberg

Pre-1962

Jasper Johns and Robert Rauschenberg meet in late 1953 or early 1954. That winter Johns also meets John Cage, at a party at artist Sari Dienes's studio on West 57th Street following a concert at the music publishing house C.F. Peters. Johns meets Merce Cunningham in late January 1954 after a performance of Merce Cunningham and Dance Company at the Brooklyn Academy of Music. In December 1954 Johns helps Rauschenberg construct his first set for Cunningham's *Minutiae*. Johns assists Rauschenberg with most of his stage work through 1960.

In October 1955 there is an evening of Cunningham/Cage performances at Clarkstown High School in Rockland County, NY, organized by film director and avant-garde producer Emile de Antonio. In 1958 Johns, Rauschenberg, and de Antonio form Impresarios Inc. Each puts up $1,000 to finance and produce a 25-year retrospective concert of Cage's music at Town Hall on May 15, 1958. On February 16, 1960, Impresarios finances and produces an evening of the Merce Cunningham and Dance Company at the Phoenix Theatre on Second Avenue, the first full program given by the Cunningham company in New York since a performance at BAM in 1957.

1962

July

Jasper Johns, John Cage, and Robert Rauschenberg examine the possibility of funding a limited-engagement Merce Cunningham season at a Broadway venue. To offset the anticipated loss of more than $30,000 for a one-week run, Johns donates *Map* (1962), valued at $15,000, to the effort; Rauschenberg offers to contribute his *Overcast II* (1962), valued at $7,500; and Cage asks sculptor Richard Lippold to return *Five Variations within a Sphere (for John Cage)* (1947), valued at $10,000, a work the composer had previously given back to Lippold. The value of the three works comes to $32,500, an amount larger than is needed. Asked what to do with the remaining $2,500, Cunningham replies that other performers are "in the same boat" and should be helped. The group decides to expand the idea by establishing a foundation and inviting other artists to contribute work.

August

John Cage visits the new Pocket Theatre at

1

2

(1) John Cage and Merce Cunningham, Black Mountain College, North Carolina, 1953 Summer Institute in the Arts. Photo: Frank Jones. (2) Robert Rauschenberg and Jasper Johns, Pearl Street, New York, c.1954. Photo: Rachel Rosenthal.

Third Avenue and Thirteenth Street, owned by Lewis Lloyd and Arthur Conescu. The 190-seat off-Broadway theater will open in February 1963. Lloyd had met Cage and Merce Cunningham by late 1960 or early 1961 while his wife, dancer Barbara Dilley, was taking classes at the Cunningham studio. (She will join the company in mid-1963.) Cage invites Lloyd to work on a planned Broadway season for Merce Cunningham and Dance Company. Lloyd and his attorney, Alfred Geller, join Cage, Johns, and Rauschenberg in the planning. It is quickly realized that a commercial arrangement will lose money, so Geller investigates incorporating as a nonprofit foundation. A number of meetings are held throughout the fall.

November 20

The Foundation for Contemporary Performance Arts, Inc. (FCPA), files for incorporation. Members of the corporation include Jasper Johns, age 32; John Cage, 50; Lewis Lloyd, 24; Alfred Geller, 31; Elaine de Kooning, 44; and David Hayes, a contemporary art collector and friend of Johns's, about 30. (Rauschenberg is uninterested in becoming involved as a director.) The certificate, filed on November 20, is recognized by the New York State Department of Education on December 28 and approved by the state on January 4, 1963. The purposes of the Foundation are given as: "To cultivate, promote, foster, sponsor, develop and encourage the understanding of, public interest in and support of performances of a contemporary nature in the fields of music, dance and drama; to promote and encourage talent and ability in composition and creation of, as well as performance of, works in each of said fields through commissions for new and original works, awards and scholarships or grants to existing organizations active in these fields; to provide a training ground to develop playwrights, composers, choreographers, performers, designers, musicians, technicians and the like in each of these fields; to institute and organize workshops where artists, writers, dancers, actors, painters, designers, musicians, can meet, study, discuss and develop techniques in each of these fields; to give recognition to experiments and achievements in each of these fields through citations, awards, scholarships and grants to individual writers, performers, organizations and the like." The articles also state that the Foundation is "not organized for profit."

November 23, 26, and 28

Telegrams are sent to 60 artists inviting them to a cocktail party on November 30 at the Allan Stone Gallery to explain the intention of the Foundation and ask for donations of works. It reads: "Foundation for Contemporary Performance Arts now being established to subsidize dance, music and other theatre events. . . . Foundation resources to be derived from tax-exempt gifts of major works of art. Questions will be answered by lawyer at party. First project to present Merce Cunningham and Dance Company Broadway Engagement. de Kooning, Graves, Johns, Lippold, Rauschenberg already committed. Desire your participation. First exhibition to be given soon."

November 30

About 25 to 30 artists attend the cocktail party. Jasper Johns and Alfred Geller explain their plans and ask those in attendance to donate works.

1963

January 9

The first "membership" meeting of the Foundation for Contemporary Performance

Founding board of directors: (1) Lewis Lloyd, Brooklyn Academy of Music, New York, c.1969. Photo: James Klosty. (2) John Cage, 225 East Houston Street, New York, c. 1968. Photo: Roberta Bernstein. (3) Elaine de Kooning, c. 1959–60. (4) Jasper Johns, 340 Riverside Drive, New York, 1964. Photo: Mark Lancaster. (5) Alfred Geller, 1976.

1

2

3

4

5

Arts, Inc., is held. Elected to the board of directors are John Cage, Elaine de Kooning, Alfred Geller, David Hayes, Jasper Johns, and Lewis Lloyd. Cage is elected president and Lloyd secretary and treasurer. Jill Jakes, 28, is hired as part-time secretary for the Foundation; she will later become a director. Johns moves that the FCPA apply for tax exemption. A formal motion is made "to have the show of paintings at the Allan Stone Galleries late in February 1963."

February 25

The Foundation's first benefit exhibition, "Exhibition and Sale of Works Donated by Artists," opens February 25 at the Allan Stone Gallery, 48 East 86th Street, New York, where it will remain on view until March 2. At what is perhaps the earliest instance of a benefit exhibition, in which artworks are donated to be sold for fund-raising purposes, 67 artists contribute 69 gifts of painting, sculpture, and works on paper, including Norman Bluhm, Lee Bontecou, George Brecht, Chryssa, Elaine de Kooning, Willem de Kooning, Sari Dienes, Jim Dine, Marcel Duchamp, Öyvind Fahlström, Sam Francis, Robert Goodnough, Morris Graves, Philip Guston, Al Held, Robert Indiana, Jasper Johns, Alex Katz, Ellsworth Kelly, Frederick Kiesler, Roy Lichtenstein, Richard Lippold, Marisol, Robert Morris, Robert Motherwell, Barnett Newman, Claes Oldenburg, Richard Pousette-Dart, Robert Rauschenberg, Ad Reinhardt, Larry Rivers, James Rosenquist, George Segal, Saul Steinberg, Frank Stella, Elaine Sturtevant, Wayne Thiebaud, Jack Tworkov, Andy Warhol, Jack Youngerman, and others. (See Appendix H for complete checklist.) Johns installs all the works except the Lippold, which the sculptor himself installs. In lieu of artwork, Mark Rothko makes a $1,000 contribution. The total value of the donated work at the time is more than $134,000.

Many paintings have Cunningham-related themes: Rosenquist's *The Promenade of Merce Cunningham* (1963); Warhol's *Merce* (1963); Elaine de Kooning's *Merce Cunningham* (1963); and Johns's *Map* (1962), which includes the name of Carolyn Brown, a founding member of the Cunningham company (Johns originally planned to use her picture, taken in a photo booth, but did not like the way it looked and wrote "machine photo Carolyn Brown" down the left-hand side instead).

Marcus Ratliff, 26, designs the exhibition poster, which features one figure for each donating artist. The Statue of Liberty image, which Ratliff borrows from an *Encyclopaedia Britannica* entry, will become the motif that the Foundation uses to this day.

Articles on the benefit appear in the February or March issues of *Arts*, *Art News*, *Arts Management*, *Art Voices*, *Dance Magazine* (see March 8 entry), and *The New Yorker*.

By the close of the exhibition, fifteen works sell: those by Bontecou, Duchamp, Graves, Johns, Ibram Lassaw, Lichtenstein, Richard Lindner, Marisol, Morris, Newman, Rauschenberg, Reinhardt, Rosenquist, Sigrid Spaeth, and Stella, totaling $34,685. After the close of the exhibition, a Sam Francis work also sells. Many remaining works are reclaimed, but most remain in the possession of the Foundation. A number will be sold over the next two years.

The exhibition firmly establishes the Foundation's roots in the community of artists.

March 8

Merce Cunningham appears on the cover of *Dance Magazine*: "Merce Cunningham Comes to Broadway." A feature article, "Paintings for Sale: Profits for Performers," describes the Foundation's goals and reproduces several works from the benefit exhibition. "Breaking

Artworks donated to first FCPA benefit exhibition: (6) Robert Morris, *Metered Bulb*, 1962, assemblage with lightbulb and meter, 18" x 8" x 8 ½". (7) Chryssa, *Unmailed Letter*, 1950, plaster relief mounted in box frame, 24 ½" x 27 ½" x 5". (8) James Rosenquist, *The Promenade of Merce Cunningham*, 1963, oil on canvas, 70" x 60". (9) Marcel Duchamp, *Box in a Valise*, 1963, assemblage with wood, cloth, and paper, 16" x 14 ½" x 3".

6

7

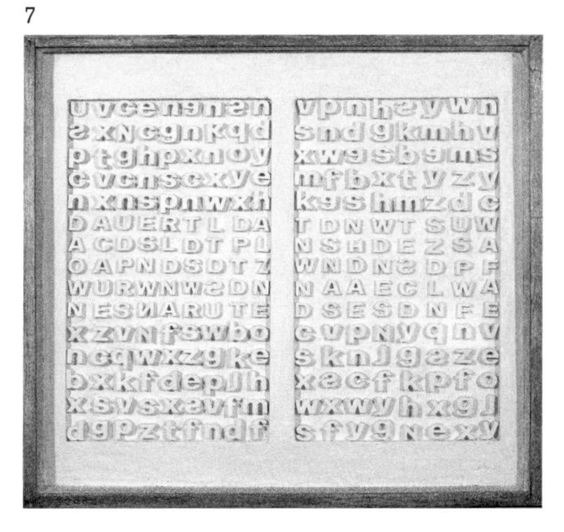

8

9

all tradition, abstract painters and sculptors have, in recent years, found themselves in a state of actual affluence. Sympathetic to the dissimilar plight of their colleagues in the performing arts—who can sometimes get financial assistance from foundations for research and preparation, but almost never for presentation—they have come up with an unprecedented offer of help."

The FCPA takes out an ad in *Dance News* that reads "1963 Spring Season at a Broadway Theatre to be Announced."

April 10
The first official meeting of the board of directors is held. Jasper Johns formally proposes that the Foundation "sponsor a one- or two-week Broadway season for Merce Cunningham Dance Group." John Cage further proposes that the board "consider sponsoring a Town Hall Concert of the music of Morton Feldman and Earle Brown and that the Foundation commission two works by both of the above Composers to be presented at the concert." David Hayes suggests that a grant be made to Judson Memorial Church for its dance performance programs. Thus, the Foundation's first grants are made, $1,000 apiece to Feldman, 37, and Brown, 36, for the commissioned works; and $500 to Judson Memorial Church for the nascent Judson Dance Theater and for the purchase of lights and permanent stage sets.

June 10
Choreographer James Waring organizes a Foundation benefit titled "The Pocket Follies," a revue of performance artists, at Lewis Lloyd's Pocket Theatre, 100 Third Avenue. Dances, skits, and "play-lets" are performed. The program consists of: Overture by The Pocket Follies Academic Festival A Cappella Group; performances and dances by George Brecht, *Transformation Artist*; Trisha Brown, *Chanteuse Excentrique Americaine*; David Gordon, *Honey Sweetie Dust Dance*, with Valda Setterfield; Fred Herko and Michael Malcé, *Cleanliness Event, with Poo-Poo Cushion Music*; Ray Johnson, *Third Nothing* (with his pet skunk Petunia); Jill Johnston and Robert Morris, *New Poses Plastiques*; Alan Marlowe, *Song Stylist*; John Herbert McDowell, "Three Pas de Deux" (from *Nine Pas de Deux & Finale*) and *Finaletto*, with Trisha Brown, Ruth Emerson, and Yvonne Rainer; Aileen Passloff, *Boa Constrictor*; and Yvonne Rainer, "Person Dance" (from *Dance for Fat Man, Dancer, and Person*); plays by Ruth Krauss, *A Beautiful Day*, directed by Remy Charlip, with Viola Farber; N.F. Simpson, *OH*, with Christine Pickles and David Vaughan; and A *Compendium of Everyone's Remarks,* Act II, overheard and made-up statements compiled and directed by James Waring, with Valda Setterfield, Ruth Sobotka, Gus Solomons, David Vaughan, and Joanna Vischer; and a musical finale, "The Love Parade," with Carolyn Brown, Trisha Brown, Viola Farber, Barbara Dilley, Sandra Neels, Yvonne Rainer, Arlene Rothlein, Valda Setterfield, Ruth Sobotka, David Vaughan, and Joanna Vischer.

Robert Rauschenberg, listed on the program as performing *Prestidigitator Extraordinary*, is a no-show.

Yvonne Rainer recalls: "Trisha Brown and I danced in a piece choreographed by James Waring. One at a time, a succession of women each made an entrance while David Vaughan sang 'A Pretty Girl Is Like a Melody.' I wore a tuxedo and Trisha wore a bikini. I found it pretty effete. Another event on the program was a duet by Robert Morris and Jill Johnston. All I remember about it was their flooding the stage with a bucket of water, which upset the rest of the participants greatly."

The event nearly sells out. With tickets at $1, $2, and $3, box office receipts are

1

PHOTO: PETER MOORE

(1) Judson Dance Theater, *Concert of Dance #8*, performance, Judson Memorial Church, New York, June, 25, 1963. Pictured: Judith Dunn, "SpeedLimit." Performer: Robert Morris. (2) Jill Johnston (pictured) and Robert Morris, *New Poses Plastiques*, performance, "The Pocket Follies," FCPA benefit, Pocket Theatre, New York, June 10, 1963. (3) Advertisement in *The Village Voice* for "New Music at The Pocket Theatre," FCPA benefits on August 19 and 26, and September 9, 1963. (4) Max Neuhaus, performing on marimba in Joseph Byrd's *Water Music*, "New Music at the Pocket Theatre," FCPA benefit, Pocket Theatre, New York, August 26, 1963. (5) Fred Herko, Edward Boagni, Philip Corner, and James Waring, "New Music at the Pocket Theatre," FCPA benefit, Pocket Theatre, New York, August 19, 1963.

2

PHOTO: PETER MOORE

$464.64; less expenses, the Foundation nets $215.26.

July 2

Robert Rauschenberg's *Overdraw*, donated to the Foundation in June, sells to Victor and Sally Ganz for $8,500, with the proceeds presumably intended to be used for the Broadway season.

August 8

Lewis Lloyd, who has become Merce Cunningham's business manager, informs company members that the Broadway season has been canceled.

August 19

The first of three "New Music at the Pocket Theatre" events to benefit the Foundation, all organized by John Cage, is held. The program consists of: La Monte Young, *Improvisation*, performed by Young, sopranino saxophone, and Marian Zazeela, voice drone; *2 Sounds;* and *Improvisation*, performed by Young and Zazeela; John Cage, *Suite for Toy Piano*, performed by Edward Boagni, piano; Al Hansen, *Alice Denham in 48 Seconds: Percussion Piece*, performed by Edward Boagni, George Brecht, Philip Corner, Malcolm Goldstein, Al Hansen, Fred Herko, John Herbert McDowell, James Waring, and La Monte Young, percussion; John Herbert McDowell, *Tragic Jelly and Slumber Music for Ratter and Miranda*, performed by Philip Corner, trombone; James Waring, mandolin; and Edward Boagni and Fred Herko, percussion; George Brecht, *Exit Music, Comb Music, and Dance Music*, performed by Fred Herko; and Edward Boagni, *СЛОН (That's not a butterfly, that's an elephant!)*, performed by Fred Herko, flute; Malcolm Goldstein, violin; and Max Neuhaus, percussion.

Lewis Lloyd recalls, "nobody came." Only 35 $2.50 tickets are sold. Total ticket sales are $84.60.

August 22

At the second meeting of the board of directors, John Cage explains that the recommendation to sponsor a Broadway season for the Cunningham dance company cannot be fulfilled as the Winter Garden venue is no longer available. (The New York newspaper strike from December 1962 to March 1963 led to a shutdown of Broadway theaters, and its resolution had created a booking backlog.) Jasper Johns suggests that, in lieu of the Broadway season, "the Foundation assist in the sponsoring of a world tour" for the company. The board agrees to subsidize the production of a booklet for the company. By the end of 1963, the Foundation will fund nearly $1,800 of the company's expenses, including advertising and the design, photography, and printing of the brochure.

The board also considers requests for funding from the Paper Bag Players and Judson Memorial Church. A $500 grant is subsequently made to the Paper Bag Players, a nonprofit children's theater group founded in 1958 by Judith Martin, 44, and former Cunningham dancer Remy Charlip, 34.

August 26

The second "New Music at the Pocket Theatre" FCPA benefit, a concert featuring contemporary American music, is held. The program consists of: Joseph Byrd, *Densities 2*, performed by Malcolm Goldstein, violin; Arthur Layzer, clarinet; La Monte Young, sopranino saxophone; Max Neuhaus, marimba; Philip Corner, conductor. Joseph Byrd, *Water Music*, performed by Max Neuhaus, percussion. Philip Corner, *High Contrast*, performed by Philip Corner, harpsichord. Joseph Jones, *Percussion for Five*. James Tenney, *Ergodos/2//3/*.

3

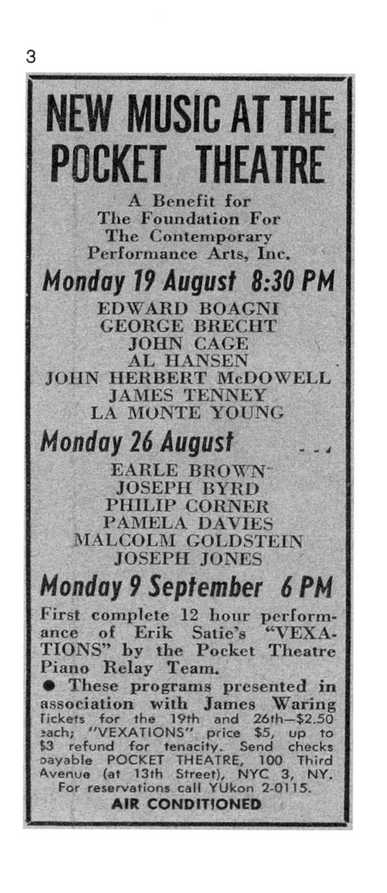

NEW MUSIC AT THE POCKET THEATRE

A Benefit for The Foundation For The Contemporary Performance Arts, Inc.

Monday 19 August 8:30 PM

EDWARD BOAGNI
GEORGE BRECHT
JOHN CAGE
AL HANSEN
JOHN HERBERT McDOWELL
JAMES TENNEY
LA MONTE YOUNG

Monday 26 August

EARLE BROWN
JOSEPH BYRD
PHILIP CORNER
PAMELA DAVIES
MALCOLM GOLDSTEIN
JOSEPH JONES

Monday 9 September 6 PM

First complete 12 hour performance of Erik Satie's "VEXATIONS" by the Pocket Theatre Piano Relay Team.

● These programs presented in association with James Waring

Tickets for the 19th and 26th—$2.50 each; "VEXATIONS" price $5, up to $3 refund for tenacity. Send checks payable POCKET THEATRE, 100 Third Avenue (at 13th Street), NYC 3, NY.
For reservations call YUkon 2-0115.

AIR CONDITIONED

4

PHOTO: PETER MOORE

5

PHOTO: PETER MOORE

Malcolm Goldstein, *Ludlow Blues*, performed by Arthur Layzer, clarinet; La Monte Young, sopranino saxophone; Philip Corner, trombone.

Tickets are $2.50 each; 28 tickets are sold, raising $66.08.

September 9–10

"New Music at the Pocket Theatre," the third Foundation benefit at the Pocket Theatre, is held. Organized by John Cage, it presents the first complete performance of Erik Satie's *Vexations* (c. 1893), played by a team of pianists. A single-page composition comprising a short theme with two harmonizations, the piece is to be repeated 840 times. Starting at 6:00 PM, the performance spans more than eighteen hours, ending at 12:40 PM on September 10. The Piano Relay Team includes Cage, John Cale, David Del Tredici, MacRae Cook, Philip Corner, Viola Farber, Joshua Rifkin, James Tenney, David Tudor, Christian Wolff, and Robert Wood, rotating in twenty-minute segments, with two reserve pianists.

Tickets are $5. The concert is advertised with a "tenacity refund": for every fifteen minutes a patron spends at the concert, five cents of the ticket price are refunded, with a twenty-cent bonus at the end of the performance. Karl Schenzer, an actor with the Living Theatre who is among a handful of people who stay for the entire concert and receive full refunds, shouts "Encore!" at the end.

The concert receives considerable coverage in the press, including the front page of *The New York Times* (which sends a team of eight critics to the event, one of whom, Howard Klein, fills in as a pianist when a member of the relay team misses his slot). Other coverage includes *France-Amérique*, the *New York Herald Tribune*, the *New York Post*, the *New York World-Telegram and Sun*, *Newsday*, *Newsweek*, *Sovetskaya Kultura*, *Time*, and *The New Yorker*. United Press and Associated Press also send reporters, and various radio stations record the event.

Aside from many reporters in attendance, 42 tickets are sold, raising $177.30.

September 23

A $200 grant is made to Judson Memorial Church for a dance concert featuring Yvonne Rainer, 28 (see 1966 Yvonne Rainer entry).

October 11

Organized and produced by the Foundation, "Music for Orchestra and Chorus by Morton Feldman and Earle Brown" is presented at Town Hall, 123 West 43rd Street, in New York. The Contemporary Chamber Ensemble, a group assembled for the event and conducted by Brown and Arthur Weisberg, and the Brandeis University Chamber Chorus, directed by Alvin Lucier, perform, with soloists David Tudor and John Cage, piano; Matthew Raimondi, violin; and Max Neuhaus, percussion. The program consists of three world premieres, commissioned by the Foundation (*Vertical Thoughts* and *Straits of Magellan* by Feldman and *From Here* by Brown), and the New York premieres of Feldman's *For Franz Kline* and *The Swallows of Salangan* and Brown's *Pentathis*. Brown's *December 1952* and *Available Forms I* complete the program. The concert marks the first time the work of both composers is presented at a major venue in New York.

Interest is only moderate; in a 1,495-seat theater, 364 tickets are sold. Priced at 99¢, $2.10, and $3.20—with one ticket selling at $50—box office receipts are $800.26.

Largely favorable articles are published in the *New York Herald Tribune*, *The New York Times*, and *The Village Voice*, both before and after the concert.

1

10 Pianists Play Same Piece 840 Times—It's 'Vexations'

By LES DENNIS

A musical work too long to put on the longest long-play- at 6 p.m. last night at the Pocket Theater, Third Ave. and 13th St. By mid-morning today the audience ... A crisis developed when one of the pianists, who played in 20-minute relays, failed to show up for the 10 a.m. shift

(1) Review of *Vexations*, *New York World-Telegram and Sun*, September 10, 1963. (2) Alvin Lucier, conducting the Brandeis Chamber Chorus, c. 1965. (3) Barbara Dilley and Robert Rauschenberg at "Feldman/Brown" concert, Town Hall, New York, October 11, 1963. (4) Merce Cunningham and Dance Company promotional brochure/program. Design by Marcus Ratliff. (5) French promotional poster, Merce Cunningham and Dance Company, world tour, 1964. (6) Merle Marsicano, 1963.

2

3

PHOTO: PETER MOORE

October 15
At the third meeting of the board of directors, it is reported that the Feldman/Brown concert production expenses were nearly $8,000. The board reviews and approves a $500 request for funds from choreographer Merle Marsicano, 40, to present a new work, but it is suggested that no further grants be made until the Foundation receives its tax-exempt status.

1964

April 11
Following the model of the Foundation for Contemporary Performance Arts, Inc., the Cunningham Dance Foundation incorporates, becoming the first nonprofit foundation in the field of modern dance.

May 5
At the fourth meeting of the board of directors, grants are proposed for the Cunningham dance company's world tour in the amounts of $2,500 to cover pre-departure costs and $17,241 for air-travel costs. Lewis Lloyd states that an additional $45,000 will be required to finance all the costs of the tour. The directors agree that "additional efforts will be made to sell paintings to raise these funds."

To support this effort Rauschenberg donates *Round Sum*, on May 1, which is sold by June 1964 to the Woodward Foundation for $7,000. Also in May, Mary Sisler, mother of FCPA director David Hayes, purchases Richard Lippold's sculpture from the Foundation for $10,000. It is not known if other paintings are sold.

The board authorizes the underwriting of a second printing of the Cunningham brochure, which will be sold as a program at their performances to raise money for the tour. In all, the Foundation will provide nearly $34,000 over the course of 1964 in grants and other subsidies to the Cunningham dance company. These are the only grants made in 1964.

June 3
The Merce Cunningham and Dance Company world tour begins in Paris. The entourage comprises sixteen people, including Cunningham, artistic director Robert Rauschenberg, musical director John Cage, and several others associated with the Foundation: FCPA director Lewis Lloyd, who shares administrative duties of the company and the tour with David Vaughan; dancer Steve Paxton and composer David Tudor, both of whom will later receive FCPA grants; and dancers Carolyn Brown and Viola Farber, who will both later serve as FCPA directors. The tour lasts six months and includes performances in Strasbourg, Paris, Vienna, Cologne, London, Stockholm, Helsinki, Warsaw, East Berlin, Bombay, Delhi, Bangkok, Tokyo, and elsewhere. The tour firmly establishes the company's international reputation.

June 22
The Foundation receives 501(c)(3) tax-exempt status.

December 15
Stating that his involvement with the FCPA was not relevant to his legal practice, Alfred Geller steps down from the board at the fifth meeting of the board of directors. He later becomes a well-known agent for various television news figures. Jasper Johns is elected president and chairman and remains so through the present.

It is noted that the funds of the Foundation are almost depleted and the directors are asked to "give serious thought to methods of additional fund raising projects."

4

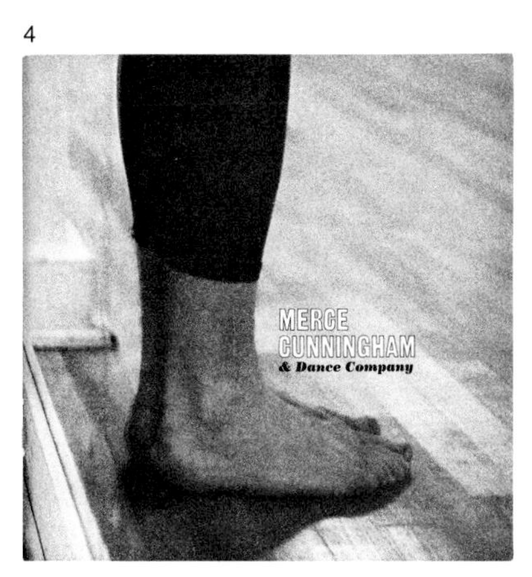

5

6

1965

January 12

"John Cage with David Tudor Present a Performance of Cage's *Variations IV*," a concert benefit for the Foundation, is held at Feigen/Palmer Gallery in Los Angeles. Largely underwritten by music patron Betty Freeman, this is thought to be Cage's first concert in a gallery setting. He presents a work that is part of his *Variations* series of "indeterminate" music, which originally premiered in Los Angeles at UCLA in July 1963. The concert takes place across two rooms—Cage in one, Tudor, 39, in the other, each playing a mix of recordings. Cage's score, in addition to a sheet of music, includes a series of black dots on a white background, which serves as a sort of map for the instruments and sound equipment.

The event draws a few hundred people, many of whom do not pay. A small number of Los Angeles art and music patrons contribute at least $205.

January 21

Included on the agenda of the sixth meeting of the board of directors are the "Sale of works of art to be contributed by California Artists; the Presentation of Show Drawings, a Series of Lectures, a Request for works of art including prints, lithographs, etc. and the Collecting of musical manuscripts from composers [to be sold] to benefit the Foundation." Elaine de Kooning suggests that "a letter be sent to all Artists who had previously submitted works to the Foundation requesting additional submissions of paintings and photographs." It is agreed that "75% of all net proceeds be retained as operating capital until $100,000 [has] been accumulated." The board, pending receipt of additional funds, approves grants of $500 apiece to 31-year-old Peter Schumann's Bread and Puppet Theater (founded 1963) for street performances in low-income urban areas and to percussionist-composer Max Neuhaus, 25.

John Cage begins to solicit donations of musical manuscripts with the intention of selling them as a collection to benefit the FCPA and for possible inclusion in a book. He sends hundreds of letters of requests to composers, visual artists, and writers.

July 10

Original board member Lewis Lloyd announces he will resign from the Foundation board and join the Cunningham board. Jill Jakes is nominated to fill his vacancy on the board and remains secretary; she will serve on the board until 1971. Lloyd goes on to manage the Cunningham Dance Foundation (CDF) with David Vaughan through the end of 1968, taking the company on international tours in 1966 and 1968 as well as handling the domestic tours. Lloyd holds other jobs at the same time, working in various capacities for the American Dance Theater, the Brooklyn Academy of Music, and the Festival Orchestra. After 1968, Lloyd resigns from CDF to oversee the dance programming at BAM, eventually becoming its general manager. Later, he will become program director for the performing arts at the New York State Council on the Arts.

September 28

At the eighth meeting of the board of directors, David Hayes, a member of the founding board, resigns. Swedish-born Billy Klüver, 37, an electrical engineer with Bell Labs, is elected to fill the vacancy (he resigns the following year). Jasper Johns reports that "the California Artists Exhibition was canceled due to lack of support from California Artists in the Project." Emphasis will be placed instead on the show of drawings

1

PHOTO: FRED W. MCDARRAH/PREMIUM ARCHIVE/GETTY IMAGES

2

3

to be held at three New York galleries in December 1965. The board also discusses preliminary arrangements for the "Lecture Series to be held at the 92nd Street YMHA in the Spring of 1966."

December 14
The Foundation's second benefit exhibition, "Drawings," opens simultaneously at Leo Castelli, 4 East 77th Street, through January 5, 1966; Tibor de Nagy Gallery, 29 West 57th Street, through December 30; and Kornblee Gallery, 58 East 79th Street, through January 5, 1966. The three-venue show, which Jasper Johns installs in two of the three spaces, is a massive undertaking. Some 221 works are donated by 216 artists, including Arman, Louise Bourgeois, Paul Brach, Christo, Walter De Maria, Niki de Saint Phalle, Richard Diebenkorn, Paul Feeley, Dan Flavin, Helen Frankenthaler, Donald Judd, Brice Marden, Agnes Martin, René Magritte, Jules Olitski, Martial Raysse, Bridget Riley, Lucas Samaras, Carolee Schneemann, Paul Thek, Wayne Thiebaud, Jean Tinguely, Cy Twombly, and many artists who had also participated in the 1963 benefit. "Drawings" nets approximately $20,000 for the Foundation.

1966

January 13
The board of directors agrees to disburse 25 percent of the proceeds from the "Drawings" benefit in grants while retaining the other 75 percent to build an operating reserve. The board also decides to award two separate grants to Judson Memorial Church: $250 toward the rental of bleachers for a performance by Yvonne Rainer, Steve Paxton, 26, and David Gordon, 29; and $1,000 for "severe deficits particularly in the Dance Theater." (A further $500 grant will be made to Rainer in July 1966.) A grant to La Monte Young "to support his activities in avant-garde music" in the amount of $1,000 is also approved.

GRANTEE FOCUS: LA MONTE YOUNG

With the grant he receives in January 1966 from the FCPA, La Monte Young, 31, realizes his idea, dating to 1963, for a "work that would be played continuously and exist as a living organism with a life and tradition of its own." The result, making its debut in September 1966, is *Dream House*, an uninterrupted sound and light composition produced with sine wave generators and consisting of live performances by Young's Theatre of Eternal Music. *Dream House* will be presented continuously for the next three-and-a-half years. Supported today by Dia Art Foundation, the *Dream House* survives at its original location, 275 Church Street, the home as well of Young and his wife and collaborator, Marian Zazeela.
—Susan Rosenberg

March 7
The board agrees to award grants of $500 apiece to choreographer Midi Garth, 50, and Max Neuhaus. John Cage reports that 90 music manuscripts have been collected and more are being gathered, with the eventual goal of selling them as a collection to raise money for the Foundation. He adds that the Library for Performing Arts in New York has agreed to mount an exhibition of these manuscripts in fall 1967, although the library will ultimately decide against doing so.

March–May
The benefit series "Six Lectures" is held over six evenings at the Poetry Center of the 92nd Street YMHA, 1395 Lexington Avenue, New York. The schedule of speakers is:

4

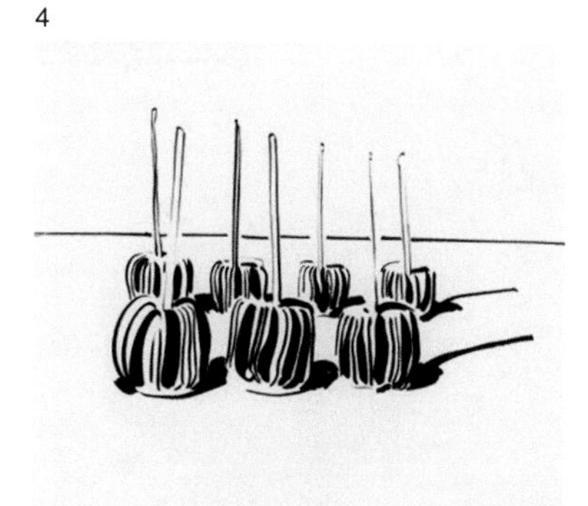

(1) Bread and Puppet Theater, *Bread and Puppet Theater Protest Vietnam*, performance, Washington Square, New York, March 15, 1965. (2) Exterior of Feigen/Palmer Gallery, 515 North La Cienega Boulevard, Los Angeles, 1963. Photo: Lillian Palmer. (3) Max Neuhaus, announcement for "Listen," from *six sound oriented pieces for situations other than that of the concert hall*, 1966–68. (4) Wayne Thiebaud, *Seven Jelly Apples*, 1964, ink on paper, 11" x 12". (5) Paul Brach, *Untitled*, 1964, paint and colored pencil, 18" x 18". (6) La Monte Young, February 26, 1966. (7) Midi Garth, New York, 1966.

7

5

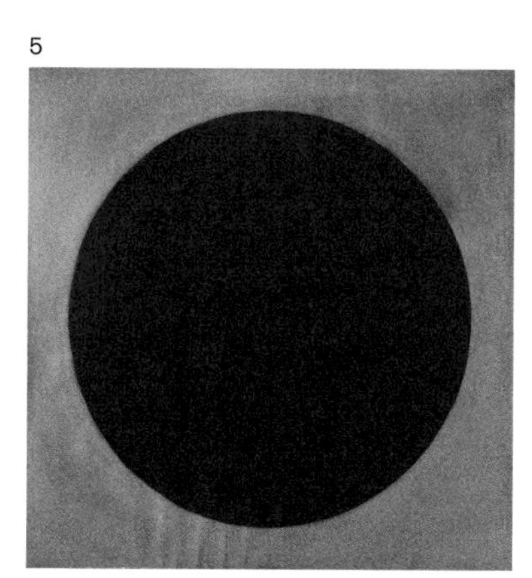

6

PHOTO: PETER MOORE

March 31: Norman O. Brown
April 7: Peter Yates
April 16: R. Buckminster Fuller
April 21: Merce Cunningham
April 28: Harold Rosenberg
May 7: Marshall McLuhan

According to the accompanying program, "Though the subjects, unannounced, are all freely chosen by the speakers themselves, the choice of speakers has been determined by an interest in positive attitudes in a period of cultural change."

The lectures of Brown, Fuller, and McLuhan are sold out (and, in the case of McLuhan, standing-room-only tickets are sold). Cunningham's and Rosenberg's lectures are 50 percent subscribed. Yates, less known on the East Coast, draws a smaller audience. Total income from ticket sales is $4,885. After $2,602 is disbursed in lecture expenses, the net income to the Foundation is $2,283.

April 24
A $2,500 grant is made to the Cunningham Dance Foundation; the specific purpose is unknown.

April 26
At a board meeting, Billy Klüver asks the directors to authorize a $1,500 "grant" to an American group of performing artists (including John Cage, Lucinda Childs, Öyvind Falhström, Alex Hay, Deborah Hay, Steve Paxton, Yvonne Rainer, Robert Rauschenberg, David Tudor, and Robert Whitman) and engineers who are invited to participate in the Stockholm Festival for Art and Technology, scheduled for September 1966. Since the funds requested have been donated to the Foundation by a supporter of Klüver's for this express purpose, it is not technically a grant. By late June, Klüver expresses concern that the Swedish organizers do not value the participation of the engineers in the project. By the end of July the Americans opt out. Klüver's original proposal will ultimately be realized in New York as "9 Evenings: Theatre & Engineering."

June 7
A $100 grant is made to Austrian composer Kurt Schwertsik, 30.

GRANTEE FOCUS: YVONNE RAINER
In September 1963, Yvonne Rainer first writes to the FCPA on behalf of Judson Memorial Church to request $200 for an evening-long collaborative project with sculptor Charles Ross and members of Judson Dance Theater. The resulting grant funds Ross's construction of the set for the November 1963 presentation of Rainer's *Room Service* at Judson Church (Concert #13). In January 1966 31-year-old Rainer premieres *The Mind Is a Muscle, Part I* at Judson Church—a program that includes *Trio A*, danced by Rainer, David Gordon, and Steve Paxton. In July 1966, she receives a $500 grant from the FCPA, the first given exclusively to her. At the time, she is developing *Carriage Discreteness* (in collaboration with engineer Per Biorn), as part of "9 Evenings: Theatre & Engineering." A later $2,000 grant will support Rainer's *Continuous Project—Altered Daily*, presented at the Whitney Museum of American Art from March 31 to April 2, 1970. This complex work involves films (a combination of Rainer's own and Hollywood features), props, text, and performances by Rainer, Becky Arnold, Douglas Dunn, Barbara Dilley, and Steve Paxton. —SR

July 21
A $4,700 grant is made to the Cunningham Dance Foundation for a new European tour.

1

PHOTO: PETER MOORE

2

PHOTO: PETER MOORE

3

PHOTO: PETER MOORE

October 13
Organized by Billy Klüver, "9 Evenings: Theatre & Engineering" opens October 13 at the 69th Regiment Armory, 68 Lexington Avenue, New York. The FCPA acts as fiscal agent for the event, accepting tax-deductible donations from the public on behalf of Klüver's Experiments in Art and Technology, Inc. (E.A.T.). "9 Evenings" comprises a set of collaborative performance works involving artists and engineers that had been developed over the previous nine months, with much of the equipment constructed specifically for the event. Participating artists are John Cage, Lucinda Childs, Öyvind Falhström, Alex Hay, Deborah Hay, Steve Paxton, Robert Rauschenberg, Yvonne Rainer, David Tudor, and Robert Whitman. In addition to Klüver, participating engineers from Bell Labs are Per Biorn, Cecil Coker, Pete Cumminski, Ralph Flynn, Larry Heilos, Peter Hirsch, Harold Hodges, William Kaminski, Robert Kieronski, Jim McGee, Robby Robinson, Herb Schneider, Fred Waldhauer, Martin Wazowicz, Witt Wittnebert, and Dick Wolff. The event is filmed by Alfons Schilling.

The program consists of: Steve Paxton, *Physical Things*, performance engineer, Dick Wolff (October 13, 19); Alex Hay, *Grass Field*, performance engineers, Herb Schneider and Robert Kieronski (October 13, 22); Deborah Hay, *Solo*, performance engineer, Larry Heilos and Witt Wittnebert (October 13, 23); Robert Rauschenberg, *Open Score*, performance engineer, Jim McGee (October 14, 23); David Tudor, *Bandoneon! (a combine)*, performance engineer, Fred Waldhauer (October 14, 18); Yvonne Rainer, *Carriage Discreteness*, performance engineer, Per Biorn (October 15, 21); John Cage, *Variations VII*, performance engineer, Cecil Coker (October 15, 16); Lucinda Childs, *Vehicle*, performance engineer, Peter Hirsch (October 16, 23); Robert Whitman, *Two Holes of Water—3*, performance engineer, Robby Robinson (October 18, 19); Öyvind Falhström, *Kisses Sweeter Than Wine*, performance engineer, Harold Hodges (October 21, 22).

E.A.T. director Julie Martin recalls that the rented bleachers seated approximately 1,500 and were always full. It is thought that more than 10,000 people attended over the course of the nine nights. At $3 a ticket, "9 Evenings" realizes about $25,000 in ticket sales. The total cost in presenting "9 Evenings" is $76,000.

December 31
Carolyn Brown, 39, a member of the Merce Cunningham company from its founding in 1953 until 1973, joins the FCPA board of directors. She serves as a director until August 2001.

1967

September
Jasper Johns creates the lithograph *Target*, in an edition of 28, at Universal Limited Art Editions, in anticipation of the Foundation's December "Prints" benefit. Throughout the Foundation's existence, Johns will donate numerous paintings, sculptures, drawings, prints, and posters to raise money for the Foundation, not only to the thirteen benefit exhibitions but in intervening years as well.

October
Jill Jakes is succeeded as secretary by David Whitney, 27, a curator and art dealer who at the time is Jasper Johns's assistant. Whitney will serve in that capacity until 1974. The board of directors also announces the move of the Foundation headquarters to the home and studio of Jasper Johns at 225 East Houston Street.

John Cage now counts 275 music

4

PHOTO: PETER MOORE

(1) Peter Yates, speaking at "Six Lectures," 92nd Street YMHA, New York, April 7, 1966. (2) R. Buckminster Fuller, speaking at "Six Lectures," 92nd Street YMHA, New York, April 16, 1966. (3) Yvonne Rainer, *The Mind Is a Muscle*, performance, Judson Memorial Church, January 10, 1966. (4) Billy Klüver, speaking at "9 Evenings" press briefing, Robert Rauschenberg studio, New York, September 29, 1966. (5) FCPA secretary David Whitney. Photo: Roberta Bernstein.

5

manuscripts, appraised at $24,915, for what will become *Notations*. A few years later, the collection will be appraised at $100,000.

December
The third Foundation benefit exhibition, "Prints: To Benefit the Foundation for Contemporary Performance Arts, Inc." is held at the Kornblee Gallery, 58 East 79th Street, December 9, 1967–January 4, 1968. It includes work by Josef Albers, Richard Anuszkiewicz, Arakawa, Robert Benson, Jim Dine, Marcel Duchamp, Adolph Gottlieb, Richard Hamilton, David Hockney, Allen Jones, R.B. Kitaj, Louise Nevelson, Barnett Newman, Man Ray, Saul Steinberg, Frank Stella, Jack Tworkov, Andy Warhol, Tom Wesselmann, Jack Youngerman, and many past participants. As with the previous two benefits—and every Foundation benefit henceforth—Jasper Johns oversees the installation. The exhibition raises approximately $8,000.

An exhibition poster is designed by Claes Oldenburg, who recalls: "I contributed a print in the shape of a punching bag in silhouette—a single one (for the exhibition poster) and a double one (for a lithograph in an edition of 90 published by List Art Posters). The images were a response to Jasper's use of the lightbulb."

1968

January
The board approves grants of $500 each to Cornelius Cardew, 31; Lucinda Childs, 27 (for a joint Judson Theater "concert" with Deborah Hay and Yvonne Rainer); and Dance Theater Workshop for presenting performances. These are the only grants awarded during 1968.

GRANTEE FOCUS: LUCINDA CHILDS

Known for solos comprising found movement, props, and text, Lucinda Childs introduces *Untitled Trio* (1968) at Judson Memorial Church in February 1968 with the assistance of an FCPA grant of $500. *Untitled Trio* underlines the young choreographer's concern with permutational structures. Following a five-year hiatus, Childs returns to New York in 1973, founds her company, and choreographs Robert Wilson and Philip Glass's opera *Einstein on the Beach*, which premieres in 1976 at the Avignon Festival in France. Childs will receive FCPA support on two subsequent projects: in 1983 for *Available Light*, commissioned for the opening of the Los Angeles Museum of Contemporary Art's Temporary Contemporary, and in 1987 to fund her first self-produced season at the Joyce Theater. —SR

GRANTEE FOCUS: DANCE THEATER WORKSHOP

Dance Theater Workshop (DTW) receives its first $500 Foundation grant in February 1968, three years after its launch as a choreographer's collective by former Anna Sokolow dancers Jeff Duncan and Jack Moore with Art Bauman. The organization provides opportunities for young choreographers of diverse backgrounds to workshop new productions. In its first decade DTW presents more than 500 works by more than 150 choreographers, including Ze'eva Cohen, Martha Clarke, Wendy Perron, Kei Takei, Linda Tarnay, and multiple-year FCPA grantees Kenneth King and Gus Solomons Jr. Programs take place at a variety of locations, including 219 West Nineteenth Street, where DTW establishes its permanent home in 2002. Following its initial 1968 grant, DTW's productions, residencies, and rehearsal opportunities for emerging artists expand and flourish, with ongoing support from the FCPA since 1981—a total of 26 grants, amounting to almost $100,000 in funding.—SR

1

2

3

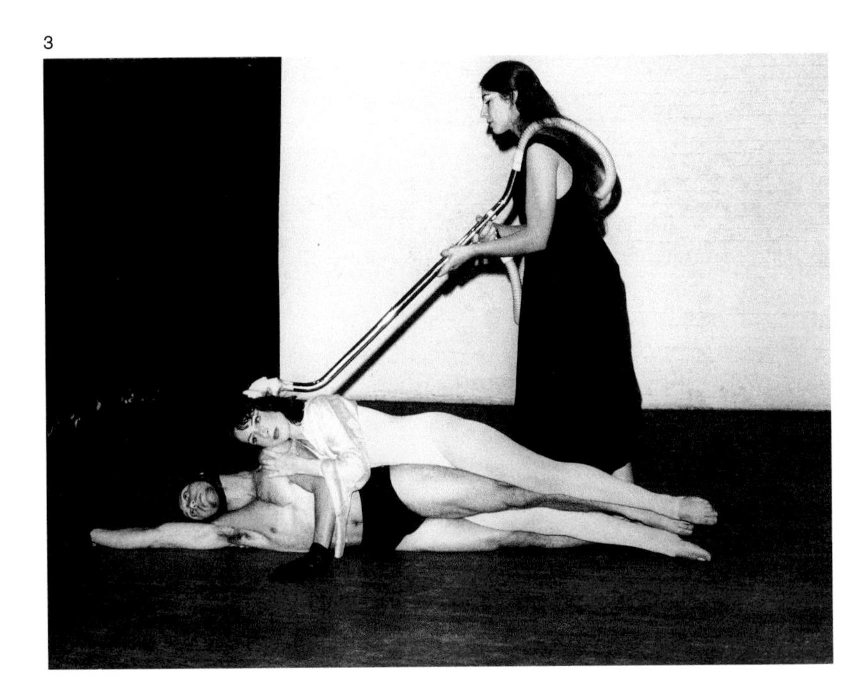

1969

circa January
Notations, a book of 269 music manuscripts collected by John Cage, is edited by the composer with artist Alison Knowles and published by Knowles's and Dick Higgins's Something Else Press. The book documents an encyclopedic range of late-nineteenth- to mid-twentieth-century musical notation, including work by the Beatles, Leonard Bernstein, Earle Brown, Elliott Carter, Aaron Copland, Philip Glass, Morton Feldman, Charles Ives, György Ligeti, Gordon Mumma, Yoko Ono, Harry Partch, Steve Reich, Erik Satie, Karlheinz Stockhausen, Igor Stravinsky, Anton Webern, Iannis Xenakis, and La Monte Young (see Appendix L for a list of contributors). The book's text and typography are determined by chance operations.

June
Alexina ("Teeny") Duchamp, the wife of Marcel Duchamp, joins the board of directors. She remains a director until 1977.

GRANTEE FOCUS: MEREDITH MONK
In October 1969, 27-year-old composer Meredith Monk receives her first FCPA grant of $200 for *Juice: A Theatre Cantata in Three Installments*. Monk's is the only grant awarded by the Foundation in 1969. *Juice* involves 85 performers and three sites: the Solomon R. Guggenheim Museum, Minor Latham Playhouse at Barnard College, and Monk's 597 Broadway loft. It is the first of four projects by Monk to benefit from progressively larger FCPA grants: *Turtle Dreams* (1983); the film *Book of Days* (1988); and her first opera, *Atlas* (1991). A three-part composition for a ten-part orchestra and eighteen voices, *Atlas* premieres at the Houston Grand Opera and is later presented at the Brooklyn Academy of Music. —SR

December
Cunningham dancer Viola Farber joins the board of directors; she serves on the board until her death in 1998.

The United States Tax Reform Act of 1969 is signed into law on December 30. The new law prohibits deductions by artists for gifts of their own work to public causes. There is concern among the directors that artists will stop donating works as they are no longer tax-deductible. There will not be another benefit exhibition until 1980.

1970

Grants totaling $8,000 are disbursed to David Tudor, Yvonne Rainer, Twyla Tharp, Grete Sultan, Kilina Cremona, and Philip Glass.

GRANTEE FOCUS: TWYLA THARP
One year after founding her first dance company, 29-year-old choreographer Twyla Tharp receives an FCPA grant in November 1970 for $1,000 to support her travel with dancers Sara Rudner, Rose Marie Wright, and Graciela Figueroa to Sullins College in Bristol, VA, where she premieres *PYMFFYPPMFYNM YPF*. Its enigmatic title is based on a misprint in *The New York Times* and was intended "to bring attention to the imperfections of organizations that were seen as the ultimate authority on a subject." Tharp announces that Figueroa's solo is to be performed topless and then bottomless as a protest against the fact that this all-women's college has a male dean. Despite threats of cancellation, *PYMFFYPPMFYNM YPF* is danced according to Tharp's plans. —SR

GRANTEE FOCUS: PHILIP GLASS
The 33-year-old Philip Glass first became

4

PHOTO: PETER MOORE

(1) Exhibition poster, "Prints," FCPA benefit, 1967. Design by Claes Oldenburg. (2) Lucinda Childs, *Untitled Trio*, rehearsal at Trisha Brown's and Joseph Schlicter's studio, New York, winter 1968. Performers: Joseph Schlicter, Lucinda Childs, and Sally Gross. Photo: Robert Propper. (3) Dance Theater Workshop, West Nineteenth Street studio, c. 1976–80. Photo: Philip Hipwell. (4) Meredith Monk, *Juice*, performance, Solomon R. Guggenheim Museum, New York, 1969. (5) FCPA board member Teeny Duchamp, c. early 1960s. (6) FCPA board member Viola Farber with Merce Cunningham, outside Sadler's Wells theater, London, July 1964.

5

6

known at the end of the 1960s through his ensemble's performances at Film-Makers Cinemathèque, the Whitney Museum of American Art, the Solomon R. Guggenheim Museum, and the Paula Cooper Gallery, where his *Music for Voices* (1970) accompanied a Mabou Mines production. Performed on a 1970 tour in Europe, which the FCPA supports in December 1970 with a $1,000 grant, *Music for Voices* joins other compositions that Glass considers aptly described as "minimalist": *Music in Contrary Motion*; *Music in Fifths*; *Music in Similar Motion*; and *Music with Changing Parts*. The completion of this cycle occurs in 1974 with the Town Hall premiere of Glass's four-hour-long *Music in Twelve Parts*, whose realization and subsequent tour is also funded by the FCPA. —SR

1971

Grants totaling $1,660 are made to Trisha Brown, Steve Reich, Nancy Green, and Lee Guilliatt.

GRANTEE FOCUS: TRISHA BROWN

Trisha Brown, a founding member of Judson Dance Theater, had established her own company in 1970. The 34-year-old choreographer receives her first grant from the FCPA in February 1971, an award of $360 that not only funds her work but also helps cover her rent. That year, her solo program "Another Fearless Dance Concert" premieres at New York's Whitney Museum of American Art. Three years after her initial Foundation award, Brown receives further FCPA support to realize the first of many choreographic programs presented in her loft at 541 Broadway. Two decades later, a 1991 FCPA grant enables her to commission an original score by Alvin Curran to accompany *For M.G.: The Movie*, a work she later reprises, with Curran's live performance on piano, at New York Live Arts in 2011. —SR

GRANTEE FOCUS: STEVE REICH

During the summer of 1970 Steve Reich had traveled to Ghana to study drumming and to observe master musician Gideon Alorwoyie. The trip inspires him to combine his earlier explorations of electronic-tape phasing with live music in a composition for percussion and voice, *Drumming*, one of three concerts the FCPA helps support in June 1971 by awarding a $500 grant to the 34-year-old Reich. Performed by his NEXUS ensemble, the four-part composition for bongo drums, marimbas, glockenspiels, whistling, and piccolo, as well as male and female voices, premieres seven months later at three New York venues: the Museum of Modern Art, the Brooklyn Academy of Music, and Town Hall. —SR

1972

Grants totaling $3,000 are made to the Poetry Project, Monica Solem, Steve Paxton, Ken Rubenstein/Rubenstein Theater Foundation, and Dan T. Jones.

GRANTEE FOCUS: THE POETRY PROJECT

A $1,000 grant is made to the Poetry Project in March 1972 for "workshops, readings and publications." Founded in 1966, the Poetry Project at St. Mark's Church in-the-Bowery is a continuation of the various coffeehouse reading series throughout the Lower East Side in the 1960s. To this day, it promotes, fosters, and inspires the reading and writing of contemporary poetry. Since the initial 1972 recognition, the FCPA will make a total of 34 grants to the Poetry Project, providing it with nearly $100,000 in support.—Stacy Tenenbaum Stark

1

2

PHOTO: PETER MOORE

3

GRANTEE FOCUS: STEVE PAXTON
Steve Paxton, 33, danced with the Cunningham company before joining Robert Dunn's experimental workshop in choreographic composition, the forerunner of the Judson Dance Theater. In Paxton's words, FCPA "supported a 40-year exploration into the phenomena of dance improvisation, including two improvisation technical approaches, Contact Improvisation and Material for the Spine." *Magnesium* is his first public Contact Improvisation performance, presented in early 1972 at Oberlin College. In June, Paxton receives a $500 FCPA grant for a five-day performance at John Weber Gallery in New York, with nine male contributors. In 1987, Paxton will receive a $2,000 grant toward the realization of a 50-minute solo improvisation, *The Goldberg Variations by J.S. Bach played by Glenn Gould Improvised by Steve Paxton*. He will also receive a $25,000 Grants to Artists award in 1994, with which he hires a small dance company to learn his new technique, Material for the Spine. —STS

1973

Grants totaling $1,500 are made to Kenneth King, Ann Wilson, and Mabou Mines.

John Cage offers the Notations manuscript collection to the Northwestern University Music Library, Evanston, IL, in January, with the stipulation that Northwestern will pay the Foundation $100,000 for its acquisition. The collection is transferred to the university that fall, despite the fact that the school is unable to produce the funds to underwrite the purchase. The complete collection includes 463 scores by 274 composers.

GRANTEE FOCUS: MABOU MINES
When it is organized in 1970, theater company Mabou Mines, conceived principally by Lee Breuer, 36, and Ruth Maleczech, 34, includes among its cofounders Philip Glass, JoAnne Akalaitis, and David Warrilow. The FCPA contributes to Mabou Mines for the first time in June 1973, providing a $500 grant to support a project by Breuer, during his artistic consultancy to the sixteen-member American Indian Theatre Ensemble during their residency at La MaMa Experimental Theatre Club. In years to follow, Mabou Mines will receive further FCPA support, both for new productions (including the 1989 staging of *Suenos* and 1990's *LEAR*) and for Mabou Mines/*Suite*, a residency program created in 1991 as an incubator of work by emerging theater artists. —SR

1974

Grants totaling $2,500 are made to Philip Glass, David Borden, Trisha Brown, Kenneth King, and Billy Apple.

1975

Grants totaling $2,500 are made to Beth Anderson, Ralston Farina, Edwin Denby, and Kathryn Bernson.

Visual artist Mark Lancaster is appointed secretary of the Foundation in April after David Whitney resigns. In late 1981 Lancaster is invited to become a director and continues to serve as secretary. He remains on the board until 1985, when he leaves New York. Lancaster will serve as the resident designer for the Merce Cunningham and Dance Company from 1980 through 1985.

1976

No grants disbursed.

4

TRISHA BROWN COMPANY, INC.
PRESENTS
A NEW WORK WITH ELIZABETH GARREN, JUDITH RAGIR,
MONA SULZMAN & PAMPLONA STONES WITH SYLVIA WHITMAN
541 B'WAY (SPRING ST.) JUNE 4-7 & 11-14 8:30 $2.50
BY RESERVATION ONLY: CALL 925-3892 BETWEEN 9 & 5

5

A.I.T.E.
AMERICAN INDIAN THEATRE ENSEMBLE
AT LAMAMA E.T.C—OCT.25-29 NOV.1-5~10p.m.

(1) Promotional poster, Steve Reich, *Drumming*, 1971. (2) Philip Glass Ensemble, performance, January 17, 1970. (3) 1983 grantee Alice Notley, reading at the Poetry Project, St. Mark's Church, New York, 1989. (4) Promotional poster, Trisha Brown Company, *Pamplona Stones*, performance, June 1974. (5) Promotional poster, Lee Breuer and American Indian Theatre Ensemble, *NA HAAZAN* and *BODY INDIAN*, La MaMa E.T.C., New York, October 1973. (6) Steve Paxton, *Contact Improvisation*, performance, John Weber Gallery, New York, June 1972.

6

PHOTO: PETER MOORE

1977

Grants are made to the Shared Forms Theatre, Inc., Performance & Video Workshop, Kenneth King, and the Poetry Project.

Artist Elaine de Kooning, a member of the original board of directors, steps down.

1978

Grants totaling $2,000 are made to Richard Foreman/Ontological-Hysteric Theater, Cunningham Dance Foundation, Performance Workshop, and Rosalind Newman/Harvest Dance Foundation.

GRANTEE FOCUS: RICHARD FOREMAN

Founded in 1968 by Richard Foreman, the Ontological-Hysteric Theater—initially based in SoHo, and subsequently at Joseph Papp's Public Theater and St. Mark's Church in-the-Bowery—is the primary vehicle for Foreman's stage work. Foreman describes his multimedia performances as "total theater" with the goal of a "disorientation message." In October 1978, he receives a $500 FCPA grant at age 36 and collaborates with cinematographer Babette Mangolte on the feature-length film *Strong Medicine*, and also produces *City Archives*, a video-play commissioned by the Walker Art Center. Several future Grants to Artists recipients will trace their beginnings directly to their early association with Foreman and OHT, such as Richard Maxwell, Young Jean Lee, and Elevator Repair Service. —SR

1979

Grants totaling $9,500 are made to Cunningham Dance Foundation, David Lusby, Gus Solomons Jr./Solomons Company Dance, the Poetry Project, Ada Katz/Eye & Ear Theater, Inc., Mel Wong, Spencer Holst, Norman Solomon, Maryanne Amacher, and The Kitchen. The increase in grants is made possible as the artworks in the Foundation's collection begin to be sold through the Margo Leavin Gallery in Los Angeles. The Foundation also begins to make regular grants to avant-garde and experimental presenting organizations in addition to individuals.

In November, 100 scores from the Notations collection go on view in "Musical Manuscripts" at the Drawing Center, 137 Greene Street, New York.

GRANTEE FOCUS: THE KITCHEN

The Kitchen first receives an FCPA grant, of $1,000, in December 1979. In awarding a grant to the institution, founded as an artists' collective eight years earlier, the FCPA directors note that they are assisting an organization "which presents in many forms the work of interesting artists with whom the Foundation may not always be familiar." The Kitchen describes itself in its original mission statement as "a space where video artists and experimental composers and performers could share their ideas with like-minded colleagues." One of the first American institutions to embrace the emerging fields of video and performance art, it also presents new, experimental work within the fields of dance, music, literature, and film. Over the years, The Kitchen will receive 30 grants from the Foundation—more than $100,000 in support. —STS

1980

Nine grants are made, totaling $8,000. An increasing number of presenting organizations begin to receive Foundation support on a regular basis.

The Foundation's fourth benefit exhibition, "Drawings: To Benefit the Foundation

1

2

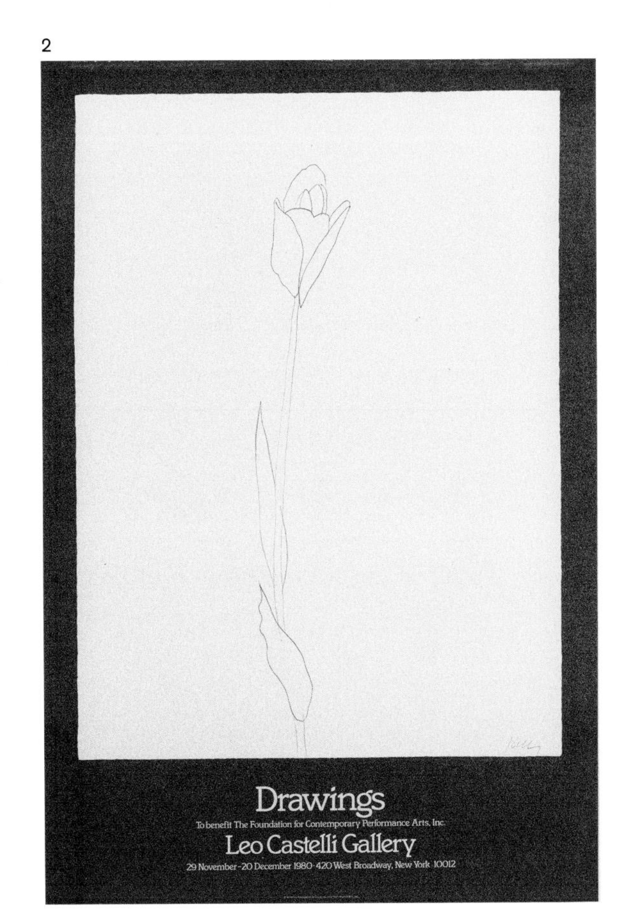

3

PHOTO: PAULA COURT

for Contemporary Performance Arts, Inc." is held at Leo Castelli, 420 West Broadway, November 29–December 20. The largest exhibition to date, the benefit includes 209 works on paper donated by 201 artists. Donating artists include Richard Artschwager, Jared Bark, Robert Barry, Jennifer Bartlett, Lynda Benglis, John Cage, Merce Cunningham, Walter De Maria, Charles Gaines, Joe Goode, Marcia Hafif, Jan Hashey, Bryan Hunt, Paul Jenkins, Joan Jonas, Lee Krasner, Mark Lancaster, Julian Lethbridge, Allan McCollum, Elizabeth Murray, Bruce Nauman, Philip Pearlstein, Ken Price, Edda Renouf, Susan Rothenberg, Julian Schnabel, Alan Shields, Pat Steir, Robert Wilson, Trevor Winkfield, and others. More than 60 drawings sell, raising over $100,000.

1981

Twenty-five grants are made, totaling $35,500.

GRANTEE FOCUS: CHARLES ATLAS

Before receiving his first FCPA grant, Charles Atlas had collaborated exclusively with Merce Cunningham, producing *Blue Studio: Five Segments* (1975–76) and working as the company's filmmaker-in-residence. After completing *Channel/Inserts* with Cunningham in 1981, Atlas, 32, a pioneer of "video-dance"—choreography created specifically for the camera—receives a Foundation grant of $1,000 in October to support his independent work. In addition to making his own films and video installations, Atlas has also undertaken numerous projects involving performing artists, including Yvonne Rainer, Michael Clark, Douglas Dunn, Marina Abramović, Diamanda Galás, John Kelly, and Leigh Bowery. In 2006, Atlas receives the John Cage Award. —SR

GRANTEE FOCUS: ROULETTE

Founded in 1978 as a venue for new music and intermedia art, Roulette receives its first FCPA grant for $1,000 in October. Roulette has presented more than 1,000 performances of experimental music by diverse composers, musicians, and sound artists, including many who would become part of the 1980s downtown music scene: Fred Frith, Bill Frisell, Christian Marclay, John Zorn, Elliott Sharp, and Yasunao Tone, the last two of whom will receive Grants to Artists awards. Roulette encourages creations by artists yet to receive attention from mainstream funding institutions. An inhabitant of lofts on West Broadway and Greene Street in SoHo for more than 30 years, in 2010 Roulette relocated to a 7,000-square-foot Art Deco concert hall in Brooklyn. Since 1981, Roulette has received 24 grants total from the Foundation, amounting to nearly $70,000 to help finance its operations and concerts. —STS

GRANTEE FOCUS: BILL T. JONES

In October 1981, the FCPA awards a $1,000 grant to Bill T. Jones and Arnie Zane to mount *Social Intercourse,* which makes its premiere at the American Dance Festival and The Space at New York's City Center. The following year, after a decade of collaboration, Jones and Zane form their dance company. The company receives further support from the FCPA in 1987, as Zane's health begins to fail in the year before his death from AIDS. A Foundation grant of $3,000 allows the company to document two new works, *Red Room* and *Where the Queen Stands Guard.* —SR

An exhibition of the Foundation's first and only fund-raising portfolio, "Eight Lithographs," is held at Leo Castelli, 420 West Broadway, November 28–December 19. A print portfolio in an edition of 50 with

4

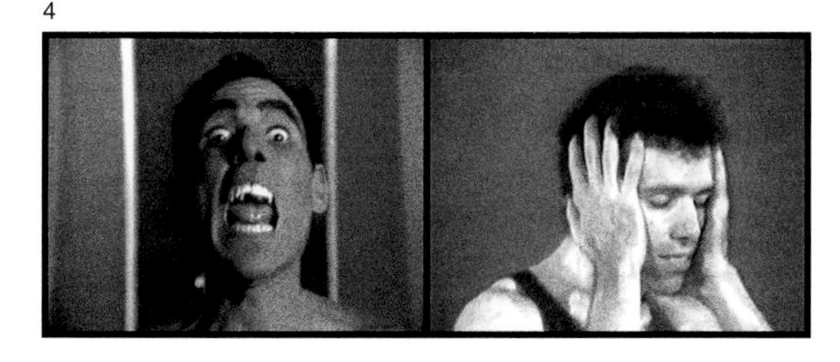

(1) Richard Foreman, production still from *Strong Medicine*, film, 1989. (2) Exhibition poster, "Drawings," FCPA benefit, 1980, design by Ellsworth Kelly. (3) The Kitchen, performance by 1985 grantee Douglas Dunn, 1980. (4) Charles Atlas, still from *More Men*, 2-channel synchronized video, 1980–82. Courtesy the artist. (5) Exhibition announcement, "Eight Lithographs," FCPA benefit print portfolio, 1981. (6) Roulette, performance by Jim Staley, 2006 grantee Ikue Mori, and Bill Frisell, 1986. Photo: Barbara Mensch. (7) Bill T. Jones, *Valley Cottage*, performance, The Kitchen, New York, 1980.

5

Eight Lithographs
to Benefit
The Foundation
for
Contemporary
Performance
Arts, Inc.
28 November-19 December 1981
Leo Castelli Gallery
420 West Broadway, New York

6

7

PHOTO: PAULA COURT

eight artist proofs is published by Gemini G.E.L., with works by Sam Francis, Philip Guston, David Hockney, Jasper Johns, Ellsworth Kelly, Bruce Nauman, Robert Rauschenberg, and Richard Serra (see page 192). Some 40 portfolios are sold, raising around $300,000. Gemini owner Sidney Felsen, who financed the project and orchestrated the participation of the seven artists other than Johns, recalls: "When the portfolio was completed, I felt it contained the highest quality of any portfolio that had ever been assembled as a fund-raiser. Each of the eight editions were examples of some of the best print works these artists created."

1982

Twenty-nine grants are made, totaling $66,000.

GRANTEE FOCUS: P.S. 122

In December, P.S. 122—a former public school on the corner of First Avenue and Ninth Street that a year earlier had introduced Avant-Garde-Arama, a multidisciplinary program of performances and classes—receives its first grant ($3,000) from the FCPA to pay administrative costs. It quickly becomes known for its spoken-word and performance-art programming, and the site of early works by Spalding Gray, Karen Finley, Ron Athey, and Eric Bogosian. Under the tenure of artistic director Mark Russell, P.S. 122 will benefit from almost uninterrupted annual FCPA funding for operating support, artists fees, and numerous initiatives, receiving 26 grants amounting to nearly $80,000. —SR

GRANTEE FOCUS: THE DRAWING CENTER

At its 1977 opening the Drawing Center's mission to showcase contemporary and historical drawing through exhibitions and education was unique in the United States. In the years to follow, the center's programming coincided with the emergence of drawing as a significant medium in contemporary art. Continuous FCPA funding, which begins with a $3,000 grant in December 1981, has served a key Drawing Center initiative: support for emerging artists through "Selections" exhibitions curated from the Viewing Program registry, a selective repository of drawing that is also accessible to the public. The FCPA will provide nearly $100,000 in grants over the years to the Drawing Center. —SR

1983

Eleven grants are made, totaling $21,200. The board votes to include visual artists "among those groups listed as possible recipients of grants. At present the suggestion is that visual artists are eligible only as collaborators with others."

GRANTEE FOCUS: EIKO & KOMA

A $2,000 grant is made to Japanese-born choreographer-dancers Eiko & Koma in July to sustain the foundering Catskills-based August Moon Festival and fund a season of a performance titled *Grain*. Since 1972, Eiko & Koma have created a theater of movement out of stillness, shape, light, and sound. Created at their Hudson Valley home and set to gamelan music, *Grain* is awarded one of the first Bessies (the New York Dance and Performance Awards) in 1984. In 1995 the artists will receive a second FCPA grant of $1,000 for a performance at the Rhinebeck Center in central New York. —STS

1984

Nineteen grants are made, totaling $29,750.

1

2

3

(1) Eiko & Koma, *Night Tide*, 1984. Photo: Beatriz Schiller. (2) P.S. 122, interior view, 1984. Photo: Dona Ann McAdams. (3) The Drawing Center, installation view, "Selections Fall '97," 1997. (4) Karole Armitage, *Paradise*, performance, La MaMa E.T.C., New York, 1984. (5) James Turrell, *Roden Crater (sunset)*, Arizona. Photo: James Turrell. (6) Movement Research at Judson Church, 1998. Performer: Karen Bernard. Photo: Barbara Mensch. (7) Artists Space, installation view, "Witnesses: Against Our Vanishing," 1989.

GRANTEE FOCUS:
KAROLE ARMITAGE
With a $2,000 Foundation grant in April, Karole Armitage, 40, presents *Paradise*, a three-act contemporary ballet "about sex, violence and destiny" with music by Jeff Lohn and lighting by FCPA grantee Charles Atlas at New York's La MaMa. It is the first of several Foundation grants to support Armitage, a former Merce Cunningham dancer who joined his company in 1976 after a three-year stint at Ballet du Grand Théâtre de Genève. Known for introducing ballet technique and pointe shoes to modern dance, Armitage will later present New York programs supported by the FCPA in 1987 and 1991, and in 2004, she receives a $10,000 Grants to Artists award. The FCPA-funded *In this dream that dogs me* premieres at the Duke Theatre the following year. —SR

GRANTEE FOCUS: JAMES TURRELL
Five years before receiving his FCPA grant, James Turrell had purchased a two-mile-wide, 400,000-year-old crater 40 miles north of Flagstaff, Arizona. In receiving a $1,000 grant in April 1984 to help found the *Roden Crater Project*, Turrell, 40, becomes the first visual artist to be awarded funding by the FCPA. (Jasper Johns recollects that Turrell's project "seemed so grand that we thought we would like to be connected to it in some way.") *Roden Crater* will again benefit from an FCPA grant in 1989. Turrell has worked since that time to transform the site into a mammoth celestial observatory. —SR

GRANTEE FOCUS: ARTISTS SPACE
A $1,000 grant is made to Artists Space in April. Founded in 1972, Artists Space began as a pilot program for the New York State Council on the Arts with the goal of assisting young, emerging artists. It quickly became active in the downtown New York alternative arts scene and evolved with the needs and concerns of emerging artists. A number of artists have been introduced to the public by Artists Space, including Jeff Koons, Peter Halley, Sherrie Levine, Robert Longo, Cindy Sherman, and Laurie Simmons. The FCPA has funded Artists Space's exhibitions and programs continuously since their first request for support in 1984—a total of 28 grants and nearly $100,000. —STS

1985

Twenty-seven grants are made, totaling $54,550.

In October, gallery owner Brooke Alexander and PS1 founder Alanna Heiss join the board of directors. Alexander will serve as a director to the present; Heiss will remain on the board until 1995.

GRANTEE FOCUS:
MOVEMENT RESEARCH
The School for Movement Research and Construction, founded in 1978 by dancers and artists teaching and performing independently in New York, is conceived as a center for new ideas in movement training and process-oriented dance composition, offering free and low-cost programs. In December 1985 the FCPA provides a $3,000 grant toward workshops, the Studies Project, Open Performance, and the Presenting Series at Ethnic Folk Arts Center, a precursor to the Movement Research at the Judson Church series. Each program enables both emerging and established choreographers to present new work in a process-oriented context. For a time it is the only artist-run dance organization in New York. Over the years, the FCPA will provide eighteen grants—and almost $40,000—in program support. —STS

Sarah Cooke Taggart is named secretary

4

PHOTO: PAULA COURT

5

6

7

of the Foundation in December. Taggart, assistant to Jasper Johns, will serve in this capacity until 2010.

1986

Twenty-three grants are made, totaling $66,200.

GRANTEE FOCUS: RHYS CHATHAM

Rhys Chatham, 33, and Joseph Nechvatal, 35, receive a joint $5,000 grant in July for their collaborative *XS: The Opera Opus* (1984–86), a protest against the Reagan administration's arms buildup. It features slide projections of Nechvatal's computer-generated paintings, singing by Jane Lawrence Smith, and dance by Yves Musard. Chatham, a student of Morton Subotnick and La Monte Young, had performed in Young's Theatre of Eternal Music in the 1970s before making his first compositions for multiple guitars in 1977, works that merged extended-time music and punk rock. Chatham will collaborate with artists working in many different media, including FCPA grantee Karole Armitage. He will receive further Foundation support for his 1990 Brooklyn Academy of Music debut, *The Heart Cries with Many Voices*, a 60-minute work for seven electric guitars and percussion, two trumpets, and chorus. —SR

GRANTEE FOCUS: RALPH LEMON

When Ralph Lemon, 33, receives his first Foundation grant of $5,000 in July, it comes at a busy moment for the choreographer: the year marks the performance of his piece *Flock* by his recently formed company at Jacob's Pillow; a new choreographic work, *En Su Llama Mortal*, realized for the Ballet Hispanico's appearance at the Joyce Theater; and the debuts of *Two*, a duet with Bebe Miller, and *And the Jungle Will Obliterate the Shrine/Seasons.* The last is commissioned by Dance Theater Workshop, where its two-week run is supported by Lemon's FCPA grant, and described by *The New York Times* as having "the aura of an ancient legend." In 2012, Lemon will receive a $25,000 Grant to Artists award. —SR

1987

Thirty-seven grants are made, totaling $79,000.

1988

Thirty-five grants are made, totaling $98,000.

In July, the Foundation moves to Jasper Johns's new home and studio at 155 East 63rd Street.

The Foundation's sixth benefit exhibition, "The 25th Anniversary Exhibition to Benefit the Foundation for Contemporary Performance Arts, Inc.," is held simultaneously at Brooke Alexander, 59 Wooster Street, and Leo Castelli, 420 West Broadway, December 8–30. The exhibition features some 83 works of painting and sculpture plus drawings and prints by 70 artists, including Carl Andre, Richard Artschwager, Arman, Donald Baechler, Jonathan Borofsky, John Cage, Francesco Clemente, John Chamberlain, Eric Fischl, Dan Flavin, Nancy Graves, Keith Haring, Donald Judd, Ellsworth Kelly, Andrew Lord, Louise Nevelson, Kenneth Noland, Robert Rauschenberg, George Segal, Richard Serra, Joel Shapiro, Frank Stella, Al Taylor, Robert Therrien, Cy Twombly, Meyer Vaisman, Andy Warhol, and others. Intended to be the last exhibition mounted by the Foundation, the benefit raises more than $2.3 million.

GRANTEE FOCUS: BANG ON A CAN

Bang on a Can started in 1987 as a twelve-hour marathon concert at SoHo's Exit Art,

1

(1) Ralph Lemon, *Two*, performance, American Center, Paris, 1987. Photo: Geneviève Stephenson. (2) Promotional poster, Bang on a Can, "Bang on a Can Festival," 1989. (3) Rhys Chatham and Joseph Nechvatal, *XS: An Opera*, Boston, 1986. (4) Exit Art, installation view of "The Green Show," 1989. Photo: Larry Lamé. (5) Installation view, "25th Anniversary Exhibition," FCPA's sixth benefit exhibition, Leo Castelli Gallery, New York, 1988. (6) The Wooster Group, *Frank Dell's The Temptation of Saint Antony*, performance, Performing Garage, New York, 1988. Pictured: Michael Stumm, Peyton Smith, Kate Valk, Jeff Webster, and Ron Vawter. (7) Franklin Furnace, Diane Torr's *Drag King Workshop*, performance at The Contemporary, New York, September 17, 1994.

2

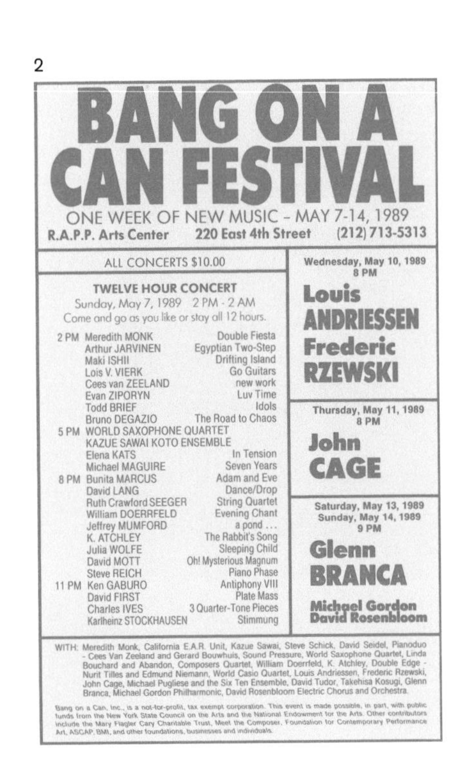

3

PHOTO: PAULA COURT

organized by composers Michael Gordon, David Lang, and Julia Wolfe. Featuring work by young artists—half of them under the age of 35—alongside that of several experimental music elders, including Milton Babbitt, John Cage, Pauline Oliveros, and Steve Reich, its long-duration format has received ongoing support from the FCPA since 1988. The festival's commitment to presenting diverse music by artists who may be unknown/emerging, midcareer, or well established has likewise endured, although its venues have come to include international, national, and local institutions, among them BAM, Henry Street Settlement, The Kitchen, Lincoln Center's Alice Tully Hall, Symphony Space, and Mass MoCA. Since its initial support, Bang on a Can has received nearly $100,000 in FCPA grants. —SR

1989

Following the success of the 1988 benefit, grant disbursements increase substantially; 67 grants are made, totaling $205,750.

GRANTEE FOCUS: EXIT ART

A $3,000 grant is made in June to Exit Art for general operating support. Founded in 1982 in a loft on Canal Street by curator Jeanette Ingberman and artist Papo Colo, Exit Art is an alternative space that presents artists whose work challenges notions of race, ethnicity, gender, sexuality, and equality. FCPA will support Exit Art with grants until the organization closes three decades later following the death of Ingberman. By 2012, its final year, Exit Art will have organized more than 200 exhibitions, events, festivals, and programs featuring more than 2,500 artists. —STS

GRANTEE FOCUS: FRANKLIN FURNACE ARCHIVE

A $2,000 grant is made in December to Franklin Furnace Archive to support the upcoming 1990 season of emerging performance artists and to increase public awareness of its programing. Founded in 1976 by artist Martha Wilson "to champion ephemeral forms neglected by mainstream arts institutions," including artists' books, temporary installation art, and performance art, it vows to make "the world safe for avant-garde art." Franklin Furnace will go on to receive nineteen FCPA grants. The 1990 season is an eventful one for the organization: in May the New York City Fire Department closes its performance space in response to a call claiming it is an "illegal social club." Not long after, it is vilified by Senator Jesse Helms for presenting Karen Finley's installation *A Woman's Life Isn't Worth Much.* —STS

GRANTEE FOCUS: THE WOOSTER GROUP

Founded in 1975 by Spalding Gray and Elizabeth LeCompte, the Wooster Group has steadily created theater, dance, and media work to the present at its Wooster Street location, the Performing Garage. The first FCPA grant is awarded to the Wooster Group in 1988, to support the LeCompte-directed *Frank Dell's The Temptation of St. Antony.* In 1989, a second, $5,000 grant helps pay for "artists' fees and production expenses for the development of the dance/music/theater spectacle" *Brace Up!*, the Wooster Group's production of Paul Schmidt's translation of Chekhov's *Three Sisters.* The Wooster Group will later be the recipient of several other grants from the Foundation for its productions and for a residency program for fledgling experimental theater companies, and in 2003 performer and fellow cofounder Kate Valk will receive a $25,000 Grants to Artists award. —STS

4

5

6

PHOTO: PAULA COURT

7

1990

Sixty-three grants are made, totaling $283,900.

1991

Fifty-four grants are made, totaling $297,250.

1992

Foundation cofounder John Cage dies on August 12 at age 79.

David Tudor is the first recipient of the John Cage Award, established in memory of the composer in November. The $50,000 award is made every other year in recognition of outstanding achievement in the arts for work that reflects the spirit of Cage; selections are made from invited nominations.

Twenty other grants are made, totaling $115,000.

1993

In March, the Foundation hires its first executive director, Mary Judge, who directs the Foundation's grants programs until 2004; henceforth the Foundation maintains its own small staff.

For the first time, the Foundation formalizes distinct grant programs, creating Grants to Individuals, Grants for Immediate Needs, and Grants to Organizations.

In December, the first Grants to Individuals for $25,000 apiece are awarded to six recipients: John Luther Adams, Paul Beatty, Steffan "Wiggles" Clemente, John Jesurun, Lois V Vierk, and Trevor Winkfield. Winkfield is the first visual artist to receive an FCPA grant since James Turrell in 1984.

In its first formal year, nine Grants for Immediate Needs totaling $18,500 are made, to artists and organizations including Bang on a Can, Bill Le Page, Pauline Oliveros, and S.E.M. Ensemble. The grants are all less than $2,000.

Fifteen Grants to Organizations are made, totaling $53,000; grants range in size from $2,000 to $5,000.

The seventh benefit exhibition, "30th Anniversary Exhibition of Drawings: To Benefit the Foundation for Contemporary Performance Arts," is held at Leo Castelli, 420 West Broadway, December 11, 1993–January 8, 1994. Some 187 artists donate 189 works, including Charles Arnoldi, Robert Barry, Nayland Blake, Ross Bleckner, Richmond Burton, George Condo, Merce Cunningham, Carroll Dunham, Eric Fischl, Dan Flavin, Richard Hamilton, Jane Hammond, Jenny Holzer, Bryan Hunt, Kim Jones, Anselm Kiefer, Barry Le Va, Tom Levine, Glenn Ligon, Richard Long, Suzanne McClelland, James Nares, Tom Otterness, Ellen Phelan, Jack Pierson, Lari Pittman, Dorothea Rockburne, Joel Shapiro, Antoni Tàpies, Dorothea Tanning, Rirkrit Tiravanija, and others. More than $400,000 is raised.

1994

Artist Julian Lethbridge joins the board of directors in January 1994; he remains a director through the present.

The Foundation's offices move to 151 East 63rd Street.

Seven $25,000 Grants to Individuals are awarded in November to David Behrman, Ondřej Hrab, Phill Niblock, Pauline Oliveros, Steve Paxton, Sam Reveles, and Trimpin.

Takehisa Kosugi is the second recipient of the $50,000 John Cage Award.

Eighteen presenting and support organizations are awarded grants totaling $55,000.

The Foundation holds its first formal grants reception to announce its annual

1

2

3

(1) Installation view, "30th Anniversary Exhibition of Drawings," FCPA's seventh benefit exhibition, Leo Castelli Gallery, New York, 1993. Photo: Dorothy Zeidman. (2) Installation view, "Prints," featuring print editions made to benefit FCPA by Robert Mangold, Richard Serra, Kiki Smith, Julian Lethbridge, and Donald Baechler, in FCPA's eighth benefit exhibition, Brooke Alexander, New York, 1995. (3) Jasper Johns, Margaret Leng Tan, and John Cage, at opening of "The Drawings of Jasper Johns," Whitney Museum of American Art, New York, February 22, 1991. Photo: George Hirose.

awards at the Drawing Center on December 8. Arts writer and memoirist Rosamond Bernier announces the grants. Margaret Leng Tan performs John Cage's *Suite for Toy Piano* (1948), and Susan Sontag and Edward Albee give readings. There is not another such reception until 1997.

By the end of 1994, ten Grants for Immediate Needs totaling $15,500 are made.

1995

In May, the directors approach artists about making a print edition for the benefit of the Foundation, to be included in a forthcoming sale of prints. Donald Baechler, Julian Lethbridge, Robert Mangold, Richard Serra, and Kiki Smith each agree to participate.

Artist Elizabeth Murray joins the board of directors in September. After resigning in March 2001 and rejoining in 2003, she will serve on the board until her death in 2007.

Nine $25,000 Grants to Individuals are awarded in November to Alex Bag, Doug Elkins, Iréne Hultman, Joan Jonas, Mary Jane Leach, Bernadette Mayer, Bob McGrath, John Moran, and Edwin Torres.

Twenty-three presenting and support organizations are awarded grants totaling $64,000.

The eighth benefit exhibition, "Prints: To Benefit the Foundation for Contemporary Performance Arts," is held at Brooke Alexander, 59 Wooster Street, December 5–29. Some 133 artists donate 141 works, including Jennifer Bartlett, Vija Celmins, Chuck Close, Merce Cunningham, Mark di Suvero, Lucian Freud, Peter Halley, Mary Heilmann, Bill Jensen, Wolf Kahn, Byron Kim, R.B. Kitaj, Robert Moskowitz, Elizabeth Murray, Chris Ofili, Richard Smith, Lawrence Weiner, Marjorie Welish, and Robert Wilson. Forty works are sold and about $67,000 is raised.

By the end of 1995, ten Grants for Immediate Needs totaling $19,000 are made.

1996

Ten $20,000 Grants to Individuals are awarded in November to Burt Barr, Paul DeMarinis, Petr Kotik, Roscoe Mitchell, Ron Padgett, David Shapiro, Patricia Spears Jones, Gary Stevens, Elizabeth Streb, and Howard S. Thies.

Christian Wolff receives the $50,000 John Cage Award.

Twenty-eight presenting and support organizations are awarded grants, totaling $65,500.

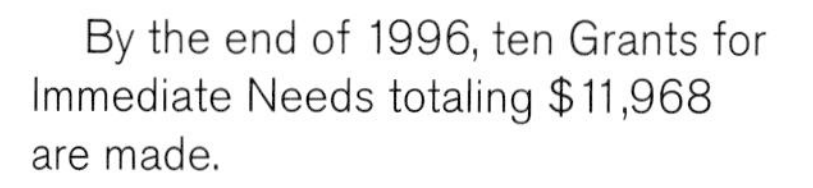
By the end of 1996, ten Grants for Immediate Needs totaling $11,968 are made.

1997

Experimental composer and 1994 grantee Phill Niblock joins the board of directors in February; he will remain on the board until 2006.

Ten $25,000 Grants to Individuals are awarded in November to Muhal Richard Abrams, Charles Amirkhanian, Zoe Beloff, Douglas Dunn, Neil Greenberg, Julian Maynard Smith, Alice Notley, Mary Oslund, Zeena Parkins, and Edward Sanders.

Twenty-nine presenting and support organizations are awarded grants, totaling $60,000.

The second formal grants reception is held at the West Village studio of artist Jennifer Bartlett on December 3. Bartlett will host these annual events for seven years. Arts journalist and critic Linda Yablonsky announces the awards with a presentation about each recipient; she will serve the Foundation in this capacity for eight years. Bang on a Can All-Stars members Mark Stewart and Robert Black perform Stewart's *Trummings* and Tom

(4) Trevor Winkfield, *I Will Not Tolerate Such Insubordination From My Pets!*, 1994, acrylic on linen, 48 ¾" x 60 ¼". Courtesy Tibor de Nagy Gallery, New York. (5) Mary Oslund, *Behavior*, Portland Institute for Contemporary Art performance series, Portland, 1997. Photo: Julie Keefe. (6) Joan Jonas, still from *Woman in the Well*, 2000, video installation, Rosamund Felsen Gallery, Los Angeles.

4

5

6

Johnson's *Failing*, and Gary Stevens performs his monologue *Threat*, a US premiere.

By the end of 1997, thirteen Grants for Immediate Needs totaling $20,250 are made.

1998

The Foundation moves to 820 Greenwich Street in June.

Attorney John Silberman joins the board of directors in October; he will remain on the board until 2003.

Thirteen $25,000 Grants to Individuals are awarded in November to Maryanne Amacher, Ann Carlson, chameckilerner—Rosane Chamecki and Andrea Lerner, Arnold Dreyblatt, David Dupuis, Peter Gizzi, David Henderson, Krzysztof Knittel, Jennifer Monson, Roger Newton, Maureen Owen, Riverbed Media—Paul Kaiser and Shelley Eshkar, and Sinan Savaskan.

Earle Brown receives the $50,000 John Cage Award.

Twenty-nine presenting and support organizations are awarded grants, totaling $64,000.

The annual grants reception is held on December 10, at Jennifer Bartlett's studio. Linda Yablonsky announces the awards. Grantee Edwin Torres reads poems from *Fractured Humorous*, and Irvine Arditti and Stephen Drury perform two works by John Cage from *Six Melodies for Violin and Keyboard*.

By the end of 1998, ten Grants for Immediate Needs totaling $19,100 are made.

1999

Now known as the Notations Project, the complete set of music manuscripts collected by John Cage in the 1960s—originally intended as a fund-raising vehicle for the Foundation—is formally gifted to Northwestern University Music Library, where it had been deposited more than 25 years before.

Fifteen $25,000 Grants to Individuals are awarded in November to Martín Acosta, Jonathan Bepler, John Bischoff, Terry Creach, Everett Dance Theatre, Rochelle Feinstein, Martin Kersels, Jennifer Lacey, Siobhan Liddell, Gary Lutz, Jaime Manrique, Stephen Petronio, Carl Stone, Paul Violi, and C.D. Wright.

Thirty-three presenting and support organizations are awarded grants, totaling $62,000.

The annual grants reception is held December 6 at Jennifer Bartlett's studio. Linda Yablonsky announces the awards. Grantee Zeena Parkins performs *Vita Futuristica*, and grantee Ron Padgett reads a selection of new poems.

By the end of 1999, ten Grants for Immediate Needs totaling $20,400 are made.

2000

Eleven $25,000 Grants to Individuals are awarded in November to Molissa Fenley, Jon Kessler, György Kurtág, Richard Maxwell, Julie Mehretu, Rubén Ortiz Torres, Wendy Rogers, Bill Shannon, Laetitia Sonami, Lorenzo Thomas, and Julia Wolfe.

Gordon Mumma receives the $50,000 John Cage Award.

Thirty presenting and support organizations are awarded grants, totaling $59,500.

The annual grants reception is held December 4 at Jennifer Bartlett's studio. Linda Yablonsky announces the awards. Cellist Maya Beiser performs Evan Ziporyn's *Kebyar Maya*. The cast of grantee John Moran's opera *Book of the Dead (Second Avenue)* performs an excerpt.

The ninth benefit exhibition, "Drawings &

1

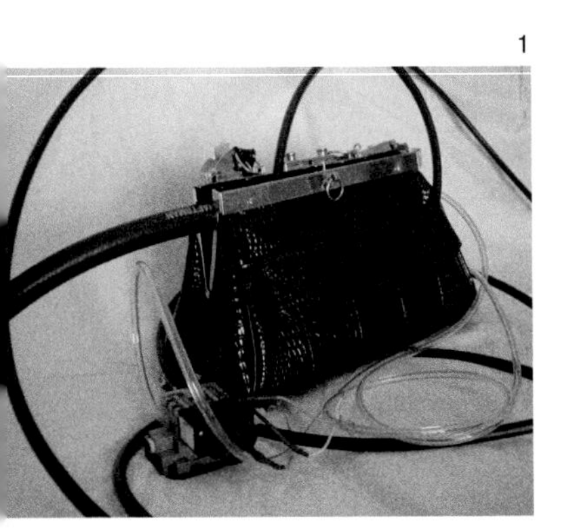

(1) Laetitia Sonami, *BAGS* (detail), kinetic sound installation, New Langton Arts, San Francisco, 2002. Photo: Brian Laczko. (2) Terry Creach, *Air Tight*, 2001. Photo: Matthew Huber. (3) Rubén Ortiz Torres, *La Infanta Elena, Mexico City,* 2001, Fujiflex, 40" x 60". Courtesy the artist. (4) Dean Moss, *board dance*, solo from *american deluxe*, performance, The Kitchen, New York, 2001. (5) Jin Hi Kim, *Self Portrait*, performance, Vancouver New Music Festival, Canada, 2002. (6) Installation view, "Drawings & Photographs," FCPA's ninth benefit exhibition, Matthew Marks Gallery, New York, 2000.

2

3

Photographs: An Exhibition to Benefit the Foundation for Contemporary Performance Arts, Inc." is held at Matthew Marks Gallery, 522 West 22nd Street, December 8–23. Some 267 artists contribute 275 works, including Donald Baechler, John Baldessari, Mel Bochner, Trisha Brown, Matthew Buckingham, Francesco Clemente, Merce Cunningham, John Currin, Rachel Feinstein, Wayne Gonzales, Andreas Gursky, Rachel Harrison, Neil Jenney, Jeff Koons, Sol LeWitt, Glenn Ligon, Elizabeth Murray, Robert Rauschenberg, Lucas Samaras, Julian Schnabel, James Siena, Keith Sonnier, Tom Wesselmann, and others. The organizing committee comprises Matthew Barney, Cecily Brown, Robert Gober, Jasper Johns, Julian Lethbridge, Elizabeth Murray, and Cindy Sherman, all of whom also donate work. Some 102 works sell and nearly $900,000 is raised.

By the end of 2000, sixteen artists or groups receive Grants for Immediate Needs totaling $42,700, including a $20,000 grant made in May to S.E.M. Ensemble for a concert honoring Earle Brown at Alice Tully Hall.

2001

Twelve $24,000 Grants to Individuals are awarded in November, to David First, Erica Hunt, Jin Hi Kim, Caden Manson, Dean Moss, Tere O'Connor, Jim O'Rourke, Mikel Rouse, Michael Schumacher, Sally Silvers, Anne Waldman, and Young-Hae Chang Heavy Industries—Young-hae Chang and Marc Voge.

The annual grants reception is held December 10 at Jennifer Bartlett's studio. Linda Yablonsky announces the awards. Grantee C.D. Wright reads from *Cooling Time: An American Prison Vigil*, and grantee Jennifer Monson performs *Atlas of Holes: Pitfall*, sound by grantee Jonathan Bepler, who also performs his own *Duet for Computer and Voice.*

Forty presenting and support organizations are awarded grants, totaling $61,000.

By the end of 2001, thirteen Grants for Immediate Needs totaling $17,265 are made.

2002

In November, ten $20,000 Grants to Individuals are awarded to Jonathan Burrows, Adam Chodzko, William Duckworth, Michael Gordon, David Lang, Douglas Messerli, William Pope.L, Paul Sietsema, Fiona Templeton, and John Yau.

Robert Ashley receives the $40,000 John Cage Award.

Twenty-seven presenting and support organizations are awarded grants, totaling $45,000.

The annual grants reception is held December 9 at the studio of Jennifer Bartlett. Linda Yablonsky announces the awards. John Cage's stories from *Indeterminancy* are performed by speakers Merce Cunningham and David Vaughan, and, on toy piano and toy instruments, Margaret Leng Tan.

By the end of 2002, nine Grants for Immediate Needs totaling $10,000 are made.

2003

Seven $20,000 Grants to Individuals are awarded in November to John Jasperse, Bill Morrison, Susan Rethorst, Elliott Sharp, Kate Valk, Rosmarie Waldrop, and Mac Wellman.

Twenty-five presenting and support organizations are awarded grants, totaling $40,000.

The annual grants reception is held December 8 at Jennifer Bartlett's studio. Linda Yablonsky announces the awards. Grantee Peter Gizzi reads poems from *Some Values of Landscape and Weather*, and

4

PHOTO: PAULA COURT

5

6

pianist Nurit Tilles performs James Scott's *Calliope Rag*, Joseph Lamb's *Cottontail Rag*, and Scott Joplin's *Maple Leaf Rag*.

By the end of 2003, six Grants for Immediate Needs totaling $7,100 are made.

2004

In March, the Foundation inaugurates a fifth, smaller funding program, the Contemporary Visual Arts Scholarship, supported by a Connecticut foundation. It awards a four-year, $40,000 scholarship annually to a college-bound senior from a local public high school planning to major in the visual arts. Since its inception, nine students have matriculated, five have graduated, and $300,000 has been awarded.

The name of the Foundation is legally changed to Foundation for Contemporary Arts in November to reflect the broader grant-making efforts, which include visual arts and poetry as well as dance, music, and theater.

Ten $10,000 Grants to Individuals are awarded in November to Germaine Acogny, Karole Armitage, Wade Guyton, Carla Harryman, Stuart Hawkins, Arturo Herrera, Marc Mellits, Harryette Mullen, Peggy Shaw, and Yasunao Tone.

David Behrman receives the $20,000 John Cage Award.

Thirty-two presenting and support organizations are awarded grants, totaling $41,000.

By the end of 2004, sixteen Grants for Immediate Needs totaling $18,000 are made.

2005

In February, the Foundation hires its second executive director, Stacy Tenenbaum Stark.

The Foundation holds a benefit performance, "A Reading to Benefit the Foundation for Contemporary Arts," at Diane von Furstenberg Studio, 389 West Twelth Street, New York, on May 25. Edward Albee reads his two-act, two-character *Edward Albee's Occupant: A Play About Louise Nevelson*, with stage actress Marian Seldes reading the role of Nevelson; it is directed by Lawrence Sacharow.

The Foundation launches a website, www.foundationforcontemporaryarts.org, in October 2005.

In November, arts philanthropist Agnes Gund and former Vassar College president Frances Fergusson join the board of directors. Fergusson will serve on the board until June 2012; Gund remains on the board to the present.

Because of a move to adopt a new timetable in which annual awards are made in January rather than December, no Grants to Individuals are awarded during 2005; the next awards will be made in January 2006.

Forty-six presenting and support organizations are awarded grants, totaling $50,000.

By the end of 2005, eighteen Grants for Immediate Needs totaling $20,620 are made.

2006

In January, thirteen $20,000 Grants to Individuals are awarded to Jonah Bokaer, Paul Chan, Norma Cole, Nathaniel Dorsky, David Grubbs, Joanne Kyger, Young Jean Lee, Ikue Mori, Michael Pisaro, Ishmael Randall Weeks, Vicky Shick, Yuji Takahashi, and Christopher Williams.

Charles Atlas receives the $40,000 John Cage Award.

The Foundation's tenth benefit exhibition, "Clarissa Dalrymple's Exhibition of Young Artists to Benefit the Foundation for Contemporary Arts," is held at Bortolami Dayan, 510 West 25th Street, February 16–25. For the first time, the Foundation's

1

2

3

PHOTO: PAULA COURT

(1) Peggy Shaw, *Miss America*, performance with Split Britches at La MaMa E.T.C., New York, 2008. Photo: Lori E. Seid. (2) Jonah Bokaer, *Charade*, performance, Chapelle des Pénitents Blancs, Avignon, France, 2006. Photo: Éric Boudet. (3) Kate Valk, The Wooster Group's *Hamlet*, performance at Public Theater, New York, 2007. (4) Installation view, "Posters," FCA's eleventh benefit exhibition, Paula Cooper Gallery, New York, 2006. (5) Allison Smith, *The Donkey, The Jackass, and The Mule*, 2008, mixed media, dimensions variable. Photo: Allison Smith and Michelle Pemberton. Courtesy the artist and Haines Gallery, San Francisco. (6) Installation view, "Young Artists," FCA's tenth benefit exhibition, Bortolami Dayan, New York, 2006. (7) Jennifer Walshe, still from *The Faerie Queene*, film by Freya Birren, 2010.

directors invite a respected curator to organize a benefit and select a group of emerging artists. Some 37 artists contribute 42 works, including Richard Aldrich, Hope Atherton, Huma Bhabha, Carol Bove, Anne Collier, Wade Guyton, Matthew Day Jackson, Matt Johnson, Nate Lowman, Adam McEwen, Mika Rottenberg, Cordy Ryman, Gedi Sibony, Kelley Walker, T.J. Wilcox, and Aaron Young. Some 28 works sell and $74,000 is raised.

The annual grants reception is held at Bortolami Dayan on February 21 during the benefit exhibition. Linda Yablonsky announces the awards. Grantee John Yau reads from his book *Ing Grish*, and grantee Jin Hi Kim performs her work *One Sky*.

Forty-one presenting and support organizations are awarded grants in July, totaling $50,000.

The Foundation's eleventh benefit exhibition, "Posters: Exhibition and Sale to Benefit the Foundation for Contemporary Arts," is held at Paula Cooper Gallery, 521 West 21st Street, December 8–20. Some 418 rare and signed exhibition posters are installed in a salon-style hang overseen by Jasper Johns. With more than 200 posters selling, $175,000 is raised.

The Grants for Immediate Needs are renamed Emergency Grants in July. A volunteer panel of visual artists is established to review the requests at monthly panel meetings. (A complete list of panelists can be found in Appendix K.) By the end of 2006, 23 Emergency Grants totaling $26,380 are made.

2007

In January, ten $25,000 Grants to Individuals are awarded to Rae Armantrout, DD Dorvillier, Douglas Henderson, Kimsooja, Clarinda Mac Low, Nathaniel Mackey, Yuko Nexus6, Pan Pan Theatre, RoseAnne Spradlin, and Jennifer Walshe.

Artist Kara Walker joins the board of directors in May.

In July, 52 presenting and support organizations are awarded grants, totaling $57,500.

By the end of 2007, 29 artists receive Emergency Grants, totaling $30,600.

2008

In January, twelve $25,000 Grants to Individuals awards are made to Kimberly Bartosik, Tamy Ben-Tor, Annie Gosfield, Cameron Jamie, Wang Jianwei, Ron Kuivila, Ohad Meromi, Sarah Michelson, Charles North, Elizabeth Robinson, Allison Smith, and Yasuko Yokoshi.

Paul Kaiser receives the John Cage Award ($50,000).

The annual grants reception is held at Brooke Alexander, 59 Wooster Street, on February 25. Dance writer and eventual Merce Cunningham Trust scholar-in-residence Nancy Dalva announces the awards. Grantee Ron Padgett reads poems from his new book, *How to Be Perfect*. Grantee Jennifer Walshe performs solo works for voice. Grantee Charles Atlas screens a video excerpt from *Berlin Mix 2007*.

In April, the Grants to Individuals program is renamed Grants to Artists.

Fifty-four presenting and support organizations are awarded grants, totaling $56,000.

Robert Rauschenberg dies on May 12 at age 82.

The Foundation's twelfth benefit exhibition, "Photographic Works: To Benefit the Foundation for Contemporary Arts," is held at Cohan and Leslie, 138 Tenth Avenue, December 11–20. The organizing committee includes Gregory Crewdson, Nan Goldin, Annie Leibovitz, Julian Lethbridge, Laurie Simmons, and Kara Walker. Some 209

4

5

6

7

artists donate 212 works, including Marina Abramović, Robert Adams, John Baldessari, Matthew Barney, Uta Barth, Bruce High Quality Foundation, Paul Chan, Lynn Davis, Tacita Dean, Liz Deschenes, Robert Gober, Katy Grannan, Timothy Greenfield-Sanders, Dana Hoey, Jon Kessler, Joel Meyerowitz, Shirin Neshat, Catherine Opie, Pipilotti Rist, Paolo Roversi, Ed Ruscha, Cindy Sherman, Francesco Vezzoli, Massimo Vitali, William Wegman, James Welling, Robert Whitman, and others. In the wake of a major economic downturn, 43 works sell and the show raises $150,000.

By the end of 2008, 31 artists receive Emergency Grants, totaling $36,000.

2009

Twelve $25,000 Grants to Artists are awarded to Mick Barr, Glenn Branca, Foofwa d'Imobilité, John Godfrey, Maria Hassabi, Elevator Repair Service, Klara Liden, Paul Etienne Lincoln, Ruth Maleczech, David Meltzer, Gedi Sibony, and Guido van der Werve.

The annual grants reception is held at Brooke Alexander, 59 Wooster Street, on February 23. Nancy Dalva announces the awards. Grantee Stephen Petronio's company performs *Prelude*, and grantee David Lang's *warmth*, for two electric guitars, is performed.

Thirty-nine presenting and support organizations are awarded grants, totaling $41,000.

Merce Cunningham dies on July 26 at age 90.

By the end of 2009, 40 Emergency Grants totaling $40,000 are made.

2010

Ten $25,000 Grants to Artists awards are made in January to Luciana Achugar, Fia Backström, Luke Fowler, Michael Gizzi, Miguel Gutierrez, Leslie Hewitt, Okkyung Lee, Rabih Mroué, Nature Theater of Oklahoma, and Pam Tanowitz.

William Anastasi receives the John Cage Award ($40,000).

The annual grants reception is held at Robert Rauschenberg Studio, 381 Lafayette Street, March 22. Nancy Dalva announces the awards. Grantee Joan La Barbara performs "Circular Song" and "Conversations," for voice; and grantee Kate Valk performs a monologue from the Wooster Group's then-work-in-progress, *Vieux Carré*.

Artist T.J. Wilcox joins the board of directors in June.

Fifty-one presenting and support organizations are awarded grants, totaling $53,000.

The Foundation's thirteenth benefit exhibition, "Painting and Sculpture: Exhibition to Benefit the Foundation for Contemporary Arts," is held at Lehmann Maupin, 201 Christie Street, December 9, 2010–January 9, 2011 and features 192 works by 190 artists. Organized by Cecily Brown, Vija Celmins, Rachel Feinstein, Robert Gober, Jasper Johns, Julian Lethbridge, Nate Lowman, Brice Marden, Julie Mehretu, James Rosenquist, Dana Schutz, Kara Walker, and T.J. Wilcox, the benefit includes their work as well as that of Tom Burr, Dan Colen, Tara Donovan, John Duff, Damien Hirst, Glenn Ligon, James Nares, Martin Puryear, R.H. Quaytman, Ed Ruscha, Frank Stella, Dan Walsh, Terry Winters, and others. Several Emergency Grants recipients also donate work, including Kerstin Brätsch, David Brooks, Joy Curtis, David Kennedy Cutler, Mia Pearlman, and Allyson Vieira. With 74 works selling, the exhibition raises $3.2 million.

By the end of 2010, 57 Emergency Grants totaling $50,000 are made.

1

2

3

PHOTO: PAULA COURT

(1) Installation view, "Photographic Works," FCA's twelfth benefit exhibition, Cohan and Leslie, New York, 2008. (2) Pam Tanowitz, *The Wanderer Fantasy*, performance, Danspace Project, New York, 2010. Photo: Julie Lemberger. (3) Maria Hassabi, *Solo*, performance, P.S. 122, New York. (4) Dona Nelson, *Hair Conditioning (front)*, 2011, acrylic and dyed cheesecloth on canvas, 82" x 78". Courtesy Thomas Erben Gallery, New York. (5) Steve Roden, *Striations* (16-mm film transferred to digital), installation view, Susanne Vielmetter Projects, Los Angeles, 2011. Photo: Robert Wedemeyer. (6) Neil Greenberg, 1997 grantee, performing *(like a vase)*, 2010, with James Kidd, FCA grants reception, Merce Cunningham Studio, 2012.

2011

Fourteen $25,000 Grants to Artists awards are made in January to Jos de Gruyter and Harald Thys, Kevin Drumm, Deborah Hay, Ryan McNamara, Jodi Melnick, Curtis Mitchell, Dona Nelson, David Neumann, Alix Pearlstein, Katie Peterson, Raha Raissnia, Steve Roden, Marina Rosenfeld, and Michael Webster.

Visual artist John Delk becomes secretary of the Foundation. Delk, who worked at the Foundation from 2002 to 2007, is an assistant to Jasper Johns.

The annual grants reception is held at Cunningham Dance Studio, 55 Bethune Street, on March 28. Nancy Dalva announces the awards. Grantee Jonah Bokaer performs an excerpt from *Prime Mover*, and grantee Elevator Repair Service performs an excerpt from work-in-progress *Shuffle*.

Artist Glenn Ligon joins the board of directors in July.

Through a major $500,000, four-year grant from the Andrew W. Mellon Foundation, which fully underwrites all grants made to performance arts organizations, 62 Grants to Organizations are made, totaling $193,500. This nearly quadruples the Foundation's support of avant-garde arts nonprofits. Most grants are either $2,500 or $5,000.

By the end of 2011, 74 Emergency Grants totaling $70,368 are made.

2012

Fourteen $25,000 Grants to Artists are awarded in January to Ei Arakawa, Justin Vivian Bond, Daniel Bozhkov, Thomas Bradshaw, Jace Clayton, Jack Collom, Rhodri Davies, Beth Gill, William E. Jones, Ralph Lemon, Tan Lin, Kate Millett, Jen Rosenblit, and Grace Schwindt.

Pauline Oliveros receives the $50,000 John Cage Award.

The annual grants reception is held at the Cunningham Dance Studio, 55 Bethune Street, on March 19. Nancy Dalva announces the awards. Grantee Neil Greenberg dances an excerpt from *(like a vase)*, 2010, with James Kidd and music by 1997 grantee Zeena Parkins. Grantee Red Light New Music performs excerpts from several works by John Cage. This is the final event to be held in Cunningham's historic Westbeth studio.

Artist Robert Gober joins the board of directors in June.

Sixty-nine Grants to Organizations are made, totaling $200,000.

By the end of 2012, 83 Emergency Grants are made, totaling $117,000.

2013

The inaugural Robert Rauschenberg Award, a $25,000, by-nomination unrestricted grant funded by the Robert Rauschenberg Foundation to honor his legacy of innovation, risk-taking, and experimentation, is awarded to Trisha Brown. This is the FCA's first endowed grant.

Fourteen Grants to Artists are awarded to Paula Court, Beverly Dahlen, Faye Driscoll, David Dunn, Robert Grenier, Ishmael Houston-Jones, Matt Hoyt, Rashaun Mitchell, MPA, My Barbarian, Matana Roberts, Wu Tsang, Toby Twining, and Kota Yamazaki.

By the time of its 50th anniversary, the Foundation will have made nearly 2,000 grants, totaling almost $10,000,000. ◆

5

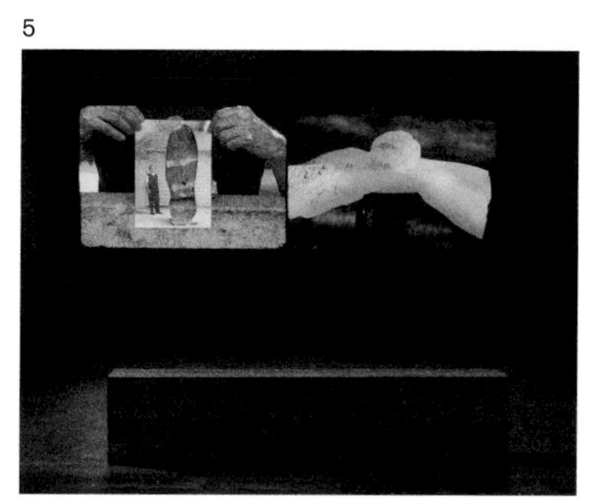

4

6

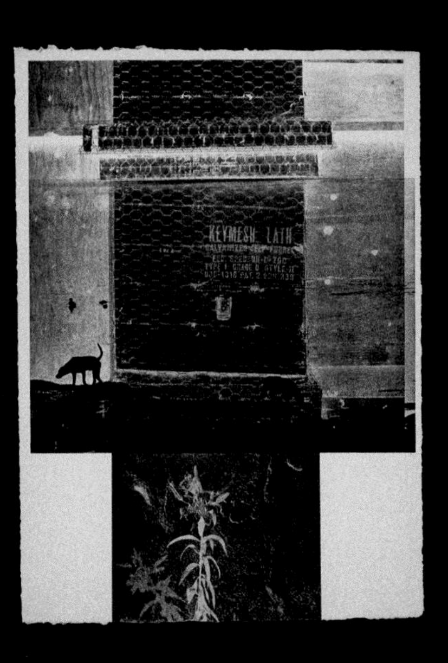

"Eight Lithographs," 1981, print portfolio to benefit FCPA, edition of 50, published by Gemini G.E.L. Clockwise from top left: Ellsworth Kelly, *St. Martin Tropical Plant*, 1981, 26" x 34". David Hockney, *Celia, La Bergere*, 1981, 24" x 35". Sam Francis, *Falling Star*, 1981, 36" x 28". Philip Guston, *Remains*, 1980, 19 1/2" x 29 3/4". Robert Rauschenberg, *Lily Scent*, 1981, 32" x 24". Bruce Nauman, *Human Companion, Human Drain*, 1981, 30" x 22". Jasper Johns, *Cicada*, 1981, 35" x 26". Richard Serra, *Out the Window at the Square Diner*, 1980, 29 3/4" x 23".

Appendix

A. Grants, 1963–1992

B. Grants to Artists, 1993–2013

C. John Cage Award

D. Robert Rauschenberg Award

E. Grants to Organizations, 1993–2012

F. Art Contributors, 1963–2013

G. Benefit Exhibition History

H. 1963 Benefit Exhibition Checklist

I. Grants to Artists Selection Committee Panelists, 2000–2013

J. Grants to Artists Poetry Readers, 2000–2013

K. Emergency Grants Panelists, 2006–2013

L. *Notations* Contributors

M. Board of Directors and Secretaries History

A

GRANTS 1963–1992

1963
Earle Brown
Morton Feldman
Judson Memorial Church
Merle Marsicano
Paper Bag Players

1964
Cunningham Dance Foundation

1965
Max Neuhaus
Peter Schumann/Bread and Puppet Theater

1966
Cunningham Dance Foundation
Midi Garth
Judson Memorial Church
Max Neuhaus
Yvonne Rainer
Kurt Schwertsik
La Monte Young

1967
No grants made

1968
Cornelius Cardew
Lucinda Childs
Dance Theater Workshop

1969
Meredith Monk

1970
Kilina Cremona
Philip Glass
Yvonne Rainer
Grete Sultan
Twyla Tharp
David Tudor

1971
Trisha Brown
Nancy Green
Lee Guilliatt
Steve Reich

1972
Dan T. Jones
Steve Paxton
The Poetry Project
Ken Rubenstein/Rubenstein Theater Foundation
Monica Solem

1973
Kenneth King
Mabou Mines
Ann Wilson

1974
Billy Apple
David Borden
Trisha Brown
Philip Glass
Kenneth King

1975
EAR Magazine/Beth Anderson
Kathryn Bernson
Edwin Denby
Ralston Farina

1976
No grants made

1977
Kenneth King
Performance & Video Workshop
The Poetry Project
Shared Forms Theatre

1978
Cunningham Dance Foundation
Richard Foreman/Ontological-Hysteric Theater
Rosalind Newman/Harvest Dance Foundation
Performance Workshop

1979
Maryanne Amacher
Eye and Ear Theater/Ada Katz
Cunningham Dance Foundation
Spencer Holst
The Kitchen
David Lusby
The Poetry Project
Norman Solomon
Gus Solomons Jr./Solomons Company Dance
Mel Wong

1980
Michael Brownstein
Collaborative Projects
Cunningham Dance Foundation
Jana Haimsohn
The Kitchen
Robert Kovich
The Poetry Project
Garry Reigenborn
James Schuyler

1981
A.I.R. Gallery
Maryanne Amacher
Charles Atlas
Collective for Living Cinema
Gail Conrad
Andrew Culver
Cunningham Dance Foundation
Dance Theater Workshop
Peter Garland
Solomon R. Guggenheim Trust (Meirkhold Fund)
Risa Jaroslaw/Roxanne Dance Foundation
Bill T. Jones
Pooh Kaye
The Kitchen
Joëlle Leandre

Linda Mussmann/Time & Space Limited
The Poetry Project
Dana Reitz/Roxanne Dance Foundation
Roulette
Jim Self
Shared Forms Theatre
Ton Simons/Third Street Dance Company
Theodora Skipitares/Skysaver Productions
Elizabeth Streb/Ringside
Whitney Museum Independent Study Program Scholarship

1982
John Bernd
Ping Chong/The Fiji Theater Company
Collective for Living Cinema
Cunningham Dance Foundation
Dance Theater Workshop
Danspace Project
The Drawing Center
Eye and Ear Theater
Vangelis Katsoulis
Kenneth King/Transmedia
The Kitchen
Joseph Kubera
David H. Macbride/GAGEEGO
Chris Mann
Charles Moulton
Rosalind Newman/Harvest Dance Foundation
Performance Space 122
The Poetry Project
PS1/Institute for Art and Urban Resources
Garry Reigenborn
Ellen van Schuylenburch
Gus Solomons Jr./Solomons Company Dance
Eva Soltes
The Squat Theatre
Symphony Space
Anne Tardos
Whitney Museum Independent Study Program Scholarship
Stefan Wolpe Society

1983
Lucinda Childs
Yoshiko Chuma and the School of Hard Knocks
Ornette Coleman
Andrew Culver
Eiko & Koma
John Giorno/Poetry Systems Institute
Martin Kalve
Takehisa Kosugi
Tim Miller
Meredith Monk/House Foundation for the Arts
Alice Notley

1984
Karole Armitage
Artists Space
David Behrman
Neely Bruce
Bill & Mary Buchen/Sonic Architecture
Cunningham Dance Foundation
Dance Theater Workshop
Danspace Project
The Drawing Center
EAR Magazine/New Wilderness Foundation
Filip Filipovic
Julia Heyward
Kim Jones
The Kitchen
The Poetry Project
Real Art Ways
James Schuyler
James Turrell/Skystone Foundation
Dan Wagoner Dance Foundation

1985
Artists Space
John Bernd
Sean Bronzell
Composers' Forum
Cunningham Dance Foundation
Dance Theater Workshop
Danspace Project
The Drawing Center
Douglas Dunn & Dancers
EAR Magazine/New Wilderness Foundation
Filip Filipovic
Peter Garland
Movement Research
Pentacle
Performance Space 122
Phill Niblock/Experimental Intermedia Foundation
The Poetry Project
Wendy Rogers/Choreographics
Roulette
Ton Simons/Third Street Dance Company
Elizabeth Streb/Ringside
Tui St. George Tucker

1986
Anthology Film Archives
Artists Space
Jack Briece
Cabrillo Music Festival
Rhys Chatham & Joseph Nechvatal
Cunningham Dance Foundation
Dance Theater Workshop
Dancing in the Streets
Danspace Project
The Drawing Center
Ralph Lemon
Performance Space 122
The Poetry Project
Dr. Mildred Pollner/Cinema Verité Foundation
Real Art Ways
Dana Reitz
Beatriz Roman
Susan Sontag
Thorpe Intermedia Gallery
Robert Wilson/Tisch School of the Arts, New York University
Dan Wagoner Dance Foundation
John Wieners
White Noise Theatre

1987
Karole Armitage/The Armitage Foundation
Power Boothe
Changing Dance Theatre/José Brown
Lucinda Childs
Collective for Living Cinema
Leatitia de Compiegne
Composers' Forum
Cunningham Dance Foundation
Dance Theater Workshop
Anthony Davis/Parabola Arts Foundation
The Drawing Center
Richard Elovich
Eye and Ear Theater
Julia Heyward
Bill T. Jones/Arnie Zane Dance Company
Kynaston McShine
Bebe Miller
Charlotte Moorman
Pat Oleszko
Steve Paxton
Pentacle
Performance Project/Worklabs
Performance Space 122
The Poetry Project
Printmaking Workshop
Real Art Ways
Nelson Rivera
The Rachel Rosenthal Company
Roulette
Ton Simons/Third Street Dance Company
Soundings Press
Standby Program at Matrix
Myron Stout Fellowship
Tellus
Fiona Templeton
Yellow Springs Institute
Bill Young and Dancers

1988
14th Street Dance Center/Emanu-el Midtown YM-YWHA
Artists Space
Bang on a Can
Composers' Forum
Gyula Csapó
Cunningham Dance Foundation
Dance Continuum
Dance Theater Workshop
Dancing in the Streets
Danspace Project
The Drawing Center
En Garde Arts
Grand Windows
Amy Greenfield
John Jesurun
The Kitchen
The Knitting Factory
Robert Kovich
Movement Research
Phill Niblock/Experimental Intermedia Foundation
Maria Nordman
Performance Space 122
The Poetry Project
Primary Performance Group
PS 1/Institute for Art and Urban Resources
Real Art Ways
Susan Rethorst
Roulette
Ellsworth Snyder/The First Unitarian Society
Elizabeth Streb/Ringside
Sun & Moon Press
Telluride Institute
David Tudor
White Columns
The Wooster Group
Bill Young and Dancers

1989
14th Street Dance Center/Emanu-el Midtown YM-YWHA
Anthology Film Archives
Artists Space
Atlantic Center for the Arts
Bang on a Can
Changing Dance Theatre/José Brown
Remy Charlip
Ping Chong/The Fiji Theater Company
Yoshiko Chuma and the School of Hard Knocks
Collective for Living Cinema
Jane Comfort Dance Company
Composers' Forum
Gyula Csapó
Andrew Culver
Cunningham Dance Foundation
Dance Continuum
Dance Theater Workshop
Brenda Daniels Dance Company
Danspace Project
Molly Davies/AM Foundation, Inc.
Dixon Place
En Garde Arts
Essential Music
Exit Art
Exquisite Corpse
Molissa Fenley/Momenta Foundation
Lisa Fox
Frankin Furnace Archive
Ruth Happel
Harvestworks
Robin Hastings
Ariel S. Herrera
Jeannie Hutchins
The Knitting Factory
Alan Kryszak
Linda Lindroth & Craig D. Newick
Lynx
Mabou Mines
MELA Foundation
Raphael Mostel
Movement Research
Jalalu-Kalvert Nelson
New Museum of Contemporary Art
Nuyorican Poets Cafe
The Orchestra of the S.E.M. Ensemble
Hank Pellissier (a.k.a. Hank Hyena)
Penguin Rep
Performance Space 122
The Poetry Project
Eliane Radigue
Real Art Ways
Dana Reitz
Michael Richardson
Ron Rocco
The Rachel Rosenthal Company
Roulette
Ton Simons/Third Street Dance Company
The Squat Theatre

Richard Teitelbaum
Telluride Institute
James Turrell/Skystone Foundation
Doug Varone and Dancers
Stefan Wolpe Society
The Wooster Group
Fred Worden
Bill Young and Dancers

1990
Anthology Film Archives
Artists Space
Bang on a Can
Johannes Birringer
Susan Botti
Rhys Chatham
Collective for Living Cinema
Ray Colmer
Cunningham Dance Foundation
Dance Theater Workshop
Danspace Project
Dixon Place
Samantha Mae Dorfman
The Drawing Center
Leah Durner
En Garde Arts
Essential Music
Phill Niblock/Experimental Intermedia Foundation
Franklin Furnace Archive
Peter Garland/Soundings Press
Keith Glassman
Malcolm Goldstein
Ain Gordon
David Gordon/Pick Up Performance Company
Harvestworks
Jerry Hunt
Jeannie Hutchins
Ken Jacobs
John Jesurun/Shatterhand, Inc.
Judson Memorial Church
John Kelly and Company
The Kitchen
Petr Kotik
La MaMa Experimental Theatre Club
Shelley Lee Dance Company
William LePage
Linda Lindroth & Craig D. Newick
Lynx
Mabou Mines
Bunita Marcus
Marzena Performance Ensemble
Mel Mercier
Meredith Monk/House Foundation for the Arts
Raphael Mostel
Conlon Nancarrow
New Museum of Contemporary Art
Nuyorican Poets Cafe
Dora Ohrenstein
Pauline Oliveros Foundation
Performance Space 122
The Poetry Project
Quartet: Iréne Hultman, Joseph Lennon, Dennis O'Connor & Ann Papoulis
Real Art Ways
The Rachel Rosenthal Company
Roulette
Ton Simons/Third Street Dance Company

Elizabeth Streb/Ringside
Telluride Institute
Volunteer Lawyers for the Arts
The Wooster Group
Bill Young and Dancers
Paul Zukofsky

1991
14th Street Dance Center/Emanu-el Midtown YM-YWHA
Alternative Museum
Karole Armitage/The Armitage Foundation
Jeffrey Arsenault
Artists Space
Robert Ashley
Bang on a Can
Martha Bowers
Sean Bronzell
Trisha Brown/Trisha Brown Company
The California E.A.R. Unit
Bruce Checefsky
Rick Cluchey/San Quentin Drama Workshop
Coffee House Press
Company Appels
Composers' Forum
Crossings
Cunningham Dance Foundation
Dancing in the Streets
Dixon Place
The Drawing Center
Douglas Dunn & Dancers
Exit Art
Phill Niblock/Experimental Intermedia Foundation
Molissa Fenley
The Field
Erin Fitzgerald
Ain Gordon
David Gordon/Pick Up Performance Company
Harvestworks
Martine Joste
Jin Hi Kim & Joseph Celli
The Kitchen
Shelley Lee Dance Company
David H. Macbride/GAGEEGO
Maxine Moerman
Meredith Monk/House Foundation for the Arts
Ken Montgomery/Generator
Movement Research
New York Studio School of Drawing, Painting & Sculpture
Bruce Odland
The Orchestra of the S.E.M. Ensemble
The Poetry Project
Real Art Ways
Roulette
Michael Rush and Co./New Haven Artists' Theater
Mercy Sidbury
Spencer/Colton (Amy Spencer & Richard Colton)
Telluride Institute
Donna Uchizono
Urban Bush Women
Volunteer Lawyers for the Arts
Dan Wagoner Dance Foundation
ZONE

1992
Artists Space
Bang on a Can
Composers' Forum
Cunningham Dance Foundation
Dance Theater Workshop
Danspace Project
The Drawing Center
Franklin Furnace Archive
The Kitchen
Los Angeles Contemporary Exhibitions
Movement Research
Nuyorican Poets Cafe
Performance Space 122
The Poetry Project
Dana Reitz/Field Papers
Wendy Rogers/Choreographics
Roulette
Telluride Institute
David Tudor
The Wooster Group

B

GRANTS TO ARTISTS 1993–2013

1993
Dance
Steffan "Wiggles" Clemente
Music/Sound
John Luther Adams
Lois V Vierk
Theater/Performance Art
John Jesurun
Poetry
Paul Beatty
Visual Arts
Trevor Winkfield

1994
Dance
Steve Paxton
Music/Sound
David Behrman
Phill Niblock
Pauline Oliveros
Trimpin
Theater/Performance Art
Ondřej Hrab
Visual Arts
Sam Reveles

1995
Dance
Doug Elkins
Iréne Hultman
Music/Sound
Mary Jane Leach
John Moran
Theater/Performance Art
Alex Bag
Joan Jonas
Bob McGrath
Poetry
Bernadette Mayer
Edwin Torres

1996
Dance
Elizabeth Streb
Music/Sound
Paul De Marinis
Petr Kotik
Roscoe Mitchell
Theater/Performance Art
Gary Stevens
Poetry
Patricia Spears Jones
Ron Padgett
David Shapiro
Visual Arts
Burt Barr
Howard S. Thies

1997
Dance
Douglas Dunn
Neil Greenberg
Mary Oslund
Music/Sound
Muhal Richard Abrams
Charles Amirkhanian
Zeena Parkins
Theater/Performance Art
Julian Maynard Smith
Poetry
Alice Notley
Edward Sanders
Visual Arts
Zoe Beloff

1998
Dance
chameckilerner, Rosane Chamecki and Andrea Lerner
Jennifer Monson
Music/Sound
Maryanne Amacher
Arnold Dreyblatt
Krzysztof Knittel
Sinan Savaskan
Theater/Performance Art
Ann Carlson
Poetry
Peter Gizzi
David Henderson
Maureen Owen
Visual Arts
David Dupuis
Roger Newton
Riverbed Media, Paul Kaiser and Shelley Eshkar

1999
Dance
Terry Creach
Everett Dance Theatre
Jennifer Lacey
Stephen Petronio
Music/Sound
Jonathan Bepler
John Bischoff
Carl Stone
Theater/Performance Art
Martín Acosta
Poetry
Gary Lutz

Jaime Manrique
Paul Violi
C.D. Wright
Visual Arts
Rochelle Feinstein
Martin Kersels
Siobhan Liddell

2000
Dance
Molissa Fenley
Wendy Rogers
Music/Sound
György Kurtág
Laetitia Sonami
Julia Wolfe
Theater/Performance Art
Richard Maxwell
Bill Shannon
Poetry
Lorenzo Thomas
Visual Arts
Jon Kessler
Julie Mehretu
Rubén Ortiz Torres

2001
Dance
Dean Moss
Tere O'Connor
Sally Silvers
Music/Sound
David First
Jin Hi Kim
Jim O'Rourke
Mikel Rouse
Michael Schumacher
Theater/Performance Art
Caden Manson
Poetry
Erica Hunt
Anne Waldman
Visual Arts
Young-Hae Chang Heavy Industries,
Young-hae Chang and Marc Voge

2002
Dance
Jonathan Burrows
Music/Sound
William Duckworth
Michael Gordon
David Lang
Theater/Performance Art
William Pope.L
Fiona Templeton
Poetry
Douglas Messerli
John Yau
Visual Arts
Adam Chodzko
Paul Sietsema

2003
Dance
John Jasperse
Susan Rethorst
Music/Sound
Elliott Sharp
Theater/Performance Art
Kate Valk
Mac Wellman
Poetry
Rosmarie Waldrop
Visual Arts
Bill Morrison

2004
Dance
Germaine Acogny
Karole Armitage
Music/Sound
Marc Mellits
Yasunao Tone
Theater/Performance Art
Peggy Shaw
Poetry
Carla Harryman
Harryette Mullen
Visual Arts
Wade Guyton
Stuart Hawkins
Arturo Herrera

2006
Dance
Jonah Bokaer
Vicky Shick
Christopher Williams
Music/Sound
David Grubbs
Ikue Mori
Michael Pisaro
Yuji Takahashi
Theater/Performance Art
Young Jean Lee
Poetry
Norma Cole
Joanne Kyger
Visual Arts
Paul Chan
Nathaniel Dorsky
Ishmael Randall Weeks

2007
Dance
DD Dorvillier
RoseAnne Spradlin
Music/Sound
Douglas Henderson
Yuko Nexus6
Jennifer Walshe
Theater/Performance Art
Clarinda Mac Low
Pan Pan Theatre
Poetry
Rae Armantrout
Nathaniel Mackey
Visual Arts
Kimsooja

2008
Dance
Kimberly Bartosik
Sarah Michelson
Yasuko Yokoshi
Music/Sound
Annie Gosfield
Ron Kuivila
Theater/Performance Art
Tamy Ben-Tor
Wang Jianwei
Poetry
Charles North
Elizabeth Robinson
Visual Arts
Cameron Jamie
Ohad Meromi
Allison Smith

2009
Dance
Foofwa d'Imobilité
Maria Hassabi
Music/Sound
Mick Barr
Glenn Branca
Theater/Performance Art
Elevator Repair Service
Ruth Maleczech
Poetry
John Godfrey
David Meltzer
Visual Arts
Klara Liden
Paul Etienne Lincoln
Gedi Sibony
Guido van der Werve

2010
Dance
Luciana Achugar
Miguel Gutierrez
Pam Tanowitz
Music/Sound
Luke Fowler
Okkyung Lee
Theater/Performance Art
Nature Theater of Oklahoma
Rabih Mroué
Poetry
Michael Gizzi
Visual Arts
Fia Backström
Leslie Hewitt

2011
Dance
Deborah Hay
Jodi Melnick
David Neumann
Music/Sound
Kevin Drumm
Steve Roden
Marina Rosenfeld
Michael Webster
Theater/Performance Art
Ryan McNamara
Alix Pearlstein
Poetry
Katie Peterson
Visual Arts
Jos de Gruyter and Harald Thys
Curtis Mitchell
Dona Nelson
Raha Raissnia

2012
Dance
Beth Gill
Ralph Lemon
Jen Rosenblit
Music/Sound
Jace Clayton
Rhodri Davies
Poetry
Jack Collom
Tan Lin
Theater/Performance Art
Ei Arakawa
Justin Vivian Bond
Thomas Bradshaw
Grace Schwindt
Visual Arts
Daniel Bozhkov
William E. Jones
Kate Millett

2013

Dance
Faye Driscoll
Ishmael Houston-Jones
Rashaun Mitchell
Kota Yamazaki
Music/Sound
David Dunn
Matana Roberts
Toby Twining
Poetry
Beverly Dahlen
Robert Grenier
Theater/Performance Art
Paula Court
MPA
My Barbarian
Visual Arts
Matt Hoyt
Wu Tsang

C

JOHN CAGE AWARD

1992
David Tudor

1994
Takehisa Kosugi

1996
Christian Wolff

1998
Earle Brown

2000
Gordon Mumma

2002
Robert Ashley

2004
David Behrman

2006
Charles Atlas

2008
Paul Kaiser

2010
William Anastasi

2012
Pauline Oliveros

D

ROBERT RAUSCHENBERG AWARD

2013
Trisha Brown

E

GRANTS TO ORGANIZATIONS 1993–2012

The directors award grants to presenting and support organizations on an annual basis by application. Grants range in amount from $1,000 to $5,000. The number of grants made varies from year to year.

1708 Gallery, Richmond, VA
651 Arts, Brooklyn, NY

Aaron Davis Hall, New York, NY
Abrons Art Center, Henry Street Settlement, New York, NY
Anthology Film Archives, New York, NY
Antonia Arts, Peekskill, NY
apexart, New York, NY
Art in General, New York, NY
ART PAPERS, Atlanta, GA
Art Resources Transfer, New York, NY
Artists Alliance Inc., New York, NY
Artists Space, New York, NY
ARTPIX, Houston, TX
Asia Society, New York, NY
Athens Institute for Contemporary Art, Athens, GA

Ballroom Marfa, Marfa, TX
Bang on a Can, People's Commissioning Fund, Brooklyn, NY
Baryshnikov Arts Center, New York, NY
Black Square Editions, New York, NY
Beyond Baroque Literary/Arts Center, Venice, CA
BOMB Magazine, Brooklyn, NY
The Brecht Forum, New York, NY
Brooklyn Arts Exchange, Brooklyn, NY
The Brooklyn Rail, Brooklyn, NY
Trisha Brown Dance Company, Choreographers' Composition Workshops, New York, NY
The Bushwick Starr, Brooklyn, NY

Cabinet Magazine, Brooklyn, NY
Cal Performances, Berkeley, CA
The Camera Club of New York, New York, NY
The Center for Book Arts, New York, NY
Center for Performance Research, Brooklyn, NY
The CENTER for Performing Arts at Rhinebeck, Rhinebeck, NY
Center on Contemporary Art, Seattle, WA
chashama, New York, NY
Chez Bushwick, Brooklyn, NY
The Chocolate Factory, Long Island City, NY
Classic Stage Company, New York, NY
Cleveland Performance Art Festival, Cleveland, OH
Coffee House Press, Minneapolis, MN
Composers' Forum, New York, NY
Creative Time, New York, NY
CUE Art Foundation, New York, NY
Cunningham Dance Foundation, Cunningham Studio Rental Program, New York, NY

Dancing in the Streets, New York, NY
Danspace Project, New York, NY
Deep Listening Institute, Kingston, NY
Diapason Gallery for Sound and Intermedia, Brooklyn, NY
Dieu Donné, New York, NY
DiverseWorks Art Space, Houston, TX
Dixon Place, New York, NY
Djerassi Resident Artists Program, Woodside, CA
The Drawing Center, New York, NY
Dumbo Arts Center, Brooklyn, NY

Echo Park Film Center, Los Angeles, CA
Elizabeth Foundation for the Arts, New York, NY
Esopus, New York, NY
Exit Art, New York, NY
Experimental Intermedia Foundation, New York, NY
Experiments in Art and Technology, Berkeley Heights, NJ

The Field, New York, NY
FiveMyles, Brooklyn, NY
The Flea Theater, New York, NY
Forever & Today, Inc., New York, NY
Franklin Furnace, Brooklyn, NY
From the Fishouse, Pittston, ME
Fusebox Festival, Austin, TX

A Gathering of the Tribes, New York, NY
Greenwich House, New York, NY

Hallwalls Contemporary Arts Center, Buffalo, NY
Hard Press Editions, Stockbridge, MA
Harvestworks, New York, NY
Headlands Center for the Arts, Sausalito, CA
HERE Arts Center, New York, NY

Incubator Arts Project, New York, NY
Independent Curators International, New York, NY
ISSUE Project Room, Brooklyn, NY

The Joyce Theater, Joyce SoHo Presents, New York, NY

KEXP, Seattle, WA
The Kitchen, New York, NY

La MaMa Experimental Theatre Club, New York, NY
LAND (Los Angeles Nomadic Division), Los Angeles, CA
LAXART, Los Angeles, CA
Light Industry, Brooklyn, NY
Links Hall, Chicago, IL
Locust Projects, Miami, FL
Los Angeles Contemporary Exhibitions, Los Angeles, CA

Mabou Mines, New York, NY
Machine Project, Los Angeles, CA
MAD ALEX Arts Foundation, New York, NY
MAPP International Productions, New York, NY
MATA (Music at the Anthology), Brooklyn, NY
Mattress Factory, Pittsburgh, PA
Mobius, Boston, MA
Momenta Art, Brooklyn, NY
Richard Move/Martha @, New York, NY
Movement Research, New York, NY

New Arts Program, Kutztown, PA
New Dance Alliance, New York, NY
New Museum of Contemporary Art, New York, NY
New York Live Arts, New York, NY
New York City Players, New York, NY
No Longer Empty, New York, NY
Nuyorican Poets Cafe, New York, NY

O Books, Berkeley, CA
On the Boards, Seattle, WA
Ontological-Hysteric Theater, New York, NY
Other Minds, San Francisco, CA
Outpost Artists Resources, Ridgewood, NY

PARTICIPANT INC, New York, NY
PAJ: A Journal of Performance and Art, New York, NY
Performa, New York, NY
Performance Space 122, New York, NY
The Poetry Project, New York, NY
Portland Institute for Contemporary Art, Portland, OR
Primary Information, New York, NY
Printed Matter, New York, NY

Rain Taxi, Minneapolis, MN
Randolph Street Gallery, Chicago, IL
Real Art Ways, Hartford, CT
Recess, New York, NY
Red Light New Music, Brooklyn, NY
Rhizome, New York, NY
Roulette, Brooklyn, NY

S.E.M. Ensemble, Beyond Cage Festival, Brooklyn, NY
St. Ann's Warehouse, Brooklyn, NY
San Francisco Cinematheque, San Francisco, CA
SculptureCenter, Long Island City, NY
Show Box L.A., Los Angeles, CA
Signature Theatre Company, New York, NY
Smack Mellon, Brooklyn, NY
The Society for the Activation of Social Space through Art and Sound, Los Angeles, CA
Socrates Sculpture Park, Long Island City, NY
Soho Rep, New York, NY
South Florida Composers Alliance, Interdisciplinary Sound Arts Workshop, Miami, FL
SPACES, Cleveland, OH
Summer Stages Dance, Concord, MA
Symphony Space, New York, NY

terraNOVA Collective, New York, NY
The Tank, New York, NY
Thread Waxing Space, New York, NY
theatreflective, Brooklyn, NY
Tigertail Productions, Miami, FL
TOPAZ ARTS, Woodside, NY
Triple Candie, Philadelphia, PA
Triple Canopy, Brooklyn, NY

Under the Radar, New York, NY

Velocity Dance Center, Seattle, WA
Volunteer Lawyers for the Arts, New York, NY

White Columns, New York, NY
The Wooster Group/The Performing Garage, Garage Works, New York, NY

Yale Union, Portland, OR
Yellow Taxi Productions, Nashua, NH

ART CONTRIBUTORS 1963–2013

Since 1963, the following artists have donated their work to benefit the Foundation for Contemporary Arts:

Sigmund Abeles
Marina Abramović
Rita Ackermann
Jeremy Adams
Robert Adams
Justin Adian
Peter Agostini
Ricci Albenda
Josef Albers
Richard Aldrich
Simon Aldridge

John Alexander
David Altmejd
John Altoon
Joseph Amar
William Anastasi
Carl Andre
Matthew Antezzo
William Anthony
Shigeo Anzai
Tateyuki Aoyama
Billy Apple
Arakawa
Kamrooz Aram
Uri Aran
Diane Arbus
Arman
David Armstrong
Charles Arnoldi
Richard Artschwager
Eve Aschheim
Dennis Ashbaugh
Hope Atherton
Edward Avedisian
Ay-O

Donald Baechler
Jo Baer
John Baldessari
Roger Ballen
Tom Bamberger
Tim Barber
Miquel Barceló
Jared Bark
Matthew Barney
Burt Barr
Robert Barry
James Barth
Uta Barth
Jennifer Bartlett
Adam Bartos
Georg Baselitz
Samantha Bass
Lillian Bassman
Mary Bauermeister
Paul Baumann
Robert Beauchamp
Lawrence Beck
Gene Beery
Lynda Benglis
Richard Benson
Robert Benson
Eva Weis Bentzon
Tanyth Berkeley
Ellen Berkenblit
Cindy Bernard
Jake Berthot
Michael Bevilacqua
Mary Beyt
Sasha Bezzubov & Jessica Sucher
Huma Bhabha
Anna Bialobroda
James Biederman
Elmer Bischoff
Carolyn Marks Blackwood
Nayland Blake
Ross Bleckner
Dianne Blell
Norman Bluhm
Erika Blumenfeld
Mel Bochner
Bruce Boice
David Bolger

Ilya Bolotowsky
Lee Bontecou
Jennifer Bornstein
Jonathan Borofsky
Richard Bosman
Corinne May Botz
Louise Bourgeois
Carol Bove
Gary Bower
Paul Brach
Joe Bradley
Dove Bradshaw
Joe Brainard
Kerstin Brätsch
George Brecht
Robert Breer
Frank Breuer
Jeff Bridges
Christopher Brooks
David Brooks
Cecily Brown
James Brown
Joan Brown
Trisha Brown
Bruce High Quality Foundation
Matthew Buckingham
Stephen Buckley
David Budd
Lee Bul
Chris Burden
Tom Burr
Richmond Burton
Andrew Bush

Miriam Cabessa
Pedro Cabrita Reis
John Cage
Peter Caine
Ernesto Caivano
Elinor Carucci
Enrico Castro-Cid
Giorgio Cavallon
Vija Celmins
John Chamberlain
Paul Chan
Jake & Dinos Chapman
Adam Chodzko
Christo
Chryssa
Francesco Clemente
Chuck Close
Charles Clough
Peter Coffin
Cora Cohen
Dan Colen
Anne Collier
George Condo
Julia Condon
Bruce Conner
Lois Conner
Billy Copley
Joseph Cornell
Will Cotton
Petah Coyne
Jessica Craig-Martin
Michael Craig-Martin
Jane Creech
Gregory Crewdson
Sarah Crowner
William Crozier
William Crutchfield
Gary Cruz

Enzo Cucchi
Merce Cunningham
John Currin
Joy Curtis

Meredith Danluck
Nassos Daphnis
Michael David
Lynn Davis
Ron Davis
Verne Dawson
E.V. Day
Sue de Beer
Nancy de Holl
Walter De Maria
Jimmy De Sana
Joe Deal
Tacita Dean
Jay DeFeo
James DeFrance
Katrina del Mar
Tony DeLap
John Delk
David Dempewolf
Agnes Denes
Richard dePeaux
Liz Deschenes
David Deutsch
Steve DiBenedetto
Jane Dickson
Richard Diebenkorn
Sari Dienes
Laddie John Dill
Jim Dine
Mark Dion
Madeline Djerejian
Willie Doherty
Hisao Domoto
Rita Donagh
Tara Donovan
Christian D'Orgeix
Roy Dowell
Rosalind Drexler
Sherman Drexler
Tyler Drosdeck
Sally Drummond
Marcel Duchamp
Trenton Duerksen
John Duff
Carroll Dunham
David Dupuis
Michael Dweck
Friedel Dzubas

Shannon Ebner
Martha Edelheit
Keith Edmier
Echo Eggebrecht
Gardar Eide Einarsson
Arthur Elgort
Stephen Ellis
Tracey Emin
Barbara Ess
Inka Essenhigh
Suzan Etkin
Donald Evans

Öyvind Fahlström
Heide Fasnacht
Richard Feaster
Paul Feeley
Tony Feher

Rachel Feinstein
Rochelle Feinstein
Robert Feintuch
Feng Mengbo
Rae Ferren
Jud Fine
Aaron Fink
Larry Fink
Eric Fischl
Louise Fishman
Daphne Fitzpatrick
Dan Flavin
Caio Fonseca
Hermine Ford
Walton Ford
Seth Michael Forman
Robert Alan Fosdick
Llyn Foulkes
Rachel Foullon
Jason Fox
Sam Francis
Richard Francisco
Luis Frangella
Helen Frankenthaler
Suzan Frecon
Jonah Freeman
Jane Freilicher
Lucian Freud
Anthony Friedkin
Katharina Fritsch
Emi Fukuzawa

Simone Gad
Charles Gaines
Ron Galella
Sally Gall
Anya Gallaccio
Jedd Garet
Anna Gaskell
Gelitin
Thomas George
Tio Giambruni
Ralph Gibson
Liam Gillick
Tina Girouard
Robert Gober
Glenn Goldberg
Michael Goldberg
Nan Goldin
Bill Goldston
Andy Goldsworthy
Dulce Gómez
Wayne Gonzales
Joe Goode
Robert Goodnough
Ron Gorchov
Daniel Gordon
Sam Gordon
Adolph Gottlieb
Amy Granat
Katy Grannan
Deborah Grant
Morris Graves
Nancy Graves
Cleve Gray
Luke Gray
Robert Greene
Stephen Greene
Isca Greenfield-Sanders
Timothy Greenfield-Sanders
Joel Grey
Michael Joaquin Grey

Joseph Grigely
Red Grooms
Robert Grosvenor
Jerzy Grzegorski
Donald Gummer
Guo Hongwei
Andreas Gursky
Philip Guston
Janice Guy
Wade Guyton

Marcia Hafif
Peter Halley
Tamar Halpern
Josephine Halvorson
Richard Hamilton
Jonathan Hammer
Jane Hammond
Lloyd Hamrol
Marc Handelman
W.A. Hansbauer
Keith Haring
Lyle Ashton Harris
Rachel Harrison
Grace Hartigan
Jan Hashey
Joseph Haske
Julian Hatofsky
Mona Hatoum
Stuart Hawkins
Todd Haynes
Phillip Hefferton
Jay Heikes
Mary Heilmann
Al Held
John Heliker
Adam Helms
Edward Henderson
George Herms
Daniel Hesidence
Todd Hido
Matthew Higgs
Stephen Hilger
Charles Hinman
Taishi Hirokawa
Damien Hirst
David Hockney
Howard Hodgkin
Dana Hoey
Christian Holstad
Carl Holty
Jenny Holzer
Hong Hao
Naoki Honjo
Kosai Hori
Roni Horn
Jonathan Horowitz
Jaya Howey
Matt Hoyt
Alex Hubbard
Judy Hudson
Peter Hujar
Greg Hull
John Hultberg
Gary Hume
Ralph Humphrey
Jacqueline Humphries
Bryan Hunt
Robert Huot
Tim Hyde

Jerald Ieans
Gerald Incandela
Robert Indiana
Gen'ichiro Inokuma
Will Insley
Patrick Ireland
Jamie Isenstein
Arata Isozaki

Robert Jack
Matthew Day Jackson
Bill Jacobson
Yvonne Jacquette
Valerie Jaudon
Paul Jenkins
Neil Jenney
Susan Jennings
Bill Jensen
Jasper Johns
Cletus Johnson
Larry Johnson
Lester Johnson
Matt Johnson
Ray Johnson
Ryan Johnson
Joan Jonas
Allen Jones
Kim Jones
Pirkle Jones
Ronald Jones
Michael Joo
Donald Judd
Tony Just

Wolf Kahn
Mitsuo Kano
Jane Kaplowitz
Dennis Kardon
Nikki Katsikas
Alex Katz
Allison Katz
Bill Katz
Craig Kauffman
Kcho (Alexis Leyva Machado)
Matt Keegan
Ellsworth Kelly
William Kelly
David Kennedy Cutler
Lisa Kereszi
Martin Kersels
Jon Kessler
Rosy Keyser
Anselm Kiefer
Frederick Kiesler
Kiki
Mokuma Kikuhata
Karen Kilimnik
Chris Killip
Byron Kim
Kimsooja
William King
R.B. Kitaj
Laura Kleger
Martin Kline
Christopher Knowles
Win Knowlton
Dorota Kolodziejczyk
Komar & Melamid
Gary Komarin
Akira Komoto
Elaine de Kooning
Willem de Kooning

Jeff Koons
Leon Kossoff
Joseph Kosuth
Joyce Kozloff
Aaron Krach
Daniel Kramer
Lee Krasner
David Krueger
Ella Kruglyanskaya
Nicholas Krushenick
Gary Kuehn
Robert Kulicke
Barney Kulok
Justine Kurland
Shio Kusaka
Robert Kushner
Guillermo Kuitca

Bruce LaBruce
Karl Lagerfeld
Gerald Laing
Mark Lancaster
Fay Lansner
H. Peik Larsen
Annika Larsson
Jonathan Lasker
Ibram Lassaw
Evelyn H. Lauder
Julian LaVerdiere
Louise Lawler
Deana Lawson
Gail LeBoff
Rico Lebrun
Leigh Ledare
Catherine Lee
Margaret Lee
Wesley Duke Lee
Daniel Lefcourt
Annie Leibovitz
Annette Lemieux
Zoe Leonard
Alfred Leslie
Julian Lethbridge
Barry Le Va
Matvey Levenstein
Les Levine
Tom Levine
Mon Levinson
Margrit Lewczuk
Sol LeWitt
Alexander Liberman
Roy Lichtenstein
Siobhan Liddell
Glenn Ligon
Linda Lindeberg
Richard Lindner
Judy Linn
Richard Lippold
Donald Lipski
Frank Lobdell
Jane Logemann
Lois Long
Richard Long
Robert Longo
Andrew Lord
Nate Lowman
Lu Shengzhong
Charles Luce
Sven Lukin
Eva Lundsager
Jim Lutes

Cassandra MacLeod
Paula Madawick
Matt Magee
René Magritte
Gerard Malanga
Janet Malcolm
Robert Mallary
Paul Manes
Robert Mangold
Robert Mapplethorpe
Conrad Marca-Relli
Marcia Marcus
Brice Marden
Helen Marden
Tom Marioni
Marisol
Mary Ellen Mark
Nicholas Marsicano
Agnes Martin
Knox Martin
Jacqueline Matisse Monnier
Taiji Matsue
Nick Mauss
Michael Mazur
Dan McCarthy
Matthew McCaslin
Suzanne McClelland
McDermott & McGough
Adam McEwen
Megan McLarney
Patrick McMullan
Maureen McQuillan
Emily McVarish
George Mead Moore
Josephine Meckseper
Julie Mehretu
Steven Meisel
Susan Meiselas
Jonas Mekas
Sean Mellyn
Ohad Meromi
Sam Messer
James Meyer
Joel Meyerowitz
Tomio Miki
John Miller
Keith Milow
Lisa Milroy
Marilyn Minter
Fred Mitchell
Joan Mitchell
Nancy M. Mitchnick
Tatsuo Miyajima
Aiko Miyawaki
Tracey Moffatt
Donald Moffett
Santi Moix
Sharon Molloy
Andy Monk
Matthew Monteith
Frank Moore
Gordon Moore
Malcolm Morley
Robert Morris
Sarah Morris
Jill Moser
Ed Moses
Robert Moskowitz
Robert Motherwell
Carrie Moyer
Reinhard Mucha
Stephen Mueller

Carter Mull
Antonio Muntadas
Tomoharu Murakami
Walter Murch
Elizabeth Murray

Peter Nadin
Laurel Nakadate
Billy Name
James Nares
Robert Natkin
Bruce Nauman
Elizabeth Neel
George Negroponte
Nelson
Jennifer Nelson
Joan Nelson
Manuel Neri
Lowell Nesbitt
Shirin Neshat
Barnett Newman
John Newman
Roger Newton
Katsuhito Nishikawa
Cady Noland
Kenneth Noland
Thomas Nozkowski

Chris Ofili
Kenzo Okada
Claes Oldenburg
Claes Oldenburg & Coosje van Bruggen
Michael Olodort
Jules Olitski
Nathan Oliveira
Karyn Olivier
Toshinobu Onosato
Catherine Opie
Julian Opie
George Ortman
Alfonso Ossorio
Barbro Östlin
Saburo Ota
Tom Otterness
Tony Oursler
Laura Owens

Paul Pagk
Nam June Paik
Roxy Paine
Harold Paris
Ji yeon Park
Erik Parker
Elizabeth Payne
Oliver Payne and Nick Relph
Debra Pearlman
Mia Pearlman
Philip Pearlstein
George Peck
Adam Pendleton
Irving Penn
Joyce Pensato
David Perry
Robert Peterson
Elizabeth Peyton
Judy Pfaff
Paul Pfeiffer
Bernard Pfriem
Ellen Phelan
Peter Phillips
Chloe Piene

Otto Piene
Jack Pierson
John Pilson
Howardena Pindell
Lari Pittman
Sylvia Plimack Mangold
Rona Pondick
Larry Poons
Bruce Porter
Fairfield Porter
Liliana Porter
Darryl Pottorf
Joanna Pousette-Dart
Richard Pousette-Dart
Zak Prekop
Ken Price
Richard Prince
J. John Priola
Rob Pruitt
Elliott Puckette
Martin Puryear
Adam Putnam

Harvey Quaytman
R.H. Quaytman
Eileen Quinlan

Raquel Rabinovich
Markus Raetz
Joseph Raffael
Sara Greenberger Rafferty
Mel Ramos
Ishmael Randall Weeks
Robert Rauschenberg
Man Ray
David Reed
Elaine Reichek
Ad Reinhardt
Edda Renouf
Andreas Rentsch
Carl Fredrik Reuterswärd
Sam Reveles
Jeanne Reynal
Guy Richards Smit
Gerhard Richter
William Ridenhour
Bridget Riley
Pipilotti Rist
Matthew Ritchie
Herb Ritts
Larry Rivers
Alex Robbins
Dorothea Rockburne
Halsey Rodman
Tim Rollins and K.O.S.
Ugo Rondinone
Mia Westerlund Roosen
Aura Rosenberg
James Rosenquist
Alexander Ross
Amanda Ross-Ho
Dieter Roth
Frank Roth
Yumi Janairo Roth
Susan Rothenberg
Mark Rothko
Mika Rottenberg
Helen Rousakis
Paolo Roversi
David Row
Heather Rowe
Nancy Rubins

Nicolas Rule
Ed Ruscha
Lisa Ruyter
Cordy Ryman

Niki de Saint Phalle
Peter Sacks
Q. Sakamaki
David Salle
Lucas Samaras
Victoria Sambunaris
Ludwig Sander
Joseph Santore
Julião Sarmento
Matt Saunders
Salvatore Scarpitta
John Schabel
Miriam Schapiro
Melanie Schiff
Katy Schimert
Mark Schlesinger
Edwin Schlossberg
Julian Schnabel
Carolee Schneemann
Lara Schnitger
Christian Schumann
Dana Schutz
Anja Schwörer
Carole Seborovski
Nikko Sedgwick
George Segal
Michelle Segre
Calvin Seibert
Jason Seley
Richard Serra
Andres Serrano
Joel Shapiro
Jack Shear
Cindy Sherman
David Benjamin Sherry
Toshio Shibata
Lior Shvil
Gedi Sibony
James Siena
Shahzia Sikander
Thomas Sills
Regina Silveira
Peter Simensky
Gary Simmons
Laurie Simmons
Jonathan Smith
Kiki Smith
Lindy Smith
Richard Smith
Sharon Smith
Tony Smith
David Smyth
Michael Snow
Keith Sonnier
Pierre Soulages
Theodoros Stamos
Doug and Mike Starn
Anita Steckel
Saul Steinberg
Amy Steiner
Pat Steir
Frank Stella
Gary Stephan
Bert Stern
Sterck & Rozo
Harold Stevenson
Ruby Sky Stiler

Rudolf Stingel
Paul Stopforth
David Storey
Kianja Strobert
Patrick Strzelec
Elaine Sturtevant
George Sugarman
Kunié Sugiura
Billy Sullivan
Peter Sullivan
Ryan Sullivan
Donald Sultan
Larry Sultan
Mark di Suvero

Philip Taaffe
Jorge Tacla
Yokoo Tadanori
William J. Taggart
Dorothea Tanning
Antoni Tàpies
Toeko Tatsuno
Al Taylor
Whiting Tennis
Paul Thek
Robert Therrien
Wayne Thiebaud
Jonathan Thomas
Mickalene Thomas
Yvonne Thomas
Sidney Tillim
Jean Tinguely
Rirkrit Tiravanija
Mark Tobey
Judy Tomkins
Thomas Trosch
Tseng Kwong Chi
Hiromi Tsuchida
Deborah Turbeville
Alan Turner
Richard Tuttle
Lane Twitchell
Cy Twombly
Jack Tworkov

Yoshihiko Ueda
Alan Uglow
P.O. Ultvedt
Keiji Usami

Meyer Vaisman
Georges Valmier
Coosje van Bruggen
Inez van Lamsweerde
Johannes VanDerBeek
Sara VanDerBeek
Francesco Vezzoli
Allyson Vieira
Jacques Villon
Massimo Vitali
Stephen Vitiello
Charline von Heyl

John Walker
Kara Walker
Kelley Walker
Star Wallowing Bull
Dan Walsh
Wang Jianwei
Andy Warhol
Oliver Wasow
Albert Watson

Robert Watts
Jeff Way
Bruce Weber
Meg Webster
William Wegman
Susan Weil
Lawrence Weiner
Matthew Weinstein
Marjorie Welish
James Welling
Will Wendt
John Wesley
Tom Wesselmann
H.C. Westermann
Stephen Westfall
Roger White
Robert Whitman
T.J. Wilcox
Hannah Wilke
John Willenbecher
Jesse Willenbring
Neil Williams
Jane & Louise Wilson
Robert Wilson
James Wines
Trevor Winkfield
George Winter
Robin Winters
Terry Winters
Steve Wolfe
Christopher Wool
William Wood
Bing Wright
Suzanne Wright
Wu Jian'an
Rob Wynne
Mark Wyse

Xing Danwen
Xu Bing

Takeo Yamaguchi
Yōsuke Yamahata
Amy Yao
Robert Yarber
Karen Yasinsky
Mie Yim
Aaron Young
Daisy Youngblood
Jack Youngerman
Mario Yrisarry
Adja Yunkers
Lisa Yuskavage

Michele Zalopany
Kes Zapkus
Marian Zazeela
Andrzej Zieliński
Elyn Zimmerman
Larry Zox
Michael Zwack

G

BENEFIT EXHIBITION HISTORY

Since 1963 the Foundation has held thirteen benefit exhibitions with the total participation of nearly 1,000 artists, who have donated some 4,000 works. Sales from benefit exhibitions raise needed funds for the FCA's programs.

1. "Exhibition and Sale of Works Donated by Artists to the Foundation for Contemporary Performance Arts"
February 25–March 2, 1963
Allan Stone Gallery
48 East 86th Street
67 artists (69 works)

2. "Drawings: Benefit: the Foundation for Contemporary Performance Arts"
December 14, 1965–January 5, 1966
Simultaneous showings at:
Leo Castelli Gallery, 4 East 77th Street
Tibor de Nagy Gallery, 29 West 57th Street (through December 30)
Kornblee Gallery, 58 East 79th Street
216 artists (221 works)

3. "Prints: To Benefit the Foundation for Contemporary Performance Arts"
December 9, 1967–January 4, 1968
Kornblee Gallery
58 East 79th Street
Number of artists and works unknown

4. "Drawings: To Benefit the Foundation for Contemporary Performance Arts"
November 29–December 20, 1980
Leo Castelli Gallery
420 West Broadway
201 artists (209 works)

5. "Eight Lithographs to Benefit the Foundation for Contemporary Performance Arts"
November 28–December 19, 1981
Leo Castelli Gallery
420 West Broadway
8 artists

6. "The 25th Anniversary Exhibition to Benefit the Foundation for Contemporary Performance Arts, Inc."
December 8–30, 1988
Simultaneous showings at:
Brooke Alexander, 59 Wooster Street
Leo Castelli Gallery, 420 West Broadway
70 artists (83 works)

7. "30th Anniversary Exhibition of Drawings: To Benefit the Foundation for Contemporary Performance Arts"
December 11, 1993–January 8, 1994
Leo Castelli Gallery
420 West Broadway
187 artists (189 works)

8. "Prints: To Benefit the Foundation for Contemporary Performance Arts"
December 5–29, 1995
Brooke Alexander
59 Wooster Street
133 artists (141 works)

9. "Drawings & Photographs: An Exhibition to Benefit the Foundation for Contemporary Performance Arts, Inc."
December 8–23, 2000
Matthew Marks Gallery
522 West 22nd Street
267 artists (275 works)

10. "Clarissa Dalrymple's Exhibition of Young Artists to Benefit the Foundation for Contemporary Arts," organized by Clarissa Dalrymple
February 16–25, 2006
Bortolami Dayan
510 West 25th Street
37 artists (42 works)

11. "Posters: Exhibition and Sale to Benefit the Foundation for Contemporary Arts"
December 8–20, 2006
Paula Cooper Gallery
521 West 21st Street
418 posters

12. "Photographic Works: To Benefit the Foundation for Contemporary Arts"
December 11–20, 2008
Cohan and Leslie
138 10th Avenue
209 artists (212 works)

13. "Painting and Sculpture: Exhibition to Benefit the Foundation for Contemporary Arts"
December 9, 2010–January 9, 2011
Lehmann Maupin
201 Chrystie Street
190 artists (192 works)

H

1963 BENEFIT EXHIBITION CHECKLIST

"Exhibition and Sale of Works Donated by Artists to the Foundation for Contemporary Performance Arts"
February 25–March 2, 1963
Allan Stone Gallery

Peter Agostini
The Wave, 1963
Plaster, gauze, and wire
74" x 37" x 30"
$3,500
Unsold
Returned at request of the artist

Norman Bluhm
Jug End, 1961
Oil on canvas
48" x 60"
$1,400
Unsold
Sold in 2007 to a private collector through James Graham and Sons, New York

Ilya Bolotowsky
White Vertical, 1960
Oil on canvas
96" x 40 1/16"
$3,200
Unsold
Sold in 1987 to Mr. and Mrs. James DeWoody, New York

Lee Bontecou
Untitled, 1963
Graphite and black pigment on muslin
36 1/8" x 36 1/4"
$950
Sold at 1963 Benefit to Adelaide de Menil, New York; currently collection of the Menil Collection, Houston

Paul Brach
Omen #3, 1961
Oil on canvas
20" x 24"
$400
Unsold
Returned at request of the artist

George Brecht
No Smoking, 1962
Assemblage with enamel, metal, and wood
7 1/4" x 10 3/4"
"Price unspecified for philosophical reasons"
Unsold
No record of later sale

George Brecht
Coat Rack, 1962
Assemblage with wood, metal, and fabric
49" x 51"
"Price unspecified for philosophical reasons"
Unsold
No record of later sale

Chryssa
Unmailed Letter, 1950
Plaster relief mounted in box frame
24 1/2" x 27 1/2" x 5"
$1,500
Unsold
Foundation for Contemporary Arts, New York

Nassos Daphnis
S-PX-5-62, 1962
Plexiglas object
32" x 9"x 2"
$750
Unsold
No record of later sale

Elaine de Kooning
Portrait of Merce, 1963
Oil on canvas
96" x 48"
$4,500
Unsold
Donated in 1996 to the National Portrait Gallery, Washington, DC

Willem de Kooning
Blue + White, c. 1960
Ink on paper; four drawings on paper mounted on canvas
19" x 22 ½"; 21" x 17"
$4,000 each
Unsold
Traded in 1970 to Jasper Johns for eight out of 60 impressions of *0 Through 9*, lead relief, 1970

Sari Dienes
Black Moons, 1960
Plaster and burnt pizza collage
35 ¼" x 15" x ¾"
$1,000
Unsold
Returned in 2005 to the Sari Dienes Foundation, Pomona, NY

Jim Dine
Child's Room #4 (Toy on a Blue Wall), 1962
Oil and metal toys on canvas
72 ½" x 60 ¼"
$1,900
Unsold
Donated in 1971 to the Greenville County Museum of Art, Greenville, SC

Marcel Duchamp
Box in a Valise, 1963
Assemblage with wood, cloth, and paper
16" x 14 ½" x 3"
$750
Sold at 1963 Benefit to Robert C. Scull, New York

Öyvind Fahlström
Performing K.K., 1963
Tempera on paper
30" x 20"
$200
Unsold
Sold in 1964 to Harry Abrams, New York

Sam Francis
Untitled, 1957
Egg tempera on paper
20" x 25"
$1,800
Sold in 1964 to a private collector

Jane Freilicher
The Ridge, 1961
Oil on canvas
51 ½" x 49 ½"
$1,200
Unsold
No record of later sale

Michael Goldberg
Bank Café, 1960
Oil on canvas
45 ¼" x 50"
$1,000
Unsold
No record of later sale

Robert Goodnough
The Voyage, 1962
Oil on canvas
28" x 36"
$1,000
Unsold
Returned at request of the artist

Morris Graves
In the Moonlight, 1939
Gouache on paper
24 ½" x 31"
$3,000
Sold at 1963 Benefit to the Woodward Foundation, Washington, DC

Philip Guston
Untitled, 1960
Ink drawing
Dimensions unknown
$1,000
Unsold
No record of later sale

Al Held
Untitled, 1961
Oil on canvas
82" x 66 ½"
$1,800
Unsold
Sold in June 1963 to Arnold Maremont, Chicago

Robert Indiana
Tilt, 1962
Oil on canvas
36" x 36"
$600
Unsold
Sold in 1964 to Harry Abrams, New York

Jasper Johns
Map, 1962
Encaustic and collage on canvas
60" x 93"
$15,000
Sold at 1963 benefit to Mr. and Mrs. Frederick Weisman, Los Angeles; currently collection of The Museum of Contemporary Art, Los Angeles

Wolf Kahn
Mysterious Vessel, 1962
Oil on canvas
26" x 36"
$650
Unsold
No record of later sale

Alex Katz
Don and Marisol 1, 1961
Oil on linen
71 ⅛" x 49"
$1,200
Unsold
Returned at request of the artist

Ellsworth Kelly
Red White, 1963
Acrylic on canvas
36" x 26"
$1,000
Unsold
Sold in 1964 to Bud Holland, New York; currently collection of Barney A. Ebsworth

Frederick Kiesler
Any Title, 1960
Pastel on paper
45" x 28 ½"
$1,500
Unsold
Sold in 2006 to Lawrence Dubin, New York

Ibram Lassaw
Enclave, 1963
Welded steel, copper, and bronze
13" x 7" x 9"
$1,000
Sold at 1963 Benefit to Ned Pines, New York

Rico Lebrun
In 8 Drawings for Three Penny Novel (The Peach sitting on Lap of Jack the Knife), 1962
Ink wash on paper
40" x 29 ½"
$700
Unsold
Returned at request of the artist

Alfred Leslie
Lady with Apple, Strawberry, and Chinese Apple, 1963
Wood sculpture
48" x 72" x 32"
$5,000
Unsold
Returned at request of the artist

Alfred Leslie
Harry Sultans Paper Bag, 1953
Collage, framed in aluminum and Plexiglas
13" x 12 ½"
$800
Unsold
No record of later sale

Alexander Liberman
IOTA I, 1961
Oil on canvas
50" x 30 ½"
$1,200
Unsold
Donated in 1971 to the Greenville County Museum of Art, Greenville, SC

Roy Lichtenstein
Flatten—Sand Fleas! 1962
Oil and Magna on canvas
34 ½" x 44 ½"
$675
Sold at 1963 Benefit to Leon Mnuchin, New York

Richard Lindner
Untitled, 1949
Oil on canvas
108" x 144"
$350
Sold at 1963 Benefit to Alfred Ardover, New York

Richard Lippold
Five Variations within a Sphere (for John Cage), 1947
Brass wire, steel, silver wire, and copper wire
Dimensions variable
$10,000
Unsold
Sold in 1964 to Mary Sisler, New York; currently collection of Museum of Modern Art, New York

Robert Mallary
Falling Man, 1963
Polyester and tuxedo
73" x 60" x 57"
$2,500
Unsold
No record of later sale

Conrad Marca-Relli
Untitled, 1963
Plastic collage
10 ½" x 13"
$900
Unsold
No record of later sale

Marisol
Untitled, 1962
Construction paper and wood
35" x 35" x 9"
$425
Sold at 1963 Benefit to Robert Mayer, Winnetka, IL

Nicholas Marsicano
Summer Black, 1960
Oil on canvas
51 ½" x 66 ½"
$2,000
Unsold
Sold in 2009 to Mark Patnode, New London, CT

Fred Mitchell
Pool, 1958
Oil on canvas
46" x 34"
$700
Unsold
Sold in 2005 to a private collector, New York

Robert Morris
Metered Bulb, 1962
Assemblage with lightbulb and meter
18" x 8" x 8 ½"
$200
Sold at 1963 Benefit to Jasper Johns, New York

Robert Moscowitz
Untitled #45, c. 1963
Collage and oil on canvas
72" x 60"
$700
Unsold
No record of later sale

Robert Motherwell
Night Beside the Sea, 1962
Oil on paper
29" x 23"
$2,500
Unsold
Returned at request of the artist; currently collection of Audrey and David Mirvish, Toronto, Canada

Barnett Newman
Untitled, 1960
Lithograph ed. 30/30
Dimensions unknown
$350
Sold at 1963 Benefit to Jill Kornblee, New York

Constantino Nivola
Motel Couple, 1962
Two terracotta sculptures
11 1/12" x 10 ¾" x third dimension unknown; 6 ½" x 6 ¾" x 4 ½"
$1,200
Unsold
No record of later sale

Claes Oldenburg
Funeral Heart, 1961
Cloth dipped in plaster on wire armature painted with enamel (bas relief)
57" x 39 ¾" x 5 ½"
$1,200
Unsold
No record of later sale; currently collection of San Francisco Museum of Modern Art, San Francisco

George Ortman
Star, 1958
Collage, oil, and plaster on Masonite
48" x 48"
$1,750
Unsold
Sold in 2006 to Jay Stark, New York

Barbro Ostlihn
Fan, 1962
Oil on canvas
27" x 30"
$600
Unsold
Returned at request of the artist

Richard Pousette-Dart
Untitled, 1962
Oil on Masonite
24" x 30 ½"
$2,500
Unsold
Returned at request of the artist

Robert Rauschenberg
Overcast II, 1962
95" x 72"
Oil and silk-screen ink on canvas
$7,500
Sold at 1963 Benefit to Vera List, New York; currently collection of Mr. and Mrs. Graham Gund

Ad Reinhardt
Abstract Painting, 1960
Oil on canvas
22" x 22"
$1,000
Sold at 1963 Benefit to the Woodward Foundation, Washington, DC

Jeanne Reynal
Tears of the Hero, 1959
Mosaic
60" x 20"
$800
Unsold
Returned at request of the artist

Larry Rivers
Blend, 1963
Oil on canvas
72" x 48"
$5,000
Unsold
No record of later sale

James Rosenquist
The Promenade of Merce Cunningham, 1963
Oil on canvas
70" x 60"
$2,200
Sold at 1963 Benefit to Mrs. John de Menil, New York; currently collection of the Menil Collection, Houston

Salvatore Scarpitta
Sphinx, 1961
Canvas relief
18" x 23 ¼"
$600
Unsold
No record of later sale

Miriam Schapiro
Shrine for J.J., 1963
Oil on paper
15 ½" x 22 ½"
$250
Unsold
Returned at request of the artist

George Segal
Crouching Woman, 1961
Sculpture of burlap dipped in white plaster
49" x 46" x 24 ½"
$1,400
Unsold
Foundation for Contemporary Arts, New York

Thomas Sills
Dreams, 1959
Oil on canvas
40" x 40"
$450
Unsold
Returned at request of the artist

Sigrid Spaeth
Still Life, 1962
Pencil and crayon on paper
15" x 19 ½"
$85
Sold at 1963 Benefit to Mrs. John de Menil, New York

Saul Steinberg
Sam, c. 1963
Ink and watercolor
14 ¼" x 22 ¾"
$350
Unsold
No record of later sale

Frank Stella
Newburyport, 1962
Oil on canvas
30 ⅜" x 60 ¾"
$1,200
Sold at 1963 Benefit to the Woodward Foundation, Washington, DC; currently collection of Yale University Art Gallery, New Haven, CT

Elaine Sturtevant
Pontificate, 1962
Charcoal and oil on canvas
31" x 43"
$350
Unsold
No record of later sale

Wayne Thiebaud
Windtoys, 1962
Oil on canvas
24" x 36"
$600
Unsold
Returned at request of the artist

Jack Tworkov
Abandoned, 1962
Oil on canvas
45" x 47"
$4,500
Unsold
Sold in 1979 to a private collector through Margo Leavin Gallery, Los Angeles

Andy Warhol
Merce, 1963
Silk-screen ink and black spray paint on linen
82" x 81 ½"
Price unknown
Unsold
Returned to Stable Gallery per request of Eleanor Ward

Jane Wilson
Shade, 1962
Oil on canvas
36" x 30"
$900
Unsold
Sold in 2012 to a private collector through DC Moore Gallery, New York

Jack Youngerman
Little Yellow Green, 1962
Oil on canvas
16" x 13"
$700
Unsold
No record of later sale

Adja Yunkers
Drawing Ink and Crayon I, 1962
Ink and crayon
16" x 21 ¾"
$250
Unsold
Sold in 1980 to Lawrence Dubin, New York

*The following artists are listed on the exhibition poster but did not ultimately exhibit works:
John Chamberlain
Joseph Cornell
Niki de Saint Phalle
Grace Hartigan
Paul Jenkins
Wifredo Lam
Isamu Noguchi
Mark Rothko
Jean Tinguely
Mark Tobey

I

GRANTS TO ARTISTS SELECTION COMMITTEE PANELISTS 2000–2013

David Behrman
Johanna Burton
Christoph Cox
Nancy Dalva
Molly Davies
Carroll Dunham
Boo Froebel
RoseLee Goldberg
Annie Gosfield
Neil Greenberg
David Grubbs
Clay Hapaz
Matthew Higgs
Anthony Huberman
John Jasperse
John Jesurun
Laura Kuhn
David Lang
Margaret Leng Tan
Ruth Maleczech
Brice Marden
Carla Peterson
Scott Rothkopf
Jay Sanders
Valda Setterfield
Debra Singer
Fiona Templeton
Laurie Uprichard
Kate Valk
T.J. Wilcox
Christopher Williams
Martha Wilson
Julia Wolfe

J

GRANTS TO ARTISTS POETRY READERS 2000–2013

Bill Berkson
Charles Bernstein
Anselm Berrigan
Mónica de la Torre
Larry Fagin
Forrest Gander
Peter Gizzi
Jorie Graham
Ann Lauterbach
Ben Marcus
Harryette Mullen
Charles North
Ron Padgett
Elizabeth Robinson
David Shapiro
Patricia Spears Jones
Rosmarie Waldrop
Marjorie Welish
Trevor Winkfield
C.D. Wright
John Yau

EMERGENCY GRANTS PANELISTS 2006–2013

Robert Bordo
Cecily Brown
Anne Collier
Moyra Davey
Liz Deschenes
John Duff
Stephen Ellis
Rachel Feinstein
Kate Gilmore
Jane Hammond
Oliver Herring
Jacqueline Humphries
Michael Joo
Miranda Lichtenstein
Glenn Ligon
Suzanne McClelland
James Nares
Paul Pagk
Paul Pfeiffer
Ellen Phelan
James Siena
Amy Sillman
Emily Sundblad
Nari Ward
T.J. Wilcox
Trevor Winkfield

NOTATIONS CONTRIBUTORS

The following composers and artists contributed to a collection compiled by John Cage and published as a book in 1969.

Murray Adaskin
Samuel Adler
Hugh Aitkin
Gilbert Amy
Eric Andersen
David Andrew
Hendrik Andriessen
Louis Andriessen
István Anhalt
Theodor Antoniou
Robert Ashley
Larry Austin
Ay-O
Milton Babbitt
Claude Ballif
François Bayle
The Beatles
John Beckwith
David Bedford
David Behrman
Gunnar Berg
Arthur Berger
Luciano Berio
Leonard Bernstein
Sir Arthur Bliss
Ernest Bloch
Suzanne Bloch
Karl B. Blomdahl
Lars-Gunnar Bodin
Benjamin Boretz
André Boucourechliev
Pierre Boulez
Paul Bowles
Carl Bowman
Henry Brant
George Brecht
Stanley Brouwn
Earle Brown
Herbert Brün
Richard Gavin Bryars
Sylvano Bussotti
Joseph Byrd

George Cacioppo
John Cage
Jacques Calonne
Cornelius Cardew
Elliott Carter
Niccolo Castiglione
Graciela Castillo
Carlos Chávez
Giuseppe Chiari
Barney Childs
Chou Wen-Chung
Henning Christiansen
Aldo Clementi
Wilson Coker
Michael Colgrass
Edward T. Cone
Anthony Conrad
Aaron Copland
Philip Corner
José E. Cortés
Manuel Cortés
Ramiro Cortés
Henry Cowell
Lowell Cross
George Crumb

Ingolf Dahl
Luigi Dallapiccola
Ton de Leeuw
Norman Dello Joio
Luís de Pablo
Franco Donatoni
Matt Doran
James Drew

Pedro Echarte
Tom Ehrlich
Merrill Ellis
Rudolf Escher
Franco Evangelisti

Morton Feldman
Carl Fernbach-Flarsheim
Luc Ferrari
Robert Filliou
Albert M. Fine
Ross Lee Finney
Michael Fleisher
George W. Flynn
Lukas Foss
Harry Freedman
Ken Friedman

Kenneth Gaburo
Gerardo Gandini
Roberto Gerhard
Miriam Gideon
Pia S. Gilbert
Alberto Ginastera
Jimmy Giuffre
Aylmer Gladdys
Peggy Glanville-Hicks
Jack Glick
Vinko Globokar
Malcolm Goldstein
Pelle Gudmundsen-Holmgreen

Alois Hába
Cristóbal Halffter
Bengt Hambraeus
Charles Hamm
Al Hansen
Lou Harrison
Roman Haubenstock-Ramati
Josef Matthias Hauer
Bici Hendricks
Geoffrey Hendricks
Juan Hidalgo
Dick Higgins
Lejaren A. Hiller
Alan Hovhaness
Jerry E. Hunt
Karel Husa
Scott Huston

Toshi Ichiyanagi
Andrew Imbrie
Charles Ives

Terry Jennings
Ray Johnson
Ben Johnston
Betsy Jolas
André Jolivet
Charles Jones
Joe Jones

Mauricio Kagel
Allan Kaprow
Udo Kasemets
Milko Kelemen
Jack Frederick Kilpatrick
Leon Kirchner
George Kleinsinger
Bengt af Klintberg
Milan Knížák
Alison Knowles
Gottfried Michael Koenig
Rudolf Komorous
Arthur Køpcke
Takehisa Kosugi
Peter Kotík
Ernst Krenek
Philip Krumm

Frederic Lieberman
György Ligeti
Noël Llinos
Anestis Logothetis
Alvin Lucier
Otto Luening
Witold Lutoslawksi

Jackson Mac Low
William R. Maginnis Jr.
Walter Marchetti
Tomas Márco
M. Lourdes Martins
Salvatore Martirano
Max Mathews
Richard Maxfield
Walter Mays
Toshiro Mayuzumi
George McKay
Colin McPhee
Wilfrid Mellers
Arne Mellnäs
Josep Maria Mestres Quadreny
Gertrud Meyer-Denkmann
Darius Milhaud
Ilhan Mimaroglu
Francis Miroglio
George Montana
Douglas Moore
Robert Moran
Jan W. Morthenson
Richard Moryl
Gordon Mumma
Frederic Myrow

Conlon Nancarrow
Isaac Nemiroff
Max Neuhaus

Pauline Oliveros
Yoko Ono
Hans Otte

Nam June Paik
Harry Partch
Benjamin Patterson
Hansjörg Pauli and Rolf Liebermann
Vincent Persichetti
Jon Phetteplace
Henri Pousseur

Folke Rabe and Jan Bark
Gene and Francesca Raskin
Gardner Read
David Reck
Steve Reich
Roger Reynolds
Josef Anton Riedl
Wallingford Riegger
Rainer Riehn
Terry Riley
George Rochberg
Ned Rorem
Dieter Roth
Jerome Rothenberg
Carl Ruggles
Gerhard Rühm
Terry Rusling
Frederic Rzewski

Michael Sahl
Eric Salzman
Erik Satie
Henri Sauguet
Richard Saylor
Pierre Schaeffer
Tomas Schmit
Dieter Schnebel
Carolee Schneemann
Gunther Schuller
Kurt Schwertsik
Ralph Shapey
Conrado Silva
Gianni-Emilio Simonetti
Netty Simons
Roger J. Smalley
Sydney Wallace Stegall
Karlheinz Stockhausen
Igor Stravinsky
Soulima Stravinsky
Richard Swift

Yugi Takahashi
Toru Takemitsu
Simeon Ten Holt
James Tenney
Alan Thomas
Virgil Thomson
Michael Thorpe
Virgilio F. H. Tosco
David Tudor

Horacio Vaggione
Edgard Varèse
Wolf Vostell

Robert Watts
Ben Weber
Anton Webern
Adolph Weiss
John H. Whitney
Frank Wigglesworth
Emmett Williams
Richard Winslow
Christian Wolff
Stefan Wolpe
Charles Wuorinen

Yannis Xenakis

La Monte Young
Jōji Yuasa

Gerd Zacher

M

BOARD OF DIRECTORS AND SECRETARIES HISTORY

Founding Directors
Jasper Johns
John Cage
Lewis Lloyd
Alfred Geller
Elaine de Kooning
David Hayes

Directors History, in Chronological Order
Jasper Johns, 1963–present
John Cage, 1963–92
Lewis Lloyd, 1963–65
Alfred Geller, 1963–64
Elaine de Kooning, 1963–77
David Hayes, 1963–65
Jill Jakes, 1965–71
Billy Klüver, 1965–66
Carolyn Brown, 1966–2001
Alexina Duchamp, 1969–77
Viola Farber, 1969–98
Mark Lancaster, 1982–85
Alanna Heiss, 1985–95
Brooke Alexander, 1985–present
Julian Lethbridge, 1994–present
Elizabeth Murray, 1995–2001; 2003–2007
Phill Niblock, 1997–2006
John Silberman, 1998–2003
Frances Fergusson, 2005–2012
Agnes Gund, 2005–present
Kara Walker, 2007–present
T.J. Wilcox, 2010–present
Glenn Ligon, 2011–present
Robert Gober, 2012–present

Secretaries History
Jill Jakes, 1963–1967
David Whitney, 1967–1974
Mark Lancaster, 1975–1984
Sarah (Cooke) Taggart, 1985–2010
John Delk, 2011–present

CONTRIBUTORS

Eric Banks
Eric Banks is a writer and editor based in New York. He is formerly senior editor of *Artforum*, and in 2003 he relaunched *Bookforum*, of which he was editor in chief until 2008. He has contributed articles and reviews of books and art to numerous publications, including *The New York Times*, *The New York Times Book Review*, the *Financial Times*, *Slate*, *W*, and *The Chronicle of Higher Education*. He is currently president of the National Book Critics Circle.

Mark Beasley
Mark Beasley is a freelance curator, producer, and writer based in New York. He has served as a curator with the Performa biennial and Creative Time and, as an independent curator, he organized "Electric Earth: Film and Video from Britain" for the British Council (cocurated with Colin Ledwith); "Infra Thin Projects" with Book Works, London; and "Sudden White (After London)," at the Royal Academy of Arts. He has contributed articles and essays to numerous exhibition catalogues and journals including *Dot Dot Dot*, *Artforum*, and *Frieze*.

Nancy Dalva
Nancy Dalva is the producer and writer of the Web series "Mondays with Merce" and the Scholar-in-Residence of the Merce Cunningham Trust. Her work has appeared in *The New Yorker*, *The Atlantic Monthly*, *The New York Times*, *Town and Country*, and the *New York Post* and on air via WNYC and NPR. Her work has been anthologized in *Reading Dance* (Pantheon, 2008), and she is a contributor to the Oxford University Press *International Encyclopedia of Dance*. Dalva has served as a nominator and panelist for the FCA's Grants to Artists program.

Eva Díaz
Eva Díaz is assistant professor of contemporary art at the Pratt Institute. She received her Ph.D. at Princeton University in 2009 for her dissertation "Chance and Design: Experimentation in Art at Black Mountain College." Her writing has appeared in magazines and journals such as the *Art Bulletin*, *Art in America*, *Artforum*, *Cabinet*, and *Modern Painters*, exhibition catalogues, and numerous monographs and books, and her essay on the influence of R. Buckminster Fuller on contemporary art recently appeared in *Grey Room*. Díaz is currently at work on a book about Black Mountain College, to be published by the University of Chicago Press later this year.

Rebecca Y. Kim
Rebecca Kim is associate academic specialist in music history at Northeastern University. Her research focuses on American music of the twentieth century, particularly the works of John Cage. She received her PhD in musicology from Columbia University, where her dissertation "In No Uncertain Musical Terms: The Cultural Politics of John Cage's Indeterminacy" was a finalist for the Society for American Music's Wiley Housewright Dissertation Award. She is currently at work on a book on Cage's indeterminate works. At Northeastern, Kim is organizing the Department of Music's 2013 symposium on composer Earle Brown.

Joseph Logan
Joseph Logan is a New York–based book designer. After many years as a commercial art director (Baron & Baron, French *Vogue*), he served as design director of *Artforum* from 2005 to 2010. He has designed numerous art books, including *Wade Guyton OS* (Yale University Press, 2012); *Whitney Biennial 2012* (Yale University Press, 2012); *Taryn Simon: A Living Man Declared Dead and Other Chapters* (MACK, 2011); and *Ellsworth Kelly Plant Drawings* (Schirmer/Mosel, 2011).

Julie Martin
Julie Martin has worked with Experiments in Art and Technology since 1967 and is executive producer of ten films on the performances at "9 Evenings: Theatre & Engineering." She coedited the book *Pavilion* (Dutton, 1972), documenting the Pepsi Pavilion at Expo '70, and wrote *Kiki's Paris* (Abrams, 1989) with Billy Klüver. She is currently coordinating producer of Robert Whitman's performances and communications projects and is editing Klüver's writings on art and technology.

Susan Rosenberg
Susan Rosenberg is associate professor of art history at St. John's University, New York. A former curator at the Philadelphia Museum of Art, she contributed to exhibitions and publications on Alice Neel, Gabriel Orozco, and Christian Marclay and worked with Trisha Brown to realize "*It's a Draw/Live Feed*," (2003) at Philadelphia's Fabric Workshop and Museum. Her writings on Brown have recently appeared in *TDR* and *October*, and she is at work on a book on the choreographer for Wesleyan University Press.

Irving Sandler
Irving Sandler is the author of numerous monographs on twentieth-century artists. In four seminal works—*The Triumph of American Painting: A History of Abstract Expressionism* (Praeger, 1970), *The New York School: The Painters and Sculptors of the Fifties* (Harper & Row, 1978), *American Art of the 1960s* (Harper & Row, 1988), and *Art of the Postmodern Era: From the Late 1960s to the Early 1990s* (Icon, 1996)—he detailed the span and ambition of postwar American art. Sandler's memoir of more than five decades in the art world, *A Sweeper-Up After Artists* (Thames & Hudson), appeared in 2004.

Debra Singer
Debra Singer is the former executive director and chief curator of The Kitchen, where she organized exhibitions, performances, and events by such artists as Alix Pearlstein, Sarah Michelson, Richard Maxwell, Ikue Mori, Maria Hassabi, Young Jean Lee, Nature Theater of Oklahoma, Pauline Oliveros, and Okkyung Lee. Prior to The Kitchen, Singer was associate curator of contemporary art at the Whitney Museum of American Art, where she co-organized the 2002 and 2004 Whitney Biennials as well as solo projects by such artists as Paul Sietsema, Sarah Sze, Paul Pfeiffer, Arturo Herrera, Tom Burr, Miranda July, and William Pope.L

Stacy Tenenbaum Stark
Stacy Tenenbaum Stark has been the executive director of the Foundation for Contemporary Arts since 2005, following a career as an executive in the beauty industry. She oversees the FCA's staff, programs, finances, development, communications, and events. Stark received her MA in art history from the Courtauld Institute of Art. Her thesis, "The Triumph of 'The New American Painting': MoMA and Cold War Cultural Diplomacy," was published in *Artists and Patrons in Post-War Britain* (Ashgate, 2001).

CREDITS

Every effort has been made to trace copyright holders and to obtain their permission for the use of copyright material. The publisher apologizes for any errors or omissions in the list below and would be grateful if notified of any corrections that should be incorporated in future reprints or editions of the book.

Photographs

Courtesy Allan Stone Gallery, New York: p.50; © The Richard Avedon Foundation: p.24; Courtesy Bang on a Can: p.182; Stephanie Berger: p.13; Roberta Bernstein: pp.164, 173; Linsey Bostwick: p.14; Éric Boudet: p.188; Tom Brazil: p.157; Courtesy Carolyn Brown: pp.39, 56, 57, 175; Courtesy Trisha Brown Dance Company: p.177; © Dan Budnik: p.58; Rudy Burckhardt: p.51, courtesy Leo Castelli Gallery Records, Archives of American Art, Smithsonian Institution; Sheila Burnett: p.144, courtesy Maureen Paley, London; Witjak Widha Cahya: p.187; Hunter Canning: p.155; Bob Cato: p.48, courtesy John Cage Trust; Julieta Cervantes: p.160; Jocelyn Chase: pp.16, 17; © Paula Court: pp.15, 147, 151, 178, 179, 181, 182, 183, 187, 188, 190; Jessica Craig-Martin: pp.16, 17; Ellen Crane: p.159; Courtesy Jade Dellinger: p.65; Ian Douglas: p.150; Courtesy The Drawing Center: p.180; Todd Eberle: p.16; Brad Farwell: pp.17, 191; Courtesy Richard Foreman: p.178, scan Fales Library & Special Collections, New York University; Courtesy the artist and Franklin Furnace Archive, Inc.: p.183; David Fullard: p.9, courtesy Eiko & Koma; Gianfranco Gorgoni: p.9, courtesy Steve Reich; Lois Greenfield: p.9; Timothy Greenfield-Sanders: p.162; David A. Henderson: p.138; Philip Hipwell: p.174; George Hirose: p.184, courtesy Jasper Johns Studio; Anja Hitzenberger: p.12; John Houck: p.17; *Houston Chronicle*: p.154, courtesy Tere O'Connor; Matthew Huber: p.186; Douglas H. Jeffrey © V&A Department of Theatre & Performance: pp.54, 56, 57; Frank Jones: p.163, courtesy North Carolina State Office of Archives and History, Raleigh, North Carolina; Courtesy Jill Jakes: p.32; Ros Kavanagh: p.14; Julie Keefe: p.185; © James Klosty: inside cover jacket, pp.1, 7, 38, 43, 164; Brian Laczko: p.186; Larry Lamé: p.183, courtesy Papo Colo, scan Fales Library & Special Collections, New York University; Mark Lancaster: p.164, courtesy Jasper Johns Studio; © Julie Lemberger: p.190; Geneviéve Stephenson: p.182; Courtesy Lewis Lloyd: p.31; Édouard Lock: p.157, courtesy La La La Human Steps; Courtesy Alvin Lucier: p.168; © Babette Mangolte, all rights reserved: p.9, courtesy Trisha Brown Dance Company; Barbara Mensch: pp.179, 181; Courtesy Jacqueline Matisse Monnier: p.175; Dona Ann McAdams: p.180; Fred W. McDarrah/Premium Archive/Getty Images: pp.28-29, 30, 170; PatrickMcMullan.com: p.17; Yasuo Minagawa: p.45, courtesy Jasper Johns Studio; © Jack Mitchell: p.4, courtesy John Cage Trust; Peter Moore © Estate of Peter Moore/VAGA, NYC: pp. 6, 52, 70, 85, 86-87, 88, 91, 92-93, 94, 95, 123, 166, 167, 168, 171, 172, 173, 175, 176, 177; p.6, courtesy House Foundation; Courtesy Ikue Mori: p.145; Ryan Muir: p.16; Ugo Mulas: p.3 © Ugo Mulas Heirs. All rights reserved; © Hans Namuth: p.60; New York City Players: p.153; Boru O'Brien O'Connell: p.14, courtesy Alix Pearlstein; Jerald Ordover: p.16; Lillian Palmer: p.170, courtesy Feigen/Palmer Archives; Steve Paxton (attributed to): pp.40, 56, courtesy Robert Rauschenberg Foundation Archives ; Courtesy The Poetry Project: p.176; Robert Propper: p.174; © Robert Rauschenberg Foundation/Licensed by VAGA, New York, NY: p.57, courtesy Robert Rauschenberg Foundation Archives; Rachel Rosenthal: p.163; Beatriz Schiller: p.180; Lori E. Seid: p.188; Vivian Selbo: p.9, courtesy The Poetry Project; Carl Skutsch: p.152; Allison Smith and Michelle Pemberton: p.189, courtesy of the artist and Haines Gallery, San Francisco, collection Indianapolis Museum of Art; Luke Stettner: pp.10, 11, 18, 33, 34, 46, 57, 68, 72, 76, 79, 82, 84, 96, 169, 171, 174, 176, 178; © Anna Stöcher/Burgtheater Wien: p.15; Rob Strong: p.156; Courtesy SUNY Buffalo Music Library: p.71; Paul Taylor: p.154; Val Telberg: p.171, courtesy 92nd Street Y Archives; Stacy Tenenbaum Stark: p.189; James Turrell: p.181, courtesy Skystone Foundation; Courtesy Wang Jianwei: p.14; Robert Wedemeyer: p.191, courtesy Susanne Vielmetter Projects, Los Angeles; Yi-Chun Wu: p.143; John Wulf: p.6, courtesy The Paper Bag Players

Artworks

Alex Bag: p.146, courtesy the artist and Team Gallery, New York; © Paul Brach, 2013 Artists Rights Society (ARS), New York/VG Bild-Kunst, Bonn: p.171, collection Foundation for Contemporary Arts; Chryssa: p.165, collection Foundation for Contemporary Arts; © Elaine de Kooning Trust: p.37, collection National Portrait Gallery, Washington, DC; Marcel Duchamp © 2013 Artists Rights Society (ARS), New York/ ADAGP, Paris/Succession Marcel Duchamp: p.165; David Dupuis: p.12, courtesy Derek Eller Gallery, New York; Sam Francis © 2013 Sam Francis Foundation, California/ Artists Rights Society (ARS), NY and Gemini G.E.L.: p.192; © The Estate of Philip Guston and Gemini G.E.L.: p.192; Wade Guyton: p.161, courtesy of the artist and Petzel Gallery, New York, collection Charlotte and Bill Ford; © David Hockney and Gemini G.E.L.: p.192; © Jasper Johns/ Licensed by VAGA, New York, NY: p.36, collection The Museum of Contemporary Art, Los Angeles; © Jasper Johns and Gemini G.E.L./ Licensed by VAGA, New York, NY: p.192; © Ellsworth Kelly: p.36, collection Mr. Barney A. Ebsworth; © Ellsworth Kelly: p.178; © Ellsworth Kelly and Gemini G.E.L.: p.192; Jon Kessler, photo © Tom Powel Imaging, New York: p.12; © Estate of Roy Lichtenstein: p.37, courtesy Roy Lichtenstein Foundation, private collection; Richard Lippold © 2013 Estate of Richard Lippold/Artists Rights Society (ARS), New York: p.37, collection Museum of Modern Art, New York, Mary Sisler Bequest; Ryan McNamara: p.148, courtesy the artist and Elizabeth Dee Gallery, New York; © Julie Mehretu: p.145, photo Cameron Wittig, private collection; Ohad Meromi: p.15, courtesy the artist and Harris Lieberman, New York; © 2013 Robert Morris/Artists Rights Society (ARS), New York: p.165, collection Jasper Johns; © 2013 Bruce Nauman/Artists Rights Society (ARS), New York and Gemini G.E.L.: p.192; © Claes Oldenburg: p.174; Ruben Ortiz Torres: p.186, courtesy the artist; Dona Nelson: p.191, courtesy Thomas Erben Gallery; William Pope L.: p.158, courtesy the artist and Mitchell-Innes & Nash Gallery, New York, photo BF crew; Raha Raissnia: p.14, courtesy the artist and Miguel Abreu Gallery, New York; © Robert Rauschenberg Foundation/Licensed by VAGA, New York, NY: p.37, collection Mr. and Mrs. Graham Gund; © Robert Rauschenberg Foundation/Licensed by VAGA, New York, NY: p.82, photo Luke Stettner; © Robert Rauschenberg Foundation/Licensed by VAGA, New York, NY and Gemini G.E.L.: p.192; Steve Roden: p.191, courtesy Susanne Vielmetter Projects, Los Angeles; © James Rosenquist/Licensed by VAGA, New York, NY: p.165, collection The Menil Collection, Houston, formerly in the collection of Christophe de Menil, photo D. James Dee; © 2013 Richard Serra/Artists Rights Society (ARS), New York and Gemini G.E.L.: p.192; © Wayne Thiebaud/Licensed by VAGA, New York, NY: p.171, private collection; © 2013 The Andy Warhol Foundation for the Visual Arts, Inc./Artists Rights Society (ARS), New York: p.36, private collection; © Trevor Winkfield: p.185, courtesy Tibor de Nagy Gallery, New York, private collection

Music Scores

Courtesy Dunvagen Music/St. Rose Music: p.6; Courtesy Fondation Satie/Archives de France/Archives Imec.: p.65, scan Lewis Lloyd Collection, Beinecke Rare Book and Manuscript Library, Yale University; © C.F. Peters Corporation. Used by kind permission. All rights reserved: p.69; © Robert Moran: p.75, courtesy John Cage Notations Project Manuscript Scores, Northwestern University Music Library; © Éditions Alphone Leduc: p.76; © The Beatles: p.79, courtesy Sony/ATV Music Publishing; © John Beckwith, composer and James Reaney, author: p.79; © Alison Knowles: p.80, courtesy John Cage Notations Project Manuscript Scores, Northwestern University Music Library

Texts/Lectures

© Calvin Tomkins/New Yorker Magazine/Condé Nast: p. 5; Courtesy Alison Knowles/Something Else Press: pp.76, 79; © The Estate of R. Buckminster Fuller. All rights reserved: p.113; © Rae Armantrout, "Simple," *Versed*, Wesleyan University Press, Middletown, CT 2009. Used with permission: p.146; © Patricia Spears Jones, "GHOSTS," *Femme du Monde*, Tia Chucha Press, Los Angeles, CA, 2006: p.161; © The Estate of Harold Rosenberg: p.124, courtesy Patia Yasin; © The Estate of Peter Yates: p.107, courtesy Peter Yates; © The Estate of Corinne McLuhan: p.129; Carolyn Brown, *Chance and Circumstance: Twenty Years with Cage and Cunningham*, Alfred A. Knopf, New York, NY © 2007: p.122

Ephemera

Lewis Lloyd Collection, Beinecke Rare Book and Manuscript Library, Yale University: pp. 6, 40, 42, 50, 56, 63, 66, 167, 169; *The Village Voice*: p.6; Reprinted with permission of Dance Magazine, © 1963: p. 62; Courtesy 92nd Street Y Archives: p.94; Courtesy Sylvia Neuhaus: p.170; Courtesy La MaMa E.T.C. Archives: p.177

The FCA Acrostics

August 2012

Fragments
Collect
Ambiguity.

Free
Cognition--
Alleluia!

Flop
Click,
Acerbic.

Feeling
Confident
(Alas?).

"Failures"
Come
Alive.

(Frugal
Calvinists'
Anathema.)

Fish*
Cormorants*
Ahhh*.

Flight
Continuously
Arrives.

Frolics of
Cosmological
Ants.

Fresh,
Clean
Allegoricals.

Flashing
Carboniferous
Anger.

Finally
Crushed:
Assumptions.

Finding
Concurrence in
Articulation.

Fuck
Cunt
Asafoetida.

Fine-tuned
Color
Aggregation.

Flesh:
Conditional
Amazement.

Fiddling
Copies
Agriculture.

Flinging
Consecutive
Acrobats.

Fools
Can? cannot?
Argue.

France!
China!
Atlantis!

Freakishly
Compounding the
Arts.

NOTE: If the one beginning "Fuck" were deemed inappropriate for reproduction, here's an alternative suggestion:

Fridge
Containing
Abracadabra.

Jack Collom

Jack Collom, 2012 grantee, "The FCA Acrostics," 2012. Courtesy the artist.

FOUNDATION FOR CONTEMPORARY ARTS

Mission

The Foundation for Contemporary Arts was started in 1963 by visual artists in a spirit of community, hoping to assist and encourage innovation, experimentation, and potential in the arts. Since then, exhibitions and sales of works donated by nearly 900 artists have made possible our program of non-restrictive grants to individuals working in dance, music/sound, performance art/theater, poetry, and the visual arts. Grants are also given to presenting organizations, and we maintain a fund to help artists with unexpected emergencies related to their work.